Feasting on the Word®

Editorial Board

Feasting on the Word®

Preaching the
Revised Common Lectionary

Year B, Volume 3

DAVID L. BARTLETT and BARBARA BROWN TAYLOR

General Editors

WJK WESTMINSTER
JOHN KNOX PRESS
LOUISVILLE · KENTUCKY

© 2009 Westminster John Knox Press

Book design by Drew Stevens
Cover design by Lisa Buckley

First edition
Published by Westminster John Knox Press
Louisville, Kentucky

This book is printed on acid-free paper that meets the American National Standards Institute Z39.48 standard. ♾

PRINTED IN THE UNITED STATES OF AMERICA

11 12 13 14 15 16 17 18 — 10 9 8 7 6 5 4 3

Library of Congress Cataloging-in-Publication Data

Feasting on the Word : preaching the revised common lectionary / David L. Bartlett and Barbara Brown Taylor, general editors.
   p. cm.
  Includes index.
  ISBN 978-0-664-23098-2 (v. 3: alk. paper)
  ISBN 978-0-664-23097-5 (v. 2: alk. paper)
  ISBN 978-0-664-23096-8 (v. 1: alk. paper)
  1. Lectionary preaching. 2. Common lectionary (1992) I. Bartlett, David Lyon, 1941–
II. Taylor, Barbara Brown.
  BV4235.L43F43 2008
  251'.6—dc22   2007047534

Contents

Publisher's Note

Feasting on the Word: Preaching the Revised Common Lectionary is an ambitious project that is offered to the Christian church as a resource for preaching and teaching.

The uniqueness of this approach in providing four perspectives on each preaching occasion from the Revised Common Lectionary sets this work apart from other lectionary materials. The theological, pastoral, exegetical, and homiletical dimensions of each biblical passage are explored with the hope that preachers will find much to inform and stimulate their preparations for preaching from this rich "feast" of materials.

This work could not have been undertaken without the deep commitments of those who have devoted countless hours to working on these tasks. Westminster John Knox Press would like to acknowledge the magnificent work of our general editors, David L. Bartlett and Barbara Brown Taylor. They are both gifted preachers with passionate concerns for the quality of preaching. They are also wonderful colleagues who embraced this huge task with vigor, excellence, and unfailing good humor. Our debt of gratitude to Barbara and David is great.

The fine support staff, project manager Joan Murchison and compiler Mary Lynn Darden, enabled all the thousands of "pieces" of the project to come together and form this impressive series. Without their strong competence and abiding persistence, these volumes could not have emerged.

The volume editors for this series are to be thanked as well. They used their superb skills as pastors and professors and ministers to work with writers and help craft their valuable insights into the highly useful entries that comprise this work.

The hundreds of writers who shared their expertise and insights to make this series possible are ones who deserve deep thanks indeed. They come from wide varieties of ministries. But they have given their labors to provide a gift to benefit the whole church and to enrich preaching in our time.

Westminster John Knox would also like to express our appreciation to Columbia Theological Seminary for strong cooperation in enabling this work to begin and proceed. Dean of Faculty and Executive Vice President D. Cameron Murchison welcomed the project from the start and drew together everything we needed. His continuing efforts have been very valuable. Former President Laura S. Mendenhall provided splendid help as well. She made seminary resources and personnel available and encouraged us in this partnership with enthusiasm and all good grace. We thank her, and look forward to working with Columbia's new president, Stephen Hayner.

It is a joy for Westminster John Knox Press to present *Feasting on the Word: Preaching the Revised Common Lectionary* to the church, its preachers, and its teachers. We believe rich resources can assist the church's ministries as the Word is proclaimed. We believe the varieties of insights found in these pages will nourish preachers who will "feast on the Word" and who will share its blessings with those who hear.

Westminster John Knox Press

Series Introduction

A preacher's work is never done. Teaching, offering pastoral care, leading worship, and administering congregational life are only a few of the responsibilities that can turn preaching into just one more task of pastoral ministry. Yet the Sunday sermon is how the preacher ministers to most of the people most of the time. The majority of those who listen are not in crisis. They live such busy lives that few take part in the church's educational programs. They wish they had more time to reflect on their faith, but they do not. Whether the sermon is five minutes long or forty-five, it is the congregation's one opportunity to hear directly from their pastor about what life in Christ means and why it matters.

Feasting on the Word offers pastors focused resources for sermon preparation, written by companions on the way. With four different essays on each of the four biblical texts assigned by the Revised Common Lectionary, this series offers preachers sixteen different ways into the proclamation of God's Word on any given occasion. For each reading, preachers will find brief essays on the exegetical, theological, homiletical, and pastoral challenges of the text. The page layout is unusual. By setting the biblical passage at the top of the page and placing the essays beneath it, we mean to suggest the interdependence of the four approaches without granting priority to any one of them. Some readers may decide to focus on the Gospel passage, for instance, by reading all four essays provided for that text. Others may decide to look for connections between the Hebrew Bible, Psalm, Gospel, and Epistle texts by reading the theological essays on each one.

Wherever they begin, preachers will find what they need in a single volume produced by writers from a wide variety of disciplines and religious traditions. These authors teach in colleges and seminaries. They lead congregations. They write scholarly books as well as columns for the local newspaper. They oversee denominations. In all of these capacities and more, they serve God's Word, joining the preacher in the ongoing challenge of bringing that Word to life.

We offer this print resource for the mainline church in full recognition that we do so in the digital age of the emerging church. Like our page layout, this decision honors the authority of the biblical text, which thrives on the page as well as in the ear. While the twelve volumes of this series follow the pattern of the Revised Common Lectionary, each volume contains an index of biblical passages so that all preachers may make full use of its contents.

We also recognize that this new series appears in a post-9/11, post-Katrina world. For this reason, we provide no shortcuts for those committed to the proclamation of God's Word. Among preachers, there are books known as "Monday books" because they need to be read thoughtfully at least a week ahead of time. There are also "Saturday books," so called because they supply sermon ideas on short notice. The books in this series are not Saturday books. Our aim is to help preachers go deeper, not faster, in a world that is in need of saving words.

A series of this scope calls forth the gifts of a great many people. We are grateful first to the staff of Westminster John Knox Press: Don McKim and Jon Berquist, who conceived this project; David Dobson, who worked diligently to bring the project to completion, with publisher Marc Lewis's strong support; and Julie Tonini, who has painstakingly guided each volume through the production process. We thank former President Laura Mendenhall and former Dean Cameron Murchison of Columbia Theological Seminary, who made our participation in this work possible. We thank President Steve Hayner and Dean Deborah Mullen for their continuing encouragement and support. Our editorial board is a hardworking board, without whose patient labor and good humor this series would not exist. From the start, Joan Murchison has been the brains of the operation, managing details of epic proportions with great human kindness. Mary Lynn Darden, Dilu Nicholas, Megan Hackler Denton, and John Shillingburg have supported both her and us with their administrative skills.

We have been honored to work with a multitude of gifted thinkers, writers, and editors. We present these essays as their offering—and ours—to the blessed ministry of preaching.

David L. Bartlett
Barbara Brown Taylor

A Note about the Lectionary

Feasting on the Word follows the Revised Common Lectionary (RCL) as developed by the Consultation on Common Texts, an ecumenical consultation of liturgical scholars and denominational representatives from the United States and Canada. The RCL provides a collection of readings from Scripture to be used during worship in a schedule that follows the seasons of the church year. In addition, it provides for a uniform set of readings to be used across denominations or other church bodies.

The RCL provides a reading from the Old Testament, a Psalm response to that reading, a Gospel, and an Epistle for each preaching occasion of the year. It is presented in a three-year cycle, with each year centered around one of the Synoptic Gospels. Year A is the year of Matthew, Year B is the year of Mark, and Year C is the year of Luke. John is read each year, especially during Advent, Lent, and Easter.

The RCL offers two tracks of Old Testament texts for the Season after Pentecost or Ordinary Time: a semicontinuous track, which moves through stories and characters in the Old Testament, and a complementary track, which ties the Old Testament texts to the theme of the Gospel texts for that day. Some denominational traditions favor one over the other. For instance, Presbyterians and Methodists generally follow the semicontinuous track, while Lutherans and Episcopalians generally follow the complementary track.

The print volumes of *Feasting on the Word* follow the complementary track for Year A, are split between the complementary and semicontinuous tracks for Year B, and cover the semicontinuous stream for Year C. Essays for Pentecost and the Season after Pentecost that are not covered in the print volumes available on the *Feasting on the Word* Web site, www.feastingontheword.net.

For more information about the Revised Common Lectionary, visit the official RCL Web site at http://lectionary.library.vanderbilt.edu/ or see *The Revised Common Lectionary: The Consultation on Common Texts* (Nashville: Abingdon Press, 1992).

Feasting on the Word®

DAY OF PENTECOST

Acts 2:1-21

¹When the day of Pentecost had come, they were all together in one place. ²And suddenly from heaven there came a sound like the rush of a violent wind, and it filled the entire house where they were sitting. ³Divided tongues, as of fire, appeared among them, and a tongue rested on each of them. ⁴All of them were filled with the Holy Spirit and began to speak in other languages, as the Spirit gave them ability.

⁵Now there were devout Jews from every nation under heaven living in Jerusalem. ⁶And at this sound the crowd gathered and was bewildered, because each one heard them speaking in the native language of each. ⁷Amazed and astonished, they asked, "Are not all these who are speaking Galileans? ⁸And how is it that we hear, each of us, in our own native language? ⁹Parthians, Medes, Elamites, and residents of Mesopotamia, Judea and Cappadocia, Pontus and Asia, ¹⁰Phrygia and Pamphylia, Egypt and the parts of Libya belonging to Cyrene, and visitors from Rome, both Jews and proselytes, ¹¹Cretans and Arabs—in our own languages we hear them speaking about God's deeds of power." ¹²All were amazed and perplexed, saying to one another, "What does this mean?" ¹³But others sneered and said, "They are filled with new wine."

Theological Perspective

The Day of Pentecost is sometimes called "the birthday of the church." The Holy Spirit came on the day of Pentecost, after the ascension of Jesus (Acts 1:6–11), to empower the disciples and "devout Jews from every nation" who were assembled in Jerusalem. They "began to speak in other languages, as the Spirit gave them ability" (Acts 2:4). This is seen as the fulfillment of Jesus' command and promise that disciples would "receive power" when the Holy Spirit came upon them (Acts 1:8). They spoke in other languages and heard in their own "native language" (Acts 2:6). Using the words of Joel 2:28–32, Peter proclaimed that in the "last days" God will pour out the Spirit of God "upon all flesh" so that sons and daughters, young and old, and "even" slaves, "both men and women" shall see visions and prophesy; and "everyone who calls on the name of the Lord shall be saved" (Acts 2:17–21).

Theologically, the Christian church begins to take shape when the Holy Spirit fills those who believe in Jesus as the Messiah, enabling them to proclaim the gospel and to witness to the Christ "to the ends of the earth" (Acts 1:8). The church emerges by the Holy Spirit, who dramatically establishes a fellowship of faith, calling believers into the household of God to be witnesses to what God has done in Jesus Christ for the purposes of salvation.

Pastoral Perspective

Preaching on Pentecost may not seem as important as preaching on, say, Christmas or Easter. The festival day marking the birth of the church does not have the familiarity of glad tidings and alleluias, nor does it have secular holiday traditions to accompany it. Perhaps this is just as well, because the focus of Pentecost is aimed directly at us, the community of disciples known as the church. It is the story of how, through the power of the Holy Spirit, the church is gifted with an identity and an authority centered in the proclamation of the gospel.

Ironically, this miraculous gifting of the Spirit to the church in Acts can be a dispiriting passage to preach about year after year. After all, the contemporary church does not much resemble the early church. Even the most faithful Christian will occasionally express a nagging feeling that the church is a sorry shell of its awe-inspiring birth, that somehow the church has lost its thunder, that it no longer acts with conviction, that schisms and infighting have stripped it of its unity and vitality. We speak of the church at the end of Christendom and of its decline in the face of an ever-increasing secularization of culture. Even the most encouraging signs of spiritual growth, church renewal, and evangelism seem tepid compared to Pentecost's infectious energy. How can our typical

14But Peter, standing with the eleven, raised his voice and addressed them, "Men of Judea and all who live in Jerusalem, let this be known to you, and listen to what I say. 15Indeed, these are not drunk, as you suppose, for it is only nine o'clock in the morning. 16No, this is what was spoken through the prophet Joel:

17'In the last days it will be, God declares,
  that I will pour out my Spirit upon all flesh,
    and your sons and your daughters shall prophesy,
  and your young men shall see visions,
  and your old men shall dream dreams.
18Even upon my slaves, both men and women,
  in those days I will pour out my Spirit;
    and they shall prophesy.
19And I will show portents in the heaven above
  and signs on the earth below,
    blood, and fire, and smoky mist.
20The sun shall be turned to darkness
  and the moon to blood,
    before the coming of the Lord's great and glorious day.
21Then everyone who calls on the name of the Lord shall be saved.'"

Exegetical Perspective

Literary Context. The narrative of Luke's Gospel is resumed in Acts by recapitulating the resurrection and ascension of Jesus (Luke 24; Acts 1:1–11). Then Luke's account of the apostolic age, prefaced by the report of Matthias being chosen to replace Judas (Acts 1:12–26), commences with the coming of the Holy Spirit on Pentecost. This epiphany of wind [*pnoē*] and fire fulfills the prophecy of John the Baptist, that Jesus would "baptize with the Holy Spirit [*pneuma*] and fire" (Luke 3:16), as it also fulfills the Father's promise, transmitted through the risen Christ, that the disciples would soon be "baptized with the Holy Spirit" (Acts 1:4–5). After Peter's speech to the crowd (Acts 2:14–36) he exhorts them to be baptized and "receive the gift of the Holy Spirit" (Acts 2:38). Luke uniquely describes Jesus' ministry as "bringing fire to the earth"—the heated conflict within which he will experience the "baptism" of his suffering and death (Luke 12:49–50). Thus Luke figuratively describes the coming of the Holy Spirit as a baptism—conversely linking baptism with reception of the Holy Spirit—and associates both with the image of fire.

This Lukan literary context creates a thematic framework that conditions the interpretation of the Pentecost episode in the following ways: (1) Because the dramatic manifestation of the Holy Spirit fulfills

Homiletical Perspective

Acts 2:1–21 is so freighted with significance that it can overwhelm the thoughtful preacher, just as the Spirit overwhelmed the devout Jews who witnessed the outpouring of the Holy Spirit at Pentecost. The "signs and wonders" that occur in Jerusalem stir awe and doubt—rushing wind, tongues of flame, and the miracle of speaking in foreign tongues (xenolalia). Peter's sermon, based upon the words of the OT prophet Joel, fills the air with Spirit-filled visions and dreams involving "blood, and fire, and smoky mist" (v. 19). "God's deeds of power" (v. 11) echo around the walls of the preacher's study long after she has analyzed the passage. So much is going on that the preacher may wonder along with the Jews if those first Spirit-filled Christians weren't filled with "new wine."

The preacher who puts the text into conversation with the congregation and wider world will discover numerous directions for the sermon. First, there is the sheer mystery of the event. Ours is a consumer-driven and technologically saturated world that has been drained of mystery. The sights and sounds of Pentecost can quicken the sense of the sacred for preacher and congregation. Imaginatively retold from the pulpit, the outpouring of the Holy Spirit at Pentecost can restore wonder for a mystery-starved people. Aided by the Spirit, a sermon based upon

Acts 2:1-21

Theological Perspective

Pentecost is the "big bang" event that sets the events of the book of Acts into motion.

The Spirit for the World. The language of the Pentecost experience, with its images of "wind," "spirit," and being "filled" with the Spirit or the "breath" of life, is reminiscent of God's initial creative activity (Gen. 1:2; 2:7). Here, however, the emphasis is not so much on creation or God's works in history as on direct contact with the Spirit of God, who is now filling the world in a new way. The roll call of nations and languages points to the universality of the Spirit's work for the whole world. God's Spirit is the divine energy that now enables an eternal life to be real for those on whom God's Spirit is poured and in whom the Spirit dwells (cf. Rom. 5:5).

Even more, linking the Pentecost events with the prophetic word about "last days" (Acts 2:17) points forward to the ultimate consummation of God's reign in a "new heaven and new earth" (Rev. 21:1). The coming messianic age has already begun with Jesus as the Christ (Messiah; Acts 2:31–36). Now the Spirit is the presence of the risen Christ throughout the world. The Spirit works in and for the world as history moves toward the future fullness of God's reign (kingdom). So wherever we see signs of the coming age—in works of love, peace, and justice—we know God's Spirit is at work. The creation itself is "groaning" toward its future redemption, even as those who have received the "first fruits of the Spirit" (Rom. 8:23) live into hope.

The Spirit for the Church. Pentecost is a foundational theological event for the church because the Spirit is sent by God to incorporate people, universally, into the body of those who acknowledge Jesus as the Christ. It is God who initiates Pentecost, as God initiates salvation. God's Spirit calls a people to faith and comforts, challenges, and guides the church. The reality of the Spirit's presence is the church's guide to living as faithful servants of God in the world and faithful witnesses to Jesus Christ.

There is a rabbinic tradition that says that when the law was given at Sinai, the Ten Commandments were given with a single sound, yet when the voice went forth it was divided into seven voices and then seventy tongues, so that "every people received the law in their own language."[1] In later Judaism, the day of Pentecost, as the fiftieth day after the presentation

1. F. F. Bruce, *The Book of Acts,* New International Commentary on the New Testament (Reprint, Grand Rapids: Eerdmans, 1980), 60.

Pastoral Perspective

accoutrements of Pentecost Sunday—red paraments in the chancel and red balloons in the courtyard for coffee hour—compete with tongues of fire? How can singing a hymn in Portuguese, Xhosa, or Korean compete with strangers from many languages speaking to one another with understanding?

The good news is that such comparisons are unnecessary. The story of Pentecost is not meant to be a benchmark of what the church should look like on any given Sunday. Rather, it seeks to communicate how important the church is and how inseparable it is from Christ. Pentecost serves as a catechetical instruction that continues to tradition the church into its identity and purpose. Every year, on the Day of Pentecost, we are reminded of who we are as a church, what we proclaim, and the source of that proclamation. It is a message to the church from the church, passed down through millennia to each generation.

The voice of the Pentecost story is infused with miraculous energy and enthusiasm. Through the power of the Holy Spirit, the church receives the authority to proclaim the gospel of the risen Lord. Even Peter, the disciple who publicly denied Christ, becomes a bold preacher. The gospel is intended for everyone; repentance and forgiveness are offered to all who call on the name of the Lord. The heavens open, something new and surprising is afoot. Throughout Luke–Acts, the presence of the Holy Spirit announces a fresh inbreaking of the kingdom of God. Theophanies such as Christ's baptism (Luke 3:16), his miracles, and the tearing of the temple curtain at his crucifixion (Luke 23:45) demonstrate God's intention to break open, tear down, and make new. The mighty wind and the tongues of flame that fall upon the disciples in Acts 2:2–3 are continuations of this work. In Acts, the work of the Holy Spirit is to call individuals into community as the body of Christ.

Pentecost emphasizes the centrality of Christ to the church's identity, authority, and proclamation. This christological focus at Pentecost is essentially ecclesiological, and it affords an opportunity for pastors to preach about the church in its many dimensions. The first, and most important, dimension of the church is its universality. We confess this each time we recite the Apostles' Creed: "I believe in the holy catholic church." The Holy Spirit gifts the church to proclaim the Good News to the ends of the earth. Pentecost reminds us that, even though all our faith practices are rooted in local contexts, the church's identity extends beyond every

Exegetical Perspective

prophetic promises, it attests Jesus' resurrection and designation as the Messiah (Acts 2:36). (2) This formative experience of the first disciples is relived by subsequent disciples in their baptism. (3) When disciples are baptized into the apostolic fellowship, their reception of the Holy Spirit is manifest in a particular form of communal life (Acts 2:42–47). Living together in this way, they are empowered to witness (Acts 1:8) not only by preaching, but also by imitating Jesus in their creative endurance of conflict.

Textual Analysis. The narrative describes the impact of the Holy Spirit's coming in two phases, first on the assembled disciples (Acts 2:1–4) and then on the gathering crowd (Acts 2:5–21). The occasion for the assembly of the disciples is the festival of Pentecost or Weeks, celebrated fifty days following the festival of Passover. Pentecost, originally a harvest festival, eventually came to commemorate the giving of the law at Sinai. The Spirit's manifestation as wind and fire recalls similar images of YHWH's theophany and agency, particularly in creation, exodus, and covenant making (e.g., Gen. 1:2; Exod. 15:8; Pss. 18:7–15; 104:4; Exod. 19:18–19). Emphasis on the forceful sound of the wind and the tonguelike shape of the flames prefigures the expression of divine energy in speech. The Spirit animates a diversity in language that contrasts with the homogeneity of the disciples in every other respect: they are *all together* in the same place, the wind fills the *whole* house, *all* are filled with the Spirit, and although the fiery tongues are individually allocated, *each and every* person has one. Thus the Holy Spirit reinforces the unified fellowship of the disciples as it enables them to express their unity in culturally diverse forms.

As the disciples begin speaking all at once, the noise attracts a crowd consisting of "devout Jews from every nation under heaven." Second Temple Judaism was a cosmopolitan religious movement, and the holy city of Jerusalem would attract Jewish residents originally from many different regions. Pentecost, one of the Jewish calendar's three major pilgrimage festivals (Exod. 34:22–23; Deut. 16:1–17), would also attract international visitors. The astonishing thing is not that the covenant community could come to include an ethnically and culturally diverse membership—it already does—but that members from one group can readily make understandable to members from other groups their message concerning "God's deeds of power." This will eventually lead to the recognition that Gentiles can also belong to the covenant community, as they

Homiletical Perspective

this text can usher the entertainment-bloated but spiritually undernourished congregation into the presence of the true, life-giving God. It can recall that the resurrected Christ is always present to the believing congregation through the miraculous gift of the Holy Spirit. We do not have to manufacture "spirit," usually understood as charged emotions, in Christian worship through tricks and the latest worship gimmicks; rather, the Spirit-led preacher will open the eyes of the congregation to the astounding gifts of the Holy Spirit that are fully available to those who believe.

A second approach for this Sunday might center on the speaking and hearing in foreign languages that occur at Pentecost. This is not the unknown tongues (glossolalia) that Paul encounters in Corinth (1 Cor. 12–14). The language event at Pentecost causes no divisiveness among the speakers or hearers, though it does stir some initial skepticism. The text states clearly that Jews from all parts of the Middle East are each able to hear in their own native languages. Like a gathered conference of the United Nations, each delegate hears the proceedings in his or her own tongue. What could be a more timely message for twenty-first-century Christians? The Word of God not only transcends cultural barriers, but it arrives in the particular language of each listener. Pentecost verifies Christmas. All wrapped up in human form, God comes to us in our very own bodies; God speaks to us our very own language(s). In an age of increasing cultural diversity, religious pluralism, and the perpetual rubbing of shoulders across lines of nation, race, and class, God offers authentic human communion. Through ordinary human speech, the Holy Spirit establishes unity amid diversity, a fulfilled promise that even the most divided congregations and communities can take to heart.

A third path into the Pentecost sermon leads to the prophetic dreams and visions of Joel that Peter interprets for the congregation. Luke determines that Peter and the early church are fulfilling the salvation story of Israel set down in Hebrew Scripture. Only now, within the context of Jesus' death and resurrection, the prophecy of Joel does not presage the arrival of God's judgment upon the enemies of Israel in "the Day of the Lord." Rather, the pouring out of the Spirit upon all flesh signals the empowering of Jesus' disciples to proclaim the resurrected Christ to all the nations. A new day has come for those who follow the resurrected Christ. God has bestowed upon them a bold and prophetic

Acts 2:1-21

Theological Perspective

of the first sheaf of the barley harvest, was also considered the anniversary of the giving of the law at Sinai. The law was meant to express God's will and guide the people of Israel. So now, with the giving of the Spirit on Pentecost, the church receives God's Spirit to guide and help and indwell the people of God as they seek to live out God's will, known in Jesus Christ.

The Spirit for All People. Luke associates the pouring out of the Spirit on Pentecost with the prophet Joel who announces the coming Day of the Lord when God's righteousness and mercy will be revealed and enacted. The messianic reign is marked by the reception of the Spirit by "all flesh." The Spirit is for all people who are united by the Spirit in the praise of God in prophecy, visions, and dreams. Humans are now united in their diversities of age, gender, and social status by the great outpouring of the Spirit.

Sometimes Pentecost is seen as the reversal of the effects of the tower of Babel (Gen. 11:1–9), when the languages of the world were "confused" and people were scattered. Peter's association of the Pentecost event with the outpouring of the Spirit foretold by Joel means that there is now a new community of women and men where the one Spirit bestows many gifts—on all people, regardless of who they are. As Jürgen Moltmann put it, "In the kingdom of the Spirit, everyone will experience his and her own endowment and all will experience the new fellowship together."[2] The church is the place where this new fellowship begins to take shape as it recognizes the gifts of the Spirit in and for all people. To realize that "all flesh," all people, receive the Spirit, enables us to watch and participate in God's work in this world with a wide-open vision. We live in eager anticipation of the Spirit's work in our midst as we join with all others to accomplish the Spirit's purposes.

DONALD K. MCKIM

Pastoral Perspective

congregation, denomination, and cultural tradition. Pentecost celebrates the face of Christ throughout the world in all its theological, cultural, and liturgical diversity. It also challenges North American Christians to engage the emerging vitality of the church in the Southern Hemisphere.

A second dimension of the church is the local congregation. Speaking of the church universal can make some local churches feel small and insignificant, especially those that struggle with declining membership or with the anxiety that they do not measure up to the ever-extending criteria of congregational success. Here is an opportunity to speak of every congregation's participation in the work and worship of the entire church. It is also an opportunity to speak of congregational renewal. The book of Acts testifies to the filling of the Holy Spirit as an ongoing gift, not just a onetime event, and the church is constantly changing, according to the Spirit's leading. The book of Acts also reminds us that such change is rarely easy or harmonious. Pentecost challenges churches to live into the promise that Christ is present and alive in the midst of change.

Finally, Pentecost has something to say to individuals who do not feel that belonging to the body of Christ is necessary for personal Christian discipleship. It also speaks to those who feel discouraged, disillusioned, or excluded by the church. From the very beginning, Christ calls individuals into community as the church. Pentecost allows us to speak boldly to the church as we are and about the church Christ would have us be. The many dimensions of the church's identity—global, local, and personal—are interrelated and essential. None can exist apart from Christ or from the others.

Liturgically, the Day of Pentecost completes the cycle that begins with Ash Wednesday and continues through Lent and Holy Week and into Eastertide. It is the capstone of a liturgical journey that moves symbolically from ashes to fire. Pentecost sums up the gospel with simplicity and audacity: Jesus Christ offers salvation to all, and the church exists to proclaim it. Pentecost is an appropriate time to reaffirm congregants' participation as disciples in the body of Christ, to challenge a congregation to live into its promise, and to celebrate the global witness of the church.

KRISTIN EMERY SALDINE

---

2. Jürgen Moltmann, *The Spirit of Life: A Universal Affirmation*, trans. Margaret Kohl (Minneapolis: Fortress Press, 1993), 239.

Exegetical Perspective

also experience a "pentecost" (Acts 10:44–48). At this point, however, the issue is mutual understandability despite the diversity within the Jewish community. And the dramatic demonstration of this possibility evokes both perplexed wonder and sarcastic accusations of drunkenness.

After countering these accusations, Peter explains what has happened as the fulfillment of an oracle prophesied long ago. According to the prophet Joel, God would one day empower all classes of the community to become prophets by pouring out the Spirit in a theophany of wind and fire, so that all who call on the name of the Lord will be saved (Joel 2:28–32a). The disciples have all become prophetic in the sense that (1) they can see the deeds of power still being performed by God; (2) they have a common understanding of God's purpose in performing them; and (3) they proclaim this to people who speak all sorts of different languages. God's deeds of power (Acts 2:11) include the sending and raising of Jesus (Acts 2:22–24), and God's purpose is the salvation of all (Acts 2:21, 40).

Summary Conclusion. When this pericope is interpreted in relation to its literary context for those who have been baptized, it invites them to recapitulate the reception of the Holy Spirit in their baptism in light of the first disciples' primal experience of the Holy Spirit. More specifically, it raises the question of whether the Spirit is actualized in their form of communal life. Does their fellowship have a discipline that engenders the prophetic capacity to discern what God is doing, to reach a common understanding of God's purposes, and to proclaim this by words and actions that are readily understandable to people of different cultures? A key element in developing such a capacity is a prophetic approach to Scripture, which seeks to discover patterns of divine action in the past that are still evident in the present and future. On the basis of such patterns, God's people can discern where and how God is still active in the paradigmatic ways that are evident in the history of Israel and the life of Jesus—in the renewal of creation, in liberation from oppression, in the beneficial ordering of life together, and in the creative endurance of conflict.

MICHAEL H. FLOYD

Homiletical Perspective

Spirit, with Peter as emblem bearer, to spread this good news.

Significant for preaching from this text is the radical social equality of those who receive the Holy Spirit. This becomes even clearer as the story in Acts unfolds (e.g., 2:42–47). Old and young, women and men, slave and free all receive the power of God to prophesy, see visions, and dream. Occasionally God anoints big dreamers who with their lives and words paint upon a global canvass, renewing visions for human community—dreamers like Martin Luther King Jr. But God also anoints ordinary believers like the ones who sit in the pews before the preacher. They too see visions and dreams that can move the church and its surrounding community a little closer to the "Lord's great and glorious day" (v. 20). On Pentecost Sunday, sermons might name the visions present within the congregation, which lead to the fulfillment of those dreams.

Finally, a word of caution for the preacher who prepares the Pentecost Sunday sermon. The responsible interpreter will wrestle with the tension in the text, especially as we read beyond verse 21, between the Jews who believe the proclamation of the resurrection and lordship of Jesus Christ and the Jews who disbelieve. Peter's sermon speaks plainly of these matters. But it would be a theological and social mistake of the worst kind to interpret Peter's sermon as anti-Jewish. Christians who are blessed by the Holy Spirit, the fruits of which are love and wisdom, can ill afford to cast others as "enemies" of the gospel. That way lies Christian triumphalism. Peter is speaking as a brother of the Jewish family to beloved family members. He notes that Jews and Gentiles alike rejected Jesus (v. 23). He pleads his case not for the condemnation of Israel but for her own salvation.

With respect to faithfully hearing and responding to its own revelation, the Christians today are in a similar position to the Jews gathered in Jerusalem. We need not look beyond ourselves to find scoffers and sincere disbelievers, much less to cast blame upon others for our own inability to hear the good news. Peter proclaims that "*everyone* who calls on the name of the Lord shall be saved" (v. 21). It is a proclamation spoken not in judgment but in love to all.

G. LEE RAMSEY JR.

Psalm 104:24-34, 35b

²⁴O Lᴏʀᴅ, how manifold are your works!
In wisdom you have made them all;
the earth is full of your creatures.
²⁵Yonder is the sea, great and wide,
creeping things innumerable are there,
living things both small and great.
²⁶There go the ships,
and Leviathan that you formed to sport in it.

²⁷These all look to you
to give them their food in due season;
²⁸when you give to them, they gather it up;
when you open your hand, they are filled with good things.
²⁹When you hide your face, they are dismayed;
when you take away their breath, they die
and return to their dust.

Theological Perspective

In the Nicene Creed the church confesses that the Holy Spirit is "the Lord, the giver of life." This psalm, which makes reference to a highly significant "sending" of the Holy Spirit prior to the day of Pentecost, contributes to a deeper understanding of what that confession might mean. It raises important questions about the relationship between creation and redemption.

Psalm 104 is sometimes referred to as a "nature" psalm, because of its extraordinary attention to the natural world. But, more accurately, it's a hymn to God the Creator, who brought all things into being and who, through the Spirit, continues to animate and sustain all of life.

The passage begins with the psalmist's wonderment at the scope and diversity of God's handiwork. The early part of the psalm has already furnished a list of the abundant features, phenomena, and wildlife that make up the created order. God's greatness is declared not just in bringing all of this into being, but in protecting it and allowing it to flourish in the face of the chaotic forces that might otherwise overwhelm it (vv. 5–9). More than being merely some kind of clever inventor who makes things and moves on, God is with this creation, alongside it, allowing it space to be, creating the conditions for growth and freedom.

Pastoral Perspective

The reading of Psalm 104 always brings to my mind my experience of Joseph Sittler, by then an aged and near-blind preacher, at the front of a small stone chapel with wooden pews in a building connected to the university. He was reciting the psalm from memory. I was stunned, first by the fact of his recitation, unprecedented in my experience, especially in its virtuosity; next by the power of the specificity and intimacy of the images of the creator God's relationship with that which is creation and with us, God's people. And the sermon that followed, on the sacredness of creation and our human place and role in it—it is one of those few sermons that I recall, even thirty years later. That day was born in me an appreciation for the power of the psalms that was not present before and that has never left me.

The reading for Pentecost Sunday begins midway through the psalm and is a tribute to the wisdom of Creator God, who made the earth skillfully and well, with both craft and grace. In it God placed the creatures, among whom we are. We love the playful image of whalelike Leviathan "sporting" in the sea ("Yonder is the sea! . . . There go the ships!" vv. 25–26) for its childlike wonder and its tone of whimsy and pleasure. The intensity of the psalm's personalization of the relationship between the Creator and the created is, simply, incredible and

³⁰When you send forth your spirit, they are created;
and you renew the face of the ground.

³¹May the glory of the LORD endure forever;
may the LORD rejoice in his works—
³²who looks on the earth and it trembles,
who touches the mountains and they smoke.
³³I will sing to the LORD as long as I live;
I will sing praise to my God while I have being.
³⁴May my meditation be pleasing to him,
for I rejoice in the LORD. . . .
³⁵Bless the LORD, O my soul.
Praise the LORD!

Exegetical Perspective

Psalm 104 is a hymn to God as the *creator* and *nourisher* of the world and all that is in it. The psalmist in the first twenty-three verses of the hymn takes the reader through a poetic litany of God's handiwork. Light is God's garment, the heavens are God's tent. The clouds are chariots upon which God can ride the wings of the wind. Fire and flame are the ministers of God. God set the earth on its foundations and called back the waters and set the mark beyond which the waters may not pass. God makes springs gush forth in the valleys to provide drink for the wild animals. God waters the mountains from God's lofty home. God causes the grass to grow for the cattle. God gives plants for people to use to make food and wine to gladden the heart. The Lord keeps the trees alive and strong that the birds may build their nests. The mountains give shelter to the wild goats and coneys. God sets the moon in the sky and tells the sun when to rise so as to mark the seasons and the days. Even darkness is a gift to the animals of the forest who creep out into the night and to the young lions who roar their evening prayers for food. Daytime too is a gift that allows people to do their work. God has fashioned a world that is both to God's glory and a rich and endless store of sustenance for all God's creatures.

The remaining verses of Psalm 104 may be divided into four sections: the Bridge (v. 24); the Sea and

Homiletical Perspective

Psalm 104 is traditionally read on Pentecost because of its reference to the life-giving spirit (v. 30), but how often is it preached? Part of the preacher's difficulty may be in the way the lectionary "edits" the psalm, which quashes its spirit.

For the psalm is *one* marvelous song. Can we begin where the lectionary does, "How manifold are your works!" (v. 24), without the catalog of works in the preceding verses? Can we understand the sea (v. 25) without having heard the hymn to water that takes up much of the psalm? Indeed, water is the central image of the psalm.

Then, there is the "deletion" of 35a. Can we leave out that half verse, because it doesn't make us feel good? If we do, aren't we ignoring the psalmist's "blessed rage for order," not to mention how this psalm flows from the preceding psalm?

"Blessed rage for order," the title of theologian David Tracy's 1975 volume, comes from the poem by Wallace Stevens (1879–1955), "The Idea of Order at Key West." The poet is walking by the sea with philosopher Ramon Fernandez, listening to the song of the woman; and they find that her words give meaning to "the meaningless plunges of water and wind," that her passion for order has "mastered the night and portioned out the sea." That woman might be the psalmist (or the psalmist that woman), for the

Psalm 104:24-34, 35b

Theological Perspective

And it is clear that God takes delight in what has been made, rejoicing at this plethora of life (v. 31) There is an element of innocent playfulness in the creation of the mighty Leviathan, which seems to have been made simply to sport and gambol in the great oceans (v. 26).

It is noteworthy—and should give serious pause for thought—how little mention there is of human beings in Psalm 104. They are present, but as one part of a rich and varied community of creatures, not its focus. Nor is there any command to exercise dominion over the earth (cf. Gen. 1:28); and if such is to be inferred here, it must be qualified by, and understood in the light of, God's intense delight and pleasure in biodiversity. God's interest in and involvement with the created order is certainly not limited to the human race. In this psalm it is as though humankind's primary calling is to lead the doxology, to give voice to creation's praise (vv. 33, 34).

According to Psalm 104, the fundamental truth about the life of every creature, including every person, is that from moment to moment our lives are directly in God's hands (vv. 27–30). We live because we have breath/spirit that has been breathed into us by the Spirit of God (cf. Gen. 2:7). We die when God "takes our breath away" and stops breathing breath/spirit into us (v. 29). New life is created when the Spirit is sent forth and renews "the face of the ground" (v. 30). The Holy Spirit continues God's great work of creation.

Human beings are no different than other creatures with respect to this "breath of life." Ecclesiastes tells us that "the fate of humans and the fate of animals is the same; as one dies, so dies the other. They all have the same breath. . . . All are from the dust, and all turn to dust again" (Eccl. 3:19, 20). We share with the animals in what has been called "the solidarity of the 6th day"[1] of creation. We all depend on something that is not our own, but that comes to us from outside of ourselves as a gift. None of us can live without the Spirit:

> When you hide your face, they are dismayed;
> when you take away their breath, they die
> and return to their dust. (v. 29)

Since God can—and does—stop breathing into us, it is, as Barth observes, a precarious thing to be a human being.[2]

Pastoral Perspective

cannot fail to speak to us of the joy that faithful people take in our dependence on the One who sets the worlds on their courses. When we hear and picture God's open hand, full of food *for us*, it echoes in our spirits God's provision of manna to the chosen people Israel and moves us to affectionate gratitude. We feel wonder and love at the picture of God's face so close to ours that we can feel the breath of God upon us, as a loving parent breathes upon the face of a little child when it snuggles and sleeps on the shoulder. It is no surprise that we are dismayed when we feel this loving God turn from us. Our entire being depends upon our Creator, who sustains us so completely, so closely, and so lovingly that God is intimately involved in even these most basic aspects of our lives. We acknowledge that dependency and return thanks when we hear these verses. Who can help but be moved to devotion?

But we hear something different in the rest of the reading, where a sense of the divine majesty replaces the intimacy and familiarity of the previous lines. We hear a God of glory and might, so powerful that a glance or a touch can make the earth tremble and smoke. The God of love is also a God of power; we feel awe at knowing our relationship to such a being. And so we join the psalmist in the blessing of a joyful heart: "Bless the LORD, O my soul. Praise the LORD!" (v. 35).

Given the vicissitudes of life, even for faithful people and communities, it would be hard to assert that this psalm would stand up to serious scrutiny of the details of its poetic theology of creation, providence, and the dependence of the creation on the One who made it all. We do not always feel so cared for by God, nor do we recognize God's hand so clearly and closely in our doings, nor do we appreciate it every time we do. Bad things happen to us and to the world. Those we love and trust betray us. We are heedless of the good or resent our dependency. Communally, the most faithful congregations may be the ones struggling the most to live in difficult situations and circumstances. Fidelity to God is no guarantee of closeness or gratitude, and if that same God rules the universe with power, it makes things all the more confusing. Someone will no doubt hear this psalm and ask: Where is that loving Creator? Why do I feel distant? Such questions leave us in the dark. Perhaps they can be answered only with a hymnic assertion of trust such as this, and a life that is lived against the seeming grain.

Coming as it does on the Day of Pentecost, the psalm offers a reminder to the gathered community

---

1. Helmut Thielicke, quoted in Ray S. Anderson, *On Being Human: Essays in Theological Anthropology* (Grand Rapids: Eerdmans, 1982), 22.
2. Karl Barth, *Church Dogmatics*, III:2 (Edinburgh: T. & T. Clark, 1960), 362.

Exegetical Perspective

Leviathan (vv. 25–26); Life, Death, and Renewal (vv. 27–30); and Bless the LORD, O My Soul (vv. 31–35).

The Bridge (v. 24). The psalmist echoes the declaration of the creation story from Genesis, when God looks out over God's creation and sees that, indeed, it was very good. With jubilant confidence the author looks out into the world and declares with God, "O LORD, how manifold are your works! In wisdom you have made them all; the earth is full of your creatures." This verse summarizes and propels the reader forward.

The Sea and Leviathan (vv. 25–26). The psalmist turns our attention to the sea. These verses are reminiscent of the fifth day of creation, when "God said, 'Let the waters bring forth swarms of living creatures.' . . . God created the great sea monsters and every living creature that moves, of every kind, with which the waters swarm" (Gen. 1:20, 21). The sea is teeming with the fullness of God's creative handiwork.

Verse 26 begins with a short phrase "There go the ships." This insertion onto the canvas of God's natural world of a human-made vehicle serves as a reminder that even the most accomplished of human ventures floats upon the goodness of God's gifts. Ships, no matter how grand, are useless without the sea. All things—naturally occurring in creation or made by human beings—are ultimately dependent upon God.

The second half of verse 26 is ". . . and Leviathan that you formed to sport in it [the sea]." Leviathan is a sea monster and in other parts of the Psalms is considered an enemy to God. Psalm 74:14 reads, "You [God] crushed the heads of Leviathan; you gave him as food for the creatures of the wilderness." In Psalm 104, however, Leviathan is a plaything for God. The fear of chaos is often attached to the sea and to the largest fish and animals in the sea, who are innocuous parts of God's good creation. God in God's wisdom is the creator of all things big and small, and all of God's creation is good and not to be feared!

Life, Death, and Renewal (vv. 27–30). According to the hymn writer all living things on earth look to God for sustenance. Not only is God the creator of all that is, God is also the One who sustains life and fills the creatures of the earth with good things. There is an implied interdependence among all the creatures of the earth, but the undergirding connection for all beings is an absolute dependence

Homiletical Perspective

words of the psalm also portion out the sea—or show how God has done that.

I have said that water is the central image of the psalm. Among water's chief properties is that it flows into the shape of its container. But at the beginning of the psalm, water is uncontained, at least on earth. God may have covered the earth with a protective tent (v. 2), and built a palace on the waters above (v. 3), but on earth itself, ironically, "the deep" has covered the heights (v. 6).

Immediately God rebukes the waters, and what was uncontained becomes contained, what was disordered is ordered. The water flees at God's command, but it does not flee pell-mell; rather it goes to the place God has appointed for it. And around that place, God sets a boundary, that the waters may not pass.

It is not so difficult for us in these days of hurricane and tsunami to imagine a world in which the boundaries between sea and land are ruptured. But the psalmist, who lives among a people of the land—definitely *not* a seagoing people—imagines a world even more terrifying, in which there are no boundaries at all. Yet God puts boundaries where there were none. Next, when the chaotic water is in its place, God makes use of it. God turns what was only frightening into a good, springs and streams and rain, which give drink to wild animals and tame, and food and drink to humankind (vv. 10–16).

The water nourishes grain and vineyards and olive trees; it nurtures trees, which provide homes for the birds. This reminds the psalmist that God has provided homes for all God's creatures, both in terms of space to live and time to be active (vv. 17–23). These are some of God's manifold works, evidence of God's wisdom (v. 24). So, returning to the theme of order: here is the earth, and *yonder* is the sea (v. 25).

Again, one cannot simply begin reading the psalm here and grasp its poetic meaning. Only if we have imagined a world in which there is no boundary between sea and land, can we imagine *how* frightening the sea is to a people who are land people (though the first chapter of Jonah and the movie *The Perfect Storm* may give us a hint). So, in something of a humorous aside, the psalmist remarks, "Yonder is the sea," filled with creeping, creepy things. Ships may go there—the ships of fools and fleeing prophets—but surely they will encounter monsters. Or, the psalmist reflects, they would, had not God made *the* monster, Leviathan, his bath toy.

And the psalm turns once again to its theme: God has ordered the world. Even the farthest, most

Psalm 104:24-34, 35b

Theological Perspective

It is a central aspect of biblical anthropology that we cannot understand ourselves or the nature of reality apart from the Spirit. Anthropology is rooted in theology. All of life, including human life, is grounded in and sustained by God. This does not mean that we become one with God or a part of God. Unlike pantheism or certain kinds of mysticism, in biblical thinking there is real differentiation between God and human beings. We are not gods. We remain creatures—often rebellious, ungrateful and even unaware of our true origins—and, as is made clear in this very psalm, God allows us the space and creates the conditions in which our distinctive forms of creatureliness can flourish or fester. But the fact remains that we are utterly dependent on God for our existence.

This is why it is impossible for the human race to be truly godless. We may deny God with our lips, but the very breath we employ to do so is granted us by the Creator. The breath of the Spirit leaves its traces deep within.

Psalm 104 raises the question as to what is so special about the day of Pentecost. The Holy Spirit was and is already close to every person on the planet—as close as their own breath. What need is there of another, different sending of the Spirit? If it's true, in the memorable words of Vatican II's *Pastoral Constitution on the Church in the Modern World*, that "without the Creator the creature vanishes,"[3] is not the Spirit's continuing activity in creation already an act of redemption?

Whatever happened in Jerusalem on the day of Pentecost—and there is no doubt that something remarkable and world-changing did indeed happen after the resurrection and ascension of our Lord Jesus Christ—it must be understood in the light of what the Holy Spirit was already doing throughout creation, and not separate from it. God's sustaining grace is part of the history of salvation. God preserves the world in order to save it. The Spirit-empowered mission of the church, which we celebrate on this day, finds its true origins in the mission of the Triune God, Father, Son, and Holy Spirit, the movement of the Creator toward the creature in grace and mercy.

IWAN RUSSELL-JONES

Pastoral Perspective

of believers that the very existence of the church depends upon the love and life-giving power of God's Spirit. As the Creator gives life to the world, so the Spirit gives life to the church, a new community in which we disciples of Christ are called (in John 13:34) to "love one another, as I have loved you." If our God delights to love us so wonderfully, ought we not in community to love one another as well? And so we ask: Is the church at rest in God? As a body, is it appropriately humble, dwelling in its dependence, trusting in and thankful for God's sustaining grace? Or are there rumbles of anxiety, or echoes of the sin of self-sufficiency? This reading might call us once again to account for the idolatry—or the faith—that is within us, church as well as individuals.

Finally, the psalm calls us strongly to remember the created order that God so loves. If the creation is the holy handiwork of God, and if all aspects and parts are soaked in God's care as intimately as the psalm says, then do we not have the responsibility to care for the creation as well? It ought not to be possible for us to treat so carelessly that to which God gives so much love. A reminder to God's people of their stewardship over earth is in order.

Theological questions aside, as a love song of a people to their Creator God, isn't it marvelous? This is a psalm that I deeply enjoy reading aloud in the sanctuary, for God's people to hear and relish as I once did.

MARK MILLER-MCLEMORE

---

3. Quoted in *Catechism of the Catholic Church* (Liguorí, MO: Liguori Publications, 1994), 49.

Exegetical Perspective

on God for abundant life in the created order. When "you [God] open your hand, they are filled with good things" (v. 28).

Yet, when God hides God's face, the creation groans in dismay. The One who gives is the One who can take away. God gives and takes away food and God gives and takes away breath. "When you [God] take away their breath, they die and return to their dust" (v. 29). God is Lord of life *and* of death.

And yet again, God is the Lord of new life. God is a God of renewal. Verse 30 connects this psalm to the Christian celebration of Pentecost. "When you [God] send forth your spirit, they are created; and you renew the face of the ground." This claim of "renewing the face of the ground" connects to the "dust" of the previous verse. God is a God of creation, sustenance, death, *and* a God of renewal. Nothing is lost in God's spiritual economy. The dead can be made to breathe again. The bones dried up to dust can be revived. The parched earth is made to teem again with living creatures upon the return of God's spirit.

Bless the Lord, O my soul (vv. 31–35). Psalm 104 concludes with an act of praise. Verse 35b sums up these final five verses: "Bless the Lord, O my soul!" The lectionary omits the first part of the verse (35a), but the omitted portion gives interpretation to the last few verses and to the whole psalm. The prayer of the psalmist in verse 35a—"Let sinners be consumed from the earth, and let the wicked be no more"—can be thought of as a prayer for harmony within God's good creation. The poet envisions a time when sin and wickedness shall be gone from the earth, a time when all will sing praises to God, and the Lord will forever rejoice in the works of creation.

ROBERT WARDEN PRIM

Homiletical Perspective

frightening stretches of it belong to the Lord, whose glory will endure forever, so that "all look to you" (v. 27)—not only the "creeping things innumerable" of the sea, but *all*: the wild asses, the birds of the air, the cattle, people, the stork, wild goats and coneys, even the sun and the moon; these are also *creatures* of God (v. 24). Moreover, God's ordering of the world is not only past; it is present (vv. 27–28), and it is future (vv. 29–30). So the psalmist will sing praise to God as long as he lives.

Will not you all join in? That is what happens at the end of the previous psalm (103:20–22). But not here. It may be the psalmist's devoutest wish—and ours—but it is not the truth of the world we live in. There are those who do not sing God's order, who in fact court chaos, who hymn disorder, who teach wickedness. Is it wrong to wish them gone and the world whole?

Finally, to call on the spirit of God is to call on a spirit that desires order, that has provided places and times for all created things and that delights in them in their times and places. We may imagine the spirit of Pentecost as powerful and explosive—as powerful as an earthquake, as explosive as a volcano (v. 32); Acts describes it as wind and fire (as the psalmist describes God, riding the wind with fire as his ministers, vv. 3–4); but we do God's spirit wrong if we imagine it as wild. God's spirit may be as exuberant as the psalm itself, but it is not out of control. God is in control; so even the most frightening of possibilities need not frighten us. We are never whistling in the dark, we are singing in the light that is God God's self (v. 2).

RICHARD S. DIETRICH

Romans 8:22-27

²²We know that the whole creation has been groaning in labor pains until now; ²³and not only the creation, but we ourselves, who have the first fruits of the Spirit, groan inwardly while we wait for adoption, the redemption of our bodies. ²⁴For in hope we were saved. Now hope that is seen is not hope. For who hopes for what is seen? ²⁵But if we hope for what we do not see, we wait for it with patience.

²⁶Likewise the Spirit helps us in our weakness; for we do not know how to pray as we ought, but that very Spirit intercedes with sighs too deep for words. ²⁷And God, who searches the heart, knows what is the mind of the Spirit, because the Spirit intercedes for the saints according to the will of God.

Theological Perspective

Paul speaks here about "the whole creation" and opens our eyes to the astonishing world around us. We see birds in the air, fishes in the water, animals on the ground, creatures big and small. Some we can see only in the zoo; others we meet often. They hum, run, or crawl around us. They are encompassed by the world of plants, which is no less marvelous. This is "the whole creation," which we humans, unfortunately, think we may use or misuse without hesitation for our own purposes. Indeed, we think there is no other way than to sacrifice some of these creatures for our benefit, even if we inflict great pain on them. We may need them for food, or we may need them for medicinal purposes. But have we ever really seen them with the eyes with which the apostle perceives them? Albert Schweitzer learned to see them this way. He wrote about this in his ethics, which was focussed on the idea of "reverence for life." Even if we are unable to avoid such sacrifices, we should have a compassionate connection with "the whole creation," about which the Bible speaks here, and this means especially a sense "that the whole creation has been groaning in labor pains until now" (v. 22).

However, are not believers who are children of God saved from this anguish, this groaning in travail? Is this not simply the sign of their

Pastoral Perspective

The characters in Raymond Carver's "A Small Good Thing"[1] live "with sighs too deep for words" (v. 26). This short story by one of America's greatest writers is about Scotty, who is hit by a car while walking to school the week of his eighth birthday. His mother, Ann Weiss, has already gone to the local bakery and ordered a special cake for the birthday boy. Everything had seemed right in the world of Ann and Howard Weiss.

Everything changes in the Weiss family's world as Scotty is taken to the hospital and slips deeper and deeper into a coma. Raymond Carver takes the reader into the pain and bondage of the Weisses' agony, an agony that Paul knew as he wrote to the church in Rome. In Romans 8:22–27, the apostle foretells a future glory but is mindful of the "groaning" and "sighs" that belong to the "children of God" in the present age. Paul asserts that "the sufferings of this present time" are "not worth comparing with the glory about to be revealed to us" (8:18). Clearly, Paul knows that pastorally he cannot focus solely on the future glory. It is the present suffering that is on his mind as he writes to the Christians in Rome—particularly in this brief passage.

1. "A Small Good Thing," in *Listening for God*, ed. Paula J. Carlson and Peter S. Hawkins (Minneapolis: Augsburg Press, 1994), 74–93.

Exegetical Perspective

Today's reading carries forward the themes of "suffering" and "the glory about to be revealed in us" (my translation) from Romans 8:18–21.

Creation and God's Children (vv. 22–23). To buttress his claims in 8:19–21 regarding creation (*ktisis*), Paul draws on knowledge he shares with the Romans, namely that creation "groans together (*systenazō*) and shares in agony until now" (v. 22, my translation). God's children also groan (*stenazō*) and thereby share in the suffering of creation (v. 23). Paul's perception of the inseparable connection (in groaning) between humans and creation diverges sharply from the gnostic ideal of the human's separation from materiality.

An additional parallel between creation and God's children is that the potential for redemption exists for each. Creation expects (*apekdechomai*) the "revelation of the sons of God" (v. 19, my translation) and God's children expect (*apekdechomai*) "adoption, the redemption of our body" (v. 23, my translation). This reference to adoption as a future event is puzzling given its description in verses 12–17 as a *past* experience.[1] Romans 6:12–13 and 12:1–2 may clarify what "redemption of the body" involves.

---

1. This apparent conflict likely explains the word's absence in some manuscripts. Translating *huiothesian* as "adoption," rather than "sonship," obscures its connection with "sons of God" (v. 8:19; cf. vv. 14–15).

Homiletical Perspective

As we celebrate Pentecost Sunday, many of us may wonder what the Spirit is doing today. It is one thing to read about what the Spirit of God did in the first century. But is that Spirit alive today, and in what ways is the Spirit manifest among us? The eighth chapter of Romans assures us of the activity of the Spirit in the lives of believers, and this particular pericope offers concrete hope to those who are 2,000 years removed from the vibrant activities of the second chapter of Acts.

"We know," says Paul, "that the whole creation has been groaning in labor pains until now" (v. 22). He is referring again (as in chap. 5) to the fallen state of creation. Creation waits, along with all believers, the fulfillment of God's plan for the world, including our final adoption as the sons and daughters of God and the full redemption (that is, resurrection: cf. 6:5) of our bodies (v. 23). In other words, when Christ returns, the standing of believers as heirs of God's reign (v. 17) will be made complete.

The return of Christ seemed imminent to Paul. It feels less so today. The groans of creation that he described continue in our time and perhaps even increase as pollution, overpopulation, and inequitable distribution of food and resources continue. The groans of believers also continue as we await a consummation of faith. If we tried to put

Romans 8:22-27

Theological Perspective

redemption that they live rather luckily and contently because they already possess what the others still do not have? But it is Whitsun, and let us go to the school of the apostle Paul! He stands all this on its head. He does not deny that we are already children of God. He says indeed that we may be already "saved" (v. 24). But then he adds an important qualification. It is true that we are saved, but we are saved in the hope of redemption. We live in the light of a good promise, but we do not live in the fulfillment of that promise. "Beloved, we are God's children now; what we will be has not yet been revealed" (1 John 3:2).

John Calvin stressed this insight. "Though Christ gives us the spiritual goods in present fullness by the gospel, their enjoyment is hidden below the care of the hope, until we have given up our mortal body and we are transformed into the glory of him, who led the way for us. We cannot enjoy Christ in another way than that we seize him under the cover of his promises."[1] Christians who live in the light of this promise are still *waiting*. They are not yet at the goal. They are on the way, like pilgrims. They "wait for it with patience" (v. 25); that is, they wait with perseverance and with the certainty that what they hope for will happen. Above all, they discover that they wait with "the whole creation" for the redemption of their bodies and for their adoption as children of God (v. 23). Certainly they are not forgotten by their creator and redeemer. God is with them, but often they do not see this. They have to wait and to yearn for it.

Their waiting is evident in their behavior when they are sensitive to the living and suffering of other humans and other creatures. It makes them weak and perhaps lonely. They may be depressed by the thought that they are abandoned by God. Their suffering may also stem from a feeling of powerlessness. Furthermore, they know that in this world all things perish. But they also know that the cross of Jesus Christ stands in the midst of this lonely, forsaken world, and this cross is the sign of hope. Easter proclaims that at the end of our possibilities God creates a new beginning. Therefore we may say to all humans that they are not deserted by God, even if they think that God is not with them. In this situation God comes to them and stands by them and resides with them. God strengthens them by his Holy Spirit and gives them energy to resist the world's principalities and powers.

1. John Calvin, *Institutio Christianae religionis*, II 9,3.

Pastoral Perspective

Paul confirms that his readers "have the first fruits of the Spirit"; yet they and we "groan" because we in every age await the "redemption of our bodies." Once again, Paul navigates the choppy waters of now and not yet, of the present time and the time when all that plagues the "children of God" will be conquered "through him who loved us."

The apostle acknowledges that "in hope we were saved" (v. 24). We hope for that which is not seen, and "we wait for it with patience" (v. 25). Most pastors know firsthand that the followers of Jesus do not often wait "with patience." In Raymond Carver's poignant story, there is no patience. The baker is anxious for Scotty's birthday cake to be picked up and paid for; the Weisses are full of anxiety as they hope for what they do not see in their coma-bound young son; and the medical staff impatiently searches for answers. All of Carver's characters are hopeful, but none is patient. So it is with most of our members.

Pastors, like the apostle Paul, know that it is no comfort to the faithful to deny present suffering by focusing on the hoped-for future glory. In an ironic way, reflections on the future must be postponed, even as it is the hoped-for future that pulls the Christian through this present time with all its "groaning," pain, "weakness," and "sighs too deep for words." In most pastoral care and conversations, it is not the future but the present that demands our most careful listening as pastors. Pastors do not pass over the present; rather, they pass through it as they face with their flocks the "hardship, distress, persecution, famine, nakedness, peril, and sword" that are named in the compelling crescendo of Romans 8.

As pastors listen and walk with their flocks through the darkest valleys, they boldly claim in faith, hope, and love that the "Spirit helps us in our weakness" (v. 26). This strong assurance comes to the faithful even when "we do not know how to pray as we ought" (v. 26). When we cannot find words, the Spirit, according to Paul, is one with us in our "sighs." The presence of the Spirit in the time of the present suffering is an ever-present reminder that God is present with the faithful always. Paul anticipates fully the work of the Trinity: God searches the heart, loves us in Jesus Christ, and knows the mind of the Spirit. Finally, in our weakness God is present with us in the one "who died, yes, who was raised, who is at the right hand of God, who indeed intercedes for us" (v. 34).

The pastor is likewise one who intercedes—one who both stands with the faithful in their groans and

Exegetical Perspective

Precedents for the interconnectedness of creation and humanity exist in the Jewish Scriptures (see Isa. 24:4–7; Hos. 4:1–3). That God's redemption is not restricted to humanity finds expression in John 3:16, which speaks of God's love for the *kosmos*. Paul has already portrayed creation as a vehicle of divine revelation (Rom. 1:20). Byrne notes rightly that Romans 8:18–22 "offers rich hermeneutic possibilities in view of current concern for the Earth."[2]

Hope (vv. 24–25). Paul specifies (three times) that hope is not dependent on that which is seen (vv. 24b, 24c, 25a). Succinctly put, "hope seen is not hope" (v. 24b). Rather than hoping for what one sees, one hopes for what one does *not* see (vv. 24c–25a).

Paul's understanding of hope is illuminated by his discussion of Abraham (Rom. 4:16–21). Abraham's hope entails trusting (*pisteuō*) God's promise that he will become "the father of many nations," notwithstanding the overwhelming physical evidence to the contrary. Despite his old age and Sarah's barrenness, Abraham was "fully convinced that God was able to do what he had promised" (4:19–20, my translation). Hope thus requires a willingness to risk trusting in that which is not empirically verifiable (God's promise), even when physical evidence suggests that doing so is foolish. One who hopes considers the unseen world of God's promises to be more real (and dependable) than the material world.

Though often maligned in our post-Enlightenment worldview, hope is for Paul a cherished virtue. It occupies pride of place alongside faith and love (see 1 Cor. 13:13; 1 Thess. 1:3). Paul speaks of the "God of hope" and prays that the Romans may "abound in hope by the power of the Holy Spirit" (Rom. 15:13).

The "hope" in 8:22–27 likely refers to the expectations regarding the revelation of the children of God, the potential freedom of creation (vv. 19–21), and "the redemption of our body" (v. 23, my translation). Yet the expectation that these events will occur might prove difficult, given the sufferings mentioned in 8:18. Since hope *is* unseen, it requires endurance (v. 25), two motifs Paul frequently links (Rom. 5:3–4; 15:4; 1 Thess. 1:3). Hope also plays an integral, albeit undefined, role in salvation (v. 24a). This is the only time in Romans that Paul uses the verb "to save" in the past tense (cf. 5:9, 10; 9:27; 10:9, 13; 11:14, 26).

Paul envisions suffering or trials as a necessary prerequisite for hope. The cause-and-effect chain that

Homiletical Perspective

those groans into words, we might articulate a long list of things we are dissatisfied with in our broken world. Any brief review of the current news will give concrete examples: global terrorism, wars raging around the world, sexual exploitation of women and children, modern-day slavery, oppressive regimes, gang crime, drug and alcohol abuse, marital and family distress, incurable diseases, pandemics. It is nearly impossible to state all of the problems to be met by people of faith. Perhaps the best we can do is groan and sigh and hope.

If this is the place we find ourselves, Paul assures us that we are on the right track. We hope for what we have been promised in faith, but do not yet see (v. 24). We pray, but often inarticulately, given the weight of our concerns. When they overwhelm us, the Spirit is there to carry our burdens for us (8:26), interceding with God on our behalf. The Spirit knows both what we need and what God's will is for us. What the Spirit does for us today is to bring our concerns and the will of God into harmony.

On the day of Pentecost, the Holy Spirit was seen as tongues of flame atop the disciples' heads, and was heard both in the sound of a rushing wind and in the outpouring of speech in many languages. Such physical manifestations of the Spirit are uncommon in most places today. They occur occasionally in some churches and in places in the majority world where a first-century type spread of faith is sometimes expressed in extraordinary ways. Witnesses in Africa and Asia, for example, report miracles, exorcisms, and strange abilities of missionaries suddenly to communicate in native tongues without benefit of translators or study of local languages. Many of us would like to witness these pronounced workings of the Spirit. But, like Paul's readers, we may not receive the visible signs of hope that we desire. Hope that is seen, Paul reminds us, is a limited kind of hope, for if we can see manifestations of it, it is certain to be limited to what we are able now to behold. Something greater is in store for believers, something that makes all present groaning and suffering pale in comparison (vv. 18, 24).

Those who preach on this text will be concerned about the location of its promise. At first glance, it seems full of angst: groaning and travail, unfulfilled longing, unseen hope, concerns too deep for words. But the hope here can be put in terms of what Peter Storey[1] has called the *great nevertheless of God*. He

2. Brendan Byrne, *Romans*, Sacra Pagina (Collegeville, MN: Liturgical Press, 1996), 255.

1. See Peter Storey, *With God in the Crucible: Preaching Costly Discipleship* (Nashville: Abingdon Press, 2002).

Romans 8:22-27

Theological Perspective

The Holy Spirit is indeed the presence of God among us. In the Holy Spirit, God becomes our intercessor. The Spirit of God is the power by which God "helps us in our weakness" (v. 26). We are still poor creatures who are powerless before the principalities and powers if the Spirit of God does not enter our hearts and lives. When the Spirit enters our lives, we do not become despondent and passive. We find ourselves given courage and hope. The Spirit empowers us so that we do not resign ourselves to what is, but live in hope for God's future. The Spirit gives us "fresh legs" and lifts us up. The Holy Spirit must be given to us anew every day. We pray that God's Spirit will lift us, straighten us up, and empower us. And we may pray this with the certainty that God will answer us.

If it is clear that we are dependent on the help of the Holy Spirit, then we also must stress that Paul does not write that "it" prays in us, but that when we pray, it is *we* who pray. And then we can understand what Karl Barth wrote about Romans 8:26: "To pray, that is *the* free human action, in which the human concedes the precedence of the freedom of God over its own freedom, but in which the human follows the freedom of God freely." And in this sense the prayer is "the archetype of all human actions of freedom."[2]

EBERHARD BUSCH

Pastoral Perspective

weakness and proclaims the good news of God's future in Jesus Christ, even in the present age. Raymond Carver's short story ends with Scotty's death and a vision of the redemption and wholeness that will characterize God's future. Scotty's grieving, anger-filled parents find redemption and wholeness, at least for a moment, at the bakery in a late afternoon visit with the baker who had been phoning over and over again, requesting that they pick up and pay for Scotty's birthday cake. The baker apologizes for the incessant calls and breaks open a rich dark loaf of bread. Ann and Howard partake of the rich dark bread, and the baker tells them that eating is a "small good thing" in a time of groaning, in a time of "sighs too deep for words." The baker listened to Scotty's parents, and they to him.

As pastors, we are called to sacramental acting and listening when faithful people struggle with living now, as they await a hoped-for future. Hoping for what is not seen, faithful pastors in the present act and listen patiently with courage and proclaim boldly with assurance the good news of Jesus Christ, the one who lived in times like these and who now lives eternally with the God of our future hope.

Denise Levertov in her poem "A Cure of Souls" has written both poignantly and powerfully of the role of the true pastor.[2]

In the poem the pastor's job is to lead the sheep through their mundane lives, though the pastor has also caught an echo of a reality beyond the present—a promise toward which even the most ordinary pastoring always leads. The "bell tolling" is the hoped-for glory. But now, in this time of groaning and sighs, the pastor remembers that the flock is "hungry" and needs "the grass, today and everyday."

J. BARNEY HAWKINS IV

2. Karl Barth, *Kirchliche Dogmatik* I/2, 782. *Church Dogmatics*, I/2, ed. G. W. Bromiley and T. F. Torrance (Edinburgh: T. & T. Clark, 1956), 698.

2. "A Cure of Souls," in Denise Levertov, *O Taste and See* (New York: New Directions Books, 1962).

Exegetical Perspective

ultimately produces hope begins with suffering (5:3–4). That Paul is concerned with suffering in 8:22–27 is clear from 8:18 and 8:35 (cf. 12:12). Turmoil may not always produce hope, but hope cannot emerge apart from it. Paul acknowledges the reality of suffering, yet insists on finding hope in its midst. In doing so, he rejects the extremes of Pollyanna and pessimism as viable options for the community in Rome. Without ignoring the reality of suffering, hope insists that suffering does not have the final word.

The Spirit (vv. 26–27). The Spirit partners with the Romans by assisting in their "weakness" (v. 26a). Though Paul later refers to specific segments of the Roman community as "weak" (see 14:1–2; 15:1), he applies the term here to everyone (including himself), stressing the commonality of "*our* weakness" (cf. Rom. 5:6). Depending on one's translation, such weakness entails either not knowing *how* one ought to pray or not knowing *for what* one ought to pray (v. 26b).

In any case, the Spirit lends assistance by "interceding (*hyperentynchanō*) with unspeakable groanings" (v. 26c). The importance given to the Spirit's role as an intercessor is evident in its repetition by Paul, who notes that the Spirit "intercedes (*entynchanō*) with God on behalf of the saints" (v. 27b). As an advocate for God's children, the Spirit engages in the same activity as Christ Jesus who also "intercedes (*entynchanō*) on our behalf" (Rom. 8:34). Luke Johnson suggests the spirit's intercession (8:27b) may refer either to childbirth imagery (v. 22), the "Abba! Father!" prayer (8:15), or glossolalia.[3]

With its groanings (*stenagmoi*) the Spirit participates in the same activity as creation and God's children (vv. 22, 23, 26). One might say the Spirit sympathizes (in the literal sense of the word) with people and indirectly with creation. As with people and creation, God's Spirit is neither untouched by, nor removed from, experiences of suffering. The Spirit's willingness to "suffer with" coheres with the model of Jesus who suffered also.

Nor does the presence of the Spirit protect God's children from suffering with creation. Paul is adamant that life with the Spirit does not immunize one from suffering: "but even we ourselves, although we have the first fruits of the spirit, *even we ourselves* groan in ourselves" (v. 23), a groaning that may be a tangible expression of the hope to which Paul earlier refers.

MATTHEW S. RINDGE

3. Luke Timothy Johnson, *Reading Romans: A Literary and Theological Commentary* (Macon, GA: Smyth & Helwys, 2001), 140.

Homiletical Perspective

developed this idea while serving as bishop of the Methodist Church in South Africa during the struggle against apartheid. Even while surrounded by the strong-armed agents of repression, Storey knew that the Holy Spirit was active in his nation. The government had all the power; *nevertheless*, God was with the poor in South Africa. The South African regime did not hesitate to use force in order to stop rebellion; *nevertheless*, Storey, along with Desmond Tutu and others, led the black South Africans in a peaceful revolution. The odds were heavily against the peaceful revolution; *nevertheless*, with God on their side, they were victorious. In the end, there was strong temptation to retaliate; *nevertheless*, God gave them a means of forgiving enemies and forming a reconciled nation. No matter what the odds, if God is in something, no obstacle can block the great nevertheless of God.

This passage gives us the same kind of hope. We may live in difficult times; *nevertheless*, God is guiding creation through the pains to a future fulfillment of promise. We do not see the hope that we hold to; *nevertheless*, it is this hope that saves us and for which we are given patience to endure. The Spirit is not always as visibly active in the church as we might desire; *nevertheless*, the Spirit is unceasingly attentive to our pleading, even to the point of bringing our prayers home to God when we are unable to articulate them for ourselves. We may not know what God has in store for us; *nevertheless*, the Spirit knows the mind of God and leads us toward the will of the One who made us for God's own purposes. Such things are promises worth reiterating on the day we celebrate the birth of the church.

CLAYTON J. SCHMIT

John 15:26-27; 16:4b-15

26"When the Advocate comes, whom I will send to you from the Father, the Spirit of truth who comes from the Father, he will testify on my behalf. 27You also are to testify because you have been with me from the beginning. . . .

4b"I did not say these things to you from the beginning, because I was with you. 5But now I am going to him who sent me; yet none of you asks me, 'Where are you going?' 6But because I have said these things to you, sorrow has filled your hearts. 7Nevertheless I tell you the truth: it is to your advantage that I go away, for if I do not go away, the Advocate will not come to you; but if I go, I will send him to you. 8And when he comes, he will prove the world wrong about sin and righteousness and judgment: 9about sin, because they do not believe in me; 10about righteousness, because I am going to the Father and you will see me no longer; 11about judgment, because the ruler of this world has been condemned.

12"I still have many things to say to you, but you cannot bear them now. 13When the Spirit of truth comes, he will guide you into all the truth; for he will not speak on his own, but will speak whatever he hears, and he will declare to you the things that are to come. 14He will glorify me, because he will take what is mine and declare it to you. 15All that the Father has is mine. For this reason I said that he will take what is mine and declare it to you."

Theological Perspective

The promise of the Spirit arises within the context of the collision of the love of God for the world, and the hatred of the world for the love of God. The love of God for the world is first of all present and revealed in Christ, the only Son of God. However, the disciples are chosen by Christ (15:16), and are called to abide in Christ, which will necessarily mean abiding in his love, and the love of the Father for him (15:9). The disciples abide in the love of God and the love of Christ when they love one another, even to the point of laying down their lives out of love (15:12–13). However, by abiding in God's love for Christ and Christ's love for them, the disciples will also share in the world's hatred of Christ, which is ironically the world's hatred of love. Precisely because they believe in Christ and abide in the love of God, the world will hate them, because they no longer love what the world loves, and thus no longer belong to the world (15:19). Thus the love of God for the world is viewed by the world as an attack on itself, on the things that the world values the most. Because the disciples belong to Christ, they will be seen as part of the same attack on the world, and will be hated accordingly (15:20).

Christ promises to send the Spirit of truth to the disciples to strengthen them for the trial and even scandal that this collision will create for them.

Pastoral Perspective

The Promised Helper Comes. One of the losses we humans feel most keenly is that of human companionship. When a person we have been close to leaves "for good," we experience grief and sorrow. In John's Gospel the essence of love is to be connected to and share deeply in the presence and work of Jesus. In Jesus' farewell discourse we see him dealing with the disciples' love and sorrow at his impending departure. Jesus, anticipating the grief they will inevitably feel, prepares the disciples for his return to the Father. Although it is time for him to leave them physically, he will continue to be with them spiritually through the presence of the Holy Spirit. The language used to describe this person is full of significance—Paraclete, Advocate, Helper, Comforter—One who by coming alongside gives strength, encouragement, and ability. Our text divides into three sections, each emphasizing a particular aspect of the work of the promised helper.

Truth-Telling Witness (15:26–27). The One who will replace Jesus' physical presence in the world will be the "Spirit of truth" who will speak truthfully and bear testimony on his behalf. Because the Spirit, sent by Jesus, will come from the Father, he will continue the work of both Father and Son. What he says will be precisely what Father and Son have said. He will

Exegetical Perspective

The Spirit, Pentecost, and Easter. We are totally dependent on Luke's story in Acts 2:1–21 for the specific account of Pentecost Sunday. Among NT writers, only Luke tells of the empowering gift of the Holy Spirit at the Jewish festival of Pentecost. Several NT writers speak of the Holy Spirit, including Paul in Romans 8:22–27 and John in our text, but none of them refers to Pentecost. The differences point to the rich diversity of NT descriptions of the Spirit.

In John, Jesus gives the Spirit to the disciples, not on Pentecost but on Easter, when the risen Christ breathes on them and tells them, "Receive the Holy Spirit" (John 20:22), empowering them for mission. This story resonates with Genesis's description of God's breathing "into [human] nostrils the breath of life" (Gen. 2:7). Jesus promises the disciples the Spirit at his Last Supper (John 14–16). It would be well for the preacher to read through all of these chapters to see the full literary context of our text. In these chapters Jesus explains the purpose of the Spirit before breathing the Spirit on them on Easter day. A wordplay on *pneuma* occurs with its multiple meanings as spirit, breath, and wind (note John 3:8).

John's Unique Name for the Spirit. Except for 1 John 2:1, John's Gospel is the only place in the NT to employ the name "Advocate" (*paraklētos*), sometimes

Homiletical Perspective

Because Pentecost is the occasion when the church celebrates the coming of the Holy Spirit, we are tempted to read these verses from the Gospel according to John too quickly, as if we know their subject already. We could easily say that the Holy Spirit is promised to the followers of Christ, that the wind that blows through and animates the church was given on this day in history and is promised to all members of the church. But such a claim would be a superficial reading, superimposing the overall New Testament picture of the Spirit on a passage that presents a unique aspect of the Holy Spirit, the Paraclete.[1]

It is an oversimplification of this text to equate the Spirit of truth, the Paraclete, with the Holy Spirit. The Paraclete is the Holy Spirit in a special, personal role. The Paraclete is the presence of Jesus when Jesus is absent. "It is to your advantage that I go away," said Jesus, "for if I do not go away, the Paraclete will not come to you" (John 16:7). Had we been there, we might have argued that Jesus' absence is no advantage at all; for we know all too well what

---

1. As Raymond E. Brown notes: "[T]he Johannine portrait of the Paraclete cannot be simply equated with the general NT picture of the Spirit—the Paraclete is the Spirit under a particular aspect" (*Gospel according to John XIII–XXI*, Anchor Bible 29a [New York: Double Day, 1999], 699); and "[t]his does not mean that the Paraclete is simply the same as the Holy Spirit" (1140).

John 15:26-27, 16:4b-15

Theological Perspective

Without the Spirit, the disciples will not be able to stand with Jesus when his collision with the world comes to its fruition in his condemnation and crucifixion, for even Peter will deny that he belongs to Christ (18:15–27). However, the Spirit will not be given to them to comfort them in light of this betrayal and abandonment, but will rather thrust them out into the world to bear witness to Christ, thereby engendering the same hatred for themselves that was directed toward Christ. The Holy Spirit does not override human agency of the disciples, but actually sets it in motion, so that they are able to testify to Christ in spite of the world's resistance, opposition, and hatred, having clearly experienced the truth that without the Spirit they could only betray, deny, and abandon Christ, through fear of the world's animosity.

The lectionary leaves out a crucial aspect of the conflict that will be perpetuated by the testimony of the Spirit, one that will give rise to the possibility of offense for the disciples; that is their excommunication from the synagogues (16:2). The Spirit will not protect the disciples from this opposition, but by powerful testimony will actually lead their opponents to destroy them to protect the true worship of God (16:2). The expulsion of the disciples from the synagogues should raise a permanent possibility of offense for all subsequent believers, for how can Christ be the revelation of the love of God for the world if his own people reject him and his followers? Unfortunately, the possibility of offense has grown even more since that day, as Christians have expelled one another from their own communities of worship and have even killed one another as an act of worship to God, all in the name of the love of God in Christ, and all in the power of the Spirit of truth. How are we to understand the testimony of the Spirit of truth today, when the testimony of Christians arouses the opposition and hatred, not only of the world, but of countless other Christian communities?

Christ goes on to add to the anxiety and sorrow of the disciples by telling them that he is going to return to God and will no longer be with them (16:5). However, he assures them that it is to their advantage that he goes away, for if he did not, he could not send the Spirit to them. However, once again the Spirit does not protect the disciples from the hatred of the world, but further provokes it, by attacking the very values by which the world secures for itself its highest life and meaning. The greatest sin is not to violate the laws and ideals that the

Pastoral Perspective

strengthen the community of believers and enable them to speak the truth about what they have experienced of Jesus the Son. The testimony of the Spirit within the disciples and in the community of the church will empower them to testify in word and deed to what they have witnessed in the life of Jesus from the very beginning.

From Grief to Prophetic Proclamation (16:4b–11). Jesus does not fail to acknowledge the sorrow and pain of his disciples. However, Jesus argues that his leaving has its advantages. Far from being all bad, his departure will give room for a greater engagement with the whole world. Although the community of faith may initially grieve the loss of his physical presence, they will be imbued with power from on high and will become a courageous community unafraid to confront the world with the truth of the Word of God. There are three areas of confrontation between the community of faith and the world. Each is theological, having to do with the truth of the Word of God: sin, righteousness, and judgment.

Sin is not so much a moral failure as a theological one. As in the garden Adam and Eve chose not to believe the word of God, so in the world sin lies in our human failure to believe the word of God. *Righteousness* also is not so much a moral as a theological category. The truth of the Word of God is seen in the vindication of Jesus. Unbelieving eyes see his death as a defeat. However, the eyes of faith see his resurrection as a vindication, a victory over the world, made known by his promised triumphal return to and embrace by the Father, who sent him into the world in the first place. *Judgment* has to do with who has the ultimate and final say—the power of evil in the world or God. In Jesus' life, death, and especially his resurrection, the eyes of faith can see the overthrow of the power of evil. The ultimate truth is made plain, even before the end of time. The Spirit of truth will not only help the believing community see and understand these ultimate truths, but also impart the courage to bear witness to them before an unbelieving world. The Promised Helper will inspire spiritual insight and moral courage. Throughout history, when people of faith have seen truth that others cannot see, they have often found the grace to courageously live and bear witness to it. Such courage is inspired by the Holy Spirit.

The Helper as the Teacher Who Has More to Give from the Same Source (16:12–15). The Blessed Paraclete is the link that keeps alive the relationship

translated "Counselor" or "Comforter." The literal translation is "one called alongside" to take Jesus' place after his physical absence and to testify on Jesus' behalf. Jesus says, "I will ask the Father, and he will give you another Advocate, to be with you forever. This is the Spirit of truth. . . . You know him, because he abides with you, and he will be in you. . . . [T]he Advocate, the Holy Spirit, whom the Father will send in my name, will teach you everything, and remind you of all that I have said to you" (John 14:16–17, 26). In our text he says, "When the Advocate comes, whom I will send to you from the Father, the Spirit of truth who comes from the Father, he will testify on my behalf" (John 15:26). "I tell you the truth: it is to your advantage that I go away, for if I do not go away, the Advocate will not come to you; but if I go, I will send him to you" (John 16:7).

John's Historical Context. When the Gospel of John was written, probably toward the end of the first century, the prior, first generation of Christians had expected the final coming of Jesus and the end of the world in their time. It did not happen. The second generation, including all of the Gospel writers, had to deal with this disappointment, each in their respective contexts. How long would they have to wait for Jesus' coming? John's answer is the Advocate, the Holy Spirit, the Spirit of truth. Jesus' disciples do not have to live with Jesus' absence. The Spirit brings his presence every day and continues the task of interpreting him in new historical settings. Jesus says, "I will not leave you orphaned; I am coming to you. . . . Those who love me will keep my word, and my Father will love them, and we will come to them and make our home with them" (John 14:18, 23; the same Greek word, *monē*, is translated "home" here and "dwelling place" in John 14:2). John has a twofold understanding. On the one hand, the Spirit overcomes the distant past by making the historical Jesus present for John's community. On the other hand, the Spirit overcomes the distant future by making the not yet of Jesus' coming already present.

The Work of the Spirit of Truth. John defines the Advocate as the Spirit of truth (see John 14:17; 15:26; 16:13). John's Gospel uses the word truth (*alētheia*) at least twenty-five times and defines Jesus himself as the truth (John 14:6). In our text Jesus says, "When the Spirit of truth comes, he will guide you into all the truth. . . . He will glorify me, because he will take what is mine and declare it to you" (John

life without him is like. But Jesus is assuring us that he will indeed remain alive in the community, and not just in the community. Rather, the Paraclete will be Jesus' presence in the individual Christian. Jesus is promising to send the Spirit of truth to make a home within us, to become, as Brown notes, "a way of life or something that penetrates [our] very being."[2] How, then, might we describe the turn toward a new direction for gospel living, the calling to discover what is deepest in the human soul in order to find God in the midst of life?

A summons to a way of life that allows the Spirit of truth to penetrate our very being is a call to a continuous process of *alētheia*, the Greek name for truth. *Alētheia* means unconcealing, uncovering such as is done in theological reflection, an art that one could argue is 5 percent our effort and 95 percent the guidance of the Paraclete. Such an effort on our part requires openness to learning the truth and personal engagement with the mystery of grace, an attitude of receptivity and a sense of awe. The trouble is, we live in a culture that offers us little assistance in the art of seeking truth and grace in life.

Some would contend that in this country there is very little schooling that is education in its primary sense of leading or drawing out. What we do instead is plaster over—not *un*covering but covering a topic. Learning must be useful, many say; education is for employment, they go on; instruction in the arts is superfluous, so funding for art and music is slashed when public school budgets must be tightened. At best our Puritan work ethic and the spirit of capitalism that ethic engenders have shaped the cultural values of our nation from its beginnings, but that work ethic also has a tendency to take a practical view of all learning. For example, how many women have listened to Mozart while pregnant because they were told that the complexity of Mozart's music would be good for the brain development of their unborn child? Some people have even gone so far as to play Beethoven to stimulate growth in house plants. This functional view of music sees it as useful only because it makes children better at other, *more* useful things.

A revelatory view of art, on the other hand— whether that art be painting or music, creative writing or theological reflection—sees these arts as shafts of light cast on the reality that is God. The revelatory approach to life looks on these modes of unconcealing as forms of truth and sees them not as

2. Ibid., 1138.

John 15:26-27, 16:4b-15

Theological Perspective

human community devises for itself, but to reject the love of God in Christ, which calls us out of the world to seek our security in the love of God alone. Righteousness is not vindicated by success and achievement in this world, but is found in the apparent defeat of Christ in his death, whereby he returns to the Father. Judgment is not the future vindication of the world's laws and ideals over against its enemies, but rather the decisive defeat of the adversary of God, accomplished already in the crucifixion of Christ.

Christ has more that he would tell the disciples, but he cannot tell them until after he departs, when he will teach them by the Spirit, for only then will they be able to understand (16:12). This does not mean that Christ has more revealed doctrine to teach them later by the Spirit, but rather that he cannot strengthen them in their suffering until they have been taught by that suffering itself, beginning with their abandonment of Christ in his suffering. The Spirit will guide them into the truth that is in Christ by directing them to the future (16:13b). This future is one that promises increasing opposition and hatred for the disciples, but by the Spirit the disciples will abide in the love of God in Christ by loving those who hate them, so that those who now hate Christ may one day come to love him, through the witness of those who once denied Christ out of fear, and who are now willing to lay down their lives for Christ out of love.

RANDALL C. ZACHMAN

Pastoral Perspective

between the past and the future. The Holy Spirit connects the creative genius of the Father with the redemptive love of the Son and the courageous witness of the church. There is a bond that keeps history, current experience, and future hope together in Christian faith. Anglican Bishop John V. Taylor described the Holy Spirit as the "Go-between God": the God who connects past and future in a present that is full of meaning. For Taylor, what is spiritual about us is our capacity for relationship that lies at the heart of our being.

There were things Jesus wished to share with the disciples that they were not yet ready to receive. These things are not out of character with what he did share. However, part of the work of the Spirit has been to continue the work of Christ through the life of the church. The Spirit still speaks through the church and people of faith. This living word of God glorifies Christ in that it is an elaboration and application of the life and word of Jesus, not a contradiction or denial of it. The Spirit will help make plain and visible the presence of God in the church and the world. The life-giving presence of God manifest in creation, reestablished in the life and death of Christ, will be seen and heard anew in the church through the power of the Spirit. The community of Christ's faithful people will be connected to God and one another by the Spirit's work of guiding, leading, revealing, and reminding. Through the power and presence of the Spirit, the church is enabled to be a faithful witness to the presence of God. Through the enabling presence of the Spirit, every need for care and support we have in all of life's difficult and painful circumstances can be met. The church can draw upon the empowering presence of the Spirit to be a community that cares for and supports all persons in their times of need.

EMMANUEL Y. LARTEY

16:13–14). The Gospel of John is itself a product of the continuing work of the Spirit—the Paraclete, guiding disciples into and glorifying the truth in Jesus. What is the heart of the truth in him? When Pilate asks Jesus, "What is truth?" (John 18:38), Jesus gives no verbal response. The answer is the glory (*doxa*) of the cross, the self-giving love of God for the world (note John 3:16). The truth is not finally verbal proclamation but God's loving action, unfolded in John's Gospel until the final "It is finished!" of the cross (John 19:30).

The work of the Spirit of truth confronts misunderstandings of "sin and righteousness and judgment" (*hamartia, dikaiosynē, krisis,* John 16:8–11). The Spirit confronts the world with the sin (singular) of not receiving the love of God at work in Jesus, of not recognizing God's right-making work (i.e., God's righteousness) and the integrity of relationship between God and Jesus, and of not realizing that what God has done in Jesus brings judgment (*krisis*), a crisis of decision condemning the world's choice of evil (see John 12:31 and John 3:19).

A Concluding Word. Our text speaks powerfully about the work of the Spirit of truth. But what are the disciples to do? Jesus says that when the Spirit of truth comes, "he will testify on my behalf. . . .You also are to testify because you have been with me from the beginning" (John 15:26–27). Because Jesus will breathe the Spirit upon them at Easter, the Spirit's testimony will be theirs as well, and it is a testimony that includes loving action (see John 15:12–17).

PAUL L. HAMMER

just affirmative and pretty, not as commercially viable, but as visions of reality so deep as to reflect some aspects of God. The image given vivid expression by the painter's stroke of color forms truth. The tone emerging from silence that brings into being the sound conceptualized by the music's original composer is truth. The life unveiled by the pen of a creative writer is a sketch of creation, an etching of the nature of God. So too with the art of theological reflection: theological reflection requires the rehearsal of the language and practices of the Christian faith in such a way as to open oneself to the place where "deep calleth unto deep" (Ps. 42:7 KJV).

Scientists too speak of awareness of something deep within reality that cannot be reached by rational analysis alone; but whatever the form of revelation in our present age, Jesus has promised that the Spirit of truth will guide us into all the truth, to a deeper understanding of the fundamental reality that underlies perceived experience.

The individual who strives to discover what is deepest in the human soul in order to find God in the midst of life finds the answer to the struggle for meaning in Jesus, who is the way, the truth, and the life (John 14:6). Jesus is not with us now; but while he is with the Father, he has left with us his presence in the person of the Paraclete, the Spirit of truth. It is the Spirit of truth who guides each generation along that way to uncover the grace and beauty in life. It is the Spirit of truth who teaches us to find God in the midst of life, to see life as Jesus taught us to see. It is the Spirit of truth who speaks in our hearts the presence of Jesus. And with that Presence we can indeed glorify God.

JUDITH M. MCDANIEL

TRINITY SUNDAY

Isaiah 6:1-8

[1]In the year that King Uzziah died, I saw the Lord sitting on a throne, high and lofty; and the hem of his robe filled the temple. [2]Seraphs were in attendance above him; each had six wings: with two they covered their faces, and with two they covered their feet, and with two they flew. [3]And one called to another and said:

"Holy, holy, holy is the LORD of hosts;
the whole earth is full of his glory."

[4]The pivots on the thresholds shook at the voices of those who called, and the house filled with smoke. [5]And I said: "Woe is me! I am lost, for I am a man of unclean lips, and I live among a people of unclean lips; yet my eyes have seen the King, the LORD of hosts!"
[6]Then one of the seraphs flew to me, holding a live coal that had been taken from the altar with a pair of tongs. [7]The seraph touched my mouth with it and said: "Now that this has touched your lips, your guilt has departed and your sin is blotted out." [8]Then I heard the voice of the Lord saying, "Whom shall I send, and who will go for us?" And I said, "Here am I; send me!"

Theological Perspective

Isaiah's dramatic temple vision is rich with theological meanings. The passage can be approached from many angles. At points, Calvin used it to deal with God's incomprehensibility, the Trinity, the nature of proper worship, the mystery of election and reprobation, and the authority of the church in the Old and New Testaments.[1]

Church lectionary use of this passage for Trinity Sunday appropriately focuses on the theological aspects of the Christian doctrine to which Isaiah 6:1–8 points. The traditional hymn "Holy, Holy, Holy! Lord God Almighty!" echoes the continuing praise of the seraphs who use this "threefold *sanctus*" to worship the "thrice holy" God whom Isaiah encounters in the temple. The hymn cements the connection with the Trinity through the twice-repeated line: "God in three persons, blessed Trinity."[2]

The Trinity. The doctrine of the Trinity is notoriously hard to understand. It is a human attempt to explain who the Christian church has understood God to be, on the basis of Scripture. The biblical bases for the doctrine are important. They

1. See David Steinmetz, *Calvin in Context* (New York: Oxford University Press, 1995), 97.
2. *The Presbyterian Hymnal*, ed. LindaJo H. McKim (Louisville, KY: Westminster/John Knox Press, 1990), #138.

Pastoral Perspective

Preaching on Trinity Sunday is a challenge. How can we even begin to describe the mysterious dynamic of God's inner being? Even more important, how can we make it seem relevant to the everyday lives of our listeners? Trinity Sunday invites us to attend to many facets of God's nature, but it is probably best to focus on only one of them. The text from Isaiah 6:1–8 emphasizes God's radical holiness. In his vision Isaiah encounters the first person of the Trinity, the Lord of Hosts, the Divine Other lifted so high in glory and splendor that even the seraphs must cover their faces. "Holy, holy, holy is the LORD of hosts;" they proclaim, "the whole earth is full of [God's] glory."

These first eight verses of chapter 6 describe one of the best known of Isaiah's prophetic visions. Summoned to the throne of God and surrounded by the awe and terror of the Lord, Isaiah is struck with the realization of his own unworthiness and that of his people. He is not worthy to stand before the Lord, yet here he is in the presence of the Lord. He knows he is unworthy to serve, yet what other option does he have here at the throne of God? This is not the time to say no; it is the time, in Isaiah's words, to say woe. "Woe is me! I am lost." There is a deep mystery at work here, and it profoundly upsets Isaiah's equilibrium. But in the upsetting, Isaiah is

Exegetical Perspective

Literary-Rhetorical Context. Isaiah 6 reports a vision in which the prophet is commissioned to deliver a message—a prophecy that will keep Judah from recognizing what really threatens them, so that they will inevitably suffer the consequences as YHWH's judgment. The fulfillment of this prophecy is described in Isaiah 7–8, as Isaiah fails to convince Judah that the danger seemingly posed by their neighbors will soon fade. If they overreact, they will set in motion Judah's eventual destruction by a far more dangerous and distant foe. Only a small remnant will be spared to begin anew when this enemy is finally ousted. The text presupposes readers who know that these things have happened. It models for them how to recognize authentic revelations of God's involvement in potentially confusing historical situations, defining a pattern of divine action that subsequent sections of the book see recapitulated in events long after Isaiah's time.

Historical Context. Isaiah saw this vision "in the year that King Uzziah died," about 740 BCE. This may have initiated his prophetic calling. In any case, it was a formative event in the earliest phase of his prophetic career. During the reign of Uzziah's son Jotham (742–735), Syria and Israel began to make advances against Judah (2 Kgs. 15:37). These culminated in the

Homiletical Perspective

Ministers gravitate to this text on Trinity Sunday like a compass spinning to true north. It is a paradigmatic call story within the Old Testament in which preachers—no matter how many times we read it and preach from it—discover afresh the mystery, power, and surrender at the heart of our vocation.

There in the temple with Isaiah, in fear and trembling, we lift our eyes to behold "the LORD sitting on a throne, high and lofty" (v. 1). Seeing the angels attending God, hearing their voices echo around the cavernous sanctuary ("Holy, holy, holy is the LORD of hosts"), sensing in our joints the shaking of the foundations, and smelling the smoke upon the altar, we come undone. Before this God we cry out our unworthiness among an unworthy people. Cleansed of our guilt, we hear the very voice of God, "Whom shall I send, and who will go for us?" (v. 8). Stunned, stammering, pushing the words of response out through our burned lips, we yield, "Here am I; send me." God calls. That's scary enough. We answer, and the real trouble begins.

The faithful frequently wonder about vocation. How does God call the believer? How does one listen for the call of God, and how do we know if what we hear is the voice of God? Preachers can fashion a sermon from this text around the holiness of the call

Isaiah 6:1-8

Theological Perspective

are pointers to what the church has been led to say in confessing that God is one and that this one God is three persons at the same time: Father, Son, and Holy Spirit. As the church hammered out this doctrine through the early centuries, a number of theological statements were proposed—many of which were rejected as not expressing what the church believed to be the biblical witness to God. These statements often did not safeguard what the church considered most important: that God is "one"—over against all forms of "polytheism" or the establishing of rival (or dueling!) gods; and that God is known to us in three persons—distinguishing God's eternal being as Father, Son, and Holy Spirit, all of whom are equally "God" and who, biblically and historically, are distinctively at work in the world. God's work in "three persons" is still the work of the "one God," since the Godhead cannot be "divided" or "separated." The three are one; the One is three. God is one God in three persons. How this is possible, is a mystery. Yet the church affirms the Trinity as its basic belief about God.

Isaiah's Vision. From early times, this passage has been viewed as pointing to what later became the Christian doctrine of the Trinity. The passage itself, of course, does not "lay out" a full-fledged view of God as eternally existing as three coequal persons. But taken with other biblical passages (especially from the New Testament) it anticipates what the early church gradually came to understand as the doctrine of the Trinity, given expression at the Council of Nicaea (325 CE).

There are references to Isaiah 6 in the New Testament. Christian interpreters believed the evangelist in John 12:39–41 regarded the revelation of God in the temple to Isaiah as being in some sense a revelation of Christ (John 12:41). Paul is said to regard the voice speaking to Isaiah as the voice of the Holy Spirit (Acts 28:25). Given these canonical connections, interpreters have seen Trinitarian "pointers" in the Isaiah passage. These dimensions are coupled with the question posed by the Lord, "Whom shall I send, and who will go for us?" (Isa. 6:8). This is reminiscent of the use of the plural in the creation account: "Let us make humankind in our image" (Gen. 1:26).

Theological Interpretation. Calvin's handling of these issues is instructive. In his commentary on Isaiah, he linked the revelation of the Lord to a vision of Christ (as with John 12:41) but did not favor applying this

Pastoral Perspective

able to confess his sin, be cleansed of his guilt, and receive a clean heart. Only then can he hear God's call with clarity.

Isaiah's vision is intended for earthly readers just like us, and the narrative accentuates at least three characteristics of God's relationship with us: God encounters us in our historical context, God's word is revealed in our worship, and God calls us to serve.

First, the importance of Isaiah's own particular context is noted in the very first verse: he receives the vision in the year that King Uzziah died. According to 2 Chronicles 26, Uzziah was the king who ruled Judah for fifty-two years, bringing the kingdom to new heights of economic prosperity, military power, and political influence. But Uzziah forgot that he was an earthly king. He challenged the sacred worship of the temple and lost. As mighty as he was, Uzziah was no match for the Lord, and his arrogance led to his death.

Prophets are often called to speak the word of the Lord to those who have forgotten the distinction between holy and human. The sudden shift from the historical reference to Uzziah to the heavenly throne of God is meant to set us on edge: God is holy; we are not. This is the sad realization that hits Isaiah with such overwhelming force. We are sinners, we dwell among sinners, and we live in sin-filled times. Too often we do not recognize this until it is forced upon us, and there is nothing like an encounter with the divine to shatter our self-centeredness and bring us to our knees in lament. Yet it is this realization that opens Isaiah to the possibility of forgiveness. He is touched by divine intervention and made clean. Isaiah is now free to answer when God calls.

Second, Isaiah's journey through confession, forgiveness, and commission occurs in the context of the worship of the Holy. Isaiah describes the Lord of Hosts as completely and divinely Other, the God who alone is worthy of eternal adoration, glory, and praise. Other prophets have had similar visions at the foot of God's throne (1 Kgs. 22, Ezek. 1–2, Rev. 4), and all share a similar theme: wherever God dwells, there is worship; God's praise never ceases. In the Christian faith, we understand our worship to be a place where God is revealed to us through Word and sacrament. Indeed, the order of our Lord's Day worship is similar to that of Isaiah's experience before the Lord. We come together to praise the almighty God, confess our sin, and seek forgiveness. We ask God to allow us to hear the Word with discernment and respond to the good news. Our worship matters, just as it matters in the courts of heaven. The elements of our worship—gathering,

Exegetical Perspective

Syro-Ephraimite crisis of 735, as Jotham's son Ahaz began his reign (735–715).

Isaiah tried to convince Ahaz to resist these advances, but Ahaz decided instead to rely on Assyria. This superpower invaded and defeated Syria and Israel, thus relieving Judah of any threat from these neighbors, but also imposed on Judah an alliance that eventually soured. During the reign of Ahaz's successor Hezekiah (715–687/6) Assyria invaded and took nearly all of Judah, but mysteriously abandoned its siege of Jerusalem midcourse, so that the city did not fall (2 Kgs. 18:13–19:27). In hindsight all this was seen as fulfillment of Isaiah's prophecy that Judah would not perceive the real stakes in the Syro-Ephraimite crisis, and that this would finally result in their destruction by the Assyrians—all but a small remnant in Jerusalem. YHWH would then take hegemony from the Assyrians, so that this remnant could grow and prosper.

This retrospective interpretation of the events leading up to the retreat of the Assyrians, in light of Isaiah's prophecy, provided a template for the interpretation of subsequent events by editors who added to the book of Isaiah. Isaiah himself had analyzed YHWH's involvement in the near-but-not-total destruction of Judah by the Assyrians at the end of the eighth century. This became the analogy by which later editors analyzed YHWH's involvement in the similarly near-but-not-total destruction of Judah by the Babylonians in the sixth century (Isa. 36–55). Thus the commission in Isaiah 40:1–11 to prophesy the return of the exiles echoes in key respects the commission in Isaiah 6:1–13 to prophesy that restoration is possible after a remnant endures Judah's desolation and exile.

The Scene (vv. 1–4). Jerusalem's royal temple is imagined as the earthly representation of YHWH's heavenly throne. Because the temple is the axial point at which heaven and earth come together, Isaiah can see from this location into the throne room above. Isaiah is surrounded by the smoke from burning sacrifices and incense, and by the noise from a festive throng of worshipers. This mirrors the praise of the heavenly attendants—represented by the seraphim—that surround YHWH's throne (cf. Ps. 29:1–2, 9b–10).

Such imagery connotes power structures that define the world order. The throne and the royal term used for "temple" (*hêkal*) imply the political power exercised by the Davidic king as YHWH's vice-regent (cf. Ps. 2). The "holiness" and all-pervasive "glory" attributed to "YHWH of hosts" reflect the priestly power that maintains sacred space and regulates its

Homiletical Perspective

as reported in Isaiah but sifted through the minister's own personal experience. The sermon, if carefully constructed, invites the congregation to hear and see in the Isaiah account how God calls the believer: from an awareness of the mysterious (and frightening) presence of God, to conviction and confession of sin, to reception of forgiveness, and, finally, to surrender to God's direction. This is not to say that God's call and our response always takes this identical shape. But Isaiah's report and the many that have followed, from Paul on the Damascus road to Augustine in the garden, suggest a pattern that some contemporary listeners will find instructive. It may possibly change the life of someone in the congregation if the hearer, like the preacher, finds herself personally addressed.

Commentaries rightly note that worship is the setting of Isaiah's call. Belief, theology, and vocational calling take wing out of worship. Isaiah's call in worship invites a sermon that that attunes the listeners to the voice of God who speaks throughout Christian worship, not just in the sermon. Preachers who value the sermon as a piece within the whole of Christian worship will find a wealth of material to develop a teaching sermon on worship as the meeting ground between God and humanity. [1]

Some biblical scholars interpret verse 8—"Whom shall I send, and who will go for us?"—as indicative of the triune nature of God. Since this is the designated text for Trinity Sunday, the First Sunday after Pentecost, preachers may elect to interpret the passage through the lens of this Christian doctrine. If so, the responsible preacher will need to work hard to bring down to earth this abstract yet theologically central doctrine of the faith. If we are not careful, the richness of the Isaiah call story within its original Jewish setting could be lost among the philosophical thickets that surround the Christian interpretation of the Trinity.

While the lectionary text ends with verse 8, the preacher knows that the verses that follow (vv. 9–13) get Isaiah into a mess of trouble. Rather than a call to a settled ministry, God summons Isaiah to prophetic engagement with faithless Israel. By the end of chapter 6, God commands Isaiah to prophesy until Israel lies in "waste" and "the land is utterly desolate." Like a scene from Cormac McCarthy's apocalyptic novel, *The Road*, all is destruction except

1. See Geoffrey Wainwright, *Doxology: The Praise of God in Worship, Doctrine, and Life* (New York: Oxford University Press, 1984); Marva J. Dawn, *A Royal Waste of Time: The Splendor of Worshiping God and Being Church for the World* (Grand Rapids: Eerdmans, 1999).

Isaiah 6:1-8

Theological Perspective

unequivocally, since he believed that Christ is the "image" of the invisible God (Col. 1:15; cf. John 14:9). The revelation of God to Isaiah somehow involves the whole Trinity. Calvin recognized that ancient interpreters saw the "Holy, holy, holy" (Isa. 6:3) language as "proving" the Trinity. Yet while he had no doubt the seraphs are describing one God in three persons, he believed there are more compelling passages that should be used to indicate the doctrine of the Trinity. Calvin did not want to argue the Trinity on the basis of the Isaiah passage, because "heretics," he said, can provide other explanations for this language. Calvin did, however, approve of interpreting the phrase "Who will go for us?" as pointing to the three persons of the Godhead.

What is instructive here, from Calvin, is to recognize a relationship between the biblical texts (Old Testament) and Christian doctrine (the Trinity). To appropriate this Isaiah passage for Trinity Sunday in the Christian church is to see that the context for the passage is not just the theology of the book of Isaiah, or the theology of Isaiah as reinterpreted in the New Testament. Rather, it is, as David Steinmetz has written, "the theology of the Christian church in the whole sweep of its historical development. God did not become a Trinity at the Council of Nicaea, though Nicaea clarified what had always been true." The God whom Isaiah encountered "was and is one God eternally subsisting in three Persons. Therefore it is not anachronistic to detect hints of the Trinitarian nature of God in the vision of Isaiah. . . . it is simply sound exegesis. The hermeneutical key to the Old Testament is the *regula fidei* [rule of faith] of the Christian church."[3]

A sermon on the doctrine of the Trinity can refer to the Isaiah passage in the same way that the hymn "Holy, Holy, Holy! Lord God Almighty" gathers up the Isaiah images and provides an opportunity for doxology. In preaching, the nature and character of the triune God can be expounded. The vision and call of Isaiah is one illustration of the way the triune God has been at work in history, as attested by the Scriptures. The Isaiah passage does not "prove" the Trinity. Instead it is a witness, pointing to the triune God's revelatory actions in calling Isaiah, and in the continuing biblical story of salvation.

DONALD K. MCKIM

Pastoral Perspective

praising, confessing, praying, hearing, and responding—are all appropriate responses to the holy God who claims us.

Third, Isaiah's encounter with the living God teaches us that there is no way to know God without being changed. That kind of transformation almost always leads to service, to work and witness in God's name. This requires that Christians practice a discipline of prayerful discernment, of listening for God's call in their lives. This is not just an individual endeavor but also the corporate practice of a worshiping community.

Preachers who choose Isaiah as the primary text for the day might want to emphasize the connection of Isaiah's vision with the pattern of our own worship: praise, confession/forgiveness, listening to the Word, and responding to the Word. Hymns, prayers, and litanies would be chosen to follow that movement. The prayer of confession could be written with special attention to Isaiah's lament in verse 5. We are invited, before God, to confess our sin and the sin of the world. We should not be afraid to name the sins of our time, just as Isaiah did when he condemned Judah for her acts of political arrogance, spiritual pride, and economic injustice. But the assurance of pardon should be as strong as, if not stronger than, the confession. Think of the image of the seraph cleansing Isaiah's lips with a live coal. That is how vibrant and powerful God's forgiveness is. God's forgiveness draws us into service rather than away from it. The response to the Word should include prayers of intercession that draw our attention to the needs of the world beyond our own. This Sunday would also be an appropriate time to commission church members to specific ministries and to recognize those who have particular callings within the community of faith.

KRISTIN EMERY SALDINE

---

3. Steinmetz, 105, 106.

Exegetical Perspective

relation to the purity system. The power of male sexual dominance is also implicit in the euphemistic reference to the covered "feet" of the seraphim (i.e., their genitals), and perhaps also in the reference to YHWH's *šûlîm* (NRSV "hem of his robe," v. 1), a term that can be associated with (un)covered genitals (e.g., Jer. 13:22; Nah. 3:5; cf. Exod. 28:33, 34, 42). This convergence of power structures is initially overwhelming but turns out to be short lived.

The Action (vv. 5–8). Seeing all this, Isaiah senses that he has violated a life-threatening taboo (cf. Exod. 33:20; Judg. 13:22). "Unclean lips" is a metaphor—like "uncircumcised lips" (Exod. 6:12, 30)—that likens false speech (e.g., Pss. 12:2–4; 140:3, 9) to a violation of purity rules. Judah is guilty of lies that misrepresent the reality of their situation and Isaiah is therefore unfit to stand in the presence of the Holy One. Because the convergence of political, priestly, and sexual power is so spectacular, Judah has spoken as if their structures had unconditional divine approval. As a Judahite, Isaiah is implicated in this lying, but his own guilt is meta-phorically burned away by the seraph. Thus he can remain in the heavenly assembly and hear the call for a messenger—a call he readily answers. The message reinforces Judah's incomprehension that YHWH will let them be destroyed. Only afterwards will they understand what happened to them. Thus YHWH's power as creator and ruler of the world transcends human structures and wisdom.

Conclusion. Isaiah's vision has significant theological implications. (1) The mythic image of the heavenly council affirms that although God is one, God is not a monad. Divine judgment is a collaborative process. (2) Although divine power is manifest in historically contingent local structures, they are continually sub-ject to the test of whether they truthfully represent God's larger purposes for all creation. (3) God some-times lets people suffer the consequences of their self-delusion to learn how self-deluded they have been. By pondering these cases, God's people can learn to reckon with their capacity for self-delusion in discerning God's intentions.

The mythic image of the heavenly council is the antecedent of trinitarian thinking. By holding the concept of the Trinity accountable to its roots, Christians are reminded that such a notion of God points not to an intellectual conundrum, but to a mysterious divine-human encounter with sociopolitical consequences.

MICHAEL H. FLOYD

Homiletical Perspective

for God's voice through Isaiah.[2] If the preacher decides to incorporate this disturbing second half of chapter 6, she will have no trouble communicating the perils of saying yes to God. She may lead the congregation to confess and lament the destructiveness of contemporary culture and the idolatries of the church before pointing toward the slender shoot of hope in the stump and holy seed of verse 13.

Finally, a different look at the passage suggests another direction. A stumbling block can become a stepping stone in the sermon: God's silence. Whenever we preach about God's call, especially in the dramatic terms of Isaiah 6, it is likely that some within the congregation will feel left out. They are not necessarily skeptics who doubt the veracity of Isaiah-like mystical encounters with the living God, but their own religious experience does not include thunderous voices and winged messengers. In fact, for some of them God is silent. Rather than urge upon them an audible encounter with God, which the preacher cannot manufacture, the sermon might explore the God who dwells in silence—the Holy One who resides in silence before and after Isaiah's call. As Barbara Brown Taylor points out, there are many good reasons why contemporary believers have difficulty hearing God.[3] Some listeners will be reassured by a sermon that tries to clear away the cacophony of contemporary sounds that obscure the voice of God—the jangling of cell phones, the screeds of talk radio, the blasts of wartime, the deafening drones of leaf blowers, and the ugly shouts of partisan politics. When those marauders are named and cleared away, many listeners will be quickened by the quiet, pastoral suggestion that in true silence, the holy God draws near.

G. LEE RAMSEY JR.

2. Cormac McCarthy, *The Road* (New York: Alfred A. Knopf, 2006).
3. Barbara Brown Taylor, *When God Is Silent* (Cambridge, MA: Cowley, 1998).

Psalm 29

¹Ascribe to the LORD, O heavenly beings,
   ascribe to the LORD glory and strength.
²Ascribe to the LORD the glory of his name;
   worship the LORD in holy splendor.

³The voice of the LORD is over the waters;
   the God of glory thunders,
   the LORD, over mighty waters.
⁴The voice of the LORD is powerful;
   the voice of the LORD is full of majesty.

⁵The voice of the LORD breaks the cedars;
   the LORD breaks the cedars of Lebanon.
⁶He makes Lebanon skip like a calf,
   and Sirion like a young wild ox.

Theological Perspective

Out at sea a storm gathers strength, moving across the waters with immense, uncontrollable power. It hits land, and trees snap like matchwood before it. Forests are stripped bare, and mountains shake. The whole earth is caught up in a great elemental convulsion.

It is a scene that arouses a mixture of terror, awe, and wonder: terror, because we know it can destroy us in an instant; awe, because this is totally out of our control; wonder, because we are confronted with something tremendous, majestic, utterly unfathomable.

The grandeur of the storm, the tempestuous energy of the waves, the ferocity of the wind—all are called upon as images, metaphors, evidence. God is like this, says the psalmist. God is *in* this—"the God of glory thunders, the LORD, over mighty waters" (v. 3).

Some claim that this ancient psalm began as a Canaanite hymn to Baal. It is possible. The tempest is no respecter of religion and culture. Even modern, Western societies, cocooned in technology, inoculated against nature, cannot shut out the storm. It breaks in with cataclysmic, world-changing results. Terror, awe, and wonder are universals, they know no boundaries.

But whatever the distant origins of this text, Psalm 29 is not some thinly disguised promotion for

Pastoral Perspective

This majestic hymn-poem is made for reading aloud in the setting of congregational worship, especially on Trinity Sunday. What a wonderful testimony to the Creator-God! The psalm helps to enlarge the picture of God in the other texts for the day and reminds us that the divine power lives in the created world, as well as in the incarnation of Jesus and the sustaining power of the Spirit. The delightful language of the NRSV helps to convey God's rule, to declare in written and spoken word that God, glorious and strong, is enthroned over all of creation and its mighty forces. Finally, the psalm assures us that this God is *our* God.

Certainly, the theme of coronation and kingly power is evident in both the opening and closing stanzas (vv. 1–2, 10–11), in which the Lord YHWH sits in splendor above all other "heavenly beings." All creatures are called to acknowledge the power of YHWH God, and to worship, but the focus of the poem is on the role of YHWH in nature. Our God is a storm God, who resides high above the waters. The Lord's voice thunders with devastating effect. Even stout cedars splinter before the force of its wind, and the ground shakes and rolls beneath. The oak trees whirl and spin in the gale, and their branches are laid bare of leaves by the force of God's voice. The poem's use of alliteration in verse 7 (NRSV) is

^{7}The voice of the Lord flashes forth flames of fire.
^{8}The voice of the Lord shakes the wilderness;
the Lord shakes the wilderness of Kadesh.

^{9}The voice of the Lord causes the oaks to whirl,
and strips the forest bare;
and in his temple all say, "Glory!"

^{10}The Lord sits enthroned over the flood;
the Lord sits enthroned as king forever.
^{11}May the Lord give strength to his people!
May the Lord bless his people with peace!

Exegetical Perspective

Psalm 29 is a hymn to the power (raw power?) of God. The guiding image in the psalm is a thunderstorm that rolls off the Mediterranean Sea onto the coast of Syria-Palestine and then into the wilderness. There is scholarly consensus that this psalm originated outside of Israel and was reworked for use in Israelite worship. This leads some scholars to propose that this hymn is one of the oldest in the Psalter. The hymn could be heard as a polemic against worshipers of Baal, the Canaanite god of weather and fertility. Thunderstorms were thought to be the work of the Canaanite god, but here it is declared over and over again that the storm is "the voice of the Lord." Whether or not the hymn is polemical toward Canaanite religion does not alter the basic message: *The Lord, the God of Israel, is all-powerful and the sovereign God above all beings in heaven and on earth!*

The psalm breaks into three distinct sections: An Invitation to Submissive Worship of the Lord; The Voice of the Lord in the Thunderstorm; A Prayer to Be Heirs of the Lord's Power and Peace.

(A liturgical note: it would be appropriate within the theological framework of the psalm to use verse 10 as a refrain that would be said or sung before verses 1, 3, 5, 7, 10, and then again after verse 11. All the verses of Psalm 29 illustrate the declaration of

Homiletical Perspective

Psalm 29 may be the Psalms' equivalent of T. S. Eliot's *The Wasteland*—not because the poems have similar content, but because neither can be read without footnotes, for both are filled with mythological references. The psalm, most critics agree, is a victory song. The Lord is a storm over the waters, a storm thundering onto the land—breaking the mighty cedars of Lebanon, shattering the mountains to the north, shaking the wilderness to the east.

So the victory is the Lord's over the sea and the land, but it is also a victory over the Canaanites and over their gods. For the sea and the mountains, the forests of cedar and oak, and the wilderness of Kadesh represent those "foreign" gods (the god of the sea, the mountain god, the god of the forest, the wilderness god). The land itself represents these gods. There is even a sense in which the land was theirs before it was the Lord's. At least, it belonged to their people, before the Hebrew people came into the land and dispossessed them. But now they have been dispossessed, because God, the Lord of all things, was *not* on their side.

Does the God of all things take sides? This is one of the questions the psalm raises. And its answer is abundantly clear. It sings praise and thanksgiving to the God who promised to make of Abraham "a great nation," to "bless those who blessed" him and "to

Psalm 29

Theological Perspective

the pagan gods of thunder, fire, and rain. The God proclaimed here is no muscle-bound, testosterone-fueled, force of nature, bellowing incoherently above the storm. This is a psalm soaked in the life-giving paradox of the biblical revelation of God—a God who Christians believe must be understood in Trinitarian terms. It speaks of a being so majestic and transcendent that all creatures in all places are called upon to cry, "Glory!" (vv. 1, 2, 9), yet whose mighty power is also directed towards sustaining, affirming, and blessing human life (vv. 10, 11).

The psalm begins with a celestial vision of God worshiped by the heavenly congregation. Words like "glory," "holy," "strength," and "splendor" are used of the one at the center of the action. They remind us of a similar scene in Isaiah 6:3, where the seraphim call out to one another, "Holy, holy, holy is the Lord of hosts: the whole earth is full of his glory." It is a majestic vision that continues through the epiphany in the storm (vv. 3–9). To catch a glimpse of God in this way is to experience awe. It is to be reminded that we inhabit a world that we did not make, that we are unable to control, and that we cannot dispose of as we wish.

The great Jewish thinker Abraham Heschel thought the recovery of a sense of awe was vital for our civilization: "Forget your sense of awe, let your conceit diminish your ability to revere, and the universe becomes a market-place for you." Awe is much more than a spiritual high, a religious trip, he wrote: "It's a way of understanding, insight into a meaning greater than ourselves."[1]

God is majestic. God is mighty. God is awesome. This much the worshipers of Baal may know. But there is more to the self-revelation of God in Scripture than this, and it is good news. As Karl Barth put it, "God is not imprisoned by his own majesty."[2] Instead of remaining remote from human experience, God has chosen to be alongside us as our redeemer and friend. In Isaiah this God declares: "For thus says the high and lofty one who inhabits eternity, whose name is Holy: I dwell in the high and holy place, and also with those who are contrite and humble in spirit, to revive the spirit of the humble, and to revive the heart of the contrite" (Isa. 57:15). God above us. God with us. God in us and for us.

After the awesome revelation in the storm, the psalm ends, as it begins, around the throne of

Pastoral Perspective

simply too good not to read aloud: "The voice of the Lord flashes forth flames of fire." It needs to be fixed in the imagination of Christians.

The poem is filled with repetitions and parallelisms that increase its cumulative impact on the ear and the mind and heart. The imagery is stunning: lightning flashes, trees explode, the ground heaves like a young calf skipping, the whirling winds strip the trees. These are forces beyond all human power, strength, or imagining. But God wields them with ease. The poem needs to be read aloud in worship, so that its force can be felt as well as heard.

The poem is hypnotic, so powerful aurally that it almost makes us forget the theological implications and questions it raises. To be sure, we mortals stand in awe of a God who is so powerful that even the storms obey. We are drawn to this power, to worship it. We see, many of us, the handiwork of God in the natural world. As we stand at the edge of the ocean and watch the waves, as we look over the edge of the Grand Canyon, as we smell the fragrance in a forest of pines or see mountains climbing from the horizon, we contemplate the immense forces that brought these things to being. We know our finitude in the face of the infinite Creator. As we thank God for the gentle sun and rain and soil that bring forth food from our fields and gardens, as we watch the care with which birds feed their young, as we rejoice in fall colors or fresh snow or spring leaves, we think of the love of God that watches over us through benevolent provision of "brother sun and sister moon." We are drawn to a loving Creator, and we give thanks.

But this psalm also reminds us that these forces are not always so benign. This is not Elijah's God (1 Kgs. 19) of a "still, small voice." In that story, there is no God in the earthquake, wind, or fire, and many times we are driven to a similar understanding. These immense forces also bring destruction and death. Who among us or in our churches has not seen incredible images of the desolation wrought by forces of nature in recent years? Tornados, hurricanes and typhoons, tsunamis, fires, drought, and floods—all raise the specter of an uncaring or capricious God, if God is ruler of all nature. Even the echo of the Genesis flood in verse 10 recalls this reading; the flood that God sent to cleanse the earth, also destroyed.

There is an unavoidable ambiguity to a creator/nature god, especially one of such vast force and power. Sometimes nature blesses. Sometimes it curses. How do we make meaning of that? A God

1. Abraham Joshua Heschel, *Who Is Man?* (Stanford, CA: Stanford University Press, 1965), 88, 89.
2. Karl Barth, *Evangelical Theology: An Introduction*, trans. Grover Foley (Edinburgh: T. & T. Clark, 1979), 10.

Exegetical Perspective

verse 10: *The LORD sits enthroned over the flood; the LORD sits enthroned as king forever.*)

An Invitation to Submissive Worship of the Lord (vv. 1, 2). The hymn begins by demanding submission from all heavenly beings. These "heavenly beings" may be the deposed gods of Baal or perhaps they are angels or the Lord's heavenly council. Whoever these heavenly beings are, the psalmist makes it perfectly clear that they are underlings. The poet says, "Ascribe . . . ascribe . . . ascribe to the LORD glory and strength, . . . the glory of his name." The psalmist declares the unparalleled splendor and glory of this Lord, and the absolute necessity of bowing down in worship before this One who is about to display a torrent of power. These first two verses insist on giving due credit to the Lord, the source of all strength.

These heavenly beings who are called on to ascribe to the Lord glory and strength may be thought of as the seraphs of Isaiah 6, who call to one another, "Holy, holy, holy is the LORD of hosts; the whole earth is full of his glory" (Isa. 6:3).

The Voice of the Lord in the Thunderstorm (vv. 3–9). These verses draw a picture of a storm that gathers over the waters (the Mediterranean Sea) and then moves onto land (Syria-Palestine) with hurricane fury. There is a sevenfold use of the term "The voice of the LORD," which has poetic and literal connotations of claps of thunder. "The voice of the LORD" is of such power that it hovers over the water to harness the energy of the sea, and then "the voice of the LORD breaks the cedars." "The voice of the LORD" is so overwhelming that even the mountains of Lebanon and Sirion (the Phoenician name for Mount Hermon) tremble at the tumult of God's voice (see Ps. 46). "The voice of the LORD flashes" (lightning!), "shakes the wilderness," and "whirls" the oaks and "strips the forest bare." "The voice of the LORD" fills the earth with God's majesty and power and therefore demonstrates the Lord's awesome dominance over all things, even those things that wrought destruction on earth. "The voice of the LORD" causes all the heavenly beings to acknowledge with humble adoration, "Glory!" (v. 9).

The sevenfold repetition of this phrase "The voice of the LORD" may symbolize completion (as in the days of creation, Gen. 1–2). It is also a poetic way of declaring God's control over everything and everyone. It may allude to the slaying of the seven-headed Leviathan, a sea monster of Canaanite mythology. The message is a majestic declaration

Homiletical Perspective

curse the one who cursed" him (Gen. 12:2–3). But the psalm goes on to "up the ante." Having taken sides, does God go to war? And having gone to war, does God *destroy* the enemy? Does the Lord burn the enemy's forests, dynamite his mountain fortresses, and scour the wilderness in which he is forced to flee? Finally, is this how God brings peace to God's people (v. 11)?

The evidence—historical *and* biblical—is (at best) mixed, if victory is the criterion. The bad guys win as often as the good guys. The sons and daughters of Abraham and Isaac and Jacob—of Sarah and Rebekah and Rachel and Leah—receive God's promise, then face famine. They are rescued by Joseph, only to become slaves in Egypt. Led by Moses, they are released from their bondage, but to wander the wilderness. Led by Joshua, they do take the land from the Canaanites, but they are never completely, peacefully settled in it. They are constantly threatened by rumors of war, and war itself makes most of the rumors true. And in those wars, the chosen ones are defeated as often as they are victorious. They are dispossessed of the land and taken into exile. When they come back—those who do come back—they hardly live in peace.

Nor do we, their descendants by adoption. Still there are rumors of wars and still there are wars. Sometimes—often—we war among ourselves, father and son, mother and daughter, brother against brother, sister against sister. Then, is God on our side? When we win *this* war—whichever war it is: the Hundred Years' War, the Franco-Prussian War, the Great War, the Second *World* War, the "war" on terror—will the Lord finally "bless his people with peace"?

In the meantime, what? Do we argue—as we have sometimes argued—that God has actually blessed us with war, because God is on our side? That is right, is it not? Does not the psalm say as much?

Walter Brueggemann's *Theology of the Old Testament* reminds us that if we sing, "The LORD sits enthroned over the flood," we sing the Lord who is over *all*, for in the world picture of the psalmist, the earth is surrounded by the waters that are above and beneath as well as those encompassing the dry land. If we sing "the LORD sits enthroned as king forever," we sing the God that is not only over all but king over always. And if we sing that the Lord *is* king over all and over always, we remember that there can be no other.[1] That does not mean that in our singing

---

1. See the discussion, "Yahweh as King," in Walter Brueggemann, *Theology of the Old Testament: Testimony, Dispute, Advocacy* (Minneapolis: Fortress Press, 1997), 238 ff.

Psalm 29

Theological Perspective

YHWH. And it is now clear that this glory and majesty are not intended to smash, subdue, and subject. They are directed toward men and women for their good and well-being: "May the LORD give strength to his people! May the LORD bless his people with peace!" (v. 11). The peace promised here is not some inner tranquillity or even a cessation of hostilities between warring parties. *Shalom* is more radical and far reaching than that. It is a social and political condition, a state of just and right relationships between people, and with God—a community united in the solidarity of love. The God who sits majestically enthroned above the flood (v. 10) turns all that glory, all that holiness, toward the human race. *God is not imprisoned by majesty.*

The clue to understanding something of the mystery of this paradoxical God surely lies in the central section of the psalm (vv. 3–9) where it is repeatedly stated that the means whereby this awesome power is exercised is "the voice of the LORD" (vv. 3, 4, 5, 7, 8, 9). This is not some primitive way of referring to inexplicable noise, however majestic or awe-inspiring. God's sound is not an animalistic roar or an elemental crash. It's a voice—personal, articulate, demanding, relational. But it is dynamic.

The term takes us right back to Genesis 1. *In the beginning God said, "Let there be!" and there was.* A word is spoken and things spring into being. When God speaks, God acts. To exist, to be, is to obey the command of creation. As Jacques Ellul has pointed out, God creates through that which is "primarily a means of relationship."[3] From the very beginning, the majestic voice of the Lord is not just an explosion of energy. It is an invitation to a relationship.

Psalm 29 bears witness to a God who speaks—creatively, articulately, and meaningfully—and who draws human beings into the conversation. It points to the Trinitarian God who is transcendent *and* immanent, revealed in the earthquake *and* the still, small voice, present at Sinai *and* Bethlehem, Lord of heaven *and* earth.

IWAN RUSSELL-JONES

Pastoral Perspective

who rules over even the storms and the earthquake partakes of that ambiguity, and deeper consideration of Psalm 29 will raise questions in the minds of thinking Christians. They will hear this ambiguity in terms of the larger forces around them, but also in terms of their own and others' individual lives and personal meaning making. As pastors, we should be prepared for someone to be so affected. At the least, we should be honest in reply and acknowledge the ambiguity. Such a God rules and blesses, but bad things happen to good people anyway.

We likely have no final or even satisfying answer to the big questions or to the personal ones. There is a complex relationship between created and Creator around benevolence and evil that has never been settled, within the canon (Job) or outside (Voltaire's *Candide*, among many). The NRSV concludes this psalm with a hopeful petition in verse 11: "May the LORD bless his people with peace." Other translations (KJV, NIV) conclude the psalm on a more assertive note and offer the assurance, "The LORD will bless (or "blesses") his people with peace." This is the reading I prefer, for it offers within the text itself a sense that, despite the ambiguity, God stands with God's people, even in time of trial.

This is a psalm to be read aloud and treasured, as it pronounces God's power, as it raises hard questions, and as it assures us of God's grace, strength, and peace.

MARK MILLER-MCLEMORE

---

3. Jacques Ellul, *The Humiliation of the Word* (Grand Rapids: Eerdmans, 1985), 50.

Exegetical Perspective

through earth-rattling thunder that the Lord of Israel is Lord of all beings in heaven or on earth! There is no heavenly or earthly being who is not under the thumb of the Lord of Israel.

A Prayer to Be Heirs of the Lord's Power and Peace (vv. 10, 11). The thunderstorm described by the poet is a manifestation of God's power. The storm emanates from the waters upon which God sits enthroned in the heavens. God is king over the flood waters; God is sovereign over all things in and above the earth. The Lord is pure power that turns even the home of chaos, the storm and the flood, into a royal seat. The Lord is master of all things in heaven and on earth, both now and forevermore!

Now that the psalmist has established the absolute and overwhelming power of the Lord and the enthronement of the Lord above all beings in heaven and on earth, the poet then prays that God will share some of this thundering power with those whom the Lord has chosen, the people of Israel. For the first time in this psalm, the people of earth are brought into the picture. Heretofore the hymn has demanded adoration from heavenly beings. Now, however, the poet prays to the Lord that the people of God's own choosing be heirs of God's own power and peace. The poet prays that the Lord, who is enthroned over the flood, who is enthroned as king forever, will bless the people with *shalom*. The psalmist trusts that God's power, as awesome and destructive as that power may be, is power that will be used for the well-being of the Lord's people.

ROBERT WARDEN PRIM

Homiletical Perspective

we are removed from the present state of war—wherever that is taking place—in the Middle East or the horn of Africa or fill in the blank. It does not mean that we are uninterested in those places, nor that we, whoever we are, do not have interests in those places and they in us. But so to sing to the Lord is to acknowledge that all our interests—even our *best* interests—are parochial. They are *our* interests, and we place ourselves in peril—because we place our relationship with God in peril—if we identify our interests with God's interests.

We may never be able to avoid that completely. It may simply be too frightening to think, God is *not* on our side; or worse to think, God may be on *their* side. But even as the psalmist sings a song of victory—beat up those cursed Canaanites, yeah!—the psalmist also remembers and stops: Whose is the glory . . . no matter what happens? God is the "king of glory" (Ps. 24). From where does any strength we have come? "God is our refuge and strength" (Ps. 46).

It is that God, who is "enthroned over the flood" and over all, who is "enthroned . . . forever" and over always—it is that God who gives us true strength. May the Lord bless us also with true peace—not as we know peace or even as we wish to know peace, for our peace is always partial and parochial. No, this Trinity Sunday may the Lord bless us with the perfect peace and joy God knows in God's self, Father, Son, and Holy Spirit.

RICHARD S. DIETRICH

Romans 8:12-17

¹²So then, brothers and sisters, we are debtors, not to the flesh, to live according to the flesh— ¹³for if you live according to the flesh, you will die; but if by the Spirit you put to death the deeds of the body, you will live. ¹⁴For all who are led by the Spirit of God are children of God. ¹⁵For you did not receive a spirit of slavery to fall back into fear, but you have received a spirit of adoption. When we cry, "Abba! Father!" ¹⁶it is that very Spirit bearing witness with our spirit that we are children of God, ¹⁷and if children, then heirs, heirs of God and joint heirs with Christ—if, in fact, we suffer with him so that we may also be glorified with him.

Theological Perspective

What a wonderful, great promise that we are allowed to be God's children! "See what love the Father has given us, that we should be called children of God" (1 John 3:1). We should understand this in the right way. We are not told we are deities. We are and remain human beings, and we are all too "human." It is God's kindness that makes us children of God. The same promise was given by God to children in the past and will be given to children in the future. And we live with other children today to whom the same promise is given. What a welcoming experience, when we discover that we and they are all children of God. When we see these others as God's children too, we communicate with them differently. They are for us no longer simply problematic contemporaries, but also children of God. They may behave poorly, but, like us, they are also God's children. They may be a needy people, but they are near us because they are children of God. In a sermon Calvin spoke of his encounter with a stranger and said, Although we could not speak a word with each other, "our Lord shows us today that we will be brothers, because Christ is the peace of the whole world and of all its inhabitants. Therefore we must live together in a family of brothers and sisters, which Christ has founded with his blood."[1]

1. John Calvin, *Sermo Deuteronomium* 125, CO 28, p. 16sq.

Pastoral Perspective

In this summary passage, "So then, brothers and sisters," Paul restates emphatically his earlier assertion that "with my mind I am a slave to the law of God, but with my flesh I am a slave to the law of sin" (Rom. 7:25). Paul bluntly writes that the flesh means death, whereas the Spirit means life. He directs the followers of Jesus in Rome to "put to death the deeds of the body" and to have a relationship with God of adoption not slavery, of acceptance not fear. He reminds those to whom he is writing that, if led by the Spirit of God, they are children of God: "if children, then heirs, heirs of God and joint heirs with Christ" (8:17). Almost as an afterthought, Paul notes that being an heir with Christ will involve glory but first suffering.

In the apostle's theology, there is an "even now," just as there is an end of history. They are not separate, but the end is woven into the even now, the daily life where the faithful struggle with flesh and the Spirit. Ever present for Paul was the suffering of this present age, a suffering embodied and yet longing to be free of the body.

Paul's way of dealing with the problem of flesh and the Spirit may be easier to write about than to live out in pastoral relationships. The war with the flesh is as old as creation, and the people with whom we serve as pastors know the persistent struggle all

Exegetical Perspective

Today's reading is suffused with spirit (*pneuma*) language. Readers of Romans 8:12–17 discover that the Spirit enables us to put to death the deeds of the body (v. 13); that all who are led by God's Spirit are children of God (v. 14); that we have received a spirit of adoption and not one of slavery (v. 15); and that when we cry, "Abba, Father," this same Spirit bears witness with our spirit that we are God's children (v. 16).

Paul's pneumatology has implications for how his readers/hearers are to live. A consequence of God's indwelling Spirit (Rom. 8:9–11) is that Paul and his audience are "debtors *to live* not by the flesh according to flesh" (8:12, my translations). Such living is possible since the Spirit who raised Jesus from the dead "dwells" among Paul's audience, and through this Spirit "the one who raised Christ from the dead will give life" to their bodies (8:11). The new life Paul describes is thus not dependent on moral exertion but on the power of God's indwelling Spirit.

Using a chiasm, Paul describes two divergent types of living: "For if you live according to flesh (*sarx*), you are about to die; but if by spirit you put to death the deeds (*praxeis*) of the body (*sōma*) you will live" (8:13). In light of Romans 8:4b–9a, flesh (*sarx*) is to be understood here as antithetical to Spirit (*pneuma*). Setting one's mind on the flesh is "death," whereas setting one's mind on the Spirit is

Homiletical Perspective

The liturgical concern for Trinity Sunday is the interrelationship of Creator, Redeemer, and Holy Spirit. This lesson gives us one indication of how the Three-in-One work together. First, note that Paul is forcing our hand in terms of traditional language for God. Without our present-day sensitivities to such things, Paul here speaks of God as Father (literally, *Abba*). The role of the first person of the Trinity is as a divine parent. All who believe are sons (and daughters) of God. How so? The Spirit lives in us (8:9) and testifies with and through us (8:16) that we belong to God's family. Having been made children of God by the working of the Spirit, we become siblings to Christ and fellow heirs of all that Christ has. What we inherit is both a share of his glory and his suffering. While this sounds ominous, Paul assures the reader in the verse following this passage that whatever believers may suffer, it pales in comparison with what believers ultimately stand to gain.

One means of dealing homiletically with this passage is to attempt to teach about this rich interplay of divine personages. Yet understanding doctrinal issues is usually not at the top of believers' list of biblical interests. The majority of those who listen to sermons on this day will want to know how these theological ideas relate to the everyday concerns that face them. Fortunately, there is much

Romans 8:12-17

Theological Perspective

Such a claim does not mean we are God's children by nature. God himself has given us this status as a gift. God has elected us and by his Spirit has made us his children. The Holy Spirit is the mysterious presence of God in us and the power by which God opens himself for us and is present in our midst. Without God we are "flesh," Paul says. Without God we are tempted, even seduced, by what surrounds us: secular power, fashion, egoism, wealth or "mammon" (Matt. 6:24). We live in a time in which these temptations are pervasive in every part of our society; for instance, they can be found on every page of the daily newspaper. These temptations lure us to a fatal precipice: "If you live according to the flesh, you will die." What can save us? Only *God*. And when we trust in God and make God the center of our lives, we turn away from "the deeds of the body." We say goodbye to what has governed us until now. We declare that these authorities, these principalities and powers, have lost their power to reign over us. We are no longer led by them; we are led by the Spirit of God.

As the presence of God in the midst of us, God's Spirit connects us to God—not only for a passing moment and at a distance, but eternally and intimately. It is the Spirit who makes us children of God. God's Spirit confers on us the spirit of adopted "sonship," not the spirit of "slavery" in which we "fall back into fear." God's Spirit gives us confidence to live before God as children live with their parents.Then we may address God as "Abba," which means "Dad" or "Mom." But once more: We are not God's children by nature. The Spirit, who makes us God's children, is the Spirit also of the Son of God. Calvin writes: "By the blood of Christ the door was opened; now we are allowed to praise loud and clear that we are God's children. . . . Now the promise is fulllfilled (Hos. 2:25): I will say to them: 'You are my people,' and they will answer: 'Thou art my God.'"[2] It is fulfilled in the One who has prayed in the dark hour in the garden of Gethsemane: "Abba, Father, for you all things are possible" (Mark 14:35). The Holy Spirit gives us the right to address God with the same title. So it is said by Paul, "God has sent the spirit of his Son into our hearts, crying, 'Abba! Father!'" (Gal. 4:6). Now we *may* associate with God in a new and intimate way.

But is this really a possibility? Must we not fall down before God in fear? "For if you will live according to the flesh, you will die." We are *sinners*.

2. John Calvin, Commentary to Rom. 8:15.

Pastoral Perspective

too well. Paul's either/or solution—either the flesh or the Spirit—may not be easy for most people to hear. Is the flesh or the body always bad or evil? Paul's vision of the new life in Christ with its suffering and glory may be a goal for many, but it is far from reality for most. What does it mean to suffer with Christ?

The people we encounter at the front door of the church on Sunday mornings, or as we stand beside a hospital bed, live not fully in the flesh, nor fully in the Spirit of God. Rather, most people who attempt to follow the Christ live with fear and anxiety in between the flesh and the Spirit. Faithful people have heard it said that if we struggle with the flesh and somehow slough it off, then we will be free to live in the life of the Spirit and to become children of God. In sacred texts and sermons we hear over and over again that we are to be one with Christ, a "joint heir" with him before God who is our Father, "Abba."

Daily living, however, often collides with theological truths. What does it mean to live daily as a "joint heir" with Christ? Many of the people with whom we share ministry are not simply slaves to the flesh, nor do they know themselves to be heirs with Christ. It would be easy to feel defeated by Paul's stark contrast between the flesh and the Spirit, the body and the mind; this world—even now—and the next—the end of history and the reign of God. Does Paul's either/or solution leave room for the inevitable conflict that most people have with living in this world and following Jesus Christ? Paul presents pastoral challenges but also offers pastoral hope.

Paul's conclusion that our choice is either the flesh or the Spirit is not very helpful. We are both flesh and the Spirit in this earthly journey. We cannot literally, once and for all, separate ourselves from the world and "put to death the deeds of the body." The apostle's either/or solution leaves no room for ambiguity or for the tension that is at the heart of the Christian life.

Throughout Christian history, there have been individuals and religious groups who have sought to separate themselves from the flesh and from the world in order to be pure, undefiled, and one with the Spirit of God. The hermit approximates the ideal that Paul held up; and the separatist groups, such as the American Shakers, ultimately find that being of this world is an inevitable consequence of being human. Finally, those who take Paul literally and without critique may resort to the end of history, the coming of the Christ, or the rapture as the sure way to solve the problem of the flesh and the Spirit. These are the people who place on their cars the

"life and peace" (8:6). The mind set on the flesh is both "hostile to God" and can neither submit to God's law nor please God (8:7–8). The phrase "about to die" may refer to a physical death, a symbolic one, or both (Paul uses the verb "die" in both senses). Nor is it clear what Paul means by "deeds of the body" (since *sōma* is usually not used negatively in Romans). The textual variant "flesh" (*sarx*), which typically is used negatively, removes the difficulty posed by the ambiguity of *sōma*.

Paul seeks to instill within his readers/hearers an awareness of their identity as children of God. God's children (literally, "sons," *huioi*) are "all who are led by God's Spirit" (8:14). Paul's audience has become God's children by means of a spirit of adoption/sonship (*huiothesia*). Paul contrasts this particular spirit that his addressees "received" (in baptism? cf. Rom. 6:3–8) with a "spirit of slavery" (8:15). Whereas the latter connotes fear, the spirit of adoption enables people to cry out, "Abba! Father!" (8:15). When this cry is uttered, the spirit of adoption "bears witness" with our spirit that "we are children (*tekna*) of God." The status as God's "son" or "child" is significant, given the numerous times Paul refers to Jesus as God's Son (Rom. 1:3, 4, 9; 5:10; 8:3, 29, 32).

The cry "Abba! Father!" likely refers to a specific prayer with which the church in Rome was familiar. If so, Paul encourages his audience to consider their status as God's adopted children each time they cry, "Abba! Father!" Paul similarly connects this same prayer to the status of the Galatians as God's adopted children (Gal. 4:5–7). The Aramaic word *abba* (literally, "daddy") highlights the intimate relationship Paul envisions between God and the church in Rome, an intimacy that precludes fear and a "spirit of slavery."

Being children of God entails unity among members of the community and between this community and Christ. Those who are God's children are also God's heirs and joint heirs with Christ, a relationship made possible by adoption (8:16–17). One sign of unity with Christ is the practice of praying the same prayer ("Abba, Father") Jesus prayed during his time of distress (Mark 14:36).

Unity is also established among members of the church in Rome. Seen within the broader argument in Romans, identity as children of God implies an equal status for Jews and Gentiles. As adopted children, neither group occupies an elevated status over the other. As a sociocultural equalizer between Jews and Gentiles, Paul's metaphor of adoption

to be explored in this text that speaks to the life of believers.

The main thrust of this text is not so much to explicate Trinitarian theology as to draw Paul's readers into the family of God. Note the repetition of these themes: sons (meaning sons and daughters) and sonship, God as Father, believers as God's adopted children, children as heirs of God and coheirs with Christ. Paul's purpose generally in chapter 8 is to explain what it means for Christians to live life through the Spirit. In this pericope, he focuses specifically on the Spirit drawing believers into God's family. This is an issue that is perennially ripe for homiletical exploration.

Everyone senses the need to belong. Psychologists tell us that the most basic human need is for security. Children need to know whom to trust, whom to call "Mommy" or "Daddy," and where they can feel safe. We have heard about those studies showing that orphan babies have died from lack of human contact. Even when given excellent food and care, they suffer for want of the most elemental needs: to belong to a family, to have someone hold them, to know the presence of a loving parent. All people have the same basic need for belonging: people to call friends and family, relationships that are safe and rewarding, places that feel like home. Robert Frost captured this human characteristic in a poem about Old Silas, an unreliable farmhand who, though no longer welcome, returned to a certain farm to die. The farmer's wife said he had come home, but the farmer said that because Silas had left when he was most needed, he was certainly not returning to a place he could call home. His wife countered, "Home is the place where, when you have to go there, they have to take you in."[1]

Everyone needs to know where they belong. Jesus, who knew no permanent home, surrounded himself with people he felt at home with. He even assigned them nicknames (James and John were the Sons of Thunder) and spoke of intimate things with them. He drew them into his most intimate relationship, the one he had with *Abba*, to whom he frequently prayed.

Paul is also drawing on this relationship. It belongs, he says, to everyone who follows Christ. He even uses the same intimate term that Jesus used. It was such a fitting way to speak about the parental nature of God that the earliest followers of Jesus

1. Robert Frost, "The Death of the Hired Man," in *The Poetry of Robert Frost*, ed. Edward Connery Lathem (New York: Holt, Rinehart, and Winston, 1969), 34–40.

Romans 8:12-17

Theological Perspective

Nice, normal people are also malicious, arrogant, and lazy. We flee from a righteous God while we continue to think of ourselves as religious. Like the first parents in paradise (Gen. 3) or the prodigal son (Luke 15), we desire to be like God, and then we live in misery. How could God possibly want to have anything to do with us? And yet God forgives us our sin. God forgives because Christ's sacrifice gives us access to our Father in heaven. God forgives us by involving us in the story of the sacrifice of Christ. Thereby he makes us "fellow heirs," adopted children of God. In this way God says yes to us and takes us in his arms as he does the prodigal son.

When we celebrate the festival of the Trinity, we do so with adoration and thankfulness that God is *this* God who by his Spirit dwells in us. And his Spirit teaches us to call God "Abba," the same God who reigns above us and over all things. And Christ, God's only Son, forgives us our sin in his sacrifice for us and overcomes our sinful separation from God. This Christ is God himself. God is the one who is in these three figures and who in these three figures is the one God. We do not believe in three gods. We believe in the *one* God. The doctrine of the Trinity tells us that fully the *same* God is above us in the heaven and comes in the depths of the life on earth and enters our hearts. God *alone* cares for this. The doctrine of the Trinity is deeply connected with the doctrine of pure grace. We adore this triune God, and we do so with thankfulness and with hope in him.

EBERHARD BUSCH

Pastoral Perspective

bumper sticker "This car will be driverless at the rapture."

Perhaps the tension of living in the flesh and yet longing for the Spirit of God is at the center of what Paul means by suffering with Christ. To suffer with Christ is implied in the baptismal covenant, and in pastoral care we should not overlook the reality of spiritual suffering that is at the core of Christian living for individuals and congregations. For those who come to us for pastoral care, the present is most often the primary focus. This may be a challenge when reading Paul, who seemed always drawn into the future by the decisions of the present. Paul's letter to the Christians in Rome is also difficult in pastoral circumstances because of his assertions about being "children of God" and suffering with Christ, "so that we may also be glorified with him."

In a pastoral visit or conversation, it would be important to name the truth that we are children of God, not because of a decision we make about the flesh or the Spirit, but because in Christ we are God's adopted children. That we are beloved children of God invites gratitude more than a tension between the flesh and the Spirit. Faithful people in today's church seek a pastoral exploration of their life in Christ. In pastoral encounters if we encourage gratitude more than guilt, then we will have served God, the church, and the world well.

J. BARNEY HAWKINS IV

Exegetical Perspective

functions like his egalitarian statement in Galatians 3:28. Paul stresses the inclusive nature of God's family by noting that God's children are "*all* who are led by God's Spirit" (8:14). God's family is not a hierarchy but a group of fellow heirs (and joint heirs with Christ).

The participatory nature of the life among community members and between the community and Christ is reflected in Paul's repetition of "together/with" (*syn*). The Spirit testifies *with* our spirit; we are *fellow*-heirs of Christ since we suffer *together* so that we also may be glorified *together*. Moreover, every verb Paul uses in 8:12–17 (to refer to his audience) is plural ("we are debtors," "we cry out," "we are God's children," "since we suffer with," "that we also might be glorified with," "if *you* live . . . *you* are about to die," "if *you* put to death . . . , *you* will live," "*you* did not receive . . . but *you* received," "all led by God's spirit, these are God's sons"). Individuals do not participate in the new life of Christ on their own, but rather as partners in community.

Suffering is the primary way through which the community participates together with Christ (8:17). Rather than shielding one from suffering, the "privileged" position as God's heir is contingent on the fact that one suffers with Christ. *Eiper*, translated by the NRSV as "if, in fact," is closer to "since," implying that the suffering of which Paul speaks is not hypothetical but a reality in the church in Rome. Paul's reference to "present sufferings" in the following verse (v. 18) confirms this suspicion. Paul interprets the suffering of the community as an indication of their identity as heirs of God and fellow heirs with Christ. The result (or purpose?) of such suffering is glorification of the community with Christ. Paul's understanding of Jesus' life (movement from death/suffering to life/glorification) thus becomes a template for the community in Rome. The community participates with Christ by following (t)his pattern.

MATTHEW S. RINDGE

Homiletical Perspective

used it too and refrained from translating it from Aramaic into Greek. When Paul speaks of the family of God here, he says that by the Spirit, we also "cry, '*Abba!*'" When we do this, "it is the Spirit himself bearing witness with our spirit that we are children of God" (8:15, my translation). The benefits of this relationship are that Christians become heirs of all God has to offer, even fellow heirs with Christ. This is a Trinitarian relationship that bears immediately upon people. The Three-in-One establishes a home for us.

This should come as refreshing news to people who are searching for identity and belonging. Perhaps most striking are the ways that young people carry themselves as they attempt to fit into society. Some buy the latest clothes or shoes, others shave their heads or wear hair colors once seen only on emergency vehicles or have their bodies tattooed. The more desperate mutilate their bodies with studs and razors. But, the young are not alone in this. Many adults still believe you cannot be too rich or too thin. The cost of our houses and cars remains a sign of our place in the world. Whether we belong to a street gang or a country club, we drape our flesh in symbols of those groups that provide us a sense of belonging.

Paul identifies a more certain identity. It has nothing to do with what we wear or how we decorate or mutilate our flesh. In fact, when we are in the Spirit, things of the flesh—whether fashion or food, self-expression or sex—are put into perspective. The basic things of life—food, clothing, relationships—are needed and enjoyed by all people. But they should not define or consume us. Christian identity is found in relationship to God. The intimate relationship of faith is richer than others because it is established by the Spirit of God and will not fail. And even if it leads us into threatening or challenging circumstances as we share in Christ's suffering, we have the assurance of God's parental love, the Spirit's power, and presence of our brother Christ.

CLAYTON J. SCHMIT

John 3:1-17

¹Now there was a Pharisee named Nicodemus, a leader of the Jews. ²He came to Jesus by night and said to him, "Rabbi, we know that you are a teacher who has come from God; for no one can do these signs that you do apart from the presence of God." ³Jesus answered him, "Very truly, I tell you, no one can see the kingdom of God without being born from above." ⁴Nicodemus said to him, "How can anyone be born after having grown old? Can one enter a second time into the mother's womb and be born?" ⁵Jesus answered, "Very truly, I tell you, no one can enter the kingdom of God without being born of water and Spirit. ⁶What is born of the flesh is flesh, and what is born of the Spirit is spirit. ⁷Do not be astonished that I said to you, 'You must be born from above.' ⁸The wind blows where it chooses, and you hear the sound of it, but you do not know where it comes from or where it goes. So it is with everyone who is born of the Spirit." ⁹Nicodemus said to him, "How can these things be?" ¹⁰Jesus answered him, "Are you a teacher of Israel, and yet you do not understand these things?

Theological Perspective

Nicodemus continues to be a controversial figure in the Christian theological tradition. We cannot come to the story of his discussion with Jesus one night in Jerusalem without his having been shaped already in our imaginations in some way. For John Calvin, Nicodemus was judged by the company he kept, namely, Joseph of Arimathea, whom John describes as "a disciple of Jesus, though a secret one because of his fear of the Jews" (19:38). Calvin took this to mean that Nicodemus was also a secret disciple who visited Jesus at night out of fear of the Jews. Calvin therefore labeled all those in France who were evangelicals at heart but Roman Catholics in practice "Nicodemites," for they were secretly disciples who acted out of fear of the Roman Catholic authorities. Søren Kierkegaard described Nicodemus as an admirer of Jesus, as opposed to a follower. Like Calvin, Kierkegaard saw Nicodemus as someone who only partially associated himself with Jesus, but who held back from a full and public commitment to him because of his fear of persecution from his own people. Both of these pictures of Nicodemus may be supported from the text, but they lose sight of the fact that John also tells us that Nicodemus argued with the Sanhedrin against arresting Jesus on the grounds that he had not been given a fair hearing (7:50–51), which sets him publicly at odds with the

Pastoral Perspective

Nicodemus, religious leader and teacher of the law, was most likely a public figure of no mean standing in his Jewish community. He had recognized something significant and noteworthy about the charismatic young new teacher to whom the crowds were flocking. Nicodemus had come to realize that the presence of God was very clearly with Jesus: "we know that you are a teacher who has come from God" (v. 2). Yet Nicodemus's social and religious standing did not allow him to be seen openly consulting the untutored Jesus. Like Nicodemus, we discover that some of our most profound understandings about life come from conversations and consultations with people we talk to "at night," people we are often afraid to be seen associating with.

Our familiarity with this text and our associations with the language of rebirth can stand in the way of an appreciation of the conversation between these two religious teachers. Wordplay, symbolic language, misunderstanding, and confusion, common in John's writing, are very much in evidence.

Nicodemus comes to Jesus because of "the signs" (v. 2)—those acts and words of Jesus that are pointers to the inbreaking of God's reign in the world. Jesus immediately confronts Nicodemus with a riddle. The only way you can see or understand God's realm is for you to be born *again*. Nicodemus,

¹¹"Very truly, I tell you, we speak of what we know and testify to what we have seen; yet you do not receive our testimony. ¹²If I have told you about earthly things and you do not believe, how can you believe if I tell you about heavenly things? ¹³No one has ascended into heaven except the one who descended from heaven, the Son of Man. ¹⁴And just as Moses lifted up the serpent in the wilderness, so must the Son of Man be lifted up, ¹⁵that whoever believes in him may have eternal life.

¹⁶"For God so loved the world that he gave his only Son, so that everyone who believes in him may not perish but may have eternal life.

¹⁷"Indeed, God did not send the Son into the world to condemn the world, but in order that the world might be saved through him."

Exegetical Perspective

The Trinity and the Bible. Trinity Sunday celebrates the tri-unity of God. Although there is no *doctrine* of the Trinity in the Bible (that is a later development), the reality of God, Christ, and the Spirit permeates the NT. Two NT texts do join them in a threefold formula of Father, Son, and Holy Spirit in baptism and benediction (Matt. 28:19; 2 Cor. 13:13). Further, the NT readings for this Trinity Sunday (Rom. 8:12–17 and our text from John 3:1–17) also refer to Father, Son or Christ, and Spirit. The same God is at work in today's reading from Isaiah 6:1–8, part of sacred Scripture for Paul and John, as well as for Jesus and Nicodemus.

The Historical Context for the Nicodemus Story. As a Pharisee, Jewish leader, and teacher, Nicodemus becomes a distinctive link to Jesus' own Hebrew heritage. However, given the highly symbolic character of the Gospel of John, he reflects more the period when this text was written toward the end of the first century than the earlier time of Jesus himself.

After the destruction of Jerusalem and its temple by the Romans in the year 70 CE, rabbinic Judaism emerged, with its emphasis no longer on temple sacrifice but on synagogue teaching ("rabbi" means "teacher"). It was a time of conflict between those Jews who believed in Jesus as God's Messiah and

Homiletical Perspective

The Gospel according to John presents special challenges to the preacher, for here is a work of unique theological reflection upon the good news the author has received. Put another way, this Gospel is second-order contemplation, a step removed from burgeoning announcement. The author has already taken delivery of information, meditated upon that information, and distilled it. What we have received as a result of that distillation process is a work of concentrated theology.

Because of this theological concentration, it is far easier to follow the task of exegesis with the delivery of an analysis or lecture, rather than a sermon. Certainly, teaching is a function of the sermon, but instruction on what the author of this Gospel intends by the use of various devices can easily overwhelm the homiletical perspective. So the question of how we teach this text, share the results of this author's reflections, but bring its truths to bear on the realities of our world is especially acute. Fortuitously, that is precisely the message of this passage. Out of the darkness of night, the domain of ignorance and misunderstanding, we bring our questions, and those questions are addressed by the Word made flesh, bringing words of new life and fresh perspective. "You must be born from above," he says, and the Spirit will make this new life possible.

John 3:1-17

Theological Perspective

rest of the Sanhedrin. Nicodemus also brought the spices to prepare the body of Jesus for burial (John 19:39). Hence Nicodemus is a complex figure who may not be reduced to a hypocritical believer or an admirer, but may rather be seen as a work in progress, on his way from being intrigued by Jesus to believing in Jesus.

Nicodemus is a Pharisee and leader of the Jews, a member of the Sanhedrin. He comes to Jesus at night to let him know that, in his judgment, the Sanhedrin has reason to acknowledge him as a teacher who has come from God. This acknowledgment of Jesus will become the point of contention, as Jesus challenges Nicodemus to reconsider what it means to be "a teacher who has come from God" (3:2). Nicodemus takes this to mean that the signs that Jesus does reveal the presence of God in Jesus. We have already been told that Jesus "would not entrust himself" to people who believe because of his signs (2:23–24), so this already casts a cloud over Nicodemus's validation of Jesus as a divinely sanctioned rabbi. However, the point at issue in this passage has to do with the way Nicodemus and the Sanhedrin know that Jesus is a teacher who has come from God, namely, by fitting Jesus into what they already know from their interpretation of the Law of Moses. Jesus does not have his origin as teacher from Moses, but from God, for he has descended from God in order to declare what he knows of God, before he returns to God (3:11–13). Jesus therefore responds to Nicodemus by telling him that he cannot see the kingdom of God without being born again, without being born from on high. Nicodemus shows his attempt to understand Jesus based on what he already knows to be true, by ignoring the possibility of being born from on high, and showing the impossibility of being born again (3:4). Jesus responds to this misunderstanding by highlighting the source of the birth from on high, which is the Spirit.

Contrary to Nicodemus's attempt to fit Jesus into his previous understanding of the world, the birth from above is beyond anyone's control and is subject to the mysterious freedom of the Spirit. Those who think in earthly categories do not know where the lives of those born from above come from or where they go, even as Nicodemus does not see Jesus as the teacher who has come from God in order to return to God. The description of the new birth as "of water and Spirit" has been interpreted by the church to mean baptism. However, as Zwingli rightly pointed out, this would actually frustrate the whole point that Jesus is making, namely, that the new birth of the

Pastoral Perspective

familiar with disputation about words and texts, goes first for the plain, literal meaning of what he has just heard. Jesus continues on the symbolic, nonliteral plane. To enter God's realm one has to be born "*from God's realm.*" So often our misunderstandings and disputes arise because the interlocutors are not speaking the same language. Jesus is using symbolic, spiritual, analogical language; Nicodemus is looking at the plain, literal meanings. Nicodemus sees birth as "of the flesh"; Jesus speaks of spiritual realities: "What is born of the flesh is flesh, and what is born of the Spirit is spirit" (v. 6). Rebirth is a spiritual experience available to all, but perhaps most needed by religious people who might think they do not need it. Religion often becomes a matter of the correct observance of particular practices. When these practices become routine, they may actually serve to hinder spiritual sensitivity. A spiritual transformation in such situations is very much needed.

In fact, to be in tune with God's reign and presence we all need a transformative overhaul of our traditional ways of seeing and being. We need a transformation of our whole way of knowing and experiencing the world. When this happens, it is as if we have begun life all over again. Nicodemus's confusion deepens because he is unable to leave the realm of literal thinking to join Jesus on an imaginative, spiritual level. It is not possible to use literal, physical interpretations to encompass the spiritual truths Jesus is alluding to. "The wind (spirit) blows where it chooses and although you may hear the sound of it, you have no idea where it originates and where it is going." The spiritual is often in contrast with the flesh. In Romans 8:5–8, Paul argues that conflict between the flesh and the Spirit characterizes the Christian life. The Spirit is active in Christ Jesus. In Romans 8:9 the Spirit of God is the Spirit of Christ. Jesus speaks about the spiritual truths he knows and can bear testimony to. Nicodemus at this stage is not yet able to grasp these truths. For Nicodemus, there is confusion, not enlightenment.

In the context of this conversation, Christ's divine origins (v. 13, "from heaven") are revealed. His manner of suffering and death (v. 14: "lifted up" on the cross) are also alluded to. All this is for a purpose. Christ descends from above to bring the truth from heaven to humankind. He is indeed truth incarnate. He comes to be a source of healing and salvation, much as Moses's bronze serpent, lifted up on a pole in the wilderness (Num. 21:8–9), brings healing to anyone who looks up at it in faith. Jesus

those who did not. The texts in John that precede today's show a Passover context, Jesus' cleansing of the temple, and the assertion that among Jews "many believed in his name" (John 2:23; note also 8:30). At the Council of Jamnia in the 80s, an official announcement declared that anyone who believed in Jesus as the Messiah would be excluded from the synagogue. The Gospel of John reflects this separation three times (9:22; 12:42; 16:2). When this Gospel speaks of "the Jews," it is Jewish Christians referring to those Jews who did not believe in Jesus and who remained in the synagogue. John's Gospel is a massive attempt to encourage belief in Jesus as God's Messiah (note its stated purpose in 20:30–31).

Today's Gospel story presents Nicodemus as one who is trying to make up his mind about Jesus. The great Roman Catholic NT scholar of blessed memory, Raymond Brown, suggests that Nicodemus represents secret disciples of Jesus (he does come "by night"). We do know that he appears twice more in this Gospel. He defends Jesus, asking that he be given a hearing (7:50–51), and he joins with Joseph of Arimathea, a disciple of Jesus, to bury Jesus (19:38–40). In John, Nicodemus comes to Jesus near the beginning of his ministry, defends him in the middle, and is with him at the end. Is this not what a disciple would do?

The Kingdom and Being Born from Above. Our text often is used by those who speak about being "born again." This hinges on the translation of an ambiguous Greek word (*anōthen*), which can be translated "again" or "from above." It is Nicodemus who misunderstands and speaks of being "born again." It is Jesus who says one must be "born from above." For John, Jesus affirms that entering into God's reign is not a manipulation of the flesh (i.e., of humans shaping forms of religious experience). It is a gift of God's Spirit, unshaped by human hands but "blowing" where it will "from above." The story connects Spirit with water because, in the symbolism of John, Jesus brings God's gift of "living water" (4:10). Further, "'out of the believer's heart shall flow rivers of living water.' Now [Jesus] said this about the Spirit, which believers in him were to receive" (7:38–39).

The Inclusion of "We" Testimony. Though Jesus continues to speak in verses 11 and 12, the conversation with the seeking-to-understand Nicodemus is over, and the "we" of John's community joins in: "[W]e speak of what we know and testify to what we have seen; yet you do not

This first discourse in John's Gospel is a dialogue on two levels at once, a conversation from two different perspectives, an exchange whose result is misunderstanding. But the misunderstanding is purposive: The function of misunderstanding is to catch us, the readers, at work in our accustomed rut. Like Nicodemus, we collect pennies from heaven when what is being offered is unimagined wealth. That wealth is the very kingdom of God. In this passage, the only time the word "kingdom" is used in the Gospel according to John, Jesus is telling Nicodemus, and us, that God's kingdom is here. The kingdom of God is not some far-off goal to be attained, for there is nothing we can do to attain it. The kingdom is present now, as a gift from God. Only God can gift us, can beget us as a totally new being in a new world.

Why should we be so significant? Why should God even care? "The wind blows where it chooses" (v. 8) is an image of God in search of humanity, a vision of God's decision to turn toward humankind, to search for us, and to reveal God's self to us in that activity. Why? Because it is the nature of God to be in relationship. On Trinity Sunday we celebrate that most fundamental element of faith and practice: Christian relationship. The doctrine of the Trinity teaches us of the communal inner life of God: God the Father is with the Son who is with the Spirit who is with the Father, self-communicating, self-giving, self-receiving. When we profess the Trinity, we affirm that it is of the essence of God to be in relationship. But we also acknowledge that it is the nature of God to take the initiative in search of communion, to reveal God's self as the source of life itself, to pursue us, to come to us to reveal God's self as the source of all creation, the salvation of all God has created, the sustainer of all life. Here is One who is vulnerable to us in every way, yet cannot be possessed, utterly basic to our existence, yet beyond our reach.

"How, then, is God's relationship with the world possible?" we ask. We turn again to Scripture: "God so loved the world that he gave his only Son, so that everyone who believes in him may not perish but may have eternal life." The unknowable One has made himself known. The incomprehensible One has made himself heard. God is speaking; and the more nearly the divine approaches, the more we acknowledge we cannot know and cannot comprehend where the Holy comes from or where it goes. Yet something of that mystery is turning to us.

God searches for us to complete the revelation of God's being. God searches for us to participate in

John 3:1-17

Theological Perspective

Spirit is not subject to human control and cannot be coordinated with the rest of what we know of this world. Nicodemus does not understand how these things can be, which leads Jesus to question how he can view himself as a teacher of Israel.

Jesus goes on to teach Nicodemus more fully about the birth from above, which is based entirely on what God is doing in him. Even as Jesus comes from God and speaks what he knows of God, so Jesus is returning to God, but only by being lifted up on the cross. Just as Moses lifted up the serpent so that all who suffered from the venomous bites of the serpents would be spared (Num. 21:4–9), so all who turn in faith to the lifting up of the Son of Man on the cross may have eternal life, which is a synonym for the birth from above. Thus the birth from above will take place by faith in the death of the Son of Man, which is even more paradoxical than birth by the freely given wind of the Spirit. Faith receives eternal life from the death of the Son of Man, because in it is found the self-giving love of God for the world. However, the Father's gift of the Son for the eternal life and salvation of the world also plunges the world into the strife of decision and judgment, for the alternative to faith in the Son is to perish and to be condemned. The self-giving love of God in Christ cannot be accepted without illuminating our lives from the inside out, revealing to us that our old life not only is from below but also is filled with deep darkness that opposes the light of the love of God. Those who cannot bear to have themselves revealed before God in this way refuse to come to the Son, and therefore perish.

RANDALL C. ZACHMAN

Pastoral Perspective

too is to be lifted up on the cross, so that whoever looks up at him in believing faith will be saved. This is no coincidence. It is in the will and purpose of the loving God who wishes all to have eternal life. God has a salvific purpose in mind through all of Christ's life and death. God gives God's only Son to save the world. Believing in him becomes the means for obtaining eternal life. "Eternal life" is more a different quality of life than merely an elongation of life. It is a spiritual, transformative quality of life that transcends the vicissitudes of this physical life.

God's desire in sending God's Son is not condemnatory. Rather, it is redemptive. The whole mission and purpose of God in Christ is to rescue and recover humanity, from being deeply embedded in self-defeating pursuits in a physically absorbed life. God in Christ wishes to reclaim, rename, and reauthor the stories of our lives with a new life empowered by the grace of God and made manifest in the life, death, and resurrection of Christ.

We are glad to note that by the time we encounter Nicodemus again in John's Gospel (7:45–52), he is more convinced about the mission of God in Christ and is arguing for Jesus in public. He is no longer afraid to be identified as a follower of Jesus. Such is his "coming out" that by 19:38–42 he is identifying himself with Christ in his death by providing spices to embalm his dead body.

God was in Christ, reconciling the world to God's self. Anyone who is in Christ is a new creation (born from above); everything old has passed away, everything has become new (2 Cor. 5:17–19). All of this is accomplished by the creative love of God, the redemptive offering of Christ, and the empowering presence of the life-giving Spirit. And these Three are One.

EMMANUEL Y. LARTEY

receive our testimony." This is their witness to their brothers and sisters in the synagogue at the end of the first century. It proclaims that those who do not believe in the earthly and tangible "word made flesh" in Jesus cannot understand the heavenly and intangible glory that is in him. Here the argument draws on two figures in the Hebrew heritage of the hearers: God's new-world-bringing Son of Man (see Dan. 7:13–14) and the Moses-lifted-up healing serpent (Num. 21:9). The testimony is that now Jesus is that descending-ascending Son of Man, and his lifting up on the cross brings God's healing and new life. In John, "eternal life" is not only a quantity of life beyond death, but a quality of life already lived out of God's gift of love.

The Gospel of Love. In the other three Gospels, love language is rather sparse. In the Gospel of John, love language occurs more than forty times. Its use in our text probably is the most familiar of all NT texts. "God so loved the world that he gave his only Son." Here love (*agapē*) is not a sentiment but an action that seeks the good for the beloved. That self-giving love reaches its "finishing," lifted up on the cross and intended to draw all to itself (12:32). Jesus' resurrection puts God's affirming stamp on the cross as love lifted up to reign over the world and to be the source of life "from above" for all who receive it.

God's intention is never to condemn but to save, that is, to make life whole. Salvation language is health language, God's health for all the world in all of life's relationships. That love is ever constant, but never coercive. It is invitational and hopes for a response, to complete the circle of love and share in the interconnectedness of the creating, liberating, healing Holy Trinity.

PAUL L. HAMMER

God's life. God's seeking is not brought about by our circumstance, our worthiness, our sufficient understanding. Rather, that seeking derives from the anguish of God, God's longing for the work of God's hands. God did not send the Son into the world to condemn the world, but in order that the world God created might be saved. So how might we live in that kingdom where life is reborn?

In the rain forest of Olympic National Park in Washington State stand groves of towering trees, the source of whose life is not visible, yet is apparent. The roots of these trees fan out like ribs of an umbrella, seemingly embracing the air for support, for these trees were given birth by nurse logs. Nurse logs are fallen trees, left to lie on the earth until they crumble into dust. But before they disintegrate, something else transpires: A seed falls on the downed log, draws nourishment from the log even as that log decays, and creates roots that ultimately surround an empty space through which the wind blows.

The snapshot of a tree with ribbed umbrella roots above ground embracing only the wind takes us behind such a picture to contemplate origins and interpret reality with new eyes, eyes that expect the unexpected, look to new truths, and come to understand the world in new ways. Such contemplation suggests the offer of a kingdom of communion whose realm we can realize only if we accept it, trust in a relationship between death and life beyond our imagination, new life bestowed by the giving of life, a Giver as real as the wind. Living with faith in this God's reality, we have and will have life eternal.

JUDITH M. MCDANIEL

Hosea 2:14-20

¹⁴Therefore, I will now allure her,
  and bring her into the wilderness,
  and speak tenderly to her.
¹⁵From there I will give her her vineyards,
  and make the Valley of Achor a door of hope.
There she shall respond as in the days of her youth,
  as at the time when she came out of the land of Egypt.

¹⁶On that day, says the LORD, you will call me, "My husband," and no longer will you call me, "My Baal." ¹⁷For I will remove the names of the Baals from her mouth, and they shall be mentioned by name no more. ¹⁸I will make for you a covenant on that day with the wild animals, the birds of the air, and the creeping things of the ground; and I will abolish the bow, the sword, and war from the land; and I will make you lie down in safety. ¹⁹And I will take you for my wife forever; I will take you for my wife in righteousness and in justice, in steadfast love, and in mercy. ²⁰I will take you for my wife in faithfulness; and you shall know the LORD.

Theological Perspective

The book of Hosea portrays the relationship between God and Israel in strong, emotional ways. God and the nation are personified in a marriage relationship. God has been faithful to the people God has chosen; the nation has been unfaithful. The people have been apostate, pursued other gods, and broken the covenant relationship God established. From this unfaithfulness, abuses in worship, politics, and society have emerged. God's judgment is announced, taking the form of defeats by enemies and the destruction of the nation.

But in the midst of it all, God's faithfulness leads to promises of redemption and salvation. God's unwearied love will not give up on the people God has called to share in a covenant relationship. The great eleventh chapter of Hosea is a poignant description of God's steadfast love that pursues the wayward people and forestalls their ultimate destruction.

Today's passage is a preview of God's ultimate announcement of redemption for the people. After displaying Israel's infidelity and the punishment the nation deserves (2:1–13), a remarkable note of salvation emerges. The language is rich in theological content, evoking words and themes that pervade the Hebrew Scriptures as a whole and that spread into the New Testament. They are ways God deals with

Pastoral Perspective

The Old Testament lectionary text for this Sunday is a beautiful reaffirmation of God's covenant with humankind. The verses speak of God's intent to renew right relationship with a people who have been unfaithful. The list of Israel's sins, both corporate and individual, is long; idolatry and injustice have rent the political and religious fabric of the nation. Israel faces destruction from within and without, and God is under no obligation whatsoever to act on her behalf. Yet God takes the initiative and reaches out, once again, to woo Israel back, reaffirming the eternal promise of the covenant. Hosea uses the metaphor of marriage to describe this vow. "I will take you for my wife forever," God declares, "I will take you for my wife in righteousness and in justice, in steadfast love, and in mercy" (v. 19).

Taken on its own, this passage is an exquisite articulation of the love of God. Yet as beautiful as the imagery is, it is also a part of a larger pericope that many pastors choose to avoid. The problem stems from Hosea's use of the marriage metaphor to equate his own marriage to Gomer, his unfaithful wife, to God's relationship with unfaithful Israel. Gail Yee observes that Hosea's nuptial metaphor is theologically troubling on several levels. The typology equates God with the male, sin with the female, and

Exegetical Perspective

Literary Context. This pericope is an integral part of a soliloquy spoken by YHWH (2:1–23) in the presence of bystanders previously introduced in 1:2–11, namely, Hosea's wife, Gomer, and their three children. Despite occasionally addressing them directly, YHWH is mostly speaking about them to an audience that overhears him. Thus this is not the typical kind of prophetic speech, which confronts a particular person or group with the prospect of doom or salvation in historically specific circumstances. It is a prophetic text written for the instruction of readers (see 14:9) so that they can vicariously identify with the characters described in YHWH's speech, in order to discern the state of their relationship with God.

YHWH's description of these characters has implications for the God-human relationship because of an allegory implied in the children's names (1:6–9). A son is called Lo-ammi ("Not-my-people") and a daughter is called Lo-ruhamah ("Not-pitied"), which makes the rocky relationship between Hosea and his family analogous to the covenant between YHWH and Israel. As Gomer deserts Hosea to pursue paramours, Israel deserts YHWH to pursue other lords ("Baal"). As Hosea punishes and divorces Gomer for her adultery, hoping that someday she will return, YHWH lets his people be defeated and exiled, hoping that someday

Homiletical Perspective

Preachers who are squeamish about human passion, intimacy, and the language of love—love fulfilled and love denied—will find it difficult to preach from Hosea. Though this Sunday's reading finds the relationship between God and Israel on the mend, today's text is surrounded by R-rated material. There is enough of adultery, prostitution, and threats to give any country musician plenty of material to work with when composing the next country hit.

The book unfolds on the basis of an extended analogy between Hosea and his prostitute wife, Gomer, whose relationship is analogous to that between God and the faithless Israel. Israel (Gomer) is blatantly accused of "play[ing] the whore" (2:5), while God (Hosea) plays the role of the angry, spurned husband ("I will punish her for the festival days of the Baals") (v. 13). There is plenty here to offend: Israel's promiscuous cavorting with other gods in third-rate motels is only a little less disturbing than the violent response of God: "I will . . . kill her with thirst. Upon her children also I will have no pity" (vv. 3–4). Some preachers will find the whole tawdry affair too much to handle. But for the preacher who is unafraid to wade into the real muck of human and divine relationship, Hosea provides a rowdy Saturday night followed by a blessed Sunday morning.

Hosea 2:14-20

Theological Perspective

pervasive human sin. The depths of the divine love burst forth in the promises to a covenant people who have been indicted for sins they have committed and who face the just results of their actions according to divine law. But this text averts that ultimate judgment, to hold forth redemption for the people and restoration of the original relationship God intended to have with the people, through God's reconciling actions.

A New Hope. Hosea proclaims God will court Israel, bringing the nation into the wilderness again— reminiscent of the years after the exodus from Egypt. God will "speak tenderly" and give "vineyards" to "make the Valley of Achor a door of hope" (vv. 14–15). Salvation history is beginning again, and Israel is receiving the land again, as a gracious gift of God. "Valley of Achor" literally means "valley of trouble." It points to the dramatic difference Israel experienced when it emerged from the wilderness. Now God reaches out in restoration to promise hope in the most dreadful situation of alienation and woe. Now a life of promise is extended, a future not burdened by the pain of the past. Israel responds to this hope as the nation did when God brought them out of Egypt.

God offers hope, even when sin is most horrible and real. God's way of relating to Israel is to open a "door of hope" to the people, as their ancestors had experienced when they emerged from the wilderness into the Valley of Achor. This promise of hope is a constant characteristic of the God of the Bible, so graphically portrayed here. No situation is too terrible and beyond redemption. No person is beyond the pale of being redeemed by the hope that promises new life, as Israel is again promised the land. This God of hope for the people of Israel is the same God of hope who comes to us in Jesus Christ (Rom. 15:13).

A New Covenant. The restoration of hope for the people is made possible by God's promise of a covenant. The promise of hope is in the salvation God brings by moving through sin and judgment to a new beginning through a covenant. When the people turn away from the deities of the day, the gods of the land ("Baal," v. 16), and recognize their true God to be the one who has redeemed and liberated them, then blessings will abound. God's covenant with the people includes a harmony even with beasts and birds. Even more, the sword and war will be abolished so the people may "lie down in safety" (v. 18).

Pastoral Perspective

justifies a husband punishing a wife "for her own good."[1] In the previous verses of chapter 2, Hosea punishes Gomer for her unfaithfulness in a way that would now be considered abhorrent spousal abuse. The relationship is a nightmare. Hosea publicly accuses Gomer of adultery, shaming her and their children. He strips her, isolates her, and attempts to control her. He threatens to kill her with thirst and make her body a wilderness, all the while justifying his violence as morally right and fully deserved.

When we reach the beginning of this Sunday's lectionary lesson in verse 14, the anger subsides and a much gentler tone takes over. The husband/Deity speaks lovingly and compassionately in an attempt to woo the wife/Israel back. The promises are tender and sweet. Even so, the beauty of the wooing is scarred by the cruelty of the verses that precede it. Pastors know full well the patterns of spousal abuse that cycle between such violence and contrition.

The good news of this text is that, through divine love, relationship with God is possible even after judgment. But how can pastors preach the promise of this text without perpetuating the pain and damage of domestic violence? Perhaps the problem is not with the theology of the text, but with the metaphor used to communicate it. Bruce Birch suggests that we need to understand the limitation of metaphor and the limitations of the cultural context in which a metaphor originates. For Birch, the language of abuse attributed to God in Hosea may tell us something about ancient Israel's attitudes toward women, but it does not tell us a truth about God. We can reject the metaphor of domestic violence used earlier in Hosea 2 without losing the power of the vision proclaimed in the remaining verses.[2] This is not to say that we can avoid the word of judgment altogether. There is no escaping the prophet's rebuke of the individual and corporate sin that has befallen Israel. Hosea's reproach is still valid, calling us to account for our cultural accommodation, self-serving political and religious institutions, and social injustice. God's word of judgment must be rightfully spoken, but as vs. 14–20 declare, God's love prevails.

The vision of renewal Hosea describes in the last half of chapter 2 is nothing less than stunning. God's covenant faithfulness encircles the entire earth. Human society thrives in peace, security, and justice.

1. Gail Yee, "Hosea," in *The New Interpreter's Bible* (Nashville: Abingdon, 1996), 7:211.
2. Bruce C. Birch, *Hosea, Joel, and Amos,* Westminster Bible Companion (Louisville, KY: Westminster John Knox Press, 1997), 35.

Exegetical Perspective

they will return. Lo-ammi can then be renamed Ammi ("My-people"), and Lo-ruhamah renamed Ruhamah ("Pitied").

The allegory takes on an ecological dimension because the oldest son (1:4–5) is named Jezreel ("God-sows"). As Hosea impregnates his wife with his seed, YHWH the Creator sows and fertilizes the land with rain. As Gomer runs after paramours because they can seemingly provide her with luxuries, Israel runs after Baal because he can seemingly provide it with agricultural abundance. As Hosea decides to punish Gomer's adultery by stripping her bare, YHWH decides to punish Israel's unfaithfulness by stripping the fields—sending drought and letting wild plants and animals overrun the cultivated land. A chastened Gomer realizes that her real husband could give her better support than her paramours, and a chastened Israel likewise realizes that its real Creator could give it more agricultural abundance than Baal.

Historical Context. The parallel progress of Hosea's relationship with his family and of YHWH's relationship with Israel implies a narrative sequence corresponding with developments in Israel's history: marriage and children / covenant and land; punishment and divorce / defeat and exile; and remarriage / restoration. However, the sequence of the temporal perspectives in chapter 2 is not linear. Sometimes punishment / exile lies in the future; at other times this has already happened. Although the text presupposes readers who know that exile has happened, they are also invited to imagine hearing the message of Hosea from preexilic perspectives, when the northern kingdom was threatened, or after it had fallen and the southern kingdom was similarly threatened. Readers, therefore, can consider whether their situation is more like the preexilic period, when the issue was whether Israel/Judah might change its ways and avoid punishment, or more like the postexilic period, when the issue was whether Judah might learn from its punishment how to consummate a restoration. Even if readers discern that they now face a fate analogous to exile, they can also see that beyond exile there lies a real possibility of restoration. Our lectionary pericope (2:14–20) is YHWH's explicit affirmation of this hopeful possibility.

Remarriage/Restoration. The restoration of the YHWH-Israel covenant (2:14–20) has two phases, analogous to Hosea and Gomer's courtship and remarriage. Courtship (2:14–15) is described as a recapitulation of the exodus and entry (through "the Valley of Achor") into the promised land. The

Homiletical Perspective

A sermon on this text will be enriched if the preacher sets the stage properly. She will allow the congregation first to see and hear the broken marriage between God and Israel. But after the two-timing behavior of Israel is exposed, and after God breaks a few dishes and slams a few doors, God waits on the porch brokenhearted long into the night. God remains hopeful, not just that Israel will return of her own accord, but that God can woo Israel to return. "I will now allure her . . . and speak tenderly to her" (2:14). Where Israel had sinned at the Valley of Achor (Josh. 7:20–26), God will set up "a door of hope" (2:15). Israel will once again call God, "My husband" (v. 16), and God will make Israel "my wife forever" (v. 19). God speaks of this marriage renewal in the future tense, but the words are so tender, the promise of reconciliation so sure, that the action already seems to be a realized future. God's love for Israel, and through Israel for all creation, is so full of compassion that in time we will all "lie down in safety" in God's arms (v. 18).

Just as the text reveals the covenantal nature of God's love for humanity, it invites a sermon on covenant within human relationships. Our age is long on contracts and short on covenants. Contracts of all sorts—legal, economic, political—are easily changed to fit the needs of the moment or to satisfy those who hold the most power. Contracts have their place. But humans hunger for covenants sealed by God—covenants where both partners share equally in the relationship and where both are committed to the greater good of the other. Such relationships are marked by righteousness, justice, steadfast love, mercy, and faithfulness (vv. 19–20). These are not abstract principles but daily virtues. Practiced enough, with plenty of room for forgiveness of failure, they forge the bonds between persons and institutions that lead to wholeness, *shalom.*

In God's renewal of the covenant with Israel (v. 18) the whole creation is brought into the promise. The wild animals, the birds, the creeping things of the ground, all find their place within the covenant, as God abolishes "the bow, the sword, and war from the land" (v. 18). Here is pay dirt for a sermon that connects creation and covenant. Such a sermon will help the congregation of the twenty-first century imagine and act upon our yearning for environmental protection and restoration—for clean rivers and air, reduction of global warming, and reforestation of the planet—while sounding a call for the end of human warfare. It turns out that God wants not only to renew a marriage with Israel but to renew the covenant with all creation.

Hosea 2:14-20

Theological Perspective

Israel receives peace as the gift of God's grace. It is not a reward for obedience, but the gracious sign God has reestablished the covenantal relationship that binds God to the people and the people to God. Though judgment has been imminent, God does not give up on the love that binds God and the nation together. This covenant promise has future dimensions and, as Calvin wrote, "God's favour, of which the Prophet now speaks, is not restricted to a short time or to a few years, but extends to Christ's kingdom, and is what we have in common with the ancient people."[1] God's new covenant in Jesus Christ is the ultimate expression of the covenant of peace, promised to God's people (cf. 1 Cor. 11:25).

A New Way of Living. God promises a new marriage with the nation, marked by a new way of living. Here the promise is forever and unconditional, going beyond the covenant of Sinai and a "rewards for obedience" structure of life (vv. 19–20; cf. Lev. 26). Now God's attitudes and actions provide ways by which interactions will be carried out, a quality of living in the covenant relationship of reconciliation. The terms here are tremendously rich: righteousness, justice, steadfast love (Heb. *ḥesed*), mercy, and faithfulness. These are marks of the way Israel is to relate to God; but even more, they are what God promises to be and do for the people.

This new way of living, grounded in the covenant and introduced by hope, is an act of God's great and unexpected grace. God overcomes faithlessness and restores the people with the promise that they shall "know the LORD" (v. 20). This embraces the whole response of the people so their total life is grounded in what God has revealed and done. To "know the LORD" is the great goal of life, in this age and the age to come. The promise here is reminiscent of Jeremiah's future vision of a new covenant when all people shall "know me" (Jer. 31:34).

This passage offers overwhelming hope by conveying God's desire to overcome sin and faithlessness. God's deep covenant loyalty opens redemption and salvation. God gives the people of Israel a vision of new life, marked by the most profound ways the reconciled people should relate to each other and to God.

DONALD K. MCKIM

Pastoral Perspective

The environment is healed and natural creation prospers under human stewardship. Still, preachers are left with the problem of how to communicate this amazing promise without resorting to the unsuitable image of Near Eastern patriarchal marriage. Is there another metaphor in the text that is more fitting and pastorally sensitive? One suggestion is the geographical image of wilderness in verse 14. God will woo Israel into the wilderness, back to the memory of the exodus and the formation of God's chosen people. Throughout Scripture the wilderness image is tied to rigorous spiritual questing, and it is here that reconciliation begins. Interestingly, the Valley of Achor is identified as the specific location for this healing, a place that was itself a location of severe judgment in Joshua 7:20–26. Yet this is where God beckons Israel to return in order to go forward. This is a fitting image to proclaim the promise: the Valley of Achor becomes the doorway of hope.

Hosea 2:14–20 speaks about what it means to be a people claimed by God's love, a people who stumble and fail and yet are redeemed by God's great faithfulness. The word of grace prevails over the word of judgment. All of this is conveyed through the language of God's covenant, especially in the references to the exodus, wilderness, sin, repentance, forgiveness, and divine promise of salvation. This covenantal language is also the language of baptism, and it would be appropriate to include the sacrament of baptism or a liturgy for the renewal of baptism for this Lord's Day service. Baptismal liturgies often include an extended prayer that recounts salvation history from creation to Christ, an account that includes the flood, the exodus, and the witness of the prophets. This is the great and continuing story of how God calls us, loves us, and still seeks us, even when we have turned away. For this Sunday, the prayer could be written to emphasize Hosea's particular theme as it relates to the Good News: through Christ God's grace opens a doorway to hope and salvation.

KRISTIN EMERY SALDINE

---

1. John Calvin, *Commentary on Hosea* 2:18.

Exegetical Perspective

covenant originally instigated "in the wilderness" at Sinai is now being reinstigated, including a renewal of fertility (restored "vineyards"). It is ironic, though, that Israel will "respond as in the days of her youth" when the Hebrews came out of Egypt. At that time they broke the covenant as soon as it was solemnized, so that it had to be immediately repaired (Exod. 32–34). Thus even though renewal is now possible, YHWH is under no illusion that this new covenant will be any more durable than the original.

Remarriage (2:16–20) is predicated on Israel's recognition that YHWH, not Baal, is its real "husband"—clever wordplay exploits the fact that *baal* can also mean "husband" (see 2:7b–8). By abolishing war, YHWH forgoes the right to punish Israel's infidelity as he has in the past. YHWH's inclusion of other creatures (2:18) plays upon the ecological dimension so as to reaffirm that the YHWH-Israel relationship is subsidiary to the covenant with creation (Gen. 9:1–17). As Israel's infidelity entailed ecological disaster, Israel's renewed fidelity entails creation's restoration.

Conclusion. Here God is portrayed as a long-suffering marriage partner whose love and readiness for reconciliation withstand even adultery. This is a powerful image with significant theological implications: (1) divine energy is manifestly erotic, and God is experienced primarily in the flow of erotic desire that permeates all creation (see Song of Songs); (2) covenant renewal is an ongoing process in which God's continual willingness to forgive and the people's continual repentance engender a profound transformation of both; (3) covenant renewal entails renunciation of war and restoration of creation's ecological balance. Interpretation of the NT image of Christ as bridegroom (Mark 2:18–20, etc.) can become distorted unless seen typologically in light of such Old Testament antecedents. Hosea's portrayal of God as an aggrieved husband likens YHWH's treatment of Israel to the public battering of a woman, unfortunately implying the legitimation of such abuse.[1] It should be noted, however, that in this case YHWH finally renounces such violence as a means of reeducation (2:18), just as YHWH renounced the undoing of creation after the flood (Gen. 8:20–22). This responsive aspect of the divine character is what makes God the object of loving desire, eliciting repentance from covenant partners and empowering them to make a difference in the struggle for ecological justice and peace.

MICHAEL H. FLOYD

1. See,. e.g., Renita Weems, *Battered Love: Marriage, Sex, and Violence in the Hebrew Prophets* (Minneapolis: Augsburg, 1995).

Homiletical Perspective

One important caution should check the preacher before the sermon is cast. Commentators warn that Hosea has been used in previous eras and in some congregations today as a warrant for domination by husbands over their wives.[1] Since Israel, by analogy, is construed in Hosea as the faithless wife, some readers might mistakenly take this as license to "keep women in their place," by force when necessary. This would be egregious on three counts.

First, the passage is an extended analogy of the love between God and Israel, not a literal account or blueprint for domestic relations. To use the passage to reinforce male privilege and power is itself an abuse of the text. As contemporary readers and interpreters, we can name the patriarchal social structures and customs that informed the original composition of the text, and as a living Word, allow the text a new hearing.

Second, when it comes to God and human beings, there is enough faithlessness (idolatry) on everyone's part to go around. Men and women cheat on God; men and women cheat on one another; men, women, and God all get angry when violated. The passage primarily explores humanity's (Israel's) relationship with God. In God's forgiveness and faithfulness to Israel, we learn of God's desire for our relationships with each other.

Third, the passage does not end with submission by Israel (the wife) to God (the husband). The passage culminates in a grand vision of heaven and earthly harmony based upon justice, righteousness, steadfast love, mercy, and faithfulness by both partners—God and Israel. We find here no basis for dominance and submission in human relationships and no preference for the rights of men over women in marriage. To the contrary, in the final verses of the passage, we find God's relationship with Israel as a model for the blessing of relationships between men and women, parents and children, who walk together in steadfast love.

G. LEE RAMSEY JR.

1. See Gale A. Yee, "The Book of Hosea," in *The New Interpreter's Bible, A Commentary in Twelve Volumes*, ed. Leander E. Keck et al., vol. 7 (Nashville: Abingdon, 1996), 197–297, esp. 223–29.

Psalm 103:1-13, 22

¹Bless the LORD, O my soul,
  and all that is within me,
  bless his holy name.
²Bless the LORD, O my soul,
  and do not forget all his benefits—
³who forgives all your iniquity,
  who heals all your diseases,
⁴who redeems your life from the Pit,
  who crowns you with steadfast love and mercy,
⁵who satisfies you with good as long as you live
  so that your youth is renewed like the eagle's.

⁶The LORD works vindication
  and justice for all who are oppressed.
⁷He made known his ways to Moses,
  his acts to the people of Israel.

Theological Perspective

To theologians, pastors and congregations alike, Psalm 103 is a powerful reminder that the proper center of theology, preaching, and life itself is the living God. It seems such an obvious point. What other focus could theology and preaching and the life of the people of God properly have? Yet the history of the church is marked by periods in which God has, in effect, been elbowed out of its life by all kinds of worthy human interests, concerns, and ideas that are given apparently impressive theological justification. In times such as these, Psalm 103 sounds forth both as the guilty conscience of the church and as a great call to renewal.

The themes of this tremendous hymn of faith relate to the primacy of God in our lives, and the character and identity of this One who is worthy of praise. The psalm begins with a simple, but utterly radical summons to the self: "Bless the LORD, O my soul" (v. 1). It is radical precisely because this is a declaration at the heart of one's life, the very core of one's being, that the self is not preeminent. God comes first. It is a reminder, a restatement of the first commandment: "You shall love the LORD your God with all your heart, and with all your soul, and with all your might" (Deut. 6:5). We cannot begin with our own needs, aspirations, and desires and build the world around what we want. God has prior claim

Pastoral Perspective

This is a song of elation. When read in worship, it bubbles with joy for the immense redeeming and blessing power of God. A preacher would want to attend to the joy of blessings and why they come—not because we are special, but because we are not, and we know it. We know our right place in relationship with God.

The reading begins with very personal blessings: forgiveness, healing, love, mercy, good, youthfulness—one blessing piled upon another. Then it moves toward more communal considerations. Not only does God save and redeem us as individuals; God blesses the people as well, as in the exodus God led Israel out of oppression. The reading concludes with a blessing of the Creator by all God's creatures.

The psalm recounts the blessings and satisfaction of knowing that one is living in right relationship with God and with the world. A term familiar from the Hebrew Bible's wisdom tradition is key: those who "fear" God (vv. 11, 13). In the wisdom tradition, especially captured in Proverbs 9:10, "the fear of the LORD is the beginning of wisdom." Fear of God on our part is not dread in the face of the divine judge. More, it is an inner sense that we relate rightly within the created order. Those who fear God know their appropriate place in relation to the Creator and to the creation and to one another, and in response

⁸The Lord is merciful and gracious,
　　slow to anger and abounding in steadfast love.
⁹He will not always accuse,
　　nor will he keep his anger forever.
¹⁰He does not deal with us according to our sins,
　　nor repay us according to our iniquities.
¹¹For as the heavens are high above the earth,
　　so great is his steadfast love toward those who fear him;
¹²as far as the east is from the west,
　　so far he removes our transgressions from us.
¹³As a father has compassion for his children,
　　so the Lord has compassion for those who fear him.
....

²²Bless the Lord, all his works,
　　in all places of his dominion.
　　Bless the Lord, O my soul.

Exegetical Perspective

There are several scholarly opinions as to how to classify this hymn. For some the psalm is a song of thanksgiving that celebrates the poet's recovery from illness. From this perspective verses 3–5 represent the primary event that gives rise to the whole psalm. The psalm is a prayer of thanksgiving for healing that invites the whole community to acknowledge the redeeming activity of the Lord in the poet's life. If the psalm is primarily about an individual's restoration from illness, then the hymn can be understood as moving from the particular to the communal.

Other scholars place this hymn of praise in the category of a celebration of God's activity within the whole people of God. Understood this way, the benefits categorized are the experiences of all the children of Moses, all the people of Israel (v. 7). Taken this way, the psalm invites the individual to recognize God's activity in his or her own life as a reflection of the communal experiences of God.

There can be no certainty regarding the exact origins of Psalm 103, but for our purposes we will consider the psalm a hymn of praise to God for God's steadfast love and compassion offered to the people of God. The psalm is framed by a Call to Praise the Lord (vv. 1–2, 22). The verses used in the lectionary reading can be divided into two sections:

Homiletical Perspective

The psalmist of Psalm 103 is a poet; moreover, the psalmist knows it. The psalm makes full use of a number of poetic devices, not to be showy, but because language itself is insufficient to the task at hand: imagining God, even how God is at work in the life of the psalmist and God's people.

Poetry makes use of various kinds of rhythm, and in every good poem, there are rhythms that escape translation, and there are rhythms that transcend translation. In Psalm 103 there is at least one grand rhythm—a rhythm of all in all, if you will—that cannot escape translation and should not be overlooked by the preacher.

One way to begin to see this rhythm is to go through the psalm and circle every "all" (vv. 1, 2, 3, 6, 19, 21, 22). To sense how the rhythm works, however, imagine the psalm in three movements. In the first (vv. 1–5), the psalmist calls up "*all* that is within me" to praise YHWH. In the second (vv. 6–18), the psalmist imagines God's "vindication and justice for *all* who are oppressed." And in the third movement, the psalmist calls on "*all* [God's] works, in *all* places of his dominion" to join in praise and thanksgiving.

The first and third movements are straightforward and clear. The second movement, which we will consider last, breaks the rhythm, as the psalmist

Psalm 103:1-13, 22

Theological Perspective

over us. We understand who we are, our own reality, the very meaning of our existence, not by self-analysis and introspection, but by responding in blessing to God, the Lord of life.

The soul and "all that is within me" are called to bless the Lord because the Lord knows what goes on in the deep places of the human heart. In his reflections on this psalm, Augustine of Hippo said that "when there is no man to hear thee, there is never wanting one to hear all that is within thee."[1] For Augustine, our most secret thoughts are never hidden from God. The soul always has an audience.

George Stroup has observed that "according to the Bible human life is lived *coram Deo*—before God. Human beings are created to live before the face of and in the sight of God." However, in contemporary culture this idea is now foreign to most people—including many churchgoers. As he points out, it is not that we lack a sense of spirituality. Statistics show that the overwhelming majority of us believe in the existence of a "higher power." We simply do not share Augustine's belief in the soul's audience. We do not have a sense that our lives are lived out before a God who has any kind of claim upon us.[2]

In this culture, the call to bless the Lord comes as a shock and a scandal. It comes into conflict with widely held religious belief. We find it hard to entertain the suggestion that our inmost thoughts and motivations could be known to anyone but ourselves or should be turned to anyone's praise but our own.

So who is this God whom the soul is called upon to bless? Here we venture ever deeper into strange and unfamiliar territory. This is YHWH, whose name is known only because YHWH has revealed it. This is the God of the covenant with Israel, the relationship with a people who once were not, but now are, God's people. This is not a God who is the product of the imagination or social construction or philosophical word games or ideological power play. The soul stands before a God whom it did not invent. This is a truth that theologians and preachers and disciples need to discover and rediscover afresh every day. We are always the servants, never the masters, of the Word. YHWH, the Lord, is revealed through self-revelation in history: "He made known his ways to Moses, his acts to the people of Israel" (v. 7).

Pastoral Perspective

to this knowledge they act in wise and good ways. Things go well for them and with them, and they prosper and are blessed. Therefore they rightly turn to God with the joy and satisfaction this psalm expresses.

All of us know such joy personally at certain special moments: enjoying the beauty of the created world, watching a particularly lovely sunset, or leaving the first footsteps in new fallen snow, or hearing Canada geese flying in a V overhead with the quiet air-stirring hum of their wings. We know that joy at times when all seems right with the world, and with us in it, and when we know the presence of God: at a time of discernment of a call or clarity about a path; at the finding of a life partner or the celebration of a marriage; with tears of joy at the birth of a child; in our hearts' pride at a child's accomplishments, small or large; in the satisfaction of good work recognized or good deeds done in anonymity; at anniversaries of relationships that are deeply marked by love; at the ending of a life well lived. At such moments, we know that we have received a blessing, and it may be hard to repress a smile. As the hymn says, "It is well with my soul." People in our congregations will think of times such as these when they hear the opening of the psalm.

Those who fear God and are part of the people of God may know such moments of joy in community as well, even though our often individualistic and competitive culture may make them harder to apprehend. In terms of communal joy, our culture knows best the rowdy raucousness of huge crowds at stadium sporting events, but that at which we are pointing is not like winning the World Cup or a political convention. It may be hard for us to imagine such satisfaction and joy as these within our churches. In fact, many people lament that life in the community of faith is drab in comparison—and perhaps it is. However, we may know ceremonies of covenant celebration, when all in a worshiping community together signify their willingness to work toward common aims for the realm of God. We may know the powerful presence of God around a committee room table, when we ask God to be with us in our deliberations and discernment. We may experience together the same type of generative joy as a parent, when our congregation sends forth one of its own into ministry or mission and service, or when we give birth to a new congregation, or see the results of our support for mission work elsewhere. Churches may feel the blessing of satisfaction when they celebrate the dedication of a

---

1. Augustine, "Psalm 103," *Expositions on the Psalms*, in *Post-Nicene Fathers*, series 1, vol. 8, ed. Philip Schaff and Arthur Cleveland Coxe (1888, New York: Cosimo Classics, 2007), 503.
2. George W. Stroup, *Before God* (Grand Rapids: Eerdmans, 2004), 1, 4.

Exegetical Perspective

Personal Benefits Given by the Lord (vv. 3–5) and People of God Benefits Given by the Lord (vv. 6–13).

One of the words used throughout the psalm is "all." The poet wants to convey the totality of God's restorative activity. The hymn writer wants us to respond to God with our "all" (vv. 1, 21, 22) because God has forgiven "all" iniquity (v. 3), healed "all" diseases (v. 3), works vindication for "all" who are oppressed (v. 6), and because God's reign is over "all" (v. 19). The fact that there are twenty-two lines in the poem—the number of letters in the Hebrew alphabet—may also point to the author's intent to symbolize the totality of God's benefits and the totality of God's claim upon our allegiance.

Also of note, when this psalm is taken as a response to the first reading in the lectionary, Hosea 2:14–20, the dominant theme that presents itself is God's willingness to forgive the iniquities of God's people. Hosea 2:1–13 includes strong words of judgment against the idolatrous ways of the people of Israel. God, it seems, is ready for a divorce from a promiscuous people; God is ready to punish the wayward wife. Yet Hosea 2:14 begins a love song that speaks of divine compassion, forgiveness, mercy that shall lead to peace. God's anger does not last forever (see Ps. 103:9). God is ready to restore the marriage between God and God's people. Psalm 103 is a beautiful response to this reading from Hosea, because it echoes the yearning of God to separate the people from their transgressions "as far as the east is from the west" (v. 12). The psalm echoes Hosea's conviction that God abounds in "steadfast love" for God's people.

Call to Praise the Lord (vv. 1, 2, 22). The psalmist is calling upon himself, herself to worship the Lord, to bless the Lord, with all that he or she is. The use of the term "soul" is not meant to convey a duality between body and the inner self; rather, "soul" represents the totality of a human being. This soulful worship of the Lord is to be head-to-toe, heart-to-mind, limb-to-limb, and sense-to-sense expressions of adoration to God, who is the giver of good gifts.

There is a connection between verse 2 and the rest of the psalm, particularly verse 7. The poet encourages the worshiper to "not forget all [God's] benefits," and then the poet reminds the worshiper that God "made known his ways to Moses" (v. 7). The human activity of *memory* holds this psalm and, indeed, God's people together. The people of God are a people of *memory,* who always are ready to call to mind and heart all that God has done to bring

Homiletical Perspective

moves from creature and creation to the Creator and seeks to express what is inexpressible. So the psalm in its movement reminds us that God's mercy, God's grace, God's steadfast love to us, all are both apparent *and* beyond our comprehension. But how do we explain what we cannot comprehend? We do not. The psalmist does not explain, nor should the preacher.

Movement 1 (vv. 1–5). The psalmist will praise God with *all* that he is. The psalmist will bless the Lord for *all* the blessings the Lord has given him—forgiveness and healing, even redemption "from the Pit." For it is not only the psalmist's soul and body that are made whole; it is as if he has been brought back from the dead. Here begins a series of spatial metaphors that actually move beyond space. (The psalmist will also make use of temporal metaphors that go beyond time.) All that held the psalmist down, all that holds us down, that weighs us down—so that we are so heavy we are no longer standing on the ground, but we have sunk into the earth as if into quicksand, and the sand, the earth, has closed over our heads, and still we are sinking—all that is lifted away; so suddenly we are flying on eagle's wings, up and up and up until we catch a draft and disappear into weightlessness.

Movement 3 (vv. 19–22). After the psalmist contemplates what God has done for him and what God has done for God's people, after the psalmist considers God's all-encompassing goodness—which, as we shall see, encompasses *more* than all there is—the psalmist realizes the insufficiency of one individual's praise, even if it is with all that is within him; and so the single singer calls all in heaven and earth to join the song. If the Lord rules over all, let all join in God's praise.

Movement 2 (vv. 6–18). The second movement is less straightforward, because the psalmist is trying to describe what cannot be described—because it cannot be comprehended. So the poet turns to metaphor—of several different kinds. If God cannot be described in terms of who God is, then perhaps we can begin to understand God in terms of what God is not. Thus God is *not* as we imagine, dealing with us according to our sins, repaying us according to our iniquities: God will not remain angry or accusing (vv. 9–10). Rather, "as the heavens are high above the earth"—or as high as the heavens are above the earth—so great is God's love. The psalmist

Psalm 103:1-13, 22

Theological Perspective

And what are these ways? This God forgives, heals, redeems, crowns, satisfies, vindicates, works justice for the oppressed (vv. 3–6). These are acts of costly, covenantal love, of blessing. We bless the Lord who has already richly blessed us; we speak of a God who has already spoken to us; we seek a God who has already sought and found us.

According to this psalm the central human calling is to bless the Lord and not to forget all the goodness that has been lavished upon us. The Reformers understood the essence of sin as falling back on ourselves—*incurvatus in se*—curving in on ourselves rather than responding in love and obedience to the Lord before whom we stand. Sin is an egotistical forgetfulness that leads to ever diminishing human possibilities. But it is a reality in human life that arouses intense anger in God (vv. 9–10). Happily for us, God's mercy and grace and reliable, "steadfast" love are greater than our claustrophobic self-obsession, opening up a huge space in which human beings can live: "For as the heavens are high above the earth. . . . as far as the east is from the west" (vv. 11–12).

Walter Brueggemann suggests that a profound anthropological claim is being made here in Psalm 103: "Everything depends on this relation to the One who is utterly reliable. This utterly reliable One is the primary truth about human personhood."[3] We are an indebted people who can only ask with the psalmist, "What shall I return to the LORD for all his bounty to me?" (Ps. 116:12). Ethics flows out of our praise. In blessing the Lord with all our being, we testify to the primacy of God, the source of blessedness, holiness, and wholeness. Authentic existence begins, not in belief or affirmation of doctrine or in a correct worldview or subscription to a set of values and morals, but in gratitude.

IWAN RUSSELL-JONES

Pastoral Perspective

sanctuary after years of temporary quarters in a school. They may feel a resigned rightness when they bring the organized life of a faith community to an end and close a church, distributing its assets to other ministries or giving its building to another congregation. Or they may know the blessing of God's forgiveness when they experience reconciliation and powerful new beginnings after seasons of conflict, or when someone in the community experiences healing, or when they celebrate together at the time of a death the "homecoming" of a good soul who was a special part of their community, or simply when the quality of worship is great. These moments of communal exhilaration, satisfaction, and joy are powerful and entirely real, even if they may be more rare in our experience and harder for most listeners to call to mind. They are the blessings that come to those communities who "fear God" daily by knowing and practicing a life together centered around the Source of life—in holy covenant, in wisdom sought and found, in mission discerned, in lives dedicated in commitment and service to others, in accomplishment and completion in Christ's name, in grateful praise and worship that connects.

Much of human life is troubled by misunderstanding or overestimating or forgetting our place and our powers. Many communities are marked by practical idolatry, by sins of seeking after power or prestige. This reading joyously reminds us of the personal and communal blessings we realize when "God's in his heaven and all's right with our world." For these special times, how else can we respond but with thankfulness?

MARK MILLER-MCLEMORE

3. Walter Brueggemann, *Theology of the Old Testament: Testimony, Dispute, Advocacy* (Minneapolis: Fortress, 1997), 488.

wholeness and peace to the children of the covenant (see vv. 17–18).

Personal Benefits Given by the Lord (vv. 3–5). The first benefit listed is forgiveness. God is, first and foremost, a God of mercy who forgives sins. It may be that the poet connects the power of God's forgiveness to the healing of diseases and to deliverance from death. As we experience the compassion and mercy of the Lord, our bodies are made well and our lives are allowed to flourish (see Ps. 32:1–5). To live in our sins is to be sick and finally to die (to go to "the Pit"), but to live in God's forgiveness is to have a life bejeweled with love and mercy. To live under the weight of sin is to have a life that is drained of vitality, but to live under God's forgiveness is to have wind under our wings so that we sail like an eagle. Those who know God's mercy and steadfast love are forever young in the Lord.

People of God Benefits Given by the Lord (vv. 6–13). The Lord has set an oppressed people free (v. 6). The Lord has shown the people how to live (v. 7). God has shown God's ways to the people of Israel (v. 7), but the people have not followed in that way; yet the Lord is in love with the people of God. God's love is greater than the distance between heaven and earth. God removes transgressions from the people as far as the east is from the west. God loves God's people as a parent loves a child. Even though the people of God have fallen away, they are not dealt with according to their sins; rather, God's steadfast love endures forever.

ROBERT WARDEN PRIM

not only mixes metaphors but turns to hyperbole, though the hyperbole exaggerates what cannot be exaggerated.

It may help at this point to remember that all metaphors are a form of exaggeration *and* paradox. Metaphor itself is a paradox, a lie that tells the truth. For example, the poet says of her beloved that "his eyes are stars." They are not. The sun is a star, a bright ball of fiery gas so large a million earths would fit into it and so hot they would be consumed by it. His eyes are nothing like that—except that they are.

Throughout this second movement the psalmist uses metaphors that exaggerate—especially that *stretch*—time and space. How great is God's love? Look up: as high as the heavens above the earth—farther than you can see. To what extent does God forgive us? Look around: as far as the east is from the west—not only farther than you can see, but farther than you can imagine seeing.

What can *we* see anyway? The psalmist uses metaphors of impermanence—partly to "explain" eternity, which cannot be explained. In terms of time, we can see nothing. We are "dust" (v. 14)—specks in both time and space. Moreover, our "days are like grass"; we live no longer than "a flower of the field," a single spring before we are blown away by hot summer winds (vv. 15–16).

And again comes the question: how great is God's love? (v. 17, cf. v. 11). From everlasting to everlasting. We could say that it was from before time was, and we could say that it will continue after time has ended, except what has "before" or "after" to do with what is beyond time? Then our dilemma is the dilemma of the psalmist. We begin to understand why, if we choose to preach on Psalm 103, we must also make use of the paradoxes of poetry to say what cannot be said.

"My God is an awesome God." The words of the praise song are true, but they are not enough, nor is there enough, even if all creation joins the song.

RICHARD S. DIETRICH

2 Corinthians 3:1-6

¹Are we beginning to commend ourselves again? Surely we do not need, as some do, letters of recommendation to you or from you, do we? ²You yourselves are our letter, written on our hearts, to be known and read by all; ³and you show that you are a letter of Christ, prepared by us, written not with ink but with the Spirit of the living God, not on tablets of stone but on tablets of human hearts.

⁴Such is the confidence that we have through Christ toward God. ⁵Not that we are competent of ourselves to claim anything as coming from us; our competence is from God, ⁶who has made us competent to be ministers of a new covenant, not of letter but of spirit; for the letter kills, but the Spirit gives life.

Theological Perspective

Paul writes to the congregation of Christ: "Show that you are a letter. What you say and do as Christians is a letter. You have not written it. Your task is only to carry the letter to its destination. The letter has an address. And you are responsible to see that the letter reaches its goal: your neighbors, your friends, your enemies. Even though you have not written this letter, you are responsible for delivering it. At the same time, you know two things, because you have already received a similar letter from the same sender. First, the letter will contain a *surprise*, because its contents are not known in advance to the addressees. For them the letter will be a big piece of news—far more, it will be *the* great news. And second, this news will be for them a *good* message. It is good, even if it must address an earnest and serious word to them. In any case, the message is good, because it encourages them and sets them straight."

But where does this letter come from? Paul answers: "You are a letter, prepared by *us*," that is, by the service of the apostles. What he meant is this: the first witnesses and messengers of the gospel in the New Testament, together with the prophets of the Old Testament, are the couriers of Jesus Christ to us. The word of Jesus is related to them first and funda-mentally, as it is written in John 20:21: "As the Father has sent me, so I send you." The consequence of this is

Pastoral Perspective

Paul writes with considerable confidence, a confidence "we have through Christ toward God." The apostle makes it clear: the competence that accompanies the "ministers of a new covenant" is not self-initiated but is God-given. Both confidence and competence are named as marks of the "ministers of a new covenant." How do pastors wear such gifts in their caring and counseling?

Paul distinguishes between the "ministry of death" and "the ministry of the Spirit." The "ministry of death" is chiseled in letters on stone tablets, whereas the "ministry of the Spirit" represents a "greater glory" and is written on the human heart. In pastoral conversations, is it helpful to dwell on the distinctions between Jew and Gentile that are implied in Paul's two conflicting ministries? Do pastors need to denigrate one path in search of the truth in order to describe another path in search of the truth? It may be more helpful to focus on Paul's theology of ministry in Jesus' name—without drawing attention to his critique of the "old covenant." Such a focus, however, will not be easy to maintain, because the apostle returned often to the theme of the "new covenant" versus "the old covenant." It may not be possible to consider the "new covenant" without a consideration of the "old covenant."

Exegetical Perspective

Paul rejects the notion that he needs to provide the Corinthian church with letters of recommendation or receive such letters from them (v. 1).[1] Recommendation letters were used in Greco-Roman culture as a means of introducing or commending someone. Paul himself utilizes this practice on different occasions, as both the author and the subject of such letters. Certain believers "wrote to the disciples" so that Paul would be welcomed upon his arrival in Achaia (Acts 18:27). Paul recommends Phoebe to the church in Rome (Rom. 16:1–2), using the same word, "commend" (*synistēmi*), that is in 2 Corinthians 3:1. The letter to Philemon may be read as Paul's letter of recommendation on behalf of Onesimus. Paul even acknowledges that "some" do need letters of recommendation (2 Cor. 3:1). If Paul is not opposed to the practice in principle, why does he resist providing the Corinthians with such letters?

Lives as Letters. Paul redefines the notion of a recommendation letter by using an extended metaphor of a *life* as a letter (vv. 2–3). Paul does not reject the need for a letter; he claims that he already has such a letter—the Corinthians themselves (v. 2)!

---

1. Although Paul *and Timothy* identify themselves as the authors of the letter (2 Cor. 1:1), I refer to the author as Paul.

Homiletical Perspective

The Sundays after Pentecost bring us lectionary texts that pertain to the growth and upbuilding of the church of Christ. This lesson from 2 Corinthians gives us two issues relating to growth in faith. The first has to do with "letters of recommendation."

The letters Paul speaks of here are both literal and figurative. Literally, there were outsiders who came to Corinth with letters of recommendation in their pockets in order to subvert Paul's authority (v. 1). Paul says he ("we" in the text, Paul's guarded way of referring to himself) needs no letters of recommendation. By way of explanation, he turns to the figurative sense: "You yourselves are our letter, written on our hearts, to be known and read by all" (v. 2). What need is there of a letter of recommendation for him, when the faith of the church and its apparent ministry speak for themselves? Paul brought the faith to these incorrigible people, and the fruits of his ministry are showing. Paul is reveling here in his reestablished role as the chief theological authority in this church he founded. He is even magnanimous to the key troublemaker in Corinth: "you should forgive and console him," Paul says (2:7).

There may not be strong parallels between Paul's problems with the church in Corinth and our present-day churches. But there are surely parallels between the faithful service that he describes as

2 Corinthians 3:1-6

Theological Perspective

that we Christians who are born later have to read the writings of the first messengers, the Holy Bible, with its two testaments, repeatedly. Therefore we cannot celebrate divine services, in public or in private, without listening to the Bible and letting it speak to us. Paul now adds a decisive remark: "Not that we are competent of ourselves to claim anything as coming from us; our competence is from God" (v. 5). What the first witnesses write in the Bible is not invented by them, but given to them. And it is given to them in order that they may pass it on to us.

Who gives it to them? Paul now takes a further step, and writes that the letter comes from *Christ*. "You are a letter from *Christ*." And therefore you are a quite different letter from one written by humans. You come from him. He stands at the beginning of your life, and he rules your life up to this moment. According to Paul, Christ is the Savior, of whom he confesses: "For our sake [God] made him to be sin who knew no sin, so that in him we might become the righteousness of God" (2 Cor. 5:21). God forgives sin in such a radical way that he takes sin upon himself, in order to eliminate it completely. But what does it mean that Christians are allowed to live because of this great gift and to think, and to speak, and to act as the receivers of this gift? Paul answers by quoting from Jeremiah 31:31–34 and Ezekiel 36:26–29, which he understands in the light of Jesus Christ.

Thus the difficult problem Paul confronts becomes clear: You are a letter "written not with ink but with the Spirit of the living God, not on tablets of stone but on tablets of human hearts" (v. 3). Paul recalls here the prophetic promises that God "will make a new covenant with the house of Israel," not like the covenant which they broke; in this new covenant: "I will put my law within them, and . . . they shall all know me, from the least of them to the greatest, says the LORD" (Jer. 31:31–34). And Ezekiel writes: "A new heart I will give you, and a new spirit I will put within you; and I will remove from your body the heart of stone and give you a heart of flesh" (Ezek. 36:26).

Let us clarify what Paul says about the promises in the Old Testament! By doing so, we clear up two misunderstandings of 2 Corinthians 3: Paul does not set the two parts of the Bible in contrast to one another when he speaks about the written code that kills, and the Spirit who gives life. And he does not call a literal understanding of the holy Scripture stupid, and recommend a "spiritual" interpretation. Paul's concern is that if we disregard Christ as we

Pastoral Perspective

In verses 12–16 Paul writes of Moses, who personifies the people of Israel. Unlike Moses, the "new" ministers will not put a veil over their faces, and "their minds" will not be hardened. In Christ, the veil is "set aside"; indeed, "when one turns to the Lord, the veil is removed." Paul suggests that with the "new covenant," there is a relationship with God that is unhindered and is new in Christ. There is nothing between God and God's people in the "new covenant," save Jesus Christ himself, who is our mediator and advocate. With Jesus Christ, the veil is removed once for all, and the encounter with God is a new relationship, a "new covenant" that is confirmed by the death and resurrection of Jesus.

This passage provides critical insight into Paul's theology of pastoral leadership and ministry. From the first verse, it is clear that ministers or pastors do not serve without flocks or congregations. Ministry is always about context. Each member of the flock is a "letter of Christ." The members are "prepared by us" (v. 3), or prepared by the pastoral leaders. The flock becomes, as does each member, an outward and visible sign of the "Spirit of the living God" (v. 3).

Pastors are called to be celebrants of congregations made up of "letters of Christ." For Paul, this special relationship of Christians with God and their pastors was not to be assumed, nor was it a natural occurrence. Rather, almost as an afterthought, Paul holds up the catechetical role of the "ministers of the new covenant" to "prepare" the congregation as a "letter of Christ" (v. 3). Pastors guide, listen, and care. They also instruct and "prepare." Pastors educate and enlighten the faithful by God's grace. They speak, not out of their own confidence and competence, but out of the truth of Scripture and tradition, interpreted for the present time. Pastors do not worry about their own authority but trust in the authority of the One who calls them. This passage from Paul's second letter to the church in Corinth emphasizes the importance of acceptance and education in the church's pastoral leadership.

Paul also invites the "ministers of a new covenant" to a "ministry of justification," not a "ministry of condemnation" (2 Cor. 3:9). Was the apostle, in more modern terms, suggesting that the "new" ministers would be more about acceptance than exclusion? In pastoral care, it would be wise to draw attention to the fruits of a ministry of justification. For the apostle, at the heart of a ministry of justification was the ministry of the Spirit. Implicit in Paul's theology is that the ministry

Exegetical Perspective

The lives of the Corinthians are a more reliable indicator of Paul's credentials than written letters. Their lives trump Paul's resume as an accurate reflection of his character and (apostolic) ability.

Throughout his letter Paul draws attention to the importance of how lives are lived. The substance of Paul's boast is that he has "behaved" both in the world and toward the Corinthians in specific ways (2 Cor. 1:12). He likewise instructs the Corinthians to behave in concrete ways (forgiveness, comfort, love) toward a particular member of their community (2:5–11). It is the "obedience" of the Corinthians that causes Titus's heart to go out to them (7:15). Paul fears that when he visits the Corinthians he may mourn over those who have failed to repent of specific sexual practices (12:21). Paul's emphasis on "right living" is no doubt connected to his perception of the future judgment as an event in which "recompense" will be given for "what has been done in the body, whether good or evil" (5:10). Regarding the superapostles (see 11:5), he similarly claims that "their end will match their deeds" (11:15). Sublimating Paul's emphasis on deeds to a *sola fide* doctrine constitutes a failure to listen to, and appreciate, the distinctive voice of *this* letter.

Old Testament Allusions. Both Paul's metaphor of lives as letters (3:2–3) and his reference to the "new covenant" (v. 6) contain allusions to the Old Testament. Obedience to God is a significant motif in each of the texts to which Paul alludes.

Paul's description of "tablets of stone" (*plaxin lithinais*) (v. 3) employs the same term used to describe the "stone tablets" given by the Lord to Moses on Mount Sinai (Exod. 31:18; 34:1, 4; Deut. 9:9–11; cf. Exod. 24:12). Immediately following the giving of the tablets in both Exodus and Deuteronomy is the account of the worship of the golden calf (Exod. 32; Deut. 9:12–29). Jewish authors cited the golden calf incident as an archetypical example of disobedience to God. Jeremiah and Ezekiel associated God's first covenant with disobedience and envisioned a new covenant that would enable God's people to obey.

Jeremiah envisions the Lord giving a "new covenant" (*diathēken kainēn*) to Israel that will differ from the one they broke after they came out from Egypt. God will "write" such a covenant "on their hearts" (Jer. 31:31–33).[2] In Ezekiel, God promises to

Homiletical Perspective

letters written on people's hearts by the Spirit of God and the kind of faithful service given by people in our churches today. To preach on this pericope and to relate this section of it to our own circumstances will allow us to examine the kinds of fruitfulness evident among the faithful. What are those signs that can be "known and read by everybody"? (3:2) They are signs of active faith as people are involved in "adoration and action."[1] As Miroslav Volf describes it, there is a two-pronged thrust to worship: what takes place within the church as the adoration of God, and what takes place in the world as the active work (action) of the people of God. The first we sometimes refer to as liturgy, classically understood as the work of praise people do in worship. The second could be called the living liturgy of discipleship, the acts of praise made manifest in Christian service. As preachers look out over their congregations, they might ask, what are those signs of faithfulness that are worth noting and raising up as examples of the kind of "letter" Paul refers to with pride in this passage?

The preacher may wonder, however, what the purpose is of reviewing the goodness and faithfulness of the congregation in the sermon. Where is the challenge to further faith growth and discipleship? We can answer that question by describing how the Corinthian church survived various challenges. The difficulties faced by the Corinthian church are legendary: laxness in morality, fighting among various factions, following after interloping leaders, arguing over spiritual gifts, and abusing the Lord's Supper. Still, Paul is pleased with them here and reads their hearts as his own letters of recommendation about his work with the church. For churches in upheaval, this message may bring hope and direction. Even in difficulty, people can grow in faith, mature in discipleship, and become people with whom pastors, perhaps even Paul, might be pleased.

A second homiletical purpose might be to challenge people to continue or to expand their Christian service. To proceed in this direction, the preacher must move toward the second portion of the text.

The second issue relating to growth in faith comes in verses 4–6. Here Paul says that the competence for faithfulness comes from God alone. This is a good theme both for congregations actively

---

2. This reference is to the Hebrew version of Jeremiah. The Greek version (LXX) is chapter 38.

1. Miroslav Volf, "Worship as Adoration and Action: Reflections on a Christian Way of Being-in-the-World," in *Worship: Adoration and Action*, ed. D. A. Carson (Carlisle: Paternoster, 1993), 203–11, 251–52.

2 Corinthians 3:1-6

Theological Perspective

begin reading the Scriptures, then we will understand the text as a mere "letter" that will allow our life with Christ to die. Then the "letters" will seem to us perhaps interesting, or a matter of research for scholars, but they will not give us the life that braves death, nor the life that we need to survive.

Paul shows us we have to read Scripture in another way. He says that God has made us competent to be ministers of a new covenant, not in a written code but in the Spirit (v. 6). We read the Bible in this way and not in another because the Bible is the signpost to Jesus Christ. And when we read it in this way, then we are—in spite of our weaknesses and doubts—in fact a letter of Christ, for the welfare and salvation of many of our contemporaries. Only God can give us what we need for this. But he does give it to us. We may have confidence in God because of Christ's support for us (v. 4). He delivers us from death by sending "the Spirit of the living God" (v. 3) into our heart and into our life, and he makes us alive so that we really are a letter of Christ.

EBERHARD BUSCH

Pastoral Perspective

that claims us is not our own ministry. The ministry that is "ours" is always "of the Spirit" (2 Cor. 3:18). So we share and continue Jesus' ministry in the world. This means that in pastoral care and counseling we proclaim a "new" day, a "new covenant," even a new "ministry of the Spirit." More importantly, pastors proclaim Jesus Christ, not themselves.

In this passage Paul points on more than one occasion to the "glory" that will be. He speaks of a "greater glory" with the new covenant. He boldly claims that the ministry of justification will "abound in glory" (2 Cor. 3:9). The pastor must keep in mind this "glory," even as the pastor identifies the important work of ministry here and now. This passage will be best understood as pastors invite their flocks to consider the "ministry of justification," moments now when their flocks, both corporately and individually, are a "letter of Christ," written "not with ink but with the Spirit of the living God, not on tablets of stone but on tablets of human hearts." The pastor in preparing or educating the faithful may ask the question, What does it mean to be a "letter of Christ," a living document of the good news of Jesus Christ? If the "old" letter kills, how does the Spirit of the "new" letter give life? What does it mean in pastoral care to read the human documents?

Finally, the pastor has the opportunity to explore the radical nature of the new encounter with God wherein the veil of Moses has been removed. What does it mean to see the face of God in the face of Christ and in the face of all human beings? This is a passage of radical acceptance and transformative education—which are always at the heart of pastoral ministry.

J. BARNEY HAWKINS IV

Exegetical Perspective

give Israel "another heart" and place "a new spirit" within them. God will remove the "heart of stone" (*kardian tēn lithinēn*) and give them a "heart of flesh" (*kardian sarkinēn*). God gives these things so that "they may follow my statutes and keep my ordinances and obey them" (Ezek. 11:19–20). God also promises to give a "new heart" and a "new spirit," to remove the "heart of stone" and give a "heart of flesh." God does this so that Israel will follow God's statutes and observe his ordinances (Ezek. 36:26–27). For Jeremiah and Ezekiel, obedience is the reason that God gives Israel a new heart, a heart of flesh.

Lives of Obedience to God and Christ. Paul's references to "tablets of stone" (*plaxin lithinais*), "tablets of human hearts" (*plaxin kardiais sarkinais*), "written on your hearts," and a "new covenant" (*kainēs diathēkēs*) are explicit allusions to these texts in Exodus, Deuteronomy, Jeremiah, and Ezekiel. Utilizing the imagery of a new covenant and tablets of human hearts evokes the concern in these Jewish texts for faithful obedience to God. The Corinthians' *obedience to God and Christ* is thus the specific element of their lives that functions as a "letter of recommendation." Such obedience is made possible since, as Jeremiah and Ezekiel envisioned, it is written on their very hearts (2 Cor. 3:2, 3). Their obedience is not merely a private affair but is "to be known and read by all" (v. 2). Since the content of their letter is "Christ" (v. 3) their obedience is both to the type of life that Christ lived and to the life that Christ's Spirit engenders within them (v. 6).

Though this obedient life is "written" by God's Spirit, it is "prepared" by Paul and his ministry partners (v. 3). As a minister of the "new covenant," Paul is to prepare people for obedience to God and Christ and somehow be a "servant" of a person's potential to obey. The description of the new covenant as one "not of letter but of spirit" recalls the emphasis on obedience in the Old Testament texts cited above. Whereas the letter fails to produce obedience (and therefore "kills"), the Spirit "gives life" by making such obedience possible. Paul serves as a minister of the "new" covenant by helping to produce obedience among the Corinthians. He can be "confident" in this endeavor, since God gives competency in this ministry role (vv. 4–5). Such competency is important, given the fractious relationship between Paul and the Corinthian church.

MATTHEW S. RINDGE

Homiletical Perspective

engaged in mature discipleship and for those seeking to grow in mission and service. The mature in faith already know that the source of their capacity for faithful adoration and action is God. They will hear in Paul's words a confirmation of what they already know: "our competence is from God" (v. 5). Proclaiming this will allow mature believers to return to the source for continued inspiration and power. The good news for these disciples is that their ongoing action does not depend on their own strength. It is a gift of God who makes them competent for ministry (v. 6). For believers learning to grow in faithfulness and service, the same good news applies, but rings perhaps even more loudly. Those who are less mature in faith may assume that the ministry to which God calls them depends entirely on their own efforts and strength. Proclaiming that God provides all the competency that is required for ministry is good news, indeed, to those who see God's call as a daunting and exhausting mission. Given a moment of reflection, the believer might be convinced that he or she cannot begin to do what God asks. But the preacher can dispel such fears with these words of Paul, who reminds us that all confidence for ministry is a gift.

A final word of grace is found in this passage. Paul says that the ministry for which we are enabled is a ministry of the new covenant. We do not serve in order to satisfy the old covenant, that is, the law. We serve in ministry because we are part of something new, something that the Holy Spirit is involved in. To serve by the law is to serve futilely, for "the letter kills" (3:6). In other words, fulfilling legal obligations will earn no reward and achieve nothing in the kingdom of God. But engaging in new covenant ministry means that we are empowered by the Spirit of God to do what is required and to be filled with life in the process: "the Spirit gives life," and does not deplete it.

CLAYTON J. SCHMIT

Mark 2:13-22

¹³Jesus went out again beside the sea; the whole crowd gathered around him, and he taught them. ¹⁴As he was walking along, he saw Levi son of Alphaeus sitting at the tax booth, and he said to him, "Follow me." And he got up and followed him.

¹⁵And as he sat at dinner in Levi's house, many tax collectors and sinners were also sitting with Jesus and his disciples—for there were many who followed him. ¹⁶When the scribes of the Pharisees saw that he was eating with sinners and tax collectors, they said to his disciples, "Why does he eat with tax collectors and sinners?" ¹⁷When Jesus heard this, he said to them, "Those who are well have no need of a physician, but those who are sick; I have come to call not the righteous but sinners."

Theological Perspective

The Gospel of Mark has already established that Jesus speaks and acts with astonishing authority. When he teaches in the synagogue, the people recognize that his authority is greater than that of the scribes. Jesus' authority also gives him power, which he demonstrates by casting out the unclean spirit of the man who cries out in the synagogue, as well as by healing the sick and cleansing the lepers. The question therefore becomes, to what end is Jesus going to exercise his authority? A major indication of the nature of his authority is given in the pericope about the paralytic that immediately precedes the readings for today. The primary way in which Jesus will exercise his authority is in the forgiveness of sins, and the healing he does will be the sign that he has the authority to forgive.

The passages for today describe the controversy that arises due to the way Jesus exercises his authority. To begin with, Jesus calls a tax collector to follow him. Tax collectors were viewed as traitors to their own people, as they collaborated for their own profit with the Roman occupying power. Since Jesus "saw Levi son of Alphaeus sitting at the tax booth," Jesus could not at all be mistaken about Levi's chosen livelihood, which makes his call to him all the more provocative. However, Jesus not only calls Levi to follow him; he also goes to dinner at Levi's

Pastoral Perspective

In Jewish society at the time of Jesus, tax collectors were considered the scum of the earth. These Jews were vile traitors, since they collaborated with the oppressive Roman colonial authorities, doing, as it were, their dirty work. They were ritually unclean because of their constant interaction with their uncircumcised Gentile employers. Moreover, they were corrupt cheats because they exploited their own people to enrich themselves. Their actions and activities prevented them from conforming to the purity customs and laws of their own people. They were thus sinners of the worst kind.

In our reading today Jesus is confronted with the issues of religious, social, and cultural prejudice and acceptability.

The Calling of the Scum (vv. 13–15). Jesus seems to be at home in this crowd of social and religious misfits. In fact, in apparent flagrant disregard for the sensibilities of the religious and social order, he invites one of them—Levi—to be one of his close followers. Levi, the tax collector, must have been a man of some means, as indeed most of the "collaborators" possessed ill-gotten riches. He responds to Jesus' call to discipleship, and in turn invites Jesus to his home for dinner. Visualize the scene—Jesus the well-respected religious teacher,

18Now John's disciples and the Pharisees were fasting; and people came and said to him, "Why do John's disciples and the disciples of the Pharisees fast, but your disciples do not fast?" 19Jesus said to them, "The wedding guests cannot fast while the bridegroom is with them, can they? As long as they have the bridegroom with them, they cannot fast. 20The days will come when the bridegroom is taken away from them, and then they will fast on that day.

21"No one sews a piece of unshrunk cloth on an old cloak; otherwise, the patch pulls away from it, the new from the old, and a worse tear is made. 22And no one puts new wine into old wineskins; otherwise, the wine will burst the skins, and the wine is lost, and so are the skins; but one puts new wine into fresh wineskins."

Exegetical Perspective

From John to Mark. After texts for Pentecost and Trinity Sundays from John, the latest Gospel, we turn now to Mark, the earliest Gospel. Unlike Paul, who says little about Jesus' ministry, Mark reaches back to Jesus' baptism to include stories of his words and deeds. With no end timetable (Mark 13:32), he wants his readers to follow Jesus. Yet for Mark, there is to be no telling of those words and deeds apart from the lens of the cross and resurrection (see 9:9).

All of the Gospels are *interpreted history.* The events in Jesus' ministry come to us through the shaping perspectives of each Gospel writer. We can compare Mark with Matthew and Luke as the *Synoptic* ("viewed-together") *Gospels* because they have materials in common, whereas so much in John is unique to that Gospel, with only about 8 percent similar to the others. Our text does have parallels in Matthew and Luke, but not in John. By comparison, we see that both Matthew and Luke probably knew Mark. Though we shall not compare them here, it is interesting to see how Matthew and Luke have reshaped stories for their own new audiences.

An Inclusive Message. Stories in the Gospels show clearly that Jesus' message included in God's reign those whom some religious leaders would exclude as unworthy. Our text moves from Jesus teaching

Homiletical Perspective

Jesus has been making his way through the region of Upper Galilee, proclaiming a message. He has cured the diseases of a number of people, no doubt drawing crowds. But as he himself has declared (1:38), proclaiming the message is what he came out to do; and the power of that message is compelling. He has been preaching the coming of the kingdom of God, but in each proclamation there has been a cost. The shadow of the cross looms over the story from the very first chapters of Mark, and these verses are no exception: "I have come to call . . . sinners. . . . The days will come when the bridegroom is taken away. . . . No one puts new wine into old wineskins; otherwise, the wine will burst the skins, and the wine is lost."

Jesus is speaking of the incompatibility of the old ways with the new, signaling by his actions the presence of a new reality. He eats with the confused majority, the people of the land. Those in this crowd are poor in many ways: Some of their debts or sins are the result of ignorance of Jewish law. Some are too financially impoverished to adhere to the strict codes of purity demanded by temple authorities. Eating with this impure rabble violates pharisaic practices of table fellowship whereby withholding food from the stranger is equivalent to murder, but sitting with the stranger at table is forbidden. Jesus

Mark 2:13-22

Theological Perspective

house. To share a meal with another is to express that one belongs to this person, and is to be identified with him. Far from using his authority to demand that sinners repent before he will have fellowship with them, Jesus goes to the tax collector's house with his disciples, and shares a meal with Levi and many other tax collectors and sinners. The Pharisees are rightly scandalized by this behavior and ask the disciples why Jesus eats with tax collectors and sinners. Jesus responds by saying, "Those who are well have no need of a physician, but those who are sick; I have come to call not the righteous but sinners" (v. 17).

What does Jesus mean by saying that he has come to call sinners? We could think that he means that he has come to call sinners to repent. This might be implicit in his message, which is, "repent, and believe in the good news" (1:15). However, Jesus does not ask Levi or the other tax collectors and sinners with whom he is eating to repent, but rather desires to share the meal with them in Levi's home. This indicates that he accepts the tax collectors and sinners as they are, without judging them. Luke was clearly uncomfortable with the implications of this depiction of Jesus, for he amends the saying of Jesus in Mark in a very significant way: "I have come to call not the righteous but sinners to repentance" (Luke 5:32). Mark refuses to amend the saying of Jesus in this way, making his vocation all the more offensive—he has come to call not the righteous, but sinners.

The next pericope in Mark only intensifies the scandalous way Jesus exercises his authority. John's followers were fasting, along with the Pharisees. One would expect Jesus and his followers to be fasting as well, since John baptized Jesus and also preached a message of repentance. However, Jesus and his followers do not fast, and when people ask Jesus why, he says that people do not fast when the bridegroom is present, but only after he has been taken away (2:20). The wedding feast is a symbol for the joy of the kingdom of God (Isa. 25:6). Jesus is saying in this response that his refusal to fast, and his eating with tax collectors and sinners, manifests the presence of the kingdom of God in their midst. Jesus does not judge the tax collectors and sinners; he does not treat them as though they are problems that he is going to solve, nor does he demand that they repent or face eternal separation from the kingdom of God. Rather, he extends his call specifically to them and confirms the seriousness of his call by eating and drinking with them, and by describing these meals with sinners as the wedding banquet of the kingdom.

Pastoral Perspective

reclining on the dinner couch in the home of a despised rich crook, with many of his fellow villains in attendance. This is enough to raise the ire of the religious establishment. Indeed, as might be expected, the scribes and Pharisees are clearly outraged. They ask the disciples for an explanation of this irreligious and antisocial behavior.

Care for the Outcast (vv. 16–17). Jesus' response is striking and in sharp contrast with what the scribes of the Pharisees might have expected. He does not challenge the categorization of these people as "sinners," but redescribes them, not as unworthy and sinful, but as sick. They are not sinners but rather people who are ill. And then, far from despising them, he identifies them as those who are the purpose of his mission. Jesus appears to say, "I have not come for you who consider yourselves fine and right. I am like a physician who has come to heal the sick. I need to be with my patients. You may consider them unclean sinners, but to me they are people who suffer illness. What they need most is not rejection but rather the love and care of one who accepts them as they are and is willing to help them regain the dignity and respect they need." Social, cultural, and religious outcasts in the Gospel are both the targets and the agents of God's grace. Mother Teresa of Calcutta demonstrated by word and deed the saying of Jesus, "just as you did it to one of the least of these who are members of my family, you did it to me" (Matt 25:40). The sick, the outcasts, lepers, and all those who are excluded on grounds of preconceived notions of acceptability are the very people who are the recipients of God's unfailing grace. Outcasts of every age and society reflect and need God's grace.

New Circumstances Require New Approaches (vv. 21–22). There *is* something new and different about this rabbi. His disciples do not seem to observe the ritual of fasting, generally practiced for spiritual preparation for high religious festivals and seasons, as the disciples of other religious leaders did. The questioners invoke the example of John's disciples and that of the Pharisees. Is there not something wrong with this new religious movement? Are they not completely out of line both religiously and culturally? Very often we are caught up in observing and criticizing the religious practices of others, instead of interrogating the motives and reasons for our own practices. Our spiritual practices run the risk of becoming an imitation of, or else a

(v. 13) to the act of his inviting Levi, a despised tax collector, to follow him (v. 14). In that culture, tax collectors often were Jews who collaborated with the Romans. They were allowed to add their own take to the tax and thereby often became wealthy. Jesus does not countenance such corruption, but he sees into the person involved and calls him to a new life. Further, Jesus participates with his disciples in a dinner party at Levi's house. It included other tax collectors and sinners, that is, those who did not keep the many religious laws. Good religious persons simply do not eat with such folk.

The "scribes of the Pharisees," the official scriptural interpreters of the very meticulous law-keeping party of the Pharisees, raise objections to Jesus. The Pharisees are good people who seek to live holy lives. Jesus is not against law-keeping, but he challenges them that they "have neglected the weightier matters of the law: justice and mercy and faith" (Matt. 23:23). In our text, Jesus responds to their objection by saying that a physician is not there for the healthy but for the sick. He has come to articulate and embody the outreaching, inclusive character of God's reign to those whom others have neglected and excluded. He has come to welcome them to a new and healed relationship with God.

A Time for Celebrating. Religious obligations then included prayer, almsgiving, and fasting. The scribes ask why the disciples of John the Baptist and the disciples of the Pharisees are fasting but not Jesus' disciples. Jesus responds with a wedding analogy. When the bridegroom is present, the wedding guests do not fast. It is time for celebration. When the bridegroom is no longer present ("when the bridegroom is taken away from them," v. 20), then and only then will they fast. In Jesus' person and ministry, however, "the time is fulfilled, and the kingdom of God has come near" (1:15). It is indeed a time to celebrate the outreaching deed of God in him. With his earthly departure, there will be a time for fasting, that is, for renewal to nurture all that it means to follow Jesus. His physical presence will no longer be there to celebrate. The act of fasting will move from material food to spiritual food, so that his disciples, nourished by Jesus' spiritual presence, may face the world where they are called to live daily as his followers.

New Realities Need New Vessels. One of Jesus' distinctive teaching methods is his use of common objects as illustrations. In our text he uses old cloth

reinterprets these codes, embracing everyone in a new creation based on the coming kingdom.

Talk of the bridegroom and the dualism of two ages, new and old, is central to this passage. Using images of wedding and wine, Jesus speaks of betrothal and renewal of the world, the re-creation of the kingdom that God intended to establish from the beginning; but this good news is threatening. The impending separation of old ways of thinking from the new hovers like a shaft that will pierce the earth, a cross that will divide humankind, one from another. Yet despite the catastrophic tone of his declarations, the crowds continue to follow, pressing, crushing in on him. Why such urgency? Because they are drawn to the authority of Jesus' utterances (1:27), the power of the word of God; and they want to hear more.

There is a sense in which you and I cannot hear the word of God because we are no longer equipped to hear. We live in a culture that drowns us with countless words, words that flatten out the fact that there are real distinctions to be made between religious beliefs. The Sundays after Pentecost, the season of the church, invite us to consider anew what it is and who it is that call us to identify ourselves as Christian.

It is ironic but true that in an era which has been dubbed the information age, we are becoming incapable of gleaning from the Christian Bible its critical information. Not only are we becoming less and less biblically literate as a society, but when some of us do read the Bible, we examine the text with secular eyes. We look for historical examples or literary prototypes or stories that can be tested in scientific terms. Substituting manageable categories of analysis for transcendent perspectives, we attempt to make the biblical story relevant to our lives, rather than looking at our world through God's eyes.

Perhaps the safest thing to say about religion in America is that what is venerated is our right to worship as we please, that American culture no longer constructs its questions and answers on the basis of the existence of the God of the Christian Bible, that the message of the God who proclaimed the coming of the kingdom by dying on a cross is somehow more inaccessible to us.

If ever we could have claimed that America is a Christian nation, we cannot make that claim now. Pluralism of worship is accepted in American society, and confusion of claims about God necessitates clarity on the part of the Christian preacher. For example, we commonly hear Jewish, Christian, and

Mark 2:13-22

Theological Perspective

This kind of behavior simply cannot be made to fit into the world—especially the religious world—as we understand it. We are convinced that the purpose of any religious community is to make people better, to change them from collaborators, traitors, and sinners, into righteous and obedient saints. We are convinced that if we accept the invitation of Jesus to come unto him, to follow him, this of itself makes us better people, and we take great delight in comparing our moral and spiritual superiority to the disgusting and dissolute drug dealers, cocaine addicts, prostitutes, and terrorists who have not accepted the invitation of Jesus to follow him. We lament the fact that others will not improve their lives to meet our standards, so that we might have fellowship with them, so that we might eat and drink with them. It never occurs to us that it is precisely our willingness to see ourselves as the standard that others need to meet—to see ourselves as the judges before whom others stand or fall, to see ourselves as the gatekeepers of the banquet of the kingdom of God—that excludes us from being invited to the kingdom of God. We Christians are no more able to understand why Jesus came to call sinners, and to eat and drink with them in the banquet of the kingdom, than were the scribes, Pharisees, and followers of John. Our communities continue to be the old wineskins that cannot hold the new wine that Jesus came to bring, the wine of the heavenly banquet with tax collectors and sinners, the wine of the forgiveness of sins.

RANDALL C. ZACHMAN

Pastoral Perspective

competition with, others. In a competitive social environment we may fall into the trap of comparing ourselves, even in the realm of spirituality, with others, instead of presenting ourselves and our spiritual activities to God for God's examination. The response of Jesus, once again, recasts the very premise and basis for the religious practice of fasting. Fasting is good and proper—but at the right time, not on a happy occasion such as a wedding banquet. By putting it this way, Jesus declares his presence on earth not a sorrowful, sad time, but rather one of joy and gladness. While he is present with his followers, they can only rejoice. Fasting, a means of humbling oneself before God, has been described as "mourning." A time is coming when he will be taken away—that will be the time of sorrow in which fasting will make sense.

So there really is something new and different about Jesus' religious movement. It is made up of ritually unclean and socially disregarded people who recognize their need for help and healing and so begin to follow him. His presence with them is an occasion for joy and gladness. It is a time of healing and salvation. Unlike the "old cloth," this is new and cannot simply be sewn onto the old. Like new wine it is likely to burst old wineskins, because as the new wine ferments, the gases that come forth will be more than the inelastic old wineskins can bear. When we attempt to graft new attitudes, behaviors, and ideas onto the old, the results are often disastrous. Much more radical action is required. New, flexible structures are needed. New thoughts, attitudes, and behaviors need the creation of new lifestyles and new structures capable of containing and promoting them. The old structures simply cannot cope with the power of the new. Sometimes the most caring thing we can engage in is the formation of new and different structures able to contain and sustain the new.

EMMANUEL Y. LARTEY

Exegetical Perspective

and old wineskins. He explains that one simply cannot sew new, unshrunken cloth onto old, shrunken cloth and expect it to stay intact. Nor can one put the bursting power of new wine into old wineskins and expect them to stay intact. In the one instance, the cloth will tear; in the other, the wine will be lost.

For Mark, one cannot sew the new reality in Jesus onto the cloth of old religion, nor pour him into the skins of old practices. In Jesus, God is doing a new thing that cannot be contained in the old ways. For instance, Jesus includes in God's reign those whom old ways exclude. His presence means celebrating at dinner parties and weddings, not retreating into an exclusive, religious holiness.

This is not to say that the old is bad. In the Old Testament readings for today, Hosea depicts God speaking tenderly to Israel, giving a door of hope, taking Israel as his wife in righteousness and justice, in steadfast love and mercy, in faithfulness (Hos. 2:14–15, 19–20). Psalm 103 speaks wonderfully of the God who forgives and heals, who redeems life and crowns it with steadfast love and mercy, who satisfies with good things and works justice for the oppressed (Ps. 103:3–6). This same God now does a new thing in Jesus, not abrogating God's faithful relationship with Israel, nor the law, but now embracing God's ecumenical world.

A Concluding Word. Our text moves from dinner party, to fasting, to cloth and wineskins. These parts all conclude positively: a barrier-breaking dinner party, a fast-concluding wedding, unshrunken new cloth and bursting new wine. What for Mark lies at the heart of all this celebrating? What provides the framework for telling this story? Is it not Jesus' resurrection? He ordered them to "tell no one . . . until after the Son of Man had risen from the dead" (Mark 9:9).

PAUL L. HAMMER

Homiletical Perspective

Islamic faiths identified as the Abrahamic traditions. While it is possible to agree that whenever people speak of God, they are referring to the One true God, only Christians worship a triune God. So Christian preachers take care not to confuse the referent [God] with the description [God in three Persons] of the object of our adoration.[1] Put another way, the Christian faith differs from other Abrahamic traditions by definition: Christianity stands or falls on the identity of Jesus and his salvific work on the cross.

Lacking the marker of the cross, we might read this Gospel as we would any other piece of prose; and if we did so, we would miss its meaning. Finding it increasingly difficult to read this sacred text and hear what first-century listeners heard, we would lose not only the depth of its meaning. We would lose something more important: We would lose the capacity for Christian religious experience, the capability of living in the kingdom Jesus proclaims. Hearing only the messages of our society, unable to quell the fear inside, we cry, "I have done all I can. I have done my best. There is nothing left." But still he calls us, just as he called Levi; and he says to each of us, "When the totals of your plans and of your life's experiences do not balance out evenly, I am the unsolved remainder."[2] "I am the vastness of new life, and I am with you."

Hearing that word, on the strength of that promise, we can drink the wine that ferments in the veins of God and reimage, reconfigure, even redesign our lives, putting new wine into fresh wineskins and discovering new life, a kingdom of new possibilities with Jesus, Christ our Lord.

JUDITH M. MCDANIEL

---

1. I am indebted to a conversation with Dr. Katherine Sonderegger, professor of theology at Virginia Theological Seminary, for this distinction.
2. Karl Rahner, *The Eternal Year*, trans. John Shea (Baltimore: Helicon, 1964), 25.

1 Samuel 3:1-10 (11-20)

[1]Now the boy Samuel was ministering to the LORD under Eli. The word of the LORD was rare in those days; visions were not widespread.

[2]At that time Eli, whose eyesight had begun to grow dim so that he could not see, was lying down in his room; [3]the lamp of God had not yet gone out, and Samuel was lying down in the temple of the LORD, where the ark of God was. [4]Then the LORD called, "Samuel! Samuel!" and he said, "Here I am!" [5]and ran to Eli, and said, "Here I am, for you called me." But he said, "I did not call; lie down again." So he went and lay down. [6]The LORD called again, "Samuel!" Samuel got up and went to Eli, and said, "Here I am, for you called me." But he said, "I did not call, my son; lie down again." [7]Now Samuel did not yet know the LORD, and the word of the LORD had not yet been revealed to him. [8]The LORD called Samuel again, a third time. And he got up and went to Eli, and said, "Here I am, for you called me." Then Eli perceived that the LORD was calling the boy. [9]Therefore Eli said to Samuel, "Go, lie down; and if he calls you, you shall say, 'Speak, LORD, for your servant is listening.' " So Samuel went and lay down in his place.

[10]Now the LORD came and stood there, calling as before, "Samuel! Samuel!" And Samuel said, "Speak, for your servant is listening." [11]Then the LORD said to

Theological Perspective

This is dramatic narrative, fetching in its many realistic, very lifelike, human details. The young boy Samuel, placed under the care of the aged priest Eli in the Shiloh sanctuary of the ark of the covenant, is roused from bed repeatedly (three times!) by a voice calling to him by name. There are elements of mystery and fear. A first-time, unwary reader wonders, like young Samuel himself, what is going on.

There are tender elements too. Eli, roused from sleep and at first quite at a loss about the situation, is no mean and nasty faith-based institutional ward keeper from a Dickens novel. He is kindly and, although slow on the uptake, offers the boy sound counsel. Also tender in its persistence and its tone is God's call to Samuel, by name. This is not thunder, fire, whirlwind, or "wizard of Oz" or "raiders of the lost ark" pyrotechnics.

The narrative itself has neither provoked nor decided any major theological disputes in the history of Christian doctrine. Yet it has not been insignificant. On the contrary, the boy prophet Samuel declares God's remorseless abandonment of the priestly house of Eli, and this prophecy of condemnation presages Samuel's later career as God's spokesperson in the making and breaking of monarchs. This passage is, then, but the first episode in the canonical account of the transitions from the movable ark to fixed temple

Pastoral Perspective

The Bible abounds in call stories, from the Creator's "Where are you?" in the garden of Eden, to YHWH's addressing Moses out of the burning bush, to Isaiah's vision in the temple, to the voice declaring its delight in Jesus as he was washed in the Jordan by John. But today's story of the call of the boy Samuel is one of the most memorable and charming in all of Scripture. Just as Luke seems to have used Samuel's mother Hannah's song as a template for Mary's Magnificat, so also the narrative of the boy Samuel's nighttime visitation by God in the temple at Shiloh seems to have shaped the telling of the only narrative we have of Jesus' boyhood from the end of Luke 2. This is the beguiling story of his parents losing the twelve-year-old Jesus during the Passover festivities and their frantic three-day search and eventual discovery of him sitting among the teachers in the Jerusalem temple. Luke ends this little interlude with the comment that Jesus "increased in wisdom and in years, and in divine and human favor" (Luke 2:52), while of Samuel it had been written centuries earlier, "Now the boy Samuel continued to grow both in stature and in favor with the LORD and with the people" (1 Sam. 2:26) and "As Samuel grew up, the LORD was with him and let none of his words fall to the ground" (1 Sam. 3:19). A good call story is worth retelling.

Samuel, "See, I am about to do something in Israel that will make both ears of anyone who hears of it tingle. [12]On that day I will fulfill against Eli all that I have spoken concerning his house, from beginning to end. [13]For I have told him that I am about to punish his house forever, for the iniquity that he knew, because his sons were blaspheming God, and he did not restrain them. [14]Therefore I swear to the house of Eli that the iniquity of Eli's house shall not be expiated by sacrifice or offering forever."

[15]Samuel lay there until morning; then he opened the doors of the house of the LORD. Samuel was afraid to tell the vision to Eli. [16]But Eli called Samuel and said, "Samuel, my son." He said, "Here I am." [17]Eli said, "What was it that he told you? Do not hide it from me. May God do so to you and more also, if you hide anything from me of all that he told you." [18]So Samuel told him everything and hid nothing from him. Then he said, "It is the LORD; let him do what seems good to him."

[19]As Samuel grew up, the LORD was with him and let none of his words fall to the ground. [20]And all Israel from Dan to Beer-sheba knew that Samuel was a trustworthy prophet of the LORD.

Exegetical Perspective

In order truly to appreciate the historical and textual context of 1 Samuel 3, it is necessary to be familiar with the chapters that both precede and follow the lectionary reading. First Samuel 1–2 describes the unusual circumstances surrounding Samuel's birth, and 1 Samuel 4:1ff. describes the capture of the ark, the demise of Eli and his family, and Samuel's role as a priest, prophet, and judge. This was a pivotal time in biblical history, as it marked the transition from the old tribal confederacy—in which Israel understood itself as a theocracy led by charismatic judges—to a monarchy led by Saul, David, and Solomon respectively. The Israelite defeat at the hands of the Philistines and the capture of the ark of the covenant—which immediately follows the lectionary reading (1 Sam. 4:1ff.)—constituted one of the great political and theological crises recounted in the Hebrew Bible. Although Samuel's judgeship is ultimately rejected by the people in favor of the kingship of Saul (1 Sam. 8:4ff.), Samuel continued to function as the most important religious leader of his time. Most would agree with Bernhard Anderson's assessment that Samuel was "unquestionably Israel's greatest spiritual leader since the time of Moses."[1]

1. Bernhard W. Anderson, with Steven Bishop and Judith H. Newman, *Understanding the Old Testament*, 5th ed. (Upper Saddle River, NJ: Pearson/Prentice Hall, 2007), 190.

Homiletical Perspective

Let us speak first of the use of parentheses in lectionary texts. Today's parentheses, for instance, take a wonderful familiar story and cut it in half. To what purpose? Well, perhaps there is some advantage to ending the reading on a dramatic note: "Speak, for your servant is listening." Indeed, this is a great theme for a sermon, and it carries a message for all who care to ponder what it means to listen for God's voice. Never mind that God does not speak to most of us these days in an audible human voice. It seems that God was not saying much then, either. "The word of the LORD was rare in those days;" our text tells us, "visions were not widespread" (v. 1). May we pause for a moment to consider what it would be like to experience widespread visions?

Ending at verse 10, however, means that the preacher must sacrifice the succulent image of God doing something in Israel "that will make both ears of anyone who hears of it tingle" (v. 11). Not just one ear; *both ears*! The church would be so much the poorer without Hebrew narrative like this. Why chop it up into parenthetical sections? This story is best told in its entirety, from verse 1 through verse 20. No drama is lost, and there is much to gain.

How do we hear God's call? How do we discern the meaning of the call? What should be our response? Some, like Jonah, pack up and run the

1 Samuel 3:1-10 (11-20)

Theological Perspective

and the age of judges to the age of kings—and so as well the Bible's lengthy canonical course from alpha to omega, first to final things.

The religious-political implications of the larger narrative were of special interest to theologians of late antiquity, the Middle Ages, the Reformation era, and early modern times, who were regularly called upon to address contests between rival rulers claiming divine-right legitimacy and disputes of church and state. This reading's special call to this boy launches a career as prophet-judge that legitimates monarchical-authoritarian rule but protests and chastises it as well.

No less theologically significant, and far more widespread and lasting, have been theological reflections on the pattern of reward and punishment running throughout the books of Samuel and the entire complex today known as Deuteronomistic History. The pattern's deceptive simplicity has always held distinct theological appeal: goodness gains God's blessing; wrongdoing triggers just retribution. Against it, however, are plaintive cries of distress— why do such bad things happen to good people?— that at times mount to the level of dark-night-of-the-soul struggles over theodicy, from that of the book of Job, to the Augustine of *The City of God*, to post-Holocaust theologies of current times. Also to be considered are those biblical testimonies of God's refusal to give up on love, even if it is unrequited, and God's unconditional promises of care and mercy for the "lost" as well as the least of us.

The lectionary reading itself stops a moment short of the prophetic word of doom that Samuel must pronounce on "the house of Eli." Highlighted instead are merely the run-up verses, God's "call" to Samuel. It is one of several models of calling that carry over prominently into theology's accounts of God's call to faithful Christian service, and ordained ministries in particular. Many aspects of the model are so rich, and wholesome, that theological quarrelsomeness seems, in effect, unbecoming. Here, for example, God turns not to those who are first, high, and mighty in the world's ways but to one of the least likely of servants. God is mercifully persistent in calling out. Samuel's "Here I am" is no calculated or calculating career move on his part but an openhearted, vulnerable, and presumably open-ended willingness to hear God's message. Christian teachings of vocation, call and calling, and ordination frequently lift up these themes—and doctrine of this sort is probably one, as the phrase goes, "that will preach too."

Pastoral Perspective

We worship leaders like to think that we do the invoking of God.[1] But the truth of the matter is that we have no power to call God into our midst, as if God is lurking somewhere else waiting to be alerted to our need for the divine presence. The reality is that it is God who in-vokes us in the sense of *invocare*, a Latin word meaning literally "to call into." It is God who calls us into the divine presence and who co-missions us ("apostles us," in Greek), sending us out with a calling or what we have come to call a "vocation." As we pray in one of the classic prayers of the church, "Lord God, you have *called* your servants to ventures of which we cannot see the ending, by paths as yet untrodden, through perils unknown. Give us faith to go out with good courage, not knowing where we go, but only that your hand is leading us and your love supporting us; through Jesus Christ our Lord. Amen." So it certainly was with Samuel.

The Harvard Old Testament scholar Paul Hanson has called Samuel "a person of pivotal significance" in Israel's history, who is both the last judge and also portrayed as the first prophet.[2] Add Samuel's training as a priest under the tutelage of old Eli, and clearly we have here a triple-threat, well qualified to kick-start, even if reluctantly, Israel's monarchy and midwife the story of God's covenanted people into its next political incarnation under kings Saul and David. But today's story concerns Samuel's call, and we had best attend to its enchanting narration.

The story begins with what we might well hear as a narrator's disclaimer regarding the oddness of the tale about to be told, a warning we can be forgiven for nodding our heads in sympathy: "The word of the LORD was rare in those days; visions were not widespread" (v. 1b). No one was expecting what now is about to happen. The boy Samuel, we are told, "was lying down in the temple of the LORD, where the ark of God was" (v. 3), a spooky place for a young lad to be expected to sleep. Little wonder that he began to hear voices, or more specifically, a voice calling his name, "Samuel! Samuel!" "Here I am!" the boy answered, running to the bedside of his ancient, priestly mentor, Eli, whose sleep he interrupted not once or twice but three times. Until the last time, Eli, finally getting it, "perceived that the LORD was calling the boy" (v. 8b). Whereupon the voice called yet a fourth time, "Samuel! Samuel!" and the boy answered as the old priest had directed him, "Speak,

---

1. See my article "Invoking in Public," *Perspectives: A Journal of Reformed Thought*, October 2006, 12–14, for a reflection on the oddity of such a practice.
2. Paul Hanson, *The People Called* (Louisville, KY: Westminster John Knox Press, 2001), 97.

Exegetical Perspective

Although the events described in the early chapters of 1 Samuel are generally dated to about 1050–1020 BCE—that is, from the fall of Shiloh to the rise of king Saul—determining the time at which this account was actually written down has long been an issue of scholarly debate. Some ancient Talmudic traditions held that the book was written by Samuel himself. It seems more likely that the name of the book was derived from the fact that Samuel is one of the principal characters in the text rather than from his having been the original author.

In his groundbreaking work *A History of Pentateuchal Traditions*, the German scholar Martin Noth[2] argued that 1 Samuel and Joshua, Judges, 2 Samuel, 1 and 2 Kings were the product of a single historian (i.e., the Deuteronomistic Historian, often abbreviated Dtr or DtrH), writing during the Babylonian exile around 550 BCE. Today an increasing number of biblical scholars argue that the first version of Deuteronomy was produced in the late seventh century BCE during the reign of King Josiah.[3]

Eli and Samuel are the only two characters (in addition to YHWH) mentioned in the 1 Samuel 3:1–10 text. The son of elderly parents, Samuel was "dedicated to YHWH" at an early age and taken to the central sanctuary at Shiloh to be mentored by the priest Eli. The setting for the story in the lectionary reading is the tabernacle at Shiloh, with Eli sleeping by the entrance and Samuel sleeping within the tabernacle near the Holy of Holies where the ark of the covenant was located. Shortly before dawn, Samuel hears his name being called and, assuming it is Eli, reports to Eli, only to be told that Eli had not called him. After this scenario occurs twice more, Eli perceives that YHWH is calling Samuel and instructs Samuel that the next time this happens, he should simply respond, "Speak, YHWH, for your servant hears" (v. 9, my translation). Samuel follows these instructions and in verse 10 YHWH actually steps forth—apparently visible this time—calls Samuel's name, and Samuel indicates his willingness to "hear" or "obey" (Heb. *shama*ʿ). This is a typical account of a prophetic call that shares similarities with the call of Moses (Exod. 3:1–15), Isaiah (Isa. 6:1–13), and Jeremiah (Jer. 1:4–10), but it is unusual in that neither Eli nor Samuel at first recognized it as a call from God. One might excuse

2. Martin Noth, *A History of Pentateuchal Traditions* (Englewood Cliffs, NJ: Prentice-Hall, 1971).
3. P. Kyle McCarter Jr., *1 Samuel: A New Translation with Introduction, Notes & Commentary*, Anchor Bible 8 (Garden City, NY: Doubleday & Co., 1980), 12–27.

Homiletical Perspective

other way, and some of us have tried to emulate his response down through the centuries. Others struggle for years, even lifetimes, to figure out just what God is calling them to do. Still others seem to hear God's call with absolute clarity; they know right away exactly what it is they are to do, and they set out to accomplish it.

In the church we speak of a "sense of call" among both clergy and laity. Many churches emphasize that *all* are called to be in ministry in some way or another, and that there is a multitude of avenues for serving the gospel. Certainly, most clergy feel called to their vocation. Many church members also feel called to be in ministry in a variety of ways. The prophetic call narratives in Scripture perhaps provide a model by which we think of ourselves as called by God, although most of our personal call narratives are not nearly as dramatic as Samuel's. But they are nevertheless every bit as unshakable and every bit as real to us.

And yet, without belittling any of this, there seems to be a greater intensity somehow in the biblical prophetic-call narratives. There is more heat, more urgency, and invariably more at stake. The biblical narratives portray the prophetic call in mythic proportions; we serve on the ordinary plane of everyday human existence. Furthermore, our calls to serve in ministry in our time have, in many instances, taken on the trappings of career choices. Decisions to respond to God's call today are often made based on means, convenience, resources, available opportunities, job listings, desire to relocate or not, admission to one's choice of college and seminary. Rarely, if ever, are we dropped off on the temple doorstep by our mother, who dedicates us to service in God's name.

Here is another reason for reading and preaching this text through verse 20. In the Bible, every instance of the prophetic call from God entails the commissioning of the prophet for some crushing burden. There is bad news to deliver, there are armies massing on the borders, there is a foreign ruler preparing to invade, there is the current local king who has abandoned the God of Israel and gone chasing after other gods, there are people who have turned their backs on God and who are about to be called to account. The biblical call to the prophetic vocation is charged with a magnitude that burns in the heart of those who hear God's voice.

Our text is framed by family tragedy (Eli and his sons) and a disastrous war in which the Israelites are defeated by the Philistines and, in the process, lose

1 Samuel 3:1-10 (11-20)

Theological Perspective

The passage raises some theological issues regarding calling nonetheless. It is a peculiar, prophetic call coming in a theophany, so extraordinary as an unmediated one-on-one encounter with God, that its general applicability to the ministries of the laity and ordained is far from evident. The church's history is rife with individuals who present themselves to congregations, church judicatories, and "the world" claiming to have been called by the voice of God, quite personally and directly and when no one else was around, to declare the word of God—believe it or not. Contrariwise, untold numbers of otherwise dedicated Christians have shied away from lay leadership or preparation for ordained ministries because they received no stunning, late-night, Samuel-like "special call." The former have on occasion caused churches harm and grief and high-profile bad publicity, nearly as extraordinary as their supposed callings. The latter, however, are, in numbers and by their untapped resources, the greater loss to the ministry of the church at large. It is theologically unwise to praise Samuel's call as if this is how it always is or how it ought to be.

Paul—whose own claims of calling as an apostle troubled a good many in the churches—elaborated an image of one body composed of many members, called and gifted by the Spirit for diverse services of faithful ministry. The "prophets" were among those members. But a communal context was central, and along with it the full equality, complementarity, and interdependence of every member of the body—for the proper functioning of the whole. Doctrinal discussions of Christian vocation and the meaning of ordination have in large measure tried to blend what is considered the "best" features of various biblical models of authorization for leadership. Results, of course, have themselves been diverse, and today's ecumenical dialogues and proposals for the "mutual recognition and reconciliation of ministries" reflect ongoing concern to think and rethink *together* about the meaning(s) of calling to Christian service, along with the ways it comes, the means by which to test and approve it, and the multiple forms it takes.

The lectionary reading of young Samuel's call is closer to the first than the last word on the subject of "vocation" in the history of Christian doctrine. But it is far too poignant and weighty to pass by without serious consideration.

JAMES O. DUKE

Pastoral Perspective

LORD, for your servant is listening." The exact content of what the Lord had to tell Samuel need not concern us here, even though it was enough to "make both ears of anyone who hears of it tingle" (v. 11). The story, rather, connects for the following pastoral reasons. You are invited to add your own.

Notice that the boy Samuel, priest-in-training, dedicated to the service of God by his grateful mother, is already a part of the faithful, worshiping community when his special call comes in the nighttime. Notice that he does not recognize God's voice when it comes. God is sufficiently patient to call several times, and even then it takes the special discernment of Eli, Samuel's mentor, for him to recognize whose voice it is. The emphasis in the story is clearly on listening—"deep listening," we might call it—as in at least three hymns that come immediately to mind: the lively Tanzanian gathering hymn "Listen, God Is Calling," "Open Your Ears, O Faithful People" sung to a lilting Hasidic melody, and Fred Pratt Green's "How Clear Is Our Vocation, Lord." But then comes the faithful response of the hearer, as in the refrain of Dan Schutte's familiar hymn "Here I am, Lord." Favorite, compelling call stories worth retelling are those of Albert Schweitzer, Martin Luther King Jr., and Reynolds Price.[3]

All these stories remind us to listen deeply too.

JOHN ROLLEFSON

---

3. Schweitzer, *Out of My Life and Thought* (New York: Mentor, 1933), 70; King in David J. Garrow, *Bearing the Cross* (New York: Vintage, 1988), 56–58; Price, *A Whole New Life* (New York: Scribner, 1982), 43, 80.

Exegetical Perspective

Samuel's lack of discernment, due to his young age and the fact that "Samuel did not yet know (or "know intimately" from the Heb. *yada'*) YHWH" (v. 7a). Eli's initial lack of perception may be explained as a result of his advanced age or the fact that YHWH had rarely spoken or sent visions in these days, both of which are emphasized in verses 1–2.

If one stops reading at verse 10, it is clear that YHWH seeks to convey a message to Samuel, but the content of that message is unknown until one reads the remaining eleven verses of the chapter. For this reason, it is a good idea to read, or at least summarize the content of, the later part of this chapter to put the lectionary reading in context.

YHWH's message to Samuel is surprisingly negative, announcing the impending doom of Eli and his legacy due to the sins of Eli's sons, whom he has failed to constrain. The ethos of the story at this point is intense. Samuel, who appears to have great respect and affection for his mentor, is reluctant to reveal the message he has received. At Eli's insistence, Samuel recounts the message, Eli accepts it with apparent resignation, and the chapter concludes by stating that Samuel was established as a prophet throughout all Israel (vv. 15–21).

Not many of us have experienced a call as dramatic as that of Samuel, but we all have been called to be disciples of Christ. We can identify with Samuel's experience of becoming aware of injustices and having to decide whether or not to speak out. The temptation is to take the safe route and say nothing. The suggestion of the 1 Samuel and other lectionary readings is that we, like Samuel, must remain faithful to our calling to speak the word of the Lord, even when that message contains bad news.

DAVID W. MCCREERY

Homiletical Perspective

the ark of the covenant. Into this crucible of harsh judgment, war, and loss comes the word of God, rare in these times as we have been told. And God speaks not to the learned, nor to the religious leaders, nor to the powerful, but to an unsuspecting boy who thus far knows nothing of such things. As always, God does the unexpected, and one thinks immediately of the boy Jeremiah, and Amos the farmer, Sarah and Ruth, the young Mary, fishermen and tax collectors and sinners, and many others.

Here God raises up a prophet in the midst of trouble. Here God prepares once again to speak the divine Word into a world still bent on ignoring it. Down through the ages, God has raised up prophets in desperate times—men and women who seem to suddenly appear out of nowhere, yet who seem to have been called for a particular time and place. We know some of them by name, and others carry out their missions in obscurity and anonymity.

Samuel grows up and goes forth to play a pivotal role in the rise of the ancient Israelite monarchy. He anoints Saul, then David, but not before he warns the people of the inherent dangers in subjecting themselves to imperial rule: "He [the king] will take your sons and appoint them to his chariots and to be his horsemen, . . . He will take your daughters. . . . He will take the best of your fields and vineyards . . . the best of your cattle and donkeys . . . and you shall be his slaves" (8:10–17). Indeed, these words have not yet fallen to the ground (3:19).

BERT MARSHALL

Psalm 139:1-6, 13-18

¹O Lord, you have searched me and known me.
²You know when I sit down and when I rise up;
    you discern my thoughts from far away.
³You search out my path and my lying down,
    and are acquainted with all my ways.
⁴Even before a word is on my tongue,
    O Lord, you know it completely.
⁵You hem me in, behind and before,
    and lay your hand upon me.
⁶Such knowledge is too wonderful for me;
    it is so high that I cannot attain it.

....

¹³For it was you who formed my inward parts;
    you knit me together in my mother's womb.

Theological Perspective

No single psalm has been more consistently cited as the bedrock for classical Christian doctrine concerning the defining attributes of God than Psalm 139. Indeed, even more precisely, it has been a source of theological discussion about the *absolute* attributes of God—those attributes that are said to describe aspects of the divine reality as it is in itself. Such *absolute* attributes have traditionally been contrasted with those considered as God's *relative* attributes—the divine characteristics that bespeak God in relation to the universe God has made.

In light of this history of interpretation of Psalm 139 there is a remarkable caveat to be noted. While the psalm can rightly be said to deal with the traditional *absolute* attributes of God classically termed omniscience, omnipresence, and omnipotence, it does so in a subversive manner. It speaks of these *absolute* characteristics in a manner that undermines the very distinction that traditional theology has drawn between the *absolute* and *relative* attributes of God.

Though the framers of the lectionary had their own reasons for omitting verses 7 through 12 from this selection of the psalm, it is impossible to reflect on the theological discussion this particular psalm has engendered in the history of the church without considering all its parts. In speaking of God's

Pastoral Perspective

Psalm 139, in its entirety, runs the gamut of religious sentiment from soaring words of praise and confidence to a vehement call for destruction of the wicked and bloodthirsty enemies of God. While pastoral experience confirms that human beings are indeed capable of such emotional polarities, the lectionary here has spared the preacher the difficulty of dealing with them. The issue in these excerpted verses is the singer's intimate relationship with the Creator of all things—God's utter familiarity with every aspect of the psalmist's existence. Amazement, awe, and adoration form the only appropriate human response: we are, in the words of Charles Wesley's hymn, "lost in wonder, love, and praise."

For believers in the act of worshiping God, this psalm has power to lift us like children in the arms of loving parents. We are known, comprehended, understood; for the innocent child, that is a place of complete security. Our needs are anticipated, our desires are foreseen, even our thoughts are no mystery—and all this at an intensely personal level. Even in a context of corporate worship, the first-person singular tends to override any thought of community: in the words of the psalm, we become aware of God's loving creativity and constant care focused on us, and the feeling of confidence is overwhelming. The One who watches over us from

¹⁴I praise you, for I am fearfully and wonderfully made.
   Wonderful are your works;
   that I know very well.
¹⁵ My frame was not hidden from you,
   when I was being made in secret,
      intricately woven in the depths of the earth.
¹⁶Your eyes beheld my unformed substance.
   In your book were written
      all the days that were formed for me,
      when none of them as yet existed.
¹⁷How weighty to me are your thoughts, O God!
   How vast is the sum of them!
¹⁸I try to count them—they are more than the sand;
   I come to the end—I am still with you.

Exegetical Perspective

Majestic Text and Mysterious God. Psalm 139 is an exquisite composition that falls broadly into two main sections: verses 1–18 (often subdivided into vv. 1–6, 7–12, 13–18) and 19–24. The first major section consists largely of elements of praise where the psalmist confesses that divine knowledge is "too wonderful for me" (v. 6) and "how weighty are [God's] thoughts" (v. 17). The second section might best be described as a complaint that petitions God to "kill the wicked" (vv. 19–20). The discordant tone between the two sections—leading one to ponder what kind of God is met in Psalm 139—is easily heard and may invite readers to engage the pieces separately, ignoring one in favor of the other. However, the psalm is framed by references to YHWH's "searching and knowing" (vv. 1, 23), and is driven throughout by the tone of individual address to God—both of which urge interpreters to struggle with the text as a whole.[1] The psalm offers no easy settlement between praise and complaint.

Searched and Known (vv. 1–6). The psalmist's initial words acknowledge God as one who searches and knows, and at the same time establishes the poet as

1. See the extended discussion in Leslie C. Allen, *Psalms 101–150*, Word Biblical Commentary (Waco: Word Books, 1983), 254–60.

Homiletical Perspective

Writing at the dawn of the twentieth century, the French sociologist Emile Durkheim diagnosed in his society what he called a crisis of anomie: an ever-increasing confusion about social norms and expected behaviors that was developing as social consensus fragmented into a multiplicity of personal or sectarian viewpoints, leading individual members of society to feel isolated, alone, and unable to discern a purpose for their lives. It was the beginning of the trend we call postmodernism, and if it was hard to discern the place of the individual a century ago, it is all the harder now. On the one hand, we are all too accustomed to the invasion of our privacy: our pictures and bios posted on the Web sites of workplaces or social networking Web sites; our preferences and online purchases duly captured and analyzed by the engines of marketing; our political role assigned to an advertising category, be it "soccer mom" or "brie-eating progressive." And yet we remain perhaps less known than at any point in history: distanced from friends by an economic system that requires its workers to be mobile, our lives fragmented between work and home and sport, our civic identity reduced to a Social Security number, until many find their most intimate forms of communication online, with "friends" they have never even met in person. Into this confusion come

Psalm 139:1-6, 13-18

Theological Perspective

knowing, presence, and power, Psalm 139 never does so abstractly and speculatively. It always does so concretely and existentially. The psalm does not distinguish between features of God in Godself and features of God in relation to the world. Rather it understands that God's reality, while disclosive of who God really is, always discloses God in relation to the creation—and especially to the particularity of the psalmist himself. Moreover, while susceptible to being analyzed into several discrete features having to do with God's knowing, presence, and power, all of these features are finally part of the one reality of God with whom the psalmist and we have to do.

The theme of omniscience leaps out in the opening six verses of the psalm with the personal and existential dimensions to which we have been referring. God's knowledge is precisely knowledge of the psalmist in the everydayness of his sitting down, rising up, walking, stopping, and speaking: "You know when I sit down and when I rise up; you discern my thoughts. . . . You search out my path and my lying down, and are acquainted with all my ways. Even before a word is on my tongue, O LORD, you know it completely" (vv. 2–4). God is understood as the encompassing reality of the psalmist's life, surrounding him behind and before, thus laying a divine hand on a life that cannot be rightly understood apart from being known by God (v. 5). This theme is reintroduced in verse 16 and carried to a new place. In addition to knowing all the particularities of the psalmist's existence, of which that psalmist has direct knowledge as well, this knowing God also grasps what the psalmist could not and cannot yet know about himself—as God's eyes beheld his unformed substance and as God's book recorded "all the days that were formed for me, when none of them as yet existed" (v. 16). God's intimate knowledge of the self is not simply God's coknowledge of all that we experience, but also God's comprehensive knowledge of what has not yet appeared to us as the truth of our own experience.

It is this encompassing knowledge of us by God that naturally leads the psalmist into the meditation on God's presence. For the God who knows what has not yet existed for us is the God whose presence is both everywhere and nowhere—or at least not-yet-where. Verses 7 through 10 explore the presence of God as it pervades everyplace that we go—"heaven," "Sheol," "the farthest limits of the sea." Even in places where we have not imagined going, there is a happy inescapability from this God. Not only is God copresent to what we experience in life, but God is

Pastoral Perspective

the moment of our "being made in secret" until we "come to the end" knows us better than we know ourselves; we are safe. We belong.

Human beings yearn to belong. To share our lives with others, to love and be loved, to feel valued, are needs secondary only to being fed, clothed, and sheltered. This psalm displays a concentrated sense of belonging: being searched and known by God, every thought and action understood beforehand, hemmed in "behind and before" by One who lays loving hands upon us and will never abandon us— we could not escape if we wanted to! This is cause for rejoicing, for giving thanks and praise, for marveling at the rich depth of such belonging.

Sometimes, however, we find that the intimacy of truly belonging is difficult to maintain or endure. Guilt for things done or left undone, or shame for some perceived defect in ourselves—or both—wash over us, swamping us in a sense of our unworthiness to stand before the God who creates and loves us or even before another human being. Just as we push God away and hide from God's presence, so we push away those who love us, whose judgment we fear, and flee from their presence (as in v. 7). We evade the piercing vision that sees our heart and forget that those who love us, like God, might just see us through the lenses of forgiveness or mercy.

The speaker in Psalm 139 seems to know he belongs to God. In fact, if the original speaker is a person who has been accused of apostasy or idolatry, as a number of scholars suggest, the words are a testimony to the speaker's innocence. God's omniscience allows no falsehood to stand; evasion is impossible. The psalmist even claims God's enemies to be his own in the (omitted) vitriolic final verses, negating any accusation of breaking faith. Instead, the verses before us are a paean of praise, enumerating the wonders of God's love in tones of awe. Whatever doubts or fears the singer may have are erased in the limitless concern of God, who is with everyone, everywhere, now and always.

But how can this song be sung by twenty-first-century people who have studied biology and psychology? Is it only gorgeous metaphorical poetry? We know the facts of gestation and birth; what is the point of pretending we do not, of talking nonsense about being knitted together or "intricately woven in the depths of the earth" like some kind of magical fabric? There will likely be those among the listeners who take this approach, dismissing the metaphors without examining them for deeper truth. They must not themselves be dismissed, for that would set

the object of divine action: "you have searched *me*." This is important for interpreting the psalm, for whatever claims it may make about God come directly from YHWH's *relationship* with the poet. In contrast to what is sometimes believed, the psalm has little to say about notions of omniscience and omnipresence if one means by those terms some abstract description of the Divine Being apart from creation itself. Even the emphatic structure of verse 2, which literally begins, "You, *you* know . . ." does not diminish the relational character of the psalm. What is claimed about God arises in relation to the psalmist's sitting and rising, thinking, walking, lying, and speaking (vv. 2–4). The psalmist is the object of God's attention and poetically describes the sense of being surrounded by God (v. 5). Just as the psalm itself is "surrounded" by God who searches and knows (vv. 1, 23), so too the poet feels "hemmed in." That kind of knowledge is beyond the reach of the psalmist, too high to attain (v. 6).

While the first unit focuses largely upon God's knowledge of the psalmist, the next unit (vv. 7–12—not a part of the lectionary text) concentrates upon divine presence. By means of the literary device *merismus*—the expression of a totality by means of naming its contrasting parts—the psalmist affirms that no place is devoid of God's presence: heaven or Sheol; east or west; day or night, and everything in between. God is waiting for the poet in all places and times.

Created and Known (vv. 13–18). Jeremiah discerned that before his birth God had called him to be a prophet (Jer. 1:5). He also discovered that there would be no dodging that vocation as an adult. In this third unit of Psalm 139, the psalmist similarly claims that God was active in creating (*qanah*, v. 13) and observing the poet's life before birth. In verse 15 the poetic language shifts from prenatal to terrestrial imagery. "Womb" (v. 13) is replaced by "earth" (v. 15), evoking the image of life being fashioned from the earth (cf. Gen. 2:7, 19; Ps. 104:29–30). This shifting imagery should caution interpreters against reading verse 13 in particular as a biological text. There is rather a theological claim made here and throughout this unit. In hyperbolic, poetic language the poet claims that whether womb or dust, there is no place absent of God. Such discernment again leads to the affirmation, "Wonderful" (v. 14), that follows verse 13 and introduces verse 15. Indeed, God even knows the days that are to come for this yet-to-be person: "in your book [they] were written"

the promises of Psalm 139, a clarion reminder that we are neither alone nor forced to scrounge the crumbs of barren relationships, but may always dwell in the true intimacy of God.

Who, then, is the preacher? The preacher is the representative of the Good Shepherd, the One who knows all God's sheep by name, the One to whom we are not anonymous beings or subjects to be exploited for gain, but consciously created children to be loved. The promise of God in this text is the promise of true community: of a pastor who knows his or her flock, of a congregation that is a safe space to be fully known, of a God in whom we can be intimately held in the incarnate face of Love (cf. 1 Cor. 13:12).

For all its overwhelming beauty, this text may be hard for people in the twenty-first century to hear. The tender images of creation in verses 13–16 press the boundaries of contemporary struggles over the proper spheres of religion and science, and particularly raise concerns about abortion, genetic intervention therapies, and other start-of-life issues. People conditioned to think of life in terms of scientific laws and natural processes may have trouble getting beyond a simplistic literal understanding of these verses to grasp the power of the poetic insight. Parishioners who have had an abortion or who suffer from a severe genetically induced condition (or who live with such a person) may be angered or troubled by readings which suggest "God caused it or made you that way." The preacher might want to raise such issues explicitly, in order to suggest to the congregation theologically rich ways to consider them.

A different set of concerns would arise in the case of persons who have been raised in a theology that sees human beings primarily as fallen and broken sinners; for such persons, being known by God could feel more like a threat of vengeance than a promise of love. (Indeed, that ambivalence is hinted at in the omitted vv. 9–11, which could describe someone hiding from the face of God as easily as an exile seeking it.) The preacher might wish to raise the issue of shame here, to elucidate what is really meant by the "fear of the Lord," or to discuss the judgment and mercy of God in the context of other passages (such as God's revelation to Job in the whirlwind [Job 42:1–10], or the call of Isaiah [Isa. 6:1–8]) that exhibit the same tension between shame and restoration/renewal in the presence of God. (The same set of listeners might react to the suggestion of predestination in vv. 4 and 16; the preacher might

Psalm 139:1-6, 13-18

Theological Perspective

also present to what is to be—thus more intimately part of our life than we can yet be ourselves (see v. 16 again). It is not difficult to see why profound Christian interpreters have seen in such a psalm comprehensive testimony that we belong to God because God holds us actually and eternally in God's knowing, thus being always and forever present to us.

Finally, the meaning of this "omnipresence" of God is gathered into the psalmist's account of God's "omnipotence." The power of God to which the psalmist testifies is the power that makes light out of darkness (vv. 11–12), the power that accomplishes the marvelous work of creation (cf. Gen. 1) in the specificity of the psalmist's own creation as one "fearfully and wonderfully made" (vv. 13–14). The power thus celebrated reflects not only the sovereignty of power, but also the sovereignty of love, since the psalmist heralds a creation by artistic, caring hands that intricately weave his being in the depths of the earth (v. 15). Scriptural testimony such as this has given rise to some of the grandest assertions of the Christian tradition.

One of these is found in the Heidelberg Catechism, which trumpets this omnipotent God as the One who caringly encompasses our lives, whatever the predicaments in which we find ourselves. In response to the question of what it means to believe in "God the Father Almighty, Maker of Heaven and Earth," the catechism echoes the testimony of Psalm 139 saying that in the face of any evil that may visit us in this mortal life, God may be trusted to turn it to our good, "for he is able to do it, being almighty God, and is determined to do it, being a faithful Father."[1]

In the poetry of Psalm 139 the knowledge, presence, and power of God are not separately analyzed but together affirmed as leading to unavoidable praise of God's mystery. God's praiseworthy mystery encompasses us by knowing us more fully than we know ourselves, by being present to us in the wonder of God's embrace now and eternally, and by manifesting the power of a marvelous and wonderful creation, summoning us and all things into being.

D. CAMERON MURCHISON

Pastoral Perspective

them outside the fellowship of the faithful and undermine the powerful message of belonging. Instead, the preacher might look for concrete ways to bring the metaphors to life in an age of doubt, fear, and terror.

The cycle of life is implied throughout the psalm; from conception to "the end," the activities of daily living are here. Are there milestones to be marked among the worshipers? For a couple expecting or celebrating the birth of a baby, verses 13–16 speak powerfully to their experience and emotions. Recent graduates might be reminded of God's thoughts, "weighty," "vast," and uncountable, as they give thanks for their education and look to their future—always in God's care.

These verses also lend themselves wonderfully to individual meditation. In acknowledging that God has "searched me and known me," I may become aware of ways in which I need to know myself or God more deeply. A preacher who is a pastor has unique license to encourage Sabbath keeping, self-examination, and disciplines of prayer or meditation to the flock at any time; here is a beautiful meditation, ready-made, on the creativity and omnipresence of God. Taking the time to listen like Samuel for God's call in the Sabbath quiet helps to strengthen us for the path ahead. Even in our fear-filled times, these intimate truths hold the promise of healing and peace.

The lectionary offers this psalm for our consideration in early summer, in those years when Easter falls on or before April 2. Education and Christian formation programs often take hiatus about this time; families travel on holiday as the school year ends; opportunities to gather the community of faith tend to be fewer than in the busy seasons of the fall or Lent. Psalm 139 insists that wherever we go, God is there; nothing we do goes unnoticed by God. Because we belong to God, nothing—not even death—can "separate us from the love of God in Christ Jesus our Lord" (Rom. 8:39). We belong.

MARY DOUGLAS TURNER

---

1. Heidelberg Catechism, Q. 26, in *The Book of Confessions* (Louisville, KY: Office of the General Assembly, 1999), 32.

Exegetical Perspective

(v. 16). Rather than asserting some notion of determinism or fatalism, the poet is again stretching for images to convey the unimaginable reach of God's thoughts.[2] Such thoughts are as innumerable as the grains of sand; after futilely attempting to count them, all that is left is presence: "I am still with you" (v. 18).

The final section of the psalm (vv. 19–24—again, not a part of the lectionary) is crucial for understanding all that has gone before. The prayer takes a vindictive turn that asks for the destruction of those who are deemed enemies of both the poet and God. In terms as stark as imaginable, the psalm distinguishes between the wicked and the poet and petitions God to continue to search the psalmist's life. No guilty person, goes the logic of the psalm, could withstand such scrutiny. This section of the psalm suggests that the entire composition may have arisen as a response to false accusations of the "wicked" by asserting that the searching and knowing God is present to vindicate the psalmist. To hear the psalm in this way is, yet again, an important reminder that all of the claims made about God's knowledge and presence are not to be taken as abstract formulations about divine attributes. Rather, the poet speaks out of a concrete context and experience of divine presence.

While recognizing that Psalm 139 likely arose as a response to a particular situation helps guard against hearing it as an abstract philosophical text, Psalms scholar James Mays advises us to hear the psalm as the discourse of "the self in relationship to God."[3] As such, Psalm 139:1–6, 13–18 (along with the rest of the psalm) invites readers to be open to the inscrutable presence of God in ways, places, and times that seem too wonderful to imagine. God is not aloof, but rather seeks us and desires intimate relationship, even in moments of adversity. Surely that is good news for the days in which we live.

V. STEVEN PARRISH

Homiletical Perspective

want to abstain from this topic unless he or she can address it usefully.)

One more way to approach this passage would be in the context of its implications for the life of prayer. What this text seeks, above all, is the formation of persons of integrity. Its emphasis on the constant presence and perfect knowledge of God destroys forever our belief in the possibility of pretense, either in withholding issues from God because we are afraid that God will "zap" us if God knows what we are really like (God does), or in terms of trying to live one way before one's fellow human beings and another way before our God. People who lived into the divine reality described in this psalm would be transparent in offering all they are up to God for completion or transformation. They would approach God with perfect trust in their creator, and would be open to the wonder of the world around and within them, responding with awe and humility to the love of God present and incarnate in themselves. Thomas Keating, the monk and teacher of centering prayer, wrote that "the notion that God is absent is the fundamental illusion of the human condition."[1] Psalm 139 reminds us that "in [God] we live and move and have our being" (Acts 17:28).

Nor is this without its ethical implications, for the psalmist stands in the place of every human being, and the great gift that *each* listener has received (being personally created, known, and loved by the God of all the earth) is the gift that *every* listener has received. We cannot take the words of this psalm seriously without being moved to awe, not only at the work of God in ourselves, but also at God's handiwork in one another.

DEBORAH ANNE MEISTER

2. See Hans-Joachim Kraus, *Psalms 60–150* (Minneapolis: Augsburg/Fortress, 1989), 517.

3. James L. Mays, *Psalms*, Interpretation (Louisville, KY: John Knox Press, 1994), 428.

1. Cited by Cynthia Bourgeault, *Mystical Hope: Trusting in the Mercy of God* (Boston: Cowley Publications, 2001), 41.

2 Corinthians 4:5-12

⁵For we do not proclaim ourselves; we proclaim Jesus Christ as Lord and ourselves as your slaves for Jesus' sake. ⁶For it is the God who said, "Let light shine out of darkness," who has shone in our hearts to give the light of the knowledge of the glory of God in the face of Jesus Christ.

⁷But we have this treasure in clay jars, so that it may be made clear that this extraordinary power belongs to God and does not come from us. ⁸We are afflicted in every way, but not crushed; perplexed, but not driven to despair; ⁹persecuted, but not forsaken; struck down, but not destroyed; ¹⁰always carrying in the body the death of Jesus, so that the life of Jesus may also be made visible in our bodies. ¹¹For while we live, we are always being given up to death for Jesus' sake, so that the life of Jesus may be made visible in our mortal flesh. ¹²So death is at work in us, but life in you.

Theological Perspective

Paul has just described, in exalted language, how the Corinthians themselves are his letter of recommendation, written on human hearts by the Spirit of God.

Christians have often emphasized inward illumination and transformation by the Spirit. Sometimes they claim that their spiritual gifts give them insights not shared by other people. Understandably this has been a point of controversy. Is inward illumination sufficient by itself?

As we move into chapter 4, this question is answered as Paul adds four important qualifiers that were scarcely mentioned before.

1. While the focus had been on the Spirit, it now shifts to Christ. Paul had suggested that all Christians, like Moses, behold the glory of God "with unveiled faces" and are being transformed into God's image (3:18). Now he makes it clear that Christ is the only one who can be called "the image of God" without qualification (4:4), the only one whose "face" permanently reflects the glory of God (4:6).

Adam, although he is never mentioned by name, may be lurking in the background, for he was traditionally thought of as being created with not only the "image" but the "glory" of God. There had been various Jewish speculations about the glorious state of Adam before his sin. Paul ignored all of this,

Pastoral Perspective

Paul's assertion in Romans 10:17 that faith comes by hearing may reasonably raise the question as to whether a preacher can be moved to faith by overhearing herself. This is not to ask only whether one who speaks the word can appropriate it for his own life, though it is routinely observed how often we who proclaim grace to others seem ourselves to live anxiously and driven. It is also to consider whether there is saving truth that we uncover for ourselves only when we speak seeking to affect others. Can there even be a *saving* word prior to its being uttered in relationship? Relational speech, including God's word, is inevitably rhetoric and not just content: it cares about and intends the response of the other. It wants to be heeded. Can it be then that we ourselves—as pastors but also simply as real people—will learn from our own rhetoric what we had not yet fully understood?

In this reading, Paul has what might be called a rhetorical problem, the issue of his authority, and he uses a rhetorical strategy to address it. That strategy bears rich theological fruit and has indeed become gospel for us. But how much of it was there for Paul before the rhetoric, before he chose to say it, or before he heard himself saying it?

Both Corinthian epistles evidence a struggle to claim and maintain authority. In Galatia Paul had

Exegetical Perspective

To interpret individual passages in 2 Corinthians, it is necessary to understand the whole letter in the context of Paul's troubled relationship with the church in Corinth. The relationship appears to have intensified over the years since his first visit to Corinth, circa 49–51. In the correspondence in 1 and 2 Corinthians and in the other letters mentioned within these texts (1 Cor. 5:9; 1 Cor. 7:1; 2 Cor. 2:3–4), Paul defends his authority and his identity as apostle. Both subject and rhetorical style communicate his sense of urgency as he battles those who challenge him. Paul closely identifies his own ministry with the gospel, so his defense applies to both. The two rhetorical strategies of apologetic and polemic overlap; he is both defending and attacking. The rhetorical style presents the preacher with challenges. One is whether to work with the intensity and oppositional nature of the rhetoric—to emphasize the errors of Paul's opponents and their theology—or to resist and to "de-escalate" the polemic. A second is whether to identify Paul's words with his own unique experience or to understand him as speaking more broadly of the communities with whom he shared the ministry of followers of the crucified Lord.

This passage occurs within the second main part of the body of the letter, which stretches from 2:14 to 7:4

Homiletical Perspective

After a tree falls into the water, a slow process of disintegration begins. David James Duncan observes, "The fallen tree becomes a naked log, the log begins to lead a kind of afterlife in the river, and this afterlife is, in some ways, of greater benefit to the river than was the original life of the tree." While a living tree provides shade on the river and shelter for animals, a tree that has snapped in two and has fallen into the water "creates a vast transfusion of nutrients . . . a river feast." As these immersed trees break apart they assume an appearance similar to rocks. Duncan remembers as a child he called them "river teeth."[1]

As we seek to serve Jesus Christ we can often fall from the shore, break into two, and tumble into the flowing waters of ministry. Call us "river teeth." Or just call us "broken." The demands, criticisms, and breakneck pace of ministry can topple even the most grounded pastor, church leader, or volunteer.

Yet, as Paul reminds us, it is often in our brokenness, within our submerged selves, that new life bursts forth. How? Paul believes the resurrected Christ actually resides in the apostles. We might say through the power of the resurrection Paul and the apostles are now Christ's own "river teeth."

1. David James Duncan, *River Teeth* (New York: Bantam, 1996), 1–2.

2 Corinthians 4:5-12

Theological Perspective

simply treating Adam as the source of sin and death (1 Cor. 15:21–22, 45–49; Rom. 5:12–21). Now all humans fall short of "the glory of God" (Rom. 3:23) and are captives of sin and death (Rom. 7).

The grandeur that had been associated with Adam is shifted to Christ, who for the first time fulfills the potentialities offered to the human race. Adam made the wrong decisions and brought disaster; by contrast Christ, even though he shares human weaknesses, makes the right decisions and through suffering repairs the human relationship with God.

2. How does one gain access to Christ and his "face"? Only through the gospel (4:4), the entire story of Jesus, climaxing in his death and resurrection. While the gospel opens the door to renewal for those who believe, Paul also acknowledges that "his gospel," the gospel as he proclaims it, may be veiled (4:3) because of unbelief.

3. Jesus' "glory" becomes evident chiefly through his resurrection and exaltation as Lord. This was especially true in the case of Paul, who had no contact with the earthly Jesus and at first responded negatively to what he heard about him, until he received a vision of the exalted Christ. Starting there, Paul worked his way to the "background" earlier in Jesus' life. When he did this, his usual emphasis was on Jesus' humility and self-emptying (2 Cor. 8:9, Rom. 15:1–3, and especially Phil. 2:5–11). These passages are often taken to refer to preexistence and incarnation. It is more likely that they refer to the human (or divine-human) Jesus; they are themes that often appear in Christmas carols and legends. The focus is not on Jesus' origin in heaven but on his task on earth, and his special role as Lord comes only after he follows this lonely path to its end (Phil. 2:9).

4. Christ's followers are depicted not as spiritual giants but as vulnerable human beings. Once again we are reminded that God acts in ways that do not fit the world's criteria (see 1 Cor. 1:20–25). "We have this treasure in clay jars," Paul says (2 Cor. 4:7). The treasure, of course, is the gospel, which brings a new and totally different kind of enlightenment and wisdom.

"Earthen vessels" is the elegant way the King James Version put it; "earthenware jars" or "clay pots" or the NRSV "clay jars" is more accurate. These were purely utilitarian; they were not repaired but thrown away. Paul contrasts the fragile vessels with the priceless treasure they carry. It is one more way of differentiating Paul's own unimpressive behavior from that of the "superlative apostles," who certainly would not have characterized themselves as "clay

Pastoral Perspective

likewise been opposed and his right to be an apostle challenged, but there he had been able to point to his priority as founder and teacher (Gal. 1:6–9). Passionately and aggressively, he had defended his apostolicity. In Corinth, however, several others, all with their own devotees, seem to compete with him for leadership. (There is apparently even a faction that claims itself independent of mere mortal leadership and names itself the party of Christ.) Unable to claim preeminence (1 Cor. 1:10–13), Paul has had to adopt a very different line of argument.

In this setting, Paul has moved in the opposite direction, relativizing his own authority and thus also, cleverly, that of his rivals. By pointing to the danger of factionalism, warning against the charismatic and winsome rhetoric that could so easily feed prideful division, and insisting on humility, forbearance, and mutual respect, Paul not only offers sage advice to a young and fractious community; he lays out an ecclesiology where his words can be heeded, not because he has pride of place, but because we need to listen to the other, not least to the humble and the despised. Paul's words of gracious wisdom about diversity and conflict in the Corinthian community are more than wise; they are also politically and rhetorically clever. They claim authority by refusing it, or rather by subordinating it to the authority of the one who chooses the despised over the strong and attractive.

Paul's rhetoric of humility and self-deprecation, of course, lies in tension with a rather strong ego and a confidence in his own correctness. When in 1 Corinthians 3 he wrote that some build on the foundation with good materials and others with rickety ones, it was quite explicit that he did not think of himself as a shoddy workman. Still, the line of his argument there was to point to the common foundation, one that would allow even the inferior builder to be saved (1 Cor. 3:15). Paul had to argue for, and out of, whatever humility he could muster. And, of course, Paul had a valuable resource in this regard, for alongside all the confident conviction that was so naturally within him was the memory—his own and that of the church—of where such righteous self-assurance could lead: out of such certainty, he had persecuted the church of Christ. That guilt served the apostle repeatedly in the tempering of his pride, but it did not invariably and immediately come into play. Sometimes he forgot.

The context of this reading, then, is the same kind of argument, but intensified in 2 Corinthians as the attacks upon and the doubts about Paul appear more

Exegetical Perspective

and whose subject is Paul's apostleship. In this lection the first two verses (4:5–6) conclude the movement of argument that begins in 4:1 and describes apostolic ministry. The reference to God as the source of light shining in our hearts contrasts with the image of the "god of this world" who blinds the minds of the unbelievers in 4:4. Paul's argument here is playing with the difference between the veiling (3:12–18) that interferes with those who hear the reading of the old covenant, the blinding of unbelievers, and the direct action of God who illuminates the hearts of Paul and those who share his faith.

The first person plural pronoun "we" occurs frequently in the letter and can mean all people, all Christians, all the apostles, Paul and his immediate coworkers, or Paul himself. Here the "we" is closely identified with Paul and refers to his own ministry, which he is defending. He denies that the subject of the proclamation is "ourselves"; rather it is Jesus Christ as Lord, one of the earliest confessions of the community. The Lord (*kyrios*) possesses and rules over the slave (*doulos*)—here translated as "servant." Paul says that he and his colleagues are subordinate to those to whom they preach for the sake of Jesus. To speak of himself as "your" slaves, rather than as "slaves of the Lord," as he does elsewhere, emphasizes selflessness.

The concluding verse claims that God has illuminated "our hearts." To characterize God, Paul quotes God as saying "let light shine out of darkness." Not an exact quote, the phrase may refer to the story of creation in Genesis 1:3 or to the prophecy from Isaiah 9: "The people who walked in darkness have seen a great light; those who lived in a land of deep darkness—on them light has shined." The imprecision of the quote opens up its range of connotations to include both creation and the coming of the Messiah. Light shining in darkness is a vivid image for divine creativity and for deliverance from darkness and danger. God shining in our hearts may allude both to Paul's individual illumination (Gal. 1:12) and to the experience of illumination of all believers. The light is described as that "of the knowledge of the glory of God in the face of Jesus Christ." The word "glory" recalls the argument about Moses and veiling in 3:7–18. Paul stresses the intensity and directness of this illumination.

Paul now uses the memorable image of "treasure in clay jars" to describe apostolic ministry. "Treasure," used only here in Paul's letters, in Greek as in English, summons up riches. "Clay jars" keenly evokes the contrast between the fragility and

Homiletical Perspective

A sermon might consider how this good news speaks to our ministry, namely, how as Christ's "river teeth" we can draw upon what the church has historically called *fortitude*—a trait Paul references when he writes, "We are afflicted in every way, but not crushed; perplexed, but not driven to despair; persecuted, but not forsaken; struck down, but not destroyed" (vv. 8–9). Or as paraphrased by J. B. Phillips, "We may be knocked down, but we are never knocked out!"

A sermon might explore how the cultivation of fortitude can address the ups and downs of ministry. For example, a preacher might reference that the Catholic Church considers fortitude a cardinal virtue or that Scripture offers repeated stories of individuals like Adam and Eve, Abraham and Sarah, Moses and Miriam, and especially Paul, who fall from the shore and must draw upon inner spiritual resources to be "resurrected."

In other words, Paul offers a steady and faithful word of encouragement to all who have fallen into the turbulent waters of congregational life, those who have been bruised in body and spirit by the church and feel snapped in two. Such faithful folk discover in this passage a reminder that fortitude grounded in Jesus' resurrection enables us not only to survive turbulent waters but to be transformed by the experience.

On a trip to Israel, I met Father Elias Chacour, who like many Palestinians had been evicted from the land his family had farmed for thousands of years and had been forced to live as a refugee. Yet, through his faith in Jesus Christ, Father Chacour discovered an inner fortitude to swim through the waters of adversity.

The story that shaped his life and ministry occurred on Palm Sunday when he was about to pronounce the benediction. As he gazed upon the congregation and was poised to speak, all he could see was in deep division. Two sisters had not spoken in years. Neighbors fought. Everyone hated the policeman in town. Suddenly, Father Chacour was compelled to stride down the aisle, lock the front doors, and return to the pulpit. "The doors of the church are locked," he said. "Either you kill each other right here, or you use this opportunity to be reconciled. If this reconciliation happens, Christ will truly become our Lord." After what seemed like hours, the policeman slowly walked to the center aisle and asked for forgiveness. Tears ran down his face, and he stretched out his arms to hug Father Chacour, who said, "I will hug everyone and

2 Corinthians 4:5-12

Theological Perspective

jars." We are cautioned, then, not to make inflated claims for the ministers of the gospel, not even for bishops and popes; we are even authorized to analyze the church and its ministries in down-to-earth sociological terms, as James Gustafson did in his classic book *Treasure in Earthen Vessels: The Church as a Human Community* (1961).

Paul goes on to catalog the hardships he had faced, both in generalities (4:7–10; 6:3–10; 12:9–10) and listing the particulars (11:23–29). Unlike the Stoics, who felt confident that they could overcome any and all circumstances through their own inner strength, Paul admits his feelings of despair; endurance comes not from himself but from God. Paul cannot avoid connecting his own hardships with Jesus' sufferings (1:5) and dying (4:10); previously he had said, even more vividly, that he bore the stigmata of Jesus on his body (Gal. 6:17). The connection, of course, is that Paul's own sufferings are the result of proclaiming the gospel. The positive side is that "the life of Jesus" will also be manifested in his mortal flesh (4:11). This could mean Jesus' resurrection life, but his earthly mode of life should not be excluded; just as "dying" has a broader meaning, so does "life."

Paul's point is paralleled elsewhere in the New Testament. The disciples, seeing Jesus transfigured on the mountaintop, want to stay there and celebrate the occasion (Mark 9:2–8; Matt. 17:1–8; Luke 9:28–36); instead, Jesus leads them back down into the valley, where other disciples are having trouble casting out demons. After his resurrection they expect him to "restore the kingdom to Israel," but instead he tells them that they are to be his witnesses "to the ends of the earth" (Acts 1:6–8).

Throughout Christian history there are many examples of grandiose expectations being humbled and brought back down to earth. We have also seen many movements that imitate Christ's humility, service, and readiness to suffer. The Franciscans are best known, vividly making the point that property and ambition are not the way toward fullness of life, for it can be found in a wandering life of service and proclamation (cf. Matt. 10:7–15). Many communities of Catholic women have served the world by operating orphanages, hospitals, and schools. And we can think of many contemporary movements of Christian witness along the same lines.

EUGENE TESELLE

Pastoral Perspective

ad hominem and personal. Paul's weaknesses, his failures, his unimpressive self all seem reasons to reject him. If he were worthy of listening to, truly an apostle of God's future, really what he claimed, would not God have granted him greater success, more advantage, less suffering, fewer setbacks? Such are the questions he is up against. And so again Paul has adopted this strategic response: it is his *weakness* that validates his authority. It *is* in such fragile clay that the treasure is carried. The suffering, rejection, and struggle—all that seem to diminish him as a human leader—actually serve to reveal the "extraordinary power" of God. Paul's authority is not a personal lordship but that of their slave *for Jesus' sake.* This is brilliant, not just because it is much harder to reject than the claim of the proud and overweening; it also invites his readers and listeners deeper into the meaning of the gospel.

But, to take a step back from the particulars now, there seem to be two common ways of thinking about the rhetoric of Paul's argument here. The apparently more pious one holds that Paul knew and believed this and here gives expression to it; the more cynical view is that this is "just rhetoric," a sly strategic argument whereby a fundamentally arrogant man deploys a theology of humility to his own ends. I think neither of those readings gets it quite right, but would instead suggest that what Paul wrote as rhetoric and argument also taught *him* something that might otherwise have been only inchoate and unseen.

Remember, he had a way of using the imagery of clothing and of armor, of "putting on Christ." If we take that seriously, does it not suggest also that what he and we "put on"—the stances we adopt, the rhetoric we use, the ways that we present ourselves to others and to God—can in fact teach us what we do not yet know and help us to be what we have not yet become? We are shaped by what we wear. Pedagogically, psychologically, ethically, and spiritually, that principle has much to teach us.

JOHN K. STENDAHL

Exegetical Perspective

ordinariness of the earthenware and the permanence and value of the treasure. This ironic and strange juxtaposition of treasure in cheap jars, Paul explains, is "in order that" the power of God may be shown to be God's and not from us. "Extraordinary power" points to the theme of power and weakness so central to this letter (see 2 Cor. 12:1–10). The fragility of human vessels points to the divine source of the power.

Listing their sufferings in order to underscore their credibility was a common rhetorical technique among philosophers. Stoics often claimed to respond to suffering with nobility and equanimity. Jewish writing also emphasized the suffering that the righteous underwent at the hand of the unrighteous and the unfaithful. The lyrical phrases "afflicted . . . but not crushed, perplexed, but not driven to despair; persecuted, but not forsaken; struck down, but not destroyed" bear a resemblance to both traditions. The series of statements about the reality of suffering followed by denial of their permanence gives voice to both pain and hope. Suffering is described as more visceral and personal in verse 10 with the phrase "carrying in the body the death of Jesus." "Death" (*nekrōsis*) here is a rare word meaning "deadness" or "process of dying." Its purpose is that "the life of Jesus may also be made visible in our bodies." Verse 11 states this idea in a parallel form, repeating the phrase "be made visible." The verb "always being given up to death" (*paradidōmi)* links the suffering of apostles to the story of Jesus.

Paul's argument in these verses juxtaposes the ecstatic and joyful visionary experience of members of the church with the relentless hardships they face. These sufferings are transformative for those who undergo them, just as the vision of the glory of the Lord transforms those who see (3:18). The extraordinary power of God in their midst is contained in weak clay jars, vulnerable to damage and destruction. Not only does the death (*nekrōsis*) of Jesus change those who carry it, but it becomes revelatory for those who see the paradoxical expression of weakness and power manifested in the ministry of Paul and those who share this apostolic work.

CYNTHIA BRIGGS KITTREDGE

Homiletical Perspective

everybody will hug each other." Then the sisters made amends and a spirit of reconciliation and resurrection rippled through the congregation. Since that day, the church vowed never to close its doors again. As years have passed, they have also reached with a resurrection spirit into their community and built schools for Christians, Jews, and Muslims that now serve over 3,000 children and youth.[2]

As Duncan writes, while a living tree provides shade on the river and shelter for animals, a tree that has snapped in two and has fallen into the water "creates a vast transfusion of nutrients . . . a river feast."

Simone Weil volunteered in the Spanish Civil War despite her poor health. Throughout her life, she struggled with the meaning of suffering and pain. In her book *Waiting for God*, she reveals that her courage to endure and continue with her work emerged after she learned that "when an apprentice gets hurt, or complains of being tired, the workmen and peasants have this fine expression: 'It is the trade entering his body.' Each time that we have some pain to go through, we can say to ourselves quite truly that it is the universe, the order, the beauty of the Word and the obedience of creation to God that are entering our body."[3]

I hazard a pastor's guess that Paul would agree with Weil's observation—that our faith in Jesus Christ does not mean we will never experience adversity, but rather that such adversity will grant us the opportunity to discover and come to trust that by God's grace light is always brighter than the darkness, life stronger than death, and what resides inside our broken, apprenticed bodies is the glory of a resurrection waiting to burst forth.

MARK BARGER ELLIOTT

2. Elias Chacour with Mary E. Jensen, *We Belong to the Land* (San Francisco: HarperSanFrancisco, 1990), 121–45.
3. Simone Weil, *Waiting for God* (New York: Harper & Row, 1951), 131–32.

Mark 2:23-3:6

23One sabbath he was going through the grainfields; and as they made their way his disciples began to pluck heads of grain. 24The Pharisees said to him, "Look, why are they doing what is not lawful on the sabbath?" 25And he said to them, "Have you never read what David did when he and his companions were hungry and in need of food? 26He entered the house of God, when Abiathar was high priest, and ate the bread of the Presence, which it is not lawful for any but the priests to eat, and he gave some to his companions." 27Then he said to them, "The sabbath was made for humankind, and not humankind for the sabbath; 28so the Son of Man is lord even of the sabbath."

1Again he entered the synagogue, and a man was there who had a withered hand. 2They watched him to see whether he would cure him on the sabbath, so that they might accuse him. 3And he said to the man who had the withered hand, "Come forward." 4Then he said to them, "Is it lawful to do good or to do harm on the sabbath, to save life or to kill?" But they were silent. 5He looked around at them with anger; he was grieved at their hardness of heart and said to the man, "Stretch out your hand." He stretched it out, and his hand was restored. 6The Pharisees went out and immediately conspired with the Herodians against him, how to destroy him.

Theological Perspective

The passage for this Sunday concludes several stories depicting Jesus' conflict with Pharisees. Christians have often used passages like this one to interpret the relationship between Christianity and Judaism, casting contemporary Judaism in the role of the misguided and violent Pharisees. This approach is of dubious historical value and has contributed to our shameful legacy of anti-Semitism. Jews have never permitted observing Torah to override decisions to save life. In a recent story on National Public Radio, a Jewish man remembers being on the train to a Nazi death camp as a young child. His mother buys them food but all that is available is nonkosher meat. Her son asks her why she is crying. She tells him that she has kept kosher all of her life but now she is going to die, and she is crying because her children are young and have not had a chance to live. This mother was not a great scholar, but she shared the wisdom of the historical Pharisees and knew that Torah is made for humanity: her children were starving, and it was her duty and right to feed them what she could. Another approach to these stories of conflict would be to understand the "Pharisees" in terms of religious typology and notice the contrast between the "good news" of Jesus and a more rigid way of understanding religion to which many Christians—then and now—fall victim.

Pastoral Perspective

What are we to make of a Gospel that begins the story of Jesus Christ with conflict? If this is the "good news" Mark is intent on proclaiming, these incidents are disturbing, if not disorienting. This passage places side by side the only two conflicts over the Sabbath that appear in Mark.

Immediately we find ourselves in the midst of Jesus' counterpoint to religious rules and regulations. Here it takes the form of his disciples' apparent Sabbath breaking—walking through a wheat field picking grain for eating. Then Jesus is portrayed healing a man with a crippled hand. Both are occasions for the Pharisees to raise eyebrows and questions. As Mark would have it, the Galilean ministry of Jesus barely begins before he is on a collision course with religious authorities. This, as we read on, is just the beginning.

It would be too easy, of course, to say, "This shows that Jesus was a religious and political radical—attacking Sabbath-keeping," or "Jesus has no respect for the Torah or for the religious leaders of his day." Much more is here than Jesus the religious and moral nonconformist. There is much more at stake for Christian communities who seek to follow him than his antagonism toward the Pharisees. This is why the term "counterpoint" is useful. Whatever else Mark's terse opening scenes

Exegetical Perspective

Escalating Controversy. Mark 2:1–3:6 portrays a series of five controversies, each raising the level of conflict. The escalation can best be appreciated by reading the complete segment. Chapter breaks aside, the vocabulary of Mark 2:23–3:6 confirms this as one coherent section, containing the only two Sabbath controversy stories in Mark. Mark 2:23–28 is linked to Mark 3:1–6 by two major themes: (a) what is permissible (or lawful) to do on the Sabbath; and (b) the relationship of humanity (*anthrōpos*) to the Sabbath.

The earlier controversy stories call attention to table fellowship (2:13–17), fasting (2:18–20), wine and wineskins (2:21–22). Now Mark 2:23–26 speaks of bread. First-century Christians listening to Mark's account probably heard these stories within the context of their experiences of controversy about table fellowship, fasting, breaking bread and sharing wine in worship.

What Is Permissible on the Sabbath? (2:23–24). On a Sabbath, the disciples are leading (not following) through a field of grain. The evangelist may have intended the act of "making their way," a phrase usually associated with the serious work of road building, as an allusion to and partial fulfillment of Mark 1:2–3. While traversing the field, the disciples pluck some of the heads of grain, a practice permitted to hungry travelers by the law (cf. Deut. 23:25).

Homiletical Perspective

How does one preach on this text when the idea of the Sabbath seems so irrelevant to our work-oriented, consumer-dominated culture? I grew up with the "blue laws" enforcing the Sabbath. These laws fell away, and now we have laptops, cell phones, and all kinds of technological equipment that define us as belonging to a consumer society rather than belonging to God. At first glance, Jesus seems to endorse this stripping of the power of the Sabbath when he proclaims that "the sabbath was made for humankind." Is our culture what he intended? Was Jesus dethroning the Sabbath? Was he deconstructing the idea of the Sabbath so that he could build it up again? Or was he using the struggle over the Sabbath to point to a new reality, a reality that he sought to illuminate in his life?

Jesus generates great conflict in this passage, and by the end of the story several opposing groups are collaborating to kill him. On one level, the conflict seems to be over the observance of the Sabbath. Jesus allows his followers to pick grain and eat it on the Sabbath, comparing himself to the great King David. He also seems to take an "in your face" attitude when he heals a man in the synagogue on the Sabbath. He seems to do this as a demonstration of the challenge he presents, a nonviolent disobedience of the Sabbath laws.

Mark 2:23–3:6

Theological Perspective

Jesus has just returned to Capernaum after a rather dramatic beginning to his ministry, characterized in particular by a series of healing miracles. The emphasis on healing as central to Jesus' ministry is brought into relief by the Pharisees' anger at Jesus for a whole series of offenses: his intimacy with tax collectors and other sinners, his indifference to fasting, and, in this last scene, the question of the Sabbath. By the end of the encounter, the Pharisees are outraged and seek allies to destroy Jesus.

These passages are extremely rich conceptually and symbolically, and we could spiral through them for a long time and never exhaust their meaning. But one theme that stands out is the presentation of these two forms of piety. This gets at the heart of what it means to participate in the vision of reality that Jesus is offering to us. The conflict between Jesus and the Pharisees is a conflict that dwells in the heart of virtually every human being and operates in every congregation. The Pharisees represent the basic temptation of religion to absolutize those things that mediate faith to us. Each element of Jesus' conflict with the Pharisees has to do with basic observances that characterize not only Jewish but also Christian piety: forgiveness of sins; conventions concerning what, when, and with whom we eat; honoring the Sabbath. These are particular ways in which we sanctify time and space. Our commitment to each of these things comes to us through Scripture. The observation of the Sabbath is one of the Ten Commandments. Recent debates concerning the display of the Ten Commandments in courthouses indicate that they continue to be a divisive issue in American culture.

In contrast to living Judaism, these Pharisees are portrayed as obsessed with religious authority, traditional observances, and righteousness. Apparently immune to Jesus' healing power, his charisma, his intimacy with outcasts, they are enraged by his indifference to religious customs. Their love of Scripture and tradition make them blind to the compassion and joy that pour off of Jesus toward all of humanity. Foreshadowing the contemporary conflation of religion and politics, they seek alliance with political parties in order to "destroy him" (3:6).

But in defense of these Pharisees, notice that Jesus seems to be deliberately provoking a confrontation. This story is not about how urgent need permits us to break rules. That understanding of faith is as old as Scripture itself, as Mark indicates by quoting the

Pastoral Perspective

achieve, they sound the unexpected rhythms and discordant elements in what is yet to come in the whole Gospel.

What is at stake in the Pharisees' accusation that the disciples' actions constitute a violation of Sabbath? Sabbath rest was, after all, a deeply significant value and practice for the Jews. It was intimately connected to Jewish identity. Should we be so hard on the Pharisees for pointing this out? In fact, Jesus never denies or rejects the significance of the Sabbath. Something other than a simple iconoclastic response is at stake. It is about what constitutes "work" on the Sabbath, in view of humanity's life before God. It is about the very meaning of Sabbath itself. Jesus, under the figure of "Son of man," here claims lordship over the Sabbath. Whatever else Shabbat means for the followers of Jesus, it always points in the direction that the life and love of Jesus signify.

What was the intention of "Sabbath" in the first place? Here we recall that it was a day of rest directly related to the holiness and the goodness of creation. It also carries the resonance of liberation from captivity and slavery. If Jesus counters the pharisaic objection found in Mark by claiming the Sabbath was made for human beings, not the other way around, then we begin to understand that Jesus is actually calling for liberation and restoration of the meaning of Sabbath. The "day of rest" and its attending shalom are not intended to be a matter of such strenuous human observance that the worship of God is eclipsed. While the Puritan and other dissenting Christian traditions established Sunday as "Sabbath," tendencies toward making restrictive laws to be obeyed in order to keep the Sabbath "pure" were present from the beginning.

Without collapsing the biblical Sabbath into Christian Sunday, we might well understand here the need for a restoration of the way in which Sunday—day of resurrection—asks Christians to engage the goodness and holiness of creation in light of the "new creation" signified in Christ crucified and risen. It turns out that profound human needs are indeed touched in the meaning of Sunday as the "Lord's Day," such as the need to hold the whole of life before God, and the need for sheer delight and enjoyment. The gift of the Lord's Day allows the contemplative side of our humanity to flourish.

The conflict with the Pharisees intensifies in Mark's account of Jesus healing a man with a withered hand on the Sabbath. This time his accusers are actively plotting and watching for a time when he

Exegetical Perspective

Some Pharisees confront Jesus about the disciples' behavior, arguing that they were reaping on the Sabbath, in violation of the prohibition against work. No clue is given about how the Pharisees observe Jesus' disciples in the grain field. Jesus, the master responsible for his students' conduct, is asked to defend his disciples' nonpermitted actions on the Sabbath. Jesus' response is not about the disciples, but about David (and by extension, the Davidic Messiah, i.e., Jesus).

Jesus Appeals to David as Example (2:25–26).

The appeal to David's eating the holy bread is both problematic and illustrative. The situations in 1 Samuel 21 and Mark 2:23–24 are not parallel. In 1 Samuel 21, David is alone. The disciples' plucking a few heads of grain falls short of David's act of appropriating the bread of the Presence (see Lev. 24:5–9). Mark's reference to Abiathar is historically inaccurate. David interacted with Ahimelech, Abiathar's father. That inconsistency is variously explained as Markan error or as deliberate allusion to the parallels between Abiathar and the Christian community's persecution by Jewish authorities during the Great Revolt (66–73 CE).

The awkwardness in these verses, however scholars explain them, invites our listening to a prime example of early Christian appropriation and transformation of Old Testament texts in order to make bold claims for Jesus and his community. Jesus' answer does not provide a logical response to the Pharisees' question, but makes a theological point about the relationship of Jesus and his communities to Sabbath. Mark's account prepares the way for the early Christian community to establish its distinct identity and alternative Sabbath-keeping ways in order to distinguish itself from its Jewish parentage.[1]

The Sabbath Was Created for Humanity (2:27–28).

I translate these verses as follows: "And he said to them, 'The Sabbath day was created for *humanity*, not *humanity* for the Sabbath day; so the son of *humanity* is lord even of the Sabbath.'" Mark identifies Jesus with both the Davidic Messiah and the Danielic "Son of Man" (see also Mark 14:61–62; 8:29, 31, 38). The vocabulary of this story (and of the entire Gospel) demonstrates Mark's identification of Jesus with people in the fullness of the human condition.[2] The allusion to Daniel's apocalyptic judge, traditionally translated "Son of Man,"

---

1. For a longer discussion of the emergence of an a-Sabbath or anti-Sabbath position within the early Christian churches, see Judith Hoch Wray, *Rest as a Theological Metaphor* (Atlanta: Scholars Press, 1998).

Homiletical Perspective

We must always keep our eyes on this conflict and on the fact that Jesus is provoking this conflict. What is he trying to provoke? What is so dangerous about him? Feeding his disciples? Healing a man? The conflict over the Sabbath points to a deeper and more dangerous conflict. The religious leaders are not hardhearted, repressive men hoping to send everyone to hell except themselves. We often prefer to portray them that way, but in so doing, we miss the power of this passage. The conflict begins with the issue of the Sabbath, but its roots are much deeper. The religious leaders correctly perceive that Jesus is offering a new vision of life and a new vision of God. He is proclaiming—in word and deed—a new way of understanding who God is. Jesus proclaims to his own generation—and to every generation, including ours—that God is not confined to our rules about God or to our way of perceiving God. Jesus is reconfiguring our relationship to God, not just as individuals, but in the structures of society as well. Such a reconfiguration is very threatening.

Preachers need to keep the edgy nature of this passage close at hand when they reflect on it. This lectionary text closes with a reminder of the cross. The difficult truth of the cross is that we would rather kill Jesus than be transformed by his love. Our resistance is great to his reconfiguring our relationship to God. It is one of the continuing mysterious realities of life in the church, a reality that is exposed in this passage: we prefer a dormant God who is subject to our rites and rituals to the active, category-busting God who is ever present in our lives. When God gets too close to us, challenging us as Jesus challenged the religious order of his day, we begin to construct our crosses and prepare a place for God there too. What field is Jesus walking through in our lives, plucking ears of corn from our sacred rituals? Who is Jesus healing that we believe should remain sick? What is Jesus doing in our time that makes us believe that he is foolish at best and dangerous at worst?

This passage asks of readers in every age, What are the essential categories of our lives that Jesus threatens? What have we made divine in our lives that should remain mortal and finite? Since the Sabbath is the central focus of conflict in this passage, we should look first at the concept of the Sabbath in our time, and it will not take long to find ample material to preach. In this passage Jesus tries to change the idea of the Sabbath from being an oppressive ogre, which denies food to the hungry

Mark 2:23-3:6

Theological Perspective

story of David eating consecrated bread. It would be easy for Jesus and his disciples to honor the Sabbath. By ignoring traditions for honoring the Sabbath, Jesus violates basic assumptions about the authority of revelation, on which Sabbath observation is based, and of religious practice, through which communities manifest their devotion to God. He does this arbitrarily, provocatively. His disciples are not starving. They are wandering through a field, idly plucking off the tips of grain. The man's withered hand could have been cured at sundown. Jesus is not compelled to decide between lifesaving actions and violation of a narrow and technical legalism. He is behaving with wanton disregard for simple and life-giving religious practices. By refusing to observe conventions for honoring the Sabbath, Jesus invites us into a terrifying form of faith in which time-honored practices are relativized by healing power, compassion, and joy. The rather terrible implication of this story is that normal and natural religious commitments render us indifferent to human suffering and true community. They are alien to the "good news" Jesus desires to share with us. This conflict between Jesus and the Pharisees contrasts religion that hardens hearts with the gospel that opens hearts to the ubiquitous presence of God and gives birth to compassion and joy.

Christians can be tempted to side with the Pharisees—angry and irritated with everything that seems to fall outside of a customary and familiar reading of Scripture or tradition. There are good reasons to do this: the continuity of any religion over time requires these concrete ways of living out dedication to God. But the story reminds us of the terrible price that is extracted when these commitments become idolatry; when we cherish the gifts of God, including Scripture, religious conventions, and morality, we lose the power to cherish the people of God. Jesus is described as angry and grieved by his opponents' hardness of heart. But perhaps we should have some pity for the Pharisees, because they are so much like ourselves.

WENDY FARLEY

Pastoral Perspective

would "break the Sabbath." In plain sight, as if to confront them head-on, he calls the man to stand and be healed in the midst of the assembly. Here Jesus puts the point plainly: "Is it lawful to do good or to do harm on the sabbath, to save life or to kill?" Not only is Jesus angry with his accusers, but also they are silenced by his question. The striking fact here is the place of the healing and the conflict— within the religious institution itself, the synagogue.

Mark's Jesus should startle, if not unsettle, us. The opposition to him is coming from earnestly religious persons, not from outside skeptics. His surprising vision of God's intention for the Sabbath made for humanity may upset our own habitual religious ideas. Something deeper than religious ideology or juridical thinking is here. It is so easy to forget the *spirit* of religious institutions and practices in the attempt to apply regulations with absolute human certainty. Mark has opened his account of the "good news" with a serious challenge to those of us who wish to enforce on others a narrow version of God's rule and reign. To claim divine authority on behalf of the church is itself to stand vulnerably under the living gospel, which is Christ. Good people in the name of God are capable of opposing the very good that Jesus brings. In every generation there have been human attempts to invoke the name of God on programs and policies that end up subverting the love and grace shown in Christ. History is littered with such voices, from the Inquisition to the Third Reich to many ventures in pious militarism. Christ's authority is greater than any human voice, no matter how pious, no matter how deeply entrenched in religious tradition.

DON E. SALIERS

should not preclude our seeing Mark's affirmation of Jesus as the "son of humanity" or the "Human One." The complex term *huios tou anthrōpon* includes both meanings. The Markan emphasis on the Sabbath being created for humanity provides a link backward to the challenge of what is permitted on the Sabbath and forward to the encounter with humanity-in-need in the synagogue.

What Is Permissible on the Sabbath? (3:1–6) This time the question comes from Jesus, presented as a challenge to his opposition. Only Jesus speaks. The dual claims that the Sabbath is created for humanity and that the son of humanity (Jesus) is lord of the Sabbath are demonstrated in 3:1–6. A three-step movement focuses the action: (1) Jesus *enters* the synagogue (3:1). (2) Jesus calls the human with a withered hand *to the center* (3:3). (3) The Pharisees *go out* of the synagogue and conspire to destroy Jesus (3:6).

Entering the synagogue, Jesus encounters a human (*anthrōpos*) with a withered hand. The Pharisees are lying in wait to see if Jesus would cure on the Sabbath. Non-life-threatening diseases were *not* permitted to be treated on the Sabbath.

At the center of this literary structure, Jesus moves the Sabbath question beyond the matter of his own behavior: "Is it permissible on the Sabbath to do good or to do harm, to save life or to kill?" (v. 4, my translation). The opposition is silenced. Debate or challenge is no longer possible, for those who intend to do harm have been caught in their own net.

Anger (*orgē*) is attributed to Jesus only here (v. 5) in the Gospels. Elsewhere the term refers to God's wrath (Matt. 3:7; Luke 3:7; 21:23; John 3:36). While Jesus tells the human to stretch out his hand, he does nothing that would be construed as treating or healing the person. Jesus does not touch him or even speak a word of healing. The man's hand is restored, and Jesus has maintained Sabbath observance.

The account ends with Jesus at the center of the synagogue, having demonstrated his lordship of the Sabbath, standing with the human whose hand is now restored. The accusers leave and, ironically, immediately demonstrate their own desecration of the Sabbath by plotting with the Herodians[3] to kill Jesus. The conflict has now escalated past curiosity and challenge (in Mark 2) to a conspiracy to destroy Jesus.

JUDITH HOCH WRAY

and healing to the sick, to what it was originally: a reminder that we belong to God and not to our labor, or to the money generated by our labor, or to the money spent from our labor in consuming products that make us feel so much better.

In calling us back to the original intent of the Sabbath commandment, Jesus reminds us that our lives are meant for God, not for getting and spending. In this sense, what Jesus threatens is our love of money, money that defines us and falsely promises us life. Lottery fever across the country is dominated by this idea: "if only I could win the lottery, I would . . ." In lifting up the Sabbath and how important it is (and how misused it is), this passage asks us to hear the difficult truth that we cannot imagine a life not dominated by money and work and consumption. Yet, as always, there is powerful good news here as well. At the same time that we are threatened by Jesus, our hearts long for him. Who among us does not want to be freed from our consumer lifestyle that is killing our souls and polluting the earth? This text reminds us that the journey to life goes through the cross, but that the resurrection awaits as well. Jesus did not go to the cross to tell us how bad we are, but to point us to new life. So may it be with our sermons on this text—there is life available, greater and more abundant than we ever imagined.

NIBS STROUPE

2. "Humanity" (*anthrōpos*) is consistently used throughout Mark in the context of the human condition. Where male is essential to the identification, Mark chooses "man" (*anēr*).

3. See also Mark 12:13 and 8:15. Herodians are not mentioned in any other ancient source.

Genesis 3:8-15

[8]They heard the sound of the Lord God walking in the garden at the time of the evening breeze, and the man and his wife hid themselves from the presence of the Lord God among the trees of the garden. [9]But the Lord God called to the man, and said to him, "Where are you?" [10]He said, "I heard the sound of you in the garden, and I was afraid, because I was naked; and I hid myself." [11]He said, "Who told you that you were naked? Have you eaten from the tree of which I commanded you not to eat?" [12]The man said, "The woman whom you gave to be with me, she gave me fruit from the tree, and I ate." [13]Then the Lord God said to the woman, "What is this that you have done?" The woman said, "The serpent tricked me, and I ate." [14]The Lord God said to the serpent,

Theological Perspective

Christian theologians have turned to this reading frequently, finding here a dramatic moment in the larger biblical narrative of origins (genesis), the primordial beginnings of things. The larger narrative complex has long played an integral role in Christian theological reflections on God's design and purposes for all creation. Its depiction of how things were at first, as God's fresh handiwork, invites comparisons and contrasts with things as they have come to be here and now—and also as they are yet to become when God's will is ultimately done on earth as it is in heaven. For this reason the text has been of enduring significance in fashioning Christian teachings of creation, sin, salvation, and eschatology.

This text has figured prominently in the history of Christian doctrine in discussions of life in paradise, original sin, the fall, free will and predestination, total depravity, promises of salvation, and covenant and dispensational theologies. Allusions to the reading loom large as well in the many-sided debates of historic Augustinianism, Pelagianism, Arminianism, and theological variations on those positions.

It is also, as part of the Adam and Eve story, one of the all-time most familiar biblical materials, referenced and embellished in countless artistic works, both visual and literary, jokes of high and low culture, and crass ad campaigns. Its reliability as

Pastoral Perspective

Sicut Deus—the serpent's crafty "you will be like God" (Gen. 3:4b)—is the cunning appeal, the "religious" trick, according to Dietrich Bonhoeffer, that leads to humankind's fall (some prefer "leap") into rebellion against the Creator's Word. To be "like (*sicut* in Latin) God," knowing good and evil, would seem, on the face of it, a good thing—even, perhaps, a godly thing. And so a "pious serpent" becomes the inexplicable agent of sin's infection of the creation, as humankind manifests its discontent with "merely" being created in God's image and likeness. Why not eat of the forbidden tree and cut out God the "middleman" entirely, knowing good and evil without the mediation of God's Word? And so is set in motion what the early church would come to sing of in the chanted Proclamation of the Easter Vigil as the *felix culpa*, the "fortunate (or at least necessary) fault," that by God's eternal will resulted in the salvation wrought through the death and resurrection of the Word made flesh in Jesus the Christ.

According to Old Testament scholar Samuel Terrien, the narrator's intention in the telling of this story was "simply to show the religious situation of humankind" and to depict "the sin of hubris par excellence as a lust for self-deification." Of pastoral significance is Terrien's observation that "ritual acts and moral virtue tend to become techniques for

"Because you have done this,
  cursed are you among all animals
  and among all wild creatures;
upon your belly you shall go,
  and dust you shall eat
  all the days of your life.
¹⁵I will put enmity between you and the woman,
  and between your offspring and hers;
he will strike your head,
  and you will strike his heel."

Exegetical Perspective

The narrative context of this passage is clearly identified as the garden of Eden shortly after the creation of the world. Those who take this passage as an accurate historical account often follow the conclusion of the seventeenth-century archbishop James Ussher, who calculated the date of creation to be October 23, 4004 BCE. Today, most scholars agree with the assessment of Hermann Gunkel, that the first eleven chapters of Genesis should be characterized as "legends" or "faded myths" that are essentially devoid of historical content. "Primeval history" is another phrase often used to describe these early chapters of Genesis. To assert that Genesis 3 is not a historical account in no way detracts from its value as an important religious text, just as New Testament parables are viewed as valid tools for teaching one form of truth.

Over the past 100 years, the view that Moses wrote the first five books of the Bible has given way to the conclusion that the Pentateuch had multiple authors. Following the analysis of Martin Noth, most scholars today attribute Genesis 3:8–15 to the J (Jahwist/Yahwist) tradition, usually dated to about 950 BCE. Recent studies have tended to favor a later date, while also emphasizing its reliance on much older oral and written traditions.

The author of the J tradition delights in the use of wordplays, which are very transparent in the

Homiletical Perspective

What might the Lord God walking in the garden sound like? A rustling of leaves, the snapping of twigs, the swishing of tall grass? Sandals touching the earth perhaps, or bare feet? Feet? There is great possibility in imagining the sounds of God. The God of the written word is silent—trapped on a page, read silently in studies and offices, on desks and kitchen tables, wherever the preacher prepares to preach. What, indeed, does God sound like? How might your congregation respond to this question? Sometimes when you ask, you will get answers: a baby's cry, a voice in song (male *and* female!), thunder, the roar of a lion, someone's grandmother, the ocean. In what ways do we hear the sound of God in the world?

In this dazzling mythical account of human origins, having encountered the crafty (not evil) serpent, the man and the woman now encounter, for the first time together, their Maker. And they do what many of us ordinary mortals would do: they hide. In fact, they hide so well that this God does not seem to be able to find them and has to call out: "Where are you?" At this point, the man makes the first of several critical mistakes. Having hidden well enough to escape divine detection, he gives away their hiding place by responding aloud to the question. One has to wonder what would have

Genesis 3:8-15

Theological Perspective

sound history has emerged as a Christian wedge issue in today's modern, or postmodern, times. So too have its implications if any for understanding human sexuality and gender relations. All told, the challenge to the reader-preacher is probably less coming up with something to learn, preach, and teach than deciding on something of theological substance and hence helping people avoid aimless wanderings and knee-jerk reactions.

The emergent Christian movement drew on this Genesis text in several ways. One persisting trajectory of reflection was set in motion by Paul's use of "typological hermeneutics," contrasting how things were because of Adam with how they are because of Christ Jesus. Another application was stressing the genealogical, even lineal, descent of Jesus from the house of David and then beyond from Adam, in keeping with proof-from-prophecy methods of scriptural interpretation. A third use was the resolve of antignostic Christians to affirm, like Judaism at large, the goodness of creation itself and its Creator God by fixing sin's origin in the sphere of human history and decision making, rather than in God's compulsion, inadvertence, or inability to do better.

All three theological concerns became commonplaces of emergent Christian orthodoxy and powerful influences ever thereafter. In the selected verses at hand, several themes are prominent in the church's doctrinal heritage.

One is a weighty tradition of interpreting verse 15 as God's preannouncement of gospel promise coming to pass when Jesus Christ, "offspring" of the woman, is understood as victor, though not without wound or pain, over "serpent" as symbol or synonym for the tempter and agent of sin. This theological reading, fashioned early on in church history, survives despite later objections on historical-critical and myriad other grounds. So too, however, readings and preaching against this reading of this text are inviting indeed.

At the theological bottom line are understandings of Christianity's gospel. What does it mean to speak of our human condition as "in Adam" or "in Christ" or "as in creation" and "as in new creation"? Does the comparison of terms and depictions of this sort help make plain and afford fresh insights into God's good news of great joy? The classic debate in theology is whether God's promise of salvation involves a return to human innocence, as in Edenic paradise *before* temptation and sin, or an advance to a yet "better" state, on the far side of human trial and error, made possible by God's merciful forgiveness of sin that finds its goal in the reconciliation of all creation.

Pastoral Perspective

man-initiated salvation" and that "the use of morality as a substitute for a humble response to grace represents the ultimate idolatry." He concludes that this "ancient narrative" does not intend to tell the history of the originating act of original sin. Rather it is a "true myth" in the sense that it "has never happened, but it happens every day."[1]

But if Latin is not your idiom, and the intricacies of what came to be called the "doctrine of original sin" is not your choice of focus for preaching on this "fabulously" rich text (see also Elaine Pagel's *Adam, Eve and the Serpent* [New York: Random House, 1988] for a stimulating if controversial reconsideration), consider the pastoral implications of the Creator's first direct address to humankind: "Where are you?" God's first word to humankind is posed as a question that, interestingly, will become, for the Word-made-flesh in Jesus of Nazareth, a characteristic interrogatory mode of teaching and proclamation. God's originating address exposes humankind's futile attempt to hide while fleeing from the implications of its own actions. This eventuates in the tragicomic handing on of blame from man to woman to the snake, a traditioning that still lies at the heart of our practice of living in fear of the Creator rather than obedient trust, as Adam himself confesses (v. 10). Sin also alienates us from one another and gets expressed in our sense of shame at our very creatureliness (v. 11).

Old Testament scholar Walter Brueggemann suggests that we might think of the serpent in the story as the creation's first theologian, who convinces humankind to trade obedience to God's Word for theology *about* God. As such it's a story that warns that "theological talk which seeks to analyze and objectify matters of faithfulness is dangerous enterprise." Further, this also is a story that addresses the pressing pastoral issue of anxiety. Referencing Jesus' understanding of anxiety in his Sermon on the Mount (Matt. 6:25–33), Brueggemann observes that our story from Genesis reveals how "anxiety comes from doubting God's providence, from rejecting his care and seeking to secure our own well-being." The serpent seduces humankind into believing there are securities apart from the reality of God, and so "failure to trust God with our lives" proves to be "death."[2]

The Yale literary critic Harold Bloom insightfully considers this not at all a "moral tale" but a wry

---

1. Samuel Terrien, *Till the Heart Sings* (Philadelphia: Fortress Press, 1985), 24–27.
2. Walter Brueggemann, *Genesis* (Atlanta: John Knox Press, 1982), 47–48, 54–55.

Exegetical Perspective

Hebrew text but rather obscure in the English translation. For example, Genesis 2 ends with verse 25, "And the man and his wife were both naked (*'arummim*), and were not ashamed." In the next verse, Genesis 3:1, the serpent is described as "more subtle" or "more crafty" (*'arum*) "than any other wild animal." The author seems to be implying that the "cunning" serpent—who himself is among the most naked of animals, lacking fur—is about to take advantage of the "nakedness" (i.e., innocence and vulnerability) of the man and woman. The naming of the woman (*'ishshah*) by the man (*'ish*) in Genesis 2:23 is another example of J's playful use of words to evoke reflections in the minds of those who hear the story.

After the man and woman eat the forbidden fruit, God speaks to the serpent, "[C]ursed (*'arur*) are you among all animals and all wild creatures" (3:14), recalling Genesis 3:1, where the serpent is described as "more crafty than any other wild animal." It is important to note that although the man and the woman are reprimanded, they are not cursed, as the serpent is.

From the time of Irenaeus in the second century CE, many Christian theologians have interpreted the curse of the serpent as a *protoevangelium* or "first messianic promise." According to this reading, the serpent represents Satan or the devil, whereas the woman's "seed" (*zera‘*) is understood as a prophetic reference to the Messiah or Christ. Although this interpretation persists today, most modern commentators follow the lead of Chrysostom, Augustine, Jerome, Calvin, and many others, arguing that the passage speaks about a real snake—not Satan—and that the woman's seed refers to her "offspring" (that is, all humankind), rather than a particular messianic figure in the distant future. This view is supported by the fact that in Hebrew, the word "seed" always refers to one's collective descendants rather than an individual, except when used to describe a descendant of the next generation. The modern scholarly consensus therefore is that this passage is an ancient etiological legend intended to explain, among other things, the animosity that exists between humans and serpents.[1]

As with most familiar texts that we assume we understand, we often read into the text and extrapolate ideas that are not there. For example, the

1. Donald E. Gowan, *From Eden to Babel: A Commentary on the Book of Genesis 1–11*, International Theological Commentary (Grand Rapids: Eerdmans, 1988), 57–58. Gerhard von Rad, *Genesis: A Commentary*, rev. ed., trans. John H. Marks, Old Testament Library (Philadelphia: Westminster Press, 1973), 91–93.

Homiletical Perspective

happened if he had remained silent. In any case, the man then reveals his knowledge of their nakedness and, to make matters even worse, he blames the whole thing on the woman. This, of course, has the unintended benefit (for him) of deflecting the whole problem onto the woman down to this very day, in spite of the fact that the woman distinguishes herself with a straightforward, honest answer to her questioning God. "The serpent tricked me, and I ate," she says, in one of the most spectacular understatements of all time.

There are abundant, delicious ideas in this text, ideas that probe the depths of our understanding of the divine/human relationship, the nature of God, the nature of human existence, the origins of human life as we know it. Most people wonder about these things. Congregations are generally receptive to the preacher's invitation to take on the "big questions." In this text, one scarcely knows which way to turn or where to begin! Each verse has the potential to ignite a lively, engaging sermon. As a whole, the text works on several levels. First, this is one of the great stories of our faith tradition; as such it lends itself exceedingly well to imaginative retelling. Simply inviting people into this story world can lead to deeper understanding, surprising revelations, and enduring transformations. Second, this is a prime example of biblical humor—in particular, the punning wordplay in Hebrew: *'arum* ("crafty") and *'arom* ("naked"). Third, in addition to the big questions mentioned above, there is also the question of God's omniscience versus human free will; that is, did God really *not know* where the humans had hid themselves, or was God just testing them? Did God *not know* that the humans had encountered the serpent and eaten from the tree? How are our perceptions of God affected by this? Are our lives fixed and known, or are we truly free beings whose thoughts and actions unfold in their own moments—awaiting the response of a God who chose not to know from the very beginning? Clearly, it seems, the text portrays a God who has turned loose a species beyond divine control.

There is more. One might ask, in the context of preaching, what would have become of humanity if the woman had *not* plucked the fruit from the tree. Everything hinges on this, and our text today deals with the chaos that ensues from—dare we say it?—her act of courage (or defiance—however you wish to characterize it). Everything turns on this, because without it, humanity remains docile, numb, obedient, and forever trapped in the garden of

Genesis 3:8-15

Theological Perspective

Equally classical but of distinctly heightened sensitivity in much contemporary Christian doctrine are questions with regard to the nature of human sinfulness—or, perhaps better put, the *dynamics* of sin, sinning, and sinfulness. God's questions, curses, and afterward the expulsion from paradise follow upon violating an explicit command, a matter of law. Understanding sin as a legal or quasi-legal infraction has served perhaps as Christianity's historic default position, prominent if not dominant in the biblical and doctrinal tradition.

Today's reading, however, suggests as well an additional, qualifying or countervailing, theme. God goes walking in the cool of the evening, as usual, to visit friends—the down-to-earth imagery is surely among the Bible's most poignant anthropomorphisms. The narrative setting tilts doctrinal discussion from strictly legal toward personal—indeed interpersonal, I/Thou—considerations. Is sin *at base* a rule breaking or *at heart* a betrayal of trust and love? This theme—sin as broken relationship, alienation, or estrangement of God and humanity—is a hallmark of the Pauline-Augustinian theological tradition. It has been of vast influence over the centuries, though never uncontested and often limited to countercultural minority status in the churches.

The broken "vertical" relationship of God and humanity spells the breaking of "horizontal" relations too, as shown by the triple-play blame game that follows, moving from Adam to Eve to the serpent. These "free will" responses to God, including the eloquent serpent's sudden silence, are lame, no-honor-among-thieves excuses, at the "gotcha, come-clean, tell it like it is" moment of reckoning. Protests of feminist and other theologies against the historical bias, injustice, and misogyny of blaming Eve (= woman in particular) are certainly apt. Adam not only sets the blame game in motion but turns it into a theodicy issue: blaming *God*.

No creature is guileless. Deception and self-deception appear in paradise. Nor is God deceived about that point. This was already the case earlier on, when God's quasi-legal command was violated. Thus theologians have had cause to inquire into features of sin and sinfulness far deeper and more multidimensional than "I didn't do what I was told to." In any case, considered theologically, the blame game itself is the telltale sign of broken relationship, alienation, estrangement—with God and with one another at the same time.

JAMES O. DUKE

Pastoral Perspective

"children's story that ends unhappily." "When we were children," he surmises, "we were terribly punished for being children." This might be called the "essence" of this story of humankind's first disobedience. It is not at all a "Fall but a wounding estrangement . . . an expulsion from home, from a garden where Yahweh, who is both mother and father, likes to walk about while enjoying the cool breezes of the evening." What begins as a "family romance" gets "transformed into a family tragedy."[3]

Interpretation of Genesis 3 obviously varies widely. For me the truth, taught in the old doggerel quoted in reading primers of an earlier generation, "In Adam's fall/we sinned all," is simply, if finally inexplicably, that there is something wrong, something screwy, about us human beings at our core—not necessarily bad or evil, but amiss. It is not that the *imago dei* has been erased from our DNA but that deep within ourselves we are not fully what we are meant to be and, what is more, we know it. We sense that there is an estrangement from our essential, created selves that is rooted in our alienation from our Maker and gets expressed in behaviors that alienate us from one another. And what is more, as Reinhold Niebuhr made the basis of his widely influential public theology of realism, evil lies closest at hand when we are most intent on doing right and most certain of our righteousness. While the quest to distinguish between the relative good and the relative evil may be an innate human need, pretending to a "knowledge" of good and evil is an act of idolatry that leads not to *theosis* but Babel, the overweening desire to storm heaven's gate. (See such critically acclaimed movies as *Crash* and *Babel* for contemporary cultural analogues.)

JOHN ROLLEFSON

3. Harold Bloom, *The Book of J* (New York: Random House, 1990), 185–86.

Exegetical Perspective

names "Adam" and "Eve" are not to be found in the text. The first man is referred to as simply "the man" or "the human," and the first woman is referred to as "his woman" or "his wife." She is not assigned a name until Genesis 3:20. As noted above, the serpent is identified as one of the animals God created, rather than as Satan as later allegorical interpretations asserted. It should be remembered that throughout much of the ancient Near East, the serpent was venerated for its powers of fertility, wisdom, and even immortality.[2] Since the serpent was the animal symbol for Asherah, the great Canaanite fertility goddess, one can detect here a not too subtle polemic against Canaanite religion.

In order to understand this lectionary reading in its textual context, it is important to be familiar with the passages that precede and follow it, that is, Genesis 2:4b-3:7 and Genesis 3:16–24. As has been noted by Gowan[3] and other scholars, this lectionary reading is an "archetypal story." It is a story not so much of what happened to our first ancestors but of what happens to each one of us. Our loss of innocence as we grow up and become more aware of the world around us, our alienation from our fellow humans and the animal world, our yearning for independence, and our fear of and alienation from God are all addressed in this passage. This being the case, it is not surprising that this passage lends itself to a typological interpretation in which Christ is understood as the new Adam who transforms our experience of alienation into one of reconciliation.

DAVID W. MCCREERY

Homiletical Perspective

sameness and blissful ignorance. This place, as it turns out, is no paradise. No differences, no opposites, no innovation, no creativity, no diversity, no rebellion, no need for grace or redemption. You can see where that path leads.

Why do the humans' actions elicit such an overreaction from God? Would not this seem to be a nice place for God to practice a little primordial forgiveness and mercy? Test them out? See how they work? What is it that the serpent has done to invoke such wrath, other than—ironically—speak the truth? And the man, for his part, was little more than a bystander as the woman ascended center stage. Yet he does not escape the divine wrath either. Such a quirky God indeed—uncanny, imponderable, unpredictable, beyond human definition or comprehension; a good lesson for all of us. The theological obstacle course herein is a good remedy for those who think they have God pinned down and neatly figured out.

For preacher and congregation, there are no answers here—only some of the most tantalizing questions you will find anywhere in the universe. Share them, by all means, along with a sense of ancient delight and an irresistible playfulness. Invite your listeners to encounter an extraordinary mind, tuned in to the beginning of everything, wondering how it might have been, spinning a timeless sacred tale that somehow touches on so many of life's greatest mysteries. To hear this story as a literal historical account is to trivialize it beyond recognition, to deny it its depth, and power, and truth, to confine it to the realm of silliness. God and serpent, man and woman, garden and wilderness, blessing and curse—these are the very elements of our existence and the objects of our lifelong quest for understanding and enlightenment.

For the gathered congregation here are a story for the ages, theological manna, and the sound of God walking in the primeval garden.

BERT MARSHALL

---

2. Nahum M. Sarna, *Genesis: The Traditional Hebrew Text with the New JPS Translation*, JPS Torah Commentary (Philadelphia: Jewish Publication Society, 1989), 24.
3. Gowan, *From Eden to Babel*.

Psalm 130

> ¹Out of the depths I cry to you, O LORD.
> ² Lord, hear my voice!
> Let your ears be attentive
>   to the voice of my supplications!
>
> ³If you, O LORD, should mark iniquities,
> Lord, who could stand?
> ⁴But there is forgiveness with you,
> so that you may be revered.

Theological Perspective

This classical psalm of penitence and lament groans out of the chaos of human existence, addressing God in hope. It speaks personally and comprehensively of the universality of sin in several important respects. It testifies that human iniquity is ubiquitous, threatening not just occasional persons but the entire human family with separation from God. It acknowledges that this same human sinfulness is not only a matter of transgression against God, but also results in oppression within the human community.

The psalm also speaks personally and comprehensively of the steadfast love of God mediating forgiveness and redemption. It asserts that God's hand of forgiveness reaches over the apparently impenetrable barriers erected by human iniquity. Moreover, it promises that the great power of God will salvage God's project with Israel despite the floodgates of oppression its sin has opened.

The "depths" from which the psalmist speaks in the opening verse of Psalm 130 are not limited to the anguish of the sinful person alienated from God by his or her own action or inaction. It refers in Scripture more broadly to all those places of pain, depression, and alienation that leave humans in deep despair, drowning in watery chaos. Nonetheless, in this psalm the writer does articulate the reality of personal sinfulness as a factor in finding oneself in

Pastoral Perspective

Psalm 130 is labeled, along with Psalms 120–134, as "A Song of Ascents." While we cannot be sure of their original uses, many scholars suggest that together they constitute a kind of songbook for pilgrims on their way "up" to the temple in Jerusalem (or up the fifteen steps from the Court of the Women to the Court of Israel in the temple itself), especially at the time of the harvest festivals prescribed in the Torah. The pilgrim journey was spiritual as well as geographical and required preparation in heart and mind for the encounter with YHWH, the king of heaven, in worship and sacrifice.

Centuries later, long after the temple had been destroyed, the Christian church grouped this psalm together with six others (Pss. 6, 32, 38, 51, 102, and 143) as a different kind of devotional booklet, collectively known as the Penitential Psalms. By the medieval period, they had come into common use in the sacrament of penance. This was, of course, a similar sort of pilgrimage, from deep awareness of sinfulness to a sense of absolution and grace, again through an encounter with God. Throughout Christian history God's people continued to use these Penitential Psalms as a pathway toward grace.

Hardly anyone will have much difficulty in calling to mind a time when the opening verses of this psalm could have been his or her own. We all have

^{5}I wait for the LORD, my soul waits,
    and in his word I hope;
^{6}my soul waits for the Lord
    more than those who watch for the morning,
    more than those who watch for the morning.

^{7}O Israel, hope in the LORD!
    For with the LORD there is steadfast love,
    and with him is great power to redeem.
^{8}It is he who will redeem Israel
    from all its iniquities.

Exegetical Perspective

A Psalm among Psalms. Psalm 130 is the eleventh
among fifteen psalms (Pss. 120–34) that are introduced by the title "A Song of Ascents." These texts are
frequently understood to be pilgrimage psalms, that is,
psalms travelers may have sung while en route to a
festival at Jerusalem. Recent studies of the shape of the
book of Psalms suggest some plausibility for this
view.[1] While Book One of the Psalter (Pss. 1–41)
begins with a high affirmation of monarchy (Ps. 2),
the third book of the Psalter (Pss. 73–89) ends with a
lament about the demise of monarchy and loss of
Jerusalem. The final two books of the Psalter (Pss.
90–106; 107–50) offer various responses to that loss—
one of which may be pilgrimage from Diaspora lands
(Pss. 120–34). Also, the frequent references to Jerusalem among the Songs of Ascents, along with their
general brevity, suggest the sort of songs that may have
been easily intoned while traveling dusty roads.

Along with the Psalter's grouping among the
Psalms of Ascents, Psalm 130 is also stationed as the
sixth of seven texts identified by Christian tradition as
Penitential Psalms (Pss. 6, 32, 38, 51, 102, 130, 143). In
addition to their significance for individuals at

1. For summaries of this approach, see Nancy deClaisse-Walford, *Reading
from the Beginning: The Shaping of the Hebrew Psalter* (Macon, GA: Mercer
University Press, 1997); or V. Steven Parrish, *A Story of the Psalms: Conversation, Canon, and Congregation* (Collegeville, MN: Liturgical Press, 2003).

Homiletical Perspective

Any fool can see evidence of sin in our world, but
only through the eyes of faith can we begin to see
signs of redemption. Psalm 130 plays within this
space, standing in the black night of despair and
scanning the horizon for the bare glow of hope.

In order for this text to be preached effectively,
the preacher and the psalmist should be one. The
poem is written primarily in the first person, and
that "I" should guide the preacher. Just as the
psalmist becomes the spokesperson for all forgiven
sinners, so the preacher is invited to stand within the
confines of his or her frailty and lead the hearers
into the territory of gratitude to Christ, just as Paul,
in another place, boasts of his weakness (2 Cor.
11:30) and reminds his hearers of his own tarnished
past in persecuting the faith in order to demonstrate
the power of God working for redemption in his life
(1 Cor. 15:9–10) and proclaim that "this extraordinary power belongs to God and does not come
from us" (2 Cor. 4:7). Thus, the preacher's life
becomes the pattern of repentance and hope, just as
the psalmist's does.

This psalm lends itself to two very different (and
somewhat opposed) homiletical choices. First, it is
almost unparalleled in its ability to extend hope to
addicts, people with depressive mental illnesses,
people who have experienced the loss of a job or the

Psalm 130

Theological Perspective

the depths. The burden of this supplication to God is not Job's attestation of innocence, but rather the claim that the members of the human family share a tragic resemblance. The claim is framed as a rhetorical question: "If you, O LORD, should mark iniquities, Lord, who could stand?" (v. 3). Thus the one who makes the supplication at once acknowledges both sin's personal expression in the psalmist's own case and its universal ricochet through the human experience.

The second, and in many respects the more important, assumption that the psalm makes about human iniquity, is that it releases an oppressive dynamic in human communities that makes prisoners of everyone. Human sinfulness is not just individual, transgressive behavior that "good people" will disapprove. It is a powerful, enslaving force that requires an outside liberator. Thus the simple assertion that closes the psalm, "It is he who will redeem Israel from all its iniquities," embodies the understanding that iniquity has enslaving consequences that can be countered only by a power that is capable of reclaiming—thus redeeming—all that sin has bound.

Warfare, ancient and modern, is the most obvious illustration of the oppressive power unleashed by human iniquity. Though often couched in the rhetoric of justice and liberation itself, war is inevitably the assertion of certain self-interested perspectives and values over others. As such, it is an illustration of Psalm 130's testimony to the universality of human sin. But even more, war illustrates the oppressive results of such sinfulness as communities and nations are caught in the spiral of force and retaliation that binds everyone into an imprisoning reality from which there is no obvious escape, from which there is no liberation, and for which there is no redemptive power.

But no sooner than the psalm speaks of this ubiquitous human iniquity with its oppressive consequences, it also speaks of the pervasive character of God providing hope in the face of all the despair with which sin litters the landscape. Indeed, the power of the psalm comes not so much in its theological anthropology, as salient and pertinent as it is, but in its theology—that is, in its eloquent testimony to the character of God. Three characteristics of God are stressed: forgiveness, steadfast love, and redemptive power. The middle term, steadfast love, may be understood as the defining center of the divine reality. In light of that defining center, the other two characteristics describe

Pastoral Perspective

our own dark understanding of "the depths" in human life; the metaphor is visceral, the definition specific to some painful personal experience. Personal experience can broaden out into community understanding when shared: a bad season for farming or fishing, for instance, affects many others besides the actual fishers of the sea and tillers of the soil. The life of the community suffers at every level or in good seasons is buoyed by hope for the future. The psalmist's community would have shared the image of the watery depths as a place of chaos, as in the beginning at the creation—a place from which God is essentially absent, a place to be feared. A cry to God from such a place is natural, perhaps desperate. Part of the preacher's work here is to remind the listeners of their own depths without losing them there. God's people have come to hear a word of solace and pardon in a world where hurt and blame abound. The joy of "hope in the Lord" shines the brighter when the shadows of grief, pain, or guilt are visible but not overwhelming.

Here the psalmist's cry is uttered in confidence that God will hear and respond: it is the prayer of a hopeful person more than one who is lost in despair. In calling out to God in verses 1–4, the singer names her downcast state in terms so broad that they encompass the essence of the human condition. Whether the singer experiences the depths because of circumstances beyond her control or because of her own iniquities, she is caught in her humanity, needing God's help. Noting the overwhelming sinfulness of humankind, for which there is no excuse before the Lord, she affirms God's merciful nature in a subtle, indirect request for forgiveness and carefully includes a promise of the thankful reverence that is indeed God's due. The rather subservient tone of these verses springs from genuine humility and absolute trust in God.

Humility and trust, to say nothing of subservience, tend to be scarce among affluent Americans. We are generally sure of our own talents and strengths, proudly self-reliant as individuals and independent as congregations. Pushing our knowledge of the depths of the human condition to the back of our minds, we rarely see ourselves as pilgrims reaching out for an encounter with or a deeper knowledge of God. Likewise, the notion of waiting patiently for the Lord's forgiveness is foreign to people who rarely sit still but take on multiple tasks at once, whirling from one appointment or demand to the next without pause or reflection.

What does it mean, in contemporary culture, to wait for the Lord? The psalmist evokes an image of

particular moments, these psalms have been of special importance for the life of the church in those liturgical moments that call for contrition and penitence.

Although the debate continues in scholarly literature, Psalm 130 is likely best understood as one of the laments, or complaints, that so frequently occur in the Psalter. While various structural arrangements have been suggested, one helpful way to approach the psalm is to see in it four brief parts: verses 1–2; 3–4; 5–6; 7–8.

From the Depths. The psalm begins at a specific place: "Out of the depths" (v. 1). Yet it is a place that transcends its own specificity. "The depths" (*ma'amaqim*) is an expression that evokes images of the watery abyss that God subdued to establish an ordered world (Gen. 1). It is a chaotic realm that, while fundamentally circumscribed, periodically splashes over into Israel's experience and threatens to undo all that God has established. It is a realm whose waves have been felt by many people throughout the ages, whether Israel in Babylonian exile or people along the Gulf of Mexico in the wake of Hurricane Katrina. From this place of unimaginable chaos the psalmist cries the only explicit petition in the psalm: "Lord, hear my voice" (v. 2). The psalmist invokes God as the One who listens, knowing that the listening God once heard the outcry of Egyptian slaves and delivered them from their chaotic condition and brought them to freedom.[2]

Verses 3–4 associate sin ("iniquities") with the chaos introduced by verses 1–2. This is not uncommon for the Old Testament, as a quick glance at Psalm 32 or a reading of the book of Job will show—texts that, each in its own way, relate sin and conflict. However, Psalm 130:3–4 does not necessarily claim that "depths" are the result of "iniquities." This unit is, rather, an acknowledgment that should God "watch" (*shamar*, translated as "mark" in the NRSV) and "keep" every human deed, no one could withstand divine scrutiny. In a tone akin to Isaiah 6:5 the psalmist admits to being a sinner among sinners, who trusts in a forgiving God (v. 4). As a sinner, from the depths, the poet prays. Indeed, the very affirmation of God as a forgiving God stands as a reminder to the Merciful One to act in character.

Waiting and Watching. The Hebrew text of verses 5–6 has challenged interpreters, although its basic

failure of a marriage, or any who feel that their errors in life have cast them into a dark pit of despair from which there is no visible escape. Such persons can immediately identify with the psalmist—"Out of the depths I cry to you, O LORD" (v. 1)—and enter into the urgency of his or her plea. For such an audience, the preacher can preach this "straight up," leading the congregation through the territory of spiritual desolation and into the possibility of forgiveness. It might be useful to illustrate this path by reference to Chuck Colson, Moses or Augustine, or to any other repentant sinner who made good.

Second, this sermon might also touch upon the sudden turning at the end of the psalm, where the very God who has been cast as the potential accuser in verse 3 becomes the agent of forgiveness and redemption in verses 7–8, bridging in God's very being the immense gulf between Sheol (the netherworld, the bottomless pit) and the perfection of God. The preacher might choose to make use of the suggestion in verse 4 that forgiveness is extended in order that sinners might be able to revere God (as in the cleansing of Isaiah in 6:5–8), and explore the dynamic of forgiveness and gratitude in the life of the Christian.

There is a danger in the possibility that members of the congregation may be tempted to impute sin to themselves in circumstances (such as the death of a child) in which they have not erred. The preacher might consider exploring our innate instinct to blame ourselves for anything really bad that happens in our lives, and examine that assumption in the light of passages of Scripture that impute illness and failure to sin, and of other passages (such as the book of Job and the passion of Christ) which demonstrate that pain also enters the life of those who are blameless.

But the security and prosperity of our culture have also created a group of people who are alienated from the sense of their own sin, people who have stayed on the path of conformity to basic decency, who have attained tolerable success in most of what they have attempted, who have never been severely tested by any trial (as, in an earlier generation, they almost certainly would have been tested by war, poverty, hunger, or death). Such persons are likely to feel that this psalm was written for someone else, and possibly even for someone whom they hold in the unreflective contempt that those who succeed without really trying can have for those who have failed. A sermon addressed to this

2. On associations between Psalm 130 and Exodus, see J. Clinton McCann, "The Book of Psalms," *The New Interpreter's Bible*. vol. 6 (Nashville: Abingdon, 1996), 1204–7.

Psalm 130

Theological Perspective

God in response to the two dimensions of human iniquity already named.

Steadfast love is probably the Hebrew Bible's word for grace, in that it proclaims the core reality of God's abiding loyalty to all that God has made. This is the God who does not abandon the divine intention, even when what God has made willfully and wantonly disrespects that intention. This core loyalty of God to the creation in general and to the human creation in particular is a love that does not let go, but abides. Grace, loyalty, steadfast love—together they describe the God Psalm 130 cries to from the depths and waits for "more than those who watch for the morning" (v. 6).

The God of steadfast love is thus a forgiving God toward all who stand before God in sinfulness and shame. Indeed, the worship of God arises from this unconditional acceptance by God of those who are unacceptable in their own right (Tillich). "But there is forgiveness with you, so that you may be revered" (v. 4). Utterly aware of the self-interested and prideful characteristics that should by all rights keep the human family sequestered from God's gracious presence, the psalmist is disarmingly impertinent in the claim that "there is forgiveness with you." But it can scarcely be otherwise with the God who is defined by loyalty and love. To the extent that anyone feels shut off from God by their sinfulness, mired in depths of self-loathing, disappointment, or shame, Psalm 130 speaks the only word of gospel that there is: "If you, O LORD, should mark iniquities, Lord, who could stand? But there is forgiveness with you, so that you may be revered" (vv. 3–4).

Beyond this, the God of steadfast love is also a redeeming God toward the mass of humanity victimized by the oppressive power of human sinfulness. Because the effect of human sin binds people in tragic cycles of violence and exploitation, God's steadfast love goes far beyond a readiness not to "mark" iniquities. It includes as well both the power and the determination to "redeem from" iniquities, to undo and overcome—in real time—the vicious power of communal alienation that no other power can accomplish.

For this God of loyal love, who forgives sin and brings the power of redemption from sin's consequences, the psalmist waits in hope, inviting all who know the cry from the depths to do the same.

D. CAMERON MURCHISON

Pastoral Perspective

body and soul on tiptoe, breath held, tense with eagerness to greet the Lord, waiting like a sentry who searches the darkness of night for the first sign of dawn. We might see something of that eagerness in a family (especially the mother!) awaiting the impending birth of a child, or in a person who is in the process of discerning his vocation. Or how might a very elderly person or one who is extremely ill or dying await the coming encounter with God? In what word of God does such a person find hope? And for the majority of folk who may not see themselves in such a life situation, what reason can the preacher offer for the intensity of feeling found in this psalm?

If the first four verses are a prayer, the last four are a combination of creed and sermon. Verses 5–6 assert the hopeful waiting stance of the psalmist, whatever her reasons or life situation might be. In the final two lines, her eagerness to share her faith overflows in an exclamation exhorting the community to join her in hope. In the New Testament lection, Paul refers to psalms of this sort, where in the midst of troubles the psalmist's faith impels her to speak out: "But just as we have the same spirit of faith that is in accordance with scripture—'I believed, and so I spoke'—we also believe, and so we speak" (2 Cor. 4:13).

This is a prophetic word, to Israel in the original setting, to the Corinthians in Paul's time, and to congregations in the twenty-first century. Can the eager, patient faith of one individual spur the community to look again at its beliefs and the life that arises out of them? One voice may indeed be sufficient to remind God's people of God's amazing "steadfast love" and of God's "great power to redeem." Whose voice speaks that word of hope? Whose ears need to hear it?

MARY DOUGLAS TURNER

Exegetical Perspective

meaning seems reasonably clear. Following the affirmation in verse 4 that God is a forgiving deity, the psalmist assumes the stance of waiting. Indeed, the entire *being* of the poet (*nephesh*, "soul" in NRSV) is committed to waiting. It is a hopeful waiting that anticipates the outcome of a merciful God's engagement in the conflict between psalmist and depths. The stunning combination of style and imagery even evokes the mood of waiting.[3] Repetition of the word "wait" in verse 5 (not actually found in the Hebrew of v. 6), coupled with the repetition of "watch[ing] for the morning," actually mimics the experience of waiting. Further, the image of watching for the morning qualifies the character of waiting by hinting at the anxiety of threats that may come in the night and simultaneously anticipating the safety that arrives with the break of day.

Watching and waiting spill over into affirmation in verses 7–8. In the present form of the psalm, the poet seems to turn from individual concerns to enjoin the larger community to hope in the constantly loving and redeeming God. Some interpreters contend that the tone of these verses means the psalm should be understood as a thanksgiving that is offered after the psalmist's deliverance, instead of as a lament. However, there is no clear indication in the psalm that the poet has moved from "watching in the night" to "walking in the light." It may well be that the psalmist, who has cried out to a listening God, still struggles with threatening depths and battles to discern what lies ahead through the murky shadows of the night. Day is yet to dawn. However, engagement with YHWH has both engendered and strengthened faith, so that the psalmist, from the very depths of fear and despair, is able to shout to the community, "Hope in the LORD . . . who will redeem Israel from all its iniquities." What a message for pilgrims in exile!

V. STEVEN PARRISH

Homiletical Perspective

audience might probe the structural causes of failure in our society, addressing how issues such as poverty, illness, unequal education, and even parents who have to work three jobs to make ends meet can create situations in which the ordinary path to success may be closed. Such a sermon might seek to help people understand that their apparent success is not the result of their own efforts alone, but a gift from a gracious God, thus inviting empathy to replace scorn or pity for God's more visibly broken children. Or the sermon might seek to deepen the congregation's understanding of sin (often understood as committing a series of horrid deeds) as a fundamental orientation away from God. Such a sermon might help them imagine what a world would look like in which everyone dwelled in mercy, in contrast to our own society. They might realize that they too have turned away from God and been forgiven in Christ Jesus. While the first sermon would seek to form a hard-pressed group of people into a community of hope, the second would seek to form a hard-hearted group into a community of mercy.

Another challenge the text highlights is the contrast between the pace of the spiritual life and that of the modern world. The striking image in verse 6, that "my soul waits for the Lord more than those who watch for the morning, more than those who watch for the morning," implies the patience that is required in the gradual unfolding of the spiritual life. This can be hard to grasp for those who have grown accustomed to instantaneous communication through cell phones, text messaging, and information accessed through ever-faster Internet connections. Exploring this theme in terms of pastoral care (such as the patience of waiting by a hospital bed), in prayer (the slow disciplines of sanctification), and in the life of Christ (dealing with pig-headed disciples, or in the passion, whose Latin root links the ideas of patience and suffering) might provide real food for reflection to a twenty-first-century congregation.

DEBORAH ANNE MEISTER

3. See McCann, 1205.

2 Corinthians 4:13-5:1

¹³But just as we have the same spirit of faith that is in accordance with scripture—"I believed, and so I spoke"—we also believe, and so we speak, ¹⁴because we know that the one who raised the Lord Jesus will raise us also with Jesus, and will bring us with you into his presence. ¹⁵Yes, everything is for your sake, so that grace, as it extends to more and more people, may increase thanksgiving, to the glory of God.

¹⁶So we do not lose heart. Even though our outer nature is wasting away, our inner nature is being renewed day by day. ¹⁷For this slight momentary affliction is preparing us for an eternal weight of glory beyond all measure, ¹⁸because we look not at what can be seen but at what cannot be seen; for what can be seen is temporary, but what cannot be seen is eternal.

¹For we know that if the earthly tent we live in is destroyed, we have a building from God, a house not made with hands, eternal in the heavens.

Theological Perspective

After reducing Christians' expectations from the grandiose to the realistic and showing how God's power is manifested in human weakness, Paul turns to something less dramatic: the entirely human act of preaching, which has already been anticipated in his mention of the gospel.

In searching the Bible for passages about the proclamation of the truth, Paul found a verse in the Greek version of the Psalms: "I believed, and so I spoke." He would engage in similar reflections in Romans: salvation comes from believing with the heart and confessing with the lips, but prior to both of these there must be proclamation and hearing of the gospel (Rom. 10:9–17).

In this context he makes much use of the verb for "making manifest" or "bringing to light." Possibly it was used first by his opponents, who claimed greater inward illumination than Paul. If so, Paul turns it around, claiming greater truthfulness—what we today like to call "transparency." He locates it, furthermore, in the "public" or interpersonal realm; this illumination does not remain hidden within the human spirit. Sometimes Paul applies the verb to his own actions: he "openly states" the truth to everyone's conscience (2 Cor. 4:2, my translations; cf. 5:11); he bears Jesus' dying so that Jesus' living might be "manifested" (4:10–11); he has "made it plain"

Pastoral Perspective

There is of course a philosophical critique against the dualism that can be seen both undergirding and emanating from this text, this old set of qualitative distinctions between the inner and the outer, the visible and the invisible, the temporary and the eternal. We have, many of us at least, come to think more holistically and with a certain "Hebraic" resistance to these more "Hellenistic" habits of thought. Our anthropology does not assume such categories nor does our theology stake itself upon Plato or Aristotle. But Paul, like so many Jews of his time, *did* use this vocabulary, and not just, I think, to communicate with his Gentiles. It seemed, in fact, to fit rather well with many of the dualities at work in Jewish law and interpretation. The worlds that Paul bridged as "apostle to the Gentiles" were of course importantly different, but they were not as utterly distinct as the more modern schema of Hebrew vs. Greek has been understood to entail.

Yet we attend to Paul not as the spokesperson for a particular philosophical view or synthesis. We listen to him as a brother and ancestor in the faith, speaking in his own way about something we assume to be true and important, invested by and for the generations of our community with such a worthiness to be heard. We listen for some word of God within his words.

Exegetical Perspective

Paul continues his defense of his ministry and returns to the subject of "speaking" begun in 2 Corinthians 4:2 ("open statement of the truth") and "proclaiming" in 2 Corinthians 4:5. Paul's rhetorical style, with its arresting imagery and carefully crafted structure, offers rich resources to the preacher.

In order to underscore the connection between speech and belief, Paul quotes Scripture, "I believed, and so I spoke," the opening part of the Septuagint version of Psalm 115:1. While this citation is an exact quote from that psalm, the previous reference (2 Cor. 4:6) is a loose paraphrase of Genesis 1:3. For preachers it is most important to attend to how Paul roots his argument in an ongoing conversation with Scripture. Exact word-for-word quotation is not as important to the early churches as it has become for some modern Christians. For Paul, living conversation with the stories of creation and with the Psalms fuels his argument and strengthens its effect. Reading Scripture is one of the sources of wisdom and insight for the early Christian assembly, or *ekklēsia*. Other sources are visionary experience, such as the illumination, described in the previous lection (2 Cor. 4:6), and the proclamation of early traditions.

Paul cites one of these traditions, a formula believed, recited, and preserved in the community. The words "we know" and "that" in verse 14 indicate

Homiletical Perspective

In 1934 two heavyweights took a few intentional swings at each other—think of perhaps Muhammad Ali vs. George Foreman. The opponents were not professional boxers with gloves sparring in a ring but two testy European theologians, Karl Barth and Emil Brunner, who traded jabs of the pen. At stake was determining once and for all the *Anknüpfungspunkt* (namely the "point of contact") between God and human beings.

Emil Brunner believed the point of contact was located inside of us, while Karl Barth saw the point of contact as truly beyond us. To generalize many pages of argument, Brunner believed there were echoes of Eden still inside our heart, soul, and mind, while Barth staunchly argued God was nothing like us, but instead distant and ultimately "other."

In the fourth chapter of 2 Corinthians, Paul suggests, amidst the travails of life and ministry, we can take comfort that a resurrected Christ lives inside of us. Like Brunner, Paul locates the *Anknüpfungspunkt* at first as inside rather than outside of us. He writes, "Even though our outer nature is wasting away, our inner nature is being renewed day by day" (2 Cor. 4:16).

Bede Griffiths is a Benedictine monk who in his travels around the world asked various people of faith, "Where is God?" Hindus and Buddhists in the East, he

2 Corinthians 4:13–5:1

Theological Perspective

that he is not untrained when it comes to knowledge of God's truth (11:6). Sometimes he applies it to the effects of those actions: the Corinthians themselves "show" that they are a living letter (3:3); as more people trust in the grace of God, the fragrance of the knowledge of Christ is "known everywhere" (2:14–16), increasing thanks to God (4:15). Sometimes he applies it to the last judgment: all must "appear publicly" before the judgment seat of Christ (5:10), when all the secrets of the heart will "come to light" (1 Cor. 4:5).

The church since the second century has taken this same approach when it is overwhelmed with claims of secret traditions and private revelations. It looks only to what has been received publicly by the whole Christian community, which means specifically the New Testament writings ascribed to the apostles and the summary that they called the "apostolic proclamation" and we know as the Apostles' Creed. Paul identifies with the psalmist: "the same spirit of faith" is in both of them. Notice what he is saying. The psalmist and many others in ancient Israel share the same faith as Christians. This means that Paul's derogatory language about the Jews in chapter 3 must be set in a more positive context. The faithful people of ancient Israel shared the same faith, the same grace, the same promises, even though it was communicated in different forms. Moses really beheld the Spirit (2 Cor. 3:16); Abraham was justified by faith (Rom. 4:1–25); Isaac was a child of the promise, a symbol for all who inherit the Jerusalem above (Gal. 4:21–31). The basic contrast, then, is not between Israel and the church, Jews and Christians, but between two attitudes: the "oldness of the letter" (Rom. 7:6), obeying the written commandments out of fear, and the "newness of the Spirit," doing good out of love for God. What makes the difference is how one interprets revelation. Even the gospel can be "veiled" if "the god of this world" blinds the perceptions of unbelievers (2 Cor. 4:3–4). It, too, must be received with spiritual insight.

Paul's reflections along this line were continued by Augustine, the medieval church, Calvin, and Barth. While they acknowledged the contrasts between Israel and the church, they also looked at the continuities from one to the other, even their similarities, making the contrasts much less stark and much less demeaning to the Jews. Yes, the books of Moses and the whole "old" testament are "veiled" in many rituals, events, and images that seem different from the Christ they prefigure. But the

Pastoral Perspective

We need not entirely share Paul's philosophical categories to listen to him that way, nor need we agree with his logic. Sometimes his argument leaves the modern reader either scratching her head in confusion or protesting to the long-dead author that it just ain't necessarily so. Sometimes Paul argues points from Scripture in imaginative forms of midrash that have little or no relationship to the text's plain or historic meaning. Sometimes he draws on theories of nature and biology that no longer hold for us. As a debater for our age, Paul can sometimes seem far off the mark. He does not convince us; there is a gulf between us, centuries of difference.

And yet we listen. We listen partly because we are canonically bound in community to do so, but also because we have found that what the community has promised can and does happen: there *are* wisdom and insight and passion and spirit here, and he speaks to *us* after all, when we eavesdrop on him speaking to others.

What then might we hear in these words, as Paul again uses as much voice as he can in order to be heard? He employs a royal or magisterial *we* in place of a humble first person singular: he and his companions, he and his other communities, he and his God and his Christ, in whatever or every unspecified way. He addresses the community of the Corinthians as their numerical equal, not one man making an argument to the many, but *we* proclaiming something to *you*. This is not uncommon in Paul's writing, and it might be thought mere habit of speech or epistolary style, but it is nonetheless emblematic of his eagerness here to be heard and heeded. It defies those who would belittle and marginalize him.

That spirit of defiance is key in the working of this text and it gives us a way of understanding, assenting to, and, more importantly still, being addressed by, this text for the good of others, regardless of our philosophical disagreements. For Paul here voices that bold contrariety that can be the spirit of faith, that defiance of the realities that lie nearest to hand. That existential refusal to cede authority to the powers of time and space is an act of faith independent of the metaphysical vocabulary with which it is expressed. We find that defiance in the language of different layers and genres of Scripture; we find it in the narratives of the Gospel; we find it in faithful saints and martyrs into our own times.

For Paul, this spirit of faith is understandably connected to the defiance of those norms that would

that a quotation follows—here the tradition is "the one who raised the Lord Jesus will raise us also with Jesus." Jesus' resurrection inaugurates and promises the resurrection of the community of believers, the reunion of "we" and "you" and Jesus into the presence of God. The inclusion of the phrase "with you" in "will bring us with you" underscores the relationship between Paul and the audience and stresses that the promised raising will include those whom Paul includes in "we" with those he calls "you." Just as what "we know" is corporate, so is the transformation that is the result of that knowledge.

This scenario fits within Jewish eschatological apocalyptic thinking, which anticipated the climactic coming together of the righteous with God at the end times. The variety of New Testament accounts of the end times (1 Thess. 4:17; 1 Cor. 15:23–28) is evidence of a diversity and fluidity among visions of how Jesus' believers imagine this end time event. Although some commentators say this description represents Paul's speculation about his own death, it is more likely that he is speaking of the hope and expectation of all the saints about their future.

The promised reunion "with you" leads to the emphatic statement that "everything is for your sake" (4:15). This affirmation repeats the claim of 4:5 that Paul and his coworkers are "your slaves for Jesus' sake." This passage is reminiscent of Romans 5:15–17, where grace is said to abound for many, a multiplication of grace that results in the glory of God. The statement may be a doxology; that is, it gives thanks and praise in a liturgical fashion. Like 4:5, "Jesus Christ [is] Lord," it may reflect phrases used in the worship or prayers of the church. The presence of such liturgical elements in Paul's letter shows that while Paul employs logical arguments, his communication with the congregation is not strictly discursive, but colored by passion and praise.

In the next verses Paul makes a series of contrasts: between the outer nature wasting away and inner nature being renewed, what is light and temporary as opposed to what is heavy and eternal, and the visible and the invisible. The stress lies on the positive affirmation in the second half of each contrast. The series of juxtapositions assures the readers in the midst of their suffering of the reality of the inner nature, of the eternal weight of glory, and of the reliability of what is unseen.

Paul's language is at home in the Hellenistic thought world that values the unseen over the seen and the eternal over the temporal, a point of view that remains prevalent in some kinds of spirituality

discovered, would typically point to their heart while Jews, Christians, and Muslims in the West would point outside of themselves to the heavens.[1] A sermon on this passage might begin by asking a congregation to imagine where they believe the intersection occurs between God and their own life. Inside or outside? Up or down? A sermon could continue by delving deeper into the passage and reflecting on Paul's claim that our inner nature is being renewed. This renewal will also eventually draw to a close when "the earthly tent we live in is destroyed" (5:1). Paul's point is that at some point we will all die—that in time everything human will crumble and perish, whether it is a city, a home, or even our own life. In the face of our death, and the struggles of life and ministry, Paul then steers his readers to the hope found in "eternal" things. What does he mean? Like an inner nature grounded in a resurrected Christ, there also exists, says Paul, divinity "outside of us," another reality to restore us, but one not easily seen. So we might say that if Bede Griffths happened to meet Paul and asked his question, "Where is God," Paul might have pointed at first to his heart, and then with his other hand to the world and the stars above.

When I ask people in a Sunday school class to describe their experience of God, they often begin by referencing moments they cannot fully explain but that somehow hint at a spiritual dimension in this world. Celtic Christianity describes such moments as "thin places." I have found church members often describe them as coincidences or *déjà vu*.

In his book *The Sense of Being Stared At*, Rupert Sheldrake observes how some animals have a sixth sense. Sharks and birds, for example, have a magnetic sense to enable them to respond to the earth's magnetic field. Sheldrake goes on to suggest human beings may not have this sixth sense, but have what he calls a seventh sense—a spiritual awareness that connects us to each other, to the world, and to the realm of the spirit. For example, he observes how a majority of us believe we have sensed people staring at us even though our backs were turned at the time. Sixty percent of us claim to have experienced telepathy. Sheldrake guides his readers to the skaters Jayne Torvill and Chris Dean, who dazzled us during the Olympics, and how, according to Dean, the reason they could skate together so fluidly and beautifully was telepathy. "There's simply no other way to explain it," says Dean.[2]

1. Wayne Teasdale, *The Mystic Heart* (New York: New World Library, 2001), 79.
2. Rupert Sheldrake, *The Sense of Being Stared At* (New York: Crown Publishing, 2003), 24.

2 Corinthians 4:13-5:1

Theological Perspective

veiling is for the sake of an unveiling, a revealing, in the "new" testament.

Because of this "spirit of faith," which is basically trust in God's grace and promises, Paul has hope. While we are outwardly wasting away, inwardly we are being renewed, directing our attention not to what is transient but to what is eternal (cf. the "straining upward" of Phil. 3:13). Then Paul spells out what is hoped for. He mixes his metaphors: body, tent, building, garment. His point is that this inheritance is already secure, quite unlike the changing and insecure situation at present.

Just as in chapter 4, Paul's expectations are sobered and become more realistic. Earlier he had assumed that he would be alive at Christ's return (1 Thess. 4:13–17; 1 Cor. 15:18, 20, 51). Now he considers the possibility that he might be among those who die. In that case, he would be "with Christ" (2 Cor. 5:8, Phil. 1:23). But that would not yet be the fulfillment he hopes for. He will not receive his resurrection body until Christ's return. Until then he "groans" for a transformed body (2 Cor. 5:2, Rom. 8:22–23), when mortality will be "swallowed up" in life (2 Cor. 5:4, 1 Cor. 15:54). In the meantime he expresses a certain indifference about whether he lives or dies (2 Cor. 5:9; Rom. 14:8), because neither condition is the final goal.

Paul thus sets the tone for Christians who for twenty centuries have wondered when the end will come: very soon? in the more distant future? not at all in the literal sense? Paul teaches us how to live in a "between time," when the new age has been inaugurated in Christ and renewal has begun, but the old age persists.

In many ways hope remains unfulfilled. And yet the new has already begun. Paul's best explanation is that the faithful have received the Spirit as an *arrabōn*, an earnest, a down payment, a guarantee of what will be conferred in full at a later time (2 Cor. 1:22; 5:5). Life in the presence of Christ is not yet possessed. But the Spirit is a guarantee that all God's gifts are to be possessed in the future (cf. Rom. 8:18–27).

EUGENE TESELLE

Pastoral Perspective

link his dignity and authority to external success or power. What is worthy, he argues, is not the seen but the unseen. The external material of life is passing and changeable, but there is something within that abides. We can defy what we suffer because it is part of this transient world and we know of something else, something glorious, something that will abide. The dualism in this passage is not unlike that in John, in that it is not so much descriptive as a call to decision. Yet it is a gentler exhortation than in John, not so much to a stark choice between life and death as a word of encouragement and comfort, a reminder that the things still unseen will abide. "So we do not lose heart" (4:16).

Near the canonical beginning of the Corinthian correspondence, in 1 Corinthians 1:27–29, Paul spoke with the same kind of defiance. There his language was in one regard even more radical: "God chose what is foolish in the world to shame the wise; God chose what is weak in the world to shame the strong; God chose what is low and despised in the world, [*even*][1] things that are not, to reduce to nothing things that are, so that no one might boast in the presence of God." The chosen instruments of God for the shaming of the proud and the annihilation of the powerful are here not just the humble and weak; they are even "things that are not." Imagine possibly such nonexistent but powerful things as our stories and dreams, our songs and fictions, the truths we tell that are not yet facts. Imagine also *our* words of defiance, our refusals to be discouraged, even our bravado in spite of all that would convince us to despair or betray our God.

JOHN K. STENDAHL

1. The NRSV translators chose not to include the *kai* found in some versions at this point in the text.

Exegetical Perspective

and theology today. The dualistic language here confronts a preacher with the dilemma of how to harness the positive power of these contrasts without reinforcing a severely dualistic anthropology that would ultimately undercut the spirit of this passage.

One way to challenge a radically dualistic interpretation of this passage is to recognize that Paul assumes the continuity of the process between the wasting away and being made new. The process of preparation takes place in the tension between outer and inner, present and future, seen and unseen. The value of the present is not denigrated. The phrase "day by day" indicates the small, everyday steps of renewal in the present.

"Beyond all measure" (4:17) is another pleonastic phrase expressing excessive abundance. The eternal *weight* of glory stands in contrast with the *lightness* of the present affliction (the adjective translated as "slight" can also mean "light"). The original Hebrew root of *kabod,* glory, means "weight." Contemporary hearers might imagine glory, not as an abstraction, but as a substance or compound with weight. The idea of weight conveys profundity, as in the English word, "weightiness." Another connotation is "heaviness" with its implication of "burden," as the Greek word *baros* is translated elsewhere. The glory that awaits them is like material with heft and texture.

The final images compare a temporary dwelling with an eternal, heavenly building. "Earthly tent" (5:1) could refer to the Hebrew tent of meeting. It could mean the physical body of individuals. The phrase could also allude to the Jerusalem temple that would be replaced by one "not made with hands," as in Mark 14:58 and John 2:19. The different possible interpretations point to an important insight: in the imagination of the New Testament writers Mark and Paul, the meaning of house as individual body and house as community overlapped. A body possessed by a spirit was like a house occupied by a demon. An exorcism of an individual might mirror the cleansing of a land (Mark 5:1–13). Those who believed in Jesus as Lord expected in the age to come both a transformation of their own bodies and a renewal of the body of the community, the body of Christ.

CYNTHIA BRIGGS KITTREDGE

Homiletical Perspective

A sermon might ask: "Have you ever thought of someone right before the phone rang, and then heard that person's voice? Have you ever woken up before the alarm rang? Or before your baby started to cry?" In our passage Paul seems to indicate that just as Elijah heard a still, small voice, and Moses climbed a mountain to see God's glory, we can discover God's presence all around us—inside and out—if we have the eyes of the heart to see.

There is an old story about a disciple and his teacher, a story Paul might have liked. "Where shall I find God?" a disciple once asked. "Here," the teacher said. "Then why can't I see God?" "Because you do not look." "But what should I look for?" the disciple continued. "Nothing. Just look," the teacher said. "But at what?" "At anything your eyes alight upon," the teacher said. "But must I look in a special kind of way?" "No, the ordinary way will do." "But don't I always look the ordinary way?" "No, you don't," the teacher said. "But why ever not?" the disciple pressed. "Because to look, you must be here. You're mostly somewhere else," the teacher said.

The Pauline theologian J. Christiaan Beker once summed up the canon of Paul's thought as underscoring "the triumph of God." Beker believed the triumph of God is discovered when we come to understand, "the Christian already lives in the dawning of God's coming reign . . . [and] since the coming of Christ and his victorious resurrection, suffering becomes all the more tolerable."[3] Perhaps Paul would have said both Brunner and Beker were right, that God's presence and triumph is both internal and external—as the resurrected Christ renews us from the inside out, but also as God continues to birth in our midst, and before our very eyes, a new heaven and earth.

MARK BARGER ELLIOTT

---

3. J. Christiaan Beker, *Paul the Apostle* (Philadelphia: Fortress Press, 1980), 366–67.

Mark 3:20-35

²⁰And the crowd came together again, so that they could not even eat. ²¹When his family heard it, they went out to restrain him, for people were saying, "He has gone out of his mind." ²²And the scribes who came down from Jerusalem said, "He has Beelzebul, and by the ruler of the demons he casts out demons." ²³And he called them to him, and spoke to them in parables, "How can Satan cast out Satan? ²⁴If a kingdom is divided against itself, that kingdom cannot stand. ²⁵And if a house is divided against itself, that house will not be able to stand. ²⁶And if Satan has risen up against himself and is divided, he cannot stand, but his end has come. ²⁷But no one can enter a strong man's house and plunder his property without first tying up the strong man; then indeed the house can be plundered.

Theological Perspective

One way to read this passage is as a drama portraying the difficulty of the discernment between good and evil. What the passage seems to say is that this discernment is not easy and that we often are siding with Satan when we think we are being faithful to God.

The setting is a house in which Jesus is attempting to eat dinner after a long day. The lectionary reading begins mid-sentence, recalling the huge, frenzied crowd of Jews and Gentiles desperate to get close to the man reported to possess power over sickness and demons. Jesus' family is on the way to the house in order to bring him home because they are afraid he is mad. The scribes from Jerusalem are also after him, believing him to be in league with Satan. Jesus responds to this accusation with a series of short images. The first set shows that something divided against itself cannot stand: a kingdom, a house, Satan himself. A second image, perhaps more opaque than the first, is about tying up a strong man in order to plunder his house. Jesus condemns his detractors in very strong terms. At this point, a message is conveyed that Jesus' mother and brothers are outside. Jesus responds with a chilling rejection: they are not my family. Looking around him at the crowd of misfits, crazies, and his relentlessly undiscerning disciples he says, "This is my family." (In Mark's

Pastoral Perspective

With this strange Markan juxtaposition of attempted family intervention and the accusation that Jesus himself is demon possessed, we come to understand that the conflict between Jesus and the religious authorities is increasingly serious. In fact, that conflict threatens to become deadly. Accusations that Jesus was not simply misguided, but under the power of the ruler of demons, convey something of the amazing impact of both rumors and true witnesses that spread around him. No wonder his family set out to get him under control, if not out of fear for his life, at least to remove their own embarrassment because of the rising public tumult.

The beginning of the pericope (vv. 20–21) and its conclusion (vv. 31–35) carry deep implications for the theme of Christian discipleship. On the surface there is something harsh about Jesus' response to his family's request to reach out to him. This image of Jesus seeming to turn his back on his own mother and siblings simply does not fit with our pious picture of him. What is going on here? We do well not to think of this incident as the general attitude Jesus has toward family life. Yet it clearly has to do with a Christian understanding of "family." Quite apart from whether the relatives were his natural siblings, the text confronts the church with a central

^{28}"Truly I tell you, people will be forgiven for their sins and whatever blasphemies they utter; ^{29}but whoever blasphemes against the Holy Spirit can never have forgiveness, but is guilty of an eternal sin"— ^{30}for they had said, "He has an unclean spirit."

^{31}Then his mother and his brothers came; and standing outside, they sent to him and called him. ^{32}A crowd was sitting around him; and they said to him, "Your mother and your brothers and sisters are outside, asking for you." ^{33}And he replied, "Who are my mother and my brothers?" ^{34}And looking at those who sat around him, he said, "Here are my mother and my brothers! ^{35}Whoever does the will of God is my brother and sister and mother."

Exegetical Perspective

Whose House Is Divided? Who Is Outside and Who Is In? Each Gospel writer, including Mark, edits oral and written traditions about Jesus in the context of the social and political realities of the churches to whom the Gospel is sent. To hear the message most clearly, listen both for (1) What is the story? and (2) Why is the story told in this way?

This pericope is quite carefully crafted, with house and family both framing and central to Jesus' encounters. Literary structure provides clues to understanding the passage. Chiastic structures, common literary devices of the time, organize a literary unit in variations of the form of A—B—C—B'—A'. Look for A and A' to be related, for B and B' to be related, and for C, or the center of the chiasm, to be the highlight of the story.

	3:19b–20.	Setting: Jesus at home/house, great crowds, cannot eat bread.
A	3:21	Jesus' family
B	3:22	Jesus accused of being possessed by Beelzebul
C	3:23–27	Parables: A house divided and the strong man's house
B'	3:28–30	Blasphemy against the Holy Spirit
A'	3:31–35	Jesus' family

A key word is established at the beginning— "house." The passage, then, is about houses: Jesus'

Homiletical Perspective

This passage sounds strange to modern and even postmodern ears. Beelzebub? Satan? Demons? What is this passage about? How can we preach it in a world which seeks to cast out both angels and demons? Do we need to return to a premodern mind-set in order to make this passage credible? Or is there a profound reality lurking here, waiting to be excavated from layers of tradition?

Jesus takes seriously the realities of Satan and other demonic powers, including Beelzebub, whose name means "lord of the flies." Did Jesus believe that a personality named Satan actually existed? He likely did, and that makes this passage difficult to preach. Yet we should also look for the reality signified by the name "Satan." Satan does not necessarily mean a personality with horns and a red tail, but it does name a demonic power that is actively engaged against the compassionate and reconciling love of God. This is the reality that Jesus names here, and whether we believe in a person named "Satan" is not as important as hearing about our captivity to the powers of evil signified by "Satan," powers that continue to seek our allegiance.

Stated in this way, the reality of Satan and Beelzebub become disturbingly clear. They name the forces and configurations of power that capture us and cause us to hurt ourselves, to hurt others, and to

Mark 3:20-35

Theological Perspective

Gospel, the disciples almost always get it wrong, up to the last sentence when the women, who alone have seemed to understand Jesus, run away in terror.)

It is easy to identify with the family and with the scribes. The "family values" agenda defends strong, traditional families and attributes their defense to a biblical perspective. It is also natural to identify with church authorities. If we are preaching in a church or sitting on committees, choosing hymns, organizing Sunday school and potlucks we are part of the church authority. Christianity usually puts Christ at the base of these structures and uses his authority to bolster theirs. But this story demands a different perspective, because it is these very people that are condemned for failing to recognize who Jesus is.

It is disturbing to consider that these authorities are not evil. They are committed to maintaining domestic and religious life in the midst of troubled times. And yet from Jesus' perspective these familiar and essentially benign institutions are beyond the pale of his ministry. It is an odd feature of Jesus' ministry that he is open to everybody: Gentiles, Jews, the poor, the demented, the sick, working class, women, tax collectors, sexual outcasts. The only people who provoke Jesus' intolerance are his family and the normal, law-abiding scribes. The ones closest to him, his family and those who are—like him!—dedicated to a life of piety, are those that are also farthest from him. They are least able to make the leap from dedication to religion to openhearted love of God's beloved, disfigured humanity. For these people, Jesus' disordered love of humanity feels like falling off a cliff into chaos best symbolized by the demonic or insanity. The passage displays the difficulties of telling madness and evil from the inbreaking of the Holy Spirit and implies that it is especially difficult for domestic and ecclesial authorities. Though the text does not give many clues about what precisely the good news is, it is embedded in a series of stories about healing, the hostility that this healing generates, and Jesus' anger and frustration over this hostility.

If we transpose this theological vision into our own time, instead of lepers and demoniacs crowding around Jesus, we might see the strange bodies of the disabled. We might see soldiers with three-fourths of their bodies burned from a firefight in Iraq or other soldiers in prison reflecting on the horrors they witnessed and committed. We might see legless Afghan or Palestinian children. We might see a group of men reeking of cigarettes and coffee at an AA meeting. We might see a lesbian mother with a

Pastoral Perspective

reality of being a follower of Jesus' way. This is as true of our day as it was for Mark's community.

The answer to Jesus' question, "Who are my mother and my brothers?" (v. 33) is found in his saying, "whoever does the will of God" (v. 35). Thus even those who were not among the explicit disciples are indeed followers if they do what God wills.

Far from a harsh rejection of his immediate family (who were not called to be among the apostles), this opens the truth claims found elsewhere in the Gospels. Whoever is "not against us is for us" (9:40); whoever receives a child in mercy welcomes Jesus (9:37); whoever prays with faith will be heard (11:23). These examples show something of the mystery and the demand of discipleship in Mark's picture of Jesus.

Internal to the pericope, of course, is the enormous tension created by the scribes' charge that Jesus is full of sorcery and demon possession. Mark heightens the stakes in any claim that Jesus is of God. Here we encounter the striking character of Jesus' rhetorical rejoinder. He asks them how Satan can cast out Satan if it is the case that he is possessed. But this rhetorical question creates a dilemma: If no, they have no case; if yes, a divided Satan will fall. The stunning point comes when Jesus charges *them* with the sin of blasphemy. The "unforgivable sin" against the Holy Spirit is here focused on a denial that Jesus' work of healing and releasing from captivity is of God. This in itself may be a corrective to overly zealous uses of lists of sins against the Holy Spirit that has come up from time to time in Christian circles.

Of central importance to the Christian community today is the manner in which the strong christological claims are made by Mark. He does not give us a systematic or dogmatic account of Christology. Rather, as other commentators have observed, we see discipleship and the lordship of Jesus Christ fully integrated in what Jesus says and does. How are we today to "read" the teachings and the actions of Jesus in light of his death and resurrection? What does the testimony of the New Testament witness, and especially in Mark's tensive account of Jesus, actually show us about the rule and reign of God? How does Jesus manifest resistance to the power of evil?

Can we now understand that what Jesus said and did, he continues—crucified and risen—to speak and to enact in the world, and that he will do so until the rule and reign of God comes in fullness? What then makes Jesus the master of an undivided "house," which functions as a symbol for the church; and the demonic, divided house over which Jesus' power has been demonstrated.

Verses 20–21. In the NRSV, the assigned pericope begins in the middle of a sentence. Read from verse 19b: "Then he went home; . . ." "Home" is literally "into a house." The house metaphor will reappear in the center of this pericope. Seeing Jesus at home with crowds recalls the events in 2:1–12, echoes of which will reappear throughout 3:21–35: home, crowds, forgiveness of sins, scribes, accusations of blasphemy. "They could not even eat" (literally, eat bread). All other references to eating bread in Mark have eucharistic overtones, and there is no reason to think this text is any different.

Jesus' family serves as a literary tool to introduce several key themes. The antecedent of the pronoun translated as "people" (v. 21) in the NRSV is unclear, and probably indicates Jesus' family as the ones who were saying, "He has gone out of his mind." "Out of his mind" is literally, "he has stood outside." (Compare today's idiom, "he is really out of it," or the RSV "beside himself.") The question of who is *outside* arises again and again. In verse 31 the family is standing outside, in contrast to their saying in verse 21 that he "has gone outside," that is, out of his mind.

Verses 23–27. Having established the setting and structure, begin at the center and work outward. At the center are two parables. In verse 22 Jesus has been accused of casting out demons (cf. 1:21–27) by Beelzubul. The parables challenge the logic of that charge, again in the form of a chiasm:

C   How can Satan[1] cast out Satan?
c   a kingdom divided cannot stand
c′   a house divided cannot stand
C′   Satan divided cannot stand

Therefore, if the charge is true that by demons Jesus has cast out demons, then Satan is finished! Any kingdom/house/demon that is divided—that is, stands outside of and against itself—will come to an end.

In Mark 1:7, John the Baptist has identified Jesus as "the stronger one." In 3:27 Jesus is the Stronger One who has the power to tie up and plunder the strong man's house (Satan's house).

Verses 28–30. The chiastic literary structure alerted us to expect that verse 22 will be explained further in

---

1. In Job 1–2, Satan simply means "adversary." Here, Satan becomes identified with the "ruler of demons."

hurt God. To name a few of these, there is the power of race, which tells us to believe that one group is superior to another simply because of skin color or cultural heritage. There is the power of patriarchy, which tells us that men should dominate women. There is the power of materialism, which roars at us that money gives us life. And the power of militarism—the belief that weapons and war bring us peace and security—causes us to kill one another, often in the name of God.

In these verses in Mark, Jesus indicates that the power of these categories must be recognized and confronted in our lives if we are to experience the gracious and stunning love of God. He uses the metaphor of tying up the strong man in order to plunder his property. In using this parable, he speaks of the need of the gospel to expose our captivity to the "strong men" of our lives. In so doing, he seeks to free up our imaginations, which have become the property of Satan. Our captivity to Satan must be exposed in order for us to begin to discover the glorious freedom of the children of God, as Paul puts it so powerfully in Romans 8:21.

How do we come to be captive to the powers and forces signified by the name "Satan"? In this passage Jesus names one central source of our captivity and demonstrates how deeply captive we are and how difficult this process of discovery is. Jesus' family comes to take him home because people are saying (and his family may also believe) that he is insane. In his reply to his family's request to see him, Jesus stings his family by almost disowning them: "Who are my mother and my brothers? . . . Whoever does the will of God" (vv. 33–35). This is not the only time that Jesus wrestles with his family. At the age of twelve, according to Luke, he dismisses his parents' anxiety about his disappearance for three days with what seems to be a typical teenager's response: "Why were you searching for me?" Early in his ministry in John's Gospel, he is irritated when his mother seems to urge him to take care of the wine problem at the wedding in Cana. In the twelfth chapter of Luke, he makes it clear that he came to bring division rather than tranquility. In his response to his family's request to see him in this Mark passage, he is reminding them (and us) that those who take care of us, love us, and nurture us also help bind us to Satan.

I want to name one of my experiences as a demonstration of this process. I grew up in the Deep South in Arkansas on the Mississippi River Delta in the 1950s and 1960s, part of that generation of white Southerners who wrestled with the civil rights

Theological Perspective

baby on her hip and gay men holding hands or holding their adopted child. We might see scruffy members of a mining community singing old-time hymns. When we think about who is near Jesus, it is not the morally perfect. It is just the diverse mess of humanity, with all of its moral, physical, spiritual beauty and imperfection. The only ones not in the picture, the ones not pressing in at the doors and windows, desperate and aching to be near Jesus, are the ones who think they know what religion and family life is supposed to look like. Jesus, infinitely patient with the crowd, blasts away at these people. Everyone will be forgiven, except people who blaspheme the Holy Spirit. The inability to tell the difference between the power of the Holy Spirit and the demonic is an *unforgivable sin.*

For most of us, this is pretty bad news. Like the Jews of the first century, we live in troubled times and try our best to figure out how to be faithful. The Holy Spirit is wild and disturbing and comes to us in unfamiliar forms. Is same-sex love a breeze from the Holy Spirit or a sign of a disintegrating society? Are feminine images of the divine crazy, demonic, or healing? What if we make the wrong discernment? Perhaps if we pay attention to the theme of healing that runs through these stories, we might find a way to orient ourselves. It was the desire for healing that drew people to Jesus. Perhaps if we had compassion for our own wounds and the wounds of others, we might find ourselves in the crowd devoted to Jesus, instead of in the "legitimate" family that Jesus rejects.

WENDY FARLEY

Pastoral Perspective

household in a world where demonic powers still remain? Regrettably our churches appear all too often to be divided houses, subject to powers of hostility, recrimination, and even enmity between ideological groups. Communities so badly divided desperately need to find the deeper source of wholeness than our present debates allow. Jesus, the one who can exorcize the demonic, should be called upon to do his work of healing in our midst.

The clash with religious authorities is central to Mark. We do well to heed the implications of how Mark's own hearers must have heard and "read" him. For us, however, the issue is how we now understand the relationship between discipleship and Christology. More than simply "understand" intellectually, it seems crucial for the churches today to seek to live out that understanding. Living out the form of discipleship Christ bids us follow means a new solidarity with all of humanity. It requires that we learn with him to weep with those who weep and to rejoice with those who rejoice. It asks us to live into the densities of human joy and suffering. It calls us to find ourselves precisely in our willingness to give up our self-absorption. This is a demanding task, requiring a willingness to follow him into a new solidarity with God's whole family.

Is the love we see in Jesus stronger than death and the death-dealing ways of so much of the political and military world? Perhaps we can yet sing with Archbishop Desmond Tutu: "Goodness is stronger than hate." Christ's love is stronger than the illusions and deceptions of evil—including our own needs to project onto others our own unresolved struggles with the demonic. Jesus comes to dedemonize us— to free us from both our inner and outer captivities!

DON E. SALIERS

Exegetical Perspective

verses 28–30. Having debunked the accuser's logic with the two parables (vv. 23–27), Jesus returns to the consequences of the false accusation in verse 22.

"Amen, I say to you . . ." (v. 28, my translation) provides a major transition and a special claim of authority for the following word about "the children of humanity." "People" is a weak translation of this all-inclusive phrase, especially when affirming that for these children of humanity "all will be forgiven," including all blasphemies. A pause is appropriate here—to appreciate the power of this claim . . . before it is interrupted by one apparent exception.

Mark 3:29 is one of the most problematic and misused texts in the Gospels. The literary structure clearly invites us to hear that accusing Jesus of being possessed by Beelzubul is equivalent to blasphemy against the Holy Spirit. Those who falsely accused Jesus (in v. 22) committed an unforgivable sin. (Cf. Mark 2:6–7 where the scribes accuse Jesus of blasphemy.) For Mark, blasphemy against the Holy Spirit consists of calling the work of God's Holy Spirit evil.

Remember that naming the accusers as those who cannot be forgiven is spoken to a church harassed by both religious authorities and government. The conflicts may have also been internal. A look at Matthew 12:22–32 suggests that this pronouncement about the sin against the Holy Spirit raised major theological discussion in the early churches; so Matthew "clarified/modified" Mark's pronouncement. Remembering to ask why the story is told in this way and returning to Mark's clear affirmation of the inclusivity of God's forgiveness (v. 28) may bring the church closer to a responsible hearing of the text.

Look Who Is Outside Now! (vv. 31–35). The pericope ends where it began, with Jesus' family. His mother and his brothers are outside and call to him. Jesus responds with a question that he himself answers: "Whoever does the will of God is my brother and sister and mother."[2] Insiders and outsiders are now defined, not by blood, but by commitment to doing God's will. Meanwhile, the tension between the proclamation of God's inclusive love and the natural human (and church) proclivity to define outsiders and insiders persists.

JUDITH HOCH WRAY

Homiletical Perspective

movement. I was resistant to that movement because I had been taught white supremacy and the racism that undergirds it. I had accepted this ideology, and I had been taught it, not by mean and terrible people, but by loving and caring people such as my mother and my church leaders. They taught it to me, not because they were evil—quite the contrary, they were wonderful people in my life—but because they were captive to racism and had come to accept that racism was the way to find and maintain life.

As I came to hear other voices from God's Spirit—voices that told me that racism was not God's will—I began to be in internal conflict with my family and my community. It was a struggle and continues to be a struggle at some points.

I began to appreciate why Jesus calls the configuration of these forces "Satan," and I understood why he had indicated that his family might be part of the problem. In this passage, Jesus is not being antifamily and individualistic. In John's Gospel, as he dies on the cross, he makes certain that care will be provided for his momma after his death. And, for my own part, my greatest earthly resource is my mother and the church that nurtured me as a boy. This is a difficult passage, rooted in conflict and danger. It reminds us of the difficulty of following Jesus, but it also reminds us of the great possibilities that we will glimpse in the next lectionary passage from Mark's Gospel: if we have only the smallest amount of faith, great results can pour out from that.

NIBS STROUPE

---

2. Some think that Joseph's death explains the absence of a father among the family. See also Mark 10:30, which omits fathers.

Ezekiel 17:22-24

²²Thus says the Lord God:
  I myself will take a sprig
    from the lofty top of a cedar;
  I will set it out.
  I will break off a tender one
    from the topmost of its young twigs;
  I myself will plant it
    on a high and lofty mountain.
²³On the mountain height of Israel
  I will plant it,
    in order that it may produce boughs and bear fruit,
    and become a noble cedar.

Theological Perspective

These verses, like those of many other prophets, roll through the history of Christian theology as testimonies of hope born of trust in promises of God. The passage is appealing because of the vivid imagery in the larger complex embracing it. Here appear soaring eagles, the transport of sprigs and seeds to faraway, inhospitable locales where they blossom or perish, a wildlife refuge for birds of every feather in the mighty cedar's shade, and surprising reversals when high trees fall while low trees rise and green trees wither while dry trees sprout anew.

All of this is explicitly termed "allegory" and "riddle" (17:2). The allegory is explained by references to power politics of ancient Israel's rulers, who maneuver amid superpower threats. Historical-critical research has much to say about this matter. Yet riddle remains, and invites theological reflection. What hope, if any, is there for anyone, even people of faith, when the politics of our presumably savvy power politicians fail and yet another tsunami of disaster looms?

How to identify the content and thrust of the passage is itself something of a theological challenge. Two of the most popular uses of the text in theology's history fall considerably short of doing full justice to it. One all-too-familiar line of interpretation is to draw out only the most obvious

Pastoral Perspective

"Tergiversation" is one of those words that crossword puzzle addicts look for opportunities to use in conversation or that people like my old friend Nels—who is suffering the onset of Alzheimer's but still manages to beat me at Scrabble—delight in using to cover a triple-word score. The word itself is of Latin origin and means "desertion of a cause" or "apostasy" or, alternatively, "evasion" or "subterfuge." I will leave it up to my colleagues responsible for the exegetical and theological perspectives to describe the exact nature of the historical allusions found in our text, which involve both Babylon and Egypt and a couple of Judah's kings. Let me instead reflect pastorally on the point of the fable of the cedar sprig that has to do with the sovereignty of God in relation to the contending sovereignties and realpolitik of this world. It turns out to be a tale of Judah's chronic tendency to tergiversation.

When he uttered his clever head-scratcher of an answer to the Herodians and Pharisees sent to entrap him, "Give to the emperor the things that are the emperor's, and to God the things that are God's" (Mark 12:17), Jesus may well have had Ezekiel's fable in the back of his mind. The concluding verses of Ezekiel 17 that are our appointed reading for today narrate only the end of this chapter-long riddle or allegory, as it is referred to in the text itself (17:2).

Under it every kind of bird will live;
  in the shade of its branches will nest
  winged creatures of every kind.
²⁴All the trees of the field shall know
  that I am the Lord.
I bring low the high tree,
  I make high the low tree;
I dry up the green tree
  and make the dry tree flourish.
I the Lord have spoken;
  I will accomplish it.

Exegetical Perspective

The historical context for the ministry of Ezekiel is well documented by the text itself. Although not all of the oracles (including Ezek. 17:22–24) can be dated precisely, dates are given for fourteen oracles indicating that Ezekiel was active between 593 BCE (1:1) and 571 BCE (29:17). This was a turbulent and bleak time in biblical history. In 598 BCE, the Babylonians attacked Jerusalem and deported a number of Judah's leading citizens—Ezekiel among them. The devastating destruction of Jerusalem in 587 BCE occurred six years after the prophet's call and the latest documented oracle dates to 571 BCE, sixteen years into the Babylonian exile.

Scholars have long noted the careful organization of the book of Ezekiel, although there has been much debate regarding how much of the book stems from Ezekiel himself and which passages might be attributed to his later followers.[1] For the most part, the first twenty-four chapters of the book of Ezekiel are directed against Judah and speak of the coming destruction of Jerusalem. In chapters 25–48 the mood shifts, with a series of prophecies of salvation in the form of denunciations of Judah's regional enemies (25:1–32:32), visions of the restoration of

1. Walter Eichrodt, *Ezekiel: A Commentary*, trans. Cosslett Quin, Old Testament Library (Philadelphia: Westminster Press, 1970), 18–22.

Homiletical Perspective

You begin at the beginning: the prophet sitting by the river among the exiles, the heavens opening up, hallucinatory visions flashing forth. You see wind and fire, four living creatures with four faces and four wings; then a wheel, four wheels, tall and awesome, full of eyes, moving when the spirit moves—a crystal dome and a sapphire throne, gleaming amber, loins with fire streaming downward. "Like the bow in a cloud on a rainy day, such was the appearance of the splendor all around" (1:28). Ezekiel falls on his face at the sight of all this, and the reader wonders if this narrative is biblical or something from Hesse's *Steppenwolf*. The prophet is called by God, has another vision concerning a scroll, and is then lifted up by the spirit and borne away to Tel-abib (3:15), where again he sits, stunned, with the exiles.

These are, of course, the exiles who were carried off into captivity in Babylon after the destruction of Jerusalem in 587–86 BCE. Their suffering was great and their questions were many. The opening chapters of Ezekiel's book place those fantastic visions and rumors of glory alongside the crushing defeat and unfathomable suffering of his people. A provocative juxtaposition, to be sure—especially when you remember that the prophet attributes the Israelites' defeat to their own faithlessness and lifts up King Nebuchadnezzar of Babylon as an

Ezekiel 17:22-24

Theological Perspective

view of meaning and reduce the message to an aphorism: God is doing—or is about to do—something new. So it is that individuals, groups, and movements over the Christian centuries have trotted the passage out to proclaim that *they* and *their* cause *are* "the new thing" God is doing. In countless other cases of recent times, the message is more or less drained of all content and reduced to a free-floating hopefulness akin to pop-culture advice like "look on the sunny side of life," "tomorrow is another day," or "optimism pays off." A serious-minded theologian hearing such talk has counterquips ready at hand: "is this all there is?" or "where's the beef?"

There is more. The reading is a climactic moment in the prophet's word of God's own, as it were very personal, promise to act and power to fulfill the promise. Human hopes figure in here only if and when they happen to align with the promises of the God who is altogether capable of—and is here altogether intent on—bringing low anyone or anything high, global superpowers included, and exalting what is low. Thoughts such as these have been taken up into Christianity's doctrinal tradition from early on, inspiring teachings and fueling debates about the meaning of God's universal sovereignty over world affairs and all creation.

Application, or transfer, of Ezekiel's proclamation from bygone days to Christ Jesus and good news of God's reign emerged in early Christian communities. They are amply attested in writings of Apostolic Fathers. Proof-from-prophecy, typological, and varied dispensational and canonical hermeneutics have featured such theological uses of the materials, which in any case have become a common, though often contested, legacy over the sweep of the history of doctrine. Over the course of Christianity's history, from the age of Constantine on, faith convictions in God's own ultimate, universal sovereignty and its exercise have often been linked with—or confused by—a trickle-down "logic of sovereignty" from God to Christ to *Christian* rulers of church or state.

Unfortunately but not very surprisingly, theological contests and protests over the logic of sovereignty have focused more often on who benefits from it than on its biblical and theological adequacy. There are exceptions, though. There are theologians—Luther is a notable case—who adhere to proof from prophecy but reflect on the odd, counterintuitive "logic" of the theology of the cross rather than theology of glory. Kierkegaard's discussion of Christ as paradox strikes a similar chord, as does his blistering critique of smug, self-

Pastoral Perspective

But it does proclaim the prophetic Word that God's sovereignty is comprehensive, transcendent, and inclusive of all other sovereignties that, at God's discretion, still may have their role to play. And so Ezekiel, like his contemporary Jeremiah, does not pretend to be neutral regarding the political choices facing his people and their rulers, but clearly opts for honoring the preexisting treaty with Babylon that some fellow believers viewed as treasonous.

Still, while daring to speak God's word into the messiness of the politics of his day, Ezekiel concerns himself with the even deeper matter of asserting the new and lasting thing that God is doing both through and despite the political intrigues in which Judah is enmeshed. For this is a messianic prophecy through which God promises, "I myself will take a sprig from the lofty top of a cedar. . . . I myself will plant it on a high and lofty mountain . . . in order that it may produce fruit, and become a noble cedar." The result will be that "all the trees of the field shall know that I am the LORD," a prophetic echo of the promise to Abraham of old, whose progeny are destined to be a blessing to "all the families of the earth" (Gen. 12:3b) and as a near-contemporary prophet would put it, "a light to the nations" (Isa. 42:6b). While Ezekiel no doubt understands the messianic "sprig" of his prophecy to mean a future Davidic king (similar to Jeremiah's language regarding a "righteous Branch" for David [Jer. 23:5] and Isaiah's image of "a shoot . . . from the stock of Jesse" and "a branch . . . out of his roots" [Isa. 11:1]), Christians cannot but hear in these words a foreshadowing of Jesus of Nazareth as the ultimate messianic fulfillment of Ezekiel's "sprig" become "noble cedar."

Not to be ignored is the universalistic thrust in verse 23b: "Under it every kind of bird will live; in the shade of its branches will nest winged creatures of every kind." I cannot help visualizing here the lovely stylized Navajo weavings that depict the "Tree of Life" teeming with birds. It also prefigures the prophet of the return's memorable words "for my house shall be called a house of prayer for all peoples" (Isa. 56:7b), a prophecy that forever stands as challenge as well as promise to the obdurate exclusivisms of so many of our faith communities. Marty Haugen's hymn "All Are Welcome" sings memorably of God's inclusive welcome.

God's avowal "I bring low the high tree, I make high the low tree; I dry up the green tree and make the dry tree flourish" finds its echo in the Magnificat of Mary, which of course finds its own inspiration in the exilic community (Ezek. 37), the restoration of the Davidic Dynasty (Ezek. 34), and the rebuilding of the Jerusalem temple on a grand scale (Ezek. 40–48).

The lectionary passage, Ezekiel 17:22–24, presents some interesting problems in its current literary context. Unlike the first seventeen verses of this chapter, which employ folkloric and metaphorical images to describe the impending exile of the "house of Israel" and death of "the king" (v. 16), verses 22–24 shift the emphasis dramatically and speak— still metaphorically—of the coming restoration. Due to differences in style, language, and theological emphasis, scholars have suggested that verses 1–21 and verses 22–24 were originally independent units, with verses 1–21 coming from late in the reign of Zedekiah and verses 22–24 having been produced later, during the exilic period. Although these passages may well have been independent literary units, the present position of verses 22–24 follows the familiar pattern in biblical prophecy of punishment for failure to keep God's covenant, followed by restoration.

As has been noted by the eminent biblical scholar Walther Zimmerli[2] and others, a wide variety of literary forms and genres is employed throughout the book of Ezekiel. Ezekiel 17:2 alerts the reader that what follows is a "riddle" (*chidah*) in the form of a "parable" or "allegory" (*mashal*), directed toward "the house of Israel." The parable is set forth in verses 1–10, followed by its interpretation in verses 11–21. To the modern reader, the references to eagles, cedar trees, and vines taking on human characteristics is bizarre, but these are fairly common motifs in ancient Near Eastern fables, where plants and animals often take on anthropomorphic characteristics. The interpretation offered in verses 11–21 clarifies matters somewhat, indicating that the two eagles represent Babylon (eagle #1) and Egypt (eagle #2), while the fickle vine (Zedekiah) that reaches out for help to Egypt, rather than to YHWH, will be uprooted by YHWH. Because the king of Judah has broken his covenant with both YHWH and Babylon, he will be snared like a bird, his troops slaughtered, and the survivors scattered.

It is interesting to note that in the lectionary reading (vv. 22–24), no mention is made of the eagles (i.e., Babylon and Egypt), but instead it is *YHWH* himself who will take "a young tender twig" from the "topmost shoots" of a "lofty cedar" and

instrument of God! Tough words from a tough prophet in tough times.

We do not know anything like these times, like Ezekiel's times. We know nothing of being invaded, forcibly removed from our homes, and carried into exile in a foreign land. We know nothing of seeing the very foundations of our religion—our land, our temple, our sacred objects—laid waste by a rampaging army. We know nothing of siege warfare, starvation, open fighting in the streets, death and dying all around, the end of our civilization as we have known it. But most of all, we know nothing of being a subjected people, small and powerless, bloodied, repeatedly beaten down, trampled, invaded, occupied by the reigning superpower in the region. And yet the primary biblical narratives, all of them, are in some way about this: a small people, of no account, chosen by God for special care and attention, yet who become—in spite of this divine attention, or perhaps because of it—the pawns of every major imperial power during the biblical period. The patriarchs, the Hebrew slaves in Egypt, the wilderness wanderers, the early settlers in Canaan—even the monarchies of David and Solomon—were small and insignificant in their time by world standards. The people of Israel and later the early Christians were *all* minor historical players in the unfolding drama of world empires and their conquests. Jesus himself is hardly mentioned in the historical accounts of his time.

We practice the art of preaching in a land of great wealth, privilege, and power. When the biblical narratives speak of us, it is almost always as adversary, as oppressor, as other. We represent the empire in which the exiles are held captive. We are the power to whom the prophetic truth must be spoken. Our people are not Ezekiel's people. Western Christianity has grown accustomed to the comforts of affluence and the entitlements of empire. Preaching from the standpoint of Ezekiel's people is a difficult task. It is not easy to be on the receiving end of the prophetic word.

How extraordinary, then, with defeat and exile as background, is our text! How poignant, how unbearably touching. Is there a text anywhere in Scripture in which God is portrayed with such tenderness? "I myself will take a sprig from the lofty top of a cedar." God's startling word of consolation leaps from the page at precisely the moment when the national catastrophe is recounted by the prophet (17:11–21). From the depths of humiliation and despair comes this surprising recitation of God's

2. Walther Zimmerli, *A Commentary on the Book of the Prophet Ezekiel, Chapters 1–24.* trans. Ronald E. Clements (Philadelphia: Fortress Press, 1979), 25–40.

Ezekiel 17:22-24

Theological Perspective

righteous Christendom—a term of shame hardly restricted to last century's Denmark. Strands of Christian pacifism and nonviolent resistance to evil likewise take up how God wills the exercise of sovereign power in comparison and (stark!) contrast to worldly sovereigns we know all too well.

In modern and current (postmodern?) theologies, the ancient-world, royalist cast of the prophetic message has demanded attention, as a rule far from favorable. Numerous and quite diverse theological initiatives have sought to extract the enduring force of this prophecy regarding God's promise and human hope from the context of monarchialism, and with it idealizations of hierarchical subordination of "inferiors" to "superiors" of any sort. Liberation theologies— African American, feminist, womanist, and global— often press such concerns. "High and low" as defined by the norms of this world's powers and principalities are not God's final word, which is yet to be enacted.

Parable research of the mid-twentieth century, particularly in "new hermeneutic" scholarship, addressed similar concerns in differing form. Here (re)discovery of multivalent biblical-theological discourse focused on surprising reversals of conventions and expectations governed by "the way(s) of this world." The Jesus parable of the Mustard Seed, for example, is a (nonmonarchical) replay of Ezekiel's message. By this account, God's promised action comes *after* all else claiming and seeming to be of great promise—as grand as eagles, great rulers of great nations, and yet still worldly— has failed. Those who (in)vest hope in God's promise are not making a hedged bet; they are asked to commit to a hope beyond their already dashed hopes. In so doing, however, they undertake a real risk too, a risk of faith.

How to capture the theological thrust of the passage without spiritualizing it away, on the one hand, or using it to promote some absolutist worldly power, on the other, emerges as a key theological issue. Equally challenging is the theological point scored by the reach of God's shade tree. Here the refuge is not that of birds of a feather flocking together, but of winged creatures *of every kind.* Taken as normative for Christian theology, or even as an eschatological hope beyond already dashed this-worldly hopes, this image raises questions about the current reach of the church's congregational, ecumenical, and interfaith relations.

JAMES O. DUKE

Pastoral Perspective

the song of Hannah. The point is that our sovereign God is in the business of upsetting normal expectations. Ours is a God of surprises, of reversing expectations, as Jesus will make a career of doing in disappointing long-held views of how the Messiah was to be identified. Jesus' own disciples, it seems, shared in this general misapprehension of the topsy-turvy character of this "culture of God" (a fresh translation of *basileia tou theou* that I have come to like) that Jesus came to announce and inaugurate in his life, death, and resurrection. Rory Cooney's widely available "Canticle of the Turning" puts Mary's revolutionary lullaby in fresh and vigorous contemporary language.

Ezekiel's prophetic imagining gives encouragement for us pastors to recognize (if not embrace too enthusiastically!) our own calling to proclaim God's Word into the midst of the political and social predicaments in which our own people and nation find ourselves engaged. Perhaps we can take consolation that even the likes of Ezekiel found it necessary to use a riddle to speak God's Word, perhaps not wishing needlessly to inflame an already volatile situation (see Jeremiah!). The great preacher/teacher Fred Craddock is well known for his counsel to pastors regarding the necessary "indirectness" of the preaching task, a parabolic, storytelling mode of proclamation at which Jesus himself was adept. Or consider as an example the late William Sloane Coffin, who for many of us remains a model of prophetic preaching, who proclaimed the biblical Word into the midst of our tangled and tergiversated political landscape with humor and an unusual gift for aphorism. "Hell is truth seen too late"[1] is one of my favorites.

JOHN ROLLEFSON

1. William Sloane Coffin, *Credo* (Louisville, KY: Westminster John Knox Press, 2004), 53.

Exegetical Perspective

"plant it on a high and lofty mountain" (v. 22, my translation). There is general agreement that the cedar twig planted by YHWH represents the reestablishment of the Davidic dynasty. The "lofty mountain" (v. 22), and "the mountain height of Israel" (v. 23) are veiled but rather transparent references to Mount Zion in Jerusalem, site of both the temple and the royal palace. This vision of the future is very similar to that which is spoken of in Isaiah 2:2–4.

Although this tree almost certainly refers to the restoration of the "true" Davidic dynasty—through Jehoiachin rather than the discredited line of Zedekiah—it also has a broader and deeper meaning. This is no ordinary cedar tree, as majestic as the great cedar might be. YHWH will plant this tree so that "it may produce boughs and bear fruit," and provide shade and shelter for all kinds of birds and animals (v. 23). This tree thus appears to be a version of the tree of life (Gen. 2:9), the fabled image in religious iconography throughout the Middle East from prehistoric times.

The final verse provides the climax of the pericope: "All the trees of the field shall know that I am YHWH" (v. 24). Here "all the trees of the field" is a figurative way of saying that "all the people of the world" will be compelled to acknowledge the power of YHWH. The means by which all people will come to a knowledge of YHWH is by observing what God does. The words of verses 22–24 were addressed to a group of disenfranchised, desperate exiles whose future looked extremely bleak. The promise that God would "make high the low tree" and "make the dry tree flourish" is a message of hope for the refugees of the sixth century BCE as well as the oppressed people of the twenty-first century CE. Likewise, the promise to "make low the high tree" and to "dry up the green tree" serves as a warning to the rich and powerful of ancient and modern times, that their wealth and power are fleeting. By humbling the powerful and elevating the powerless, ultimately all the people of the earth will come to acknowledge that the destiny of the world lies in the hands of YHWH.

DAVID W. MCCREERY

Homiletical Perspective

personal intervention. And here the divine action is not to summon a great army that will swoop down upon Babylon and pulverize the captors (that happens later, in another book). Here the image is not one of power confronting power. It is of a God who prunes and plants. "I will set it out. . . . I myself will plant it on a high and lofty mountain."

Chapter 17 begins with a riddle [Heb. *chud*] and an allegory [or parable, Heb. *mashal*] about two great eagles and a vine, a vine destined to rot and wither. Our text echoes the *mashal*, but unlike the vine, God's planting will thrive. It will "produce boughs and bear fruit"; it will provide shade for "every kind of bird"—an image that resonates with Jesus' parable of the mustard seed ("it . . . puts forth large branches, so that the birds of the air can make nests in its shade," Mark 4:32). God will be known far and wide by this planting: "All the trees of the field shall know . . ." (v. 24). The chapter concludes with the anticipation that God's speech will accomplish its purpose.

The preacher cannot in good conscience detach this beautiful little text from its context. God's tenderhearted response is addressed directly to the exiles. These words derive their depth and power precisely from the background of suffering and defeat. In a situation where the powers of the world seem to have prevailed with devastating fury and finality, the prophet comes along speaking a word that God will yet have the final say. All the great powers of the world throughout history, down to this day, ought to tremble inside at the speaking of this word.

On the other hand, our congregations are not great empires bent on invasion and conquest. Our people live their lives in the crucible of the world's opportunity and violence, its good and evil, its beauty and brokenness. We can say with confidence that God plants the cedar sprig for us too, so that one day we shall all find shade under its branches.

BERT MARSHALL

Psalm 92:1-4, 12-15

[1]It is good to give thanks to the LORD,
    to sing praises to your name, O Most High;
[2]to declare your steadfast love in the morning,
    and your faithfulness by night,
[3]to the music of the lute and the harp,
    to the melody of the lyre.
[4]For you, O LORD, have made me glad by your work;
    at the works of your hands I sing for joy.

. . . .

[12]The righteous flourish like the palm tree,
    and grow like a cedar in Lebanon.
[13]They are planted in the house of the LORD;
    they flourish in the courts of our God.
[14]In old age they still produce fruit;
    they are always green and full of sap,
[15]showing that the LORD is upright;
    he is my rock, and there is no unrighteousness in him.

Theological Perspective

Psalm 92 makes a fundamental theological-ethical assertion. It claims that the moral life, exemplified in a commitment to justice and righteousness, is the key to genuine human flourishing. Such a life flourishes truly because it is rooted in the creative and redemptive work of a sovereign God. This theological-ethical awareness in the psalm results in theological testimony that takes the form of doxology.

This sovereign God comes into view in the opening chorus of praise. "It is good to give thanks to the LORD, to sing praises to your name, O Most High" (v. 1). This God "on high" is later contrasted with the merely apparent power of evildoers, as the abiding nature of God's sovereignty is described in comparison to the short-lived "sprouting" of the wicked (vv. 7–8). Echoes of Psalm 1 are easy to hear in this chorus as it chants "the wicked are . . . like the chaff that the wind drives away" (1:4). And at the conclusion of Psalm 92, God's sovereignty is expressed in the metaphor of God as "my rock" (v. 15). Thus the psalm opens and closes with the acknowledgment of God's strength greater than any other.

To be sure, God's strength is not an abstract power for the psalmist. It is instead the power of steadfast love and faithfulness (v. 2). Such accounts of God's sovereignty are rooted in what the psalm reckons as God's works. "For you, O LORD, have

Pastoral Perspective

Psalm 92 has as its subtitle (not printed above) "A Song for the Sabbath Day." The first four verses selected for the lectionary name the goodness of acts of worship: giving thanks, singing joyful praises, and declaring the steadfast love and faithfulness of God—a classic case of "preaching to the choir"—and verses 12–15 go on to describe the choir! This is a song for the faithful who celebrate their rich relationship with God; it is good news from beginning to end. At the completion of creation, "God blessed the seventh day and hallowed it, because on it God rested from all the work that [God] had done" (Gen. 2:3). Our observance of the Christian Sabbath should be nothing less than joyous and celebratory, delighted with and thankful for God's work in our lives. Every Sunday is a little Thanksgiving as much as it is a little Easter, especially if our liturgy includes a celebration of Holy Communion; the Eucharist is our Thanksgiving meal.

Like the other scriptural texts for this late spring/early summer Sunday, this psalm offers images of life that is, mysteriously, at once continuously fruitful and altogether new. How wonderful to be one of "the righteous" who flourish and grow in the house of the Lord! To participate in worship is, ideally, to renew and strengthen one's faith; to hear good news proclaimed and take it to

Exegetical Perspective

Good to Give Thanks. Psalm 92 may be approached as an individual's song of thanksgiving that contains didactic elements (e.g., vv. 6–7, 12–15) typically found in Israel's wisdom tradition (see the book of Proverbs). Additionally, there is some debate about how best to translate the verbs in verses 10–11—a section that describes the reason for thanksgiving. They can be rendered into the English as either past or future tense verbs, thus raising the question of whether thanks are being offered for divine actions completed or for deeds anticipated. Perhaps fruitful interpretation need not settle the ambiguity but instead recognize that gratitude frequently arises from a sense of what God has done in the past and in anticipation of God's future assistance.

Psalm 92 is tightly composed, making structural divisions difficult and tentative, as a quick look at various commentaries will show. One way to approach the psalm is to see in it these four units: verses 1–4, thanks and a general reason for thanks; verses 5–9, a didactic meditation on God's works and the wicked ones' inability to discern them; verses 10–11, a specific reason for thanks; verses 12–15, instruction on the righteous. The lectionary selects the opening and closing units for reading, but these are best understood in relation to the entire psalm.

Homiletical Perspective

When the Victorian poet Elizabeth Barrett Browning wanted to capture the ecstasy of romantic love, the way it draws you outside of yourself until you expend your life in constant praise of the beloved, she found herself turning to the language of the soul's relationship with God: "How do I love thee? Let me count the ways. / I love thee to the depth and breadth and height / My soul can reach, when feeling out of sight / For the ends of Being and ideal Grace."[1] Her assumption is that pondering grace and why we were made should expand the soul, make it sing for the sheer joy and delight of loving God. This overwhelming response of joy and gratitude is at the heart of Psalm 92, a love song to God from an infatuated soul.

The psalm begins with the sheer rightness of praising God, the psalmist echoing the very words that God spoke when God first gazed on creation: *it is good.* The focus is on the joy of worship, which celebrates God's love and faithfulness to God's creatures. In this context, the preacher is either a fellow worshiper or the worship leader; either way, this is the preacher's chance to communicate the act of praise that lies at the very heart of his or her ministry, the way that worship restores us to our proper place in creation and, in doing so, makes us

---

1. Elizabeth Barrett Browning, *Sonnets from the Portuguese,* XLIII.

Psalm 92:1-4, 12-15

Theological Perspective

made me glad by your work; at the works of your hands I sing for joy" (v. 4). As James Mays observes, the psalms characteristically use the term "works" as a "summary term for God's deeds in creation (8:6; 103:22; 104:24, 31) and in the history of salvation (74:12; 77:14; 90:16)."[1] So as the psalmist contemplates how God has combated the forces of chaos in fashioning the cosmos and the forces of injustice in saving God's people, the unmistakable portrait emerges of God whose love is steadfast, utterly faithful. Indeed, the declaration of God's gracious reality in the morning and in the evening (v. 2) alludes to the careful work of God in creation in which each day is framed by evening and morning (Gen. 1), even as the declaration recalls the testimony of God's people to God's mighty acts in bringing deliverance from its enemies (Ps. 77:14–15).

Based on this theological conviction about who God is, the psalmist eloquently witnesses to an accompanying ethical conviction: that this power of steadfast love and faithfulness in creation and history extends into the moral lives and experience of God's people.[2] Genuine human flourishing occurs as personal moral life is grounded in God's life, which is full of righteousness and justice. The image in which the assertion is made is one of deep contrast with the grasslike flourishing of the evildoers. Rather than exhibiting passing, effervescent growth, the righteous person is said to flourish like the palm tree or a cedar in Lebanon (v. 12).

Again the echo of Psalm 1 is unmistakable as it speaks of those who "delight in the law of the Lord." "They are like trees planted by streams of water, which yield their fruit in its season, and their leaves do not wither. In all that they do, they prosper" (1:2–3). Just so, says the writer of Psalm 92. "In old age they still produce fruit; they are always green and full of sap" (v. 14). The common, collected wisdom of the psalms is that against all the evil and injustice of the world, one may trust the call of God into a life of justice and care for creatures and creation. Whatever may appear to be the vitality of evil's force, it will prove to be a chimera. A richer and deeper vitality is to be found in the righteous life rooted in divine righteousness and justice. For these roots run all the way to the righteousness and justice that combated the forces of chaos in creation and the oppression of pharaohs and kings in God's redemption of Israel. Lives rooted truly and deeply

1. James Luther Mays, *Psalms*, Interpretation (Louisville, KY: John Knox Press, 1994), 299.
2. Ibid.

Pastoral Perspective

heart; to face the day or week ahead "full of sap" and ready to join God in the work of creation. No matter the age of the worshiper (who in mainline churches tends to be older), he or she is ("still") capable of producing fruit in the Lord's vineyard. These texts provide a perfect opportunity for straightforwardly encouraging the people whom God has planted in our congregations to grow and flourish.

What is there in the life of the parish that calls out for an application of thankfulness or trust in God's "steadfast love"? Are there family or community events to celebrate—marriages, births, major anniversaries, graduations; project beginnings or completions, pilgrimages? The possibilities are many, and words of encouragement from the pulpit can be based on biblical truth in ways the people may be surprised and glad to hear. Is stewardship flagging as the summer budget doldrums approach? The theology of stewardship is based in gratitude for God's bountiful gifts; when we invite the people to sing for joy "at the works of [God's] hands," we can invite them to respond with generosity as another mark of gladness. A focus on creation and our God-given stewardship of Earth might also emerge here. Taking a different perspective, are there individuals known pastorally to be in difficult situations of one sort or another? The images of stability and rootedness evoked by the palm and cedar trees may offer comfort to one who needs shelter and protection in one of life's storms: God's faithfulness is to be declared by night, God's "steadfast love in the morning." In short, God is trustworthy, and that is a truth worth sharing with the world.

Our secular culture, however, is marked by cynicism, fear, and despair as well as faith: declarations of faith and trust in God are often heard with suspicion or derision outside the church. Indeed, because God's people live in the world, neither the preacher nor "the righteous" in the pew are unaffected by the general skepticism. The questioning of reasonable people cannot be disallowed: a sermon that dismisses the questions or denies their existence will have little resonance inside the church doors, much less beyond them. What shall the preacher say about his own questions and fears, or about her own faith? How can one invite both the questions and the devotion of God's people?

Blind, unthinking devotion may well be blind also to genuine wonder before the glory of God. It behooves us to open our eyes, open our minds, open our souls to the deep questions, to ask them humbly and honestly, and to listen for their deeper answers.

Exegetical Perspective

Thanks to the Lord (vv. 1–4). With its opening breath Psalm 92 stakes out the claim that it is YHWH to whom thanks are due. Framed by the repeated references to the divine name (vv. 1, 4), the psalm's first unit sends notice that no other entity is praise-worthy. God has stood by the psalmist steadfastly and faithfully (v. 2), and the poet resolves to sing of God's fidelity both day and night. The references to "morning" and "night" in verse 2 need not mean exclusively certain moments in time, as, for example, liturgical periods for prayer. This is an example of the poetic device of *merismus*, the expression of a totality by means of citing its contrasting parts. God is to be praised *continually* and not just periodically. This thanksgiving and praise is thoughtful and aesthetic in that it fuses music (v. 3) and lyric—a combination attested much earlier by Miriam, who sang of her deliverance after the crossing of the sea (Exod. 15:21). Verse 4 mentions only the "work" of God as the reason for this joyous song. It is not clear what comprises this work, although the words translated as "work(s)" (*po'al; ma'aseh*) can refer to God's work both in creation and in history. Scholar H.-J. Kraus maintains that in this context the divine work in view is God's rule in Israel.[1] Kraus's suggestion makes considerable sense in view of Psalm 92's location in the canon (see below), but again it may not be wise to exclude one possibility in favor of another. Israel would have experienced YHWH's rule as consisting of both creating and redeeming roles. The point here is that these roles merge in the personal experience of the psalmist. God has been fully available for the psalmist in catastrophic times.

Although verses 5–11 are not included in the lectionary reading, they are crucial for understanding the thought of Psalm 92. The units of this section inject three elements into the psalm: the presence of wicked enemies who do not understand God's works (vv. 5–9), the centrality of YHWH's reign (v. 8), and deliverance from the enemies (vv. 10–11). Who these enemies are and what they have done are not stated. They are merely described as undiscerning "grass" doomed to destruction (cf. Ps. 37:20), in contrast to YHWH, who is "on high forever" (v. 8.). YHWH is named seven times in Psalm 92 (vv. 1, 4, 5, 8, 9, 13, 15), the fourth and middle time in v. 8, which is also the exact center of the psalm.[2] The centrality of YHWH's reign is a

1. Hans-Joachim Kraus, *Psalms 60–150* (Minneapolis: Augsburg/Fortress, 1989), 228.
2. See James L. Mays, *Psalms*, Interpretation (Louisville, KY: Westminster/John Knox Press, 1994), 298.

Homiletical Perspective

whole. The opportunity and task is to strip away the tedium that can sometimes accrue to the act of coming to church every week, sitting in the same pew, singing the same hymns, and then leaving to wonder what on earth any of it had to do with the tasks and challenges of our daily lives; the psalmist is a God-intoxicated lover, bursting into song, invoking music because it bypasses the limits of our cognitive understanding to wrap the heart in prayer. Such a sermon might ask the congregation what role joy plays in their life together: Do they embody their delight in Christ in ways that would tempt an unbeliever to want to know this God? How might they become more "contagious" in expressing their love and gratitude?

There is challenge here as well for a culture crazed with busyness until time with God is pushed to the margins of our lives (or even off the pages entirely); the psalmist invokes the ancient pattern of praying morning and evening, so that the first and last thought of the day will be of God. The preacher could use this as a framework for a discussion of the interconnectedness of love and discipline (spontaneity and careful cultivation of the soul) in the life of faith.

Verses 12–15 pose more problems for the preacher with their claim that "the righteous shall flourish like the palm tree, and grow like a cedar in Lebanon" (v. 12). They evoke the obvious objection that sometimes the righteous do not appear to flourish; anyone who has ever seen good people trapped in grinding poverty or stricken with a horrendous illness will challenge these words as mere wishful thinking. One way to approach the issue would be to explore differing concepts of well-being: both Scripture and our culture depict material prosperity as one way to flourish, but Scripture includes other concepts as well, most notably in the Beatitudes, which subvert ordinary understandings of blessedness and confront them with a blessedness of spirit that does not rely upon external factors, but enables the individual or community to persevere in wholeness through whatever may be happening in his or her life. The comparison to a cedar might allow one to pick up on the idea of growth and to ask what experiences enable us to grow in faith; often, our times of greatest growth will not be our times of tranquility!

Another challenge lies in the depiction of old age in verse 14, which contradicts many of the assumptions we make in our society and, all too often, in our faith communities: "In old age, [the

Psalm 92:1–4, 12–15

Theological Perspective

in that reality, and only those rooted thus, will finally prosper.

Such psalmic wisdom, clearly and definitively articulated in Psalm 92, is a source of those streams in Christian theology that have continued to appreciate the Law of God as a gift, rather than a burden; as a source of life, rather than a means of oppression. As the summary statement of what it means for members of the human family to live out of God's life of justice and righteousness, the commandments provide the gift of a life patterned on God's own steadfast love and faithfulness. Thus the moral life of God's people is not an arbitrary imposition designed simply to evoke blind obedience to a sovereign who relates to humanity simply for the sake of compelling allegiance. Instead, human ethical life is understood by the psalmist to arise from the knowledge of God's "works" that display God as steadfast love and faithfulness. This ethical life is therefore rendered in joy, with the singing of praises, with the music of lute and harp, and accompanied by the melody of the lyre (vv. 1, 3). Psalm 92's consummate statement of the dispositions and affections of this moral life are expressed thus: "For you, O LORD, have made me glad by your work; at the works of your hands I sing for joy" (v. 4).

Among those theologians who have reiterated this account of the moral life the psalmists articulate so clearly and well, John Calvin famously referred to the third use of the law.[3] That third use followed the first use of the law in calling all to account and confession, as well as the second use, whereby evil was restrained in some measure by a certain fear that may accompany transgression of God's law. But the third use transcends both contrition and constraint, making God's people glad and joyful, green and full of sap.

D. CAMERON MURCHISON

Pastoral Perspective

In that conversation and the study and worship that naturally surround and inform it, human beings become more keenly aware of the God we praise, the amazing universe God has created, and the kinship—the image—we share with the One who made us. Our authentic song of praise and thanksgiving springs from our genuine relationship with God, which is nurtured by prayer and contemplation both in solitude and in community and made evident in our worship and our action in the world. We can indeed claim to be the righteous, "planted in the house of the LORD" (v. 13) where we worship—rooted and grounded in God—blooming and flourishing for the entire world to see.

Christian worship is not performance; it is service, offered to God first of all in thanks and with humility and love. The styles will vary, as will the language or idiom employed, depending on the community and the individuals who comprise it, because liturgy is literally the people's work. The worship leader must never lose sight of the people's needs and longings, seeking always to help them perceive and receive the grace of God. Nor must one forget the longing of God for the beloved creatures of Earth.

With Psalm 92 as an example, how inviting the Christian community could look in its worship! Here, centered in and focused on the Lord of the universe, are so many wonderful things: thanksgiving, praise, love, faithfulness, music, joy, stability, growth, productivity, health, vigor, and all in abundance. Can these actions, emotions, and attitudes be consciously made a part of every liturgy and every sermon? They call to mind the fruit of the Spirit enumerated by Paul in Galatians 5:22–23: "love, joy, peace, patience, kindness, generosity, faithfulness, gentleness, and self-control." The Spirit's fruit, it would appear, grows on the sturdy, righteous trees planted in the house of the Lord and reflects the character of our God.

MARY DOUGLAS TURNER

---

3. John Calvin, *Institutes of the Christian Religion*, ed. John McNeill, trans. Ford Lewis Battles (Philadelphia: Westminster Press, 1960), 2.7.12.

Exegetical Perspective

major feature of the fourth book of the Psalter (Pss. 90–106) and is likely a response to the crisis of the Babylonian exile by those who gave shape to the book of Psalms. In its canonical location Psalm 92 introduces a series of psalms that affirm that YHWH, rather than kings and empires, reigns (Pss. 93, 95, 96, 97, 98, 99). Boldly the psalm proclaims that no enemy, not even foreign exile, has the upper hand on YHWH's saving power.

Like a Cedar (vv. 12–15). The final unit of Psalm 92 shifts attention away from the "enemies" (v. 11) to the "righteous" (*tsadiq*). In contrast to the wicked that are like grass (v. 7), the righteous are like verdant trees planted and nourished in the presence of YHWH (vv. 12–13). With language highly evocative of Psalm 1, the poet avows that the righteous are fruitful even in old age (v. 14). The image of lush, green, productive trees may be lost to many interpreters who live in temperate climates where such sights are the norm. But for readers in arid climates with unpredictable rainfall, for readers in regions suffering from deforestation and encroaching deserts, for readers now pondering the potential fallout of global warming and climate change, the image of an enduring green and productive tree can be powerful indeed. Such, says the psalmist, are the righteous ones who are nourished in the presence of YHWH.

The opening and concluding units (vv. 1–4, 12–15) surround the psalm—and the enemies!—with the powerful presence of YHWH. Indeed, even in the middle of the enemies stands YHWH (v. 8). Perhaps it is the sevenfold mention of YHWH, coupled with the psalmist's self-identification with the righteous (e.g., "*my* rock," v. 15), along with the open possibilities for understanding God's works, that attracted early readers to associate Psalm 92 with the Sabbath as the superscription does. It is an appropriate association, for Sabbath provides a time to ponder God who creates, redeems, and rules, and just where readers stand in relation to the Most High—even in the midst of enemies and adversities.

V. STEVEN PARRISH

Homiletical Perspective

righteous] still produce fruit; they are always green and full of sap." This image of fruitful and abundant old age comes from the wisdom traditions, which saw elders as repositories of the accumulated wisdom of a lifetime and allocated to them a prominent and valued role in the life of the community. What would it take for us, who shunt elderly people into special facilities where they will be cared for, to understand seniors as people who bear fruit and would like an opportunity to give? What kinds of support and encouragement from the church would it take for our elderly members to understand themselves as dwelling in a time of spiritual enrichment, rather than of inevitable decline and loss? What would our churches look like if we were to encourage seniors to exercise ministries rather than expecting them to be the passive and grateful recipients of visits and gift baskets? What would it take for our health-obsessed culture to recognize the spiritual gifts that can come through facing honestly the constraints of a body in decline? What would help us to release our fear of death so that we could live until we die?

This text offers a vision of a godly community that is ordered on principles that challenge our own: a community that is bound together by the worship of God, that fosters creativity in word and music (and, one can assume, in other forms as well), in which each person (young or old) has gifts to offer. It is a community rooted and grounded in the righteousness of God, not a harsh, judgmental, legal righteousness, but a life-giving blessedness of spirit that is founded in joy and "endures all things" (1 Cor. 13:7).

DEBORAH ANNE MEISTER

2 Corinthians 5:6-10 (11-13), 14-17

[6]So we are always confident; even though we know that while we are at home in the body we are away from the Lord— [7]for we walk by faith, not by sight. [8]Yes, we do have confidence, and we would rather be away from the body and at home with the Lord. [9]So whether we are at home or away, we make it our aim to please him. [10]For all of us must appear before the judgment seat of Christ, so that each may receive recompense for what has been done in the body, whether good or evil.

[11]Therefore, knowing the fear of the Lord, we try to persuade others; but ourselves are well known to God, and I hope that we are also well known to your consciences. [12]We are not commending ourselves to you again, but giving you an opportunity to boast about us, so that you may be able to answer those who boast in outward appearance and not in the heart. [13]For if we are beside ourselves, it is for God; if we are in our right mind, it is for you. [14]For the love of Christ urges us on, because we are convinced that one has died for all; therefore all have died. [15]And he died for all, so that those who live might live no longer for themselves, but for him who died and was raised for them.

[16]From now on, therefore, we regard no one from a human point of view; even though we once knew Christ from a human point of view, we know him no longer in that way. [17]So if anyone is in Christ, there is a new creation: everything old has passed away; see, everything has become new!

Theological Perspective

Paul has been drawing several contrasts: human weakness/divine glory and power; outer/inner; present/future; transient/eternal. These have come to a resolution in his description of the future that is to be awaited. Now he personalizes them with several other contrasts: away from home/at home; faith/sight; old/new; flesh/new creation.

The basic situation is that "while we are at home in the body we are away from the Lord," since "we walk by faith, not by sight." Paul was writing about his own divided situation and the attitude he is to take toward it; but Augustine found these words so convincing that he took them as the charter, the "hermeneutical key," for a comprehensive interpretation of human history, developed most fully in *The City of God*. Many since Augustine have found his perspective persuasive.

We dwell either "at home" or "away from home." Being away from home was the situation of the sojourner in ancient Israel and the Greek and Roman worlds. The metaphor of the sojourner was a perfect one for gathering up many themes in the Bible. All of us are born children of Cain, the founder of the earthly city (Gen. 4:17); but some are reborn as citizens of the heavenly Jerusalem (Gal. 4:26). Then we become sojourners in the earthly city. But that does not mean being indifferent to the earthly city.

Pastoral Perspective

It feels a bit strange to end this pericope at verse 17 if we know what follows in this chapter, how the words about a new way of seeing, a new creation, immediately roll on into that familiar yet still magnificent exposition of God's reconciling work in Christ. God reconciling the world to himself, God in Christ, God entrusting us with the ministry of reconciliation, God making us ambassadors of reconciliation—and so we bid you, for Christ's sake, be reconciled. Why should those powerful words, at once gospel and commission and entreaty, have to wait another whole week once we are on the verge of them? I want to hear them now.

Yet it is salutary to stop here, to take this pericope as it is. Rushing on could leave this part forgotten, seemingly rendered superfluous by the force of what it introduced. It is worth paying attention to the flow and context of Paul's epistle here, and the connection of what follows it to what preceded it. It is, moreover, of value to hear these final verses as a culmination and climax, rather than, as they would otherwise be, the beginning of "still more."

Sometimes we pastors make the mistake of not stopping at the right place, of thinking we need to continue, to say the "still more." For some of us it is less an assumption than an unchecked instinct, an eagerness to share the riches that we know and

Exegetical Perspective

This portion of Paul's argument pursues the interlocking issues of life and death, human physicality, and the transforming reality of Jesus' resurrection. All these themes are expressed in the arresting image of the new creation. This passage concludes with the ministry of reconciliation entrusted to the community. As the passage is divided here, the emphasis is on the exclamation, "So if anyone is in Christ, there is a new creation: everything old has passed away; see, everything has become new!" (v. 17).

Accusations of Paul's detractors may be heard softly in the background of his expressions of confidence, conviction, and commendation. Scholars differ upon how specifically to characterize Paul's critics. Paul's self-defense suggests that perhaps he has been criticized for his physical distress, for his mystical experience or lack of it, or for his outward appearance. He may have been accused of being self-serving. While Paul shadowboxes with his critics and persuades the audience of his trustworthiness, a preacher might hear him also "arguing with himself" as he reflects on his present situation in light of his faith in the one who died for all. Such wrestling can be seen in 2 Corinthians 5:6–10. The reference for "we" in these verses includes those whose faith Paul shares. Twice Paul repeats the word for "be

Homiletical Perspective

One of the most remarkable women I have ever met suffered for over fifteen years from ovarian cancer. When asked why she continued to believe in God through one debilitating cancer treatment after another, she said that if she looked really hard she could sense God's presence even in the exhausting chemotherapy treatments and the endless oncologist visits.

God was not the source of her cancer, she often said, but God was the source of her strength and determination. At her funeral the congregation sang a praise chorus with the lyric, "O my soul, claim nothing as your own. For you there is God and God alone." Many commented how this lyric summed up Lynda's life. Although battered in her struggle to defeat cancer, she discovered through the experience that she was never alone when she was in remission, or when the news was grim. Always Christ was in her and she was in Christ.

The fourteenth-century mystic Meister Eckhart once observed, "The spiritual life is not a process of addition, but rather of subtraction." What we subtract in our lives depends of course on what initially fills it—ambition, addiction, suffering, even our misgivings. In the face of all of our trials and tribulations Paul reminds us transformation is possible when we invite Christ into our lives and

2 Corinthians 5:6-10 (11-13), 14-17

Theological Perspective

Jeremiah had told the exiles in Babylon—certainly a worthy image of the earthly city, then and now!—to "seek the peace (welfare, *shalom*) of the city where you are, for in its peace you will find your peace" (Jer. 29:7, my translation). The peace of the earthly city is worth seeking, even by those who are not fully at home in it. In our own day, of course, the metaphor of sojourners has been adopted by Christians to describe their task of radical discipleship and witness within the earthly city.

Then a jarring note is sounded. Paul, who usually emphasized justification by grace through faith, mentions that all will be judged according to what they have done "in the body" (5:10; cf. Rom. 2:6–7; 1 Cor. 3:8, 14–17). In the body—not in a prior life, not in ecstatic experiences. Life in the body is real and earnest. Does Paul contradict himself? No. A righteous life is expected at the judgment. But it is accomplished not by trying to achieve a righteousness of one's own but by receiving righteousness from God as a gift (Gal. 2:16, 3:22; Rom. 3:26; Phil. 3:9). Exactly how to say this has been debated through the centuries. Catholics emphasize that good works are truly one's own and therefore meritorious, though they are made possible by grace; Protestants emphasize that good works, while expected, can never be adequate, but God treats them as though they were adequate because of Christ's own righteousness. Either way, the judge will be Christ, the one who surprised many people by proclaiming the priority of love over law and inviting sinners to receive the grace of God.

This is reinforced in four quick images.

1. Christ's love "holds together" (*synechei*, v. 14, NRSV, "urges us on") all that believers do. It contains, constrains, controls in the positive sense of empowering and giving consistency; it does not compel or confine.

2. Christ "died for all," therefore "all have died," and because of this they are able to die to self and live to Christ (vv. 14–15). For Paul the crucial question is how one can make the transition from one system of salvation (obedience to the law, which leads only to condemnation) to another (righteousness as God's gift through faith). The transition is not an easy one; it happens only through death (Rom. 6:3–11; 7:1–6). Those who are crucified with Christ die to the law through the law (Gal. 2:19–20); Scripture "consigned all things to sin" so that salvation would be through faith (Gal. 3:22).

How does this happen? The cross discredits all who claim superior righteousness, power, and

Pastoral Perspective

treasure. Or perhaps it is more an anxiety, a need to stay in control by how much we have to say and what riches we have to offer. There can be other reasons as well, good or bad or mixed, but the point is that many of us often do it, and we neither slow down nor stop, at least not until we have gotten to the best and favorite things we want to say. And perhaps the word that was most immediately needed got lost along the way, left behind. Not that it did not get said, but that we turned it into one word among many or a prologue receding behind us as we rushed ahead.

I am not in a position either to absolve Paul of such pastoral failing or to hold him up as a counterexample of careful attention to the rhythm and timing of his listeners' needs and questions. Both the epistolary form of his writing and the likelihood that these are actually multiple letters stitched together make it impossible to judge such a thing, though one could get the impression that he also was prone to run further with a topic than his hearers were interested in following.

What we have in Paul's letters is rich and multiform, and many of them are fairly long. It is good, therefore, to read them aloud in one sitting so that we have a sense of their function as letters, of their rhetoric and practicality and real relationships, and so that we are not so inclined to milk or mine their individual verses without a sense of the human voice and purpose involved. The perspective afforded by such light and quick reading will help us see what is at stake, *who* it is who is speaking and *why*. Without it, reading only in verses, chapters, or pericopes, we may not only mishear the vital word; we may also glut ourselves and our hearers with all the spiritual riches that we can mine from each piece of the text—riches that delight us but do not nourish the hungering soul.[1]

On the other hand, we *do* normally read and think about Scripture in this liturgical fashion; its richness and complexity require us to carve it up into segments. Let us then think seriously, and pastorally, about the pattern of an appointed reading, the logic of its rhythm and timing, and also about where we on this particular day would pause or find a conclusion. The same passage may, in this sense, be "punctuated" differently at different times,

---

1. Is not this a possible meaning of Matthew's version of the first Beatitude: "Blessed are the spiritually poor"? It is not a criticism of the pharisaic tradition to consider it a valuing of the spiritual riches of Torah and faithful living. But Jesus' words may be heard as an opening of the kingdom's doors to those who are not as religiously adept, educated, and blessed as we.

confident." Confidence here means not simply self-confidence in an individually focused way but faithfulness and security in believing, that confidence whose true giver and object is God. Such confidence leads to trust and boldness in preaching. Using the parallel verbs "to be at home" and "to be away from home," Paul first expresses the distance between being in the body and with the Lord. He then expresses his preference for being "at home with the Lord," and finally a promise of orientation toward pleasing the Lord in whatever relationship with "home." The sequence is reminiscent of Romans 14:8: "If we live, we live to the Lord, and if we die, we die to the Lord; so then, whether we live or whether we die, we are the Lord's." The concluding affirmation that all will be judged by the good or evil deeds done in the body reminds hearers of their accountability to Christ.

Paul states that his efforts to persuade arise out of his fear of the Lord. Paul appears to be returning to a defense of his ministry in the face of some kind of criticism. Perhaps the reason for the criticism lies behind the phrase "so that you may be able to answer those who boast in outward appearance and not in the heart" (v. 12). Paul is clearly defending his good intentions. The preceding argument states that what is not seen is of more value than what is seen; so here Paul asserts that what is "in the heart" is superior to "outward appearance."

The cultural background of this discussion is the ideal of competitive boasting. While our culture appears to disapprove of any appearance of boasting, in Paul's world, boasting was assumed; what mattered most was what you boasted about. Here Paul asserts that he is always oriented toward others. If in an ecstatic state ("if we are beside ourselves") Paul is oriented toward God, and if in a sober condition ("in our right mind") he is working on behalf of others: "for you" (v. 13). This cryptic reference to ecstatic experience is further evidence (see also 4:6) of how important and disputed such mystical experiences are in the discussion behind this letter. In the context of Christian faith, both ecstasy and sobriety should be for others, because of Christ's death for all. Again Paul cites a traditional affirmation of faith: "that one has died for all" (v. 14).

Jesus' death for others makes it possible for others to live "no longer for themselves but for him who died and was raised for them." Living for "him" in this way is living responsibly with others in the community of Christ's body. Paul's insistence both on the reality of the unseen and on the urgency of

enable him to make us a new creation from the inside out, subtracting our anxieties, doubts, and fears. As Paul writes in 2 Corinthians 5:17, "So if anyone is in Christ, there is a new creation: everything old has passed away; see, everything has become new!"

A sermon might explore how that such a transformation occurs.

As biblical scholar James Dunn observes, in Paul's theology, "Being in Christ is not any kind of mystical removal from the real, everyday world. On the contrary, it becomes the starting point and base camp for a quite differently motivated and directed life."[1] In Paul's mind our faith in Jesus does not inoculate us against the reality of hardship, but reframes our life with Christ at the center—the Christ who suffered on our behalf. When we come to discern this truth, we also discover the true source of our strength in the person of Jesus Christ.

Parker Palmer writers on matters of faith and life and how the two intersect. In his book *The Active Life* he describes going on an Outward Bound course:

I took the course in my early forties, and in the middle of that course I was asked to confront the thing I had fears about since I had first heard about Outward Bound: a gossamer strand was hooked to a harness around my body, I was backed up to the top of a 110-foot cliff, and I was told to lean out over God's own emptiness and walk down the face of that cliff to the ground eleven stories below.

I remember the cliff all too well. It started with a five-foot drop to a small ledge, then a ten-foot drop to another ledge, then a third and final drop all the way down. I tried to negotiate the first drop; but my feet instantly went out from under me, and I fell heavily to the first ledge. "I don't think you quite have it yet," the instructor observed astutely. "You are leaning too close to the rock face. You need to lean much farther back so your feet will grip the wall." That advice went against my every instinct. Surely one should hug the wall, not lean out over the void! But on the second drop I tried to lean back; better, but not far enough, and I hit the second ledge with a thud not unlike the first. "You still don't have it," said the ever-observant instructor. "Try again."

Since my next try would be the last one, her counsel was not especially comforting. But try I did, and much to my amazement I found myself moving

1. James Dunn, *The Theology of Paul the Apostle* (Grand Rapids: Eerdmans, 1998), 411.

2 Corinthians 5:6-10 (11-13), 14-17

Theological Perspective

wisdom. The "powers" that rule the world would not have crucified the Lord of glory, Paul says, if they had understood the wisdom of God (1 Cor. 2:8). One who knew no sin "was made sin," being treated as an evildoer (2 Cor. 5:21; cf. Gal. 3:13 and Rom. 15:3).

Living by the system of salvation based on the law turns out to have been a massive blunder, leading to the discrediting of the entire attitude that righteousness is gained through obedience to the law. This approach not only is unfeasible but leads to hypocrisy, self-righteousness, abuse of power, scapegoating, and unjust condemnation; God's disapproval of it is indicated by raising Jesus from the dead and exalting him as Lord and Judge. What could not be attained through the law can be received through faith in God's promises.

3. Therefore Christ is no longer known "after the flesh" (v. 16, my translation). Paying too much attention to outward appearances—his itinerant and homeless lifestyle, his eating with sinners, his emphasis on love rather the externals of the law—led some to view him as a deceiver, a lawbreaker, or a revolutionary, who received his just deserts on the cross. A massive reversal has taken place.

4. Thus there is a "new creation," since "the old has passed away and the new has come" (v. 17, my translation). This does not mean disappearance of the old and a fresh creation ex nihilo; it is more like a re-creation, a transformation of the humanity that is already created but has been subjected to sin and death. Paul has already spoken of "renewal" of the inner person while the outward person is wasting away (4:16; cf. Rom. 12:2). The point is that this renewal is as drastic as the original creation, since it can come only from God, and in an action that is voluntary on God's part, sheer grace. If we have any "sufficiency," it is from God (3:5). "What do you have that you did not receive? And if you received it, why do you boast as if it were not a gift?" (1 Cor. 4:7) We must receive it, make it our own; but if we treat it as our own accomplishment, we lose it.

EUGENE TESELLE

Pastoral Perspective

the flow of its argument given various emphases, not only as an effect of the lectionary but also of our own aliveness to both text and listener.

Now to the case in point: these verses proceed from the reflection on mortality and transience that bridges chapters 4 and 5, wonderful words of comfort and promise but also part of Paul's justification for his authority in weakness and rejection. Despite both mortality and the yearning for a life beyond it, Paul continues to live as life demands, faithful, accountable, bound by bonds of affection to those he serves, indeed sometimes crazy with love. And to do so requires for him this change of perspective, this new understanding, stemming from a death not just for his own sake but for all.

Hence the passage as we have it here builds to that powerful conclusion: we no longer regard anyone from a human point of view. That new way of seeing others becomes the point. The old has passed away; behold, everything is different now! If we also *see*, in the imagination of our hearts, ourselves, our foes, and this old world all thus transfigured by the death of Christ, will we not deal differently with each?

So it is that in *this* passage Paul's argument in defense of his own authority and ministry becomes decisively and urgently something more. It culminates in words about how he now sees others, words with profound ethical and communal implications. Paul goes on speaking, and there are still more wonderful words, but this day's pericope reaches its climax here. And perhaps it is exactly *here* that we need to pause in order to think—and *then*, perhaps, to preach.

JOHN K. STENDAHL

ministry to the visible existing body makes this passage a model of faithful realism and of realistic faithfulness.

The lectionary reading reaches its climax in the exultant affirmation of the new creation and the exclamation "everything old has passed away; see, everything has become new!" (v. 17). Early Christians imagined salvation as God's recreating the world according to the prophet Isaiah's announcement in Isaiah 65:17–25: "For I am about to create new heavens and a new earth; the former things shall not be remembered or come to mind. But be glad and rejoice forever in what I am creating." Other occurrences of this image are in Galatians 3:28 and Galatians 6:15. God promises deliverance from exile, envisioned as renewal of the land. This renewal was enacted in baptism, when believers clothed themselves in Christ (Gal. 3:27). The ongoing process of hardship and suffering—which Paul struggled with earlier in this passage—has its resolution in the transformation or new creation. Even Christ, who was known "from a human point of view" (*kata sarka*), is no longer known in the same way. Just as Christ, having died and been raised, is no longer known "according to the flesh," neither is anyone else known in that way. This new "spiritual" knowing, knowing in a way different from a human point of view, is part of the ecstatic vision to which Paul refers. The remade creation is the image for a community of people transformed in Christ. Their relationships with one another in the community of Christ's body are reshaped toward mutual concern, grounded in confidence in God. As the argument continues, the transformation of relationships in the new creation will be described with another word, "reconciliation," with one another and with God.

CYNTHIA BRIGGS KITTREDGE

slowly down the rock wall. Step-by-step I made my way with growing confidence until, about halfway down, I suddenly realized that I was heading toward a very large hole in the rock, and—not knowing anything better to do—I froze. The instructor waited a small eternity for me to thaw out, and when she realized that I was showing no signs of life she yelled up, "Is anything wrong, Parker?" as if she needed to ask. To this day I do not know the source of my childlike voice that came up from within me, but my response is a matter of public record. I said, "I don't want to talk about it."

The instructor yelled back, "Then I think it's time you learned the Outward Bound Motto." Wonderful, I thought. I am about to die, and she is feeding me a pithy saying. But then she spoke words I have never forgotten, words so true that they empowered me to negotiate the rest of that cliff without incident: "If you can't get out of it, get into it." Bone-deep I knew that there was no way out of this situation except to go deeper into it, and with that knowledge my feet began to move.[2]

Author Brennan Manning has made the observation that in everyone's spiritual journey there is that first moment when we believe, when we stand before a congregation, or privately before God, and profess our faith. But that is only the first step, says Manning, because in the spiritual life there is always a second step, when we come to trust God walks beside us through all the peaks and valleys of our lives. This is where the journey of subtraction will end, as Meister Eckhart suggests, when we are able to lean upon a God as near to us as our very breath, dwelling inside us, waiting to be discovered so that the work of re-creation and transformation can begin.

MARK BARGER ELLIOTT

---

2. Parker Palmer, *The Active Life* (San Francisco: Jossey-Bass, 1999), 32–33.

Mark 4:26-34

²⁶He also said, "The kingdom of God is as if someone would scatter seed on the ground, ²⁷and would sleep and rise night and day, and the seed would sprout and grow, he does not know how. ²⁸The earth produces of itself, first the stalk, then the head, then the full grain in the head. ²⁹But when the grain is ripe, at once he goes in with his sickle, because the harvest has come."

³⁰He also said, "With what can we compare the kingdom of God, or what parable will we use for it? ³¹It is like a mustard seed, which, when sown upon the ground, is the smallest of all the seeds on earth; ³²yet when it is sown it grows up and becomes the greatest of all shrubs, and puts forth large branches, so that the birds of the air can make nests in its shade."

³³With many such parables he spoke the word to them, as they were able to hear it; ³⁴he did not speak to them except in parables, but he explained everything in private to his disciples.

Theological Perspective

Like almost everything in the Gospels, this reading combines straightforward, accessible images with extremely opaque and dissonant elements that make it impossible to appeal to some simple, obvious interpretation. Instead, we peel off layers and walk through infinite riches of this living text.

One layer of meaning arises from an attempt to interpret the parables, both of which offer homely, familiar images to draw into view something that is anything but familiar: the kingdom of God. The first parable likens this kingdom to a feature of plants that is familiar to any gardener or farmer. The gardener can put the seed in the ground but cannot really do anything about its growing. In fact, the gardener has so little to do with making the seed grow that in the parable the gardener sleeps through the process of sprouting and maturation. The kingdom of God is like a sleeping gardener. Or perhaps the kingdom is like a gardener who slept through the growing season but wakes up in time for the harvest. In case we did not quite get the message with this parable, Jesus offers us a second one. The kingdom of God is like a mustard seed, which though the smallest of all seeds, grows into a bush so large and lush that birds can make nests in its shade.

Being a theologian, I want to make sense out of these odd little stories. The imagery of passivity

Pastoral Perspective

"Jesus told so many parables he became one." I do not know the origin of that phrase, but it seems apt for reflection on this part of Mark 4. For here in these well-known parables we confront how the teaching and the life of Jesus were one. Yet the parables remain what they are: continually breaking open our understanding of the reign of God. Elusive yet pointed, indirect yet powerfully relevant—like the very kingdom Jesus brings.

While Mark does not present, as do Matthew and Luke, an extensive body of teachings, there can be little doubt that chapter 4 presents pointed examples and the reason for Jesus' use of parables. The secret of the kingdom is contained in parabolic form. Of course even when Jesus explains the stories to the Twelve (and some others—4:10ff.) understanding requires more than the disciples themselves comprehend. All we have to think of is the pattern of the original disciples' misunderstanding also recorded by Mark. Could the most profound parable of all be the whole life and death of Jesus? Do the disciples fail to understand this most powerful parable too?

The parabolic story of seeds and the harvest leads us directly to Jesus' comparison of the kingdom of God to a mustard seed. It builds upon the earlier, more extensive parable of the sower and the harvest. In Mark there is no admonition that we should

Exegetical Perspective

Parables: Hiddenness and Growth. In chapter 4 the evangelist presents parables containing both contemporary and eschatological implications, metaphors for the growth of God's beloved community. The parables include encouragement to action, counsel to patience, and hope for the future. They speak of hiddenness and growth and end with a vision of many nations finding shelter in the kin-dom of God.

Hē basileia tou theou, found fourteen times in Mark and usually translated by "the kingdom of God" or "the dominion of God," is an ancient metaphor not easily translated into today's culture. In the first century CE, power and dominion belonged to Caesar. Early Christians preached that Caesar's dominion has been overtaken by the dominion of God. This was an in-your-face radical claim defining insiders not by Caesar's proclamation, but by relationship to the community that followed Jesus (cf. Mark 3:31–35). In various twenty-first-century cultures, the claim of radical inclusion is seeking expression in terms reflecting the egalitarian relationship of God's beloved community. To that end, we translate *hē basileia tou theou* as "the kin-dom of God."

Mark 4:26–34 assumes the parable of the sower (4:1–9), its explanation (4:14–20), and the introduction to Jesus' parables in teaching in 4:10–13. The various segments are interwoven, interpreting and informing

Homiletical Perspective

When we lived in Nashville in the early 1980s, we had some scruffy weeds in our yard. I would cut them back to the ground in January and in March, expecting that to be the end of them. Yet by May, from these little brown stumps came green shoots, and by midsummer they were growing tall again. I stood in awe of this process—from stumps in the ground to full grown bushes in July! It is this kind of dynamic power and vitality that Jesus is describing in these parables in today's text.

In order to describe the kingdom of God, Jesus often uses parables. Why? As the Greek root (*para ballō*) suggests, parables are stories thrown alongside our lives. In using these short, provocative stories, Jesus recognizes the importance of the imagination. In using parables Jesus is seeking a shift in our imaginations, a shift in the way we see ourselves, see God, and see others. Such a shift may seem small and insignificant, but here he compares it to a mustard seed, a tiny particle that can have miraculous powers.

In using parables, Jesus seeks to stimulate his audience's imagination so that they might perceive the power and presence of God in a new and immediate way. Believe it or not, sermons can be like that. They can help open windows to the biblical text, to ourselves, and to God. They can help open

Mark 4:26-34

Theological Perspective

combined with fantastic and disproportionate growth makes me think about grace. This is such a central biblical, Christian, and Reformed idea, and yet it remains so difficult to really accept or believe. Intimacy with Christ grows in us as certainly and as effortlessly as seeds grow. We have so little to do with Christ's nearness to us that we can just go to sleep. In fact it might be better if we did sleep through the whole thing, snug and safe, resting like babies in our mothers' arms. This trust so deep that we can sleep without anxiety is much more useful to us than fussing over the little seed: dousing it with pesticide, repotting it, clucking anxiously over the amount of sun it has. The kingdom is like this sleepy, restful trust. It is not like the frenetic busyness of works righteousness, and it is not like the anxious attachment to particular moral or doctrinal positions, defending which we gladly expend all our energy. Being busy and dogmatic makes a lot of sense to us. It fits with our normal way of being human. We achieve all sorts of goods by working hard and committing ourselves to our values: well-run offices, good grades, better schools, the politicians of our choice, svelte figures, neatly trimmed lawns, and so on. These are mostly reasonable things, and certainly nothing useful would happen if we did not work for it or if we remained indifferent to moral and political issues. It is just that this way of operating is not like the kingdom of God. Our difficulty arises in confusing the way of the kingdom with our ordinary way of doing things. Jesus is calling us to a very different way of being with ourselves, with one another, with the divine, by asking us to recognize that spiritual growth and intimacy with God arises as naturally as seeds growing. The harvest will come without us having to work for it, because God adores us and it is this love that is the power of growth. It is this love that transforms the tiniest and most impotent-looking seed into a lush bush that gives rest and shade to the singing birds, just as it transforms our tiny, distorted awareness of God into a magnificent luminosity in which we ourselves and all the creatures we meet can rest.

I like this theological reflection on the parables. It satisfies the "faith seeking understanding" part of me. But the text resists not just this particular interpretation but this *way* of interpreting the parables. Its familiar images seduce us with the expectation of some simple, perhaps even pat, message: the sort one might find painted on china at Stuckey's, along with pictures of kittens or flowering

Pastoral Perspective

develop faith the size of a mustard seed; it is, plain and simple, about the kingdom that provides saving space way beyond our imagining. The parable is not about us, but about the grace of God; and yet we "overhear" in these compacted stories so much about what pertains to human reception of the good news of salvation. There are clues in the plant that grows so large from so small a seed. We marvel that birds come to nest in the shade of this spacious dwelling. So shall the reign of God be. We, like the farmer, do not understand how the sprouting and the growing of such a reality take place. Yet it becomes a harvest of life, and the tree from the seed spreads out branches to be a place of rest and song and abundance.

One suspects that the early Christian communities were often as puzzled by this parabolic presentation of the kingdom as we are. These two parables that Mark stitches together have generated many theological interpretations over the centuries. Does the kingdom come slowly, over the long haul? Should we understand the harvest in due season as the future event of the eschatological time? Are we to believe that God is in control of growth and harvest, despite the evidences of the way the world is?

What strikes this reader is how religious believers and certain strands of Christian theology have stressed that the kingdom of God comes primarily in judgment of the world's wickedness. Indeed Mark's own little apocalypse in chapter 13 lends credence to this. But here there is no hint of God's anger, nor any suggestion of the kingdom of God coming with an apocalyptic ending in which everyone will get what is coming to them. Rather the mystery of the kingdom is that it is here and not here. It is already being shown in the life and death and resurrection of Jesus, while yet hidden.

This is a profoundly pastoral side of Mark's account of Jesus. These are hope-filled parables. God will not fail to fulfill the promise of salvation. It is already coming to be in this world—like the seed sown in the earth, or the remarkable growth of the tree from the mustard seed, silently but powerfully coming to be.

Even though our pericope ends with yet another reference to why Jesus told parables, it leaves a lingering tension in the air. On the one hand, it is as though Jesus uses humble human images to tells us as much as we are capable of understanding; on the other even when he "explains" the stories to those closest to him, they cannot possibly comprehend what is coming to pass. John Calvin is right in

one another. Mark uses repetition as a literary device. The outline below offers one way of seeing the chiastic[1] structure of Mark 4:1–34 and provides a sense of the relationship of this pericope to the entire chapter.

	4:1–2	Introduction: Jesus teaching to a large crowd
A	4:3–9	Listen! Parable of the Sower
B	4:10–13	Primer on parables
A'	4:14–20	The parable of the Sower explained
B'	4:21–25	Parables about what to do with what you hear
C	4:26–29	Parable of the Automatically Growing Seed
C'	4:30–32	Parable of the Mustard Seed
B''	4:33–34	Parables, as "they" can hear; explanations for disciples

Verses 26–29. The parable of the growing seed is found only in Mark. It and the next parable (vv. 30–32) are Mark's only "kin-dom of God" parables.

Verses 26–27. The task of scattering is performed by a human (*anthrōpos,* "someone" in NRSV). The "seed" has been defined as "the word" in verse 14. The phrase *epi tēs gēs* ("on the ground") occurs three times in these two parables (vv. 26, 31, 31) and is translated with three different English phrases by the NRSV. The phrase "on the earth" may best convey the ambiguity inherent in the Greek, allowing for "on the soil" and "throughout the world" to be implied simultaneously. "Sleep and rise night and day" follows the Jewish mode of reckoning time (cf. Gen. 1:5b).

Verse 28. The earth produces "of itself" (*automatē,* from which we derive "automatic"). In the OT and later Jewish texts, the term referred to that which was worked by God alone, without human effort. An ongoing theological debate among Jewish and Christian thinkers has continued from Jesus' time until now: Does the coming of the final redemption depend on God's will alone, or does human effort make a difference? Mark asserts that while humans are called to "sow" or to "scatter the seed," the growth is completely up to God. The fulfillment comes in stages—first . . . , then . . . , then. . . . For now, the one who scatters does not understand the process and can only wait patiently.

Verse 29. The vocabulary implies both action by the early church and the eschatological work of God. Mark inserts eschatological urgency with the term

windows into our hearts and minds where invigorating and life-giving air can blow in and refresh our souls. This is not so much about the relevance of sermons as it is about stirring the imagination, affirming and connecting our individual and historical story with the larger story of God's movement in our lives and in the life of the world. Jesus uses parables to say, "You count because God is in your life. Your life and your witness have energy and value because God has filled you with gifts." The parables emphasize the positive and life-giving quality of those gifts as well as the negative and death-dealing edge that those gifts can take if we abuse them. In using parables, Jesus emphasizes the power of the imagination and describes it as even more important than the power of the will.

This process seems evident in the two parables that Jesus uses in today's text. The first parable (vv. 26–29) emphasizes that the kingdom of God is dependent upon God's grace and upon human initiative. Why is Jesus telling us this? Is it to emphasize that all is not dependent upon us? Is he urging us to have the patience of a farmer? Is this a parable about God's grace, or about the growing impatience of the first generation of followers? We should also note the vitality and the dynamic power of the seed.

There is also an emphasis on the mystery and surprise of God. We live in an age when the mystery and surprise of all of life, including God's power, are being squeezed out of our consciousness. This parable asks us not to close our imaginations too quickly, because there is a dynamic, vital power that is mysteriously beyond our comprehension and our grasp. In this parable, Jesus suggests that history has been made ready, just as fields are readied to be planted. Through the life of Israel and its prophets, through the prophecy of John the Baptizer, the world has been made ready, and now God's reign has burst on the stage of history in the life of Jesus.

If the reign of God has burst into history, why does history seem so nonchalant about it? Jesus uses the second parable to speak to this. The mustard seed was a common metaphor in Palestine for "the smallest thing." The plant could grow as tall as a house, and birds seemed to love its little black seeds. Like the mustard seed, the followers of Jesus are a bunch of ragged folk, full of doubts, full of fears, unable to comprehend much of what Jesus says or does. The reign of God bursting into history rests on these kinds of folk? Jesus emphasizes, "Yes, this is the scruffy seed from which the reign of God will be

---

1. See exegetical note in Proper 5 on Mark 3:20–35, pp. 117–21, for an explanation about chiastic structures.

Mark 4:26-34

Theological Perspective

plants. But the parable moves from some tame little image to a strange, incomprehensible analogy to the central symbol and urgency of Jesus' teaching ministry.

The passage ends by saying that Jesus spoke the word only in parables to the crowd, "as they were able to hear it," but that he explained everything to the disciples. It is not really any easier to make sense out of this than the parables themselves. But if we were tempted to think that the disciples received an inside track that saved them from the pain and confusion of the gospel, the next story disabuses us of that thought. As soon as we learn that everything is explained in private to the disciples, we learn how useful this was to them. They are on the boat; a storm comes up; they are terrified. On the verge of drowning, they wake up Jesus (sleeping, like the gardener, through the tumult). He cannot understand why they were afraid. "Have you no faith?!?!?" he asks them. To Jesus, their fear is incomprehensible; to them, Jesus' calm is incomprehensible.

It is interesting to observe how frustrated Jesus gets in these stories. He is trying to convey some fantastically good news as clearly as possible, in healing, in parables, in private explanations, in his (odd, even offensive) choice of companions. But the disciples, the crowd, and 2,000 years of Christians find whatever he is trying so hard to give us incredibly hard to receive. Perhaps in working with these passages we should avoid explaining them. Perhaps we should simply let them vibrate in their strangeness so that our habituated patterns of understanding and feeling begin to loosen enough to allow something of Jesus' strange and wonderful news to break into us.

WENDY FARLEY

Pastoral Perspective

reminding us that God speaks to us in language we can understand. At the same time the mystery and the reality of the saving realm and reign of God continue to be beyond every human reality we know.

We do well to continue pondering the inexhaustible range of meanings these stories of Jesus about the kingdom generate. The saving act of God in Jesus Christ remains both revealed and veiled to us in this life, just as it remained so for the first communities. Like the disciples and like the early church, we are caught between understanding and misunderstanding. Mark's portrait of Jesus must remain a persistent factor in our attempts to understand and to live into discipleship. To follow this teller of parables is to become alive to all the paradoxes and the tensions of his life and death: goodness appears in human form, and human powers are threatened; yet death leads to life. We struggle to understand while yet standing under the signs of God's offer of life.

Jesus told so many parables he became one. He told so many because he is the very parable of God in human flesh. This is the extraordinary under the signs and words of the ordinary. So the hope is in the question: "What is God's kingdom like? To what shall we compare it?" No one answer will ever exhaust the meaning of this question, but the pulse of Jesus' words, deeds, death, and resurrection point to the secret hid from a distracted, hopeless world. This pulse is the heartbeat of God, whose rule and reign is coming with the terrible speed of mercy.

DON E. SALIERS

Exegetical Perspective

"immediately" (*eythys*, here NRSV "at once," occurs five times in Mark 4 and forty-two times in the entire Gospel). The phrase "he goes in with his sickle, because the harvest has come" echoes the apocalyptic conclusion of Joel 3:13 (4:13 LXX). At the same time, the phrase "goes in with his sickle" is *apostellei to drepanon,* literally, "he sends out the sickle," a phrase that echoes the sending out (*apostellē*) of the apostles in Mark 3:14.

Verses 30–32. The parable of the mustard seed belongs to a pre-Markan nucleus which included the three seed parables. The parable of the mustard seed is found also in Luke 13:18–19 and Matthew 13:31–32 (both based on Q) and in Thomas 20.

Verse 30. The kin-dom of God is such a mystery (cf. 4:22) that Mark names the dilemma twice.

Verses 31–32. The mustard seed is proverbial for its smallness (see Matt. 17:20). The mustard seed works because it was very common and its size was so small in contrast to the large mature plant.[2] Small beginnings can yield great outcomes.

The parable of the mustard seed also creates comic irony. The mustard plant is just a bush! Surely, a large, stately tree like the cedar would better represent the kin-dom of God. In fact, Matthew and Luke were so disturbed by the bush imagery that they changed the bush to a tree (Matt. 13:32; Luke 13:19). That change may have seemed justified by reference to Ezekiel 17:23. The reference to birds making their nests in its shade speaks of the eschatological gathering of Gentiles to the God of Israel (see also *Joseph and Aseneth* 15.6).

The parable has invited the imagination on a mysterious journey. Beginning with the smallest seed, sown in the earth, which becomes a great bush, the kin-dom of God now provides for multitudes of nations (Ezek. 3:16 LXX).

Verses 33–34. Who can understand these things? We are back to the enigmatic nature of parables. Mark accentuates his point with repetition about Jesus' speaking only in parables, that not all were able to hear. Mark claims special knowledge for the church with the comment that Jesus explained everything to the disciples in private (in spite of the disciples' tendency to misunderstand Jesus in Mark's narrative).

JUDITH HOCH WRAY

2. Pliny (*Nat. Hist.* 19:170–71) describes the mustard plant as "a hardy plant that tends to germinate rapidly and take over a garden."

Homiletical Perspective

proclaimed." Once again he lifts up the grace and power of God taking the smallest seed and transforming it into the great plant that provides sustenance for all. It is at once a humbling parable and an exhilarating parable for the followers of Jesus.

This text closes with a mystery first noted in 4:11–12: "And he said to them: 'To you has been given the secret of the kingdom of God, but for those outside, everything comes in parables in order that "they may indeed look, but not perceive, and may indeed listen, but not understand, so that they may not turn again and be forgiven."'" Jesus uses these words to punctuate the parable of the sower, yet another farming story in an agrarian setting. In his closing words to that parable, Jesus seems to indicate that he uses parables to guard against too many people comprehending what he is saying. A likely interpretation is that he is looking for hungry hearts, those longing for the bread of life, those for whom the world's answers are not adequate. In all of these parables in Mark 4, the seed is an important image, and indeed it is important throughout the biblical story. Ezekiel uses it (17:22–24); John uses it (12:24); and Paul uses it (1 Cor. 15:35–38). It is an enduring symbol of life growing out of what seems not only small but dead. Out of the most insignificant beginnings, God creates a mighty wind that will blow throughout the entire world. In these parables, Jesus invites seekers in every age and every place to consider joining in this kind of journey. So let it be in our sermons.

NIBS STROUPE

Job 38:1-11

¹Then the Lord answered Job out of the whirlwind:
²"Who is this that darkens counsel by words without knowledge?
³Gird up your loins like a man,
  I will question you, and you shall declare to me.

⁴"Where were you when I laid the foundation of the earth?
  Tell me, if you have understanding.
⁵Who determined its measurements—surely you know!
  Or who stretched the line upon it?
⁶On what were its bases sunk,
  or who laid its cornerstone

Theological Perspective

Why do bad things happen to good people? This old question has fueled vigorous discussion among Job and his friends during the previous thirty-seven chapters. Meanwhile, suspense has been building as Job keeps asking God to answer his complaint (9:32; 13:3, 15, 22, 23; 31:35). Finally God speaks. While noting the need for perseverance and patience in prayer, our theological focus concerns *how God responds to Job*.

Those of a rational, analytic bent who like clear-cut answers to specific questions are likely to be frustrated. (What is the *reason* for Job's suffering? If it is the consequence of *sin*, does the moral problem lie with Job personally or with the world generally?) Far from the judge who levies charges or defends a victim, God responds as a poet. God does not correct Job or teach him a lesson, but dazzles him with the divine glory. God stretches Job's imagination to ponder the majestic panorama of creation. The text is vivid. Job is taken on a whirlwind tour to wonder at space and time, at science and nature. The language is invitatory ("let me share with you what I have done"). This is the kind of thing to "make one gasp and stretch one's eyes," not so much in analysis as in awe. As G. K. Chesterton put it, "The riddles of God are more satisfying than the solutions of man." But riddles are

Pastoral Perspective

In the hospital room everything has its place. The IV machine, the telephone, the rolling tray that holds the Styrofoam cup and straw, the reclining chair, the nurse who writes her name on the board in case you forget who is tending to your parishioners, or your father, your child, your grandparent, or you. Inside this room, the church and its messengers also have a place: comforting the afflicted, offering prayers to our God—we are mediators between the physical and the spiritual world. This is the place assigned to us not just by the hospital, but by the expectations of the people who call on the church for support. "Pray for me, pastor." "Pray for healing in my child." "Pray for a gentle death for my mother." This is the place assigned to God's representatives: one foot inside the cold, sterile hospital room, one foot inside the mystery that governs our meaning.

But by its definition, what is mystery cannot always be arranged in the place of our choosing. Try as we might, we cannot always bring order where there is chaos. We cannot always bring explanation to confusion, we cannot always arrange the rooms of our lives the way we want them. In these places of chaos, where our heart's deep yearning shouts down our rational selves, we sometimes cry out to God.

Job raises his cry to God and gets a hearing. By some accounts it is not a good one. Overwhelmed by

⁷when the morning stars sang together
   and all the heavenly beings shouted for joy?

⁸"Or who shut in the sea with doors
   when it burst out from the womb?—
⁹when I made the clouds its garment,
   and thick darkness its swaddling band,
¹⁰and prescribed bounds for it,
   and set bars and doors,
¹¹and said, 'Thus far shall you come, and no farther,
   and here shall your proud waves be stopped'?"

Exegetical Perspective

A Solo Amid Multiple Voices. The structure of the book of Job demonstrates how the book creates a polyphonic presentation of multiple voices.[1] We find the voice of the narrator, the *satan* (the accuser), Job's friends (Eliphaz, Bildad, and Zophar), the uninvited Elihu, Job's wife, and of course Job. For most of the book the divine name lies sequestered, appearing only as a foil to the *satan* (the accuser). The polyphony of voices gives way to a solo when God takes the stage in chapter 38.

Whenever God speaks in the Hebrew Bible, the attention shifts. However, this is all the more so when it is preceded by circular conversations. The dialogue carries the narrative. When one reads the book, the lack of prose leads one to forget the strong narrative feel of the piece.

Doublespeak in a Place Not My Home. The seeming clarity masks a double message of the text: "speak up" and "know your place." Much of the earlier book has been addressing the absence of God; chapter 38 provides a decisive rebuttal of such an accusation (Job 38:1; 40:1, 6; Joel 2:19; Zech. 1:13). Earlier in

1. Carol A. Newsom, *The Book of Job: A Context of Moral Imagination* (Oxford: Oxford University Press, 2003); Robert W. Neff, *Voices in the Book of Job* (Elgin, IL: Brethren Press, 2005).

Homiletical Perspective

This lection begins the climax to the book of Job: God's dramatic answer to Job out of the whirlwind. While the figure of Job has seeped into popular consciousness, many listeners are not familiar with the details of the story as it appears in Scripture. To understand the climax, listeners need to know the contours of the whole narrative. To grasp God's answer, they first need to know Job's question.

Job's question emerges from a particular framework for understanding the world, a theory that was shared by ancient Israel and many of the surrounding cultures and one that will still sound familiar to listeners today. According to this framework, those who live a good life and are obedient to God's commands will be rewarded with good fortune—health, wealth, and other blessings. Those who sin and disobey God's commandments will meet misfortune—illness, poverty, and other woes. This legalistic moral framework, focused on right and wrong, was considered the essence of justice. People get what they deserve. They reap what they sow. When tragedies strike, as they inevitably do, consolation is found in the belief that the outcome is just, that the victims must deserve the "punishment" in some way.

Job had lived and breathed the moral framework of his culture, this particular understanding of the

Job 38:1-11

Theological Perspective

hard to understand, and it is doubtful Job feels satisfied. At the end of the first divine speech, Job is invited to respond, but has nothing to say (40:1–5).

The last chapters of Job remind us that it is not so much God who must answer to humanity, as humanity that must answer to God. For God's "answer" to Job is no solution. Rather, it consists of questions—questions we must consider rhetorical, since the mortal mind can barely fathom their depths. They render Job silent—whether in wonder or puzzlement—until the point where Job *sees* God (42:5–6). It is this theophany that becomes the decisive factor. Job is offered something more than instruction: he is assured of God's presence. This resolves Job's problems on a different level, where the old questions become redundant. The scenario challenges all human egotism, our habit of replacing the confession that our chief end is to glorify God[1] with the assumption that God's chief end is to be concerned with mortals. "We think and worship as if the only question was whether God loves us, instead of whether His love has absolute power to give itself eternal and righteous effect."[2]

The sovereignty of God is expressed through the wonder of creation, harnessing a variety of different discourses and traditions. God's speeches defy formal categorization, containing wisdom material, mythic discourse, divine-warrior imagery, royal language, and legal forms. It is hard to determine any single textual form that offers the interpretive key for the rest. What is more distinctive here are the references to God as YHWH. The specifically Israelite name of God—YHWH—is used at the beginning of each speech and in Job's response to each (38:1; 40:1, 3, 6; 42:1). Whereas the prose prologue and epilogue of the book of Job use this title, it does not appear in the central portion of the book—in the dialogues between Job and friends, or in the Elihu speeches—until God enters the fray directly here.

This has striking implications. The God of the whole world, the God whose wisdom and power are supreme over all creation and are evident in his universal works of creation, is not a nameless "force," an abstract ʾel (the Hebrew word for "god"). This God does not exist aside from his particular revelation and relationship with Israel. God reveals the name YHWH to Moses (Exod. 3) at the point where God calls Moses to lead God's people out of

1. Westminster Shorter Catechism (1647), Q. 1, in *The Book of Confessions* (Louisville, KY: Office of the General Assembly, 1999), 175.
2. Samuel Terrien, "Job," in *The Interpreter's Bible* (New York: Abingdon, 1954), 3:1171.

Pastoral Perspective

a recitation of natural mysteries that Job and our best theology cannot adequately explain, God's forceful rhetoric seems to discourage the faithful from ever questioning the persistence of injustice, or the seeming silence of God in the face of suffering, or any other conundrum of our faith that leaves us hurting or dismayed. Reading Job, some may be tempted to wave the white flag to God and give up the struggle.

Many faith journeys stumble at this place. Sometimes those journeys are stymied with the encouragement of the church. Like Job's friend, Eliphaz (Job 22), the church prefers to share what it knows from its cherished truisms: "God is good all the time" ; "God's will is sometimes hard for us to understand"; "God will not give us more than we can handle." Like Eliphaz, we do not enjoy puzzling over mysteries that we cannot easily explain.

But that is what the church does when it is at its best—it summons mysteries that are not easily explained; it invites people into these mysteries, never in control of where those mysteries will lead or of what will happen to the people caught up in them. The church introduces people to the living God, as unpredictable and volatile as the sea bursting from its womb (38:8), or the clouds, unfurling a thick darkness too expansive for us to handle (vv. 9–10). This kind of encounter is not for the fainthearted. Job must "gird up [his] loins like a man" (v. 3), prepare himself for a physically taxing encounter. Perhaps this is part of the role of the church—to prepare the questioning faithful for what can be a demanding encounter with our God.

Often, the church treats mystery as the intersection of the physical with the supernatural. Even the most skeptical of Christians will sometimes pray for the supernatural when desperate circumstances leave few other choices: prayers for healing when the doctors know the cancer will stay the course, or prayers for peace in places where violence has lived for a thousand years.

But mystery, according to Job, is located primarily not in what is exceptional, but in what is natural, regular, and known—the morning stars, the sea, the womb, the clouds. They invite Job, and us, to ponder the breadth of the depth of this God with whom we must struggle. In the world unfurled for us in the words of poetry, we find that our questions lead not to answers but to an awareness of how deep and fathomless are the mysteries of the God we struggle to understand.

The temptation of many churches, drenched in the cherished theologies of our traditions, is to give

Exegetical Perspective

the book Job had answered plenty. More than that, he requested an answer from God.

The term here translated "whirlwind" is used in the context of divine appearance (see Ezek. 1:4). The broader use of a storm as a sign of divine appearance occurs using other terms as well (See Pss. 18:7–15; 50:3; 68:8; Nah. 1:3; Zech. 9:14). Elijah was taken off in the midst of a whirlwind (2 Kgs. 2:11). The whirlwind strikes the reader as a place where the reader is not at home.

After the editor sets the scene, the text moves into a series of questions meant to explore the credentials of Job as a witness. The reader who looks at verses 4–11 sees a set of cosmological markers: the foundation of the world (vv. 4–7) and the establishment of the seas (vv. 8–11). While the unit does not stop after verse 11, the tone does continue through the end of the first divine speech. Thus a reader can take these two portions as limits that can represent the broad sweep of the entire unit (38:2–40:2).

The book of Job functions as a series of speeches and counterspeeches, sometimes referred to as a dialogue. The speech in 38:1–11 builds with a series of rhetorical questions. The first one goes to the heart of identity, "who." This is one of the most controversial verses in the passage. The debate has centered on whether the question is meant to impugn the witness of Job. The metaphor "darkens counsel" stands as a counterpoint to Job's description of divine wisdom (12:13–25).[2] The writer uses synonymous parallelism, "darkens counsel" and "words obscuring knowledge" (my translations), to depict Job as the epitome of the unwise character. The text with an ironic sleight of hand betrays its purpose. When God designates Job as the personification of the antiwisdom, one understands the movement of the text.

The imperative "Gird up your loins like a warrior" (38:3a; 40:7) in late modernity creates a stir. This could be a call to action (Jer. 1:17) that requires loose ends to be tied up (Exod. 12:11; 1 Kgs. 18:46) or physical and intellectual courage and agility.[3] Often the language of warrior (*geber*) is the language of agency. But here the agency is thwarted. Once again the use of similar gender-based shaming in popular culture can be instructive. Often when such phrases are used, the function is to coerce through shaming a type of desired behavior. Here the goal is disclosure: forced testimony.

2. J. Gerald Janzen, *Job*. Interpretation (Atlanta: John Knox Press, 1985), 231.
3. Carol A. Newsom, "Job," in *New Interpreter's Bible* (Nashville: Abingdon, 1996), 4:601.

Homiletical Perspective

world, his whole life. Then his own tragedy strikes. Chaos comes knocking at his door. Thanks to a heavenly deal between God and Satan, Job loses everything. His flocks are stolen, his servants murdered, his children killed, his health ruined. And yet Job is innocent. As Job sits among the ashes with nothing but a potsherd to scratch his skin, all the evidence suggests that Job's framework for understanding the world is inadequate. Job knows that he has not sinned or disobeyed God—and still he suffers.

Job cannot see beyond his narrow worldview. All he can perceive in his situation is injustice. He still thinks of the world in legal terms of right and wrong, even though this legal theory has failed him. Job's framework has proven inadequate, but it is the only thing left standing between him and the chaos of the world. Job is desperate for justice, not chaos, to prevail. So when this legal framework fails him, Job seeks a legal solution—a trial. In desperation, Job challenges God to a legal hearing, convinced that if only he has a chance to plead his case in court, then surely he will be vindicated. Surely justice will prevail and the chaos will be tamed. Job demands to know why he must suffer despite his innocence: "Let the Almighty answer me!" (31:35).

Job's question, of course, is also our own. This lection provides the preacher an opportunity to probe the chaos of our own lives, to name out loud the doubts and fears we normally whisper only in the dark on sleepless nights. Job invites us to examine our own frameworks for organizing the unimaginable, to see with clear eyes the constructs we use to hold chaos at bay. Like Job, we are loath to admit when our frameworks fail us, and we are unprepared for God's answer.

And God does indeed answer. Out of the whirlwind, God replies, "Where were you when I laid the foundation of the earth? Tell me, if you have understanding. Who determined its measurements—surely you know! Or who stretched the line upon it? On what were its bases sunk, or who laid its cornerstone when the morning stars sang together and all the heavenly beings shouted for joy?" (38:4–7). The lection includes only the first eleven verses, but God's response goes on for four chapters and spans the whole universe. In a fierce and beautiful poetic litany, God describes the works of creation, from the birth of the seas to the movement of the constellations, from the patterns of wind and rain to the customs of wild creatures. God's expansive answer from the whirlwind tells Job,

Job 38:1-11

Theological Perspective

slavery in Egypt. The name YHWH is inextricably tied to the God who redeems a people in trouble, sustains them through the wilderness, and brings them into the promised land. God acts through history, in fulfillment of promises made long before to a particular people, with whom God enters into covenant relationship.

Thus it is not possible to talk of a God "out there" who is sovereign over the universe without relating to the God who enters the fray of history and politics, investing fully in a people and expecting the same loyalty in return. The reference to God as YHWH here in Job reminds us (and Job) of this reality. It forces an integration of philosophy and history, of faith and life. Creation and redemption are inextricably linked. The God who magnificently created the world, who is inherently sovereign and wise, is the same God who enters into covenant and in whom human beings can trust. The naming of God as YHWH also underlines a more subtle point evident in the divine speeches: there is a parallel between the natural order and the moral order. The suffering and injustices of the moral order have their counterpart in the forces of chaos (personified by Behemoth and Leviathan, 40:6–41:34) that threaten the created order. God is sovereign over both realms.

This reinforces the monotheism evident throughout the Hebrew Scriptures. Job himself has already demonstrated the logic of Hebrew monotheism: that the God who made everything is the One to whom we must cry when something is wrong. A Hebrew name speaks of the character of its bearer, and the exodus narratives are paradigmatic here. God's self-revelation to Moses at the exodus denotes YHWH as one who hears the cry of the oppressed. At the same time, at Sinai, Israel learns (the hard way) that YHWH's nature is to show mercy and forgiveness (Exod. 33:19; 34:5–7) even as God demands exclusive loyalty (Exod. 34:14). Thus, "I AM WHO I AM" (Exod. 3:14)—the God who can be known only on God's own terms, not by analogy with anything else—whose presence is awesome, whose creation is unfathomable, whose judgment is final, is the God to whom we must cleave, and with whom we must plead, whatever the circumstances.

JO BAILEY WELLS

Pastoral Perspective

our people answers. But faith, by its very nature, is not the product of right answers. The deepest places of our knowledge of God are often those places that we cannot explain: experiences of tranquility in the presence of fear, comfort known deeply near death, the enigma of undeserved suffering visited on the life of a child—these and many other moments experienced regularly by people in the church.

These are the kinds of moments people of faith cherish, puzzle over, and pay attention to. These are the mysteries that the church cannot often explain. Most of the time people do not want an explanation. They want an experience of the presence of God, more unpredictable than they had originally hoped, more mysterious than they had first imagined, perhaps more real than the gods we all construct to our own specifications. These moments of mystery are the answers to the questions about God most of us do not know how to ask: comfort, challenge, joy, and hope, all wrapped up into moments that do come. Perhaps the church's vocation has less to do with explaining the root of that mystery and more to do with making space for that kind of mystery to be known and shared.

In the hospital room, like every other room in our lives, not everything has its place, not everything is given a meaning that we can understand. Like Job, the people of God ask for explanation, for an accounting. More often than not, what we are given are moments of mystery. The church's role is to support people in the midst of this encounter, to teach them the interpretive tasks of recognizing God's work, not just in the exceptional moments of our lives, but in the regular moments of every human life, where God can be known but never finally explained.

ANDREW FOSTER CONNORS

Exegetical Perspective

One can hardly miss the irony here. Typically the warrior embodies the least disclosive character. One could paraphrase the passage, "Gird up your loins like a man, and I will make you sing like a bird." The metaphors collapse on themselves. The superior reading observes the interlocking strategy of rhetorical questions and imperatives. The "who" question points to the previous and necessary testimony of Job, and the imperatives speak to the ongoing witness of that testimony.

Where in the World Were You? The second rhetorical question captures an English colloquialism as well: "Where were you?" Once again the question precedes an imperative of disclosure. This rhetorical question is a social discriminator, setting some in the group and others outside. Just as the whirlwind provides a way of distinguishing the divine voice from Job's, now the temporal realm becomes a discriminator between the two. The language "the foundations of the earth" harks back to creation myths as authorizing stories. The ones there at the very beginning derive benefits of longevity—financial benefits. In the case of Job the benefits are perspectival, that is to say, wisdom.

Verse 5 has two rhetorical questions set in synonymous parallelism. Once again the question is "who" and the locus is "from the beginning." Tossed into the middle of these rhetorical questions one finds the taunt "surely you know." The momentum of the passage is building like a cross-examination of a witness in a legal drama. Before the witness can give an answer, the accuser, this time God rather than the *satan*, presses on. The rhetorical questions of verses 6–7 press the absence of Job at the creation of the world, just as Job presses the absence of God during Job's suffering. Just as verses 4–7 outline Job's absence from the creation of the world, verses 8–11 testify to Job's absence in the establishment of the seas.

STEPHEN BRECK REID

Homiletical Perspective

"Your categories were far too small. You think in terms of the courtroom. I think in terms of the cosmos. Your human theories cannot possibly capture the complexity of the universe, nor can they contain the chaos. For chaos is part of creation as surely as crocodiles roam the Nile."

In all of this beautiful, lyric response, God's rebuttal never actually answers Job's question. God never explains why Job has suffered as he has. Barbara Brown Taylor observes, "Job's question was about justice. God's answer is about omnipotence, and as far as I know, that is the only answer human beings have ever gotten about why things happen the way they do. God only knows. And none of us is God."[1]

Instead, at God's insistence, Job must confront that which he fears most. He faces the chaos of the world and the immensity of the cosmos. And his blinders fall off. "I had heard of you by the hearing of the ear," Job says to God, "but now my eye sees you" (42:5). With God's answer from the whirlwind, Job's narrow moral framework gives way to a cosmic vision of the Divine. In this divine encounter, Job acknowledges the inescapable presence of the chaotic in existence. And yet he comes to recognize that despite the existence of chaos, the world rests on a secure foundation. Despite his pain and loss, God's creation will support and sustain.[2] Job's question is never answered. He is comforted not by an explanation, but by a vision—he has seen the Divine and lived.

The challenge for the preacher is to convey that vision to listeners who may long instead for explanation. For ultimately the content of God's answer to Job does not matter nearly as much as this: God answers. That is the miracle. The chaos is still there, but so is God. And that is enough.

LEANNE PEARCE REED

---

1. Barbara Brown Taylor, *Home by Another Way* (Cambridge: Cowley, 1999), 165.
2. Carol A. Newsom, "The Book of Job," in *The New Interpreter's Bible* (Nashville: Abingdon, 1996), 4:631.

Psalm 107:1-3, 23-32

¹O give thanks to the LORD, for he is good;
  for his steadfast love endures forever.
²Let the redeemed of the LORD say so,
  those he redeemed from trouble
³and gathered in from the lands,
  from the east and from the west,
  from the north and from the south.
. . . .
²³Some went down to the sea in ships,
  doing business on the mighty waters;
²⁴they saw the deeds of the LORD,
  his wondrous works in the deep.
²⁵For he commanded and raised the stormy wind,
  which lifted up the waves of the sea.

Theological Perspective

The verses assigned in this reading of the longer
psalm include an *introduction* (vv. 1–3) and a *specific
narrative* case of rescue for which thanks is to be
rendered (vv. 23–32). The two subsections of the
psalm together constitute a characteristic song of
thanksgiving in ancient Israel that expresses the
primal mood of Israel's faith, one of gratitude that
requires and evokes explicit articulation.

The introduction (vv. 1–3) is quite general and
highly stylized, and perhaps reflective of actual
liturgical use. The opening imperative, "give thanks,"
is perhaps a summons to the congregation by the
priest. The verb "give thanks" in the first instant is a
bid that Israel should verbalize (confess) in the most
specific ways the reasons it has for gratitude to
YHWH. That is, it tells the story of divine
intervention or generosity. It is likely that in
liturgical practice the *utterance* was matched by *a
bodily act* of bringing an offering to YHWH, a
"thank offering" (on which see Ps. 116:12–19; Lev.
7:11–18). The remainder of the introductory verses
provides motivation for thanks and supplies the
context for such a recital of gratitude.

The imperative that names YHWH as recipient of
thanks is followed by two conjunctions, "for . . . for,"
conjunctions that regularly introduce motivations.
Israel should thank YHWH (a) because YHWH is

Pastoral Perspective

God is surely able to be present to "*all* in need."
However, if in the morning prayers we offer a petition
for "*all* those who suffer," the object of our prayer is
beyond our ability to imagine, and God's presence is
obscured. Psalm 107 has an eloquent and helpful way
of saying "everyone." This psalm imagines God's
drawing together all those whom God has "redeemed
from trouble" and gathering them from the four
corners of the earth. The overture in verses 1–3 is
followed by four sections, which in a schematic way
reflect the complete horizon from which God calls the
redeemed. The genius of the psalm's "all" is in those
schematic four sections. They provide explicit hooks
for our sense of God's extraordinarily complex reach
toward humanity in redemption.

The first section (vv. 4–9) is about those rescued
from the desert wastes; the second (vv. 10–16) recalls
those redeemed from prison; the third (vv. 17–22)
refers to those sick and near to death; the final
section, included in the lection, refers to those
caught in a storm on the sea. Each of these receives
the redemption of God; each is called to give praise
and thanks to God for their redemption. Their
cumulative effect is to deepen our sense of the many
layers of God's mercies.

The grace described in this psalm is abundant
and specific. It is clearly a reminder to make the

²⁶They mounted up to heaven, they went down to the depths;
    their courage melted away in their calamity;
²⁷they reeled and staggered like drunkards,
    and were at their wits' end.
²⁸Then they cried to the Lᴏʀᴅ in their trouble,
    and he brought them out from their distress;
²⁹he made the storm be still,
    and the waves of the sea were hushed.
³⁰Then they were glad because they had quiet,
    and he brought them to their desired haven.
³¹Let them thank the Lᴏʀᴅ for his steadfast love,
    for his wonderful works to humankind.
³²Let them extol him in the congregation of the people,
    and praise him in the assembly of the elders.

Exegetical Perspective

Thanksgiving for God's Acts of Deliverance. This psalm takes the reader through four life-threatening experiences and acknowledges God's provision in rescuing the distressed from each situation. As a result of God's intervention, the psalmist calls upon the reader to praise God for the *ḥesed* (steadfast love) shown in each act of deliverance. Each of the four strophes concludes with the repetition "Let them thank the Lᴏʀᴅ for his steadfast love, for his wonderful works to humankind" (vv. 8, 15, 21, 31), followed by two causal statements introduced with "for" (vv. 9, 16) and two calls to action, "let them offer thanksgiving sacrifices" (v. 22) and "let them extol" (v. 32). The psalm concludes with wisdom themes that declare God's power and willingness to reverse oppressive situations in order to benefit the righteous while confounding the wicked.

The Symmetry of the Psalm (vv. 1–3). The four strophes are foreshadowed in the opening lines of the psalm by four directions from which the "redeemed" are to be gathered in order that they may give thanks to God. These four directions correspond to the four conditions out of which God redeems the distressed. Those who wander in deathly deserts, those who sit in darkness, those who are ill to the point of death, and those who survive a raging

Homiletical Perspective

"God is good," the preacher calls out, and the congregation answers, "All the time!" Like the opening verses of this psalm, this call and response forms a prayer of both gratitude for the gifts of God's grace and confidence in God's continuing activity in the lives of the believers.

"Let the redeemed of the Lord say so," calls out the liturgist, and the psalmist's answer is both gratitude and confidence as she details the way in which God has acted in the lives of God's people. At this point the lectionary reading leaves out much of what God has done. Gone are the references to the refugee without "inhabited town," food, or water; to the prisoners in their misery; to the sick. We are left only with those who "go down to the sea in ships." Even for landlubbers the description of the ship pitching and tossing—first high on the crest of the wave, then down to the trough between with water towering overhead—will bring that edge-of-the-seat-queasy-in-the-stomach feeling that comes with movie scenes of such events. It does not take much imagination to put ourselves on the deck of that ship and know what it means to the sailor to be rescued.

Perhaps the lectionary skips over the other woes that beset human beings because this great storm that leaves us without firm footing or clear vision is a powerful image for the other storms of life. I do

Psalm 107:1-3, 23-32

Theological Perspective

"good," that is, causes Israel to prosper, and (b) because YHWH is utterly faithful. The term "steadfast love" (*ḥesed*) is answered by the same term in the conclusion of verse 43, so that the entire psalm moves from "steadfast love" to "steadfast love." The two general grounds for gratitude in Israel—"good, steadfast love"—are made somewhat more specific in verses 2–3 on two counts. First, the ones who will be grateful are "the redeemed," the ones whose lives are honored and protected by YHWH, their "kinsman." The verb "redeemed" is used for exodus rescue, but also for deliverance from exile, so that the term refers to all of those contexts in which YHWH is credited with bringing Israel to well-being. Second, the grateful are the "scattered" ones who have been "gathered." This language characteristically refers to those who have been displaced and exiled. Thus the verse anticipates a great gathering and homecoming of Israelites from many places far from Jerusalem. This may refer specifically to homecoming of Jews after the sixth-century exile, on which see Isaiah 43:5 and 56:8. In Christian usage the rhetoric of "east, west, north, south" anticipates the eucharistic invitation to come from "the north and the south" to gather at the table. God is thanked for ending exile!

Verses 23–32 report a specific (though characteristic) case of divine rescue. In this psalm it is the fourth such case, preceded by reference to those rescued from desert sojourn (vv. 4–9), those emancipated from prison (vv. 10–16), and those healed from sickness (vv. 17–22). The four cases together (including our vv. 23–32) are stylized representations of all the recurring wondrous ways in which YHWH transforms danger, suffering, and death into possibilities for new life and joyous well-being. The four "case studies" follow a fourfold pattern that is highly stylized and that has close parallels to the stylized formulations of the book of Judges (see Judg. 3:7–11). The pattern is clear in verse 23–32:

a. The poetry describes a situation of threat from which the Israelites cannot extricate themselves (vv. 23–27). In this case the trouble is a storm at sea which recalls the threat that confronted the prophet Jonah (Jonah 1:4–16). The storm is described as a vigorous threat so that we sense both the danger and the wonder of YHWH, who is the powerful creator storm God. The phrase "mighty waters" in verse 23 is surely a technical phrase and refers to the primordial waters of chaos, as in Genesis 1:1. Thus the poetry passes back and fourth between *creation imagery* that attests the wondrous power of YHWH, who can

Pastoral Perspective

prayers of the people or the pastoral prayer specific and abundant in order to reflect the magnitude and expansiveness of God's steadfast love. The psalm reminds us that God's love touches the deck hands working in Maine fisheries, is a present help to those wandering in search of subsistence in sub-Saharan Africa, is at hand for the young man who is in prison on his second conviction, and reaches for the young woman whose eating disorder is secretly killing her. This psalm challenges us, when we pray, to remember the retirement consultant, the childcare worker, the ticket taker, the cabbie, the waitress, the fourth-grader, the poet, the highway patrolman—it calls forth our imagination to see how vast are God's wonderful works. This psalm's breadth leads us to see that God's steadfast love is a warm and clear call to responsibility for one, a guiding hand and sober outlook for another, a pure and completely believable affirmation for another, the gift of food from a generous foreigner for yet another.

In this psalm God's steadfast and creative love is replete with the inventiveness necessary to adapt or grow, cozy up or expand as wildly as our human conditions require. That steadfast love is not just one thing, and it is matched to the receiver's plight. It is as if it were liquid, so that it can conform itself to the shape into which it is poured, can conform itself to our need—like the cup of salvation. It is for those who come from east and west, north and south, and it can match their accents, their cultures, their challenges, and their idiosyncrasies. God's steadfast love has a redemptive gift for each of them.

And in the specific stanza (vv. 23–32) that is included in the lection, God heals the seasick. God saves them from their precarious place on the chaos of life, but also rescues them from their seasickness and lack of sea legs. The seasick: God attends to their precise malady. We can hardly imagine a God so scrupulous, so meticulous in love. The psalm provides not only a clear window on God's blessing the multitudes but an invitation to receive God's blessing of our particular uniqueness. It offers an invitation to invite God into the minutiae of our lives.

We are prone to leave certain aspects out of our relationship with God. This proper is a Sunday to confess the limitations we place on God's redemptive power for ourselves. We want to keep God out of some parts of our lives, leave just a little room for a self-indulgence: "Can't I have just a little space where you're not there, God, not luring me out into my gifts or leaving me alone to my self-pity? Can't you leave me with some of my comfortable brokenness?"

Exegetical Perspective

storm at sea are invited to gather before the Lord to testify to God's saving action.

However, we encounter a problem in understanding the last of these four directions. The NRSV translates "east, west, north, south" in an effort to provide the symmetry one might expect. But the Hebrew text uses *yam* (sea) rather than *yamin* (south). Most commentators, expecting a perfect directional symmetry, have emended the text to read "south," as have most English translations (the NJPS does not emend the text). One can argue from the movement of the psalm that the Hebrew not be emended and that we read "sea" in place of "south."[1] By so doing one enters a new world of imaginative possibilities regarding the artistry of the text.

These four correspondences do not necessarily relate to a particular experience of exile or disease but present situations of distress that appeal to the sympathetic imagination of the reader. East is the direction from which the sun rises, and the scorching heat of the desert provides no respite from suffering. The west is the direction of the sunset and the advent of darkness where dangers lurk, threatening the body and the mind. The north is often a direction from which military dangers arise and the threat of annihilation draws near. The sea is a place with which Israel has little experience as sailors, but where chaos threatens to overwhelm life and the power of the sea is to be feared. These directions are then expounded in verses 4–32. Each of the four strophes begins with the declaration that "some" have experienced these life-threatening situations.

The Structure of the Psalm. In order to understand the fourth strophe we must be aware of the features it shares with the other three. The four scenarios repeat particular words and phrases. Each of the four experiences in this psalm begins with the same expression: "some" (vv. 4, 10, 17, 23). Each also uses the same expression at the point of declaring God's deliverance: "They cried out" (vv. 6, 13, 19, 28). The same verb form is used with each statement of rescue; however, a variety of synonyms is used (delivered, saved, saved, brought out). Each narrative of trouble is concluded with the expression "Let them thank the LORD for his steadfast love, for his wonderful works to humankind" (vv. 8, 15, 21, 31).

1. See John Jarick, "The Four Corners of Psalm 107," *Catholic Biblical Quarterly* 59.02 (1997): 270–87.

Homiletical Perspective

not think the preacher would be stretching this text to use the storm as a way to enter whatever traumas her particular congregation faces this Sunday. We are sometimes afraid to raise up the pain, but it is only when we feel our own helplessness that we are ready to hear the good news.

This psalm begins, "Let the redeemed of the LORD say so." Yet how many of our good Christian folk are willing to say so? We do not talk about religion. It is not the thing to do. Why? Old Testament scholar Walter Brueggemann comments, "Praise is an act of relinquishment."[1] Think about that. Truly to praise is to admit our own lack, our own need. We relinquish our pride. We relinquish our independence. We did not accomplish this. Someone else did. Someone far more powerful than we are did what we could not. That is not a comfortable stance for citizens of the world's richest, most powerful nation. Are we willing to relinquish our own sense of self in order truly to praise God?

Perhaps this is where the image of the storm at sea is so powerful. Look to the Gospel reading for today, with Mark's account of Jesus and the disciples caught in the teeth of a howling gale. Several of them have sailed this water all their lives, but now they must relinquish their own sense of competence and admit their inability to cope on their own. When the storm is stilled, "they were filled with great awe and said to one another, 'Who then is this, that even the wind and the sea obey him?'" (Mark 4:41).

Do you remember the final verse of the Navy hymn?

> O Trinity of love and power!
> Our brethren shield in danger's hour;
> From rock and tempest, fire and foe,
> Protect them wheresoe'er they go;
> Thus evermore shall rise to Thee
> Glad hymns of praise from land and sea.[2]

In bearing his own witness, the psalmist models how to do this. He is specific. He talks about real life events—things that readers then, as now, find in their own lives or the life of their community. Likewise Paul, writing to the Corinthians in the lectionary's Epistle reading, is specific as he lists the "affliction, hardships, and calamity" that have befallen him (2 Cor. 6:1–13). By being specific in naming the storms, we are also specific in naming

1. Walter Brueggemann, *Cadences of Home: Preaching among Exiles* (Louisville, KY: Westminster John Knox Press, 1997), 86.
2. William Whiting, in *Pilgrim Hymnal* (Boston: Pilgrim Press, 1958), 429.

Psalm 107:1-3, 23-32

Theological Perspective

govern the storm, and the concrete experience of a storm at sea that in its ferociousness was an immediate sign of chaos unleashed.

b. At wit's end, the sailors, who are frightened and at risk, cry out to YHWH (v. 28a). The "cry" is one of need, desperate need in a context of hopelessness. The cry is a raw expression of pending disaster; it functions as a petition, for the cry of distress is addressed to YHWH. This "cry" is an echo of the cry of the slaves in Egypt, a cry that set the exodus narrative in motion (Exod 2:23–25). The usage is an admission of impotence and an acknowledgment that YHWH alone has power to save.

c. YHWH responds to the cry of the petitioners (vv. 28b–30). Most telling is the fact that the response of YHWH follows immediately after the cry of Israel. YHWH is a God who hears and answers, with no qualifications necessary, no explanations required (see Isa. 65:24). YHWH is credited with three acts:

He *brought them out*;
he settled the storm;
he *brought them in* (to a safe harbor).

The sequence and the verbs are reminiscent of the exodus, "*brought out* of the house of bondage," and pushed back the waters, "*brought into* a land flowing with milk and honey." The sequence of verbs recalls Israel's most familiar cadences of credo confession.

d. The sequence of verbs culminates with "thanks" (vv. 31–32). The wording returns to verse 1 concerning "thanks . . . steadfast love." YHWH's fidelity is made specific in the rescue at the sea, this miracle typical of "wondrous works." Verse 31 moves beyond the *specificity of thanks* to the more *general act of praise* whereby the entire congregation of elders and people is able to join in the thanks for a quite particular rescue.

The dramatic movement of *need, petition, rescue, and thanks* voices the epitome of Israel's faith. The sequence here is no doubt tightly stylized for liturgic use. That stylization, however, derives from the raw, lived experience of Israel. Israel inhabits a world of threat in which YHWH makes a decisive difference. Such a decisive difference evokes specific words and acts of generous gratitude in response.

WALTER BRUEGGEMANN

Pastoral Perspective

We do not want to consent to a "gospel agenda" for *every* dimension of our lives: Why not 8 miles per gallon? Why not the newest thing, even if we already have two that work? We want some arena where God just does not meddle—our sexuality, our eating habits, our good mornings to coworkers, our good nights to our children, our voting, our driving. Psalm 107 says, "You don't think God can get into healing that part of you? This God cares about your sickness and those lost in the desert, those working on a submarine, and girls deluded by their culture's distorted images of womanhood." In the psalmist's ancient way, calling on the four directions and getting specific about the wavering of those on the sea, this psalm tells us that God is there for *all* the suffering in the world.

Imagine a community that seeks to be as imaginative as this psalmist in offering grace to a world in need. Imagine a community that is bold enough to claim God's grace for all. Jim Manley, pastor and songwriter, has a lyric that goes, "Children and elders, middlers and teens, singles and doubles and in betweens, strong eighty-fivers and streetwise sixteens, we are a part of the family . . . Greeters and shoppers, long-time and new—nobody here has a claim on a pew, and whether we're many, or whether we're few, we are a part of the family . . ."[1]

This psalm begins the fifth and final book of the Psalter. That final book begins here, with praise of God's steadfast love infusing every tight and broken place in us and redeeming lives from north and south, east and west, and the book climaxes at the end of the Psalter itself: "Let *everything* that breathes praise the LORD! Praise the LORD!"

CHANDLER BROWN STOKES

---

1. James K. Manley, "Part of the Family," copyright 1983.

Exegetical Perspective

In the first two narratives of trouble, the call to thank the Lord is followed by a motive for praising God (e.g., "For he satisfies the thirsty," "For he shatters the doors"). The third and fourth narratives conclude the same call to thank the Lord with an extension of that call to praise (e.g., "And let them offer thanksgiving sacrifices," "Let them extol him"). On the whole, the movement of this psalm of deliverance is from reflection on God's action to an extended call to praise.

Deliverance at Sea (vv. 23–32). The outline of the strophe is as follows: Narrative (vv. 23–27), first refrain (vv. 28–30), second refrain (vv. 31–32). Each of the four strophes has the same outline; however, the first refrain of the fourth strophe has one more line than the other three. All four strophes share the pattern of a cry for help, a statement of the deliverance that God effected, and a call to give thanks. In the fourth strophe the experience of deliverance is lengthened. The extra verse reports the mental state of the sailors ("then they were glad") and the success of their trip ("he brought them to their desired haven").

The narrative describes a violent storm at sea. It is clear that God is responsible for the storm. God commands the wind, and the wind lifts up the waves. The magnitude of the rolling waves and the ship is emphasized by the distance they travel through the swells; up to heaven and down to the depths. The experienced sailors are helpless. Their seafaring skills fail; they are left to flounder like drunks. The danger is so overwhelming that their *hokmah* (wisdom, skill, craft) fails them (v. 27, lit. "their skill [wisdom] was in ruins"). None of their attempts to save the ship can bring it under control, so at the moment of complete despair they cry out to the Lord. Immediately, the Lord rescues them and "made the storm a whisper" (v. 29, my translation).

The sea is quieted and the sea merchants are brought into the harbor of their desire. This, the fourth of the narratives of distress, concludes the strophe with a call for praise from the congregation. The recounting of God's power and steadfast love to save is a communal event meant to evoke a sense of wonder and praise in the community.

STEVEN BISHOP

Homiletical Perspective

the praise. "This you did, God. This is where your steadfast love was seen."

There are Hebrew words that do not lend themselves to easy one-word translation. *Ḥesed* is such a word. "Steadfast love" is a good try, but seems tame compared to the determined, unrelenting love of God that will not let go, that will not be deterred.

The poet puts it this way:

> I fled Him, down the nights and down the days;
> I fled Him, down the arches of the years;
> I fled Him, down the labyrinthine ways
> Of my own mind; and in the mist of tears
> I hid from Him, and under running laughter,
> Up vistaed hopes, I sped;
> And shot, precipitated,
> Adown Titanic glooms of chasmed fears,
> From those strong Feet that followed,
> followed after. [3]

God's *ḥesed* is like that. It is a love that pursues not only you and me but all humankind. The words repeat themselves throughout the psalm:

> Let them thank the LORD for his steadfast love.
> for his wonderful works to humankind.

God's love and care is for all, and it is to all God's beloved children that the psalmist's call goes out: "Let the redeemed of the Lord say so!" As each of us bears witness to what God has done in our lives, we proclaim God's faithfulness to all God's children. Each grace bestowed, each grace declared, confirms God's promises. Others can hear our story and find hope in the midst of their darkness. Others can hear our praise and find voice to speak their words of gratitude. Each voice strengthens the other in both the hard times and the good. Then indeed the glad hymns will rise from both land and sea.

NETA LINDSAY PRINGLE

---

3. Francis Thompson, "The Hound of Heaven," in *Oxford Book of English Mystical Verse* (Oxford: Oxford University Press, 1917), 239.

2 Corinthians 6:1-13

¹As we work together with him, we urge you also not to accept the grace of God in vain. ²For he says,

"At an acceptable time I have listened to you,
and on a day of salvation I have helped you."

See, now is the acceptable time; see, now is the day of salvation! ³We are putting no obstacle in anyone's way, so that no fault may be found with our ministry, ⁴but as servants of God we have commended ourselves in every way: through great endurance, in afflictions, hardships, calamities, ⁵beatings, imprisonments, riots, labors, sleepless nights, hunger; ⁶by purity, knowledge, patience, kindness, holiness of spirit, genuine love, ⁷truthful speech, and the power of God; with the weapons of righteousness for the right hand and for the left; ⁸in honor and dishonor, in ill repute and good repute. We are treated as impostors, and yet are true; ⁹as unknown, and yet are well known; as dying, and see—we are alive; as punished, and yet not killed; ¹⁰as sorrowful, yet always rejoicing; as poor, yet making many rich; as having nothing, and yet possessing everything.

¹¹We have spoken frankly to you Corinthians; our heart is wide open to you. ¹²There is no restriction in our affections, but only in yours. ¹³In return—I speak as to children—open wide your hearts also.

Theological Perspective

One of the built-in hazards of using a lectionary is the temptation to treat Scripture as a collection of self-enclosed modules, each of which can be read, understood, interpreted, and proclaimed as though it stood alone. This passage is a prime example of the necessity to look beyond the specific reading to see it in its proper literary and theological context. In this case, the key to the integrity of the passage is metaphoric as well as thematic. The primary clue is the word "ambassadors" in 5:20, which introduces a chain of diplomatic metaphors that extends to the conclusion of our passage in 6:13. The word "therefore" (NRSV "so") in 5:20, however, is an indicator of a still broader context, for it introduces Paul's climactic appeal to the Corinthian church after having described in detail the "message of reconciliation" (5:19) in the preceding chapters. That message is concentrated in a pithy summary in the verse that immediately precedes our passage: "For our sake he made him to be sin who knew no sin, so that in him we might become the righteousness of God" (5:21).

Our reading opens with the appeal that follows from this message: God's ambassadors, having delivered their communiqué, now make their entreaty on behalf of their sovereign. The opening participle, *synergountes* ("working together"), might raise the theological specter of a Pelagian synergism

Pastoral Perspective

A text from an unknown sage that every pastor has occasion to cite somewhere in the course of parish ministry is this: "The reason that fights in churches get so vicious is that the stakes are so low." Trivial issues peripheral to the mission of the church—the color of the new carpeting in the fellowship hall, dress codes for junior high dances—consume a disproportionate share of time and energy and sometimes lead to outright conflict.

While the Christian community in Corinth likely did not struggle with decorating issues, they appear to have bickered over almost everything else. A colleague who serves a large, affluent suburban parish once confessed that she finds Paul's letters to the Corinthians disturbing precisely because they are so relevant to her setting, portraying as they do a congregation whose members were far more interested in the pursuit of personal spiritual "knowledge" than the greater good of the community. Paul may have defused a crisis in the Corinthian church through his "severe letter," but it remains a community that is divided, distracted, and self-preoccupied, reconciled with neither God nor one another.

In the midst of this narcissism, competition, and conflict, Paul proclaims that far more is at stake than the "spirituality of the week." The radical new way of life offered in the gospel of Christ, he insists,

Exegetical Perspective

Today's passage falls toward the end of Paul's complex argument describing and defending his and his coworkers' ministry to the Corinthians (2:14–7:16). In this section, Paul does not argue with a series of subarguments that hang together in a deductive sequence. Instead, he comes at the issue from a number of different perspectives, using several rich and suggestive images to communicate the nature of his and his coworkers' ministry as authoritative and divinely rooted. In 6:1–13, Paul continues the direct exhortation to the Corinthians to view their ministry properly, as embodying the work, if not the very being, of Christ, and to act appropriately in response to this grace they have received.

Paul begins and ends the passage with complementary exhortations. In verse 1, he urges the Corinthians "not to accept the grace of God in vain," and in verses 11–13, he describes his and his coworkers' disposition toward the Corinthians ("our heart is wide open" and "there is no restriction in our affections"), calling on them to reciprocate ("open wide your hearts also"). The beginning and end of this passage are complementary because Paul blurs the lines between his and his coworkers' ministry and the grace that God has offered the Corinthians. In 5:18–20, Paul declares God's reconciling work through Christ and then claims

Homiletical Perspective

The preacher coming to 2 Corinthians may feel that its treasure is buried in a clay jar. To begin with, what we now have as an epistle is a composite of fragments from different documents; it lacks the unity and coherence of the apostle's other extant letter to this same community. More importantly, it is often shrill in tone and (with all due respect) self-serving in its argument. This is ostensibly the case in our passage.

So to find the homiletic gold amid the clay, it is crucial to understand what motivates Paul to speak this way. The stakes are very high, and so too his emotions. In essence, he is writing his own letter of recommendation to a church he planted, loves, and feels betrayed by. In the past he sent them a now-lost "letter of tears" (2:4; 7:8) that pained him to write and grieved them to receive. Imagining this missing document might make a wonderful opportunity for the preacher to think creatively about Paul's troubled relations with this particular community and the crises on which he feels called to speak out.

Things have gotten better since the "letter of tears," but not entirely. While the Corinthians have always been fickle in their affections—he once asked if they belonged to Cephas, to Apollos, or to him? (1 Cor 1:12)—their allegiance is now tested by unscrupulous "super-apostles" (2 Cor. 12:11), who

2 Corinthians 6:1-13

Theological Perspective

(the doctrine that one's salvation results from a combination of human effort and divine grace), but that is clearly not what Paul is saying here. Following upon Christ's sacrifice on our behalf, the apostles are bringing that message of grace to the Corinthians by means of a direct appeal—like the appeal brought by an envoy on behalf of his king—not to receive it "in vain." In other words, Paul is begging them not to respond in such a way that God's grace in Christ will have no meaningful effect on them. Paul uses the same expression elsewhere in reference to the effectiveness of the gospel message—for example, when he says that "if Christ has not been raised, then our proclamation has been in vain and your faith has been in vain" (1 Cor. 15:14), and when he assures the Corinthians that "in the Lord your labor is not in vain" (1 Cor. 15:58).

Paul introduces his main point by citing Isaiah 49:8 in the exact language of the Septuagint, which begins, *Kairo dekto*, "At a favorable time." It is no accident that this prophetic passage opens with the word *kairos*, used repeatedly in the New Testament to indicate the appointed time for God's purpose. Mark's Gospel records the first public utterance of Jesus, proclaiming the "gospel of God," in these words: "The time (*kairos*) is fulfilled, and the kingdom of God is at hand" (Mark 1:15). Taking up the key phrases of Isaiah's prophecy, Paul goes on to proclaim, "See, *now* is the favorable time; see, *now* is the day of salvation!" (6:2b). God's *kairos* is now—in the atoning death of Jesus and in the apostolic proclamation of it. And, we may surely add, in our preaching of the same gospel today.

Paul's use of what may be termed the apocalyptic *now* strikes a note that runs throughout his letters and indeed throughout the proclamation of the earliest Christian community. God's *kairos*, God's *now*, takes place at the intersection of two worlds, two aeons, two realities. They are discontinuous and incommensurable, yet they meet in the event of the cross. All of Paul's familiar dualities presuppose this central truth: old creation/new creation, first Adam/last Adam, "according to the flesh" (*kata sarka*) "according to the Spirit" (*kata pneuma*), sin/righteousness. That is the meaning of the apocalypse that he has just proclaimed to the Corinthians: "Therefore, if anyone is in Christ, he is a new creation; the old has passed away, behold, the new has come" (5:17, RSV). The church lives at the intersection of two realities, and whenever the gospel is preached and heard, that is the *kairos*, the *now* of God's salvation, foretold by the prophets and

Pastoral Perspective

demands total allegiance, even if the cost of that allegiance is the kind of suffering he himself has willingly endured: "afflictions, hardships, calamities, beatings, imprisonments" (vv. 4–5).

The list goes on, and it makes us squirm for several reasons. We squirm first because it strikes us as unseemly for Paul to draw so much attention to his own sufferings. As pastors, we are taught to make reference to our own lives only in the form of humorous anecdotes or the occasional humble confession of personal failings and foibles. To lift one's own life up as an example for others to follow or to speak of the costs we have paid for our discipleship is perceived as bragging; placing ourselves above or apart from our congregations. In challenging the narcissism of the Corinthian community, Paul's recitation of personal hardships strikes us as narcissistic in itself.

We squirm also because, in an era when fundamentalist extremism threatens the integrity of all faith traditions, we have lost our ability to distinguish between "passion" and "fanaticism." What sort of Christians will willingly, even gladly, endure beatings and imprisonments for the sake of their faith? Extremists. Fanatics. People who fly planes into buildings or bomb abortion clinics. We have become frightened of passionate faith, faith that commands total loyalty and obedience. We maintain a safe distance from Kierkegaard's precipice, embracing instead a gospel of reason and moderation.

In the service of a gospel of moderation, the role of the pastoral leader shifts from bold proclamation to helpful facilitation: we step between the followers of Apollos (committed to blue carpet in the fellowship hall) and those of Cephas (the green carpet contingent) and suggest that a muted shade of aqua might represent an acceptable compromise. "Being pastoral" is reduced to "being helpful" or "making everybody happy." Our pastoral leadership is trivialized, and the churches we serve become irrelevant to the gospel.

Paul's pastoral message to the self-preoccupied Corinthian congregation was, in effect, "Get over yourselves!" In Christ we are a new creation, a new community: the former things, including competitive social hierarchies, have passed away. True pastoral leadership lies not so much in applying balm to wounds as it does in proclaiming the good news that each person has been declared infinitely precious in God's eyes; that a life's value and worth grow not from the status attained through wealth or position in the community but from being one for whom our

Exegetical Perspective

that they (Paul and his coworkers) were given the same ministry of reconciliation as ambassadors for Christ. To act as an ambassador (*presbeuein*) in Paul's culture would mean to act on behalf of and in place of the one who sent the ambassador. So it seems that Paul claims for himself and his coworkers (1) authority over the Corinthians that shares in Christ's authority and (2) a certain efficacy of the ministry akin to the reconciling effect of Christ's actions. For the Corinthians "to accept the grace of God" corresponds to "open[ing] wide your hearts" to Paul and his coworkers.

Paul then cites Isaiah 49:8, which is part of one of the Servant passages in Second Isaiah. The passage seems to function to communicate to the Corinthians the gravity of their actions in questioning the ministry of reconciliation that Paul and his coworkers embody. What was once a future hope for God to attend to Israel through the work of the Servant has now come to fruition in Paul and his coworkers. What lies before the Corinthians is more than just a decision to recognize Paul as their founding father; it is a decision to recognize and welcome the grace that exists in their ministry of reconciliation.

Verse 4 talks of self-commendation (*synistēmi*), one of the more interesting terms in 2 Corinthians. Paul rejects this practice in 3:1 and 5:12, but it is something that he accepts or embraces in 4:2 and here in 6:4. Why the inconsistency on Paul's part? The negative practice of self-commendation in 3:1 and 5:12 happens for one's own benefit, to prove the self-possessed nature of one's authority. But the positive practice of it becomes clear just after 6:4, when Paul gives the content of his self-commendation, which includes many hardships as well as virtuous and edifying behavior. Verses 8–10 hint at the paradoxical nature of the ministry of reconciliation, one whose ministers are treated harshly and yet gain strength from it. Two lists of hardships—verses 4b–5 and verses 8–10—couch a list of virtues, culminating in the claim to wield the power of God as weapons of righteousness (vv. 6–7). The ministry they embody paradoxically takes everything from them violently, yet it gives them everything in the power of God. This central section of the passage is linked to and conditioned by two other important passages in 2 Corinthians—4:7–12 and 11:21b–30.

Second Corinthians 4:2, the other positive self-commendation that Paul makes, functions to introduce the famous "treasure in clay jars" passage in 4:7–12. This passage functions like 6:4–10, in that it

Homiletical Perspective

have done their best to deride him personally and undermine his ministry. Paul is aware that he is coming on strong: "I do not want to seem as though I am trying to frighten you with my letters" (10:9). He rants, he raves, he boasts, he dramatizes himself in ways that, even at this remove, are embarrassing to read. Can the gospel really be all about him? (How easy it is for the preacher to let insecurities rule the day, to confuse a laudable desire to speak personally to a congregation with talking about oneself.)

Second Corinthians 6 shows Paul's effort to convince the Corinthians to accept his authority and mission among them. With help from the prophet Isaiah (49:8) he appeals to Scripture to bolster his claims: now is the acceptable time for them to listen and help *him*. How? By realizing that his labor on their behalf has been faultless; that as a servant of God he has been in every way commendable; that no matter what has befallen him—and the list of disasters is long, not only here but elsewhere in this epistle (4:8–9a; 11:21b–30)—he has more than earned their trust. His whole life has become cruciform.

Insofar as style makes the man, Paul shows us the degree to which his words compel acceptance as well as attention. Many rhetorical stops are pulled out as he answers various objections raised against him. Just think for a moment about what he has been through (vv. 4–5); about how consistently he has taken overwhelming serial adversity and prayed that it would become "purity, knowledge, patience, kindness, holiness of spirit, genuine love, truthful speech" (vv. 6–7). Whatever may be his fear of appearing foolish, of violating decorum and going "too far," he does not scruple to open his heart wide. In fact, nothing else in the rest of his correspondence approaches this level of self-disclosure.

Some may have judged him "contemptible" as a speaker in person (see 10:10 and 11:6), but there can be no doubt about his ability to harness "weighty and strong" (10:10) written language to take him (and the Corinthians) where he wants to go. One can imagine, moreover, the power of someone else's delivery of this text in Corinth, as an absent Paul holds forth through another person's performance of his words. Should even such rhetoric fail, however, guilt may end up doing the job. As we read at the conclusion of this selection, Paul presents himself as a father whose affection for the Corinthians is unlimited—quite unlike their own for him! Whatever has been the case in the past, *now* is the time for them to offer nothing less than a loving

2 Corinthians 6:1-13

Theological Perspective

proclaimed by the apostles. The free, "kairotic" grace of God in Christ Jesus may light up our own worldly reality at any point in "chronological" time.

It may not be as obvious that the metaphor of diplomacy continues in the following verses (6:3–10), but it is there, at least implicitly. For Paul, as God's emissary, having delivered the message and made his appeal, must now present his credentials. It can hardly escape any reader of 2 Corinthians that Paul is defending his apostolic vocation and message from those who have called them into question. In order to grasp the theological point of our passage, it is not necessary to delve into never-ending speculation about just who Paul's opponents were or what they were teaching, for the issue here concerns Paul's own apostolic credentials. He opens (vv. 3–4a) by saying that the apostles "commend" or "recommend" themselves, and proceeds to unroll a catalog of specifics, arranged in four groups. The first (vv. 4b–5) stresses endurance in the face of hardships; the second (vv. 6–7a) lists eight qualities or gifts of apostolic ministry; the third (vv. 7b–8a) is harder to categorize generally but consists of three phrases beginning with the preposition *dia* ("through"). The fourth and final group (vv. 8b–10), composed of seven pairs of contrasting terms, each introduced by "as" (*hōs*), underscores the radical antithesis between the old aeon and the new: from the false perspective of this world, the apostles appear as impostors and nobodies who are dying, punished, sorrowful, poor, and possess nothing; but the apocalyptic light of the gospel reveals them in fact to be truthful and well-known, ones who are living, rejoicing, bestowing riches, and possessing everything.

In the final verses of our passage (vv. 11–13), Paul appeals directly and intimately to the Corinthians—addressing them by name and (shifting to the first-person singular) calling them his "children"—pleading with them to open their hearts to the gospel and be reconciled to God. The church, in acknowledging the canon of Scripture, has accepted Paul's apostolic credentials, so that today's Christians, like those of ancient Corinth, are pledged to hear his appeal and take it to heart.

GARRETT GREEN

Pastoral Perspective

Redeemer died upon the cross; and that true joy grows not from the absence of hardship but from knowing God's grace even within that hardship.

Paul is speaking to the critical issues of how we create and sustain genuine Christian community and how authority is expressed responsibly within that community. Christian community is not formed or maintained through holding tastes and interests in common, and authority within Christian community is not to be confused with popularity. In their founding essay for *The Ekklesia Project*, Stanley Hauerwas and Michael Budde wrote: "Thomas Aquinas claimed that our ultimate destiny is to be made friends with God—a view that obviously challenges the superficial understanding of friendship that assumes friends 'like' one another. Charity, according to Aquinas, is that agent that makes such friendship possible. To be so formed does not mean that we all share a common 'experience,' but—more important—that we share common judgments. Charity, after all, is the deepest form of knowledge."[1]

Paul seeks to make of the Corinthian church a community defined by mutual charity rather than by competition for spiritual "knowledge," and he demonstrates a model of authority based not upon superior personal wisdom, but rather upon willingness to surrender comfort, safety, and personal ego (no small challenge for Paul!) in service to the gospel. Paul, however imperfectly, seeks to embody "servant leadership." Servant leadership does not claim personal power, but rather seeks to give itself away in Christian love for others. It does not employ threats or manipulation, but only the proper tools of charity: "patience, kindness, holiness of spirit, genuine love, truthful speech, and the power of God. (v. 6)" How does a pastoral leader help to build a genuine Christian community, fully reconciled with God and with one another? By loving that community unconditionally ("There is no restriction in our affections") with a love that will risk speaking the unpopular truth that the community needs to hear ("We have spoken frankly to you Corinthians," vv. 11–12).

If Aquinas is correct in saying that it is our destiny to be made friends with God, we must practice being friends to others who also seek to be made friends with God. For Christians there can be no such friendships unless they are rooted in charity.

JOHN T. MCFADDEN

---

1. Hauerwas and Budde, *The Ekklesia Project: A School for Subversive Friendships* (Eugene, OR: Wipf & Stock, 2000), 1–2.

describes the nature of the ministry of Paul and his coworkers as one that brings suffering and yet is effective because of that suffering. Paul uses the image of treasure in clay jars to show that the outward appearance of weakness is really the source of the Corinthians' life as a community, because it shows that their ministry is of the same nature as Christ's ministry. Christ's sufferings on behalf of humanity actually display God's love and give life; so also for Paul and his coworkers. They have become the embodiment of Christ for the Corinthians, so their sufferings give life to the community and actually display the love of God as Christ's sufferings did.

Second Corinthians 11:21b–30 lists many of the same sufferings that we find in 6:4b–5, 8–10. Again, Paul is arguing that the nature of their ministry is one that looks weak because of their experiences of suffering, in contrast to those "superapostles" whose ministry looks strong and authoritative because of their outward appearance and works of power. But Paul lists his sufferings as a résumé of sorts, one that proves one's ministry's real power because it reverses the traditional categories of power and weakness according to the model of Christ, whose weakness by suffering and dying on the cross was ultimately revelatory of God's power to overcome death. This is not to say that Paul and his coworkers seek out suffering; this would be masochism. But through their great endurance (*en hypomonē pollē*, 6:4) of it, they share in Christ's ministry in their very bodies (cf. 4:10, "carrying in the body the death of Jesus") and so the authority of their ministry is actually more authentic than the superapostles' authority.

In 6:1–13 Paul asserts his and his coworkers' legitimacy as ministers of Christ while, at the same time, he shows their care for the community by offering their affection and talking to them as beloved children. He mingles affection and careful argumentation about the nature of their ministry in a complex attempt to accept the grace embodied in their ministry.

STEPHEN P. AHEARNE-KROLL

filial response in kind. "In return—I speak as to children—open wide your hearts also" (v. 13).

After identifying all that is problematic in this reading, the preacher might well want to choose another text from among this Sunday's options! On the other hand, what if he or she were to give the apostle precisely what he is asking for—an open heart? Might the point be to acknowledge that Paul, like us, is a clay jar, a man often at wit's end and no one's notion of perfection (despite his standing among the Corinthians as founding father)? At the same time, precisely as an earthen vessel, he stands to offer a gift quite beyond himself. "We have this treasure in clay jars," Paul says, "so that it may be made clear that this extraordinary power belongs to God and does not come from us" (2 Cor. 4:7).

In other words, rather than turning to today's lection as a model for preaching about one's own ministry, why not call attention to the passion and sincerity with which Paul gives himself to his vocation, the exuberance with which he not only speaks frankly, but in effect gives himself away? Here is no Stoic philosopher keeping himself in reserve or rising above it all. Nor does he use his verbal brilliance merely to manipulate the Corinthians' emotions so that they might treat him better. Rather, as he says in the previous chapter—using a "we" that also encompasses his coworkers—"we are ambassadors for Christ, since God is making his appeal through us; we entreat you on behalf of Christ, be reconciled to God" (5:20). Whereas the lectionary selection for this Sunday seems to be all about Paul, appeal to the larger setting of the epistle can put the emphasis where it belongs—on the work of God in Christ. The preacher owes the apostle as sympathetic presentation of his message as possible; in the end, however, we pay attention to Paul to look beyond him.

PETER S. HAWKINS

Mark 4:35-41

35On that day, when evening had come, he said to them, "Let us go across to the other side." 36And leaving the crowd behind, they took him with them in the boat, just as he was. Other boats were with him. 37A great windstorm arose, and the waves beat into the boat, so that the boat was already being swamped. 38But he was in the stern, asleep on the cushion; and they woke him up and said to him, "Teacher, do you not care that we are perishing?" 39He woke up and rebuked the wind, and said to the sea, "Peace! Be still!" Then the wind ceased, and there was a dead calm. 40He said to them, "Why are you afraid? Have you still no faith?" 41And they were filled with great awe and said to one another, "Who then is this, that even the wind and the sea obey him?"

Theological Perspective

Three Weeks of Gospel Readings on Jesus' Kingship in Mark. Who is Jesus? What is the nature of his authority? What is the larger meaning of the claims he makes for himself, and the speculation of those who interact with him, as seen by the Gospel writer? Beginning this Sunday and stretching over two more weeks, we are presented with a collection of miracle stories intended to provide different insights onto a single, pressing question: What is the nature of Jesus' kingship? Within the framework of these stories the Gospel writer also suggests the source of the authority from which Jesus' kingship derives, his obedient faith.

How Is Jesus a King? Answer 1: Jesus Is King of the Created Order. The story, one of two calming-the-sea accounts in Mark, is notable for the contrast between the quiet confidence of Jesus and the agonized worry of the disciples. The difference between them is the quality of faith they have. Jesus is brought into the boat "just as he was"; the height of his authority requires nothing beyond the depth of his faith, no trappings, no outward symbols of power, no implements of coercion. He lies asleep, undisturbed by the tumult, while the disciples respond to the energy of the storm by expending energy of their own, vainly imagining human exertion can prove the equal of nature.

Pastoral Perspective

Fear. The visceral response of Jesus' terrified disciples in a frail storm-tossed boat resonates both in the individual lives of Christians and in their corporate life in congregations and civic communities. We are afraid of the "wind and waves" that assail our fragile vessels—our lives, our churches, our cities, and nations. We fear disapproval, rejection, failure, meaningless, illness, and of course, we fear death—our own death, the death of those we love, and the potential demise of the communities we cherish.

The overshadowing pastoral reality that these verses from the fourth chapter of Mark present to preacher and congregation is that of faithful disciples overcome with fear and Jesus' loving yet firm response to their debilitating anxiety. The sea, the storm, and the fragile craft that carry our Lord and his followers across the Sea of Galilee offer evocative metaphorical images of our life journey—the perils of some passages, the profound vulnerability of the craft that bears us on our way, and our longing for One who calms both us and the storm. Some congregations may indeed need to be given permission to pull this text into their own context in such a way, rather than simply reading it as an ancient natural miracle story.

Fear is confronted in this story, but not by a sudden burst of courage or resolve on the part of the

Exegetical Perspective

The immediate context of our reading today is the parable of the sower (4:1–34). After Jesus claims that insight into this parable and its implications for understanding the kingdom of God is limited to those "on the inside" (vv. 10–12), he nonetheless finds himself having to explain the meaning of the parable to *his* insiders, the disciples (vv. 13–20, 33–34). The subsequent encounter with nature's wreaking havoc and the ensuing miracle further reveal the shortcomings of these very same insiders.

An Evening at Sea (vv. 35–36). After a long day of teaching the crowds, Jesus needs a break. He initiates a trip across the Sea of Galilee. Although Jesus initiates the trip, he is now in the hands of his disciples, who include at least four experienced fishermen (see Mark 1:16–20). After dismissing the crowd, the disciples "took him." He is now in their realm. Yet they are not alone, for "other boats were with them." Thus the entourage of Jesus' disciples is growing.

A Great Storm (vv. 37–38). Soon, a great (*megalē*) windstorm arises, so great that the waves crash against the boat carrying Jesus and his disciples. Soon enough ("already"), water begins to fill up the boat. Such a vivid description speaks to the severity of the situation. Not even the experienced fishermen

Homiletical Perspective

Jesus' stilling the storm on the Sea of Galilee is one of the most familiar stories in the Gospels. Many can recall the event in children's storybook Bibles or pictures on the walls of Sunday school classrooms. Jesus stands on the edge of the boat with his arms outstretched over the whitecaps of the raging sea. With that image in mind, this text most often is interpreted as a miracle story demonstrating the divine power of Jesus. While it is that, it is much more. By probing more deeply into its language and imagery, we discover a number of insights for the community of faith today.

The events recorded in this section of Mark's Gospel take place on alternate sides of the Sea of Galilee. Since the most direct route between the shores was across the sea, there are several references to boat crossings in chapters 4 and 5. Scholars have noted, however, that Jesus' command to the disciples in 4:35, "Let us go across to the other side," indicates more than simply a change of venue. The "other side" represents Gentile territory, the "country of the Gerasenes" (5:1). This is Jesus' first foray in Mark to what might be considered a dangerous, even inappropriate destination. Thus, Jesus' venture into such a foreign region across the sea is a deliberate demonstration of his claim that his mission extends beyond the Jews. By carrying his ministry into

Mark 4:35-41

Theological Perspective

Elements of the literary form carry theological weight. The bruising storm is a recasting of the watery chaos from which creation is brought forth by God. It is the prerogative of the divine Creator to bring order out of the water's chaos. Further, unrestrained water is death-dealing; water contained within its limits is life-giving. Thus Jesus is to be seen through the lens of this account as *doing things reserved to God*—ordering chaos, conquering the force of death, assuring the endurance of life. "Jesus has shown godlike superiority over the elements,"[1] and from this we are meant to surmise the plain answer to the disciples' reply: "Who then is this?"

Jesus' demonstration of this authority and the disciples' reply to it point toward an embedded theological question: What is the source of the "godlike" authority by which Jesus effects control over the created order? An active debate has brewed for decades among Markan scholars as to the significance of the alternative messianic titles "Son of God" and "Son of Man" in the text, with particular focus on the potential significance of the Greco-Roman motif of the "divine man" (*theios anēr*) and the notion that the use of the title "Son of Man" may be intended to "correct" a prevailing cultural notion regarded as potentially heretical.[2] A different approach centers on a contrast between the faith of Jesus and the fear of the disciples. Jesus' faith gives him peace in the midst of chaos; his command of the elements is expressed as a rebuke of the elements, which we may see as proclaiming an absolute faith in the Creator's command of creation. In this absolute faith lies both his complete obedience to God *and* the source of his godlike authority.[3] Jesus' question to the disciples cuts to the core issue: "Have you still *no faith*?"

The response to this demonstration of Jesus' kingship on the part of the disciples (and, by extension, the whole of the church seated in the nave for the sermon) is also theologically fraught. We expect the response of Psalm 107, the psalm appointed for today: "He made the storm be still, and the waves of the sea were hushed. Then they were glad" (vv. 29–30). But the disciples are distinctly *not* glad; in the text for today they are "filled with great awe" (v. 41), but the KJV's "they feared exceedingly"

Pastoral Perspective

disciples. In the course of the storm, they never themselves pull themselves together. They do not, at least not on their own, discover inner resources they did not know they had. Rather, it is Jesus who calms both them and the storm with the power of his presence. Faithful proclamation of this text will, therefore, not so much challenge hearers to discover forgotten courage in themselves as it will invite them to turn again to the Lord of wind and wave, the one we trust to be more powerful than both Galilean storms and the storms that rage in our lives.

It is important to note that Jesus never says, "There is nothing to be afraid of." The Galilean storm was doubtless indeed fearsome, as are the "wind and waves" that threaten us. Rather, Jesus asks, "Why are you afraid? Have you still no faith?" To help understand this distinction, imagine a scene such as this. A child awakens in the dark of the night, terrified at some dream that has disturbed child-sleep, frightened of some phantom hiding in the bedroom closet. A mother rushes into the bedroom and scoops the little one into her arms and sits in a chair. She wipes sweaty locks off her child's forehead, caresses his hair, rocks her gently, and then she whispers what a thousand mothers have whispered since the beginning of time, "Hush now, there's nothing to be afraid of." The question these comforting words raise is simply this: "Is the mother telling the whole truth to her child? Is there really nothing to be afraid of?"

Although we often confuse them, saying, "there's nothing to be afraid of" is a very different thing from saying, "do not be afraid." The hard truth is that fearsome things are very real: isolation, pain, illness, meaninglessness, rejection, losing one's job, money problems, failure, illness, and death. As we grow in faith, we come to understand that even though such fearsome things are very real, they do not have the last word. They do not have ultimate power over us, because reigning over this world of fearsome things is a God who is mightier than they. Time and again in Scripture the word is, "Do not be afraid." It is, you might say, the first and the last word of the gospel. It is the word the angels speak to the terrified shepherds and the word spoken at the tomb when the women discover it empty: "Do not be afraid." Not because there are no fearsome things on the sea of our days, not because there are no storms, fierce winds, or waves, but rather, because God is with us.

The novelist Emily Brontë lived and wrote in a rectory set in the bleak moors of Yorkshire. She lived

---

1. Larry W. Hurtado, *Lord Jesus Christ: Devotion to Jesus in Earliest Christianity* (Grand Rapids: Eerdmans, 2003), 286.
2. An excellent summary of this debate is found in Jack Dean Kingsbury, *The Christology of Mark's Gospel* (Philadelphia: Fortress Press, 1983), 25–45.
3. See Javier-José Marín, *The Christology of Mark: Does Mark's Christology Support the Chalcedonian Formula "Truly Man and Truly God"?* (Bern: Peter Lang, 1991), 236–38.

can do anything about it. They turn to Jesus, presumably because of the powers that he has shown in healing sick people and exorcising demons. Maybe he can help in this situation. However, Jesus is sound asleep on a boat cushion at the rear part of the boat. Perhaps this negatively impacts the faith of the disciples, or perhaps their faith is not as strong as that of Jesus, who can sleep through this great storm, a sign of his faith in the face of calamity. Mark alludes to the story of Jonah, who also sleeps through a storm at sea (Jonah 1:5–6). Like the crew of the ship Jonah travels on, the disciples cry to Jesus, after waking him up in the midst of their panic. "Teacher, do you not care that we are perishing?" (4:38b) The deep, calm sleep of Jesus is contrasted with the utter destruction and death that this storm can bring.

A Great Calm (v. 39). In the Jonah story, the ship's crew awakens Jonah and implores that he pray to his God (Jonah 1:6). Here in Mark, the disciples awaken Jesus and rebuke him for his apparent lack of concern, given his sound sleep. (In Matthew's Gospel, the disciples implore Jesus to "save" them [Matt. 8:25]; in Luke, they inform him of their impending doom, without deploring Jesus' lack of concern [Luke 8:24a].) In Mark, as in Matthew and Luke, Jesus does not stop to pray. He immediately "rises up, rebukes the wind and tells the sea to shut up and be silenced" (my translation). Both "rebuke" (*epitimēsen*) and "be silent" (*phimōthēti*) are used against a demon earlier in the Gospel (Mark 1:25). Thus Mark invokes the Jewish and Greco-Roman mythological dimensions of storms at sea as ruled by demons, gods, and sea monsters. In the Psalms we read about YHWH as the Lord of land and sea (see Ps. 104:3–4; 107:24–32). Jesus too has power over nature and over its causes and effects. The vicious wind has caused a violent storm on the sea. Jesus rebukes one and silences the other. The result is that the wind "grows weary" and the sea exhibits a "great calm" (*galēnē megalē*). By the word of Jesus, a "great storm" becomes a "great calm."

Fear or Faith? (v. 40).[1] Once the storm abates, Jesus turns to his disciples and asks two fundamental questions that lie at the heart of this pericope: "Why are you afraid? Do you not yet have faith?" (v. 40). Again, the challenge in the parable of the Sower for

1. A phrase I borrow from Mary Ann Tolbert, *Sowing the Gospel: Mark's World in Literary Historical Perspective* (Minneapolis: Fortress Press, 1989), 164–72.

Gentile territory, Jesus reaches out to the strangers, the others, even the enemies of the house of Israel. If Jesus stands as the example for the church today, this story raises for us the question, who are the strangers, the others whom we have neglected? Who are the people and where are the places left untouched by Christian hospitality due to ancient hatreds and fears? The gospel Jesus proclaims and demonstrates represents good news for all, transcending the human characteristics we use to separate ourselves from others. This is an especially poignant and timely message for the church today as it struggles with issues of inclusion.

On the way to the "other side," the boat encounters "a great windstorm" (v. 37), not an unusual occurrence on the often-tempestuous Sea of Galilee. The disciples who accompany Jesus in the boat, especially those who fish for a living, are accustomed to the mercurial nature of the water. What they are *not* accustomed to is having a passenger who *might* have the power to protect them from harm. At this point in Mark, Jesus' identity is still unclear and the disciples' faith in him still tenuous. The event, then, becomes a moment of clarity despite the chaos of the storm: clarity as to Jesus' true identity and power, and clarity as to the desperate need of the disciples—and us—for the calming, healing power that only Jesus can provide.

In their fear and desperation, the disciples wake Jesus and raise an accusatory plea: "Teacher, do you not care that we are perishing?" (v. 38). Every preacher has heard a similar cry, even from people of faith. The natural disasters of hurricanes, tsunamis, and floods of the past few years, the tragedies caused by terrorist attacks, war, and inexplicable acts of violence, and the pain of various kinds of personal suffering leave us crying out to God, "Do you not care that we are perishing?" As the one called to give voice to the cries of the people, the preacher can name our fears and our sense of betrayal in the face of what seems to be the silence of God. Only when we have articulated those feelings—and the anger beneath them—can we be still and listen for a word from God.

Jesus speaks such a word when he rebukes the wind and the waves saying, "Peace! Be still!" (v. 39). After that, the text tells us, "the wind ceased, and there was a dead calm" (v. 39). This is hardly the first or only instance of the power of God's word, here embodied in Jesus, to do great things. God spoke and brought into being all creation out of the formless void. God spoke again, and God's word became flesh

Mark 4:35-41

Theological Perspective

is perhaps closer to the sense of the Greek *phobos megas* ("they were afraid with great fear").

Here is the conundrum: Jesus has godlike authority over the primordial chaos; he is king of the created order. Yet the immediate response to this demonstration of kingly power is not joy, not praise, not acclaim, but *fear*. Theologically, the significance of this jarring reaction is the power of Jesus' demonstration of kingly power to show up in stark contrast our *lack* of faith. Mark's anthropology, always illustrated primarily in the personalities and actions of the disciples, is distinctly and uncomfortably thin on charity here. The reaction of the storm-tossed faithful in Psalm 107 is notable by contrast: They are *glad*, they are *thankful*, they *extol* (praise) God's exercise of power on their behalf.

This is the response of faith. The disciples, for their part, are scarcely celebratory. Their reaction shows up a particular aspect of Mark's understanding of *those yet to come to faith* that may be seen in comparison with those who meet God's power with the response of faith—and, in its perfect expression, the absolute obedience of Jesus' faith, which from the ground of its obedience speaks fully the power of God in the created order. (This theme of unbelief will come around again in the Gospel text for Proper 9, p. 212.)

Note, in closing, that the rising interest of Christian theologians in ecological stewardship as an appropriate concern of the faithful suggests a nascent urgency in recapturing Mark's claim for Jesus as the king of the created order. Here, and elsewhere, in his interactions with the natural world, Jesus proceeds with gentle authority. He rebukes that which threatens life; his word to the storm does not overpower, but gives what it calls for: peace. Faithful discipleship in the pattern of Jesus' kingship over the created order must be characterized by the same qualities.

MARK D. W. EDINGTON

Pastoral Perspective

a grim tragedy with her half-demented father and alcoholic brother. Nevertheless, she was able to write words like these: "No coward soul is mine, no trembler in the world's storm-troubled sphere. I see Heaven's glories shine, and faith shines equal, arming me from fear."[1]

Instead of saying, "There's nothing to be afraid of," the whole truth would be for the mother comforting her frightened child to say, "Don't be afraid, because you are not alone." The easy part of the truth, which every child figures out sooner or later, is that some things that frighten us are real and some are not. But the rest of the truth, the deeper truth that only faith in the God who raised Jesus from the grave can teach, is that even though there are real and fearsome things in this life, they need not paralyze us; they need not have dominion over us; they need not own us, because we are not alone in the boat.

A scene near the end of John Bunyan's classic allegorical novel *The Pilgrim's Progress* finds the chief character, Christian, the archetype of a person struggling to lead a life of faith, nearing the end of his symbolic journey. This journey requires him to cross a great and fearsome river. He is desperately afraid. Together with his friend Hopeful, they wade into the waters with trepidation. Bunyan has Christian cry out, "I sink in deep Waters; the Billows go over my head, all His waves go over me." Hopeful replies with what may be among the most grace-filled words in all of literature; "Be of good cheer, my Brother, I feel the bottom, and it is good . . ."[2]

MICHAEL L. LINDVALL

---

1. Emily Brontë, "No Coward Soul Is Mine," January 2, 1846.
2. John Bunyan, *The Pilgrim's Progress* (1678), p. 1, sec. x.

seed to land on fertile ground (4:20) seems to be before the disciples. However, their faith still needs to grow. They act as if the seed of faith has fallen on rocky ground, such that "when trouble or persecution arises," their faith falters (4:16–17). Questions about faith and fear plague the disciples throughout Mark's narrative (see 5:36; 6:50; 10:32; 16:8). The Gospel of Mark ends with a note of fearfulness in the heretofore faithful women at the tomb (16:8). Such an ending challenges Mark's readers with the question of where their faith will take them—to paralysis or to action. Here in Mark 4:40, the question lies before the disciples on the boat after they have witnessed a horrific storm becalmed by the command of Jesus, their teacher: Will you exercise faith or fear?

Who Is This Man? (v. 41). The disciples' response, as they speak among themselves rather than directly to Jesus, is telling. They are "not yet" ready to come down completely on the side of faith. The narrator is hopeful that one day they will, as he emphasizes that not yet do they have enough faith. Nonetheless, a literal translation reads that the disciples remain "fearful with a great fear" (v. 41a). So instead of the "great storm" that was turned into a "great calm" becoming a sign of "great faith" for the disciples, it becomes a source of "great fear" (*phobon megan*). Translators and commentators have tried to minimize this reaction by speaking about their great "awe" or respect for what Jesus has done. Nonetheless, there is genuine fear about the meaning of Jesus' action, because the disciples, at this stage, do not really understand it, or him. They ask one another, "Who is this, that even the wind and the sea obey him?" (v. 41b). Yet even Peter almost immediately fails to understand the full implications of his confession (see 8:30–33). Even with the proof before their very eyes, the disciples still exhibit fear rather than confidence, just like the women at the tomb at the very end of the Gospel (16:8). This "fear factor" represents a challenge to Mark's readers. Will they respond to questions about the identity of Jesus with faith or fear?

EFRAÍN AGOSTO

in Jesus Christ. In between, God's word called a nation into being and inspired prophets who guided that nation. It is easy to forget that God's all-powerful word is still spoken amid the noise and chaos of our lives and world. And like Jesus' word of peace spoken over the raging storm, God's word still destroys the forces that threaten to do us harm and still calms our deepest fears. "One little word," the word "above all earthly powers," as Martin Luther's great hymn, "A Mighty Fortress Is Our God," puts it so well, can "fell" whatever darkness threatens to undo us.

The particular word spoken by Jesus in this text is a word of peace and stillness. It is a word we need to hear every day of our lives. The preacher need not look far for individual and corporate "storms" that call for a word of peace. Like the disciples, we are challenged in the midst of those storms to rediscover our faith in the promise of God's powerful word. The question Jesus poses to the disciples is the question he continues to pose to us in our moments of despair: "Why are you afraid? Have you still no faith?" (v. 40). The disciples are rendered speechless in the face of Jesus' great work. They respond with awe and with a glimmer of understanding of the nature and power of Jesus.

A photograph taken shortly after Hurricane Katrina struck New Orleans in the fall of 2005 shows the devastation of a cemetery in the historic district of the city, with trees toppled, debris covering the ground, and several burial vaults broken and smashed. But in the middle of the devastation, untouched by the storm, stands a statue of the risen Christ, arms extended wide, offering a benediction of calm amid the chaos. Such is the image conveyed by this text: the image of Christ with his arms extended wide over the chaos of our lives and world, saying, "Peace! Be still!"

BEVERLY ZINK-SAWYER

Wisdom of Solomon 1:13-15; 2:23-24

¹³ because God did not make death,
and he does not delight in the death of the living.
¹⁴For he created all things so that they might exist;
the generative forces of the world are wholesome,
and there is no destructive poison in them,
and the dominion of Hades is not on earth.
¹⁵For righteousness is immortal.
....

²³ for God created us for incorruption,
and made us in the image of his own eternity,
²⁴but through the devil's envy death entered the world,
and those who belong to his company experience it.

Theological Perspective

These few verses take us to the heart of the Wisdom of Solomon and its key themes of death and immortality. Much as the book appears to present a timeless set of proverbs and abstract aspirations, the theological issues are likely prompted by some rather urgent and very practical concerns of the Jewish community in Alexandria, Egypt, living under Roman rule, probably in the period 30 BCE–40 CE. Tensions with the Greeks lie behind the comparison of justice and injustice, of the Egyptians and the righteous, as well as the status of a human after death.

Our lectionary texts represent a beautiful example of the way in which theology happens, emerging when a new conversation between tradition and context becomes necessary. The Wisdom of Solomon is a valuable source for understanding the way Jewish thought adapted under Hellenistic influence during the first centuries BCE and CE. Here we find reflection on the concepts of immortality and incorruptibility—common themes among pagan Greek writers—now nuanced in a Jewish document. The work affirms unambiguously the idea of human immortality, but explains it in terms of the covenant faithfulness of God to the just. It is not that all humans possess an inherent expectation of or right to immortality. Although all people are created in the image of God and thus bear the possibility of

Pastoral Perspective

"The one true freedom in life," William Sloane Coffin observed, "is to come to terms with death, and as early as possible, for death is an event that embraces all our lives."[1] Death also takes center stage in the life of the church. Christian theology has, at various times and among various traditions, come to terms with death in a variety of ways. Christian theology often rejects the Greek dualism that treats the body as a temporary container for an immortal soul. A seminary professor hammered this point home ("On Saturday, Jesus was dead, dead, dead!"), emphasizing that Christians do not place their hope in the immortality of the soul, but in the power of the resurrection. Indeed, in the liturgy of my tradition, the funeral service carries the obviously didactic label, "A Service of Witness to the Resurrection."

In contrast, Wisdom of Solomon claims that the immortality of the soul is the hope of the righteous.[2] Indeed, righteousness, itself, "is immortal" (1:15). While the text affirms that God is responsible for the gift of life beyond death, this affirmation is expressed in the Greek dualistic world that created it.

---

1. William Sloane Coffin, *Credo* (Louisville, KY: Westminster John Knox Press, 2004), 167.
2. On Greek philosophy's influence on Wisdom of Solomon's view of the immortality of the soul, see John J. Collins, *Jewish Wisdom in the Hellenistic Age* (Louisville, KY: Westminster John Knox Press, 1997), 185–87.

Exegetical Perspective

Boundary Points. During the Hellenistic period Alexandria, Egypt, was a center for Jewish culture. The social context of Judaism in Diaspora, especially in as cosmopolitan a place as Alexandria, invited, almost coerced the Jewish intelligentsia to respond to the operative Greek Hellenistic philosophies. There were a number of attempts to depict Judaism as a precursor if not always a soul mate of Greek philosophy. The Wisdom of Solomon is found among the deuterocanonical books.

The deuterocanonical books were for many years labeled with the pejorative term "apocrypha," or "hidden things." In the West the books in this section are traditionally in order: Tobit, Judith, Additions to the Book of Esther, Wisdom of Solomon, Ecclesiasticus (Wisdom of Jesus ben Sirach), Baruch, Letter of Jeremiah, Prayer of Azariah and the Song of Three Jews, Susanna, Bel and the Dragon, and 1 and 2 Maccabees. Pope Damasus in the fourth century CE asked Jerome to translate the Bible into one authorized translation for all the people. The translation was given the name "Vulgate" because it was the common translation. Jerome translated not only the Hebrew Bible but also the books of the Septuagint available to him. He published these works with prefaces that made clear that they were not organically linked with the Hebrew Bible.

Homiletical Perspective

The lection from the Wisdom of Solomon paints a compelling vision of human life, shaped in the image of the Divine at creation, and bound for enduring relationship with the Divine. The opening chapters of the book contrast this vision with the perspective of the wicked or ungodly, given voice in 1:16–2:20. While these verses are omitted from the lection, they provide an essential backdrop for understanding the view commended by Wisdom's author. For this reason, the preacher may wish to follow the shape of the text itself and explore Wisdom's positive vision of life by first describing its contrast. Listeners will likely find these descriptions, written more than twenty centuries ago, surprisingly resonant with the contemporary human experience.

The philosophy of the ungodly is grounded in the belief that life happens by accident. Humans are born by chance, and life is short and sorrowful. In the end, bodies will dissolve into ashes, and names will be forgotten. Therefore, they say, live it up. Eat rich food and drink costly wine. Pour on the rich perfumes, and gather rosebuds while you may. But, Wisdom observes, the pursuit of these youthful pleasures is simply a form of escapism. It serves to mask and deny an underlying despair that *this is it.* This brief life, full of pain and injustice, is all humans get. That despair leads beyond simple

Wisdom of Solomon 1:13-15; 2:23-24

Theological Perspective

reflecting the divine life eternally, it is the ethical content of their life that determines their status in the afterlife.

This leads to a strongly dualistic mentality: the life of justice and virtue leads to immortality, whereas the life of injustice and wickedness leads to death (Wis. 1:16; 2:24; 3:4; 5:17–23; 6:17–20). It also implies an individualist ethic whereby each person is judged on the merits of his or her own decisions and actions. Yet justice and injustice are understood in classical Hebrew terms that are practical and relational: determined chiefly by one's attitude and behavior toward the weak. This is far from the more abstract Greek approach. As the intervening verses between our two texts expound (2:12–20), the wicked are those who misuse the gift of power to oppress the widow, the aged, the poor, and the just.

This is the *wisdom* of *Solomon*. In fact the focus is on the *wisdom* of God that, from creation, describes the structures of the cosmos and may also, through revelation, shape the structures of the human heart. This continues the sapiential tradition found elsewhere in the Old Testament (e.g., esp. Prov. 8), where wisdom is personified. Wisdom is not an entity separate from God, yet wisdom functions to describe the way God shaped creation and continues to shape the world. As in Proverbs, here *Solomon* represents the human ideal: someone naturally gifted in wisdom, yet also growing in this gift as he continues to grow in and be shaped by God. He was king, yet he chose the wisdom of God over wealth or fame. He serves as a paradigmatic example, therefore, of "the just." This explains the association of this wisdom with Solomon—especially in the middle section of the book—and the title of the book in the Septuagint. (Note, however, that the Vulgate calls the book simply "Wisdom."). Far from a statement concerning authorship, this affirms Jewish tradition concerning the human potential for wisdom under God, which is exhibited and illustrated in the exceptional figure of Solomon. The Old Testament views the human role of a king as a kind of moral exemplar —a person who, ideally at least, so embodies the characteristics of God that he is a faithful channel of God's rule over Israel (see, for example, Ps. 72). Solomon excels in this role, particularly by embodying the wisdom of God.

In pointing to God's endowment of Solomon, these texts represent a critique and redefinition of Greek notions of immortality. The Greeks held to the (Platonic) idea of a preexistent soul that enters (and is frequently debased by entering) a (personal, created)

Pastoral Perspective

This Platonic notion, less well accepted by official church teaching, is nonetheless more prevalent among grieving people in the pews. Standing next to Mrs. Jones at the open casket of her husband, the pastor may witness to the resurrection with all of the theological fervor she can muster, but Mrs. Jones will tell her straightforwardly that Mr. Jones is no longer in the casket. He has "gone on" someplace to be with the Lord. Mrs. Jones, of course, cares little about Platonic dualism; she simply affirms God's life-giving act in the presence of death. Taking a cue from this text, we might learn to recognize theological wisdom spoken by people in the pews, even when this wisdom is not articulated through the authorized language of the church.

In its Hellenistic framework, the text makes at least two claims: (1) death is not part of God's creation, and (2) the righteous will not experience it. "The dominion of Hades is not on earth" (1:14), and "through the devil's envy death entered the world" (2:24). Departing from Coffin's approach of acceptance, Wisdom of Solomon argues that death is the tool of God's enemy. Captivated by the finality of death, the "ungodly" approach life as though revelry, oppression of the poor and vulnerable, and violence against the innocent are of no consequence: "for our allotted time is the passing of a shadow, and there is no return from our death" (2:5). In other biblical texts (see Ecclesiastes) it is assumed that the awareness of death leads toward a savoring of what is good and true in life. Many a funeral homily, it must be admitted, charts this course. But here the awareness of death leads to unrighteousness, as the cry of carpe diem (seize the day!) takes on a dark, oppressive character.

In many ways, this elevation of the spiritual over against the temporality of the material is alarming to hear against the backdrop of North American religiosity. American history is replete with examples of oppression (slavery, the subjugation of women, wars that go unchallenged, etc.) that is nurtured when the church says to its people that life after death is of highest importance. But what happens when the scales are reversed and the material—what is here and now—becomes the almost exclusive concern of communities? Recently, I caught a bit of a sermon of a well-known contemporary televangelist. The sermon began with a biblical text, but soon shifted to discussions of tax-deferred annuities, IRA contributions, and the touching story of an entrepreneur whose faith made her wealthy and successful. Midway through the sermon, I was

Exegetical Perspective

However, over the course of time copyists deleted the prefaces and placed the deuterocanonical books where they thought best. Like many of the deuterocanonicals, the Wisdom of Solomon exists only in Greek and Latin manuscripts. The themes and language indicate a possible date as early as the second century BCE but possibly as late as the first century CE.

The Hellenistic Jews of the Greco-Roman period lived in a colonial world ruled by a single empire. The cultural work of any religious literature wrestles with its cultural and political context. This is all the more complicated during a colonial situation where the rhetorical exchanges of power dominate literary genres. Stoic and Platonic notions as well as allegorical interpretation of Scripture shape the Wisdom of Solomon, not only the genre but the subject matter. The Greek Platonic view of immortality had a significant history prior to the Hellenistic age, but the central role of immortality in the Wisdom of Solomon represents a new departure in Hellenistic Judaism.[1]

The Wisdom of Solomon consists of three parts. The first part (chaps. 1–5) focuses on righteousness and immortality. The second part (chaps. 6–9) addresses the nature of wisdom. The final part (chaps. 10–19) outlines wisdom's role in the early history of Israel. Throughout, the writer uses the three movements of the text to adapt the basic tenets of Stoicism (world soul) and Platonism (preexistence and immortality of the soul) in order to demonstrate the superiority of Jewish wisdom.[2]

Between the Devil and the Deep Blue Sea. The passage begins in verse 12 with the admonition toward immortality rather than a choice for mortality and death. The rationale for such an admonition is based on a view of the work of God. In other words, God did not create death, and the believer should therefore not traffic in death. That God did not create death affirms the goodness of God over the sovereignty of God (1:13). The idea that, for God to be good, God must eschew any appearance of being a direct cause of evil is a central doctrine in Platonism and Stoicism as well as Philo. This idea makes clear that the writer of the Wisdom of Solomon works at the intersection of Greek philosophy and Hebrew Scripture.

1. David S. Winston, *The Wisdom of Solomon*, Anchor Bible 43 (Garden City, NY: Doubleday, 1979).
2. Daniel J. Harrington, *Invitation to the Apocrypha* (Grand Rapids: Eerdmans, 1999), 56.

Homiletical Perspective

hedonism to oppression and destruction. Might makes right, the ungodly advise, so take whatever you can get, no matter what you must do. "Let us oppress the righteous poor man; let us not spare the widow," (2:10) they say. "Let us lie in wait for the righteous man" (2:12). Their nihilistic view brings forth a destructive despair which concludes that the Divine is absent and life is worthless.

For those who believe narcissism and nihilism are recent innovations in human life, the Wisdom of Solomon tells a different story. This text provides an opportunity for the preacher to explore the motivations and rationalizations behind the destructive impulses and exploitation of power still painfully evident today. It also provides a hopeful alternative.

In contrast to the view of the ungodly, Wisdom insists that life did not happen by chance and death is not the final word. The author understands life as the good gift of a creative God. Wisdom 1:14 recalls God's creative work, bringing to mind the opening chapter of Genesis. The preacher may remind listeners of that familiar litany of God's exuberant act of creation, where again and again the phrase repeats, "It is good." God forms humankind in God's own image, and at the end of the creation drama, God affirms the goodness of all creation: "God saw everything that he had made, and indeed, it was very good" (Gen. 1:31). The creation account is not intended as a scientific explanation, of course. It is a statement of faith. It tells that creation, including human life, was not accidental but deliberate, God's gracious initiative.

According to Wisdom, the goodness of creation did not end with Eden, but may still be found in its essence. Wisdom asserts, "The generative forces of the world are wholesome, and there is no destructive poison in them" (1:14). For the author of Wisdom, the goodness of creation becomes a source of optimism about the human struggle against injustice, suggests Michael Kolarcik. He writes, "Since God is the creator of all things, the existence of all things ultimately is wholesome. Injustice, though it pervades human existence, essentially remains foreign to human life. As an intruder, it dismantles what is essentially wholesome and good."[1] Injustice in creation might be compared to the annual invasion of kudzu in the southern United States, which begins its spread early each spring. The

1. Michael Kolarcik, S.J., "The Book of Wisdom," in *The New Interpreter's Bible* (Nashville: Abingdon, 1997), 5:456.

Wisdom of Solomon 1:13-15; 2:23-24

Theological Perspective

body. Wisdom 2:23 affirms the possibility of immortality—for all people—yet attributes this to God and to the idea of the soul as an image of divine Wisdom. For Plato, souls have a natural claim to immortality; in Wisdom it depends on the extent to which one has lived righteously. Thus the soul may be raised to immortality through its "enfleshment" in a body; it is not a simple assumption that the flesh corrupts the soul, or that the soul automatically enjoys immortality. That which causes corruption and brings mortality, in Wisdom, is attributed to the devil: "through the devil's envy death entered the world, and those who belong to his company experience it" (2:24). While in God's providence there is the theoretical possibility of universalism, Death has itself become a force to be reckoned with (it is personified here, as elsewhere the figure of Wisdom is personified). Even though there is restraint in the applications of these principles in chapter 2, those loyal to Death and the Devil are associated increasingly through the book of Wisdom with those who are enemies of the Jews. Rather like the ancient Egyptians and Canaanites, so those who are experienced as their equivalent contemporary oppressors, the Alexandrians and Romans, are declared by the third section of the book (chaps. 11–19) contemptible and already cursed (e.g., 12:10–11).

To modern sensibilities this is going too far: God appears "paternal towards Israel but inimical towards Egypt,"[1] apparently undermining the importance of the life of righteousness. Thus commentators such as Reider have declared here an undisguised particularism: no wonder Jerome hesitated to accept the canonical authority of the Wisdom of Solomon. Perhaps he was familiar with the dangerous path of "going too far" theologically within the Wisdom literature. Holding to some orthodox and valuable theological principles, but applying them too quickly or literally, is the error that Job's friends teach us. Seeking too readily to explain Job's predicament, they apply partial truths as if they are comprehensive truths, as if the correlation between God's justice and the world's apparent injustice is complete.

JO BAILEY WELLS

Pastoral Perspective

convinced that I was overdue for a financial advisor, but had forgotten the text that the preacher was supposedly proclaiming!

If the rich and powerful believe they have free license to run over the poor, the widows, the orphans, and those who raise questions about the ethic of carpe diem, it is because they wrongly believe that death is the end that awaits everyone. Not so, says Wisdom of Solomon. Only those who forsake a holy ethic will taste death. God's chosen will know immortality.

This is good news in a world where choosing to live by a holy ethic does not necessarily lead to the prosperity proclaimed by the televangelist. Recently, a Harvard Law School–educated, second-career Catholic priest who serves in my neighborhood was asked if it was difficult to shift midcareer from a relatively restriction-free life to one where he is instructed where to live and where to lead, and told what he will be paid. He laughed at the assumption that his lawyer world had been "restriction-free." "My previous work experience is very valuable, because I understand what it's like to be in a workplace where you are constantly asked to do things that go against your convictions."

Stay faithful, Wisdom of Solomon assures those in the real world of self-interest and domination, because life does not end the way the world presumes. Although oppressors may get their golden parachutes, six-digit salaries, and year-end bonuses here and now, they are, in fact, choosing the fast-approaching reward of death. This judgment, while admittedly harsh on the ears of a church that prefers to receive its grace with no strings attached, is according to the text, no judgment at all. God "does not delight in the death of the living. For he created all things so that they might exist" (1:13–14). Death is always less than what God wills for the living. This is good news for Mr. Jones, who is, indeed, with the Lord. Perhaps, more importantly, it is good news for the faithful who choose God's holy ethic in a world constantly enticing them to choose otherwise, because they trust that God's way leads to life.

ANDREW FOSTER CONNORS

---

1. J. Reider, *The Book of Wisdom* (New York: Harper & Bros., 1957), 142.

Exegetical Perspective

The role of immortality during the Hellenistic and Roman periods can hardly be overemphasized. Notice the verbs the writer uses for "make" (1:13) and "create" (1:14). They form a type of synonymous parallelism that is offset by the objects of each clause. The observation that God did not create death leads into an extended comment that God does not find pleasing the destruction of living creatures. The writer emphasizes the goodness of God. The writer contrasts *thanatos*, death, on the one hand (1:13), which God neither created nor takes pleasure in, and *einai*, being, on the other hand. This implementation of being serves as the birth of the cosmos. The NRSV here translates this as the "generative forces." At the same time the purpose of this generative force is salvation. Hence the NRSV uses the language of "wholesome." God does not participate in the poisonous forces (1:14b).

The summary of these observations comes in 1:15: "For righteousness is immortal" (NRSV). The writer uses the alpha-privative form with the noun for death, *athanatos*. One might say, "For righteousness is without death." The writer has established that God is about goodness, but in that assertion is the implicit observation that there must be another explanation for death and destructive poison in the world.

The Purpose of Humanity. God created human beings for incorruptibility, *aphtharsia* (see also 4 Macc. 17:12; Wis. 6:19). The writer buttresses this argument with the notion of *imago dei*, namely humans are made in the image of God (Gen. 1:26). However, here the writer makes a gloss that transforms the image of God into a de facto image of eternity. The incorruptibility of God has a passive effect on those things created by God, that is to say, they become immortal.

Giving the Devil His Due. The devil for this writer has creative powers. The devil created death through the sin of envy. However, at this point the writer has given over the idea of divine sovereignty. The demonic as the origin of evil and moral deficiencies occurs also in 1 Enoch and elsewhere. Now the recognition of the devil's creative force demands a decision from discerning people: support the demonic, or support the creative work of God. When one participates with the devil, one inherits death. On the other hand, when one participates with God, one lives absent death, according to this passage.

STEPHEN BRECK REID

Homiletical Perspective

green leaves unfurl, the vines lengthen and grab, growing at an astonishing pace. By summer's end, in some areas a sea of kudzu covers the ground, choking out indigenous plants and strangling the saplings. Kudzu is invasive and destructive. It may thrive, but it is not a native species. So it is, Wisdom suggests, with injustice. Injustice may thrive, but it is an invader to creation; it is not native to this place. Humans and all of creation were created by a loving God and called good. This understanding of creation is the basis for living in hope, rather than the despair that characterizes the wicked.

This view of human origins transforms the understanding of human finality as well. "God created us for incorruption, and made us in the image of his own eternity" (2:23). Christians often envision eternity or immortality as a perpetual state of being, like that evoked by the final stanza of the hymn "Amazing Grace": "When we've been there ten thousand years, bright shining as the sun, we've no less days to sing God's praise than when we'd first begun." The author of Wisdom has a rather different idea of immortality. Here, immortality is not so much about a state of being, with the soul continuing endlessly onward. Instead, immortality signifies a relationship, an enduring relationship with God. It was for this relationship that humans were created. Human dignity rests in our relationship to the divine. Even in the midst of pain and suffering, even surrounded by injustice, essential human nature does not change. We were created for good. We are meant for enduring relationship with God.

This text urges the community of faith to take a long view of human life—a view that begins with the creation of the universe and extends to an ongoing relationship with God that is beyond time. Such a long-term view provides hope for human life rather than despair. It frees the faithful to do things that do not make any sense in the short term: Work for justice. Give to the poor. Care for widows and orphans. Build peaceful relationships. Delight in God's presence. This, says Wisdom, is what we are created for.

LEANNE PEARCE REED

Psalm 30

¹I will extol you, O Lᴏʀᴅ, for you have drawn me up,
  and did not let my foes rejoice over me.
²O Lᴏʀᴅ my God, I cried to you for help,
  and you have healed me.
³O Lᴏʀᴅ, you brought up my soul from Sheol,
  restored me to life from among those gone down to the Pit.

⁴Sing praises to the Lᴏʀᴅ, O you his faithful ones,
  and give thanks to his holy name.
⁵For his anger is but for a moment;
  his favor is for a lifetime.
 Weeping may linger for the night,
  but joy comes with the morning.

⁶As for me, I said in my prosperity,
  "I shall never be moved."
⁷By your favor, O Lᴏʀᴅ,
  you had established me as a strong mountain;

Theological Perspective

This psalm is a song of thanksgiving. Such psalms
are regularly "narrative psalms" because they relate
the entire drama of faith from *need* and *petition*
through *rescue* and finally to *gratitude*. Thus the
narrative articulation characteristically attests to the
"before" of need and the "after" of gratitude, placing
at the center of the dramatic narrative the miracle of
YHWH's transformative intervention.

   In this psalm, the narrative of *need-rescue-thanks* is
offered, first of all, in verses 1–3. YHWH is named
three times, the God extolled (v. 1), the God addressed
in trouble (v. 2), and the God who has rescued (v. 3).
These verses identify the "before" of foes, Sheol, and
the Pit, all signs of powerless desperation. The "after"
is that the speaker is "brought up" and "restored to
life" by YHWH.

   The same narrative account of *need-petition-
rescue-thanks* is more fully articulated in verses 6–12.
Here the psalmist, in narrative mode, goes one step
further back to describe a life of *complete stability and
well-being* prior to any threat (vv. 6–7a). That initial
state of total well-being, however, is abruptly shattered
in verse 7cd; the absence of YHWH's *life-giving face*
leads to dismay and disarray. It is remarkable that
these two brief lines are all that are offered concerning
the condition of need. Trouble comes because the
speaker is denied access to the life-giving force of

Pastoral Perspective

This short psalm maps so many contours of our
emotional landscape: the exaltation of knowing that
we have been delivered from a hopeless situation, the
wonder at how things that seem so sinister can turn
to blessing, the chagrin of knowing we had been
overcontent and haughty, and the bewilderment at
seeing how things can turn on a dime; it includes a
self-affirming, winking prayer for help, quick
desperation, and utter joy dancing in praise—
exaltation, wonder, embarrassment, astonishment,
playfulness, anguish, and delight, all in twelve verses.
The psalm is less a map of our condition than it is a
cubist painting, simultaneously showing side, front,
and bottom views of our human face. The body of
Christ is a community that has all those faces at
once. This psalm reveals that complex reality, but
with that complexity come pastoral challenges in
exposing the psalm.

   The psalm's powerful and transparent language is
also its difficulty. In verses 8–9 the psalmist offers a
bargain to God, and it is bizarre to our ears.
Essentially the psalmist says, "God, who is going to
praise you, if I die and can't do it anymore? You
could use a guy like me. I'm good PR, God. You need
me." The tone is akin to that in the legend of Teresa
of Avila, who during the Thirty Years' War was
removing dead bodies from the battlefield on an

you hid your face;
    I was dismayed.

⁸To you, O Lᴏʀᴅ, I cried,
    and to the Lᴏʀᴅ I made supplication:
⁹"What profit is there in my death,
    if I go down to the Pit?
  Will the dust praise you?
    Will it tell of your faithfulness?
¹⁰Hear, O Lᴏʀᴅ, and be gracious to me!
    O Lᴏʀᴅ, be my helper!"

¹¹You have turned my mourning into dancing;
    you have taken off my sackcloth
    and clothed me with joy,
¹²so that my soul may praise you and not be silent.
    O Lᴏʀᴅ my God, I will give thanks to you forever.

Exegetical Perspective

The Ideal Thanksgiving Psalm. The mystery of illness has concerned humans for millennia. Humans find it hard to fathom being suddenly incapacitated at death's door. In times past, illness was a sign of God's displeasure and an opportunity for the less righteous to gloat over the sick person's apparent estrangement from God. This was especially true for our psalmist, who before this near-death experience was confident of God's sustaining protection. Many commentators have recognized Psalm 30 as an ideal thanksgiving (*todah*) psalm. Each movement is rich with expressions of gratitude and images of doom. In the first movement (vv. 1–3), the psalmist praises God for rescue from certain death. In the second (vv. 4–5), the psalmist turns toward the faithful (*hasidim*) and urges them to praise God. The final movement (vv. 6–12) addresses God in a rehearsal of the psalmist's plight and a final affirmation of promise always to give God thanks.

To God Who Rescues from Death (vv. 1–3). The image of God's drawing up the psalmist is one that comes from the daily life of the Israelites. In other places the same verb is used to describe drawing a bucket up from a well. The psalmist begins by attaching God's deliverance to the familiar practice of bringing life-sustaining water up from the depths.

Homiletical Perspective

Death casts a long shadow. Long before it comes for us that last time, its shadow darkens our lives with sickness or disease or scandal or one of the many other ways that it blights and discourages and dismays. Death is foreshadowed by the things that dishearten the spirit and darken life. A friend who had been through a particularly hard year commented, "The thing I missed most was my joy." She had known the shadow that blights long before it destroys. How it touched the life of the psalmist, we do not know—which is probably just as well, since it allows all the hurting folk in our world, and especially in our pews, to find their own story in the ancient words.

As we preach this text, we can find other hurting folk in the Gospel reading. Jairus, a leader of the synagogue, a man of power, is quite rightly afraid that the shadow of death will claim his daughter. In the midst of that story comes the desperate approach of the woman whose disease has made her dead to her community (Mark 5:21–43).

Whatever the event that had dismayed this psalmist is now far enough away that he can reflect on it. When we are close to a hard thing, our own pain often so narrows our vision that we cannot see the larger picture. Sometimes it takes years before we can look back and say, "That's why that happened.

Psalm 30

Psalm 30

Theological Perspective

YHWH. More important is the remembered petition in which the psalmist quotes himself and remembers what he said to YHWH (vv. 8–10). In these verses, YHWH is four times addressed. Verse 10 features three synonymous imperatives, all of which urge rescue by YHWH. That petition, moreover, is reinforced by the motivation offered to YHWH in verse 9. This "supplication" mentioned in verse 8 is quoted in verses 9 and 10. In a series of four questions, YHWH is reminded that if the speaker is allowed to die (go down into the Pit), there will be one less voice to sing praise to YHWH. Thus YHWH is assumed to have a vested interest in keeping the petitioner alive as a witness to YHWH's faithfulness. YHWH needs or desires such witnesses in a competitive world of many gods. The motivation seeks to establish that, as the speaker's life is at stake in this situation of threat, so the honor of YHWH is at stake as well.

After a pause at the end of verse 10—during which time we are invited to imagine a divine initiative that restores—the speaker attests that YHWH has indeed acted to cause restoration and well-being (vv. 11–12). The three verbs characterizing YHWH's action—turn, take off, clothe—are perhaps parallel to the three imperatives of verse 10. These three verbs assigned to YHWH signify a radical transformation enacted by YHWH. This is a transformation that evokes praise and thanks, for only YHWH could have effected such a change (see Eph. 4:22–24). Thus verses 6–12 narrate, in greater length, the same narrative drama given in verses 1–3.

Both scenarios of "before-after" are articulated in the first person singular (vv. 1–3, 6–12). These two units, however, bracket verses 4–5, which break beyond the intimate *personal mode of thanks* to a more generic *communal aspect of praise*. Here the summons of praise is addressed to the congregation of the faithful, the assembly that joins the individual voice of thanks. Now the entire community celebrates the particular transformation of the individual petitioner. In verse 5 the community of covenant keepers contrasts the "before" of *anger* and the long, durable "after" of *divine favor*, the brevity of weeping and the durability of joy. Thus the contrasts—anger/favor, weeping/joy—reflect the drama *from petition to thanksgiving*. The juxtaposition of weeping and joy is perhaps echoed in the teaching of Jesus in Luke 6:21, 24. In each case in these contrasts, the final condition of well-being as a divine gift will persist. The trouble is short term, because YHWH does come and intervenes to positive effect. In the

Pastoral Perspective

oxcart. In the midst of her work it began to stream with rain, and quickly the fields became thick with mud. She could barely move the cart. She is reported to have shaken her fist at the heavens and said, "No wonder you don't have any more friends, if you treat them like this!" The intimacy of those with a deep trust in our living God is unbound by conventional piety. The psalmist and Teresa share that intimacy; they recognize their deep collaboration in the Spirit. That intimacy allows for the psalmist's outlandish repartee with God and for great ebullience and extravagance in the next breath,

> For his anger is but for a moment;
> his favor is for a lifetime.
> Weeping may linger for the night,
> but joy comes with the morning.

The psalmists' days of rejoicing are not everyone's, but they know what to do with that extraordinary joy and whom to thank.

The psalmists complain to God with as much regularity as they praise God. Their intimacy with God allows them the expression of every facet of their inner being. Their trusting God's discerning eye on them means that they do not shy away from what is hidden within them but express it to the One they know has heard it all and can surely bear their cubist prayers.

It is precisely that ebullience, however, that leads to a pastoral difficulty in opening up this psalm. In particular are these verses—a snapshot of someone expressing their great relief and happiness.

> Weeping may linger for the night,
> but joy comes with the morning.
> . . . .
> You have turned my mourning into dancing;
> you have taken off my sackcloth
> and clothed me with joy.

These are compelling verses. They express the elation of one who has received grace abundantly and whose long night of anguish, whose years of oppressive experience are now at an end. The preacher is likely to be drawn to them, but there is a trap in them. These verses highlight the snare that the whole psalm may set for us and for all who hear this psalm.

When the trap is sprung, the pastor will hear the cry, "It is morning, but *I* have no joy! The night's weeping has flooded across my morning too. It is day, and I still have no relief!"

Exegetical Perspective

As in many other psalms, this act is seen as an act of justification in the face of enemies who would take pleasure in the psalmist's trouble. To appreciate this, we must acknowledge the connection between righteousness and blessing that existed in the minds of many ancients. Like Job's friends, this psalm reflects the conviction that righteous persons can explain their suffering only by appeal to God's anger against them.

Verses 1–3 offer a synopsis of the crisis from which God has rescued the psalmist. In this synopsis it is clear that the psalmist is not discussing an emotional trouble spot in life but is recounting a near-fatal situation. One of the great characteristics of the Psalms is their physicality. Here the psalmist praises God for healing. In verse 3 the parallel terms are soul (*nephesh*) and life (*hay*). In the psalms, *nephesh* has a more concrete meaning than our English translation allows. *Nephesh* means "neck" or "throat," and by extension, "life." When something threatens the *nephesh,* it threatens the life. The psalmist is describing a near-death experience, made more emphatic by naming the places of the dead, Sheol and the Pit.

The Faithful Are Called to Give Thanks (vv. 4–5). The psalmist turns from direct communication to God to direct communication to the community of faithful ones (*hasidim*). Rather than go into details about the experience of extreme urgency, the psalmist reminds the congregants of God's character in a creedlike statement (v. 5). It is an affirmation that God's character is marked by favor and not anger. It is a note of hope in the dark hour when the Pit looms before the faithful ones and their sense of abandonment is at its greatest.

The juxtaposition of the brevity of weeping with the promise of joy in the morning is found also in Psalm 126:5–6. It is a statement that acknowledges God's faithfulness to act on behalf of God's faithful ones. The word "joy" here appears some thirty-four times in the psalms in various noun forms, and its various uses are instructive as to the character of this joy. Uses are evenly divided between describing the act of crying out to God in prayer and crying out in joy or rejoicing. In Psalm 30 and 126 the expression is uniquely used for the weeping that is transformed into shouts of joy. The exuberance of this joy is greater than the heartache of the weeping.

Specific Cause to Give God Thanks (vv. 6–12). This final movement can be divided in two. The first half

Homiletical Perspective

Now I understand. Now I can see beyond that crisis and discern a purpose and meaning."

The psalmist begins his story before the shadow darkened his life:

> As for me, I said in my prosperity,
> "I shall never be moved."

Did you think nothing bad would ever happen to you? That you would be exempt from the hard things? For so many folk it does come as a shock that, through no fault of their own, that long shadow comes to blight their lives. "I shall never be moved." That will not happen to me. How do we warn folk that the probability is that it *will* happen to them? Especially, how does the preacher warn those wonderful bright young folk sitting in the pew that maybe the baby will be born with a handicap; that, despite the miracles of modern medicine, not all disease can be conquered; that maybe the job will be lost; that despite their best efforts the marriage might not survive; that the time will come when their parents will die, or their best friend? How do we warn them? How do we tell them that life is hard? How do we get them ready?

I remember a young bride who had come to talk about a wedding. After studying the vows, she asked how much leeway there was. Could she rewrite them? "I don't like all this negativity—want, sorrow, sickness—I don't want that in my wedding." I suggested that while we always want the best for people, the chances that she and her husband would get through life without some hard times were pretty slim. "Don't you want to know that when those hard times come, he is going to stick with you?" She could hear no part of it—and went somewhere else for her wedding. I have often wondered what she did when those inevitable hard times came. Was she powerful enough simply to deny them access to her life? I think not.

How do we warn them? Or do we simply stand ready to pick up the pieces when they come apart? Could that be what the psalmist is doing? "Can I have a witness?" calls the voice of the preacher. "Yes, here is my witness," and the psalmist speaks:

> Weeping may linger for the night,
> but joy comes with the morning.

Yes, it is hard. Sometimes almost more than we can bear, but this too will pass. Your joy will return. Here is my story, says the psalmist. I have moved from feeling that God is angry with me to believing

Psalm 30

end, both the individual petitions (vv. 2, 8–10) and the reflective commentary (vv. 4–5) become ground for gratitude (vv. 4, 12). The psalm thus reflects both personal *experience* and the *faith* of Israel.

It is worth observing, however, that there is some tension between the large communal faith claim of verse 5 and the lived personal reality of verse 7, for the petitioner in verse 7 has found YHWH to be, at least short term, less than reliable. The conviction of the general affirmation of YHWH, however, seems to overcome that lived reality. In the end it is confidence in YHWH affirmed by the community that persists, even for the individual. This psalmist has no doubt that YHWH will override trouble and make all things new. It is Israel's task to sound the petition, to watch for the rescue, and then to acknowledge that rescue with thanksgiving.

Israel's faith is concrete and concerns "the facts on the ground." One of those "facts" is YHWH's anger, which is known to cause trouble. Without flinching from this reality, Israel has deep confidence in YHWH, who moves past anger to rescue (see Ps. 103:9–10). Israel knows that divine anger is not defining for YHWH; it is, rather, always YHWH's purpose to move beyond anger to restorative favor and rescue. Thus the psalm, without flinching from candor, holds candor about trouble to the deeper reality of YHWH's attentive fidelity. YHWH's favor is as sure as the rising of the sun when morning breaks. Israel's *thanks* is a precise and appropriate counterpoint to *YHWH's generous care.* In its receptivity to YHWH's newness, Israel is not able to keep silent; Israel must sing and say its gratitude to YHWH, for life as a divine gift overrides every debilitating circumstance.

WALTER BRUEGGEMANN

Those who continue in mornings without joy can be further diminished by the celebration of grace that another has received. It is an essential word to those whose wounds are still open that we cannot extrapolate from one experience of healing to make conclusions about the proximity and grace of God to those who do not experience present healing. The redeemed may in their joy shout what seem like eternal verities—*joy comes in the morning!*—but the suffering can hear such elation as judgment. Suffering easily compounds itself with the theological fallacy that God is parceling out grace to some and heartache to others, withholding mercy from some and dishing it out generously to others. With such a psalm, the preacher needs to see ahead and avoid the trap.

We imagine the morning prayers in worship throughout the sanctuary—"For Jim's healing . . . for Amy's new life . . . for Joe's coming home from prison . . . for my deliverance from cancer . . ." On the one hand we can imagine, as above, some overhearing these prayers with pain—hearing gratitude echo throughout the sanctuary for others who have crossed from their wilderness or have found healing, and some experiencing a further sense of abandonment and alienation. And on the other hand we can imagine the great blessing to those overhearing these prayers, "If there was deliverance for them, maybe there will be some for me."

The preacher's task in opening up this psalm is to help us imagine and experience a community so bound together that, if one member suffers, all suffer together; if one member rejoices, all rejoice together—so that the mystery of God's presence and proximity is deepened in every joy and sorrow. Such a community could find ways to sing and read the psalm with great integrity, celebrating the healing of those who are joyful and embracing the sorrow of those who still weep, knowing that God is present to each and to the whole in all these modes—God the consoling Spirit in sorrow, God the glad recipient of the people's gratitude, God whose favor is for a lifetime, in joy and in sorrow, in sickness and in health, . . . God whom we would thank forever. Such a community could with the psalmist pray cubist prayers of nuance and depth.

CHANDLER BROWN STOKES

consists of the psalmist's rehearsing the specifics of the near-fatal experience, and the second an affirmation of God's action on behalf of the psalmist. Verses 6–7 establish the favored condition the psalmist once enjoyed with God, along with the faith that God's favor will never fail. God had established the psalmist like a mountain, a mountain the psalmist thought immovable. But suddenly all that changed. Without explanation, God turned away from the psalmist, hiding God's face. The Psalms often complain of God's turning away from the faithful. Even the creatures of the sea are dismayed (terrified) when God turns away (Ps. 104:29).

At this point the psalmist gives a verbatim rendition of the prayer offered out of deep distress. Some translations, including NRSV, render the euphemism of verse 9 ("my blood") as "my death." The fact that the psalmist is talking about death is clear. As in many other psalms, the pivotal power of this prayer is that God will lose a worshiper if the psalmist is dead. No one in the Pit praises God; the dust of death does not praise God or tell of God's faithfulness. If God wants to be praised, then the psalmist's life must be spared. This may seem like an appeal to God's vanity, and perhaps it is. But it is as likely, if not more so, that it is an appeal to the created purpose of humans. While we live we may praise God, for that is why we are created; we live to give God worship. Once a person sinks into the shades of Sheol, all worship of God halts.

In the second part (vv. 11–12) of this third movement we have a conclusion that grows out of the experience of the first part. The psalmist still addresses God and once again gives a synopsis of God's action. The image is a tender one. God removes the garments of mourning and outfits the psalmist in a festal garment of joy. Verse 12 poses a bit of a problem, since the word translated "my soul" in NRSV is "glory" (*kabod*) in the Hebrew. Emending the text to read *kevediy* ("my heart/liver") is the solution chosen by some translations. Indeed, if the idea is that from the innermost places of the psalmist praise breaks forth, then it is a more than satisfactory choice.

STEVEN BISHOP

that I have God's favor. I no longer see the moment, but am able to look at all my life. My weeping has been changed into joy. Whereas before I saw only the shadows of the night, now I live in the brightness of the morning. Mourning has become dancing; and rather than wear sackcloth, now I am dressed in joy. It takes maturity, hard-won maturity, to reach that point. Yet the thanks that come after such a time are far deeper, far richer, far more heartfelt. And it is such insight that will carry us through the next shadow, and the next—even through the shadow of death.

One final story. After many years apart I had a visit with an old friend and asked her, "What has happened to you in the last thirty-five years?" She began by telling me that her husband had died. I did know that, but not the rest of the story. Not long after he died, both of his parents had died. She and her husband had been high school sweethearts, so the relationship with his parents was close and long-standing. Their death was certainly a painful loss. The next year her older brother was killed in the attack on the World Trade Center, and his wife died shortly thereafter. I sat looking at the cheerful woman in front of me, stunned that she had endured so much. I asked, "How do you deal with all that loss?" The answer of a deep and tested faith came back: "You have to be grateful for what you had, not what you lost. Every day I thank God for my husband and our marriage. Every day I thank God for what I had. I was so blessed."

Death casts a long shadow, but the psalmist assures us that like the morning sun after midnight, joy returns.

NETA LINDSAY PRINGLE

2 Corinthians 8:7-15

⁷Now as you excel in everything—in faith, in speech, in knowledge, in utmost eagerness, and in our love for you—so we want you to excel also in this generous undertaking.

⁸I do not say this as a command, but I am testing the genuineness of your love against the earnestness of others. ⁹For you know the generous act of our Lord Jesus Christ, that though he was rich, yet for your sakes he became poor, so that by his poverty you might become rich. ¹⁰And in this matter I am giving my advice: it is appropriate for you who began last year not only to do something but even to desire to do something— ¹¹now finish doing it, so that your eagerness may be matched by completing it according to your means. ¹²For if the eagerness is there, the gift is acceptable according to what one has—not according to what one does not have. ¹³I do not mean that there should be relief for others and pressure on you, but it is a question of a fair balance between ¹⁴your present abundance and their need, so that their abundance may be for your need, in order that there may be a fair balance. ¹⁵As it is written,

"The one who had much did not have too much,
  and the one who had little did not have too little."

Theological Perspective

Our passage represents the heart of Paul's appeal to the Corinthian Christians to fulfill their pledge to the collection for "the poor among the saints at Jerusalem" (Rom. 15:26), a project whose great importance to the apostle is evident also from his earlier remarks to the Corinthians (1 Cor. 16:1–4) and to the Galatians (2:9–10). But "collection" (*logeia*, a term he uses only in 1 Cor. 16:1, 2), hardly captures the deeply theological significance of the enterprise, as shown by the other terms he uses to describe it in our passage and elsewhere: *charis*, "grace" (2 Cor. 8:6, 7, 9; also in 1 Cor. 16:3), *eulogia*, "blessing" (9:5), *leitourgia*, "priestly service" (9:12), and *koinōnia*, "fellowship," "participation" (8:4; also in 9:13 as well as Rom. 15:26). In words just prior to our passage, he says that this "relief work" (*diakonia*) is both a work of "grace" and an act of Christian "fellowship" (8:4), that is, a tangible gesture of gospel solidarity and love (see 8:8) between Gentiles and Jews.

The fuller theological significance of this relief effort becomes manifest in our passage as Paul's appeal to the Corinthian church unfolds. Having held up before them the example of the Macedonian Christians (8:1–5), he now addresses the Corinthians directly. Rather than trying to arouse a sense of competition with other churches, Paul reminds them of their own qualities and accomplishments. Praising

Pastoral Perspective

I am suspicious when colleagues claim that they actually look forward to preaching the annual stewardship sermon. It is one thing to preach about economic justice and the proper use of the financial resources God entrusts to us—one can hardly preach in a manner faithful to the Scriptures without visiting these topics regularly—but it is hard, on Stewardship Sunday, not to feel more like a fundraiser than a preacher, presenting the case for the proposed church budget.

I suspect that when the Christians of Corinth gathered for worship there was no six-foot thermometer indicating that they had already achieved 45 percent of their goal for the relief of the church in Jerusalem, no posters featuring heart-tugging pictures of widows and orphans. Terms we take for granted, like "budget goal," would likely have caused Paul great offense. Yet he wrote these words conscious of tensions familiar to pastoral leaders today.

The restoration of his relationship with the Corinthian church, so badly broken earlier, was still a work in progress. His apostolic authority has been accepted, but it is one thing to have your authority acknowledged and another to win back trust and affection. Any pastor who has led worship knowing that certain members of the congregation are glaring at you with suspicion can appreciate Paul's challenge.

Exegetical Perspective

This passage falls within a two-chapter section where Paul appeals to the Corinthians for money to help "the saints" (*hoi hagioi* in 9:1), most likely the churches in Jerusalem (see Rom. 15:26). Paul does not use "the saints" in any special or technical way with respect to the Jerusalem churches, since he uses the term many times to describe believers in Jesus, in general. Chapters 8 and 9 have been thought of as parts of separate letters by many major commentators over the years,[1] but if we read them as a unity, we see Paul at one of his most rhetorically skilled moments as he weaves together categories of honor and shame, devotion to the Lord, obligation, guilt, and encouragement in his efforts to motivate and persuade the Corinthians to amass an adequate sum for his collection project.

In verse 7 he calls the endeavor a *charis*, which the NRSV translates as a "generous undertaking." *Charis*

---

1. Starting in 1776 with J. S. Semler. The majority of contemporary scholars treat the status of chapters 8–9 as part of a larger argument of the unity of 2 Corinthians, and most often they argue that the letter consists of at least three different letters. Chapter 9 seems to repeat in content what chapter 8 says, so some (Betz, Thrall) have concluded that they were parts of separate letters. But in 1990, Stowers argued on grammatical grounds for the integrity of chapters 8 and 9, and Matera's recent commentary argues for the unity of 2 Corinthians and cites others who do the same. Whatever the compositional origins of 2 Corinthians were, someone earlier than Marcion in the second century presented 2 Corinthians as we have it today for some reason that made sense as a unified letter. It seems to me that making sense of the letter as it stands offers a greater but less speculative challenge than positing a reconstructed composition history.

Homiletical Perspective

Getting a congregation to dig deep into its pockets is a task as old as Christianity itself. It has never been easy. Paul faced the task squarely in 2 Corinthians 8–9 with a double-barreled effort to raise money from well-to-do people not eager to part with what they had. Because the Jerusalem "mother church" was poor, Paul urged the more prosperous Corinthians to do the right thing. The irony, of course, is that the Jerusalem church, dominated by Peter and James, was not immediately (or perhaps ever) taken with the apostle who, by his own admission, was "untimely born" (1 Cor. 15:8). After all, he had never known Jesus in the flesh, had been a persecutor of Christians, and was also in the vanguard of those who wanted to allow Gentiles into the community without having them first become Jews.

It says much for Paul that despite his antagonism to the Jerusalem-based "Hebraizers"—not to mention their suspicion of what he was up to among the Gentile churches—he took the suffering in Jerusalem to heart. His mission in 2 Corinthians was to get the more prosperous new churches in Greece and Asia Minor to provide economic assistance for fellow followers of Christ, even though he was working on behalf of people who did not approve of him and making his plea with largely Gentile

2 Corinthians 8:7-15

Theological Perspective

them for the excellence of their faith, speech, knowledge, and earnestness, he asks them to "excel in this [act of] grace also" (v. 7, my translation). The word "grace," *charis*, is more central to this passage than might appear from the English. In verse 1 it is explicitly the grace of God given to the Macedonian churches; in verse 4 the same word is used for the "favor" ("privilege" in NRSV) of their including Paul and Titus in the collection project; and in verses 6–7 it refers to the "act of grace" (ESV) or "generous undertaking" (NRSV) represented by the collection. For Paul these are all expressed in the one word *charis*, covering what we might call "grace" or "favor" or "thanks," depending upon the English context. (Modern Greeks still express their thanks by saying *eucharisto*.) But gratitude cannot be compelled, and Paul assures them that his counsel is not a command but an appeal to show "that your love also is genuine" (v. 8, my translation).

Only in the following verse, however, do we reach the real theological heart of Paul's appeal: "For you know the grace of our Lord Jesus Christ, that though he was rich, yet for your sake he became poor, so that by his poverty you might become rich" (v. 9 RSV). Here we have not only a pithy summary of the gospel itself but also a description of what has been called "the economy of God,"[1] a metaphor rooted in the New Testament (as in Col. 1:25) and developed extensively by the church fathers. The Greek word *oikonomia*, whose original meaning was "household" (cf. German *Haushalt*, "budget"), became a metaphor whose meaning extends from "economy" in our modern, fiscal sense of the word to God's universal plan of salvation, the "divine economy." But notice that Paul's statement in verse 9 encompasses both, since God's saving act of grace in Jesus Christ is also the model for our "economics" as Christians. The rest of our passage spells out the implications of this theological economy with specific reference to the Corinthians' contribution to the saints at Jerusalem. Paul first says something about what makes a gift "acceptable," starting with the "readiness" to give, which the Corinthians had demonstrated the previous year by pledging their support. But Paul would not agree with Hamlet that "the readiness is all," for he must now exhort them to complete their own act of grace by actually contributing what they have promised.

A final "economic" question remains: how much should they give? (Some have even surmised that

1. Francis Young and David F. Ford, *Meaning and Truth in 2 Corinthians* (London: SPCK, 1987), 169–71.

Pastoral Perspective

It is hard to ask for money when you know that not everyone is pleased with your leadership and that human beings are prone to voting with their wallets.

Paul was also bringing his version of "institutional goals" to this appeal. Certainly the needs of the Jerusalem Christians were real, but in Paul's mind the fragile unity of Christ's church hinged upon the success of this collection. Would there be one church for Jews, one for Gentiles, or would Christ's body remain united? Practical concerns and spiritual ideals were deeply interwoven in his appeal, again bringing to mind the annual stewardship sermon.

Those of us who have ever felt a bit chagrined for warming up the congregation with a bit of flattery may find comfort when Paul does the same thing: "Now as you excel in everything . . ." (v. 7). Yet his words are honest and accurate: the Corinthians were a bright and talented bunch, passionately committed to excelling in all matters. This passion had a dark side: their penchant for spiritual one-upmanship that had led the community into division and chaos. Like a wise parent, Paul seeks to redirect their passion for excellence to a worthy purpose.

We are reminded that sound, caring pastoral leadership sees people both as they are and as they can be: even our flaws and weaknesses are precious to God, who can transform them to virtues and strengths. Striving for excellence is a Christian virtue only when "excellence" is properly defined.

This Paul does by insisting that excellence in financial stewardship is not defined by giving a sum large enough to earn naming rights for the new wing. Rather it begins with humble gratitude for God's self-emptying in Christ—"For you know the generous act of our Lord Jesus Christ, that though he was rich . . . he became poor" (v. 9)—that prompts an eagerness to give in response. A year ago, Paul notes, many were not only setting money aside each week for the Jerusalem church, but filled with the desire to do so. Paul does not use the language so common in our churches about "honoring your pledges" but speaks instead of recapturing that eagerness to express gratitude to God. "For if the eagerness is there, the gift is acceptable according to what one has—not according to what one does not have" (v. 12). The larger gifts offered by the wealthier members of the community are not more "excellent" than the smaller gifts given by those of more modest means, for excellence in Christian giving is measured not in dollars but by the desire to give, which stems from gratitude to God.

Exegetical Perspective

shows up repeatedly in Paul's writings, but in 2 Corinthians, the NRSV translates the word variously as "grace," "generous undertaking," "favor," "thanks," "generous act," "privilege," and "blessing." In chapters 8–9 it is used eight times, five of those in 8:1–15. This is part of Paul's rhetorical strategy. Knowing the semantic range of *charis*, he uses it creatively to characterize participation in the collection as sharing in the same reality as the "*charis* of our Lord Jesus Christ" (v. 9). Along with using *charis* language to tie their potential generosity to that of Christ's act, Paul uses it to describe the way the Macedonian churches (probably in Philippi and Thessalonica) have participated (v. 1). This is his way of weaving shame into the picture. By calling what the Macedonians do a *charis*, and then describing the conditions under which they offered their *charis*, namely, during "a severe ordeal of affliction" and out of "their extreme poverty" (v. 2), Paul begins to set up his attempt to persuade the Corinthians to contribute to the collection.

Paul goes on to describe how the Macedonians begged him and his coworkers to take part in the collection (v. 4); he also tells of the Macedonians' desire to give themselves to the Lord and to Paul and his coworkers (v. 5). The result is a presentation of the Macedonians as harmonious, of goodwill, generous, sincere, deeply and fervently pious, and strongly affectionate toward Paul and his coworkers. Now that Paul has described the generosity of the Macedonian churches with respect to the collection, and the conditions under which they gave, he turns to the Corinthians (vv. 7–15). He begins with flattery, saying that they too excel in the qualities they value most— faith, speech, knowledge, utmost eagerness, and love. These qualities should drive them to give because they are in a superior position to do so in comparison to the Macedonians, and yet the Macedonians were able to give in such a way that their act was an act of piety and not just of generosity.

Paul then says directly that he is testing the Corinthians through this collection. They know the *charis* of the Lord, so how will they respond (v. 9)? Paul alludes to the notion of *kenōsis* (self-emptying; see Phil. 2:6–11) in verse 9 in order to show the way that the Corinthians directly benefited from the actions of Christ. They became rich through Christ's self-emptying poverty, so how will they respond when others who are poor need the same wealth that has benefited the Corinthians?

Paul goes on to reassure them that he is not asking for them to give so that they will be put into

Homiletical Perspective

congregations with little natural affinity for Jerusalem. Paul had his work cut out for him.

How did he take up the homiletic task? In the verses just preceding our text, he attempted to win over the Corinthians by pointing with admiration to peer churches elsewhere. Speaking generally about Macedonian Christians, he set up a standard the Corinthians should not only match but excel (v. 7). The Macedonians suffered poverty and yet displayed a wealth of generosity (v. 2). Not needing to be asked twice, they readily gave beyond their means, "begging us earnestly for the privilege of sharing in this ministry to the saints" (v. 4). Although poor in substance, they were rich in generosity—like the widow with her small copper coins at the temple treasury (Mark 12:41–44). Surely the Corinthians did not want to be outdone, shown up as lacking in Christian charity when they seemed to excel in everything else, "in faith, in speech, in knowledge, in utmost eagerness"—not to mention in Paul's great love for them (v. 7).

The preacher of this text should think twice about following literally in the apostle's homiletic footsteps. How constructive is it to exploit sibling rivalry, urge competitive generosity, or pit one group of Christians against another? Nor is it a good idea to play the special love card the way Paul did in verse 7, when he seems to have run out of other blandishments.

Paul did not follow what might well be a preacher's first impulse in the face of a crying need, as we heard from many pulpits in the immediate aftermath of Hurricane Katrina. Why not tell the Corinthians how bad the situation in Jerusalem actually was, focus on the plight of the Christians there, and then ask the congregation to demonstrate what it means to be in the body of Christ—as he did so beautifully in 1 Corinthians 12? The point should not be "Outdo the Macedonians because *you* don't want to come up wanting." Nor should he have set up a contest in virtue, as he regrettably did when he told the Corinthians, "I am testing the genuineness of your love against the earnestness of others" (v. 8). Rather, the preacher should exhort the congregation to be generous because that is what it means to be "in Christ" and "like Christ."

This christological turn is ultimately (and none too soon!) the one Paul made. Laying to rest Corinthian competition with the Macedonians—who will be most generous to Jerusalem? who will repay most fully his fatherly affections?—he ended by pointing them to the paradigmatic Giver: "For you

2 Corinthians 8:7-15

Theological Perspective

this issue might explain their delay in contributing.) Paul tells them to complete their contribution "out of what you have" (v. 11b, my translation), adding that a gift is "acceptable according to what a person has, not according to what he does not have" (v. 12, my translation), and that he does not mean that "others should be eased and you burdened" (v. 13a RSV). Then comes the key term in Paul's theological economics, *isotēs* (vv. 13b, 14), typically translated "equality" (KJV, RSV, NIV) though it can also mean "fairness" (ESV); the NRSV splits the difference with "fair balance." Calvin comments that Paul does not mean the kind of equality where "each side gives an equal amount" but rather "a fair apportioning."[2] The context, and especially the examples to which Paul appeals, best illustrate what he means. The term clearly involves a notion of reciprocity, as shown by the relationship between Jesus Christ and believers (v. 9) and by Paul's claim that "your abundance at the present time should supply their need, so that their abundance may supply your need, that there may be *isotēs*" (v. 14, my translation). Commentators differ on whether this reciprocity involves material resources only or also spiritual.

How far might this passage be applied to the relationships among Christians in the global society of the twenty-first century? Is there a reciprocity between the once-missionized saints of the global South, who are now recalling their secularized brothers and sisters in the North to the gospel, and the affluent Christians of the North, who are able to supply the material needs of the church in the developing world? Such a reciprocity of material and spiritual gifts is suggested by Paul's discussion of the collection in Romans 15:27, but it is unclear to what extent our 2 Corinthians passage is making a similar point. Finally, Paul appeals to a scriptural example of economic reciprocity by citing, nearly verbatim from the Greek Old Testament, a passage about the bread from heaven that the Israelites ate in the wilderness (Exod. 16:18): "Whoever gathered much had nothing left over, and whoever gathered little had no lack" (8:15). Here too the point seems to be not a strictly quantitative equality but rather, as Calvin writes, "such an equality that nobody starves and nobody hordes his abundance at another's expense."[3]

GARRETT GREEN

Pastoral Perspective

In addition to expressing gratitude to God, Christians are called to give out of genuine love for their brothers and sisters. As Paul insists elsewhere, Christ died for *all* persons, not just those who have responded by placing their faith in him, so we are called to love all those who are beloved by our Savior. But fellow members of Christ's body constitute a special category: if they live in need while we know abundance, the entire body is wounded.

Paul twice (vv. 13, 14) uses the phrase "fair balance," asking the Corinthians to weigh their present abundance against the needs of the saints in Jerusalem. He does not ask the Corinthians to give so sacrificially that the equation becomes reversed ("I do not mean that there should be relief for others and pressure on you," v. 13), but rather to be so claimed by charity that their deepest need is to share their abundance with brothers and sisters who are less materially blessed.

For the pastoral leader, this text serves to remind that we are called to be agents of transformation, and in no arena is this more challenging than in that of financial stewardship. Measuring worth and success through personal wealth and material possessions is not a modern invention (although one might fairly claim that we have taken its excesses to new heights); members of the comparatively affluent Gentile churches struggled with the same temptation to "give a little something" to those in need without compromising their own lifestyles, and were prone to measure their giving against their peers ("Did we give more to the relief offering than the Galatians did? Did our church make the 'top five' list?"). The task of pastoral leadership is to lead our congregations, from the crippling fear that if we share our abundance with others there will not be enough left for us, into joyous trust in the God who provides for all our needs. Paul concludes his appeal by recalling how God distributed the manna in the wilderness: "The one who had much did not have too much, and the one who had little did not have too little" (v. 15). Replacing fear with trust is the most challenging, and most rewarding, transformation of all.

JOHN T. MCFADDEN

2. *Calvin's Commentaries*, ed. David W. Torrance and Thomas F. Torrance (Grand Rapids: Eerdmans, 1964), 10:113.
3. Ibid., 10:114.

Exegetical Perspective

hardship, but so that there is "fair balance" between their abundance and the Jerusalem churches' needs (vv. 13–14). He says that the Corinthians need not go to the extent of becoming poor, as Christ did, so that the Jerusalem churches can become rich, but he is challenging the economic disparity between the Corinthians and the Jerusalem churches, and he is calling the Corinthians to correct this disparity. This is reminiscent of the way that Acts describes the idyllic communal life of the earliest group of post-Pentecost believers. In Acts 2:44–47, the early believers "had all things in common" and "they would sell their possessions and goods and distribute the proceeds to all, *as any had need.*" In Acts 4:32–37, "no one claimed private ownership of any possessions, but everything they owned was held in common. . . . *There was not a needy person among them.*" Similar to what Paul is saying in our passage, Acts describes the ideal of economic balance where all those who have needs are attended to through the generosity of the community. Paul seems to be trying to create such a dynamic among the communities he founded; he is trying to get the Corinthians to think beyond their borders so that the needs of the poor can be met through the desire of the Corinthians to give out of their abundance. He closes the passage with an appeal to Scripture to reinforce his point.

STEPHEN P. AHEARNE-KROLL

Homiletical Perspective

know the generous act of our Lord Jesus Christ, that though he was rich, yet for your sakes he became poor, so that by his poverty you might become rich" (v. 9). We are not talking about the good folks in Macedonia, who may or may not have been as exemplary as Paul claimed; we are looking to the great paradox of the faith, that the One who was rich beyond compare became as poor as any one of us so that we, through him, might become rich in love.

In this single sentence Paul left behind the strategies of his stewardship sermon in order to deliver the gospel truth that motivates any "generous undertaking" (*charis*, v. 7). We give of our substance, of ourselves, because we have ourselves been given to. All giving, therefore, is ultimately a giving back. But lest the Corinthians be scared off by the high theology of "the generous act of our Lord Jesus Christ," Paul reminded them that he was not bidding them to impoverish themselves or to make themselves miserable in the process. "For if the eagerness is there, the gift is acceptable according to what one has—not according to what one does not have" (v. 12). The preacher was not asking for the moon or exhorting the congregation to give everything away. Rather, with the needs of Jerusalem in mind, he was asking for something manageable: "a fair balance between your present abundance and their need" (vv. 13–14). Christ gave up everything for them; what portion of their abundance can they give to a brother or sister in Christ who stands in need? The body of Christ should take care of itself, whether at home (with members of the local congregation who are not so well off) or abroad (be it in Jerusalem or Macedonia). Supply and demand must be kept in "fair balance," so that, as in the manna story of Exodus 16:18, "The one who had much did not have too much, and the one who had little did not have too little" (v. 15). As it was in the beginning, let it be once again and ever more.

PETER S. HAWKINS

Mark 5:21-43

²¹When Jesus had crossed again in the boat to the other side, a great crowd gathered around him; and he was by the sea. ²²Then one of the leaders of the synagogue named Jairus came and, when he saw him, fell at his feet ²³and begged him repeatedly, "My little daughter is at the point of death. Come and lay your hands on her, so that she may be made well, and live." ²⁴So he went with him.

And a large crowd followed him and pressed in on him. ²⁵Now there was a woman who had been suffering from hemorrhages for twelve years. ²⁶She had endured much under many physicians, and had spent all that she had; and she was no better, but rather grew worse. ²⁷She had heard about Jesus, and came up behind him in the crowd and touched his cloak, ²⁸for she said, "If I but touch his clothes, I will be made well." ²⁹Immediately her hemorrhage stopped; and she felt in her body that she was healed of her disease. ³⁰Immediately aware that power had gone forth from him, Jesus turned about in the crowd and said, "Who touched my clothes?" ³¹And his disciples said to him, "You see the crowd pressing in on you; how can you say, 'Who touched me?' " ³²He looked all around to see who had done it. ³³But the woman, knowing what had happened

Theological Perspective

The Second Week of Gospel Readings on Jesus' Kingship. We reach the midpoint of three Gospel accounts focusing on the *nature of Jesus' kingship* in Mark. Last week saw Jesus' authority over the *created order*, the world of the material. Today's text gives us new insight into Mark's Christology, exploring new realms in which Jesus' kingly prerogatives are made clear. The same implicit questions are addressed, not only about the nature of Jesus' kingship, but the *source of the authority* from which this kingship derives—and, significantly, the authority that his followers share, namely, his obedient faith. We also learn about *how authority is exercised* in Jesus' kingdom—the nature of priorities in that order, and the relationship between subject and sovereign.

How Is Jesus King? Answer 2: Jesus Is King of Life and Law. The story-within-a-story structure of today's pericope has deep theological significance. Both stories center on healing. Taken together, they brilliantly illuminate Jesus' claim to kingship in the realm of life and law.

First and last, we are presented with the story of Jairus and his daughter. Jairus is an official of the synagogue; he is a person of authority in Jewish society. We are meant to understand that his authority derives from his leadership in the

Pastoral Perspective

The pair of healing stories sandwiched together in these verses present two distinct and at least one common pastoral concern. Like every healing miracle, in common they raise the personal, existential question in both preacher and hearer: "Will *I* be healed?" Questions about healing are ubiquitous among human beings. Almost all of us must confess some ailment—be it physical, spiritual, psychological, or interpersonal—in us and in our communities that aches for restoration. Equally present to both pastor and parishioners is the shared awareness that some are healed and some are not. The synagogue leader's daughter was raised, but other children die. A desperate woman plagued by years of illness was restored, but equally desperate men and women are not. A pastor must be honest about this, even as she encourages prayer in a sermon, even as in the same service he offers prayer for sick women and children. In a sermon on this text, it may be helpful to challenge the congregation toward a more nuanced understanding of what asking for healing is and what healing may mean.

I have a friend, a man of deep faith, who was diagnosed with Parkinson's disease when he was still in his fifties. He and his wife prayed that he might be healed. Twenty years later, he is in the last debilitating stages of the disease. Nevertheless, he

to her, came in fear and trembling, fell down before him, and told him the whole truth. ³⁴He said to her, "Daughter, your faith has made you well; go in peace, and be healed of your disease."

³⁵While he was still speaking, some people came from the leader's house to say, "Your daughter is dead. Why trouble the teacher any further?" ³⁶But overhearing what they said, Jesus said to the leader of the synagogue, "Do not fear, only believe." ³⁷He allowed no one to follow him except Peter, James, and John, the brother of James. ³⁸When they came to the house of the leader of the synagogue, he saw a commotion, people weeping and wailing loudly. ³⁹When he had entered, he said to them, "Why do you make a commotion and weep? The child is not dead but sleeping." ⁴⁰And they laughed at him. Then he put them all outside, and took the child's father and mother and those who were with him, and went in where the child was. ⁴¹He took her by the hand and said to her, "Talitha cum," which means, "Little girl, get up!" ⁴²And immediately the girl got up and began to walk about (she was twelve years of age). At this they were overcome with amazement. ⁴³He strictly ordered them that no one should know this, and told them to give her something to eat.

Exegetical Perspective

A Healing within a Healing. Mark 5:21–43 is one of several places Mark inserts one story into another so that they complement each other thematically (cf. 3:19–35; 6:14–29; 11:15–33). In our reading today, when a wealthy man wants Jesus to heal his daughter, he must wait for the healing of a destitute woman.

The Ruler's Request (vv. 21–24). As in 4:35–36; 5:1, Jesus crosses the sea, a "great crowd" gathers on the other side, and he teaches by the sea (5:21). A ruler of the synagogue named Jairus approaches Jesus. Such leaders are highly esteemed and often well-to-do. Jairus recognizes Jesus as a healer and honors him by "falling down at his feet" (v. 22, my translations). A man of honor, he renders unusual honor to a traveling preacher because of his dying daughter. He appeals to Jesus, saying that his daughter faces her final days (*eschatōs*). Jairus believes that Jesus can "lay his hands" on the girl and "she will be saved and live" (v. 23). In the Jewish context, sacrifice, blessing, and ordination employ "laying on of hands."[1] In Mark, Jesus repeats the practice several times for healing purposes (6:5; 8:25). "Salvation" and "life" relate to both restoration

1. Hugh Anderson, *The Gospel of Mark*, New Century Bible (London: Oliphant, 1976), 152.

Homiletical Perspective

If we were to give this text a title, it might be something like "Jesus the Multi-tasker." In our fast-paced twenty-first-century world, this story within a story might not seem terribly odd. In the context of the slower pace of the first-century world, however, the story conveys a sense of urgency, frenetic energy, and even confusion—qualities, it appears from the Gospel stories, that were neither unknown nor frightening to Jesus. Jesus' attention to the desperate needs of both petitioners portrayed in this text becomes a reminder for us of the God who is never too busy to hear our prayers and respond to our pleas in amazing and unexpected ways.

The miracles reported in this section of Mark's Gospel continue as Jesus makes his way back and forth across the Sea of Galilee. After healing a demon-possessed man in the country of the Gerasenes on the other side of the sea, Jesus has once again crossed over into Jewish territory. Amid the "great crowd gathered around him" (v. 21), he is approached by a frantic leader of the synagogue named Jairus, who falls at Jesus' feet and begs Jesus to visit his daughter, who is at the point of death, believing Jesus can heal her. Jesus does not respond with words but demonstrates his compassion for Jairus by his action of immediately following Jairus home. They do not travel alone, however, but with

Mark 5:21-43

Theological Perspective

community, his rectitude in the life of the law, and (more important for what is to come) his ability correctly to perceive who Jesus is. Just by coming to Jesus, Jairus tacitly acknowledges that whatever authority he possesses is surpassed by that given to Jesus. His *confession of faith in Jesus' authority* is implicit in his request that Jesus come "so that she may be made well, and live" (v. 23).

The movement of the story toward Jairus's house is interrupted by the story of the hemorrhaging woman. The particulars of her story have theological significance: her continuous hemorrhaging means that she is *ritually unclean*; her *poverty* (she "had spent all that she had") renders her powerless and underscores her absolute *vulnerability* within the society. In short, she is quickly established as the opposite of Jairus (privileged, powerful, accepted, male).

Yet one thing she has critically in common with Jairus: she too *confesses her faith in Jesus' authority.* This she does *privately* (unlike Jairus). She makes contact with Jesus *secretly*, fearing that her low position will not merit direct access to the Jesus whom she too believes to have kingly power over life and healing.

Here, literary structure stakes out two overarching theological claims. Jesus' power has already been demonstrated; the woman's healing has already been effected. Yet the action stops while he *seeks out relationship* with her; the relationship between sovereign and subject is not aloof. Jesus knows that his kingly power (*dynamis*) over life and health has flowed from him, but in some sense the full scope of his authority is not confirmed until he comes into relationship with the faith that brought the need relentlessly into contact with him. It is as though the whole of heaven and earth stops in its tracks until she becomes known to him.

Second, in the kingship of Jesus *the need of the marginalized and vulnerable is addressed before the need of the celebrated and powerful.* One imagines the reactions of the crowd, knowing in whose company Jesus is traveling. Here is a woman barred by law from hope of regaining her health, her safety, or her place in the community. But the message is clear: in the realm ordered by Jesus' kingly authority, those on the fringes of society have a rightful place in direct relationship with the Lord. Moreover, Jesus exercises *absolute sovereignty over the realm of law*, reaching through the purity boundaries to effect a direct encounter based on the authority not of law but of faith.

The pivot upon which both stories turns is what this woman—otherwise utterly unlike Jairus—has in

Pastoral Perspective

once told me that his prayers had been answered. He said in all sincerity, "I *have* been healed, not of Parkinson's disease, but I have been healed of my fear of Parkinson's disease." These two biblical healing stories in which people turn to Jesus for healing will raise the question in many hearers, "Does prayer work?" If we mean by this, "Do you get what you pray for?" the honest answer will be "Sometimes, but not always." Pray as they may, congregation and pastor both know that all prayers are not answered as we pray them.

In light of such pastoral concerns raised by healing stories, it may be helpful to remember that prayers for healing are not simply utilitarian. That is to say, prayer is not simply a matter of bending the vector of divine will toward my will, my needs, and my hopes. More profoundly, to ask something of God is to edge into deeper relationship with God. God's mind may or may not be changed, but I—my mind and heart—may be.

Individually, each of these healing stories also offers unique pastoral perspectives. The story of the healing of the daughter of the synagogue leader may bring to the surface the profound love and accompanying fears that many parents and grandparents in the congregation have about their children and grandchildren. A story about a dead child restored to life may well raise the fears that every mother and father has for his or her children. Indeed, any parents or grandparents in the congregation who have lost children or grandchildren may be profoundly affected by hearing this story. The culmination of the story is Jesus' compassion for desperate parents and their little girl, a love captured in the tender Aramaic words, *talitha cum*, "little girl, get up." Nevertheless, a pastor would be wise to proceed with sensitivity toward parents and their children.

The other healing story in this text, enclosed within that of the little girl, also raises unique and equally profound pastoral concerns. Hidden in this particular story is not only the reality of illness, but also the reality of isolation and social alienation. In Jesus' world, a woman with a condition like this woman's probably would have been a social outcast. Her condition made her ritually unclean, and she would have had to live her days in isolation, separated from her family and village. When people saw her coming toward them, they probably would have distanced themselves for fear that she might brush against them, for her touch would have made them ritually unclean, especially men.

of physical health and spiritual salvation. Jesus agrees to travel with the man to address his need. A large crowd also follows, which "presses upon" Jesus, his disciples, and the synagogue ruler (v. 24).

An Interrupted Journey—the Hemorrhaging Woman (vv. 25–29). Suddenly a woman appears, but not in a public way. She has suffered for twelve years "with a flow of blood" (v. 25), which implies a menstrual disorder. She has had many physicians, spent "all that she had" (v. 26), and still grows worse. She hears about Jesus and seeks him out. She perhaps has a magical understanding of Jesus' healing powers, for she says to herself, "even if I touch his garments I will be saved [*sōthēsomai*]" (v. 28). Later in the narrative Jesus says her faith makes her well and secures her salvation (v. 34, another form of *sōzō*). Whether magic or faith is on her mind, the text indicates the "immediate" (see 1:10, 12, 21, 23, 29, 30, etc.) cessation of her blood— "it was dried up" and "she knew that her body was healed from its illness" (v. 29).

Jesus' Reaction (vv. 30–34). Also "immediately," Jesus "knew in himself that a power had gone out from him" (v. 30a). The healing power of God is made available to this woman through Jesus. The exchange of power creates the opportunity for dialogue. Jesus asks the crowd, "Who touched my garment?" (v. 30b). The disciples, who generally lack insight, wonder who *has not* touched Jesus. The woman comes forward to make public her desperate, private search for healing.[2] Her illness made her ritually impure—she was to remain on the fringes of society, a private, not a public person, but now she has been "outed" by her attempt to seek refuge from a very public person. She too, like the synagogue ruler, falls at Jesus' feet in homage and seeks his mercy for her touch that should make *him* ritually impure (see Lev. 15:19–33). Jesus has already shown he is less concerned about touching the impure than about showing them mercy (see 1:41). Thus he calls this unnamed woman "daughter" and says, "Your faith has saved you" (v. 34a). Moreover, he sends her away in peace, because her faith has made her "healthy" from her illness (v. 34b). Thus Jesus provides a very public acknowledgment of a private healing.

Back to Jairus's Daughter (vv. 35–36). This public encounter with the hemorrhaging woman occurs

the ever-present crowd that awaited Jesus when he stepped from the boat. Despite having been run out of town by the Gerasenes, word of the miracle on the other side of the sea must have traveled by means of the testimony of the healed demoniac and those who were "amazed" (v. 20) by his story.

Out of the "large crowd" that follows Jesus to the place where Jairus's daughter lies near death rushes another desperate petitioner, this one "a woman who had been suffering from hemorrhages for twelve years" (v. 25). Thus begins the story-within-a-story form that in itself invites homiletical comment. Despite the urgency of the condition of Jairus's daughter and Jesus' determination to reach her, Jesus acknowledges the ill woman who has the faith—not to mention the audacity—to reach out and claim his healing power. At this point the symbolic parallels of the story begin to emerge, demonstrating the importance of preaching this pericope as a whole rather than focusing, as preachers sometimes do, on one of the two stories. The notable parallels deepen the meaning of the stories. Both victims of illness are female and ritually unclean, one as a result of death and one as a result of hemorrhage; both represent the significance of the number twelve in Jewish tradition (the twelve years of hemorrhage and the twelve-year-old girl); and both are regarded as "daughters" (the little girl being Jairus's daughter and the woman who is addressed by Jesus as "Daughter"). An act of touch restores both women to new life even as those surrounding them lack understanding.

The two stories raise interesting and important questions for the preacher. One question has to do with who—or what—claims our time and attention, and how we determine the worthiness of those people and things. Jesus' example in this text makes it clear that those who are the most deserving of our attention may be the least visible ones. The female child, despite the importance of her father, and the ill woman are not among those most highly regarded in their social contexts. Jesus acts here as he so often does, transcending social and religious barriers in order to carry out his ministry. Both women are deprived of power, but Jesus, in his compassion, sees their needs and deems them as worthy of his attention as anyone else.

Another important question raised by this text is, what does it mean to be healed? The hemorrhaging woman is healed when she reaches out and touches Jesus' robe, and the dead child is restored to life when Jesus takes her by the hand. Both stories have

---

2. On the public and private dimensions of this text, see Wendy Cotter, "Mark's Hero of the Twelfth-Year Miracles," in *A Feminist Companion to Mark*, ed. Amy-Jill Levine (Sheffield: Sheffield Academic Press, 2001), 55.

Mark 5:21-43

Theological Perspective

common with him: deep faith in Jesus' kingly authority. She comes before Jesus "in fear and trembling"—not the fear of the faithless, storm-tossed disciples, but the fear of one who knows that she is coming into relationship with God. In speaking to her, Jesus affirms her faith by pointing to it as the very source of the power by which she has been healed ("*your* faith has made you well"), just as his perfect faith is the source of his own authority. Her approach may be impetuous, even audacious, but her faith is utterly genuine. In it lies the source of the kingly power Jesus exercises on her behalf.

The action now returns to Jairus. Approaching the house, the party receives word of his daughter's death. The hired mourners are already present, and Jesus addresses them as he did the frightened, faithless disciples ("Why do you make a commotion and weep?" v. 39). Here, as before, the contrast is between the absolute obedience of Jesus, through which derive all aspects of his kingly authority, and the faithlessness of those around him ("they laughed at him," v. 40). Here, the situation presented is in extremis: the hemorrhaging woman suffered, but the child is dead. Jesus, as before, exercises kingly prerogatives *gently*; the parallel seems to be to 1 Kings 17, but the high drama of Elijah's healing of the son of the woman of Zarephath is answered here by simple gestures and direct words. Thus the Gospel writer successfully emphasizes Jesus' easy exercise of *godlike authority over life and death*, prefiguring his exercise of this same authority after the events of Golgotha.

For Mark's Christology, then, the implications of this pericope are manifold. How is Jesus a king? Jesus is king of life and law. He exercises godlike authority over life and death, health and sickness, clean and unclean. His authority is exercised gently, in direct relationship with those who come by faith. Priority is accorded to the marginal, the outcast, the silent. And within that faith—the faith of Jesus' absolute obedience, the imperfect yet insistent faith of his followers in him—lies the source of his kingly authority and its exercise on behalf of those who believe.

MARK D. W. EDINGTON

Pastoral Perspective

In this story however, she pushes her way through the crowd. She deliberately touches Jesus, a male and a popular religious figure. She should have kept her distance and called out to him from a discreet remove. Jesus' reaction is even more surprising. Mark tells us that she threw herself at Jesus' feet in fear and trembling. But instead of calling her "unclean," Jesus names her "daughter," a daughter every bit as precious as Jairus's beloved little girl. Instead of admonishing her outrageous trespass, Jesus praises her faith. Instead of justifiable anger, Jesus bids her go in peace.

Hidden in this tale is a flash of precious intimacy between two human beings who are socially very distant from each other. Their scandalous touch does not yield the anger and alienation you might expect. Rather, it brings wholeness, healing, and peace.

Let me offer a negative illustration of the power of intimacy. Psychologists long speculated about how children utterly cut off from human relationships might develop. Their speculations were tragically confirmed in the 1980s when the numerous orphanages of Ceausescu's Communist Romania were opened to the world's eyes after his fall from power. This dictator had mandated bizarre social policies that had resulted in thousands of unwanted children. Many of them ended up in vast, underfunded state-run orphanages where they were completely isolated, often receiving no love, in fact no human *touch at all*. Tragically, although the children grew into physical human *creatures*, they did not become human *persons*. They could not speak. They could not relate to others. They could not give or receive affection.

The pastoral affirmation in this biblical story is that, beyond even physical healing, acceptance, intimacy, and touch can make us whole and give us peace. We are, in fact, shaped and made human *in relationship* to other persons. Our relationships—in the church, in friendships, and in marriage—are not just something extra added on to life for distraction and entertainment, as if we would be complete human beings in individual isolation. Relationship, "touch" if you will, makes us human and whole. As the contemporary Scottish philosopher John Macmurray once phased it, "I need 'you' in order to be myself."[1]

MICHAEL L. LINDVALL

---

1. Quoted in an unpublished lecture by Andrew Purves.

before a public figure. Now news comes that Jairus's daughter has died. His household messengers play a role like that of the disciples in the intercalated story of the woman. They think the synagogue ruler must go home to grieve and "not trouble the teacher" (v. 35). The messengers do not address Jesus, a mere carpenter and healer. They address only their superior, but Jesus "overhears." He urges the ruler, as he did the woman, "Do not fear, only believe" (v. 36).

On the Way to a Healing (vv. 37–39).

When this trip begins, crowds follow (v. 24). Jesus now moves from public to private space. He takes only three of his most trusted disciples—Peter, James, and John (v. 37). When they arrive at Jairus's house, hired mourners are "weeping and wailing" with much "confusion" (v. 38a). Recognizing their lack of faith, Jesus asks, "Why are you confused and crying? The child is not dead but sleeps" (v. 39). What is the difference between death and this euphemism for death? Suggestions that the child was really in a coma do not suffice. Jesus admonishes everyone that death is not the final answer. In the presence of God's healing power, even death cannot sustain its stronghold. In comparison to death without hope, this child has hope for restored life, so she is merely "sleeping."

A Private Healing (vv. 40–43).

The mourners laugh, so Jesus kicks them out and allows only the father, the mother, and the three disciples to enter the girl's room (v. 40). The restoration evokes similar private healings by the prophets Elijah (1 Kgs. 17:17–24) and Elisha (2 Kgs. 4:32–37). Jesus takes the child by the hand and in his native Aramaic commands, "*Talitha, cum* . . . little girl, get up!" Again Mark uses "immediately" to show the instantaneous nature of God's healing power. The girl rises and walks around. She is twelve years old, having lived as long as the woman had been sick (v. 42). The private group that witnessed the healing is "amazed with great amazement." Jesus orders them to tell no one (v. 43a; cf. 1:25, 33, 44; 3:12), but the girl's funeral rites have already begun. Word will spread quickly. Mark's readers know that "messianic secrecy" fails repeatedly. Jesus demonstrates a final act of compassion when he instructs that the girl be fed (v. 43b). This demonstrates both that she is very much alive and needs sustenance, and that Jesus has concern for her humanity, as he had for the outcast woman.

EFRAÍN AGOSTO

happy endings. But that is not always the reality of life, as every preacher knows. Whenever we preach these stories, we must make it clear that not even our most earnest pleas *always* result in the answers we desire. Certainly we proclaim Jesus as Ruler over all things, the One whom "even the wind and the sea obey" (Mark 4:41), as declared in last week's Gospel text—a reality that most people of faith believe operative even in our skeptical, scientific age.

More troubling for the preacher of these stories is not the question of whether or not such miracles did or still may occur, but the question of how we hold onto faith *when they do not occur*. Every person of faith who suffers, such as the hemorrhaging woman and the desperate parents of the dying little girl, prays for—and usually believes in—the possibility of miraculous healing, but dramatic physical healing is rarely the response to those prayers. Here, then, is an opportunity to explore healing in its less obvious, less dramatic dimensions: healing as peace and acceptance in the face of disappointment, and as awareness of the continuing presence of God in our times of despair.

A related question has to do with what role faith plays in our healing. The hemorrhaging woman has the audacity to transgress a whole host of social protocols when she touches Jesus' robe without permission to claim her own healing. Talk about faith! And then there is Jairus, whose faith causes him to fall at Jesus' feet, despite how Jesus is regarded by most synagogue leaders. These examples challenge us to examine our own faith, asking how we find the strength to claim God's promises of healing and hope for ourselves, and how we empower others to do the same.

BEVERLY ZINK-SAWYER

Ezekiel 2:1-5

¹He said to me: O mortal, stand up on your feet, and I will speak with you. ²And when he spoke to me, a spirit entered into me and set me on my feet; and I heard him speaking to me. ³He said to me, Mortal, I am sending you to the people of Israel, to a nation of rebels who have rebelled against me; they and their ancestors have transgressed against me to this very day. ⁴The descendants are impudent and stubborn. I am sending you to them, and you shall say to them, "Thus says the Lord GOD." ⁵Whether they hear or refuse to hear (for they are a rebellious house), they shall know that there has been a prophet among them.

Theological Perspective

The account of God's call to Ezekiel speaks to the very nature of prophecy: "You shall say to them, 'Thus says the Lord GOD'" (v. 4). A prophet, most essentially, is someone who speaks on God's behalf. This is evident from the moment Moses is commissioned (Exod. 7:1). Aaron is appointed to speak on behalf of Moses *as God*. The theological phenomenon of prophecy—strictly, of someone speaking on God's behalf—is found supremely in the person of Moses. Subsequently in the Old Testament, and even more clearly in the New Testament, this sense is extended to include not only speaking but also *acting* on God's behalf. For example, in Luke 24:19 Jesus is described as one mighty in deed and word.

Why should there be prophecy at all? This is the theological question that lies behind Ezekiel's calling, one that is rarely addressed. The rationale is explained in Deuteronomy, the book that explains Israel's life by looking back to its foundational events in the time of Moses. The giving of the Ten Commandments is recounted in Deuteronomy 5:1–21, after which God "added no more" (Deut. 5:22). The people are overwhelmed with the experience of God's speaking directly to them, so they ask Moses to be a mediator. God approves the request and Moses is appointed (Deut. 5:31), after which the

Pastoral Perspective

"What a pity," Annie Dillard wrote, "that so hard on the heels of Christ come the Christians."[1] Reading the call of Ezekiel, one feels the same sort of disappointment. The first chapter opens with a stormy wind, flashing fire, four-faced beasts seated on omnidirectional chariots, and a heavenly throne hosting the glory of the Lord. Next to this backdrop, Ezekiel hardly seems to warrant the title "prophet." Too fearful, too weak, or too in shock to stand up on his own two feet, Ezekiel, like the church, is powerless to do much of anything. much less answer this call from God.

On the one hand, Ezekiel's mortal self can serve as comfort to people in the pews. It is God's voice that gives needed breath and spirit (synonymous in the Hebrew) to Ezekiel to be able stand on his own two feet, receive this difficult call, and follow through on it. If God can give strength to Ezekiel during one of the most difficult periods in the life of Israel, then God can give strength to the church, ill-equipped to respond to our own call today.

On the other hand, this kind of reassurance spoken prematurely can serve to reinforce the already dulled expectations we hold for the

---

1. Annie Dillard, "The Gospel according to Saint Luke," in *Incarnation* (New York: Viking, 1990), 36.

Exegetical Perspective

A Season of Trauma. The youth Ezekiel, during the period of King Josiah (Ezek. 1:1–3; 29:17), was ill prepared for the social trauma of the Babylonian exile. The Babylonian colonialism began in earnest with the deportation of a significant part of the population of Jerusalem in 597 BCE. The social structure of ancient Judah prior to that point revolved around an agrarian and traditional society, rooted in the particularities and promises of the land of Judah and Israel. Deportation put an end to all that for Ezekiel and his companions.

The structure of the book of Ezekiel is fairly straightforward. The call of Ezekiel (Ezek. 1:1–3:15) introduces the collection of vision reports and speeches that make up the broad expanse of the book. A clear break at 3:16 describes an event that took place in a different time frame. The call/vision report of Ezekiel has three major components: 1:1–28a; 1:28b–2:10; and 3:1–15. The second component begins with an introduction, 1:28b–2:2, followed by five elements, each introduced with an address to the prophet (2:3–5, 2:6–7; 2:8–3:3; 3:4–9; 3:10–11). The introduction and the first of the five elements give the reader a small taste of the chapter and invite further reading. This whole collection (Ezek. 1:1–3:15) functions as a prophetic call/vision report. This genre has certain literary conventions

Homiletical Perspective

This lection describes the commissioning of Ezekiel as a prophet. It speaks of his specific call in a particular time and place, yet it transcends context, to signal hope for all those who face experiences of exile and to provide encouragement for any who seek to be faithful to God's call.

Hope in Exile. Ezekiel was called as God's prophet at the start of the sixth century BCE. Babylonian armies had laid siege to Jerusalem, destroyed the temple, and carried off into exile in Babylon the king and many members of the elite, including Ezekiel, a priest of the temple. The exiles had endured the conquest of Jerusalem and the deaths of loved ones. They were forced to leave everything that was familiar and precious to them—family members, homes, possessions. They lost even the temple, the center of their life of faith. The temple was the place where they offered prayers and brought sacrifices, but more than that, it was considered the very dwelling place of God.

Now the exiles find themselves in a foreign land, far from their homeland and far from the temple. How could God permit such a thing? they wonder. Has God abandoned them? Has God been defeated by the Babylonian gods? Doubts plague their minds. Perhaps their YHWH is not as powerful as they had

Ezekiel 2:1-5

Theological Perspective

Sinai narrative continues with Moses relaying all that God speaks.

That the concept of prophecy is present here is confirmed by a later passage in Deuteronomy that addresses the question of what will happen to Israel after Moses goes—how will they know what God wants of them (Deut. 18:15–22)? The answer follows, "I will raise up for them a prophet like you [Moses] from among their own people; I will put my words in the mouth of the prophet, who shall speak to them everything that I command" (Deut. 18:18). This background explains precisely what is going on in Ezekiel 2. God is raising up Ezekiel to follow in Moses's footsteps as one who speaks for God. By the end of the chapter, Ezekiel has a vision of God's giving him a scroll of the words he is to receive and relay: "Eat this scroll, and go, speak to the house of Israel" (3:1).

The very notion of prophecy assumes that humanity is the normal channel for God's revelation to and communication with humanity. This may be risky, as God's warning to Ezekiel at the point of the call suggests (2:3–6). The people intended to hear the prophecy may be stubborn, impudent, and rebellious. And not only the listeners, but also the speaker: Is it possible for the divine word to bypass the corruption of humanity in its delivery? How is Israel to know that Ezekiel is a true prophet?

The Old Testament stresses the sin of humanity that extends to all; yet at the same time it demonstrates the human potential for obedience and faithfulness under God. There is no sense in which Moses obscures or corrupts the divine word as mediator at Sinai. In fact Deuteronomy 5:28–29 suggests it is better for Israel that God speaks through a prophet than directly. A faithful servant like Moses demonstrates the possibility that people may be channels for God's word. Thus Moses, and prophets like Ezekiel after him, enlarge the boundaries of human potential with respect to God. Ultimately in the figure of Jesus we find the full realization of human potential before God—demonstrated in his sinlessness, his oneness of will, and his obedience. The New Testament extends this phenomenon concerning human potential to all people. That which is limited to Moses and the prophets in the Old Testament is opened to everyone in the New Testament. The sort of relationship that Jesus has with God as Father is opened to all believers.

Ezekiel's call to be a prophet underlines the way in which God communicates with humanity. It is language that is the vehicle for divine communication.

Pastoral Perspective

community of faith. If Christians are always being reminded of just how ordinary and powerless we are, it is likely that we will fulfill our own demoralized expectations. Comfort is necessary for Ezekiel only after he experiences the awesome power and presence of God.

Christians claim that this encounter with God is at the root of our worship. Yet the evidence shows that many Christians have a hard time rolling out of bed on a Sunday morning to show up for that encounter. For those who decide not to sleep in, there is a host of other activities competing for time and energy. For many, worship has become another scheduled activity among many.

Ezekiel's testimony serves as a cautionary reminder that at the heart of the church's life is not a set of activities, but an encounter with the holy; an encounter that ought to knock us off our feet and leave us there until God gives us the strength to respond.

Out of that encounter comes a call. Once again, God's choice of Ezekiel is rather baffling. Ezekiel is to go to the people of Israel—"a nation of rebels"—and say whatever God tells him to say (v. 3). The enormity of the task—sending one person to speak to a nation—stands in stark contrast to the limitations of Ezekiel, who we are reminded more than once is simply another one of us ("mortal"). As if the call itself were not intimidating enough, YHWH goes on to say that it is likely that the people will not receive this message favorably, since they are "impudent" and "stubborn" (v. 4).

The church can stand in at least two places in this text: as proclaimer and as receiver of proclamation. Neither interpretive choice need be exclusive of the other. There are times when the church finds itself in both locations. As proclaimer, this text gives courage to a church already limping from its myriad wounds. God has chosen to send *this* church, sprawled out on the floor hardly able to move, to say to the nations, "Thus says the Lord GOD" (v. 4). According to Ezekiel, this is really all we need to know. The church often doubts this is so.

On those occasions when the church does make a witness in the public square, the proclamations and the press releases rarely seem to make much of a difference. The church has lost the political weight it used to throw around. But while these observations may be correct, Ezekiel would call them irrelevant. The church is sent to say whatever God instructs it to say. "Whether they hear or refuse to hear" is beside the point (v. 5). The role of the proclaimer,

Exegetical Perspective

(see 1 Kgs. 22:19–21; Jer. 1:4–10; Isa. 6:1–8). The divergent rhetorical devices carry the same core functions: the prophetic call/vision report outlines the divine sanction for the exercise of the prophetic vocation of a given person, in this case Ezekiel.

The Prophet as a Representative Person. One of the rhetorical devices in the book of Ezekiel is the use of the term *ben ʾadam*. The term occurs ninety-three times. There has been some confusion about this, because some have tried to connect the Ezekiel passages and the Daniel 7:13 Aramaic *kebar ʾenosh*. The NRSV uses the term "mortal" in order to capture the role of the prophet as the designate for the species.

In verse 1 the typical human being is told to stand up in order to "hear." The previous chapter accented the vision, whereas this unit focuses attention on the audition. In verse 2 the Spirit sets the human up and speaks. One can see in this passage the role of Spirit in the book of Ezekiel. The term "spirit" (*ruʿach*) occurs twenty-five times in the forty-eight chapters of the book. The writer invites the reader to fill in the gap and recognize that this is not a generic spirit or wind but rather the Spirit of the Lord (Ezek. 11:5; 37:1; Isa. 61:1). The emphasis is on divine action more than human compliance.

The Commissioning. The first commission, and the only one in this unit, contains three elements: sending (vv. 3, 4), speaking (v. 4), and knowing (v. 5). The Hebrew prophet in this case is itinerant. For Amos, the sending was from Tekoa to the northern kingdom. For Ezekiel it is to the community in Diaspora, in this case, Babylon. The writer repeats the phrase, "I myself am sending you" (vv. 3, 4, my translation), however, just as someone who paints in oil colors places layer upon layer in order to add depth and texture to the picture, the writer here does not focus on the location of the itinerant prophet but on the social location of the audience, whose perspective is affected by the disenfranchised space created by the exile.

The prophet is the direct object of the subject "God" and the verb "send," but the indirect object, the children of Israel (*bene Israel*), is no less complex. The phrase occurs more than five hundred times in the Hebrew Bible. Many of those occurrences refer to the broad expanse of all the Hebrew tribes. Nonetheless, the northern kingdom comes to take this title in the period of the divided monarchy (924–722 BCE). After the fall of the northern kingdom, the term once again

Homiletical Perspective

believed. And now, so distant from the dwelling place of God, how will God ever find them or answer their prayers? The exiles are in deep despair.

The opening lines of the book of Ezekiel answer this despair. Ezekiel reports, "I was among the exiles by the river Chebar, the heavens were opened, and I saw visions of God" (1:1). There, in a foreign land, among a displaced people, God appears! God finds them even in their exile! God seeks them out and speaks to them through Ezekiel. Ezekiel goes on to describe his dramatic encounter with the Divine and his commission from God: He is to warn the people of Israel to cease their rebellion and return to faithful living.

The River Chebar may serve as a dramatic image of those times in our lives when we experience exile. When do our listeners find themselves on the banks of the River Chebar? When do they experience doubt, disappointment, fear? When do they question God's power, feel abandoned by God, fear that God has gone away and will not return? Ezekiel's call is a sign of hope in the midst of despair. It assures us that we are never so far away that God cannot find us. Even in moments of exile, God remembers us and comes to us.

Called to Faithfulness. We live in a culture obsessed with measurements and statistics. It begins at birth, when a child scarcely out of the womb is weighed and measured, and continues throughout our lives. We measure test scores, cholesterol levels, investment portfolios. We count, we track, and we compare in almost every area of our lives. Often we make these measures because we want to be successful. We want to know that our efforts make a difference.

To contemporary ears, then, God's commission to Ezekiel may sound very strange indeed—for God seems to have a different notion of success. Ezekiel's call is to speak God's word to the people of Israel "whether they hear or refuse to hear" (2:5). The people's response is not Ezekiel's primary concern. His success will not be measured by the outcome of his preaching. His effectiveness will not be judged on how many people believe him or the number who repent instead of rebel. He will not be judged on whether the temple is raised or lost, whether Jerusalem rises or falls. Rather, Ezekiel is asked to answer God's call and speak the word of the Lord, no matter what the result.

What a challenging word for today's preachers! Many spend countless hours honing their craft in the hope of transforming lives. They hope that their

Ezekiel 2:1-5

Theological Perspective

This does not deny the possibility of other means of communication; rather it affirms that *words* have the greatest and fullest potential for understanding the mind of God. God's revelation is, normally, word based. It may involve action also—Ezekiel in particular among Old Testament prophets is renowned for "acting out" his message—but most essentially it takes the form of words. Here in Ezekiel, the call is to declare God's anger over Israel's rebellion and the threat of God's judgment. "Whether they hear or refuse to hear" (2:5), the message is delivered through speaking and preaching. It is through prophecy that we come to understand the importance of language for human and divine relations, and thus the seriousness of its debasement in our culture.

How exactly does one know the presence of a prophet? Ezekiel 2:5 suggests that "whether [the people] hear or refuse to hear . . . they shall *know* that there has been a prophet among them." According to Deuteronomy 18:21–22, true prophecy is determined by its outcome, that is, when what is predicted takes place or is proved true. This is the classic test of true prophecy—and is doubtless a key factor in the overall discernment of the prophecy of Ezekiel. With the benefit of hindsight, the book of Ezekiel has been received into the canon of Scripture. But such a test takes time, especially with events that are predicted some distance into the future. How can we discern at the time? Here another criterion is offered that has to do with the very presence of Ezekiel among his rebellious people. Jeremiah (chaps. 23–24) describes false prophets as those who speak comfort for the sake of the prophet's acceptance and popularity. Here is the reverse: Ezekiel's faithfulness is put to the test in a situation where the message and the circumstances are far from comfortable. The people will know he is a prophet sent from God when he says, "Thus says the LORD" despite their resistance and rebellion. We may conclude that the more it costs the messenger, the more likely a message is to be true. As Jesus describes it, the true way is the hard and challenging one (Matt. 7:14).

JO BAILEY WELLS

Pastoral Perspective

according to Ezekiel, is measured not by results but by whether or not we deliver the message.

But the church does not always get to embody the role of proclaimer. Sometimes we are the people in dire need of proclamation. Sometimes we are the impudent and stubborn rebels who are not likely to receive God's proclamation favorably. For those standing in need of proclamation, God sends not just the message, but also the messenger. This is an important point for people of the book, accustomed to receiving the word of the Lord only from the lectern on a Sunday morning. Certainly Christians are accustomed to the notion of God's Word embodied in the person of Jesus of Nazareth. Less often do we imagine God's word embodied in the lives of fellow imperfect human beings.

At a meeting of local pastors in the community in which I serve, a high school student from our ill-performing city school system was invited to share her experience with us. One of the pastors explained that she had listened to this young woman's story and determined that we needed to hear it too. The student told us that she had met with the school counselor and shared with the counselor her dream of going to college. When she asked for help in applying for a scholarship, the counselor replied, "You? You're not good enough for a scholarship." This normally verbose bunch of preachers fell silent. A few wiped their eyes. "I want to know," the student asked us through tears, "if the church cares about students like me." Sometimes powerful words from God are delivered not at the lectern, but in the flesh and blood of the messengers God chooses to say, "Thus says the LORD."

Sometimes the church is called to be proclaimer; at other times its role is to receive God's proclamation. In both instances, we are both unnerved and sustained by the word of God, embodied in the lives of the faithful.

ANDREW FOSTER CONNORS

becomes associated with the totality of the Hebrew tribes. It becomes an emblem of pan-Israelite nationalistic hopes. This makes even better sense in light of the colonial situation for the Hebrew exiles. Nonetheless, such an appellation might lead a reader to surmise prophetic optimism until one reads a little further. The writer designates Israel as a pagan nation, hence the term *goyim.*

The sense of divine disappointment comes through as this heathen nation, Israel, is further described as a rebel nation. The community is described as continuing to live out the rebellion. The structure parallels the rebelling of this generation with the transgression of its ancestors. The exiles likely thought that their circumstance was quite unique. The prophetic text speaks to the social dislocation through pointing to the continuity of rebellion and transgression. The Hebrew text, more graphic than the NRSV translation, states that "these children have hard faces and hard hearts," which the NRSV renders "impudent and stubborn."

Speaking to the Sleeping Congregation. The prophetic call vision reports almost never describe the commission to a successful ministry. For this reason, the commission begins with the phrase, "I myself am sending you," followed by the description of a less than receptive audience and says again the phrase, "I myself am sending you to them." Regardless of the receptivity of the audience, the prophet is charged to speak to the designated audience. One finds Isaiah's similar challenge (Isa. 6:9–10) and the aberration of Jonah's audience response. The content of the speech is the speech of God. Here the writer falls back on a formula. This is God's message through the prophet.

The Hard Knowing. The explicit message is that the reader's response presents no relevant contingency for the speaker/writer. The role of "hearing" in a traditional society indicates more than an auditory event alone; it is a holistic response to the message. In Ezekiel's case, the "hearing" of the listeners does not affect the role of the prophet, nor does it require the acknowledgment of the audience. Even if they do not "hear," they will nonetheless know that there was a prophet in their midst. Even if they (or we) use our best denial mechanism, they (and we) know a prophet has been in their (and our) midst. This was and continues to be a hard knowledge.

STEPHEN BRECK REID

words will not be in vain, but will bear fruit in the lives of their listeners. They carefully consider: What is the "take home" message? What metaphors best convey a point? What stories might touch people's hearts? These are not Ezekiel's concerns. For him, the measure of success is not the outcome, but his faithfulness. Ezekiel's commission suggests that he may plant seeds, but the harvest is up to God. This text provides a helpful antidote to human pride, in which we place the weight of the world on our own shoulders and hold ourselves responsible for every result. It reminds us that God is the one ultimately in charge. God calls each one of us to particular work, and our faithfulness to that call matters more than the outcome.

Of course, preachers are not the only ones who need this message. The church is not immune to the compulsion to measure success. This text provides preachers an opportunity to explore the ways that congregations evaluate their ministry and mission. Many churches count how many people attend worship and Sunday school; they track the numbers in their cash flow reports and benevolence giving. This information may serve valuable purposes. But to churches preoccupied with numbers and results, Ezekiel's commission encourages a return to the heart of the matter: What is God calling us to do? And are we faithful to that call?

The exiles in Babylon doubted that God will ever find them there by the River Chebar. But God has not abandoned them, and neither has God abandoned the community of faith today. This text invites the preacher to explore the call that God has for each one of us. Although that call rarely comes in visions as dramatic as Ezekiel's, God communicates with us and calls us in other ways: an inner nudging, a new sense of passion, a shared excitement about future possibilities. The measure of our success does not come from numbers and statistics but from our discernment of that call—and our faithfulness to it.

LEANNE PEARCE REED

Psalm 123

¹To you I lift up my eyes,
  O you who are enthroned in the heavens!
²As the eyes of servants
  look to the hand of their master,
 as the eyes of a maid
  to the hand of her mistress,
 so our eyes look to the LORD our God,
  until he has mercy upon us.

³Have mercy upon us, O LORD, have mercy upon us,
  for we have had more than enough of contempt.
⁴Our soul has had more than its fill
  of the scorn of those who are at ease,
  of the contempt of the proud.

Theological Perspective

This psalm is one of the loveliest prayers in all of Scripture, simple and direct, trusting and confident, spoken out of need and in much hope. It begins abruptly, "To you," but the name of YHWH is not uttered until the end of the long second verse. Before God is named, God is characterized as the one enthroned in the heavens, the creator who presides over the assembly of Gods in heaven (see Ps. 82). Thus in a simple utterance the prayer appeals to the entire liturgic drama of divine enthronement so central to the Jerusalem temple. The result is a characterization of YHWH in the most sweeping majestic terms.

Having alluded to kingship, verse 2 utters the counterterm, "servant." The relationship of the two characters in this prayer is *servant-to-king*. The verse ponders that relationship according to human analogue, servant-to-master, maid-to-mistress. The verse is organized around "as . . . as . . . so." How is it that a trusting servant looks at a master? How does a grateful maid look in the face of a mistress? Here there is no suspicion, no fear, no dread, no resentment; else the analogue would not work in the prayer. Rather, the look is one of gladness, awe, dependence, and glad submissiveness rooted in trust. The servant knows that his life is safe in the governance of the master. Such an image, of course,

Pastoral Perspective

There is simplicity not only in the length of this psalm, but also in its concise diction. The psalm evokes a transparency of need and longing. Translations provide a verb of seeing in verse 2 that is only implied in the Hebrew. More precisely the text could read (based on NRSV):

> As the eyes of servants to the hand of their master,
> as the eyes of a maid to the hand of her mistress,
> so our eyes to the LORD our God . . .

"As their eyes . . . so our eyes"—there is an invitation in the very abruptness of the language to identify with the desperation of the slave. One of the pastoral questions raised by this powerful analogy is how we can rightly identify with such abjection.

The psalmist has seen the eyes of those whose fates hang upon the will of their master—those whose lives will be determined by someone else's thumbs up or thumbs down. Where have we seen eyes like these? We may have seen them while visiting a prisoner on death row or in attending to people living and begging on the streets or while sitting with those in the waiting rooms of hospitals or with others whose lives are absolutely dependent on those more powerful than they. How can we rightly find ourselves in this psalm and not diminish its power?

Exegetical Perspective

Words of Life and Death. This short psalm is distinguished by its deep emotional appeal. The provenance of the psalm is uncertain, since its insistence on protection from "enemies" could locate it in a number of periods. To be sure, the anguished appeal for deliverance grows out of a real-life experience.

The superscription, not printed here, identifies this as a Psalm of Ascents or a Pilgrimage Song. It is part of a collection of psalms (Pss. 120–34) classified as Psalms of Ascents by their superscriptions. It is imagined that these psalms were sung by those on pilgrimage to Jerusalem for one of the three great annual festivals. The journey to the temple, the symbol of hope and a future with God, was characterized by joy and expectation at entering the sacred precincts. Like several other psalms in this group, Psalm 123 is a prayer for deliverance from unspecified enemies. It is not a song of thanksgiving or of praise, but a petition for God's protective care. Since these psalms reflect the realities of the Diaspora, the enemies might be imagined to be leftover aggressors from the Babylonian captivity or antagonists from the Seleucid period. The final verse of the psalm identifies the enemies as the "contemptuous proud." This expression is unique to the entire Old Testament, so identifying the

Homiletical Perspective

People of biblical faith do not live alone but are deeply connected to a community, a fact demonstrated yet again by this psalm as it begins, "I lift up my eyes," then quickly changes to the plural, "our eyes look." What affects one individual also affects the entire community of faith, and in turn what affects the community of faith affects the individual. So it is that the psalmist cries out on behalf of all. In so doing, she draws upon an image that is common for that world, but whose power is hard to grasp for those of us who live in the United States in the twenty-first century. Part of the challenge the preacher faces is to help the congregation understand the reality of slavery and so deepen the meaning of the psalm to our listeners.

If we go back in U.S. history, we find more than enough examples of what it was to be a slave—and "slave" really is the word to use. It means dependence and obedience and deprivation and humiliation. If you are a slave, the quality of your life is defined by the kind of master who owns you. In her autobiography, *Incidents in the Life of a Slave Girl*, Harriet Jacobs describes one of the countless small indignities that blighted slave life:

> Mrs. Flint . . . was a member of the church; but partaking of the Lord's Supper did not seem to put

Psalm 123

Theological Perspective

is not politically correct and, taken at face value, would encourage questions concerning the enslaved; but taken in context, the imagery bespeaks glad reliance upon a generous, agreeable master. The relationship is not a "democratic" one, but entails submissive trust and obedience and, consequently, freedom, joy, and well-being.

The "so" at the end of verse 2 now names "YHWH our God"; the look toward God is one of hope that awaits mercy. The "so" (also read as "just as") establishes the analogue. Like every analogue, this one is not perfect or complete, but only suggestive. The master may be busy, elsewhere preoccupied and distracted; but the petitioner is patient and knows that in due course the master will exhibit *mercy*. It is this mercy that is the ground of the prayer and the basis for the relationship. YHWH is indeed a God of mercy:

> The Lord passed before him, and proclaimed,
>> "The LORD, the LORD,
>> a God *merciful and gracious*,
>> slow to anger,
>> and abounding in steadfast love
>>> and faithfulness." (Exod. 34:6)

The term "mercy" bespeaks unconditional regard for, love that is completely gratuitous. The master gives himself over to the well-being of the servant without condition or prerequisite.

On the basis of verses 1–2 and this relationship of awaited mercy, the petition of verses 3–4 can now be uttered. The petition in verse 3a utters the word "mercy" two more times and the name of YHWH yet again, so that the *petition* of verse 3a mirrors the *praise* of verse 2a. The reason for the petition in verse 3a is given in verses 3b–4, introduced, characteristically, by "for." The reason mercy is now required is that the speaker—and his ilk, for the prayer is for "us"—has had more than a fill of contempt and scorn. The rhetoric of verses 3b–4 matches the substance twice. It is "filled to abundance" or "satiated," and three times uses the two terms for derogation. The speaker voices urgent petition out of unbearable humiliation. The petition assures a precise match between *voiced need* and *divine mercy*.

We may learn more about that contempt and scorn by noting the descriptive phrase, "those who are at ease" (v. 4). The same term in the more familiar passage of Amos 6:1 suggests that the reference is to the economically affluent who are

Pastoral Perspective

The first time I was working with homeless people, I received some valuable insight about these despised and largely overlooked residents of our cities' streets. A friend of mine, a rabbi with extensive experience working with homeless persons in Los Angeles, shared some of her wisdom. The sum of her lesson was—I paraphrase—"You see these people and see the desperation and the wild, unbalanced look in their eyes, and you begin to think that they really are not like you, that they are crazy in a way that you are not. Some of them do suffer from tremendous chemical and emotional imbalances that are not at all like yours, but if you were to spend as little as two weeks on the streets, you could easily be, if not crazy, then surely crazed. If for ten days no one looked you in the eye or said your name, you would begin to wonder just how connected to reality you were, and your eyes would take on their look."

In urban areas we have an idea what that desperate look is, since for some of those on our streets, life hangs upon the generosity of strangers. The analogy with the homeless is further strengthened in that in this psalm the petitioner's sense of identity has been abused. "Contempt" is the word that the psalmist uses. The despiser feels contempt because he or she considers the contemptible "worthless, inferior, or undeserving of respect."[1] We may already find ourselves implied in an uncomfortable way in this psalm in those who have helped to foster that look that the psalmist sees. As the rabbi taught me, even without our intending to despise, the overlooked feel contempt from those who do not meet their eyes, learn their names, or say a word. They feel despised.

The psalmist uses the image of desperate, begging servants to say, "God, this is how we come to you— abject! Our sense of self is gone! You are our only hope! We will not eat without your daily bread! Only you can remove our contempt!" As stylistically poor as it is to repeat exclamation points, that is the posture of this psalm. This psalm photographs the importunate widow wearing out the judge, the persistent supplicant bloodying his knuckles on the door of prayer, the unrelenting lobbyist harassing the senator's staff. The petitioner's persistence has been rewarded with contempt that further whittles away at her sense of identity. And the abjection of the servant here can only be redeemed by a master who delivers the slave from her abjection. The true

---

1. *Encarta World English Dictionary*, s.v. "contempt."

perpetrators is difficult. The expression is paralleled by those who are at "ease." No matter who they are, their threat comes early in the sequence of the Psalms of Ascents, and we should be clear that the threat is real. This psalm reflects the trials that accompany the sojourn of faithful living.

Images of Oppression. One immediately notices that this psalm begins in the singular and quickly changes to the plural. Rather than speaking to the community, as many psalms do, this psalmist is speaking for the community. The image of looking up to God's residence in the heavens indicates that this is a prayer of petition. The heavenly throne of God figures prominently in many psalms (cf. Pss. 2:4; 11:4; 29:10; 33:13–14; 93:2). The implied emphasis is on the sovereignty of God as ruler of the world, and thus capable of answering the petition.

Several repetitions of images and words occur in this brief psalm. "Eyes" occurs in the first and second verses. The psalmist begins with his/her own eyes lifted to God and then moves to an analogy that compares servants looking to their masters with Israel's dependence on God. The master is the protector and provider for the servant and assures that the basic needs and rights of the servant are protected. So, like a servant (note that both male and female imagery is used) the entire community looks toward God for protection.

Verse 2 ends with the psalmist declaring the intent of the community to look to God until God has mercy (ḥanan). Verse 3 begins with the imperative repetition of ḥanan ("Have mercy upon us, O Lord, have mercy upon us"). This is an imperative cry, repeated for emphasis, that God give to the community the very thing they need in their struggle against the proud and contemptuous.

Another important linguistic feature of this psalm is the use of synonyms for contempt (*buz* and *la'ag*). *Buz* has as its primary meaning to despise or hold as insignificant. *La'ag* has as its basic meaning to mock, ridicule, or scorn. *Buz* is used in verse 3 and in verse 4, while *la'ag* is used in parallel to *buz* in verse 4. Just as the abuse is heaped upon the faithful of God, so the language of this psalm heaps words for contempt upon one another. These expressions and others for "contempt" also appear in Psalm 22, a psalm of deep suffering and humiliation. This brief psalm parallels that one in intensity of feeling through the compact, repetitive language.

Finally, there is the repetition of *shava'* (vv. 3, 4), a term normally associated with nourishment and

her in a Christian frame of mind. If dinner was not served at the exact time on that particular Sunday, she would station herself in the kitchen, and wait till it was dished, and then spit in all the kettles and pans that had been used for cooking. She did this to prevent the cook and her children from eking out their meager fare with the remains of the gravy and other scrapings.[1]

In contrast is another owner:

Her religion was not a garb put on for Sunday, and laid aside till Sunday returned again. The eldest daughter of the slave mother was promised in marriage to a free man; and the day before the wedding this good mistress emancipated her, in order that her marriage might have the sanction of law.[2]

Think what a difference it made to be the slave of one and not the other!

Having entered that mind-set, hear again the words of the psalmist who looks to God as a slave looks to her master. To this God who holds the power to make a life joyful or miserable the plea is made: "Have mercy upon us, O Lord, . . . we have had more than enough of contempt." While we may not understand what it was to live as a slave, being the object of scorn is something that we can understand. Scorn and contempt wear thin very quickly. Such attitudes wear people down, attack sense of self, and are not limited to the world of the ancients. People of faith have experienced such treatment in every age. To be faithful in today's secular world is to open oneself to that age-old experience.

Not long ago my husband and I were in a social setting with some acquaintances who were intrigued by being confronted with not one, but two ministers and who were also quite determined to show us just how naive and misguided we were. I had the definite sense they were lying in wait for us. "Look at this," said one, pulling out Matthew's story of the slaughter of the babies in Bethlehem. "Why would anyone put that in the Bible?" Most of their arguments against God and faith were equally superficial, so that their comments were less threatening than wearying. It was with a sigh rather than with tears that I could repeat the psalmist's sense of having had my fill of "the contempt of the proud."

A more subtle form of pride shows itself in the folk who gladly tell me that they do not believe in

---

1. Harriet Jacobs, *Incidents in the Life of a Slave Girl* (New York, Oxford: Oxford University Press, 1988), 22.
2. Ibid., 77.

Psalm 123

Theological Perspective

arrogant, self-indulgent, and indifferent to those who have less. Amos's use of the term suggests a "servant class" exploited by those,

> who lie on beds of ivory,
>   and lounge on their couches,
> and eat lambs from the flock,
>   and calves from the stall;
> who sing idle songs to the sound of the harp,
>   and like David improvise on instruments
>   of music;
> who drink wine from bowls,
>   and anoint themselves with the finest oils,
>   but are not grieved over the ruin of Joseph!
>   (Amos 6:4–6)

The actions are of those "who oppress the poor, who crush the needy" (Amos 4:1).

The prayer is the voice of one in the "servant class" who looks to an alternative "master." What a way to think of prayer, as a recharacterization of social relationships with the new character YHWH, God of mercy, as defining reference! The prayer presents the socially humiliated turning from the ones who "are at ease" to the one "enthroned in heaven," a turn that means a *departure from contempt* and an *embrace of mercy*. The God of mercy thus is presented as alternative and antidote to unbearable relationships and social inequity.

While the psalm does not say so, we imagine that "mercy" here is not only divine attribute and intention, but also a matter of practice by adherents of YHWH, who will not engage in scorn and contempt toward the needy. The prayer is an immense act of hope, a conviction that demeaning social relationships are not the norm and need not endure. The ground of such hope is in the one addressed, the God of all hope, who will, soon or late, turn the world to well-being, even for those whom the world holds in contempt.

WALTER BRUEGGEMANN

Pastoral Perspective

deliverance is liberation, redemption, and restored identity.

The posture of the psalmist here is not far from the posture of those who pray the Lord's Prayer. The image of the Father in a patriarchal context is one of absolute power and sovereignty, like the master in the psalm. Jesus' making the Father intimate doesn't alter the absoluteness of "his" power. Our "Father God" is a jealous God, who wants us to have no other gods to intervene. And there is a genius in that absolute claim. Our God knows that only God can love us into our full stature as God's children. Other love, because it is conditional, sets limits on our souls, tethers us to lesser things. Only God's love makes us truly whole and truly free. The trust in Psalm 123 is in One who does not betray or diminish us, even or especially when we submit ourselves abjectly to that One. Indeed, we have had enough of those who hold us in contempt, who want us to be thinner, to be richer, to have shinier hair and whiter teeth before we are acceptable. We have had enough of those who want us to conform to their ideas of acceptability—a little lighter skin, a little brighter look, a little straighter hair, a little less bold—those who hold us in contempt.

In that abject posture toward God, we trust in One who will not necessarily give us what we want, but who will give us the reprieve we need. We may be begging for just enough "poisonous drink" to feed our addictions, but it may be time for us to wake up, be strong, face our demons, and abstain. The danger in our abjection is that we will turn to any power. If the sovereign we turn to is untrustworthy, we are ruined. The psalmist asserts that our Sovereign is One who can be trusted, even in our deepest vulnerability, especially in our deepest abjection. Ours is a God who hears the cry of the desperate. That is the confidence of Psalm 123.

CHANDLER BROWN STOKES

Exegetical Perspective

having one's fill of food. The Israelites were "filled" by the manna provided them in the wilderness. Here the word is used metaphorically and has the sense of being sated, completely overwhelmed by something (cf. Ps. 88:3). In this case it is the mocking contempt of those who are at ease that has overwhelmed the psalmist and the community.

All these repetitions combine to form a powerful image of a community crushed by the mocking derision of another community, one that is "at ease." The density of these images and their repetition expresses a feeling of immediate desperation. The psalmist's community needs its Master's hand to deliver it from the insistent oppression of its accusers.

On the Physicality of the Psalms. A fundamental quality of the Psalms is their use of concrete imagery to describe the sufferings of the psalmist or the community. This psalm is an excellent example of how that physicality is presented and manipulated in the imagery of the psalm. A major development in translation decisions made since the Septuagint was to translate *nephesh* as "soul" rather than "life." This decision comes by way of the Septuagint, where *nephesh* was translated with the Greek *psychē*. The Hebrew is not as metaphysical as the connotation involved in "soul."

Nephesh at its root means "throat" or "neck"; by extension it represents the life or being of a person. It does not represent an entity separate from the body. The throat or neck of a person represents the life, since the throat is the passageway for breathing. In many psalms the *nephesh* is threatened and the psalmist implores God to intervene so that life is not extinguished. In Psalm 123, if we use the primary idea of *nephesh*, we have "our throats are filled with the scorn of those that are at ease." The image of the community choking on the contempt of their enemies is concrete. Moreover, when we understand that *shava* (filled) has to do with nourishment or being sated on food, the image of the community choking on contempt is ironic. Rather than the "filling" providing nourishment and health, the community is unable to swallow the contempt that has been heaped upon them, and they are at their end.

STEVEN BISHOP

Homiletical Perspective

organized religion: "I'm very spiritual, but I don't need to go to church." It is usually said in a tone of voice that asks me to applaud them for their decision. Pondering what lies behind it, I have come to suspect a variety of issues. Laziness is one possibility. It is easier to use a vague "spirituality" as a way to avoid grappling with a demanding God. Pride is another possibility. I would rather go it on my own than submit to God as a slave to her master. Put together laziness and pride, and you do have contempt. How do we speak to such pride and contempt in a way that can be heard? Do we simply slough it off with polite words? And how do we who are preachers give the faithful in our pews the words that will enable them to respond? This is a text to remember and preach when our faith puts us in an unpopular and difficult place.

The words of the psalm trigger another question. "Those who are at ease . . ." (v. 4): what does it mean to be "at ease" before God? How can anyone be at ease when standing before "you who are enthroned in the heavens" (v. 1)? Is not this a time to be discomforted?

"Have you talked to the man upstairs?" So began a popular song from years ago. It implied that God is nothing more than the neighbor in the apartment above us. Wrong! The Creator and Sustainer of the universe is totally other, a God of power and might, the master of those whom God has created. This is the God who demands our attention and our commitment. Does that sound harsh? Why look for help to a God who is anything less?

NETA LINDSAY PRINGLE

2 Corinthians 12:2-10

[2]I know a person in Christ who fourteen years ago was caught up to the third heaven—whether in the body or out of the body I do not know; God knows. [3]And I know that such a person—whether in the body or out of the body I do not know; God knows— [4]was caught up into Paradise and heard things that are not to be told, that no mortal is permitted to repeat. [5]On behalf of such a one I will boast, but on my own behalf I will not boast, except of my weaknesses. [6]But if I wish to boast, I will not be a fool, for I will be speaking the truth. But I refrain from it, so that no one may think better of me than what is seen in me or heard from me, [7]even considering the exceptional character of the revelations. Therefore, to keep me from being too elated, a thorn was given me in the flesh, a messenger of Satan to torment me, to keep me from being too elated. [8]Three times I appealed to the Lord about this, that it would leave me, [9]but he said to me, "My grace is sufficient for you, for power is made perfect in weakness." So, I will boast all the more gladly of my weaknesses, so that the power of Christ may dwell in me. [10]Therefore I am content with weaknesses, insults, hardships, persecutions, and calamities for the sake of Christ; for whenever I am weak, then I am strong.

Theological Perspective

This passage is one of the most remarkable in the Pauline corpus, providing us with both an intensely personal glimpse into the apostle's own experience and a striking statement of a major theme in his theology. And the two are intimately connected. Our passage is the culmination of the "fool's speech" (11:1–12:13), Paul's passionate apologia for his apostolic ministry in the face of criticism by his Corinthian opponents. "Let no one think me foolish," he says in adopting this risky and awkward strategy. "But even if you do, accept me as a fool, so that I too may boast a little" (11:16 RSV). In effect he is behaving like his opponents, exposing their foolishness by parodying their methods, while at the same time ironically distancing himself as apostle from himself as fool in order to demonstrate the radically different nature of his own appeal grounded in the gospel of Jesus Christ. Returning to the theme of foolishness at the end of the speech (immediately following our passage), he exclaims: "I have been a fool! You forced me to it, for I ought to have been commended by you. For I was not at all inferior to these superlative apostles, even though I am nothing" (12:11 RSV). But all of this rhetorical tomfoolery should come as no surprise from the one who has already reminded the Corinthians that "the foolishness of God is wiser than men" (1 Cor 1:25 RSV).

Pastoral Perspective

Those entrusted with positions of leadership in church communities will find much to ponder in this text, which reminds us that leadership is often better expressed through the words we do not say than the ones that we do.

Self-professed "super-apostles" had captured the imaginations of many in the Corinthian church with tales of their personal experiences in the spiritual realm. One has only to click through the television channels to be reminded that contemporary superapostles still seek to establish their authority through vivid descriptions of personal revelations that demonstrate their privileged relationship with the Almighty. One influential televangelist has even taken to delivering an annual set of "predictions for the new year" received via his own hotline to heaven. Today, as in Corinth, some find such tales persuasive.

Like Paul, we sometimes feel we must respond to such claims, particularly when they are made by persons we believe are preaching a dangerously distorted version of the gospel. But how? Do we dismiss the validity of all claims of personal revelation? To do so would be to deny the witness of Scripture and the experience of many persons of deep and mature faith. Do we argue that such experiences are indeed possible, but that those claimed by the evangelist in question cannot possibly

Exegetical Perspective

This passage falls at the end of Paul's "fool's speech," which begins at 11:1 and ends at 12:11. In this speech, he is trying to convince the Corinthians that his ministry is qualitatively different, and therefore superior to the "super-apostles," an unknown group that seems to consist of rival missionaries to Paul who execute their ministry with elegant speech, boasting of revelations and visions, and entering into some sort of monetary relationship with the Corinthians. Paul has resisted this last action for himself, probably because he has tried to sidestep the possible complications of a patron-client dynamic that might have resulted—with its overtones of social obligation—in the Corinthians' seeing Paul as a client rather than as their "parent" (see 12:14). In the first part of the speech, in 11:1–15, Paul argues that he is in no way inferior to this group and even accuses them of deceitful work and "disguising themselves as apostles of Christ" (11:13). The second part of the speech is Paul's famous "apostolic c.v." (11:16–33), where he lists the sufferings that have resulted from his ministerial activity, and in a very rhetorically effective way. The last part of the speech is the passage at hand.

Verse 1 of chapter 12 (which is not included in the lectionary reading) is important to consider in this passage, because Paul says he is going to boast

Homiletical Perspective

In this passage the preacher finds the core of 2 Corinthians, the deposit of gold in the clay: "My grace is sufficient for you, for power is made perfect in weakness" (12:9). Not only does this verse go to the heart of the apostle and his mission, but it is the word of the Lord given to him personally—a divine revelation he shares with the Corinthians and us.

But what a torturous path Paul takes before arriving at these words of comfort! Chapters 10–12 show him knowingly playing the fool (11:1, 16, 21), acting like the jealous husband whose wife is playing around (11:1–3), talking like a madman (11:23) as he oscillates between emotional highs and lows. The Corinthians apparently find him ridiculous, and so he acts that way. Boasting about *everything*, he implores his beloved congregation to stick with him, no matter what.

The desperation of his letter suggests that he has reason to believe the Corinthians will not. Whereas he is presently at a distance, those on the scene are undermining his authority. The Corinthians have been led astray by teachers he dismisses as "super-apostles." Moreover, they are "false apostles, deceitful workers, disguising themselves as apostles of Christ," bogus "angels of light" (11:13–14). They also seem to be Hebraizers, raising suspicions about how "kosher" Paul's teaching actually is. In response, he establishes

2 Corinthians 12:2-10

Theological Perspective

Our passage really begins at 12:1, where the apostle again reminds his readers that "there is nothing to be gained" by boasting—while he goes right on doing it!—announcing that now the topic will be "visions and revelations of the Lord." Virtually everyone agrees that Paul is here describing his own experience, especially since he appears to confirm it himself in verse 7a. Why then does he describe these "revelations" as happening to someone else: "I know a man . . ." (v. 2 and similarly in vv. 3 and 5)? Karl Barth believes that the point of this self-distancing is that "only from this distance is he willing to participate in the glory that this man—he himself!—has from those high things."[1] Were he to claim this religious experience as one of his own apostolic credentials, he would be behaving like those "super-apostles" who oppose him—even though if he did he would "be speaking the truth" (v. 6). "But," he writes, "on my own behalf I will not boast, except of my weaknesses" (v. 5). What is most remarkable, and theologically significant, about this autobiographical passage, is how *little* he tells us about his dramatic religious experience! Although he was raptured right up to paradise in the "third heaven" (vv. 2–3), he says almost nothing about how he got there or what he heard ("unutterable words")—quite in contrast to other ancient reports of ecstatic heavenly journeys. Paul's reticence should be a warning to any Christian tempted to appeal to private religious experience rather than to the gospel of Christ! Paul subordinates everything, including his own "revelations," to the one revelation of Jesus Christ. In order to keep him from making this mistake, Paul says, "a thorn was given me in the flesh, a messenger of Satan, to harass me, to keep me from being too elated" (v. 7 RSV). Here too Paul's reticence is just the point—in contrast to all those who have speculated about the precise nature of his "thorn." Although he pleaded with the Lord to remove it, what he got instead was this oracle: "My grace is sufficient for you, for my power is made perfect in weakness" (v. 9 RSV). This message, which Paul tells us comes from Christ himself, brings us to the main point of our passage: the dialectic of power and weakness that lies at the heart of the Christian gospel.

"For when I am weak, then I am strong" (v. 10b RSV): this is Paul's theological point in a nutshell. "But what is his weakness?" asks Barth. "Simply what remains of his Christian existence after it is stripped of the religious experience of which he could boast

1. Karl Barth, *On Religion: The Revelation of God as the Sublimation of Religion,* trans. Garrett Green (New York: T. & T. Clark, 2006), 92. The passage can be found in the older translation in *Church Dogmatics,* I/2, 332.

Pastoral Perspective

be authentic? There are no external standards by which any person's claims to personal revelation can be evaluated.

Paul, who years earlier had been blessed with a profound vision of the heavenly realm, was clearly tempted to go toe to toe with the superapostles by offering vivid descriptions of his own (vv. 2–4). But he knew that a "my vision was better than your vision!" shouting match would only concede his opponents' argument that inward spiritual experience is a valid basis for religious authority.

Just as he had earlier affirmed that he regularly spoke in tongues but refrained from doing so in public because it did not benefit the entire community, now he alludes to his powerful vision without directly describing it. Such inward experiences deepen his faith, but they do not constitute a basis for his authority over the church. That authority rests not upon what he has experienced in an inward, private way, but on the manner in which he is living the gospel in their midst: "Look at what is before your eyes" (10:7).

Paul now moves from heavenly visions to the mortal trenches: "to keep me from being too elated, a thorn was given me in the flesh" (12:7). He has appealed to the Lord three times to remove this unnamed thorn (v. 8), but it remains. Paul does not give his thorn a name. Commentators suggest this is not a strategic omission, but rather assumes that the Corinthians are already aware of its nature. But for those of us who read this text many years later, Paul's omission allows us to filter it through our own thorns: a colleague gifted in creative interpretation is able to prove, at least to his own satisfaction, that Paul shared his malady of chronic sinus infections.

Paul understood his thorn as an agent sent by Satan to diminish the effectiveness of his mission, an agent that has backfired on the enemy because it guards him against being carried away by his transporting visions. Without the thorn, Paul could have easily fallen into the trap that ensnared the superapostles, diverted from his urgent mission by narcissistic fascination with his experiences and the sense of self-importance they bring. That which Satan sent to do harm has been transformed by grace to a good gift.

This does not give the pastoral leader license to tell cherished members of the congregation afflicted with chronic pain or debilitating illness that they are required to regard such conditions as blessed gifts from God. But it does guide us in our efforts to speak to them not only of the God who shares their

about visions and revelations. This conditions the passage, in the sense that what follows are not just reports about visions and revelations, but boasts about them, akin to the boasting that the superapostles apparently did on a regular basis. But Paul goes on to boast in a slightly different way, one that is indirectly self-referential. In verses 2, 3, and 5, Paul talks about someone he claims to know who was caught up in the third heaven and into paradise. There he heard and experienced things that "no mortal is permitted to repeat" (v. 4); it is enough for Paul to refer to these events without repeating the specific details of the experiences. Most commentators think that Paul is talking about himself in these vision reports. He does so in this indirect way in order not to fall into the pattern of boasting that his superapostle foes regularly practice. Instead, by deflecting attention away from himself, he can say that he too has had visions and experienced revelations (cf. 1 Cor. 15:8 and Gal. 1:12) worthy of any of the apostles without boasting as the superapostles do.

But in verse 6, he ceases to be so indirect, and says that he could boast if he wanted to and not sound like a fool. He refrains from it "so that no one may think better of me than what is seen in me or heard from me, even considering the exceptional character of the revelations" (vv. 6–7). What is at issue here, and what seems to be at issue throughout the letter, is for Paul somehow to show the power and authority of his and his coworkers' ministry while at the same time demonstrating that the power and authority are qualitatively different from and superior to those of the rival missionaries. All of his argumentation about this important issue has been indirectly trying to establish, to one extent or another, that the seeming weakness of Paul and his coworkers is actually what gives them power, since it participates in the power of Christ's ministry through weakness. At verse 7 he comes to the climax of his argument, and here he begins to speak in his most direct manner about this concept.

Paul begins verse 7 with the famous "thorn in the flesh." No one really knows what this thorn might have been. The guesses, and they really are guesses, range from psychological (e.g., sexual temptation [current throughout the Middle Ages], pangs of conscience over persecution of the early church, or humiliation for not getting more Jews to believe him) to external opposition (e.g., the superapostles or other rival missionary groups, those who oppose him in Corinth, or rough treatment by his enemies)

his qualification as a Hebrew, an Israelite, a descendant of Abraham (11:22).

Not enough? Paul then brings out his credentials as a martyr for Christ. While never charging the Corinthians a penny for his services on their behalf (11:8–11), he has proven his love for them by his suffering. The "super-apostles" may claim to be ministers of the Lord, but "I am a better one: with far greater labors, far more imprisonments, with countless floggings, and often near death" (11:23). He could go on—and does, with a list of calamities that culminates in the ludicrous image of himself on the run from Damascus, outwitting a king's wrath by escaping "in a basket through a window in the wall" (11:33).

He has one more card to play, albeit indirectly: as a "man in Christ" who was enraptured into paradise "and heard things that are not to be told, that no mortal is permitted to repeat" (12:4). At this point there is no further height to scale, no sign of apostolic calling left to claim. What could trump being caught up into heaven?

Thus far, the preacher on 2 Corinthians has only negative examples of how to preach from one's own experience. The excoriation of rivals, boasting about the downs and the ups, and chronic, often hysterical self-referencing do not belong in the pulpit (although the history of preaching is no doubt rich in examples of such bad behavior). Paul redeems himself, however, when he gets down to business by doing the work of an *apostolos*—when he bears witness to God rather than to himself, by sharing with us what it was that he *heard*.

The preacher will recall that Paul was "untimely born" (1 Cor. 15:8) and never encountered Jesus in the flesh; nonetheless, he heard him speak on the Damascus road: "Saul, Saul, why do you persecute me?" (Acts 9:4; see also 22:4–6; 26:9–18). So reports Luke. But when Paul gives his own version of the event in Galatians 1:13–17, there is none of this drama: no blindness, no fall from a horse, no voice from heaven. It is uniquely in 2 Corinthians 12, then, that we have those moments in his life when he was, by his own account, touched by God, both raised up to paradise ("whether in the body or out of the body, I do not know; God knows," vv. 2, 3) and thrown down to earth with the unrelenting torment of an unspecified "thorn in the flesh." His translation to the third heaven (in whatever state) was surely meant to impress the Corinthians and put the "pseudoapostles" in their place; but this agony keeps him on his knees, and no manner of earnest prayer

2 Corinthians 12:2-10

Theological Perspective

for good reason and in truth, but that means insults, hardships, persecutions, calamities for Christ's sake (v. 10). There he sees the *power* of Christ dwelling in him; there he knows himself to be *strong*; there is what he *boasts* about."[2] This theological truth applies not only to Paul's life but also to the life of the Christian church throughout the ages, and it is a truth that the church has all too often forgotten. The Christian community forgets that Christ's grace is sufficient for it every time it seeks to secure its existence in the world by means of its own strength and influence, every time it allies itself with worldly power rather than allowing Christ to be revealed in its weakness. Barth, in an excursus on the history of the church, shows in some detail how it has failed in every age to allow the Lord's grace to be sufficient for it.[3] The ancient church, once it was no longer subjected to the official persecution of the apostolic age, all too quickly succumbed to the temptation to make itself powerful in the world, to present itself as spiritually superior to the pagan religions. And after Constantine made official its worldly position, it sought in the Middle Ages to make itself the supreme worldly power, becoming "a witness to the glory of Western man" rather than to the grace of God. And in the modern period, despite the efforts of the Reformers to recall the church to the gospel, the church—including the Protestant churches!—has by and large yielded to the temptation to secure its place in the modern world by accepting "its proper place in service to the new secular splendor of Western man." We nevertheless ought not to despair, even though Christians will no doubt go right on seeking their security in strength rather than weakness, because Holy Scripture—as in this passage—recalls us again and again to the good news of the cross: "For when I am weak, then I am strong."

GARRETT GREEN

Pastoral Perspective

burdens, but of how we may discover God's grace even in our weaknesses and limitations. This is dangerous territory, to be entered into only in a spirit of deep compassion. Again Paul steers us in sound and helpful ways, even if his particulars of language and images need to be reframed. He clearly understands his "thorn" as an agent of Satan, not God: God did not *cause* his affliction any more than God causes a child to develop leukemia. But God is present even in the difficult things God does not cause, and the grace of God can be made manifest even through the afflictions that bring God—and us—grief and sorrow. For Paul, God's grace is as much a "given" as the air about him, a grace that prevails over sin, weakness, and hardship: "My grace is sufficient for you, for power is made perfect in weakness" (v. 9).

Paul boasts not of his experiences of transcendent wonder, but rather of his human weakness, his thorn. As is true in so many dimensions of faith, there is a paradox here: we express humility before God by boasting of our weakness because the love, power, and glory of God are made manifest through the good we are able to accomplish in spite of that weakness. "Whenever I am weak, I am strong" (v. 10).

Through this rich text, pastoral leaders are reminded that cultivating an inner spiritual life is important in deepening our own walk with God, but it is generally wise to speak of that inner life cautiously, if at all. Rather, that inner life should form us in ways that make our public ministries more faithful. Rather then describe our personal encounter with the risen Christ in transcendent clouds of glory, our calling is to *be* the presence of Christ to others. But we can, and should, speak humbly and honestly of our weaknesses and limitations, bragging not of our own accomplishments, but of what God is able to accomplish through our lives, despite our weakness.

JOHN T. MCFADDEN

2. Ibid., 92–93.
3. Ibid., 93–98.

Exegetical Perspective

to physical illness or disability (e.g., pains in the head, epilepsy, or opthalmia). Whatever the precise nature of this "thorn in the side," Paul sees it as functioning to remind him that his power does not come from himself; instead, it comes from the Lord.

Paul goes one step further in claiming that his understanding of his suffering comes from the Lord, as well: "'My grace is sufficient for you, for power is made perfect in weakness'" (v. 9). Paul claims a sort of process by which one is perfected through suffering. The rest of verse 9 is his clearest and most direct statement of the relationship between power and weakness in the letter. Here he claims that boasting in weakness actually results in the indwelling presence of the power of Christ. So, unlike the superapostles who boast of a power demonstrated by fancy speech and powerful visions, Paul boasts of his weaknesses, not out of false humility but as a way of demonstrating that his power can come only from Christ. His ministry is truly manifest in weakness and suffering, so it must be from Christ, because it is iconic of Christ's sufferings. Paul finishes the passage by explaining his contentedness with his weakness, a contentedness that is present only because he knows that "whenever I am weak, then I am strong."

His argument against the superapostles and for the legitimacy of his and his coworkers' ministry is almost complete; it has certainly reached its climax. Through a sustained presentation of his position, he has shown the qualitative difference between the nature of his authority and power and that of his opponents. Whether or not Paul was successful in his argumentation is something that will never be known, but his self-understanding is clear, and his care for the Corinthians is nowhere else expressed so passionately as in chapters 11 and 12.

STEPHEN P. AHEARNE-KROLL

Homiletical Perspective

will take it away. "Three times I appealed to the Lord about this, that it would leave me," he confides—but to no avail. This does not mean that his prayer goes unanswered, but only that the kind of deliverance he longs for will not be given; the thorn will not be extracted. Instead, Christ will be with him in his pain, will transform a solitary agony into infused strength. Whether in a vision or only in the still, small voice of prayer, the Lord says to him, "My grace is sufficient for you, for power is made perfect in weakness."

Let the preacher note: this is not a call to grin and bear it, let alone to wallow in "weaknesses, insults, hardships, persecutions, and calamities" (v. 10). Instead, it gives insight into what it means to be in grace, in the grip of a power not one's own, in a process of perfection that brings the sufferer into the life of Christ and therefore into "the power of God and the wisdom of God. For . . . God's weakness is stronger than human strength" (1 Cor. 1:24–25). Paul offers no escape route from pain, but rather holds up a way of "dwelling" with Christ in the midst of it.

To be sure, there are "thorns" that can be eliminated, and should be. To do less is to ignore both justice and good sense; suffering is not per se "of the Lord." But when it is inevitable, as indeed it is, weakness need be no cause for shame or abject resignation. God's power, after all, took a hideous crucifixion and turned it into grace, raised up human vulnerability in extremis and made it perfect. Now *that* is something to boast about!

PETER S. HAWKINS

Mark 6:1-13

¹He left that place and came to his hometown, and his disciples followed him. ²On the sabbath he began to teach in the synagogue, and many who heard him were astounded. They said, "Where did this man get all this? What is this wisdom that has been given to him? What deeds of power are being done by his hands! ³Is not this the carpenter, the son of Mary and brother of James and Joses and Judas and Simon, and are not his sisters here with us?" And they took offense at him. ⁴Then Jesus said to them, "Prophets are not without honor, except in their hometown, and among their own kin, and in their own house." ⁵And he could do no deed of power there, except that he laid his hands on a few sick people and cured them. ⁶And he was amazed at their unbelief.

Then he went about among the villages teaching. ⁷He called the twelve and began to send them out two by two, and gave them authority over the unclean spirits. ⁸He ordered them to take nothing for their journey except a staff; no bread, no bag, no money in their belts; ⁹but to wear sandals and not to put on two tunics. ¹⁰He said to them, "Wherever you enter a house, stay there until you leave the place. ¹¹If any place will not welcome you and they refuse to hear you, as you leave, shake off the dust that is on your feet as a testimony against them." ¹²So they went out and proclaimed that all should repent. ¹³They cast out many demons, and anointed with oil many who were sick and cured them.

Theological Perspective

The Third Week of Gospel Readings on Jesus' Kingship. In the three weeks ending today, Mark's Gospel imparts critical ideas about the *nature of Jesus' kingship* (the "what" of Jesus' kingly nature), the *source of his authority* (the "why"), and the *qualities that direct and shape the exercise of that authority* (the "how"). Today's selection adds information of christological significance in each of these categories and concludes the arc by inviting us to consider them all together, answering the question Jesus' own *landsmen* cannot: Who is Jesus?

How Is Jesus King? Answer 3: Jesus Is King of the Spirit Realm. This point is made in the framework of a seemingly bifurcated account that efficiently addresses the three principal categories of concern to Mark—the *nature* of Jesus' kingship, the *source* of his authority, and the *qualities with which* his godlike power is exercised.

The consternation of Jesus' neighbors and their inability to grasp why he speaks as he does ("What is this wisdom . . . ?" "Is this not this the carpenter . . . ?" "And they took offense at him") points toward the *source* of Jesus' authority, the thing that Mark says he possesses in perfection and they lack: absolute, obedient faith. Here Jesus' own folk stand in the role in which Mark often casts the dense disciples (and

Pastoral Perspective

These verses encompass parallel stories about mission and the rejection, or at least the potential rejection, of Christian mission and missionaries. The first six verses tell of Jesus' preaching and healing mission to his hometown and the offense the people of Nazareth take at him.

The second story, verses 6b–13, tells of the commissioning of the Twelve to go out "among the villages" in pairs to heal and preach, with instructions about how to respond to the rejection that they also will encounter. When they leave a place where they have been rejected, they are to "shake off the dust that is on your feet," a strong symbolic action recalling the tradition that Jews returning to Israel would shake off the defiling dust of the Gentile lands from whence they traveled.

Many Christian congregations have made sharp distinctions between "mission" and "evangelism"—between outreach in deeds and outreach in words—sometimes gravitating toward the former out of anxiety about doing the latter. In such a pastoral context, a pastor might explore the false "either/or" dichotomy between mission and evangelism. It is clear that both Jesus' ministry in Nazareth and that of the Twelve to "the villages" was unitary, encompassing both healing—"mission"—and proclamation—"evangelism."

Exegetical Perspective

Rejection at Home and Sending the Twelve. This reading includes two passages: first, the end of Jesus' successful healing journeys and rejection back home (6:1–6), followed by a new section in which Jesus extends his mission by sending his disciples (6:7–13), culminating in Peter's messianic confession (8:27–33). Together the passages link the limited perspectives on Jesus by people who should know him best with the unlimited potential of his new inner circle, even though up to now they too have misunderstood the meaning of Jesus' ministry.

Back Home (vv. 1–3). The place from which Jesus leaves to go "home" is the Capernaum side of the Sea of Galilee (5:21). Nazareth lies further inland. When Jesus appoints his first disciples, he tells them to follow him (1:16–20), and when he appoints twelve in particular, he does so in order that they will "be with him" (3:14). Up to now, all or part of them (see 5:37) have always been with him; here too they follow (6:1b). In Nazareth, Jesus goes to the local synagogue on the Sabbath. This passage represents Mark's version of the Lukan story of Jesus' sermon from Isaiah about good news to the poor. In that account, Jesus also gets in trouble with his hometown crowd (Luke 4:16–30). Mark has less interest in the content of the sermon. He describes the reaction of the local villagers to one of

Homiletical Perspective

What is it about familiarity that breeds contempt, as the saying goes? Jesus' rejection in his hometown of Nazareth proves that old adage to be true. After performing great miracles on both shores—and in the middle—of the Sea of Galilee, he returns to the town where he has grown up and lived an ordinary early life. He goes to the place where any Jewish teacher would go: to the synagogue, where he teaches the hometown crowd. Perhaps it is the unexpectedness of the whole event that precipitates the reaction of the people—the fact that the towns-folk are not expecting to see "little Jesus" who grew up around the corner, or "Jesus the carpenter" who had fashioned their tables and benches, in the role of wise prophet of God. Obviously his teaching astounds them but also strikes a nerve.

At first they are captivated. "Where did this man get all this?" they ask. "What is this wisdom that has been given to him? What deeds of power are being done by his hands!" (v. 2). But that is when the familiarity hits home and turns into contempt. "Is not this the carpenter, the son of Mary and brother of James and Joses and Judas and Simon, and are not his sisters here with us?" they ask. "And they took offense at him" (v. 3). In other words, they reason, it is still the Jesus we have always known—and we know he is just one of us, not any miracle worker.

Mark 6:1-13

Theological Perspective

by extension humanity). They understand that what they see is the work of a king ("What deeds of power are being done by his hands!"), but they cannot grasp the conclusion that is obvious to the narrator.

"The motive sparking their questions . . . is unbelief, for they find it incredible that one whose origins they know should be able to do such astonishing things."[1] This unbelief is not merely a passive obstacle but an active problem, misleading them into believing that Jesus' unique relationship with God is actually a danger to the health of their own confidently righteous belief; he is not merely ignored but, to their peril, rejected.[2]

The theological assertion beneath this vignette is uncomfortable, but plain: the human capacity for investing in social norms, for believing in one's own preferences, is *greater than the human capacity for faith.* In Mark's Gospel the person who acts beyond social norms through faith in God is rare. No socially constructed categories serve predictively: they may be rich and powerful (Jairus), poor and marginalized (the hemorrhaging woman), or acting selflessly on behalf of others (the paralytic's friends). Even the demons that afflict the Gerasene are quicker in their faith than Jesus' own neighbors: immediately they acknowledge his kingly authority ("What have you to do with me, Jesus, Son of the Most High God?" [5:7]). The evil spirits are not bound by the social conventions that blind Jesus' own people—and us.

The conundrum of Jesus' identity is then answered in the second half of this story. How is Jesus a king? He is *king of the spirit realm.* Calling the disciples together, he sends them out on missions of their own; in doing so, he gives "them authority over the unclean spirits." No one can give to another authority that one does not already possess. Jesus, having already magisterially demonstrated his authority over the spirit realm by dispatching the Gerasene's demons, here confidently shares this authority with those whom he has chosen—and who, in order to receive that authority, have implicitly *come to a new faith of their own.*

That Jesus cannot give authority he does not already possess is meant to make plain the *nature* of his kingship. But his commissioning of the disciples also makes a further claim about the *exercise* of his

1. Jack Dean Kingsbury, *The Christology of Mark's Gospel* (Philadelphia: Fortress, 1983), 85.
2. For more on this, see Javier-José Marín, *The Christology of Mark: Does Mark's Christology Support the Chalcedonian Formula "Truly Man and Truly God"?* (Bern: Peter Lang, 1991), 20–24.

Pastoral Perspective

Striking a balance between word and deed may require exploration of the sensitivities of many different parties in order to effectively proclaim the gospel. For instance, following the horrific South Asian tsunami that struck the day after Christmas 2004, relief poured in from many quarters, including aid from American Christians, some of whom used the opportunity to offer physical assistance (mission) to proclaim the gospel to aid recipients (evangelism). Interestingly, it was not so much local Muslims or Buddhists who were troubled by such actions, but leaders of local churches in India and Sri Lanka, who were often aghast.

A powerful illustration of the integrity and balance between "doing" the word and "speaking" the word was offered by one Hugh Thompson at the commencement exercises at Emory University several years ago. Honorary degrees were being awarded; the recipients made the requisite speeches. As is often the case, the students chatted through the whole ceremony. In fact, there was only one moment when they actually listened. "It was when a man named Hugh Thompson was speaking. Thompson was probably the least educated man on the platform. . . . He . . . did not finish college, choosing instead to enlist in the Army, where he became a helicopter pilot.

"On March 16, 1968, he was flying a routine patrol in Vietnam when he happened to fly over the village of Mai Lai just as American troops, under the command of Lieutenant William Calley, were slaughtering dozens of unarmed . . . villagers—old men, women, and children. Thompson set his helicopter down between the troops and the remaining . . . civilians. He ordered his tail-gunner to train the helicopter guns on the American soldiers, and he ordered the gunmen to stop killing the villagers. . . . Hugh Thompson's actions saved the lives of dozens of people . . . he was almost court-martialed. . . . It was thirty years before the Army . . . awarded him the Soldier's Medal.

"As he stood at the microphone, the . . . rowdy student body grew still." And then Thompson talked about his faith. Simple words. Speaking of what his parents taught him as a child Thompson said, "they taught me, 'Do unto others as you would have them do onto you.'" The students were amazed at these "words of Jesus, words from Sunday school, words from worship, words of Christian testimony . . . they leapt to their feet and gave him a standing ovation."[1]

1. Tom Long, *Pulpit Resources* 32 (January–March 2004): 39.

their own doing so well. They can hardly believe it ("they were amazed"). Jesus has a hearing in the synagogue because of the notoriety of his travels away from home, including the stories about his healings and teachings. The villagers ask, "Where did this man get these things, what wisdom was given to him, what powers come through his hands?" (v. 2, my translations). Yet upon hearing him, they remember that this is just "the carpenter, Mary's son" (v. 3a). Even if his father Joseph had died by this time, to identify Jesus as his mother's son rather than his father's might have been intended as an insult, shaming Jesus by insinuating that he did not have a father.[1] Moreover, his status as a carpenter (*tektōn*, a worker with wood) does not normally prepare one to be such a wise man and healer. The mention of his brothers and sisters highlights that this is a family the villagers know well enough to deny that Jesus could possibly be the successful preacher touted by outsiders. After all, a mere woodworker, while important to the economy of small villages like Nazareth, could not be expected to do great things. Thus, they are "scandalized" or "offended" by him (v. 3).

A Prophet without Honor (vv. 4–6). Jesus responds to their doubts with an aphorism: "Prophets are not without honor except in their own hometown" (6:4), a proverb well known throughout the Jewish and Greco-Roman world. Mark expands it to include the hometown, relatives, and the prophet's very own household. The result of this lack of faith in Jesus' abilities is a decreased number of healings that he can do. While the villagers are "astounded" at his teaching and miracles (v. 2), because of where he is from (from among them!), Jesus is "amazed" at their lack of faith (6:6a). Throughout his healing ministry, especially in the just completed set of trips across the sea and back, the faith of those he encounters secures their healing. Only disciples (4:40) and, now, fellow Nazarenes lack faith. So Jesus leaves and goes to the other villages to teach (6:6b). He cannot remain too long among those who lack faith.

Sending the Twelve (v. 7). After calling his first disciples in this Gospel (1:16–20), Jesus performs his first healing, casting out "an unclean spirit" (1:26). Now he sends out his disciples with the authority to do the same (6:7). Also at the outset of his ministry, he confronts opposition from religious leaders for

---

1. Pheme Perkins, "Mark," in *The New Interpreter's Bible* (Nashville: Abingdon, 1995), 8:592.

What prompts such a negative, outrageous response to Jesus from the neighbors in Nazareth? Exploring the reasons for the human emotions revealed in this text gives us a clue as to why Mark includes it in his Gospel and how we might preach it. Surely it is not a flattering portrait of the community in Nazareth *or* of Jesus himself. The people come across as mean-spirited, jealous, and even mocking. And Jesus responds to their fickleness with his own barbed words, words that have made their way into common parlance: "Prophets are not without honor, except in their hometown, and among their own kin, and in their own house" (v. 4). The charged exchange between Jesus and the townsfolk is a stark reminder of the humanity of *both* the neighbors and of Jesus himself.

A good question to ask when preaching a narrative text such as this one is, how would we have reacted, had we been in the position of the characters portrayed? What would we think about a neighbor whom we believed to be just an ordinary, hardworking man turning into a miraculous teacher, let alone the reputed Son of God? I venture to guess that we all would have our share of skepticism. After all, we tend to see what we expect to see and are slow to accept challenges to our preconceived assumptions. The townspeople of Nazareth expect to see the Jesus they have always known, the one who seems no different from them. When Jesus preaches with wisdom and performs deeds of power, the people of Nazareth cannot see beyond their own limited view of him. The questions posed to us, then, are, Whom do we take for granted? What wisdom, what deeds of power are we missing because we make judgments about how and through whom God's work can be done?

Because of the unbelief of the people of Nazareth, Mark tells us, Jesus is rendered powerless (v. 5). This is a troubling statement, for we know that God has endowed Jesus, as the Messiah, with God's own power. Here again, however, we are reminded of the reality of Jesus' humanity. Just as Jesus struggled against temptation in the desert at the beginning of his ministry and against the reality of his fate in the Garden of Gethsemane at the end of his ministry, here he struggles with the limitations of his full humanity: being rendered powerless by those who doubt his calling. But Jesus' powerlessness is not primarily about him but about *us*: about those who are unwilling to believe the great things God can do.

The preacher can explore examples of missed opportunities and lost blessings because of our

Mark 6:1-13

Theological Perspective

authority: Jesus *delegates kingly authority to those who come in faith.* Christology here is a case study in servant leadership. Jesus, deriving his authority (the "what") from absolute and obedient faith in God (the "why"), shares his authority willingly (the "how") with those who share in his faith.

There is a theology of discipleship here that brings Bonhoeffer to mind. The preacher is warned against construing Mark's brief report of the disciples' initial foray as missioners (v. 13) as a reward for their growing faith. It is rather a sign that faith brings authority—and *authority brings responsibility.* We respond to the gift of faith by *accepting our authority* alongside the sovereign to whom we answer, and we take up the *responsibility of disciples* to proclaim, to heal, and to claim victory over evil.

Summary of a Three-Week Arc: The Nature, Source, and Exercise of Jesus' Kingly Authority. The past three Sundays have imparted significant theological claims about the nature of Jesus' kingly authority. He has sovereignty over the *created order;* he is thus coequal with the Creator. He has authority over *life and law;* he is thus to be understood as one with the Giver of life, the Source of healing, and the Author of the law. He has power over *evil spirits;* he is therefore both regent of, and shares equally in, authority with, the God of heaven.

Seeing these qualities gives an answer to the pressing question: Who is Jesus? Jesus is "the Son of the Most High God," as the evil spirits call him. His authority derives from *his absolute obedience and ultimate openness to the will of God;* his is the quality of perfect faith, from which springs his godlike authority. Those who share in this faith share in his authority as disciples. His authority is exercised *gently* by being *in relationship with those who come in faith,* in contrast to the distance presumed by earthly leaders. His rule looks first to the marginalized and powerless; the celebrated and privileged are encompassed, but not as their social position would seem to demand. Finally, Jesus' kingly power is exercised by *sharing it freely with those who come in faith.*

MARK D. W. EDINGTON

Pastoral Perspective

Thompson's words about his faith had weight because the man had obviously "walked the talk." In the same way, the church will not be heard if what we *do* as Christians is incongruous with what we *say* about our faith.

Another present-day pastoral reality that these stories might raise for many is our anxiety about evangelism and the potential for rejection that sharing the gospel risks. Such discomfort is widespread, especially among "mainline" Christians, who may be justifiably concerned about coercive or emotionally manipulative methods of proclaiming the Good News. I once heard a story about a woman, a mainline Christian, who worked as a clerk in a bookstore. When she arrived for work one morning, she encountered a man dressed as a Hasidic Jew. After turning on the lights she said, 'Would you like any help?" "Yes," he answered softly, "I would like to know about Jesus." She directed him upstairs to the shop's section of books about Jesus and turned to go back downstairs, but he called her back. "No," he said, "Don't show me any more books, tell me what you believe. "My Episcopal soul shivered," the woman said later. But she gulped and told him everything she could think of.

God-talk outside the walls of the church makes many Christians anxious. We don't want to be pushy or to offend, and we are not sure we know the right words. Many Christians would sooner talk about *anything* else: sex, their salary, anything but what they believe about God.

But this text insists that, in spite of the potential for rejection (or at least anxiety or embarrassment), telling the story with words is part of the claim that Christ lays upon his disciples. A pastor might appropriately recognize these anxieties and offer suggestions to reticent people about speaking of their faith outside of church. A pastor might remind the congregation of the essential importance of the integrity between word and deed illustrated in the story about Hugh Thompson. Secondly, we might explore the truth that evangelism is not "to get them on our side" or even "to grow the church," but simply to tell others about the God who has come to mean so much to us. This is an action performed out of love, not competition or anxiety. Lastly, some of this common discomfort about evangelism might be relieved by reminding congregations that they need not have polished words, sophisticated theology, or fine-tuned dogma to speak of their faith. They are simply called to speak truth in love, from the heart, in their own words, and never be ashamed.

MICHAEL L. LINDVALL

healing on the Sabbath (3:1–6). Shortly thereafter, he appoints twelve disciples as apostles ("sent ones") and instructs them to be with him; later he sends them out with his authority (3:14). Now after facing opposition in his own hometown, the time has come to send out these twelve disciples without him, but two by two, to carry out the mission of healing and delivering people from their demons. Both Mark and Matthew (Matt. 10:1) focus on the command to heal and cast out demons. However, Luke includes the instruction "to proclaim the kingdom of God and to heal" (Luke 9:2). Later in the passage, Mark indicates that the disciples also "proclaimed that all should repent" (6:12).

Instructions for the Journey (vv. 8–11). All three Synoptic Gospels include instructions to the disciples about what to wear, what not to take, and how to react to their receptions. Mark includes the bare minimum: take just a staff to help you walk and ward off wild animals, wear sandals and one tunic, but not two (v. 8). In other words, itinerant preachers in the Jesus movement depend on the hospitality of settled believers in the various communities to which they travel. Moreover, when they come to one place, they are to stay in the first home that receives them (v. 10). There should be no appearance of looking for the best meals or the most comfortable bed in town! However, should their message be rejected at a home or by an entire town, they should exercise the practice of "shaking the dust from one's feet" (v. 11). Rabbis in later traditions talked of this symbolic way of returning from Gentile lands to one's sacred spaces. Followers of Jesus perhaps used the practice to symbolize judgment on unrepentant places. However, the shaking off of dust could be a hopeful sign if such people and places would thereby see the seriousness of the matter and mend their ways.[2]

Summary of Journey (vv. 12–13). Mark ends with a summary statement that indicates the disciples do in fact go out, preach, and cast out demons. People repent as John the Baptist (1:4) and Jesus (1:15) before them said they should. In addition, the traditional healing balm of oil is used to relieve "many sick people" of their infirmities.

EFRAÍN AGOSTO

limited faith. In an implicit way, Mark continues to raise in this text the question he repeatedly raises in his Gospel: who is this Jesus? When Jesus stills the storm on the Sea of Galilee, those in the boat with him wonder, "Who then is this, that even the wind and the sea obey him?" (4:41). When he brings Jairus's daughter from death to life, those who witness it are "overcome with amazement" (5:42). In this story it is not those who are encountering Jesus for the first time but those who have known him for years who are asking the same question about Jesus' identity and responding to his teaching with amazement.

The story of Jesus' own rejection at Nazareth sets up the mission of the twelve disciples. The reason for Mark's inclusion of Jesus' embarrassing experience at Nazareth at this particular point in the Gospel appears to be the preparation of the Twelve for what might be a mixed reception. The disciples are warned: "'If any place will not welcome you and they refuse to hear you, as you leave, shake off the dust that is on your feet as a testimony against them'" (v. 11). We cannot help but be reminded of Jesus' experience in Nazareth. Nevertheless, just as Jesus persists in his work by healing and curing even "a few sick people" amid the "unbelief" (vv. 5, 6) of the people of Nazareth, the disciples are commanded to persist in their own work in his name (v. 13). The word for us in this text is that we are not held responsible for the response to our ministries in Christ's name, but only for our own faithfulness. With such assurance, we can witness boldly and faithfully.

BEVERLY ZINK-SAWYER

2. R. T. France, *The Gospel of Mark* (Grand Rapids: Eerdmans, 2002), 250.

Amos 7:7-15

[7] This is what he showed me: the Lord was standing beside a wall built with a plumb line, with a plumb line in his hand. [8] And the LORD said to me, "Amos, what do you see?" And I said, "A plumb line." Then the Lord said,
"See, I am setting a plumb line
in the midst of my people Israel;
I will never again pass them by;
[9]the high places of Isaac shall be made desolate,
and the sanctuaries of Israel shall be laid waste,
and I will rise against the house of Jeroboam with the sword."

[10]Then Amaziah, the priest of Bethel, sent to King Jeroboam of Israel, saying, "Amos has conspired against you in the very center of the house of Israel; the land is not able to bear all his words. [11] For thus Amos has said,

Theological Perspective

The theological weight of this passage lies in the strong image at its beginning—the plumb line laid against a wall originally built with a plumb line, as God promises to set a plumb line in the people's midst and never to pass them by again. The note of judgment is unmistakable in the passage. God will lay waste Israel's religious and political establishment, for it is warped and has fallen beyond repair. But there is also the note of God's faithfulness to God's people—God still calls them, after all, "my people." The threat of judgment is bound up with the promise of God's presence, or, better, is the consequence of that holy presence that will not pass God's people by. In the promise of presence, however, the presence of the God who constituted this people through call and deliverance, surely there is hope in this. God, we find, has manifested God's faithfulness in Amos himself, for when God could not find a prophet to call from the decadent guild of prophets, God turned instead to a herdsman to deliver God's word.

God's promise in the passage is to set a plumb line in the midst of the people—a line that demands judgment of the wall presently in place, but that promises new construction as plumbed by the line. This, indeed, is Amos's role in the lives of the people. He not only declares the warp in the lives of the

Pastoral Perspective

Speaking truth to power has never been easy or risk free. Examples such as Thomas à Becket, Thomas More, Dietrich Bonhoeffer, and Martin Luther King Jr. serve as much a cautionary function to some as an inspiration to others. Still, truth being what truth is—and power what power is—the work remains to be done.

Abraham Heschel says that a significant aspect of the office of prophet in Israel was to remind the king that his "sovereignty was not unlimited, that over the king's *mishpat* [justice] stood the *mishpat* of the Lord—an idea that frequently clashed with the exigencies of government." While the prophets of Israel enjoyed considerable freedom to "upbraid the kings and princes for their sins," Heschel continues, "It was, indeed, an act of high treason when Amos stood at Bethel, the temple of the Northern Kingdom, and publicly prophesied, 'Jeroboam shall die by the sword, and Israel must go into exile away from this land.'"[1]

Amos poses a threat to homeland security. Like a live coal tumbling from the fireplace onto a straw mat, the Word of God has tumbled into his mouth, transforming this "herdsman" into a prophet. Now

1. Abraham Heschel, *The Prophets*, 2 vols. (New York: Harper & Row, 1962), 2:258–59.

'Jeroboam shall die by the sword,
   and Israel must go into exile
   away from his land.' "
¹²And Amaziah said to Amos, "O seer, go, flee away to the land of Judah, earn
your bread there, and prophesy there; ¹³but never again prophesy at Bethel, for
it is the king's sanctuary, and it is a temple of the kingdom."
   ¹⁴Then Amos answered Amaziah, "I am no prophet, nor a prophet's son; but I
am a herdsman, and a dresser of sycamore trees, ¹⁵and the LORD took me from
following the flock, and the LORD said to me, 'Go, prophesy to my people
Israel.'"

Exegetical Perspective

Today's passage combines one of the prophetic visions
of Amos with the only biographical information
Scripture gives us about him. The declaration of the
vision provokes a response in which Amos must assert
his authority to speak for God.

To this point, Amos's prophecies have taken the
form of the pronouncement of divine judgment
followed by an explanation for this judgment. As
chapter 7 begins, the form shifts to prophetic
visions. Today's passage includes the third of four
such visions in the book of Amos. The first two
visions, a swarm of locusts in 7:1–3 and fire from
heaven in 7:4–6, reveal scenes of impending disaster
and are followed by Amos's pleas for divine mercy
that result in God's promise to relent.

Today's text is the first of two visions in which
God shows Amos a symbolic object that reveals
God's intentions for Israel. Many preachers will be
familiar with translations that present the symbolic
object in verse 7 as a "plumb line." Most
contemporary biblical scholars, however, agree that
this translation is inaccurate. For this reason,
preachers will do well to look beyond the obvious
choice to focus on the symbol of the plumb line and
explore other aspects of today's text.

The Hebrew word ʾanak appears only here in the
Old Testament. It appears to be related to the

Homiletical Perspective

How big are we? In the verses that immediately
precede this passage, God twice relents from the
planned punishment of the northern kingdom of
Israel after Amos reminds him, "How can Jacob
stand? He is so small." When Amos is commanded
by God to confront Israel with its misdeeds, the
kingdom is living in a period of unprecedented
wealth, power, and prestige. Many of us live in a
similar context here in North America. Possessing
power in the world is an assumption we carry
around in our pocket like a driver's license. We
might not exactly call ourselves big shots but we
would probably say we call the shots in our lives.
How big are we? "Big enough to handle most of
what comes along," we reply.

In this showdown between Amos the sheepherder
and Amaziah the priest of the most important shrine
in the kingdom, the issue at stake is who does indeed
call the shots. In the third of Amos's visions God
appears before a wall. There is much good debate
about how the word ʾanak should be translated in
this section. Without a conclusive alternative
translation it will be referred to by the NRSV
translation of "plumb line." This tool of measurement
demonstrates that the people of God are not
measuring up to God's expectations. Thus, God's
judgment will be brought down upon the proudest

Amos 7:7-15

Theological Perspective

people, but he also declares the measure of their lives. "Let justice roll down like waters, and righteousness like an ever-flowing stream," he earlier proclaims (5:24). We must mark the faithfulness at the heart of this passage, or we entirely misinterpret God's use of law. It is a plumb line; it is fundamentally constructive (the law's third use, according to Calvin), and its critical dimension (its first use) is wholly at the service of this latter calling.

We grasp the depth of this understanding of the law, however, only when we note what the pericope states almost in passing—that the plumb line is set against a wall that was originally built with a plumb line. The measure against which God is measuring God's people is not foreign to them, but was integral to them from their start. One could take this to mean that God's people were formed around the law at Sinai—that this community has God's law as its founding document, and that they are called to live up to this. God, in this case, would be making a rhetorical move similar to that of Martin Luther King Jr., who called the United States to live up to the promissory note that it signed in its very constitution of itself. We could argue for something deeper here, however, and see this law as integral to God's people from their very creation—that we are people made for justice and formed for faithfulness. God's law, again, would not be foreign to us, but would be calling us back to our very life, to the truth of our being.

This passage, under this light, demands a christological reading, given its promise of God's presence, the connection of this presence to a measure of true life in the midst of the people, the fundamental faithfulness in the redemptive purpose of this measure, and, most significantly, the relation of this measure to our created integrity. It echoes strongly Athanasius's understanding of Christ's redemptive work in *On the Incarnation*.

Athanasius argues that an essential dimension of Christ's redemptive work is his reformation of God's image within us, which was deformed with our fall into sin. This image was originally imprinted upon us in our creation after the likeness of the Logos who was incarnate in Christ, and in this image lay our life. With our fall, however, we so warp this image that we are rapidly deteriorating into a heap of rubble, much like Amos's wall. Christ's incarnation, then, sets this image concretely before us, but not so that we might merely have a sketch after which we might pattern ourselves. Rather, this incarnate image itself reforms us; the draw of its life reframes the

Pastoral Perspective

the flames threaten to spread from Amos's tongue to consume everything and everyone around him, including the king. Amaziah, the priest of Bethel, tells King Jeroboam that "Amos has conspired against you in the very center of the house of Israel; the land is not able to bear all his words."

The vocation of the prophet is illuminated in this passage all the more clearly because of Amos's protest, "I am no prophet, nor a prophet's son." Amos stands without credentials. He is simply one who has heard and been claimed by the Word of the Lord. The prophet is not guided by his own convictions, as so many suppose, but is under the compulsion of "the Word God sent," to use Paul Scherer's evocative phrase. The prophet bears witness to the Word of God, even when that Word contradicts his own inclinations and experience. Amos's integrity lies in his ability, in his willingness, and ultimately in his courage to bear testimony to this Word.

And what, precisely, does the Word of God tell or show Amos? A plumb line! A true and reliable measure whereby to determine if a wall is in square—or a people are true! "Behold, I am setting a plumb line in the midst of my people Israel" (RSV).

"Behold!" There are few words in currency more distinctly biblical than the word we render in English as "Behold." It is a word straight out of the annual Christmas pageant. It does its job in places where only a miracle will do. The newer translations opt for "Look" or "See." They just do not get the message across. "Behold" points to something unprecedented, something beyond expectations. "Look" or "See" smacks too much of the street corners and film noir. Kids shout, "Look, Mom!" Gangsters say, "See." Angels, by contrast, herald, "Behold!"

The entire passage turns on this word, "Behold." The Lord shows Amos that the people will be subjected to a measure that holds true, a measure that shows precisely what does not measure up. This measure cannot be manipulated, because God cannot be manipulated. But the people have tried.

One cannot read more than a few lines of Amos without sensing divine anger coursing through the book. God has lost patience with God's people. The Lord's justice breaks forth in Amos against the king and his minions and a people willingly misled for their own gain and comfort. The Lord's justice breaks out as divine fury against injustice. If no one else will stand "for the victims of human cruelty," the Lord will.[2]

2. Ibid., 68.

Exegetical Perspective

Akkadian word for "tin." The translation of ʾanak as "plumb line" first appeared in the medieval era as conjecture in commentaries by Ibn Ezra, Rashi, and others. Ancient interpretations display a knowledge that ʾanak refers to some kind of metal and do not support the plumb line interpretation. Origen, for example, cites this text in his homily on Jeremiah 23:29, which depicts God's word as a hammer that breaks rocks in pieces. Origen wrote:

> God will seek a material stronger than the hammer which does not feel the blows from it. . . . Behold a man standing above an adamant wall holding his adamant. History records about adamant that it is stronger than every hammer striking it, remaining unbroken and unyielding. . . . You can say that the holy person who is an adamant wall or who is adamant in the hands of the Lord is not affected either by the hammer or the anvil, but the more one is struck, the brighter will his virtue shine.[1]

Another theory notes that tin was often used in the manufacture of armaments in the ancient world. The symbol of tin, therefore, could announce God's intent to destroy Israel through military invasion. Others point out that tin is a very pliable metal. By revealing to Amos a "wall of tin," God pronounces the judgment that Israel is weak, pliable, and soft, therefore deserving God's wrath.[2]

Finally, Gowan suggests that ʾanak may be a play on words. ʾAnak sounds like both ʿanah and ʿanaq, which both mean "sigh." God shows Amos ʾanak in order to reveal that God will soon set "sighing" in the midst of Israel, a time of lament over the destruction wrought by God's judgment. The fourth vision, in 8:1–3, supports this theory. In this vision, God reveals qayis, a basket of summer fruit, in order to announce that qes, the "end," has come upon Israel.[3]

No matter which interpretation one favors, it is clear from what follows that the force of Amos's words is frightening. His prophecy threatens the religious and political establishments of Israel. Amaziah, the priest at Bethel, reports to King Jeroboam that Amos has conspired against him and prophesied his death. The text does not report the king's response, so we do not know if Amaziah is

Homiletical Perspective

accomplishments of the kingdom, "the high places of Isaac shall be made desolate, and the sanctuaries of Israel shall be laid waste, and I will rise against the house of Jeroboam with the sword" (v. 9).

Amos brings us word that all of our greatest achievements, all of those things we lift up as signs and symbols of how big we are, are temporary toys easily swept away, should God so choose. Of course words that threaten such a possibility do not go unnoticed. The priest Amaziah, who stands in a position of prominence in the midst of these achievements, is quick to respond. We understand where he is coming from. If someone showed up from out of town and started announcing that God would be tearing down the First Presbyterian Church, the museum, and our court house, and then killing our mayor, we too would feel a need to respond. Amaziah does what we would do; he turns to the power structure that has served him so well. He sends word to the king about the treasonous words at hand. We do not hear of any response from the king, but Amaziah takes the bull by the horns and intervenes himself. He did not reach this position of power by being afraid to throw his weight around. He puffs his chest out, shows how big he is, and banishes Amos from the sanctuary at Bethel, telling him to make his money prophesying back in his hometown.

It is illuminating that Amaziah never once mentions God in this exchange. When he feels threatened by Amos's words, he turns to the king. When he speaks of the sanctuary at Bethel, it is not God's sanctuary but the king's. When Jacob awoke from receiving his promise of blessing from God, he said this of Bethel, "How awesome is this place! This is none other than the house of God, and this is the gate of heaven" (Gen. 28:17). How ironic that the fulfillment of that blessing, the creation of a kingdom with those many offspring, has led the people of God to a place beyond where they recognize the presence of God. The very abundance of blessings provided has distracted us from the God who provided them.

Amos responds to Amaziah's strong words with strong words of his own. He refuses to be quantified as some professional prophet, prophesying for his supper, as it were. He challenges Amaziah's order to go from Bethel with God's order for him to go to Bethel. As Amos stands before Amaziah and all of his believed power and might, he can hear the echo of his earlier words in his mind, "He is so small!" (v. 5).

We are so small. As much as we huff and puff ourselves up—especially when we huff and puff

1. Alberto Ferreiro, ed., *Ancient Christian Commentary on Scripture*, Old Testament, vol. 14, *The Twelve Prophets* (Grand Rapids: Eerdmans, 2001), 108–9.
2. Robert Martin-Achard, *God's People in Crisis* (Grand Rapids: Eerdmans, 1984), 54.
3. Donald E. Gowan, "Amos," in *The New Interpreter's Bible*, vol. 7 (Nashville: Abingdon Press, 1996), 407.

Amos 7:7-15

Theological Perspective

very construction of our lives. Christ, for Athanasius, plumbs us to our depths.

The christological sounding of this story draws out for us more strongly the meaning implicit in Amos's claims about his prophetic status as we wonder about the plumb lines that God has set in our midst today. It is too easy to accept complacently the preaching of the word accomplished by professional prophets to suffice for God's measure of God's people; God's call of a herdsman and tree-tender suggests that this passage is more demanding than that. It suggests that we must be aware that we not only are being plumbed by God's measure, but that we may be called to be that measure, ourselves. We, in some ways, are called to be Christ to one another in the measure of our lives by God's presence among us.

This would be the Franciscan reading of this passage. Francis of Assisi and his soul mate and counselor, Clare, lived lives plumbed by Christ—"walking in the footprints of Jesus" is what they called it. Clare calls on the evocative image of a mirror to depict this. Christ is a mirror in which we can gaze on our true selves, so that we can see clearly those aspects of our lives that are out of plumb and repent of them, while seeing the true angle and dimension to which we are called.[1] For Francis, this allowed us to lead true Christian lives in the world, lives that, in Calvin's words, would "express Christ." Such lives as these would have missionary significance. They would allow Franciscans to travel the world, preaching Christ even where they did not speak the language, for their lives would articulate the gospel by which we all are measured, for which all were created.

STEPHEN EDMONDSON

Pastoral Perspective

The hypocrisies of people who stand on their religion while neglecting common humanity, who have moved the boundary markers of compassion in their own hearts so they can trample the needy and bring ruin to the poor, have inflamed the anger of the Lord. The people do not even see their transgressions as sin anymore, they have so restricted the meaning of sin to cultic, religious, and narrow moral scruples.

"Behold, I am setting a plumb line in the midst of my people Israel." Perhaps the people have fooled others so long with their dissembling and secrecy that they have fooled themselves too. The plumb line will tell. The fact that the plumb line is held in the Lord's hand is what Amos "beholds." Amaziah, the priest of Bethel, pours scorn on Amos's vision, spitting the term *hozeh* ("seer") in Amos's face.[3] Amaziah serves King Jeroboam, so he seeks to undercut the prophetic message that the king and the people do not want to hear by discrediting the messenger. "Amos ["this seer"] has conspired against you in the very center of the house of Israel; the land is not able to bear all his words."

When many preachers would submit to political or religious authorities or attempt to justify their own authority by offering their resumes, Amos renounces any claim to authority beyond the Word of the Lord. Amaziah has tried to discredit the messenger. He calls Amos names, claims that he is a security risk. And Amos says, in effect: *I am neither a prophet nor a prophet's son. I do not possess any of the proper credentials. I was minding my own business when the Lord grabbed me by my collar and said, "Go, prophesy to my people Israel."*

Once the live coal has tumbled from the fireplace, once the straw mat is alight, the fire is hard to contain. A true word in the mouth of an honest person, whether credentialed or not, can bring down any power on earth; a true word can even change the hearts of a people. Martin Luther sings, "'The prince of darkness grim' does not reduce us to a puddle of anxiety, 'for lo his doom is sure, one little word shall fell him. . . . That word above all earthly powers, no thanks to them, abideth.'"

Amos could not have said it better.

MICHAEL JINKINS

---

1. "The Fourth Letter to Blessed Agnes of Prague," in *Francis and Clare: The Complete Works*, trans. Regis J. Armstrong and Ignatius C. Brady (New York: Paulist Press, 1982), 204–5.

3. Samuel Terrien, *The Elusive Presence: Toward a New Biblical Theology* (New York: Harper & Row, 1978), 101.

Exegetical Perspective

acting on royal orders or on his own initiative when, in verse 12, he commands Amos to leave Israel and seek his living as a prophet in Judah. Amaziah's words and actions uncover two assumptions. He believes that the king and his priests have the authority to dictate who may prophesy and when and where. He also believes that Amos is part of the guild of professional prophets and can easily pursue his work in another place. Amos responds with strong words that overthrow both of these assumptions.

First, Amos asserts strongly that he is not a professional prophet. He originally earned his livelihood in a manner in no way related to prophecy. Scholars debate the exact nature of Amos's original work. The Hebrew word *boqer*, "herdsman," is more commonly associated with cattle, yet the word *șo'n*, "flock," is associated with sheep. It may be that the term "flock" is a deliberate move to associate Amos with King David, whom God also called away from his flocks to fulfill God's purposes (2 Sam. 7:8). The phrase *bole șiqmim*, usually translated as "a dresser of sycamore trees," makes its only Old Testament appearance in this text. The tree called sycamore in the Near East is a fig-bearing tree. This phrase probably pertains to the practice of incising the fruit late in the growing season to hasten ripening.

Amos declares to Amaziah that in pronouncing God's judgment upon Israel, he is not simply carrying on the family business. He is acting on a call from God, who alone can command who may prophesy. The authority to prophesy comes from no one but God alone. Neither the state nor the religious establishment may decree where or through whose lips God will announce words of judgment or mercy to God's people. God calls prophets from all walks of life and empowers them to speak. The collusion of kings and priests to silence words that threaten their power cannot ultimately silence those whom God calls to the work of prophecy.

KAREN C. SAPIO

Homiletical Perspective

ourselves up—we are so small. The relative prosperity and prestige by which many of us are surrounded can be crippling to our relationship with God. In our beautifully adorned sanctuaries we can begin to believe they are for us. In our lovely homes we can begin to believe that it is we who have provided for ourselves. In the vast variety and abundance of this world we can begin to believe that somehow it belongs to us.

But we are so small. When we deny our smallness, our place as created and not as creator, we risk being unable to hear the call of God's word upon our lives. When we accept human systems as possessors of ultimate authority, we are living a lie. When we believe our position gives us the ability to control the will and movement of God through the institution of the church or any institution, we are lost. It is we who must be receptive to how God chooses to be at work in the world, not God who must conform to our systems and structures.

This text is an illustration of the idolatry of human power. When our sole focus is upon our own achievements and place in the world, we lose sight of where we are placed in this greater creation and who has placed us here. We pile up our resumes and our awards and our bank accounts and stand upon them, believing that they make us big. But what we stand upon is mere froth in front of God's measuring plumb line. We are small. What makes us inherently valuable is our identity as the children of God. When we remember this valuable truth, we are given the freedom of recognizing both how small we are and how cherished we are. From this location we have the wonderful opportunity to keep our eyes peeled to the surprising ways God may be at work in the world.

DOUGLAS T. KING

Psalm 85:8-13

⁸Let me hear what God the Lᴏʀᴅ will speak,
  for he will speak peace to his people,
  to his faithful, to those who turn to him in their hearts.
⁹Surely his salvation is at hand for those who fear him,
  that his glory may dwell in our land.

¹⁰Steadfast love and faithfulness will meet;
  righteousness and peace will kiss each other.
¹¹Faithfulness will spring up from the ground,
  and righteousness will look down from the sky.
¹²The Lᴏʀᴅ will give what is good,
  and our land will yield its increase.
¹³Righteousness will go before him,
  and will make a path for his steps.

Theological Perspective

1. The text invites the preacher to contemplate four theological issues. The first issue is *location*. The psalm fragment contained in the lectionary is eschatological in nature. The psalmist receives a vision of the day that God will come to God's people and put their world to rights. God is going to renew God's people and their land, restoring them with new joy, purpose, and delight. However, this eschatological fragment is embedded in a psalm that is written during a time when Israel experienced God as absent. A strong exegetical tradition holds the psalm to be postexilic. In the first verses the psalmist looks back at the liberation from exile. The psalmist and his people have returned to their land to rebuild Jerusalem and the temple. God seems nonetheless not to have returned with them. The psalm is therefore full of lament, longing, and expectation. The fulfillment of that expectation is foreseen in the lectionary's fragment.

Given this context, it is crucial for the preacher to realize that her location vis-à-vis this vision is different from that of the psalmist. From the psalmist's perspective, its realization is in the future. From the Christian community's perspective, this eschatological reality has been inaugurated. God has returned to the people; God's glory has dwelt in the land, full of grace and truth (John 1:14). The tone of

Pastoral Perspective

"Let me hear what God the Lᴏʀᴅ will speak, for he will speak peace to his people." Someone among the people of God listens for a word of salvation. The historical circumstance may have been postexilic, when the grand dreams of restoration had fallen short of the prophetic visions articulated while still in exile. Whether the psalm refers to this historical situation or another, the circumstance fits many occasions for the people of God in every generation. The psalmist is listening for the word of shalom that God will speak to God's people. He or she anticipates a word of steadfast love and faithfulness, of righteousness and peace. In the midst of communal distress, someone remembers the promises of God and becomes the speaker of holy promises.

Sometimes all we have from God is a promise. In the midst of injustice, Amos said, "Let justice roll down like waters" (Amos 5:24). In the face of violence, Micah imagined the day when "they shall beat their swords into plowshares" (Mic. 4:3). Trapped in exile, Isaiah prophesied, "Comfort" (Isa. 40:1). In similar fashion, the people of God gather in sanctuaries and, in the face of death, wrap ourselves in the promises of life, "I will come again and will take you to myself, so that where I am, there you may be also" (John 14:3).

To speak the promises of God in all their fullness requires speech to reach beyond that which we see

Exegetical Perspective

A Song of Peace, Judgment, and Reassurance. The relationship that exists between God and humanity is neither simple nor straightforward. One of the great benefits of the book of Psalms is that it allows its readers to explore, meditate, reconsider, and perhaps see that relationship with God in new, challenging, and hope-giving ways. Psalm 85 is just such an example. The psalm itself is composed of three distinct movements: a remembrance of God's favor in the past (vv. 1–3); a plea about present trials (vv. 4–7); and reassuring words about God's present and imminent salvation (vv. 8–13). Although the reading for this day includes only the last section, it is important that the message of the psalm as a whole is understood so that the reassuring words at the end can be fully appreciated.

A Remembrance of God's Favor in the Past (vv. 1–3). The psalm opens with a retrospective of the positive relationship that existed between God and the people in the past. The verbs in this section are all perfects (implying past completed action) and all are second-person verbs (implying that the focus is on "you," i.e., on God's actions). God was favorable to "your land" and the relationship was characterized by God's forgiveness, pardon, and suppression of divine wrath. Twice in the section, the Hebrew verb

Homiletical Perspective

"Everybody cheats. I just didn't know."

"Well, now you know."

In the 1979 movie *Breaking Away*, Dave, an avid cyclist, dreams of riding with the Italian national team. His dream comes true when the Italians race in his hometown. While riding alongside him, they toss a bike pump into his spokes, taking him out of the race and shattering his vision of their godlike status. As he recalls the story to his father, his dad does not pretend about the world. He simply replies, "Well, now you know."

Be careful for what you wish; it just might come true. The exiled Israelites yearn to return to their home, the land of promise. "When the LORD restored the fortunes of Zion, we were like those who dream" (Ps. 126:1). Having returned, they realize all is not dreamlike.

What it takes to sing the Lord's song in a foreign land is a question Israel faced in exile (Ps. 137:4). Yet what do you do when you return to the place you dreamed of, the place you hungered and yearned for, to find that it is now alien? In this psalm we hear from a community that has come home, but is still yearning.

When powers in the world conspire against human integrity, how can we believe? When we as nations and human communities talk about our

Psalm 85:8-13

Theological Perspective

the New Testament is therefore different; it is no longer one of expectant longing, but of holy optimism. The writers believe that the prayers of their ancestors have been answered, and they go out to proclaim "the news everywhere, while the [ascended] Lord worked with them and confirmed the message by the signs that accompanied it" (Mark 16:20).

Of course this is not to say that the eschatological reality has been fully realized. There is tension between inauguration and realization. Living between these two moments, the Christian community can join in saying the words of Psalm 85. Nonetheless, the location in salvation history is different for the Christian community than it was for the community of the psalmist. Since his particular location in salvation history is the source of the psalmist's prayer, the preacher will honor the psalm by contemplating her own place in salvation history and proclaiming it with holy optimism. One way in which she may do this is by meditating on how the ascended Lord is confirming the good news in her particular community.

2. The second issue to contemplate is the eschatological renewal's *object*. In the psalm, this object includes the people, their hearts and souls, but also the land, ground, and sky: the soil of Palestine and, from there, all of creation. Many of our mainline American church members' eschatological imagination does not, however, extend much further than the spiritual—"to go to heaven when you die"—as though that were the last act of the drama. Such expectation falls short of what the psalmist hopes for. His eschatological world is the one envisioned in Isaiah: this physical reality renewed, and people given new bodies to live, work, and take delight in God's new creation. If the preacher wants her people fully to grasp the promises of this psalm, it is up to her to extend her people's imagination to encompass such renewed reality. In other words, the preacher needs to proclaim not just Christ's ascension, but also the resurrection of the body.

3. The third issue to contemplate is the *means* of eschatological renewal. The psalm fragment speaks of the glory that dwells in the land; of the meeting of steadfast love and faithfulness; of justice and peace that will kiss. Many exegetes and theologians have tried to pinpoint what exactly is meant by each of these terms and how they interact. However, if it is true that the eschatological reality of which the psalm speaks is inaugurated in Christ, then for the Christian community the answers to these questions

Pastoral Perspective

and that which we know. To speak the fullness of God's promises is to speak the truth of the world as it is, as well as the truth of the world as the power of God's shalom will make it.

Perhaps it was a prophet, or maybe a priest, but someone stood up among the people of God in a circumstance of desperation and spoke the promise of salvation. Someone proclaimed the day of steadfast love and faithfulness, righteousness and peace.

The language of salvation is not simply borrowed from dreams. The confidence the promise speaker has in God's future is rooted in God's prior faithfulness. There was a day when the salvation of God was known. There were stories to tell of God's mighty deeds. Perhaps the exile is the particular moment in mind, when the faithfulness of God created a way home in the desert. Whether this moment or some other, the promise speaker is able to remember the times when God was "favorable to [the] land" and "restored the fortunes of Jacob" (v. 1). This memory of God's salvation gives the promise speaker confidence to proclaim the coming salvation of God.

Psalm 85 reminds us of the importance of memory. The testimony of the people of God through the generations is that God's salvation has been experienced. God's divine character has been revealed as one of steadfast love and faithfulness. God's dreams for creation include righteousness and shalom. During times of testing or seasons of emptiness, the psalmist calls on the people of God to remember all that God has done. God's anger has been withdrawn (v. 3). Sin has been pardoned (v. 2). This prior faithfulness of God provides reason to trust the promises of God that are yet unfulfilled. The act of memory, rather than drawing one into the past, propels the people of God to hope for God's new and promised tomorrow.

Even with these memories of God's faithfulness, confidence in the coming salvation of God is not shared by the community as a whole. They cry out, "Will you be angry with us forever? Will you prolong your anger to all generations?" (v. 5). Yet in the midst of such desperate circumstances and theological questioning, there is one who speaks of a new day. Someone remembers the faithfulness of God and boldly "rehearses the promises of God before the congregation as reassurance in their time of distress. He asks them to trust in the word of God that he has received by oral tradition."[1] Someone is able to

---

1. James L. Mays, *Psalms*, Interpretation (Louisville, KY: John Knox Press, 1994), 277.

Exegetical Perspective

shuv ("to return" or "to turn back something" or "to repent") is used: "You *restored* the fortunes (or, in other versions, "the captives" or "the exiles") of Jacob" (v. 1), and "You *turned* from your hot anger" (v. 3). Many commentators see the section as referring to the return of the exiles to the land from the Babylonian exile (586–538 BCE). Others see the psalm as referring either to the exodus from Egypt or, alternatively, to a more general "turning of fortunes" sometime in the past. The psalms are notoriously difficult to date to specific historical contexts. This is, however, also what lends them their power. Whatever its original context or referent, this section looks back at a time of peace between God and the people.

A Plea in the Time of Trouble (vv. 4–7). The present circumstance of the psalmist is not like the past, however, and out of the brokenness of the relationship the psalmist issues a plea. This section is organized with predominant imperatives at its beginning and end: "Restore (*shuv*) us . . . put away your indignation" (v. 4) and "Show us your steadfast love" (v. 7). Furthermore, the focus of the beginning and end of the section is on God's "salvation" (v. 4, 7). The center of the plea (vv. 5–6) is characterized by three rhetorical questions, all focused on the divine anger—the symbol of the broken relationship and the opposite of God's "salvation"—and the possibility for renewal.

Hopeful Words for Now and for the Future (vv. 8–13). The "peace" (*shalom*) and the "righteousness" (*tsedek*) that are the subject of the final section of the psalm are not, therefore, simply empty, optimistic words that say "things will get better . . . I hope!" The words, spoken within the troubling times of verses 4–7, are the response to the despairing circumstances the community is experiencing. The section is divided into two parts: a general introduction to the reassurance (v. 8), and a "census" of the symbolic inhabitants and produce of "our land" (vv. 9–13).

The psalmist expresses a desire to hear "what God the Lord will speak, for he will speak peace to his people" (v. 8). Commentators in the past have generally seen this verse as a reference to a court prophet or a temple prophet, whose function was often to speak comforting words to the royal house. The image that many commentaries try to reconstruct is that the prophet pronounced the divine word, "peace," and the psalmist here interprets this in the following verses.

Homiletical Perspective

interests as something over against the interests of other nations and communities, how can we hope? When we see leaders of commerce, government, and religion only interested in securing local and immediate prosperity rather than working for just and sustainable policies for the benefit of all peoples, how can we trust?

When we find ourselves honest about our own unfaithfulness, about the fears that keep us from acting, how do we act from hope? How do we sing the Lord's song when in exile, be that geographic or the exile of our souls?

The psalmist speaks of the "quartet of attributes characteristic of the way of the Lord":[1] covenant loyalty (*ḥesed*), faithfulness (*'emet*), righteousness (*ṣedeq*), and peace (*shalom*). In these, the psalmist names what full restoration looks like. We hear the disciplines and practices that are descriptive of God. We also hear the disciplines and practices of a community that wants to hope. Restoration comes from actions founded in this quartet. It is about these attributes that the preacher must speak. The preacher is encouraged to study these words in order to save the sermon from a simple and detrimental understanding of what they meant for the psalmist.

Righteousness is about our accepting and living into the mutual, vulnerable, and interdependent reality of all relationships. It is about accepting the fact that from this reality, this righteous relationship, the life of God, is experienced. It is righteousness that gives Martin Luther King Jr. the audacity to "have a dream." It is about accepting *ḥesed* as a practice to be chosen, as well as one that is required of those who would expect a future and a hope.

The task of the preacher is to ask how we as a community practice *ḥesed* both within the community and with the world about us. How and in what ways do our communal practices proclaim our belief in and commitment to *ḥesed*? Where might our practices be speaking a different commitment altogether?

The psalmist knows that if we are to find our restoration, it will be as the community practices this quartet. They know this is no small commitment of the community and the preacher does well not to undersell it either. As author Wendell Berry notes, "Hell itself, the war that is always among us, is the creature of time, unending time, unrelieved by any light or hope. But love, sooner or later, forces us out of

1. James L. Mays, *Psalms*, Interpretation (Louisville, KY: John Knox Press, 1994), 277.

Psalm 85:8-13

Theological Perspective

come not by way of a definition, but by way of a person. We know what the psalmist saw when he talked about glory's dwelling, and the meeting of steadfast love and faithfulness, because these words have become flesh and lived among us. If we want to know exactly how justice and peace can kiss, we do not start from whatever we think justice and peace are and try to determine how they can hold together. We start from how this kiss is embodied in Jesus.

This last point leads the preacher to an important theological insight. As theologians Stanley Hauerwas and William Willimon point out, if the church's account of love, justice, and peace is intimately bound up with the person of Christ, this does not mean that the church and its preacher can assume that their account is shared by all people. There are competing accounts. "After all, Pilate permitted the killing of Jesus in order to secure both peace and justice (Roman style) in Judea."[1] It is up to the preacher to discern which competing accounts might undermine her people's grasp of peace and justice as Jesus embodies them.

4. A final issue to contemplate is the *subject* of the psalm's eschatological vision. That subject is the Lord. The psalmist does not present his vision as an action plan for God's people. Their work is not "to build the kingdom." If that were the case, the psalmist would have written a different psalm. This is not to say that the preacher should refrain from presenting this eschatological vision as one that is to shape the way we live our lives. Once you have been set on the road of salvation, your behavior changes. But neither that salvation nor the way toward it are our doing; the promise of this passage is that they are God's doing. That is exactly what makes this vision one of good news.

EDWIN CHR. VAN DRIEL

Pastoral Perspective

articulate a new day when "faithfulness will spring up from the ground, and righteousness shall look down from the sky" (v. 11).

Anyone who would boldly speak the promises of God will find him or herself speaking of a day that we have yet to know. Speak of a day when the law will be written on our hearts (Jer. 31:33), as Jeremiah promised, and we speak of a day we have yet to know. Or speak of the lion lying down with the lamb, as Isaiah did (Isa. 11:6), or the hungry being filled with good things, as Mary did (Luke 1:53), and we speak of promises yet to find fulfillment. Throughout the witness of the Scriptures, the prophets and the priests, the apostles and the ordinary disciples have filled their mouths with speech from another day. Their mouths have been filled with language to describe the full salvation of God, where steadfast love and faithfulness will meet, where righteousness and peace will kiss each other (v. 10). Such promises of God, when remembered and proclaimed, have served to lead the children of God in hope-filled faithfulness even in the darkest hours.

The ones who speak with boldness the promises of God invite all to trust in these promises more than in the present circumstance. The good news is that it is God's promised future, and not any present circumstance, that governs our lives. Trust in the promises of God allows God's dreams for us to govern our lives and our interactions with one another, until the day is fully realized when faithfulness will spring up from the ground and righteousness will look down from the sky (v. 11).

TOM ARE JR.

---

1. Stanley Hauerwas and William H. Willimon, *Resident Aliens: Life in the Christian Colony* (Nashville: Abingdon, 1989), 38.

Exegetical Perspective

This is, however, by no means required or even helpful for understanding the psalm. What is the "divine word" that the psalmist desires so much to hear? What is the source of that word? Is it not the word that was pronounced at the beginning of the psalm: "LORD, you were favorable to your land; you restored. . . . You forgave . . . ; you pardoned. . . . You . . . turned from your anger" (vv. 1–3)? Looking back at the past, for the psalmist, is not simply a rehearsal of ancient history; it is, rather, the seedbed for a present hope in spite of circumstances. In spite of the broken relationship that the people experience with God now, the psalmist yearns to hear—again— that divine word of *shalom* from the past and is assured that *shalom* can be a part of the present and imminent future as well.

The final verses of the psalm provide a symbolic "census" of the land. In the past, God was "favorable to your land" (v. 1). This focus on the "land" is repeated throughout this final section. In the reading, the Hebrew verbs that are used are extremely varied, including perfects, imperfects, and infinitives. The impression is that the scenes painted by these verses are for the present, as well as for an imminent future. Although physically the land may be experiencing trouble, theologically the land has some important inhabitants and will be producing some remarkable crops.

"His salvation" is a "neighbor" (my translation; NRSV has "is at hand") to those who fear God, and "Glory" is an inhabitant in "our land" (v. 9). More-over, "Steadfast Love" (*hesed*) and "Faithfulness" (*'emet*), like God's counselors, have a meeting, and "Righteousness" (*sedek*) and "Peace" (*shalom*), like a couple, kiss. The concord between these anthro-pomorphized inhabitants has an effect on the land itself, which starts producing "Faithfulness" like a crop. "Righteousness," like a rain-producing cloud, looks down from the sky. God gives "Goodness," and the land, in response, gives its produce. The most important inhabitant of the land must still come, however. So "Righteousness," no longer simply the one who kisses "Peace" or the cloudlike provider of fertility, at the end serves as a forerunner or a vanguard, preparing the road so that God, as the primary inhabitant of this land, may finally come and dwell with the people in "our land."

ROY L. HELLER

Homiletical Perspective

time. It does not accept that limit."[2] Commitment to the practices of covenant loyalty, faithfulness, righteousness, and *shalom*, basing our actions and choices upon these, is how we break the limits of time.

How does the preacher invite this kind of hope? What feeds the hope foundational to these practices? How does the preacher invite the communal level of intimacy assumed here? How do we name the hope that is within us in a manner that is honest about the world and honest about our own frailties and spiritual infidelities? How do we as preachers, like the psalmist, hold in balance this honesty and the unfathomable *hesed* of God?

There is vulnerability for the preacher in revealing our hope. Experience suggests the congregation shares the same feeling. "Preacher, have you seen what they do to those who proclaim they 'have a dream'?" In his song *The River*, Bruce Springsteen asks if a dream is a lie if it does not come true, or might it be something worse? As one friend put it to me, "If Jesus has taken away the sin of the world, what is this around us?" How do we sing the Lord's song in a foreign land? For there will always be the experience of exile in communities who strive for, practice, and proclaim *hesed* and *shalom*.

Perhaps it is here that we as preachers must ask what we believe about the *hesed* and *shalom* of God, asking ourselves if we are hedging on that for which we hope, that for which we live? Having done so, we may be able to let the congregation in on our own wrestling with hope, as we accept the vulnerability of naming something fantastic. In this we can invite the community to do the same thing. For it is only as we have wrestled with the hope and fidelity of God, often with the ferocity of Jacob, that we will be able to believe in them.

The psalmist sees the past and the present. Amid the shakiness of the past and the ambivalence of the present, he hears of God's *hesed* and *shalom*. How do we proclaim our belief in the fullness of God? Let me hear.

TODD M. DONATELLI

---

2. Wendell Berry, *Jayber Crow* (Washington, DC: Counterpoint, 2000), 249.

Ephesians 1:3-14

³Blessed be the God and Father of our Lord Jesus Christ, who has blessed us in Christ with every spiritual blessing in the heavenly places, ⁴just as he chose us in Christ before the foundation of the world to be holy and blameless before him in love. ⁵He destined us for adoption as his children through Jesus Christ, according to the good pleasure of his will, ⁶to the praise of his glorious grace that he freely bestowed on us in the Beloved. ⁷In him we have redemption through his blood, the forgiveness of our trespasses, according to the riches of his grace ⁸that he lavished on us. With all wisdom and insight ⁹he has made known to us the mystery of his will, according to his good pleasure that he set forth in Christ, ¹⁰as a plan for the fullness of time, to gather up all things in him, things in heaven and things on earth. ¹¹In Christ we have also obtained an inheritance, having been destined according to the purpose of him who accomplishes all things according to his counsel and will, ¹²so that we, who were the first to set our hope on Christ, might live for the praise of his glory. ¹³In him you also, when you had heard the word of truth, the gospel of your salvation, and had believed in him, were marked with the seal of the promised Holy Spirit; ¹⁴this is the pledge of our inheritance toward redemption as God's own people, to the praise of his glory.

Theological Perspective

This has been a favorite text for those Christians who understand the gospel to be an affirmation of God's prevenient grace. From this perspective the gospel is not first about human beings, but about God and what God has done in Jesus Christ "before the foundation of the world." In the introduction to his commentary on this text, John Calvin describes Ephesians' first three chapters as "chiefly occupied in commending the grace of God":

> For immediately after the greeting at the beginning of the first chapter, he [Paul] treats of God's free election, so that they may acknowledge that they are now called into the Kingdom of God because they have been appointed to life before they were born. And God's wonderful mercy shines forth in the fact that the salvation of men flows from His free adoption as its true and native source.[1]

Election or predestination is a joyous affirmation of the sovereignty of God's grace, but it has also troubled many Christians, including those in denominations that traditionally have emphasized the doctrine. Does election mean a divine

Pastoral Perspective

For churches seeking affirmation that their work is not in vain, Ephesians is a resounding song of hope. Whether written by Paul or by one of his followers, whether to one church or all the "saints who are faithful in Christ Jesus," the intent is clear: to shore up and strengthen the church of Jesus Christ to be faithful in his service. We are reminded again and again of who we are and whose we are, brought back to the sheer joy of living as God's people.

Immediately the letter plunges us into a cascade of beauty and riches. Abundant blessings and glorious grace are lavished upon us, for God's own good pleasure. This is no capricious whim of God, but purposefully planned before the foundation of the world. God has adopted us as God's own children, made us to be God's own people, and has given us an inheritance in Christ. God has chosen us to be holy and blameless in love, forgiven and redeemed through Christ.

As other commentators have noted, this is "the excess of the language of worship."[1] The words flow in an endless stream of praise and wonder, as if meant to lift us to the very heights of God's presence.

1. John Calvin, *Calvin's Commentaries*, vol. 11, *The Epistles of Paul the Apostle to the Galatians, Ephesians, Philippians and Colossians*, ed. David W. Torrance and Thomas F. Torrance, trans. T. H. L. Parker (Grand Rapids: Eerdmans, 1965), 121.

1. Fred B. Craddock, John H. Hayes, Carl R. Holladay, Gene M. Tucker, *Preaching through the Christian Year*, Year B (Harrisburg, PA: Trinity Press International, 1993), 66, 342.

Exegetical Perspective

The basic historical question about this letter is twofold: who wrote it, and to whom? The words "in Ephesus" in the first verse are absent in some old manuscripts, leading some to speculate it was a general letter with the recipients filling in their own name. The one sent to Ephesus would then be the one that was included in the New Testament. The second problem is who wrote it? If it was Paul, it cannot have been addressed to Ephesus, since the author is unknown to the readers there, and Paul was well known to them. But the language and linguistic structures—long sentences, use of complementary genitives, abundance of relative clauses with a surplus of adjectives—seem to point to someone other than Paul. The content, however, is very Pauline. Perhaps the best solution is to posit a follower of Paul who wrote a general letter, and, in accord with ancient custom, attributed it to the one whose ideas he was expounding. The letter is an excellent summary of Paul's thought about the universal significance of the Christian faith, a point thematic for Paul's letter to the churches in Rome. Generations of Christians, ancient and modern, have found Ephesians useful for the life of the church, and we may confidently join them.

The body of the letter is divided into two parts after the letter opening: 1:3–3:31 and 4:1–6:20. Our

Homiletical Perspective

Entering into the world of Ephesians can be challenging for a congregation in the best of times. Its language is "thick." The first sentence of this Sunday's text is, in itself, a mouthful for the lector and surely an earful for a summer congregation more in the mood for a parable than for this densely worded phrasing. But the preacher will want to think twice before opting to preach on one of the other assigned texts for the day. Are there any in the congregation who struggle with shame, who know what it is to feel abandoned and of little worth? For that matter, does the congregation itself wrestle with despair when it faces the future? If so, this is a text well worth the challenge of hosting on behalf of the congregation that gathers to hear the word on Sunday.

Perhaps the best way to invite the congregation into conversation with the author of Ephesians is to acknowledge the thick "accent" spoken here. Encourage the church to open its heart to the powerful news that is carried in phrases like "blessed us in Christ," "chose us in Christ," "destined us for adoption as his children," "his glorious grace that he freely bestowed on us," and "the riches of his grace that he lavished on us."

Even a cursory reading of these lines reveals a letter that opens with superlatives. Paul piles one blessing upon another as if he thinks that the little

Theological Perspective

determinism that turns God into a tyrant and human beings into robots without any agency or freedom? Does election make faith moot and superfluous? Are some people the recipients of God's grace and others not? Why some and not others? That would seem to suggest God is capricious and perhaps cruel. Does election mean that the gospel is good news for some people and bad news for others? Or does election mean that all people are saved? If so, if salvation is universal, why do discipleship and mission matter? These are only a few of the theological questions this text may evoke. What does election mean?

First, for theologians like Augustine, Luther, Calvin, Edwards, and Barth, Ephesians makes clear that election is a statement about the wonder of God's grace in Jesus Christ. Election is misunderstood if it becomes primarily a question about the scope of God's grace (who is included and who is not, and how one can know to which camp one belongs). It is above all else an affirmation that the God Christians know in Jesus Christ is gracious beyond the wildest reaches of their imaginations. Election is important, therefore, because it is a part of the theological identity of Christians. It says something important about who God is and about who those people are who have freely and undeservedly received God's grace in Jesus Christ.

Second, election is about the sovereignty of God's will. Repeatedly this text affirms that God's choosing or election is rooted in the good pleasure and mystery of God's counsel and will (vv. 5, 9, 11). Calvin insisted that election is not simply a form of omniscience on God's part. It does not mean that God knows which people respond to God's grace in Jesus Christ and which do not. Election is good news because it affirms that those who are in Christ belong to God, not because they are less sinful than other people or because they have done the right things, but for no other reason than God has chosen to be merciful to them. God's grace is not a response on God's part to what human beings have done, but that which precedes (pre-venes or "comes before") faith and is its source.

Third, God's election is always "in Christ," and Christ is "the looking glass" in which Christians should contemplate their election. What Christians know in Jesus Christ is that God's sovereign will is good. At the birth of Christ the angels announce God's goodwill to the world. If election becomes an occasion for anxiety and uncertainty, then it has been misunderstood. The appropriate response to

Pastoral Perspective

The focus is on God's actions. This is not our doing; it is all gift. In fact, these verses offer no obvious imperative at all, nothing for us to do but "live for the praise of his glory" (v. 12). In the words of the Westminster Catechism, our "chief end" is to glorify God and enjoy God forever.

Pastorally, the most obvious connection for this passage is our baptism. At baptism we rejoice that God has claimed us as God's own; we remember how Christ has washed away our sins; we see the sign and seal of God's promise; we pray for the Spirit to come upon the water, and upon the one receiving this sacrament.

Even if no baptism occurs this Sunday, the congregation might renew their baptismal vows, sing baptismal songs, and celebrate the joy of living as children of God. If there is any way to evoke the mystery, the fullness, and the pleasure of this passage, the pastor would wisely embrace it.

Barbara Brown Taylor tells an evocative story from her own childhood that awakens this sense. Her grandmother, a tough, stern woman, was "an awesome presence, especially to a child." She was known most for "her shrewd business sense and her bad temper." Even her appearance was intimidating; with both legs amputated from untreated diabetes, and with her dark aviator sunglasses to protect her eyes, she looked, Taylor says, "like a handicapped bomber pilot."

But she lavished her love on her grandchildren. When they came to visit, there were special treats, piles of presents, and long, lazy afternoons together. Each child received a night of pampering. Taylor remembers:

> When my night came she treated me like long lost royalty, filling the tub with suds and then beckoning me in, where she washed each of my limbs in turn and polished my skin with her great soft sponge. After she had dried me off . . . she anointed me with Jergen's Lotion. . . . Then she reached for her dusting powder—Evening in Paris—and tickled me all over with the pale blue puff. When she had done, I knew I was precious. I was absolutely convinced I was loved.[2]

Ephesians reminds us of God's love for us, and the flowing words of our passage envelop us with that kind of love: excessive, tender, richly abundant.

Yet the language of Ephesians is not individualistic. As beloved as we are, we are lifted up

---

2. Barbara Brown Taylor, *The Preaching Life* (Cambridge, MA: Cowley, 1993), 17

passage is the opening of the first part, containing the usual Pauline thanksgiving and a summary of the basic themes of the letter.

The opening thanksgiving leaves no doubt as to the source of the blessings the readers enjoy: those blessings have their origin in Christ (v. 3), and that in turn is due to God's decision made from before the creation of the world to include the readers among those who receive them (v. 4). It is no accident that the classic Pauline formulation, "For by grace you have been saved through faith, and this is not your own doing; it is the gift of God" (2:8), occurs precisely in this letter.

Two important themes are enunciated in these opening verses: the agency of Christ for our salvation, and the initiative of God in this whole activity. They are combined in verse 5—God, according to God's loving purpose, destined us to be children through Jesus Christ.

Christ as the agent of God's purposes informs this entire passage. Spiritual blessings (v. 3), chosen (v. 4) to be God's children (v. 5), divine grace (v. 6), redemption that is forgiveness of sin (v. 7), knowledge of God's purposes (v. 9), unity of all creation (v. 10), living for the praise of God's glory (v. 12)—all of that has come to us because of the agency of Christ. But the author never forgets that it is God's initiative that has caused all this. Verse 11 comes as close to the idea of predestination as any verse in the NT: in Christ God accomplished all things in accordance with the divine will.

All of this has been accomplished and is to eventuate in two things: the unity of all humankind and the promotion of the praise of God. That unity, thought of by our author primarily in terms of the unity of Jew and Gentile, will become explicit later in the letter, but it is already introduced here in verse 10, in terms of the final unity of all creation, heavenly as well as earthly. It is also indicated by the shift from first person ("we") in verse 12 to the second person ("you also") in verse 13. This is probably not the first reference to Gentiles, even though it is the first shift in pronouns. The "we" in verses 3–10 is probably to be understood as including all Christians, Jew or Gentile; the reference to "we who *first* hoped in Chrsit" (v. 12 RSV) refers for the first time to the separation of humanity in terms of Jew and Gentile. The phrase "first hoped in him" is probably a reference to the fact that Jews became believers in Christ prior to the inclusion of Gentiles.

It is that unity, shown by our becoming children of God, accomplished through Christ, that has as its

church in Ephesus does not believe him. One suspects that this is, indeed, the case. Paul is not the only preacher who knows that his congregation struggles to believe it is beloved by God. This silent despair may indeed be the larger problem faced by contemporary preachers of this passage. Not far beneath the veneer of apparently happy and satisfied consumers of the market economy, pastors know that they will find many aching and troubled parishioners. A sermon on this opening passage in Ephesians may need to begin by setting Paul's superlatives over against the unspoken messages of pain and desperation carried into the sanctuary by the congregation. When Paul says "blessed," "chosen," "adoption," "grace," the congregation may not believe him, because it has memorized the mantra of "fated," "rejected," "failure," "shameful," "guilty." Giving voice to this silent unspoken truth may well be what is necessary if the congregation is to open its heart and soul to receive Paul's surprising news.

A sermon that opens this text up may shift at times from Paul's theological meditation to the language of narrative. The metaphors of "adoption" and "inheritance" may, for example, invite stories of families within the congregation that have grafted adopted children into their family trees. The challenge for the preacher will be to keep such stories small enough that they serve the text rather than become the text for the day.

One way to ensure that the sermon stays close to the text is to pattern the narrative flow of the sermon after the logic of the passage. Paul's language works in concentric circles, slowly moving forward in three progressions. The first two long sentences (vv. 3–8a) are thick with the language of "spiritual blessing" and "glorious grace." This first third of the sermon can name how difficult it is for us, in spite of so many material blessings, to believe that we are beloved.

In the next sentence (vv. 8b–10) Paul moves out beyond the congregation to the world and universe. He dares to announce that in Christ we see God's "plan for the fullness of time, to gather up all things in him, things in heaven and things on earth." The middle third of the sermon can take its lead from Paul, moving from a focus on ourselves to a focus on the world. As hard as it is to believe that we are beloved, it is even more difficult for us to trust that "all things" will be gathered up in Christ. We are easily tempted to believe that the earth is "going to hell in a hand basket." A sermon that lingers here with Paul will notice that a church that takes this

Ephesians 1:3-14

Theological Perspective

God's election is gratitude and doxology. According to both Calvin and Barth, those who wonder if they are included in God's election should look not within themselves, but upon Christ. Those who look first at themselves and what they find in their own hearts and souls cannot help but be discouraged. If, however, they look not at themselves but at Christ, and if they see in Christ the grace and mercy of God, they should find assurance they are included in the promises of God's grace and mercy. Barth criticized Calvin for not following the claim that election is in Christ to its proper conclusion. If election is "in Christ" that means he is the only one who is elect and that he alone is both the electing God and the elected (and rejected) human.[2] If all are in Adam by virtue of their sin, so too all are in Christ by means of his grace.

Fourth, election reminds Christians that they are adopted children of God. Those chosen by God in Christ belong to God not because of blood or family; rather, God "destined us for adoption" (v. 5). Their inheritance is utterly gratuitous. Election is not a right but a gift. All those who have been justified by God's grace, according to the Westminster Confession of Faith, are "partakers of the grace of adoption."[3] As adopted children they belong to God not by virtue of family or law, but sheerly by God's goodwill.

Fifth, God's election does not make Christians "special" in relation to other people, but calls them to specific tasks of serving God and neighbor. Those elect in Christ are called not to privilege but to discipleship and to the suffering of the cross. Bonhoeffer got it right. To paraphrase him, when God calls someone, God calls that person to come and die.

Election is the good news that God's grace in Jesus Christ precedes us, surrounds us, and sustains us, or, in the words of 1 John 4:19, "We love because [God] first loved us."

GEORGE W. STROUP

Pastoral Perspective

into something far greater than ourselves. We are blessed *in Christ,* we are chosen *in Christ,* we are destined for adoption *through Christ. In Christ* we have obtained our inheritance, and our hope is set *on Christ.* Moreover, the constant plural pronouns remind us that this gift is not an individual blessing but always for the community of Christ.

This passage offers a counter to the world's understanding of "worth." It isn't merely that we are somehow special, but rather that we have been taken up into something extraordinary and offered this gift to receive as our own. Like a pauper invited to take the place of a prince or princess, we have been invited to share in the riches of God's grace. God has accomplished all this on our behalf through Christ, so we might live as God's own children.

The grace of this passage is unmistakable. Yet the passage is not without tensions. Who is to be redeemed? Some would read this passage as a clear argument for predestination, that some persons have been chosen and some have not. While these verses say nothing about condemnation, the very use of the words "he destined us . . . according to . . . his will" (v. 5) implies particularity: *we* have been chosen, and others have not.

Others would suggest, though, that the passage argues for universal salvation, that God's plan "for the fullness of time [is] to gather up all things in him." This reading presumes that "all things" includes all persons, and that no one and nothing will remain outside God's embrace. If some are aware of their identity as God's children, it does not mean that others are not also God's children, only that some have been made aware of "the mystery of his will."

Whether or not the pastor chooses to address these arguments will depend greatly on the pastor, the congregation, and the moment in time. In most churches, it will be enough to soak in the wonder of being God's beloved. In the words of the old hymn, "All things are mine since I am his! How can I keep from singing?"

KAREN CHAKOIAN

---

2. Karl Barth, *Church Dogmatics* (Edinburgh: T. & T. Clark, 1957), II/2.3–506.
3. Westminster Confession of Faith, chapter XIV, "Of Adoption," in *The Book of Confessions* (Louisville, KY: Office of the General Assembly, 1999), 136.

Exegetical Perspective

goal the praise of God's glorious grace (vv. 5–6). That goal is also indicated by the fact that our lives—as those whose hope is awakened in Christ—are to be carried forward to the praise of God's glory (v. 12). The completion of God's redemptive plan will also result in the praise of divine glory (v. 14).

Yet all of this is inextricably linked to the agency of Christ. The unity of all people with God as their Father is accomplished through God's Son (vv. 5, 9–10), their redemption accomplished by the Son's self-sacrifice (v. 7).

Such praise and unity have yet to be visibly achieved, however. What we have in Christ is knowledge of God's final plan, one day to be fulfilled, but as yet only partially realized. Our author is not sanguine enough to delude himself or his readers that divine love has already fulfilled all it will according to the divine plan. Division continues still between Jew and Gentile, despite the fact that Christ's death and resurrection have destroyed the *basis* on which that division exists. Divisions exist still within the church, the very body of Christ, despite the fact that Christians are to be illumined by the hope and trust that God has redeemed all through the grace shown in the Son. That inevitably raises the questions: How do we know all of that is true? How do we know we are not the victims of a self-imposed delusion that seemingly fled in the face of reality?

The answer for our author—and for us—is the presence of the Holy Spirit, which itself represents a "down payment" on the ultimate inheritance of unity and peace (vv. 13b–14). Where the church praises God and confesses Christ as Lord, that Spirit is present, assuring Christians that the divine goal will in fact one day become reality.

PAUL J. ACHTEMEIER

Homiletical Perspective

text to heart cannot give up hope in anyone or any neighborhood or any nation. Naming the people and places that we assume to be hopeless and, instead, including them in the plan of God revealed in Christ for "all things" will remind both preacher and congregation of the scandal of the gospel.

The final two sentences in the passage (vv. 11–14) hint at the kind of life that is to be led by a people who know themselves to be adopted, graced, and richly blessed with a massive inheritance of love. Paul says that this inheritance is a way of life. He says it twice to make sure that the church hears. He calls this way of life living to "the praise of his glory" (vv. 12 and 14). He says it is a journey "toward redemption as God's own people" (v. 14). The words "praise" and "glory" are easily domesticated in the church. The glory of God for Paul—a rabbi by training—is the *kabod*, the weight and *gravitas* of the presence of God. Paul imagines the Ephesians living as a people known not for their praise of human institutions or idols or ideas but for their joy in what Christ is doing to redeem aching souls and a suffering world. The sermon's final move can be to imagine the shape of a congregation that is marked by its consistent focus on what God is doing in its midst and in the midst of a troubled earth. In this way the text's shift from receiving blessing to being a blessing may be mirrored not only in the sermon, but also in the congregation itself.

EDWIN SEARCY

Mark 6:14-29

14King Herod heard of it, for Jesus' name had become known. Some were saying, "John the baptizer has been raised from the dead; and for this reason these powers are at work in him." 15But others said, "It is Elijah." And others said, "It is a prophet, like one of the prophets of old." 16But when Herod heard of it, he said, "John, whom I beheaded, has been raised."

17For Herod himself had sent men who arrested John, bound him, and put him in prison on account of Herodias, his brother Philip's wife, because Herod had married her. 18For John had been telling Herod, "It is not lawful for you to have your brother's wife." 19And Herodias had a grudge against him, and wanted to kill him. But she could not, 20for Herod feared John, knowing that he was a righteous and holy man, and he protected him. When he heard him, he was greatly perplexed; and yet he liked to listen to him. 21But an opportunity came when Herod on his birthday gave a banquet for his courtiers and officers

Theological Perspective

A Biblical Tragedy? The dramatic character of the story of John the Baptist's death has almost guaranteed it would detract from the primary theological concern of this passage. Although it is little more than a story within *the* story, this potpourri of sexual lust, seduction, political ambition, scandal, and murder has provided endless inspiration for artists and writers ancient and modern. Titian, Caravaggio, and Gustave Moreau, among others, painted it; Oscar Wilde wrote a famous play about it (*Salome*) that Richard Strauss used as the basis of his very successful opera; Ken Russell and Billy Wilder incorporated it in films. Probably no aspect of the New Testament apart from the passion of the Christ has provided greater stimulation for the artistic imagination.

Is it a tragedy, in the classical Greek or even Shakespearean sense? The artists have usually made it seem so, but theology would raise questions on that score. Herod, the weak son of Herod the Great, although he is the main actor in the drama, seems too little capable of the requisite self-knowledge to be thought a tragic figure. Salome (confusedly called "Herodias" in the Markan version of the incident) seems too much a pawn of her angry mother (and her own glands!) to be regarded as tragic, although the Strauss opera gives her character something of a

Pastoral Perspective

Consider the personal and social dilemmas in which Herod finds himself in this passage. He is trying to negotiate myriad complicated relationships within his household and society and discovering that it is quite difficult to please everyone around him and still uphold his own personal standards. He is at odds with his wife over John the Baptist and at odds with John over his wife. He is eager to appear a generous and trustworthy leader among Galilean society and troubled by his daughter's request for John's execution. His relationship with John evokes mixed feelings of fear, perplexity, and protectiveness. Herod is quite conscious of how social perceptions shape one's possibilities in life, yet he is also seeking some measure of truth by which to guide his life choices. He is caught in a web of relationships that seem to render him a "reactor" rather than an "actor" in the drama of life.

Contemporary church leaders also struggle sometimes like flies caught in a sticky web of congregational politics. Different cohorts in the faith community clash over issues as theologically mundane as the color of carpet in the parlor and as theologically central as the shape of congregational worship. A community's perceptions of how well its leaders negotiate the settlement of these issues can bolster or compromise the ability of a pastor or lay

and for the leaders of Galilee. ²²When his daughter Herodias came in and danced, she pleased Herod and his guests; and the king said to the girl, "Ask me for whatever you wish, and I will give it." ²³And he solemnly swore to her, "Whatever you ask me, I will give you, even half of my kingdom." ²⁴She went out and said to her mother, "What should I ask for?" She replied, "The head of John the baptizer." ²⁵Immediately she rushed back to the king and requested, "I want you to give me at once the head of John the Baptist on a platter." ²⁶The king was deeply grieved; yet out of regard for his oaths and for the guests, he did not want to refuse her. ²⁷Immediately the king sent a soldier of the guard with orders to bring John's head. He went and beheaded him in the prison, ²⁸brought his head on a platter, and gave it to the girl. Then the girl gave it to her mother. ²⁹When his disciples heard about it, they came and took his body, and laid it in a tomb.

Exegetical Perspective

The evangelists hold that encountering John the Baptist is necessary for hearing the good news about Jesus. But John's story—like Jesus'—is not all good. John dies a violent death, the direct consequence of the way he lived, and a ruler who has the power to save is moved more by guilt, self-interest, and pride than by justice and truth.

Mark's positioning of the story is instructive. It comes between an account of the mission of the Twelve (6:7–13) and the feeding of the five thousand (6:30–44). In the preceding text, the disciples are commissioned and empowered to extend the realm of Jesus' rule. In the following text, the disciples return from their first mission and Jesus feeds more than five thousand people through the blessing of five loaves and two fish. The mightier one of whom John spoke is here (cf. 1:7; Deut. 18:15–22; 2 Kgs. 4:42–44; Pss. 37:18–19; 81:10; 132:15; Isa. 49:9–13).

Sandwiched between these pericopes, in Markan fashion (cf. 3:20–25; 5:21–43; 11:12–25; 14:53–72), are accounts of Herod Antipas's inadequate response to the question of Jesus' identity (6:14–16) along with Herod's captivity (6:17–20) and execution of John the Baptist (6:21–29). At first glance, this lengthy account of John's death may seem inappropriate for Mark's streamlined story of Jesus (cf. Matt. 14:1–12; Luke 9:7–9), but Mark places it here to

Homiletical Perspective

There is a moment in every story in which the presence of grace can be felt as it waits to be accepted or rejected even though the reader may not recognize this moment.

—Flannery O'Connor[1]

It is challenging to preach from a "text of terror." When faced with the dark side of human life, in this case Herod's adultery with his brother's wife and the imprisonment and execution of John the Baptist, it is tempting to gloss over the details and go straight to the moral of the story. In doing so, we often miss opportunities to see what is hidden in plain sight, namely, the stream of grace that flows within the deep recesses of the narrative.

Mark's account, stark and spartan, is unique in its ability to hide what is plain and reveal what is hidden. Extreme and even grotesque characters will suddenly appear out of nowhere, revealing a reality that is mysteriously cloaked yet very real. Hidden in plain sight is a world that is demon infested, and evil coexists with normal day-to-day existence, inflicting pain and chaos. No one is immune from this power, especially the innocent and the weak.

1. Flannery O'Connor, *Mystery and Manners* (New York: Farrar, Straus & Giroux, 1961), 118.

Mark 6:14-29

Theological Perspective

tragic slant ("Kill that woman!" shouts the distraught and horrified Herod after watching Salome kiss the severed head of the Baptist). Perhaps Herodias, the mother, has a tragic aspect—we do not know enough about her story; yet vengeance is hardly a sufficiently elevated motive to be thought a "tragic flaw."

As for John, his vocation as truth teller as well as his ascetic bearing and lifestyle somehow place him above the tempest. And this is instructive, because it can be argued that tragedy is not a *biblical* concept. For the tradition of Jerusalem, all history is *postlapsarian*: the great tragedy, the fall (understood not literally but existentially) has already occurred: the rest—history!—is "fall-out." Pathos, not tragedy, is the human condition; but even pathos is not the last word about the subject, for where the grace of God enters the pathetic, chaotic, and confused sphere of human striving and emotion, the outcome is always somehow (in Reinhold Niebuhr's words) "beyond tragedy."

The Great Struggle: Truth vs. Power. The real theme of this pericope, however, is not the drama of life and death, love and hate, that so easily captivates our imaginations; it is the confrontation of political power and prophetic faith. The great struggle is the struggle between the baptizer and the king. And it is a complicated tension because, far from being the usual battle between the forces of light and the forces of darkness—a theme as common in religion as in pulp fiction!—light and dark, good and evil, are mixed *in both of the key players in this drama.*

That is obvious enough where Herod is concerned. He is by no means the standard villain. There is that within him—that "Augustinian" residue of remembrance and hope—that recognizes in the witness of John the kind of human authenticity to which he too is called. The forces of self-aggrandizement and lust that are powerfully at work in his life—and all the more at work because he does not actually possess the secure power his office boasts—are nonetheless countered by a more ancient memory of the good. Like Paul, Herod too might well confess, "I find . . . that when I want to do what is good, evil lies close at hand. For I delight in the law of God in my inmost self, but I see in my members another law at war with the law of my mind, making me captive to the law of sin that dwells in my members. Wretched man that I am!" (Rom. 7:21–24).

But we do no service to biblical faith when we make John the Baptist, on the other hand, the

Pastoral Perspective

leader to minister effectively. Even spiritually centered and capable leaders may squirm when confronted with congregants determined to push an agenda to accomplish a goal they hold sacred. Most church leaders have capitulated at least once in their ministry to the vociferous demands of some individual or group in order to save face or keep the peace. As Henri Nouwen has observed, religious leaders can mistakenly confuse good spiritual leadership with the ability to "control complex situations, confused emotions, and anxious minds,"[1] when such leadership only hinders the deeper theological reflection in which the faith community needs to engage. It is only human to care what others think and to want to please those around us by minimizing conflicts. One need not be Herod to understand what Herod is going through as his birthday festivities take an unexpected turn.

Daily life also presents a series of Herod-like personal and spiritual dilemmas for persons to negotiate. For a harried mother of a toddler, there is the question of how best to love and parent a child in the face of a defiant "No!" and a full-fledged temper tantrum in aisle 6 of the grocery store at the end of a long day. For a father of three, it is the struggle to explain the importance of rearranging travel plans for a work trip so he can attend a Little League playoff game. A corporate executive wonders how her announcement of a long-awaited pregnancy will affect her employees' perceptions of her as an effective boss. A stay-at-home dad wrestles with the whispers of former colleagues that he just couldn't handle the pressures of work. Teenagers experience the angst of competing for acceptance in desirable social cliques, of serial broken hearts in the complex world of adolescent dating, of familial tensions over privileges and responsibilities. Younger children long for popular toys advertised on television, worry about parental fights and the potential (or actual) breakup of their families, and wonder if the trouble they have learning multiplication tables or basic grammar means they are stupid. Across the lifespan, persons question who they are and how they should act as life pushes and pulls them in conflicting directions. And as in the story of Herod's struggle, there are lives at stake as they decide which actions they will take.

The most obvious life at risk in the Mark text is that of John the Baptist. It is John who pays the ultimate price when Herod chooses to make the

---

1. Henri Nouwen, *In the Name of Jesus* (New York: Crossroad, 1999), 56.

unveil something more of Jesus' identity and to underscore the cost of faithfulness.

Speculations about Jesus' Identity (vv. 14–16). Herod and his associates have heard reports about the deeds and miracles accomplished by Jesus' disciples, and they have come to know Jesus' name and reputation (v. 14). Amazingly, they believe that Jesus' power comes from being a resurrected prophet of recent days or of old (6:14–15; 8:27–29)—a startling assessment within Judaism. Herod Antipas, however, was a staunch Hellenist and was notorious among religious Jews for his contempt of their religious practices. Indeed, he built his capital city, Tiberias, on an ancient burial ground, rendering the city ritually unclean to religiously observant Jews (see Num. 19:14–22). Many Jews shunned the place and Herod filled his capital with Gentiles and elite, nonreligious Jews.

Herod and his associates had many other religious traditions within Hellenism by which they could account for Jesus' power. As it is, they anchor Jesus' identity to the life and traditions of Israel (vv. 14–16, 20), but their assessment of his power is peculiar. Some Jews did hold that the righteous ones would be resurrected to new, corporal, eternal life; but resurrection would come on the last day (cf. Ezek. 37:24–29; Jer. 33:15).[1] Outside of Judaism, however, there are religious traditions that associate resurrection with an increase in the risen one's powers in the present age. The Hellenistic cults of Asclepius, Dionysus of Thebes, and Osiris, for instance, are built upon stories of a hero's death (even the hero's dismemberment), a miraculous restoration of the body to life, and the "risen" hero's exercise of greater powers in the present age.

Non-Jewish traditions such as these may provide a more fitting interpretive framework for the speculations of Herod and his associates. Even though their assessments of Jesus may appear to be wholly Jewish, they reveal a secularized "faith" shaped by the influences of Hellenism as much as, if not more than, by the texts and traditions of Judaism. Of course, it is also significant that Herod and his associates show no awareness of the relationship between Jesus and John (1:1–11). Moreover, Herod's own guilt and fear are certainly affecting his perspective of Jesus' identity and power (vv. 20, 26).

1. See also *1 Enoch* 1–36; 62:14; 2 Maccabees 7; 12:43–44; *Mishnah Tractate Sanhedrin* 11:1–2; 13:2; *Babylonian Talmud Tractate Sanhedrin* 90A-B; John 11:24; etc.

Mark is also a Gospel of extremes: on the one hand, the preaching of the kingdom is welcomed and received with great joy; on the other hand, there is resistance and outright rejection. There is very little neutral territory. There is no room to be disinterested. The reader is given little opportunity to reflect but is compelled into the action and forced to see what they do not want to see and hear what is best left unspoken.

Evil is found not only in the demonic but also in the centers of power, both political and religious. The strong, driven by the forces of sex, money, and power, "lord over" those who are weak. In this passage we are forced to face a world that is in opposition to the innocent, a world where injustice and brutal power prevail. The text opens with speculation regarding the source of the power of Jesus and his disciples and ends with John's disciples' claiming his beheaded body and burying it. The story begins with power and ends with powerlessness.

Notice the contrasts in this passage. The powerlessness of John's preaching dares to confront the political power of Herod, and the Baptist's Nazarite vow stands in opposition to Herod's indulgences of the flesh. Here are two extreme characters, each mirroring realities that are set in opposition to the other.

Herod's reaction to John is a mixture of anger, fear, and conviction. The conflicted ruler keeps John hidden in plain sight. This uneasy existence comes to a head during Herod's birthday banquet. Here what is hidden is revealed. Herod is forced to choose between the innocent and the politically expedient. His moment of choice is a palatable moment of grace, waiting to be accepted or rejected. Herod's rejection of grace results in the death of John. But the thread of grace continues in the narrative. It is a thread that is woven throughout the book of Mark, redeeming violence and suffering.

Certainly the stench of death that covers this passage foreshadows the latter passages of Mark that reveal a violence of grace in the passion of Jesus. The preaching of John offers grace to Herod, the narrative's conflicted character. Like Pilate he is unable to act righteously, and evil triumphs over good.

Preaching Mark means rescripting and reimaging a world for listeners whose day-to-day reality is without the metaphysics of evil. Our lives are not controlled by powers but are more closely managed and expressly neutral. Here the narrative of Mark helps us. Stories like the execution of John shatter

Mark 6:14-29

Theological Perspective

example par excellence of pure goodness. Wasn't there some reason both the mother and the daughter were so fatefully drawn to him? Could it not be, as it has so often been with the heroes of morality, that his heroic self-discipline cloaks a passionate libido, rendering him all the more subject to the sin of pride? And did Jesus perhaps understand that psychic ambiguity of his famous "cousin" when he sent John's disciples back to him with the enigmatic caveat, "blessed is anyone who takes no offense at me" (Matt. 11:5)?

What makes the encounter of the prophet and the king so poignant is that they understand each other well enough. The puppet king knows enough about truth to recognize his own falseness; and the prophet is sufficiently acquainted with temptation to desire his monarch's liberation from it. Their meeting could have been redemptive, but one great flaw prevented it: Herod's insatiable quest for preeminence—having it, keeping it, flaunting it. Not sexual lust but lust for power is the problem this text illuminates. That sex is prominent in the account is not surprising, for as has been said famously (by Henry Kissinger, we are told), "Power is the ultimate aphrodisiac."

Such power must resist truth—not only the small truths that reveal our small transgressions and guilty secrets, but the great truth that the claim to power itself hides, generation after generation, the truth, as Camus put it, that "Men are unhappy gods." What prophetic faith wants above all to reveal is the absurdity of our pretence to sovereignty. If biblical religion resists tragedy, it is because it resists the premise of tragic anthropology: it does not believe that we are wise enough or masterful enough to err so finally. Not the creature but the Creator determines the end toward which life moves.

DOUGLAS JOHN HALL

Pastoral Perspective

king's public image more important than regard for another man's life. The consequences of bad-faith actions are generally devastating for those most vulnerable to the vagaries of political decision making. Infants die when campaign promises to cut health-care expenses result in the closure of public health centers without alternative means for indigent care developed. On the other hand, many working families struggle to make ends meet when national debt erodes the value of the dollar and drives up prices. If they cannot afford health insurance, their children are also vulnerable. Military alliances may draw soldiers into conflicts weakly supported at home, placing young people at risk because of promises made by their elders. Conversely, persons around the world may die as a result of nationalistic "ethnic cleansing" movements if the militaries of other countries do not intercede on their behalf. "Bad faith" decision making is easier to identify in the story of King Herod because we read this story in the context of the life, death, and resurrection of Jesus and know that Herod is making a mistake. The challenge of the twenty-first century is for the body of Christ to read our own decisions in light of that same story and ask ourselves whether the choices we are making are self-protective, or part of God's transformation of the world.

Herod too is at risk in this story. His spiritual quest is threatened by a decision that destroys further opportunity for conversation with John. His guilt over putting John to death leads him to imagine that Jesus, another emergent Jewish teacher, is John resurrected. Perhaps he fantasizes that he will have a second chance to listen to John's message of repentance and will finally understand and embrace the spiritual life John was proclaiming. Perhaps this is how human beings deal with our inclination to prefer social stability and equilibrium over the messy, chaotic process of personal and social transformation that participating in a spiritual quest requires. We look for second chances and hope that we are ready to risk more of ourselves this time around. If not, we may find ourselves, like Herod, deeply grieved.

KAREN MARIE YUST

The Death of John the Baptist (vv. 17–29). More elaborately than either Matthew (14:1–12) or Luke (9:7–9), Mark vividly recounts the tragic convergence of a proud, unfaithful king, a vengeful wife, a subservient daughter, and a forthright prophet of the Lord. The result is a brief "passion narrative" of John the Baptizer (see vv. 24–25) that foreshadows the suffering and death of Jesus (15:1–32) and his followers (13:9–13).

Mark's accounts of John's death at the command of Herod Antipas and Jesus' death by order of Pontius Pilate (15:1–5) have much in common. Both rulers look favorably upon their captives, who are prominent religious figures. Each ruler desires to spare the life of his prisoner. Both care more about pleasing their constituencies than exercising justice. Both act against their "better judgment" and condemn to death innocent men. Finally, both of the victims' bodies are recovered by disciples and laid in tombs.

To be sure, first-time listeners and readers of this Gospel cannot know this connection yet, but Mark's Gospel is already preparing them for the passions of Jesus and his disciples (8:31; 9:31; 10:32–34; 10:45; 13:1–15:47). Mark is also delineating the identities and missions of Jesus and John, as the "bookend" narratives make clear. The disciples' mission (6:7–13) and Jesus' feeding the five thousand (6:30–44) form lenses for seeing John's prophetic ministry in the context of Jesus' messianic identity and mission (i.e., 1:1–11; 11:32; 15:39).

Mark's distinctive use of the title "king" for Herod Antipas is also significant (cf. Matt. 2:1, 3; Luke 1:5). Only Herod the Great managed to wrest from Caesar the title of "king," and when his son Antipas requested the title from Augustus at the urging of Herodias, he was soon dismissed and exiled.[2] It may be that Mark uses the title to reflect a local custom or simply made a mistake. Mark may also be using the title ironically to ridicule Herod Antipas for failing to secure the title that he coveted and for losing his kingdom. Of course, Mark may also be drawing a sharp contrast between the fading kingdom of the Herods—a kingdom marked by pride, jealousy, cruelty, and death—and the emerging kingdom of God under the rule of Jesus and his disciples, a kingdom marked by courageous faithfulness—even to death—as well as life and nourishing fellowship (see 1:15; 6:7–13; 6:30–44; 15:2, 26; etc.).

ROBERT A. BRYANT

the numbness and break into our managed world with vivid and grotesque images of transcendence, violence, and grace.

The execution of John forces the reader to gaze into a world of corruption, lust, and power. Herod's court is in a far country whose horizon seems so distant from ours. It is territory held by evil. Yet, however distant this land seems, it can easily invade our managed space. Most congregants remember well September 11, 2001. Almost daily the media bring into our comfortable homes images of needless deaths and the slaughter of the innocents. Our congregations are filled with people, hidden in plain sight, who are dealing with their own texts of terror: deaths of loved ones, broken relationships, and abuse.

The beheading of John shows us how to read our own tragic stories. Our worship services should, at times, open the windows and allow the stench of death to permeate the sanctuary. This passage lends itself to a service of stark visuals and calls for the congregation to tarry awhile in the darkness, inhabiting the pathos.

On these occasions the preacher is to pull back the curtain and call forth what is hidden in plain sight, namely, the fragrance of life found in margins of the text. In these moments the presence of grace can be felt—waiting to be accepted or rejected. It is a grace that does not gloss over pain or downplay the horror of evil. This grace redeems the narrative. Like John's disciples, the text comes to claim the body. It tenderly holds the broken and scarred tissue of devastated lives and, with sighs too deep for words, groans for the day of resurrection.

When this grace, this groaning and pathos-embracing power, is accepted, the fragrance of life fills the sanctuary, and worship fills the hearts of the faithful. This worship is not naive in regard to suffering. It is not escapist. It is worship that is eschatological in its knowledge that all things will be made new.

CHERYL BRIDGES JOHNS

---

2. Josephus, *Antiquities of the Jews,* 18.1.3; 9.4.

Jeremiah 23:1-6

¹Woe to the shepherds who destroy and scatter the sheep of my pasture! says the Lord. ²Therefore thus says the Lord, the God of Israel, concerning the shepherds who shepherd my people: It is you who have scattered my flock, and have driven them away, and you have not attended to them. So I will attend to you for your evil doings, says the Lord. ³Then I myself will gather the remnant of my flock out of all the lands where I have driven them, and I will bring them back to their fold, and they shall be fruitful and multiply. ⁴I will raise up shepherds over them who will shepherd them, and they shall not fear any longer, or be dismayed, nor shall any be missing, says the Lord.

⁵The days are surely coming, says the Lord, when I will raise up for David a righteous Branch, and he shall reign as king and deal wisely, and shall execute justice and righteousness in the land. ⁶In his days Judah will be saved and Israel will live in safety. And this is the name by which he will be called: "The Lord is our righteousness."

Theological Perspective

The messianic dimension of this prophecy stands as a promise and challenge to today's church. The prophecy itself is rooted in a challenge to corrupt and ineffectual government over the people of Israel—to the shepherds who have destroyed and scattered God's sheep. After pronouncing judgment on these evil shepherds, God promises to shepherd God's people Godself and then to raise up surrogate shepherds over them. In this promise we find a hope for peace, security, and prosperity—all of these rooted in the faithfulness of God as manifest in God's Messiah, the righteous Branch who will reign as king. The theological task in approaching this passage is discerning the when, who, and how of the fulfillment of this prophecy; we must resolve both in whom we are to put our hope and the manner in which our hope is to be answered. The promise and challenge of this prophecy to the contemporary church is the promise and challenge of allowing our hope and our lives to be shaped by this when, who, and how.

This prophecy is, in the first place, an eschatological prophecy. It offers a vision of God's breaking into the corrupt flow of human history, bringing that corruption to an end through the work of God's anointed one, and establishing the paradisiacal state for which the people long. The

Pastoral Perspective

Few preachers can claim to have inspired new words. Fewer still want their names attached to a word like "jeremiad." The term has been applied to everything from the pious exhortations of seventeenth-century Puritan preachers to the rantings of contemporary moral police. The *Oxford English Dictionary* defines a "jeremiad" as "a lamentation; a writing or speech in a strain of grief or distress."

Reading Jeremiah's "woes," one can understand the roots of the noun the prophet inspired. Sadness and fury infuse the passage. "Woe to the shepherds who destroy and scatter the sheep of my pasture! . . . It is you who have scattered my flock, and have driven them away, and you have not attended to them."

Like many "jeremiads," the subject of the prophet's lament are leaders unfaithful to their vocation. Indeed, this passage represents a lamentation on bad leadership. The "shepherds who destroy and scatter the sheep" are rulers who have misled the people of Judah and brought on their ruin. The hope toward which the passage points, "the righteous Branch" who "shall reign as king and deal wisely, and shall execute justice and righteousness in the land," is "the ideal king (Messiah) of the Davidic line under whose just and

Exegetical Perspective

Today's text forms the conclusion of a longer portion of Jeremiah dedicated to condemnation of the last four kings of Judah in particular and of corrupt monarchs in general. With 21:1–10, these verses form a frame for this section.

Although the oracles in this passage are relentlessly critical of unjust and neglectful rulers, they end with a positive theological stance toward kingship in general. The later oracles promise a renewed Israel and a revitalized covenant under righteous rulers whom God will raise up on the nation's behalf.

Scholars debate whether this text should be attributed to the original writings associated with Jeremiah or considered an interpolation by a later editor. Verse 3, which refers to the gathering of scattered exiles, and verses 5 and 6, which foresee the restoration of Israel under a Davidic ruler, are often cited as evidence that this passage is a late addition. The promise of a return from exile assumes the condition of exile. According to this argument, exile postdates Jeremiah's writing and experience, so this text cannot originate with him. Similarly, the full flowering of messianic expectations came much later than Jeremiah's lifetime. Therefore, the hopes expressed in the final verses of this passage for a restored Israel ruled by a king from David's line

Homiletical Perspective

Any text with an opening word of "Woe" is bound to make us wince a little as we prepare for the indictment and punishment to follow. This passage brings to conclusion the words of judgment against the kings of Judah. In the previous chapter we are told of the ways in which leaders have chosen greed and oppression over justice and righteousness, and of God's dismay at their behavior. This text does not stop at the judgment of these failed rulers, however, but continues on to a promise of redemption for the people of God.

The kings receiving divine condemnation have long left this world, and their names will not be familiar to many people in our pews. But it is clear that God has specific expectations for those who possess power. The privilege of power is always accompanied by the responsibility of attending to the people. The kings forgot that they were called to be shepherds. They forgot that their primary responsibility was to nurture and protect their flock. They forgot they needed to be out in the fields day and night watching over the needs of their sheep. Their failure has led to exile.

Very few of us have any sense of what it is like to possess the unparalleled power of a monarch, but almost all of us have power of one kind or another. Whether in the public square, in the workplace, or in

Jeremiah 23:1-6

Theological Perspective

prophecy at the same time, however, is clear that God is breaking into a history that continues. God's restoration of God's care for God's people does not bring us to the end of time, but provides for the care of these people through shepherds in the midst of time. The prophecy, in other words, embraces an eschatology that is realized, while pointing to God's final consummation of all things. It is a prophecy that points us to the already and the not-yet of God's work among us.

As such, the prophecy demands a christological reading when read in a Christian context. We can understand what Jeremiah would tell us about God's shepherding of God's people, about David's righteous Branch, and about the security that God would provide through God's Messiah only when we understand the manner in which Jesus has and has not fulfilled this prophecy. The prophecy offers hope to people in distress; in Jesus we find the shape of this hope.

More specifically, the prophecy promises a messianic king who will gather God's people, execute justice, and establish peace in the land. Given the context of Israel's history for this promise, the prophecy might lead us to expect a Messiah who will come with armies and rule with might, who will provide for peace through the ministration of war and the defeat of our worldly enemies in battle. Given the context of our world for hearing this prophecy, it is clear that we often hope for such violent deliverance from God. This is where a christological reading of this prophecy is crucial.

First, if Jesus is this messianic king, then we find that God shepherds and protects God's people not through violence, but through the offer of Godself and the nurture within us of love for our enemies. Jesus, in other words, revolutionizes our conception of the lordship of kings. "I am among you as one who serves" (Luke 22:27). Second, if we turn to Calvin's teaching on Christ's threefold office, we find a clear sense that Christ has fulfilled not only the office of the priest, so that there are no true priests offering sacrifice to God after him, but also the office of king. This means that we act falsely when we seek from our own rulers the fulfillment of God's promise of security and prosperity. This does not mean that there are no legitimate governments, but that they are true to this prophecy only when they rule in congruence with Christ's self-gift and understanding of love that permeates the gospel. This is a theological challenge for churches in a post-9/11 world.

Pastoral Perspective

victorious rule all the dynastic hopes would be realized."[1]

There are at least three "pastoral" temptations with this text: (1) to professionalize it by reallocating the term "shepherd" for ecclesiastical use, identifying the shepherds with church leaders with whom the preacher disagrees, thus forfeiting the political dimensions of Jeremiah's prophecy; (2) to privatize the text spiritually by reading it through a doctrine of justification by faith, thus ripping the text from its public context; or (3) to arrogate the text to oneself as preacher in a role that can be rightly occupied only by the Word of God. The text has a great deal more to say to us as pastors *and* as persons who are saved by grace if we allow it to speak primarily as the Lord's jeremiad against the leadership that has destroyed the nation of Judah and as a vision of how God intends God's people to live. It makes explicitly public claims on us regarding "the execution of justice and rightness in the land," lamenting the actions of those who have squandered their leadership and describing the character of the messianic leader who will restore the people to wholeness.

The text calls the preacher to stand alongside his or her hearers, under the claims of the Word of God. Even though the pastor articulates the Lord's lament, he or she must be addressed by the Word in the preaching event.

The pastoral temptation to sacrifice one's pastoral calling in the name of "prophetic preaching," and the opposite temptation to so limit the pastoral role that no uncomfortable word can be spoken, both misunderstand the character of proclamation as much as they misunderstand the cure of souls to which pastors are called. Dietrich Bonhoeffer explores a telling of "truth which is of Satan," that "wounds shame, desecrates mystery, breaks confidence, betrays the community . . . and laughs arrogantly at the devastation he has wrought and at the human weakness which 'cannot bear the truth.'"[2]

Jeremiah reminds us that the wrath of God is nothing less than the fire of God's passion turned against anything that would destroy what God loves. Prophetic preaching that does not proceed from such love—preaching that does not stand under the blast of God's passion alongside those who hear us preach—violates the spirit of proclamation. "Thus says the Lord" is not synonymous with "Thus say I." Preaching is a second hearing of the Word of God, a

1. John Bright, *Jeremiah* (Garden City, NY: Doubleday, 1965), 143.
2. Dietrich Bonhoeffer, *Ethics*, ed. Eberhard Bethge (New York: Macmillan, 1955), 366.

Exegetical Perspective

must have been inserted by others into Jeremiah's material.

Others, however, assert that there were several preliminary exiles of groups from Judah before the final exile in 587 BCE. Jeremiah was certainly aware of these, so it is by no means impossible that his writings would hope for a return of exiles. Likewise, the hope for national renewal under a ruler from the Davidic line was not unknown in Jeremiah's day. A fully developed messianism is not a necessary foundation for the hopes expressed in the final verses of this passage.[1]

Today's text consists of a prose section in verses 1–4 followed by two verses of poetry. The prose section contains three oracles. Verse 1 is an oracle of indictment against the shepherds of God's people. Verse 2 is an oracle of judgment. God cites evidence that the flock has been scattered because the shepherds did not attend to them and announces the intention to attend to these shepherds. Verses 3 and 4 are an oracle of mercy and grace. God will gather up the flock that is scattered and raise up good shepherds who will lead them in peace.

Shepherd is a common metaphor for kingship in the ancient Near East. It is found elsewhere in the Old Testament and previously in Jeremiah 22:22. It is also a relatively open metaphor that can refer to other leaders charged with oversight of the people. The force of these first two oracles is to place blame for the scattering of God's people not upon their Babylonian conquerors, but upon the rulers who have misused their power and failed to call God's people to account. The second oracle particularly focuses upon a wordplay related to the Hebrew verb *pqd*, which means literally "to pay a visit." Because these shepherds have failed to visit their flock with the vigilance and care that would have ensured their welfare, God will now visit these shepherds in judgment.[2]

The third oracle in this prose section shifts the focus to the future. God will regather the remnant of the flock from all the lands in which they are scattered. God will act as shepherd even when the human shepherds have failed. God will bring the exiles back into the fold where "they shall be fruitful and multiply." This phrase harkens back to Genesis 1, signifying that God's work on behalf of the people will mean no less than a whole new creation for Israel.

1. Peter C. Craigie, Page H. Kelley, and Joel F. Drinkard Jr., *Jeremiah*, Word Biblical Commentary (Dallas: Word Books, 1991), 329.
2. Jack R. Lundbom, *Jeremiah 21–36*, Anchor Bible 21b (New York: Doubleday, 2004), 168.

Homiletical Perspective

the home, we all have interactions every day that involve some form of power over others. We would be wise to ever link the wielding of power with compassion and a steadfast commitment to justice.

But the final word of this text is not about how humans wield their power but how God wields the ultimate power. God will do what human power has failed to do. God will gather the people "and bring them back to their fold" (v. 3). The prophecy echoes the calling bestowed upon Adam and Eve in paradise to "be fruitful and multiply." God is promising to restore all that has become broken in this creation, and that task begins with the people of God. New leaders are promised for the people, and these leaders will wield power in constructive, compassionate ways, creating a community beyond the current fears. God never speaks about the end of something without promising a greater future.

We are also given a very specific promise of a leader who will carry the very mantle given to David. This one to come will rule over all with wisdom, bringing "justice and righteousness in the land." Our Christian ears perk up, and we hear the name of Jesus, the Son of David, being announced. But we do not read this text in an effort to identify who the Messiah will be. This text brings us the promise that indeed there will be a Messiah. We are given the promise that there is a place beyond our human failure; a place beyond God's judgment; beyond exile. The final word from our God is always hope.

A quick look up from our Bible reveals that we do not currently live in the midst of this promise fully realized. Hearing this shepherd metaphor brings to mind the best-known use of it in the Twenty-third Psalm, "The LORD is my shepherd." In the psalm the promise of God's shepherding does not remove the suffering of this world: "Yea, though I walk through the valley of the shadow of death" (KJV). The existence of a shepherd is a demonstration of our need for protection from what can harm us in this world. This text acknowledges that reality in its judgment of political power used to evil ends. But how do we live knowing this will be true? How does this guarantee for the future instruct our present living? Knowing the future is a significant power entrusted to us, but we find ourselves with the same challenge of the failed shepherds in the earlier part of this text. We must use our knowledge of this powerful promise to serve all God's people.

So how do we live in response to this hope we have been promised? The receipt of this powerful gift of hope comes with responsibility. Our

Jeremiah 23:1-6

Theological Perspective

But what of this promise of a continuing line of shepherds? Calvin argues that God provides for the continual shepherding of God's people after the inbreaking of God's rule in the ministry of Jesus through the ministers of the church. He is clear that, although there are no priests or kings alongside Jesus, there is an entire company of prophets—those who are to care for the community of God's peace and prosperity. Again, however, we must note that this shepherding and this community are shaped by what we find in the ministry of Jesus. There is a tendency to hope for the fulfillment of the not-yet of this eschatological prophecy in the already of our economic and political lives. Jesus, on the other hand, reveals to us the true already of the eschaton in his call to service and table fellowship with the poor and the outcast.

We will find, moreover, a strength and security in the model of shepherding the community that was rooted in the early church. Rodney Stark has pointed out that one strength of the early church that allowed it to thrive and not be scattered in the face of its enemies was its egalitarian structure, in which all members of the church cared for one another.[1] This structure not only offered a welcome vision of the empowerment of all of God's people to a world where the gifts of the many often were neglected, but it also provided a thick understanding of leadership that allowed the church to survive when the authorities targeted its leaders for persecution. The logic of "strike the head and the members will scatter" was thwarted by a theology in which Christ was the head, and the members were each servants of one another. This mutual interdependence in the shepherding of the church allowed for a continuity of identity and mission as leaders came and went.

STEPHEN EDMONDSON

Pastoral Perspective

spoken hearing, and the preacher is merely one auditor among many when he or she preaches.

The proper role of the preacher as auditor is modeled by Jeremiah himself. The prophet has learned to weep over that which grieves God. Walter Brueggemann observes that "Jeremiah stands midway in the history of Israel's grief. Before him Amos condemned those in their self-deception who were unable and unwilling to grieve (Amos 6:6). After Jeremiah comes Jesus of Nazareth, who understood grief as the ultimate criticism that had to be addressed against Jerusalem (Matt. 23:27; Luke 19:41). Jeremiah stands midway and speaks the grief of God that Israel finally must share. Without it there is no newness."[3]

To reclaim the public dimensions of our pastoral calling in light of Jeremiah's message means to recognize the prophetic power of lamentation, the compelling office of uncovering God's grief so that it becomes a community's. This grief can have many causes. The grief may be a consequence of misplaced worship, idolatry, giving our ultimate loyalty to those things that should claim only relative allegiance. Regret, like fingers of smoke ranging over a fire-ravaged mountainside, lingers throughout Jeremiah's prophecies. The prophet walks in sorrow among burned-out stumps. His laments attend the false choices of a self-deluded people who realize too late what their decisions have cost them.

When the pastor and the people recognize their mutual complicity in the promotion of bad leadership, they have taken the first crucial step toward recovering the integrity of their community and their society. Lamentation and confession walk shoulder to shoulder, and unless the community learns to lament what God laments and confess as sin its participation in the failure of its leadership, it cannot move toward newness of life. However, when a community is led to lament and confess, it is able to recover the promise that transcends every human pursuit: the Lord is our righteousness. Thus our humility and our humanity are restored on the resurrection side of public mourning.

MICHAEL JINKINS

---

1. Rodney Stark, *The Rise of Christianity* (New York: HarperOne, 1997), 29f., 73f.

3. Walter Brueggemann, *The Prophetic Imagination* (Philadelphia: Fortress Press, 1978), 60.

Exegetical Perspective

In the final two verses of this passage, this general promise becomes more specific. The faithful shepherd God will send to shepherd the covenant people will be a descendant of King David. Expectation of a restored Davidic rule is a common theme in the Old Testament. It begins with the covenant promise made to David himself in 2 Samuel 7:1–17 and reappears often in the prophetic writings (see Isa. 11:1–9, Amos 9:11, Mic. 5:2–5 and Jer. 33:14–16). These two verses center upon the image of the "righteous" ruler. The Hebrew word is usually translated as "righteous" but could just as legitimately be translated as "rightful." The latter translation is supported by philological studies of related words in Phoenician and Ugaritic. Given the confusion in Judah at the time of the exile over who was the "rightful" king, the exiled Jehoiachin or the Babylonian puppet Zedekiah, this passage could be read as Jeremiah's condemnation of both these two as false rulers and an encouragement to the people to look forward to the time when God would establish the "rightful" ruler on the throne of David.[3] Even if the traditional translation, "righteous," is accepted, the language in this passage is in no way eschatological. Jeremiah looks ahead, not to the final fulfillment of God's promises at the end of time, but to a return from exile and a restoration of the nation in real time.

The passage ends with another wordplay. The name of the rightful/righteous ruler appointed to shepherd the returned exile will be "The LORD is our righteousness." This is the reverse of the name of the current, puppet king, Zedekiah, whose name means "My righteousness is God." In spite of the false righteousness of the current king, God will establish true righteousness to rule and guide the people. In the face of everything that points toward hopelessness—defeat, destruction, dynastic failure, and exile—God's intention is faithfulness to the covenant and salvation for the covenant people.

KAREN C. SAPIO

Homiletical Perspective

knowledge of this gift changes the entire landscape of our reality. We are no longer bound to the fears of an uncertain future. We "shall not fear any longer, or be dismayed, nor shall any be missing, says the LORD" (v. 4).

The first way we wisely use this power is by sharing it. The steadfast promise of God's deliverance is one to be shared. We are called to share our knowledge of this powerful promise by word and deed. If we believe that a shepherd is on the way who will lead us in the ways of justice and righteousness, we need to be preparing for their arrival. What better greeting would there be for this shepherd of righteousness than to be living in the ways of God's righteousness as best we can in this time and place?

Sometimes when we receive the promise that God will bring deliverance, we mistakenly believe we are removed from the pursuit of improving our current condition. On the contrary, we need to be deeply engaged in the world, doing all we can to prepare for the arrival of the shepherd. But in the midst of our very best efforts we are to be ever mindful that it is the Lord who "will raise up for David a righteous Branch." We do not approach our efforts with an arrogance that it is we who will accomplish these lofty goals. Nor do we flag in our zeal when our efforts fall far short of their desired goal. We stand strong in the promise of God's redeeming work as we seek to be faithful in the work we do for justice and peace for all God's children.

DOUGLAS T. KING

---

3. Ibid., 173.

Psalm 23

¹The LORD is my shepherd, I shall not want.
² He makes me lie down in green pastures;
  he leads me beside still waters;
³he restores my soul.
  He leads me in right paths
    for his name's sake.

⁴Even though I walk through the darkest valley,
  I fear no evil;
  for you are with me;
    your rod and your staff—
    they comfort me.

Theological Perspective

Few psalms are as well known and beloved as the Twenty-third Psalm. This makes the job of the preacher both easy and difficult. The job is easy, on the one hand, because the psalm preaches itself. The text does not need to be expounded and unfolded; people respond to it spontaneously. On the other hand, it is difficult: what is there left for the preacher to say, and how does the preacher not get in the way of a Bible passage that seems to speak so easily to people's hearts? One strategy is to help people become more explicitly aware of why this poem stirs so much response and emotion in them.

From a theological point of view, the two images of the psalm—the grazing herd of sheep and the laden table—masterfully catch a series of theological ideas that together form the framework of God's gracious relating to God's people.

First, the psalm expresses *grace*. God's people are God's sheep—and they do not have to be more than that. Luther suggests that the preacher on this psalm actually go out and learn from the traits and characteristics of sheep and their shepherds. Sheep are, in fact, not the smartest animals. They are defenseless in nature, weak, timid, shy, and likely to go astray.[1]

1. Martin Luther, *Luther's Works*, ed. Jaroslav Pelikan (St. Louis: Concordia Publishing House, 1955), 12:153–54.

Pastoral Perspective

"Love is patient; love is kind; love is not envious or boastful or arrogant or rude" (1 Cor. 13:4). For many, hearing these words immediately brings to mind memories of young women in beautiful dresses, young men in rented formalwear, and candles lighting the sanctuary. There are some Scripture texts that transport us to specific contexts. "In those days a decree went out from Emperor Augustus . . ." These words will carry us to the Christmas Eve service, with the singing of "Silent Night" while the light of the Christ candle is passed from pew to pew. The words of the Twenty-third Psalm have their familiar context as well: "*The* LORD is my shepherd, I shall not want." We hear these words and remember the smell of flowers and fresh dirt, the quiet sounds of grief, and the embrace of those who have come to comfort. These words are most often recited when the heart is weighed down with grief and we are at a loss for other words we might say. Through the generations when the faithful have walked through the darkest valley, this psalm has provided a word of comfort.

The central claim of the psalmist is that God's care is like that of a faithful shepherd. If God is described through the metaphor of the shepherd, then we are the sheep. One does not need to know much about sheep to understand the image provided

⁵You prepare a table before me
    in the presence of my enemies;
    you anoint my head with oil;
    my cup overflows.
⁶Surely goodness and mercy shall follow me
    all the days of my life,
    and I shall dwell in the house of the LORD
    my whole life long.

Exegetical Perspective

A Pastoral Psalm: Familiarity, Understanding, and Organization. Perhaps no other passage of Scripture is as well known as or more thoroughly commented on than Psalm 23. Its comforting assurances, its bucolic images, and its beautiful language all make this reading one of the most familiar and well loved in the whole Bible. Yet, precisely because this text is so familiar, any interpreter or preacher must be doubly cautious of it, lest "familiarity" be mistaken for "understanding," and lest the fact of the psalm's being "well loved" be equated with its being "quaint."

Two different organizational schemes have been suggested for the psalm. The more common approach is based on the two primary images in the psalm: God as a shepherd and God as a host. From this perspective, the metaphor of "shepherd" centers the first half of the psalm (vv. 1–4), and the metaphor of "host" centers the second half (vv. 5–6).[1]

On the other hand, the psalm can be organized by highlighting the pronouns referring to God. In verses 1–3, God is spoken of as a "he": "He makes me lie down . . . he leads me . . . he restores . . . he leads me . . ." At the beginning of verse 4, the psalmist's attention is turned to something else: "the darkest

1. See, among others, Peter C. Craigie, *Psalms 1–50*, WBC 19 (Waco: Word Books, 1983), 203–9; Patrick D. Miller, *Interpreting the Psalms* (Philadelphia: Fortress Press, 1986), 112–19.

Homiletical Perspective

"Keep your hands up and don't foul." This is about the first thing one is taught when learning to play basketball. It is elemental; there is nothing complex in the instruction. Yet it was being spoken by a coach during a time-out in the waning seconds of an NBA playoff game. I imagined hearing some insightful, complex strategy with so much on the line. And here it was: the elementals.

Is any text more familiar, more elemental, in Christian circles than Psalm 23? Indeed, one might be tempted to look to the other texts today for something seemingly more complex, more "meaty."

Why is this text also one of those most often chosen for funerals? Does this not suggest its power for us? When physical life is ending and we wish for foundational messages about life and its passing, it is no coincidence that we come to this text for refuge.

When recently wrestling with a needed course of action, I called a friend and asked him to hear my thoughts and reflect back what he was hearing. After listening to me discuss what I termed the complexities before me, he replied, "Sometimes I think we in the church make things complex because we already know what we need to do, but don't wish to do it."

Sometimes it is the "familiar," the noncomplex, we need to hear, resisting the urge to look for what seems more intriguing, more complex.

Psalm 23

Theological Perspective

Nonetheless, all God's people are asked to be is to be God's sheep. There is no pressure to be better, more inventive, productive, strong, or independent. All we are asked to do is to listen to the voice of the shepherd.

Second, the psalm expresses *hope.* The psalmist describes life as a route with a goal. Life with the shepherd Lord has an eschatological direction. The sheep live in leisure—they lie down in grassy meadows, they go beside placid waters—because they have a future. They can enjoy today because there is a tomorrow; they can live in the moment because they know that moment is not the last.

Third, the psalm expresses God's *abundance.* The psalmist believes there is nothing he wants. The shepherd God gives the sheep everything they need. From the green meadows at the beginning of the route to the prepared table at the end, the psalmist has more than he needs. His cup overflows. Without doubt, with these simple images of a table and a cup the poet alludes to a rich storehouse of eschatological icons: abundant harvest, jubilee, heavenly banquet, renewed creation; a storehouse to which the New Testament adds a wedding at Cana, feeding of thousands, Lord's Supper, messianic meal, and bread of life.

However, this belief in God's abundance is not as much comforting as it is controversial. After all, the sheep still go through the valley of death; their lives are not lived without enemies. But "here you must not be guided by your eyes or follow your reason, as the world does. The world cannot see this rich, splendid comfort of the Christians, that they want nothing. Yes, the world considers it quite certain that the opposite is true, namely, that on earth there are no poorer, more miserable, and more unhappy people than these same Christians."[2] With his life set in the context of the shepherd God's abundance and his feet on the road to the loaded table, the psalmist's wants have also been touched by the shepherd's rod; they have been reimagined, reorganized, *sanctified.* What once seemed needed, no longer is; what once seemed a danger, can now be taunted: "Death, where is your sting?" (1 Cor. 15:55). The shepherd restored the psalmist's soul; he received the gift of *faith.*

Divine abundance and the gift of faith form an antidote *against the sin of poor imagination.* In his recent book *God's Companions,* Samuel Wells, the dean of the chapel at Duke University, argues that there are two kinds of sin: the sin of perversity and

2. Ibid., 167.

Pastoral Perspective

in the psalm. This is evidenced in the popularity of this psalm. Confirmation classes memorize it. No fewer than six arrangements of the psalm are found in the hymnal of the denomination in which I serve. It is requested for services bearing witness to the resurrection. And yet, many who have uttered these words as faithful confession have known nothing about shepherds, or even seen a real sheep. Those more informed about these animals will describe them in less than flattering terms. They are herd animals. They are defenseless. They are vulnerable. Most commonly noted, sheep are unintelligent. But these are not the characteristics the psalmist has in mind when speaking of the shepherd and the sheep. The psalmist speaks of the sheep's dependence on the shepherd. Sheep cannot survive making their own way. Sheep are absolutely dependent upon the shepherd for life. Sheep can trust the shepherd. Knowing the dependence sheep have on the shepherd brings into focus the central testimony of the psalm: the shepherd is faithful.

When we bring our hearts to the edge of the grave, we know we cannot make our own way through the season of grief. When we face the end of our own days, our dependence upon the shepherd stands before us with more clarity than perhaps at other times. We are not the creator, but the created, and the prevailing reality for the creature is our dependence upon God for life. Perhaps this is why the community of faith finds Psalm 23 so comforting at the time of death. But the witness of the psalmist is that the shepherd is faithful throughout the whole of life. That which is confessed in the season of grief remains true in every season.

Sheeplike dependence would be paralyzing, save for the knowledge that the one on whom we depend is the good shepherd. This shepherd leads, restores, comforts, and prepares. In the care of this shepherd, there is no want.

Often the psalm is voiced by the community of faith during a service, but our text is not presented as a "communal credo." The editors of this volume request, for reasons of style, that writers use a minimum of first-person pronouns. Reading the Scriptures we notice that the majority of texts are written for the community of faith, not for reasons of style, but for theological reasons. There are few first-person pronouns. But the Twenty-third Psalm, like the Psalter's version of *In the Garden,* is awash in first-person singular. "The LORD is my shepherd, I shall not want." The shepherd makes me and leads me and restores me and anoints my head, and I shall

valley." When God is next referenced, it is in the second person: "You are with me . . . your rod and your staff. . . . You prepare . . . you anoint . . ." (vv. 4–5). Next the psalmist's attention is again turned to something else, "goodness and mercy" (v. 6a), and the final reference to God is back to the third person: "the house of the Lord" (v. 6b). The psalm moves from talking about God, to talking to God, then back to talking about God. Thus the psalm can be divided into three parts, with two transitional lines between the parts.

The Lord and I (v. 1). The first line of the psalm provides the rhetorical and hermeneutical starting point upon which all the other lines of the poem hang. The line is composed of two separate clauses. The first two-word verbless clause in Hebrew identifies and equates the two nouns: YHWH = my shepherd.

The second clause, "I shall not want/lack," is unusual in two different ways. First, the verb *hasar* does not have an object. Although this verb appears in this form eighteen times in the Bible, it almost always has some sort of object, even objects such as "lack *anything*" (Deut. 2:7; 8:9, my translations) or "lack *anything good*" (Ps. 34:10). Here in Psalm 23, no object appears at all! The point is that "lack" simply is not a part of the experience of those whose shepherd is God. The second unusual characteristic about the clause is that there is no explicit connection with the previous clause. There is no "so" or "therefore" between the two clauses. The fact that "the Lord is my shepherd" and the fact that "I do not lack" are so integrally connected, so inherently a part of one another, that one fact does not "cause" the other. The shepherding of God and the absence of lack are simply two sides of the same coin. They are the same thing. Throughout the psalm, the psalmist draws the focus on God and the focus on the individual so closely together that, by the end of the psalm, the comfort provided is found not just in the fortunate experience of the individual, and not just in the oversight of God, but in both together as mutually revealing realities.

The Shepherd's Actions (vv. 2–3). The clauses that explicate God's shepherding activity all have governing verbs that are third-person, and three of the four verbs have a pronoun direct object suffix: "*He* makes *me* lie . . . *he* leads *me* . . . *he* guides *me*." The exception to the pattern is the central clause: "He restores my soul" or "He causes my life to

The psalmists are no children. They know the powers of the world and have seen the effects of those powers on the people. They know how forces both inside and out war against our fidelity to God. Amid this they express supreme confidence in YHWH as their protector, their provider, their repose. They proclaim YHWH as the foundational reality of what they experience. At all points of life, it is YHWH who is to be trusted.

As one trained in journalism, I am very measured in the amount of media I consume. I am not a media basher. Instead, I realize how many media permeate my life, with twenty-four-hour news channels and news on my computer, my cell phone, even at my gas pump. As the noise of this world finds more ways to envelop me, I must make a decision: whose version of this world will I choose?

For the preacher, the task is holding before the community this question: in what do we trust? Why would we have confidence in God, particularly as news of the world is so convincing in its rebuttal? How and in what ways do we as communities of faith recall and celebrate the experienced faithfulness of God? Where do we point out our restoration as a people? Where are we courageous enough to reveal where we need the restoration of God? Where are our "tabernacles," our equivalents of those Hebrew piles of stone that mark where we have encountered God?

The imagery of Psalm 23 connotes both bedouin and monarch. It is imagery for the sojourner and the resident. In both contexts, it proclaims restoration and *shalom* of soul. Using monarchical imagery, the psalmist speaks of one who rules all with the benevolence and care of God. In this world, the psalmist has no need and fears not. And while this psalm is often heard in the first person singular, it is a song of the community.

As watchers of the sheep, we see one who is both guardian and banquet host. He makes me lie down in green pastures. This is lush imagery. The luxury of lying in a tranquil field speaks of serenity, of no anxiety, of "be still and know." I find myself reflecting on times when I give myself the freedom to do this, when I allow myself to know that there is no need for work, for anxious thoughts. It is instead a time for freedom from the need to do something amid a world of great need. Where are those places, what are the practices that give us the freedom to lie down? I am a threat to the world about me if I do not, at some level, understand this seeming paradox of rest and the need for *shalom* in the midst of a world in turmoil.

Psalm 23

Theological Perspective

the sin of lack of imagination. Perversity is the sin of those who set their face against God's gifts. Wells illustrates this with the Gospel stories about the Pharisees who conspire against Jesus (Mark 3:6), and the crowd's antipathy to Jesus when he is brought in front of Pilate (Mark 15). That is a sin going back to the sin of the serpent; there is no explanation for it. But there is also the sin of lack of imagination. It is the sin of the disciples who do not know how to feed the crowd (Mark 6:35–44) or are terrified on seeing Jesus coming to them walking on the sea (Mark 6:47–52). It is the sin of those who cannot apprehend the abundance of the world into which they are invited. Instead of abundance, they see scarcity. This sin goes back to Eve, who could not see the abundance of the garden for the apple she was lacking.[3] In a time when America's mainline churches feel death's shadow in declining membership, relevance, and authority, the Twenty-third Psalm might be well worth pondering.

Finally, in all these different notions—grace, hope, abundance, the gifts of sanctification and faith—the psalm speaks in fact of only one thing: the goodness of God. Commentators have pointed at the masterly shape of the psalm as a poem that is at once so simple, yet also profound. In reality, this goes back to the simple, but profound goodness of Godself. Evil and sin make life complicated. But in the presence of the sheer goodness of God there is peace: "The LORD is my shepherd" (v. 1). It is this divine goodness, present at the beginning, that the psalmist will enjoy for days without end (v. 6). It is the bedrock through which his life is guided to its destiny.

EDWIN CHR. VAN DRIEL

Pastoral Perspective

dwell. The psalmist offers a "song of trust of someone who knows in the midst of the vicissitudes of her or his personal life and over the course of the years that he or she has been carried in the bosom of God, sheltered from harm, and given rest."[1] The psalm is claimed less as theological confession by the community of faith and more as personal testimony to the faithfulness of God.

Lastly, the center of the psalm offers what Patrick Miller calls "the gospel kernel of the Old Testament, that good news that turns tears of anguish and fear into shouts of joy, that glad tiding given by the angelic choir to the shepherds, which itself echoes a word first given to the patriarchs and repeated again and again to Israel in moments of distress and fear: You don't have to be afraid. This is the salvation word par excellence of Scripture, Old Testament as well as New."[2]

There is perhaps no more relevant message for our time than the invitation to set aside fear. Governments trade in fear of terror or evil ones. The markets trade in fear of there not being enough. The church often trades in fear of exclusion or judgment or our numbers declining to the point of irrelevance.

And there are many things to fear. The culture increasingly expects violence to bear fruit of a new day. The environment is struggling to breathe under the growing effects of abuse. Families are fragile. Every minute of the schedule is filled to the point that Sabbath seems an unrealistic practice for many.

And yet in the midst of these struggles, the psalmist offers testimony to a gracious God, a faithful shepherd with whom we will lack nothing, and we need not fear. This is good news indeed. Surely, we hear in the testimony of the psalmist the echoes of other moments in Scripture when the messengers have said, "Be not afraid." Such a declaration in our time should sound to us, as it has to others, like nothing less than the voice of angels.

TOM ARE JR.

---

1. Patrick D. Miller Jr. *Interpreting the Psalms* (Philadelphia: Fortress Press, 1986), 113.
2. Ibid., 115.

3. Samuel Wells, *God's Companions: Reimagining Christian Ethics* (Malden: Blackwell Publishing, 2006), 23–26.

Exegetical Perspective

return." While shepherds may lead, pasture, and guide, only God can restore the vitality and life of those who are in this flock. This is no ordinary shepherd!

Transition: The Darkest Valley (v. 4a). The image is of a terrifying and dangerous place. Yet, as in the first line of the poem, here the experience of the individual is unusual. There, lack was not a part of the experience of the individual; here, fear is absent.

"Your" Presence and Actions (vv. 4b–5). The psalm turns here, precisely at the terrifying vale, to address God directly. The presence of God provides the reason for the absence of fear, and that presence is made palpable by the turn from "him" to "you." James Limburg notes that the line "For you are with me" stands in the exact center of the psalm, with twenty-six words before it and twenty-six words after it.[2] If the "shepherding" of God provides the initial basis for the psalm in verse 1, then the presence of God provides the focus here in its center. That presence, symbolized by the shepherd's rod and staff, provide comfort and security. Moreover, as in the initial stanza, where the provender was green and the water was nonthreatening, here the fare is spread out with no regard to enemies, and the drink is overflowingly abundant.

Transition: Goodness and Mercy (v. 6a). The verb for "follow" (*radaf*) is used in the Bible almost exclusively with a threatening, negative connotation (Exod. 14:4; 1 Sam. 23:28; Ps. 7:1). While enemies are still a part of the picture (v. 5), the only things that pursue now are "goodness and mercy." The image is of these relentless pursuers who now want only to provide the positive basis and consequence of relationship with God.

In the House of the LORD (v. 6b). At the end of the day, those who are shepherded by God are not left alone, nor are they even led to a sheepfold (Jer. 23:3). According to the psalm, they dwell with God inside the divine abode. And that household arrangement is not temporary, but will rather last for a long, long time (*le'orek yamim*).

ROY L. HELLER

Homiletical Perspective

The imagery of verses 2–4 can be understood as imagery of salvation history: Israel's being led through the desert, God's provision of food, protection, and direction. This language points beyond physical or material things to the place of the soul. "I shall not want" is about more than material needs; it is about our trust that "all shall be well."

"You prepare a table . . . in the presence of my enemies." Bernhard Anderson reflects upon the bedouin custom of tent hospitality. When one is received into the tent of another, particularly once the host has spread a meal, one is protected from any enemy pursuers.[1] YHWH's tent is always our refuge and security, where we are safe from all that might be pursuing us, both outside and inside of us.

What current images might help us as preachers to convey the experience of soul repose, the lushness of green pastures, and safe, still waters? What is it like to be anointed with oil, to be overwhelmed with the balm of God? Where, how, and from whom do we experience this?

One of my daughter's favorite stores is one that sells cleansers and lotions for the skin. It is a wonderfully decadent place. It is all about bodily comfort and restoration. I find myself drawn to her appreciation of it, to her expectation that life should include these rituals of balm, rituals of restoration from the elements that steal our suppleness and gentleness. How does God restore the suppleness and gentleness of our souls? What practices might rehearse that restoration?

If Jesus proclaims anything in the Gospels, it is "Fear not, I am with you." Once again we find Jesus is not so much a revolutionary as one marinated in his tradition. "I fear no evil, for you are with me."

TODD M. DONATELLI

---

2. James Limburg, *Psalms* (Louisville, KY: Westminster John Knox Press, 2000), 74.

1. Bernhard W. Anderson, *Out of the Depths* (Louisville, KY: Westminster John Knox Press, 2000), 183.

Ephesians 2:11‑22

¹¹So then, remember that at one time you Gentiles by birth, called "the uncircumcision" by those who are called "the circumcision"—a physical circumcision made in the flesh by human hands— ¹²remember that you were at that time without Christ, being aliens from the commonwealth of Israel, and strangers to the covenants of promise, having no hope and without God in the world. ¹³But now in Christ Jesus you who once were far off have been brought near by the blood of Christ. ¹⁴For he is our peace; in his flesh he has made both groups into one and has broken down the dividing wall, that is, the hostility between us. ¹⁵He has abolished the law with its commandments and ordinances, that he might create in himself one new humanity in place of the two, thus making peace, ¹⁶and might reconcile both groups to God in one body through the cross, thus putting to death that hostility through it. ¹⁷So he came and proclaimed peace to you who were far off and peace to those who were near; ¹⁸for through him both of us have access in one Spirit to the Father. ¹⁹So then you are no longer strangers and aliens, but you are citizens with the saints and also members of the household of God, ²⁰built upon the foundation of the apostles and prophets, with Christ Jesus himself as the cornerstone. ²¹In him the whole structure is joined together and grows into a holy temple in the Lord; ²²in whom you also are built together spiritually into a dwelling place for God.

Theological Perspective

Ephesians 2, like 2 Corinthians 5:16–21 and Colossians 1:15–20, is one of the New Testament's great hymns to God's reconciliation of all things in Christ and God's call to all those who are in Christ to participate in good works of reconciliation.

The first ten verses of Ephesians 2 describe a world of conflict and hostility, a world torn between death and life, sin and grace. The writer addresses his audience as those who were once dead in their sins, children of wrath living according to the desires of the flesh, who are now alive in Christ, recreated for good works. Jesus Christ is the dividing point between who they once were and who they now are. To be recreated in Christ is to have passed from death to life, from sin to grace, to be called to good works "which God prepared beforehand to be our way of life" (v. 10).

Reconciliation presupposes the reality of sin, alienation, and hostility between those who belong and those who do not, between residents and aliens, between insiders and outsiders. The good news of Christian faith, according to the letter to the Ephesians, is that in this broken world reconciliation is no longer merely a dream, a longing for what once was and a hope for what someday might be, but something that already is. At least it already is for

Pastoral Perspective

Three themes intertwine through this passage, linked by multiple metaphors of unity. First, those who were estranged from God have now been brought into the covenant. Second, they are united with those who are already part of God's covenant. Third, this unity brings peace where there was no peace. These themes culminate in the purpose of this union: to create a holy dwelling place for God.

The metaphors are rich and could be endlessly explored. We were aliens, but are now citizens of the commonwealth of God; we are no longer strangers, but members of the household of God; we are a building, with Christ as the cornerstone, and not just any building but the temple where God lives. We are "one body" for God's purpose.

Paul (or his follower) named the new reality taking shape before his eyes. Those who had been *atheos*—without God—were being swept up in a new creation brought about by God. As Pheme Perkins notes in her commentary on Ephesians, *atheos* was more than a description of nonbelief. It was an insult, implying that one was uncivilized. Those who rejected the gods and their laws were akin to anarchists, and threatened the well-being of society. Both Greeks and Jews could be accused of this: Greeks for rejecting the God of the Jews,

Exegetical Perspective

After assuring his readers that their former state of disobedience and death has been transformed through Christ, and that this salvation is purely by grace (2:5) appropriated through faith as God's gift (vv. 8–9), our author calls upon them to remember exactly what their former state was, what did happen to them in Christ, and what the result has been. The use of "we" (Jews) and "you" (Gentiles) in the passage reflects the perspective of the history of God's dealing with humanity—first the Jews as chosen people, then the inclusion of the Gentiles through Christ. Since modern readers belong not to the "we" (Jews as originally chosen people) in this passage, but to the "you" (the Gentiles) who have been incorporated only later into God's people, this passage speaks directly to us.

The overall theme of these verses may be stated this way: Christ has united what once was separated, destroying in himself (on the cross) the enmity that caused that separation. In developing this theme, the author employs a series of key word pairs, the first of which—then (v. 11) and now (v. 13)—provides the structure for the rest of passage, namely, the contrast between these two periods of time. Again, a second pair—commonwealth (exclusion of Gentiles from chosen people, v. 12) and citizenship (their

Homiletical Perspective

This text is one that every congregation needs in its repertoire. Here Paul describes the shocking nature of the church. Reading these verses, one guesses that it did not take long for the church to forget the radical nature of its life together. Yet Paul does not sound impatient. "So then, remember . . . that you were at that time without Christ" (vv. 11–12), he begins. "So, then, you are no longer strangers" (v. 19), he concludes. A sermon grounded in this passage will do well to adopt this moderate "so then, remember" tone as it unfolds the extraordinary story that it tells.

The congregation may struggle to identify itself with those to whom Paul is writing. "Remember," he writes, "that you were at that time without Christ, being aliens . . . and strangers . . . having no hope and without God in the world" (v. 12). Many in our congregations have been born and raised in the church. They may not remember a time when they were "far off" and were "brought near by the blood of Christ" (v. 13). Of course, just because we have been raised in the church does not mean that we have always been near to God. The preacher will do well to remember with the congregation the various ways in which the church itself wanders far from Christ, becoming alienated from life in the kingdom

Theological Perspective

those who are in Christ, even if it is not yet a reality for a world still torn by death, sin, and hostility. One form of that hostility is the enmity between Jews and Gentiles. On the one hand there are the Gentiles, the uncircumcised, who are strangers and aliens (and thus "far off") to Israel and the covenant promises God has made to it. The Gentiles are without hope because they are without God in the world. On the other hand there are the Jews, the children of God and the recipients of God's covenant and law. While the Gentiles are "far off" and do not know God, the children of Israel, who are "near" to God in God's covenant with them, are indicted by God's commandments and ordinances as disobedient and unfaithful. Both groups, Gentiles and Jews, for different reasons, are estranged from God. And both groups are estranged from and live in hostility toward one another.

Into this divided world brimming with hostility, Christ came proclaiming "peace to you who were far off and peace to those who were near" (v. 17). These two groups, the uncircumcised and the circumcised, are called to make peace with one another because Christ has made peace between each of them and God. Christ has made peace between the Gentiles (those who are far off) and God, and between the Jews (those who are near) and God, by means of his sacrificial death on the cross. It is his blood (v. 13), his atoning death, that now determines their relationship to God the Father (v. 18). Because Christ has already made peace between God and God's people, the Jews, and between God and those who are without God in the world, the Gentiles, all those who are in Christ are called to make peace with one another, to be reconciled to one another just as they have each been reconciled to God through Christ's cross.

But what is this peace to which all Christians are called in the one body of Christ? What is it that constitutes peace? Ephesians makes it clear that the peace to which all Christians are called is Jesus Christ himself. "For he is our peace; in his flesh he has made both groups into one and has broken down the dividing wall, that is, the hostility between us" (v. 14). Peace is not something apart from Christ, some program or policy independent of him. Christ himself, says Ephesians, Christ in his flesh, "is our peace." This means peace is not something Christians need discuss, debate, and construct. Christ himself is that peace. Christians do not apply some understanding of peace to Christ; rather, Christ himself and his reconciliation of all people to God is the true reality of peace.

Pastoral Perspective

and Jews for rejecting the state-sponsored religion.[1]

By using the loaded word *atheos*, the author evokes the strong emotional separation of Jew and Gentile. This was not merely side-by-side coexistence, but active antagonism and hostility. To remove the dividing walls was no small feat; indeed, the cost was the blood of Christ. To make these hostile groups one is nothing short of miraculous. What had been separate for generations—indeed, for the whole of covenant history—was now being made into one body. As much of the New Testament attests, this experience of the early church was one of the most profound gifts and surprises of new life in Christ.

The irony of our time is that so many battles are being fought between those who think their rivals are *atheos*. The mudslinging has not ended. While the past tense of the verbs in this passage affirms an already accomplished fact, the reality of our world stands against the peaceful images in painful juxtaposition. The hard truth is there is no peace. Unity, whether in the church or in the world, seems to exist only in our dreams. After years of work for ecumenical Christian unity, not only do some Christians condemn others as not "Christian" enough, but denominations themselves seem to be coming apart at the seams.

It seems as if the whole world is busy building walls. The United States is building barriers along its southern border to prevent illegal immigrants from entering. The Israelis continue to build a wall to separate themselves from the Palestinians. There is talk of erecting a barrier in the region between Pakistan and Afghanistan. Other territories are protected by invisible fences—demilitarized zones—to keep enemies apart.

One could argue that, in our world, strong walls make for more peace. Every child who has ever shared a room knows this. There is nothing like a dividing line across the middle of the floor—your side, my side—to keep the peace. This is your side of the closet; this is mine. These are my clothes, my toys, my books; those are yours. As long as we keep apart, we will not argue. In the words of the poet Robert Frost, good fences make good neighbors. Strong locks prevent break-ins, security checks prevent violence, and good fences prevent smuggling of weapons, drugs, and enemies.

---

1. See Pheme Perkins, "Reflections on Ephesians 2:11–22," in *The New Interpreter's Bible* (Nashville: Abingdon, 2000), 11:403.

inclusion, v. 19)—brackets the passage. In between is an excursus (vv. 14–18) that explains how the transition from the exclusion of Gentiles to their inclusion was accomplished.

Further contrasting word pairs include far (vv. 13, 17) and near (vv. 13, 17, a spatial contrast similar to the temporal "then" and "now"); peace (vv. 14, 15, 17) and enmity (vv. 14, 16); two peoples divided (vv. 14, 15, 16, 18) and one people united (vv. 14, 15, 16, 18); aliens (v. 12) and citizens (v. 19). The climax of the passage is then dominated by metaphors for building.

Thus the author portrays the contrast between the former state of the Gentile readers (strangers, noncitizens, far off, separated as part of two peoples, without God or hope) and their current state (no longer strangers, citizens, near, united as one people, having God as Father), and further portrays Christ as the agent by whom this transformation has occurred, specifically by his sacrifice on the cross (vv. 13, 14, 16). Thus Christ has eliminated the dividing law (vv. 14–15), uniting Jews and Gentiles in one Spirit (v. 18), bringing the Gentiles to the Father, and making them members of the household of God— this last portrayed as the goal of Christ's uniting work.

It is helpful to look at some individual verses, to see how the author accomplishes his purpose.

Verses 11–12 describe the hopeless condition of Gentiles prior to the coming of Christ—see Romans 1:18–32 for a lengthier description of the human condition. The use of "cosmos" (world) in verse 12 plays on the Greco-Roman view of a hostile universe populated by demons and evil spirits. It was essentially a hopeless situation.

With verses 14–18 the author introduces an excursus on how the diversity/enmity (vv. 11–12) has become a unity (vv. 19–22). The bracketing verses (11–12, 19–22) present the main theme of the passage, with the excursus (vv. 14–18) telling how this was achieved. The excursus is shaped by Isaiah 57:18–19, in which God acknowledges the evil of his people but promises to heal them (58:18) and bring them peace (58:19). Paul now tells his readers how in fact God has done this: through the sacrifice of his Son.

The "dividing wall" in verse 14 probably refers to the outside wall of the Jewish temple, where an inscription warned Gentiles not to go beyond the outer court of the temple (Court of the Gentiles) lest they be immediately put to death for profaning the holy place. In verses 14–15, that dividing wall is defined as the enmity between Jews and Gentiles, represented by the Jewish law that demanded separation and its implied enmity.

of God and estranged from the ways of Jesus. It is not only those outside the church who live without hope and without God. This journey from far off may remind the preacher and congregation of the parable of the Prodigal Son (Luke 15:11–32) and reinforce Paul's contention that the church is a holy experiment in reconciliation.

The heart of the text is Paul's reminder that in Jesus Christ the two distinctive peoples—Jews and Gentiles—have become "one new humanity" (v. 15). The powerful image of the dividing wall of hostility being broken down provides the preacher with direct links to the hostilities and division that emerge in the reconciled community called the church even now. Encampments form, and the dividing wall of hostility is reconstructed in spite of our best intentions. Instead of "Jew" and "Gentile," it is now right and left, orthodox and progressive, mainline and evangelical. We fall into habitual battles, dreaming of the day when "our side" is finally triumphant. But the text dreams of another day. It says that Christ has already "made both groups into one" (v. 14), "putting to death that hostility" (v. 16).

A sermon that announces this text will not implore the congregation to break down the dividing wall in order to end the hostility between us. Such a sermon might instead reframe the rite of passing the peace of Christ, reminding the congregation that it is not a simple greeting. Instead, the peace of Christ is a shocking new reality in which former enemies who would not touch or eat with one another now reach out to one another in recognition of their common humanity. The deconstruction of the "dividing wall" that has been accomplished by Christ is good news for our divided selves, divided households, and divided workplaces.

The sermon, like the text, will remind the church of the message it carries in its life together when it remembers its shocking origins. When the neighbors in ancient Ephesus saw who was eating together in the little church, they were shocked. And when the preacher in that infant congregation saw those shocked faces, all that needed to be said in the sermon was, "You are witnesses to God's kingdom come, God's will done."

Perhaps the contemporary sermon will be like that. Perhaps the preacher will point to the places in the congregation's life where the dividing wall of hostility is being broken down. Paul's rhetorical style suggests that the preacher not cajole or berate but instead encourage and remind. This tone can keep the congregation open and receptive, not closed

Ephesians 2:11-22

Theological Perspective

Furthermore, peace is not simply the cessation of hostilities, the disappearance of enmity. Peace, as Ephesians describes it, is not a truce or a cease-fire. Because Christ "is our peace," true peace is not a matter of those who are estranged coexisting. Christ is our peace because he has created "in himself" one new humanity in place of two. There is now something more important than being Jewish or being Gentile that gives all Christians their true identity and reconciles them to one another. As Paul puts it in Galatians 3:28, "There is no longer Jew or Greek . . . for all of you are one in Christ Jesus." That oneness, and the peace and reconciliation that issue from it, is a oneness in Christ and a oneness that does not exist apart from him.

Because Christ is our peace, we as Christians understand peacemaking differently than do many other people. We recognize that peace has already been made, even if the rest of the world does not. Peace has already been made, even though hostilities and bloodshed continue, in the same sense that death is no more, even though people continue to die. The peace Christians have in Christ enables us to engage boldly, perhaps even foolishly, in what may appear to the rest of the world to be hopeless situations. Christians know it is not our task to bring peace to the world. God has already done that in the person of Christ. Luke reports that as Jesus approached Jerusalem and his passion, he wept and said, "If you, even you, had only recognized on this day the things that make for peace! But now they are hidden from your eyes" (Luke 19:42). For those who are in Christ, the things that make for peace are no longer hidden.

GEORGE W. STROUP

Pastoral Perspective

One could argue that the laws and the commandments were themselves peacekeeping fences. Human beings need boundaries both for self-protection and to prevent interference with their neighbor's life. "Do not kill, do not steal, do not commit adultery" all define boundaries. *This* is yours, and not *that*. To love one's neighbor is to honor their boundaries. Why would God, in the name of peace, abolish the law with its commandments and ordinances, the law that was created to protect people?

Eliminating boundaries does not in itself create peace. Peace comes only by eliminating the hostility behind the dividing walls. God does not merely tear down walls, but unites people in the One who is our peace, creating one new humanity.

Lest we lose hope, we would do well to remember the day the Berlin Wall came down. Most of us never expected it to happen in our lifetimes. The feelings of euphoria, surprise, and possibility were palpable. If this wall could fall, what else? The end of apartheid in South Africa brought even more hope and excitement. The divisions of black, white, and colored were falling, and reconciliation became possible.

Archbishop Desmond Tutu of South Africa believes that God's hand was in that miracle:

> God saw our brokenness and sought to extricate us from it—but only with our cooperation. God will not cajole or bully us, but wants to woo us for our own sakes. We might say that the Bible is the story of God's attempt to effect atonement, to bring us back to our intended condition of relatedness. God was, in Christ, reconciling the world to God. God sent Jesus who would fling out his arms on the cross as if to embrace us. God wants to draw us back into an intimate relationship and so bring to unity all that has become disunited. This was God's intention from the beginning. And each of us is called to be an ally of God in this work of justice and reconciliation.[2]

Rather than building walls that separate us and keep us safe, these images from Ephesians urge us to let ourselves be built into a temple where God can dwell. Christ is the cornerstone. In him we are no longer *atheos*, but one.

KAREN CHAKOIAN

2. Quoted in a sermon by John Buchanan, "Dividing Walls," preached at Fourth Presbyterian Church, Chicago, July 20, 2003.

Exegetical Perspective

The result of the destroying of the law (v. 15) is not to bring Gentiles into the Jewish nation, but to create a new reality in which both Jew and Gentile participate, that is, the church. This is further pointed to in verse 19, where the opposite of being separated from the commonwealth of Israel (v. 12) is not to belong to that commonwealth but to be members of the household of God with all the saints (= Christians).

Thus (vv. 15–16), Christ both makes peace between Jews and Gentiles, making one humanity (or a "third race," as some early church fathers called it) out of them, and reconciles them to God, the only true basis of any unity among humankind. The one body (v. 16) in all likelihood refers to the church (the body of Christ), created by Christ's act on the cross. The participle "killing" may here be instrumental: Christ achieves the reconciliation by killing the enmity with his own death on the cross.

Verses 17–18 summarize and complete the thought of the excursus begun with verse 14: by his death Christ brought peace, eliminated the categories "near and far," and gave both Jews and Gentiles access to the Father by the same (Holy) Spirit.

The illustration of building a house (v. 20) occurs elsewhere in the NT (e.g., 1 Cor. 3:10–15; 1 Pet. 2:4–6) and early Christianity. The word order in the reference to the foundation consisting of apostles and prophets could point to Christian rather than OT prophets (for Christian prophets, see Agabus, Acts 21:10; 1 Cor. 11:10), or the word order may simply indicate the order of precedence: the apostles are more directly the foundation of the Christian faith, and only through the apostolic word do the OT prophets form part of the foundation.

In verses 20–22, the building is seen metaphorically in personal terms—apparently each Christian is a building currently being built, with the foundation consisting of the prophets and apostles, Christ being the keystone of the arch (not the cornerstone of the foundation; the foundation has already been named). That building/Christian is finally to be a temple, intended as a dwelling for God by (or through) the Spirit. In that way the church, illumined by the Spirit, is formed.

PAUL J. ACHTEMEIER

Homiletical Perspective

down or turned off, as the sermon moves to the surprising twist that concludes the text.

Having broken down the dividing wall that is the hostility between us, Christ is now the crucial building block (or keystone) of a new structure—a holy temple in the Lord. The final verses of the text imagine this new holy place to be built not of stones but of people. It may be difficult for congregations to imagine Paul writing to a community that has no conception of the church as a building. Contemporary congregations will need help in imagining a time when the word "church" does not mean a building but is, instead, a synonym for a reconciled community. In such a time, the word church—*ekklēsia*—means this odd group of aliens and strangers who have become "citizens with the saints and also members of the household of God" (v. 19). When Paul describes this church as a building "built upon the foundation of the apostles and prophets" (v. 20), he intends for the Ephesians to wonder whom the space is for.

In a surprising twist, Paul says that this community exists to be "a dwelling place for God" (v. 22). The sermon turns at its conclusion to reimagine the church not as a place for parishioners to come into, but instead as the household where God chooses to live. People who live together after hostility form the kind of community in which God abides. So says Paul. This surprising ending may push both preacher and congregation back into the text to note a verse that slipped quickly by, unattended. There Paul describes Christ's peace as reconciling "both groups to God" (v. 16). We imagine that reconciliation involves two parties. We forget that human schisms cause an even greater separation than the hostility between clans, tribes, and nations. They alienate us from God. Our reunion in Christ reunites us not only with one another. It is the path to our reunion with God.

EDWIN SEARCY

Mark 6:30-34, 53-56

³⁰The apostles gathered around Jesus, and told him all that they had done and taught. ³¹He said to them, "Come away to a deserted place all by yourselves and rest a while." For many were coming and going, and they had no leisure even to eat. ³²And they went away in the boat to a deserted place by themselves. ³³Now many saw them going and recognized them, and they hurried there on foot from all the towns and arrived ahead of them. ³⁴As he went ashore, he saw a great crowd; and he had compassion for them, because they were like sheep without a shepherd; and he began to teach them many things. . . .

⁵³When they had crossed over, they came to land at Gennesaret and moored the boat. ⁵⁴When they got out of the boat, people at once recognized him, ⁵⁵and rushed about that whole region and began to bring the sick on mats to wherever they heard he was. ⁵⁶And wherever he went, into villages or cities or farms, they laid the sick in the marketplaces, and begged him that they might touch even the fringe of his cloak; and all who touched it were healed.

Theological Perspective

Two *fundamental* questions emerge today from the welter of global religious striving: (1) How does your God view the world?—the basic theological question; and (2) How does your God ask *you* to view the world?—the basic ethical question. These are really two parts of the same question, for people's attitudes toward the world invariably mirror their underlying conceptions of deity—or the lack thereof. In technical terms, ethics flow from theology.

This passage of Scripture contains, in its briefest and most contextually pertinent form, the answer that Christians give—*or ought to give!*—to this two-sided question. It is stated with extraordinary forthrightness in this one key verse: "he saw a great crowd; and he had *compassion* for them, because they were like sheep without a shepherd" (v. 34). The term "compassion" is explicitly used of Jesus' attitude toward human beings in at least eight Gospel references, and it is *implicit* in the entire witness to his life, including his healing ministry that is prominent also in this text. Since for Christians Jesus, supremely, is revelatory of God and indeed God's unique representative in history, compassion must be said to be of the essence of the One who created us and before whom all life is lived.

This is no mean claim, to be brushed over lightly! For, as religious history demonstrates, compassion is

Pastoral Perspective

"For many were coming and going, and they had no leisure even to eat" (v. 31). Is this not a succinct description of the lives of many people today? Too busy to pause for a real lunch, young professionals munch on vending-machine fare while working at their desks. Teens grab a bagel for breakfast on the way out the door to school. Parents and children drive through a succession of fast-food restaurants between after-school lessons and sports practices. Commuters sip double lattes on the early morning drive, gnaw on baby carrots between meetings, and pick up takeout on the way home. Toddlers graze on cereal pieces and other portable finger foods so that meal schedules need not control the timing of family shopping trips. We are a people besieged by activities and responsibilities that reshape even basic functions of life such as eating. Our busyness prevents us from gathering for family meals, and we may even forget that we enjoy stopping to eat together, especially when we find pleasure and fulfillment in many of the other activities that make up our day.

But what happens if Christians become too busy to come away and break bread together? This text suggests that gathering as a faith community to rest from our labors and partake of a common meal is an important part of life together. Jesus offers a cautionary word to his disciples and the

Exegetical Perspective

Today's readings appear transitional—even inconsequential—against the miracle stories they frame, but these accounts are treasures and aptly merit focused attention. Bracketing Mark's lengthy accounts of Jesus' feeding the five thousand (vv. 35–44) and walking on water (vv. 45–52) are three brief accounts: the disciples' first "homecoming" with Jesus after their initial efforts in ministry (vv. 12–13, 30–31), a journey with Jesus that does not turn out as expected (vv. 32–34), and their unanticipated arrival with Jesus to the region of Gennesaret, where much healing is needed and received (v. 53–56). In stark contrast to erroneous speculations about Jesus' identity and mission (vv. 14–16), there is widespread recognition of Jesus among the needy in Galilee, at least in part. Here Jesus' compassionate purpose and divine power to restore life are made clear.

The Twelve Return (vv. 30–31). This passage concludes Mark's story of the mission of the Twelve (vv. 7–13). Jesus gives his disciples his own authority and sends them out—two by two—to extend the realm of his rule by doing the very things he is doing: preaching, teaching, casting out demons, and healing the sick and injured. It is an effective mission, and many people are healed—physically,

Homiletical Perspective

Most people in Western Christianity see the story of their life as a self-sufficient text. This text may intersect with others, but for the most part it reveals a narrative that is self-contained, self-grounded, and self-made. Pastors sometimes get to glimpse beneath these public narratives. Here we see different stories filled with anxiety, fear of failure, and loss of control. The difficult task of preaching is to connect to those hidden narratives while at the same time honoring the "public faces" of people.

Passages like those found in the Gospel of Mark provide opportunities to cut through the façade and connect to the hidden worlds of human pain. Mark's textual landscape reveals the deep neediness of humankind. The author's use of extreme characters holds up mirrors to people who are weak, over-whelmed by evil forces, and unable to sustain a viable existence.

In Mark 6, people are everywhere—they are coming and going—and they are not just following Jesus; they proactively anticipate where he is headed and hurry ahead of him. As Jesus and his disciples arrive at the place where they should find rest, there is a great crowd of people waiting for them. Later, at Gennesaret (vv. 53–56), the same scenario unfolds: people rushing to see him, bringing with them the sick.

Mark 6:30-34, 53-56

Theological Perspective

not the most common or popular concept that human beings have used to describe their sense of the divine attitude toward the world. Far from it! For many religions, both primitive and recent, deities have been regarded, to one degree or another, as ominous, wrathful, vengeful, angry, vindictive—approachable, therefore, only through carefully devised and guarded ritual supervised by a priestly caste. Christianity has itself been no stranger to such theologies. One should even be careful, in this connection, of terms like "holy" and "just," for they are often insufficiently informed by the primary Christian, suffering-love [*agapē*] category, of which "compassion" is a synonym or extrapolation.

It is no accident that this word is used so naturally of Jesus. For it is of the very essence of the prophetic traditions of ancient Israel, which Abraham Heschel named "divine pathos": "To the prophet . . . God does not reveal himself in an abstract absoluteness, but in a personal and intimate relation to the world. He does not simply command and expect obedience; He is also moved and affected by what happens in the world. . . . God is concerned about the world and shares its fate. Indeed, this is the essence of God's moral nature: His willingness to be intimately involved in the history of man."[1] The *passio Christi*—passion of the Redeemer—is nothing more or less than the incarnation of the *pathos* of the God of Israel, the Creator.

But if we would critique the conceptions of deity that neglect this foundational claim, we should also beware of cheapening the claim as such! "Compassion" must not be turned into "cheap grace" (Bonhoeffer): "God has pity on us—what else would God do?"; "God will pardon me, that's His business" (Heinrich Heine). Against all such presumption and sentimentalism, we need to consider the meaning of compassion. We might begin with the word itself. English, with its latinization of basic human experiences, obscures (for most of us) the picture behind this word. German is much more direct. The German word for compassion is *Mitleid*—quite literally, "with-suffering." Of course, that is the literal meaning of "compassion" too, but most of us do not hear it. We think it a synonym for pity. Pity is something you can manage from afar—at a once-remove! Not compassion. You do not have compassion, really, unless you *suffer with* those to whom you refer. The precondition for compassion is unconditional solidarity with the ones for whom you feel it.

Pastoral Perspective

contemporary church. We need times when we return from our individual activities—even those activities done in the name and for the sake of Jesus—and re-form ourselves as the body of Christ. Otherwise, we may be broken and poured out so often that we struggle to be useful as Christ's hands and feet in the world. We may become so caught up in the busyness of ministry that we forget to spend time with the One who would direct our preaching, teaching, healing, and justice-seeking endeavors.

It is curious that Jesus' attempt to draw the disciples apart is foiled by the crowds of people who are following him. This would be a nice text for arguing the importance of Sabbath keeping if not for the turn of events in verse 33! When Jesus and the disciples try to retreat, instead of an out-of-the-way place for a leisurely meal and communal rest, they find still more people in need of ministry. Astute congregations know that for every outreach activity on their calendar, several equally pressing societal needs go unattended. Jesus' response to the crowd he encounters suggests that faith communities should attempt to address all those needs known to them, out of compassion for those who seek guidance and assistance. Thus the message of verses 30–34 is ambiguous: set yourselves apart for divine and physical sustenance, and at the same time, set aside your own retreat when others are in need of spiritual sustenance. How does a congregation shape its life together to honor both of these teachings?

The reflections of an eighteenth-century spiritual director might be helpful as we wrestle with this question. Jean-Pierre de Caussade wanted to understand how Christians might know what God would have them to do in each moment of every day. He taught that God reveals Godself in each moment, but that Christians must learn to pay attention to God's presence and surrender themselves continually to God's will. Such surrender requires that Christians trust God to provide for all their needs, whether through times of spiritual retreat or through God's ministry to the minister during outward-directed activities. De Caussade writes, "Everything turns to bread to nourish me, soap to wash me, fire to purify me, and a chisel to fashion me in the image of God. Grace supplies all my needs."[1] While God calls us to renewal through communal practices of Sabbath keeping, Eucharist, and theological reflection, God also pledges to

---

1. Abraham Heschel, *The Prophets* (New York: Jewish Publication Society of America, 1962), 223–24.

1. Jean-Pierre de Caussade, *The Sacrament of the Present Moment* (New York: Harper & Row, 1982), 71–72.

Exegetical Perspective

spiritually, and relationally. The realm of Jesus' influence is increasing. Now in this passage, the disciples—called "apostles" ("sent ones")—return to be with Jesus and report all that they have done and taught. Curiously, teaching is not part of Jesus' explicit charge in Mark, but encouraging people to listen (v. 11) and preaching for repentance (v. 12) are here interpreted as teaching, which is a distinctive element of Mark's account of their mission and highlights Mark's emphasis on Jesus' teaching ministry too (e.g., v. 6).

During their reunion, Jesus calls them to join him "alone" or "apart" in a "wilderness place," a place of refuge and solitude where they may rest. Preaching, teaching, and healing are tiring work, and their work is following them home. Even as they are meeting with one another, people continue coming and going and the apostles have "no leisure even to eat" (v. 31). Mark's repeated reference to Jesus' invitation to retreat with him to a "wilderness place" (NRSV "deserted place") is significant (vv. 31–32). Not only is rest the completion of their mission, but throughout Israel's life the wilderness is a place of struggle and testing (see 1:12–13; Deut. 8:2), even as it is also a place where God often encounters the faithful and provides sustenance, protection, renewal, and direction (e.g., Exod. 3:1f.; 13:20–21; 1 Sam. 23:14; 1 Kgs. 19:4f.; Ps. 63). In the wilderness, God formed a new community (Exod. 32:10; 33:13).

The Compassionate Shepherd (vv. 32–34). In the second portion of today's reading, which repeats the phrase "wilderness place" (v. 32), a new exodus is underway as a new community gathers around a new deliverer. Jesus and the disciples leave by boat for a deserted place in order to rest, but the people from the surrounding towns and villages recognize them and flock to the shore where the boat is landing. The disciples may have left with Jesus for a restful place, but their journey does not turn out as they expect. They arrive on shore only to face another crowd, one much larger in number and needs than the one they left behind.

In Mark, as in Matthew (14:14), Jesus looks at the great crowd and is moved to show compassion. Jesus has been acting compassionately toward his disciples, but at this point, Jesus' concern for the crowd seems to take precedence over his concern for his disciples. Mark notes, however, that Jesus is moved because the people are like "sheep without a shepherd" (v. 34). The comparison is striking, because Moses used this analogy in his appointment

Homiletical Perspective

We do not want to be like these people! In their desperation they lack public decorum. In order to find healing and deliverance, they will cry out, beg, push through crowds, and suffer humiliation. Mark reveals a world wherein desperation overcomes order. People do not just come up to Jesus; they push through crowds in order to touch his garment. They do not walk to see him. No, they run on ahead of him, so that when he arrives they will have a good chance of contact.

While we acknowledge that oppressed people in the majority world may "need" the kind of Christianity that allows for such behavior, for the most part, our liturgies are designed for people who are able to be in control of their lives. We place a high value on order and things done decently. We like to see ourselves in the "ordered crowd" sitting on the grass in small groups while the disciples hand out bread and fish. What is difficult to imagine is the rushing after Jesus without bringing a picnic lunch! Even more difficult to imagine is running on foot to cut Jesus off before he gets away.

The feeding of the multitude is a vivid snapshot of the press of humanity upon the ministry of Jesus. In the midst of these desperate people stands "the One" who is able to meet the demands of "the many." His compassion leads him to teach when he is weary, touch and heal when he wants to be alone, and feed thousands when he himself is hungry. In this text he is pictured as standing above the fray. Note the visual imagery: he looks to heaven, blesses and breaks the bread. From this broken bread, thousands are filled. This iconic image shows up again in Mark 14:22, when Jesus, celebrating the Passover with his disciples, takes the bread, blesses it, and gives to his disciples, saying, "Take; this is my body."

The preacher faces the task of lifting up this eucharistic image of Christ to congregations who are already filled. In fact, their lives seem running over with "the many." They are involved in many things; they own many things and share in many activities. Our congregations are not the desperate crowds of Mark 6. They are not rushing to get to church ahead of the preacher. Nor do they feel compelled overtly to push through crowds for the morning bread and wine. Church is only one of the many activities that fill modern lives. This does not mean that they are not hungry, or that desperation is not present.

Ironically it is "the many" that reveal the desperation. In our preoccupation with many things, we know that our resources are too few. We ourselves are in need of "the One." In this, we are not that

Mark 6:30-34, 53-56

Theological Perspective

But here we are at the very center of our faith! Jesus' compassion for the crowd, sheep without a shepherd, is not condescension. It is the mark of his *identification* with his kind, and it will not achieve its full expression until, at Golgotha, he has gone all the way—identifying with our lot not only in birth and life, but also in death. For Christians, this is not just a "statement" about a good, generous, and loving human being, Jesus of Nazareth. It is a statement about God—namely, the Source of our lives and of all life, the One before whom we live out our days and are accountable. *And are accountable!*—for the ethic flows without a break from the theology: As recipients of such compassion, we contradict our own being—our "*new* being"—if we fail to enact the same compassion vis à vis others (see, e.g., Col. 3:12).

In her recent, powerful study *The Great Transformation: The Beginnings of Our Religious Traditions*,[2] Karen Armstrong argues that the great religions of our world had their foundations in an "Axial Age," the ninth century BCE. In the midst of the extreme violence of that epoch, religious sages advanced prototheological beliefs that were to flower in subsequent centuries as rabbinic Judaism, Christianity, and Islam. At the core of these original beliefs she finds the concept of divine compassion. This is such a radical notion that it is subject to constant doubt and manipulation, and in our time it is threatened once again by violent human impulses that find their inspiration and outlet in fundamentalist and exclusivistic religion. Our only hope as a civilization, Armstrong argues, is to return to the depths of theological wisdom that were explored in the Axial Age and subsequently at points of crisis and renewal.

I am not qualified to judge the historical aspect of this generalization, but I am in entire agreement with the "lesson" Armstrong draws from it for the present critical age. Christians today tend to look askance at Islam for having substituted for divine compassion a militant and perhaps inherently violent conception of the Deity. But "the time has come for the judgment to begin with the household of God" (1 Pet. 4:17). Christians too must ask not only whether we have grasped the full radicality of belief in a compassionate God, but whether *as church* we are ready to live that compassion in our profoundly threatened world.

DOUGLAS JOHN HALL

Pastoral Perspective

sustain us when the needs of others interrupt our plans for retreat.

Verses 53–56 encourage faith communities to recognize the extent to which the world is suffering and in need of Christian practices of healing. The Gospel of Mark speaks of people rushing and begging for an opportunity to be made whole through an encounter with God. This is not how a contemporary congregation typically experiences the neediness of the world of which it is a part. Persons in search of healing are far more likely to seek out therapists, physicians, self-help books, and prescription drugs than to enter a church building. Perhaps this is because persons outside the church do not recognize Christ's healing presence within communities of faith. The people described in this passage recognize Jesus as a healer and respond accordingly. If the church today is unrecognizable as a place of healing, then we need to reflect on what our mission and purpose in the world are and how we communicate the good news of God's healing grace in this time and place.

Both segments of this text suggest that the church belongs in the world rather than in cloistered in church buildings set apart from the hustle and bustle of daily living. Jesus and the disciples encounter people in need as part of their movement from place to place, not by establishing a central location and waiting for people to make their way to them. Healing takes place when the faith community and those with whom they minister reach out to one another in mutual need. Just as persons come to the church in need of God's grace, the faith community engages in ministry because it needs to live as Christ has commanded, as the body of Christ sent into the world to help God repair the brokenness caused by sin. By embracing its role as the fringe of Christ's cloak, the church can expect to have a healing effect on all who reach out to Christian communities with the desire to be made whole.

KAREN MARIE YUST

---

2. Karen Armstrong, *The Great Transformation* (New York: Alfred Knopf, 2006).

Exegetical Perspective

of Joshua to lead the people in the wilderness (Num. 27:17), and Moses announced God's promise of a future prophet—the Messiah—whose words would all come to pass (Deut. 18:18). Moreover, Ezekiel prophesied the coming One who will be the shepherd of his sheep, seeking the lost, bringing back the strayed, binding up the crippled, strengthening the weak, and feeding them justice and food (Ezek. 34:16–31; see also 34:1–15; Ps. 28:9; etc.).

These stories are integral to Israel's life and foundational to its hope. Moreover, they form an indispensable context for understanding today's lectionary texts and the feeding narrative that follows. The multitude and the disciples in the "wilderness" are emerging as a new Israel gathered around God's Shepherd, Jesus, who is exercising compassion by teaching "at length" the ways of the kingdom of God. Soon he will feed their hungry bodies (vv. 35–44), but presently he feeds their hungering spirits, while his disciples appear to rest (v. 35).

The Healer Is Here (vv. 53–56). The third portion of today's lectionary reading comes after Mark's accounts of the great feeding in the wilderness and Jesus' walking on the sea. It recounts the disciples' unanticipated arrival with Jesus in the region of Gennesaret, where much healing is needed and given. The town of Gennesaret was located on the western shore of the Sea of Galilee, between Magdala and Capernaum, where numerous hot mineral springs had attracted the sick and the injured for centuries. Little wonder that Jesus' and the disciples' healing ministry draws such attention there (see 1:28; 6:1, 7, 13). Now as Jesus travels, people bring to him those who need healing (see 1:32–34; 2:1–12, etc.). They recognize Jesus as the healer (vv. 54; cf. v. 33), one whose power is so great that healing would come to the needy even by touching a tassel (*kraspedon*) upon his cloak (v. 56; see also Num. 15:38f.; Deut. 22:12). Is it superstition? Not according to Mark, for as many as touched it or him (the Greek text allows either) are restored to health. Even more, there are no references to Jesus' preaching or teaching or to their faith as conditions for healing. For Mark, this healing story is an epiphany of Jesus' divine power, even if his divine nature is not understood.

ROBERT A. BRYANT

Homiletical Perspective

different from the desperate people portrayed in the Gospel of Mark. In fact, we may be one natural disaster away from homelessness and hunger. The images of Katrina were disturbing in many ways. In particular, they brought desperation too close to home.

Dare we hear the words of Jesus to the "filled" people of the church at Laodicea: "For you say, 'I am rich, I have prospered, and I need nothing.' You do not realize that you are wretched, pitiable, poor, blind, and naked" (Rev. 3:17). These words, which are spoken pastorally and prophetically, reveal a true knowledge of what lies beneath the surface of public image.

It is a great mystery how preaching can call to remembrance the ministry of Jesus, recapitulating his service of salvation, healing, and deliverance. It is this ministry that sacramentally cuts through the façade of public demeanor and reveals the starkness of human hunger. The meeting of human hunger and the outstretched hands of Jesus create the possibilities for miracles of grace. It is possible for the grace of "the One" to come into lives overwhelmed by "the many."

Preaching Mark offers opportunities to make these connections and to offer an image of Christ as the one fully able to take into his hands the "not enough" of human finitude and make it complete. The question looms before those who are not desperate: "How many loaves do you have?" However many we have, it is not enough to fill the deep hunger for the bread of life. Quiet desperation reaches out for the hands of Christ to provide food for the journey home.

CHERYL BRIDGES JOHNS

2 *Kings 4:42-44*

⁴²A man came from Baal-shalishah, bringing food from the first fruits to the man of God: twenty loaves of barley and fresh ears of grain in his sack. Elisha said, "Give it to the people and let them eat." ⁴³But his servant said, "How can I set this before a hundred people?" So he repeated, "Give it to the people and let them eat, for thus says the Lᴏʀᴅ, 'They shall eat and have some left.' " ⁴⁴He set it before them, they ate, and had some left, according to the word of the Lᴏʀᴅ.

Theological Perspective

This pericope concludes a chapter, early in the story of Elisha, that explores the miraculous power of God at work in and around the prophet. It would be easy in reading this chapter to localize the power in the prophet—Elisha, for example, as the one who multiplies the food so that all have enough—but two strands that define the chapter as a whole and are evident in our passage militate against this reading. The first, more obvious of these is the emphasis on these miracles as the work of God. As Elisha explains, it is the Lord who says, "They shall eat and have some left." But coupled with this emphasis on God's work is the understanding that Elisha is intimately bound up to the community that surrounds him. Elisha's story follows that of Elijah, the consummate outsider who attacks the political, religious, and popular establishments of his day. Elisha, on the other hand, is seen in this fourth chapter as one whose life is consistently surrounded by community, whether it be the company of prophets, the regular fellowship that he enjoys at a household in Shunem, or the nameless, and hence assumed, crowd who is fed in today's story.

If we take this chapter as an exposition of the way of life in the community gathered around the power of God, then its concluding passage offers in summary form a catalog of the qualities that define

Pastoral Perspective

The challenge to preaching this text is simply to allow it to speak for itself, to have its own integrity in the church's proclamation. The passage, describing a miraculous feeding by the prophet Elisha of "a hundred people," is easily overshadowed by the Gospel text for this day, John 6:1–21, which describes Jesus' feeding of five thousand on a mountain near the Sea of Galilee.

In order to hear the Kings text on its own terms—in order to hear it as word of God to us today—and specifically to hear it from a pastoral perspective, we must take seriously the fact that 1 and 2 Kings, as Iain Provan observes, serve "a didactic function . . . encapsulated in the ancient Jewish description of these books as 'The Former Prophets.'" These texts do not tell us a history merely to satisfy our curiosity about a distant past, but to exert God's claim on us in the present.[1]

The claim of God, both past and present, takes on particular force in these texts from 2 Kings. Whether we construe them as proclaiming, as my colleague Kristin Saldine says, "God's abundance in a time of scarcity," or as Terence E. Fretheim describes them, as recounting "miracles of life in the midst of death,"

1. Iain Provan, *1 and 2 Kings* (Sheffield: Sheffield Academic Press, 1997), 24–25.

Exegetical Perspective

The opening chapters of 2 Kings seek to establish Elisha as Elijah's legitimate successor, heir to Elijah's prophetic authority. This text's account of the multiplying loaves is the last in a series of four miracle stories that witness to Elisha's wonder-working deeds. A destitute widow receives quantities of oil that relieve her poverty and preserve her family. A couple's only son is restored to life and health. Poisonous gourds are made fit to eat. Finally, a small offering of bread and grain feeds a crowd of one hundred.

Each of these stories has a parallel in the Elijah cycle, primarily in 1 Kings 17:8–24. This helps draw the connection between Elijah and Elisha. The stories involve humble settings and ordinary needs: a widow's household, a farmer's field, a community meal. The point of making these connections is not to bolster the reputation of either prophet but to bear witness to the power of God at work. Even in the worst of times, God will not leave the people without a witness. As rulers come and go and kingdoms rise and fall, God continues to raise up prophets who not only speak but perform God's word in the world, particularly among the poor, the grieving, and the vulnerable.

It is also significant that in each story the response of those among whom the miracle is

Homiletical Perspective

This story of Elisha's feeding the people demonstrates two universal truths. The first is that there is suffering and need in this world, in this case, in the form of hunger. The second is that God's blessings are more abundant than we often realize. A congregation hearing this story read will naturally fast-forward to Jesus' feeding of the five thousand, so it is important to provide a context for this story.

Elisha, the prophet who receives his authority by receiving Elijah's mantel, serves in a time of much strife. His prophetic work occurs in the midst of wars between Syria and Israel. There is much in flux and many reasons to live in fear. The name Elisha means "God has granted salvation." This was probably a hard message for the people to trust in the midst of what they faced.

Scarcity was the rule of the day. This gift of the man who came from Baal-shalishah was a wonderful demonstration of faithfulness and generosity, which was no doubt particularly difficult in such a context. He brought the best of what he had, "the first fruits" before God's prophet. Elisha chooses not to receive this gift himself but to offer it to God's people in need. But in the midst of so much need, how could it possibly help? Elisha instructs his servant to distribute it among the people. The servant surveys the crowd of one hundred people and the twenty

2 Kings 4:42-44

Theological Perspective

the life of that community: stewardship, hospitality, and an expectation of abundance. We will see that these qualities are grounded in a faith in God's power—confidence that a faithful life emerges from the life of faith—and that each informs the others. The virtues of a holy life are interdependent, and from this emerges their rich texture.

Our pericope opens with the exercise of *stewardship* by the man from Baal-shalishah. He brings a portion of his first fruits to Elisha; presumably the remainder of the first fruits were offered to God in some other context, given the thrust of the story as a whole. The significance of this act, of course, is underlined by the definition of his gift as the first fruits. He not only offers to God's people his best, but also the initial product of his labor, trusting that there will be more with which he can feed and support his family. As a whole, then, this act embodies his faith in God's provision and his genuine thanksgiving for it. These two virtues, faith and thanksgiving, will be the root of the life lived in the presence of God.

From this act of stewardship springs a life of *hospitality*. From the initial gift comes the impetus to feed the gathered multitude—as we must assume that it was a multitude, given the question of whether such a generous gift would suffice. The hospitality reflected in this story catches up a theme that originates in Abraham's willingness to entertain the three travelers in the desert (Gen. 18) and is echoed in the story of the woman from Shunem, whose relationship with Elisha begins with her provision of a roof and meal for him in his travels (2 Kgs. 4:8–37). Hospitality, the act of caring for one another, either out of our abundance or out of our pittance, is the life force that creates community. A lasting relationship between Elisha and the Shunammite family is born of the woman's hospitality—and that allows it to thrive; from Abraham and Sarah's hospitality to the travelers, he and Sarah are blessed.

From these acts of stewardship and hospitality flows *the abundance of God*. The abundance of the great feast of our pericope answers the abundance of the opening story of the chapter, where a widow finds that her small container of oil has sprung into a fountain, so that from the proceeds of her windfall she can rescue her family from debt. This passage, then, promises God's abundance. It is important to note that the abundance is both the fruit of our stewardship and our hospitality—they have some to eat and more left over only because the gift of the feast was given and offered to all—and the motive

Pastoral Perspective

the point of these texts is not to glorify Elisha as a miracle worker but to articulate the power of "God's life-giving word" to those who are in greatest need.[2] Elisha performs miracles, like his predecessor Elijah, "that demonstrate the strength of God, heal the vulnerable, and pronounce judgment upon the wicked."[3] The first pastoral message of this text, therefore, is compelling and compellingly clear in the face of the practical Docetism (the version of gnostic thought that distrusts the Christian claim that the material world is God's fundamentally good creation) that rages in so much contemporary Christianity. God's power cannot be relegated to a disembodied spiritual realm but extends to all of life; God's claim upon our humanity is coextensive with God's creative power in the here and now.

Another closely related pastoral message in this text is more classically "prophetic," reminding us that these two roles, the pastoral and the prophetic, need not be seen as two contradictory offices perpetually at odds, but as distinct, indispensable, and often complementary aspects of the church's proclamation. God takes up the cause of those most vulnerable in society—those who are most in need, who are most neglected by the powers of this world. God's power effectively calls into question the unchecked powers of the mighty upon these vulnerable ones. There is a persistent strain of resistance that runs through the Elijah and Elisha cycles, a strain that, in the first instance, challenges the ninth-century BC Omrid dynasty in the name of the Lord and on behalf of the oppressed, and ultimately calls every dynasty and every people to account for their treatment of the most vulnerable in their midst. The God on behalf of whom Elisha acts and speaks cares for those who suffer and will not be thwarted by human empire.

There is no more pastoral message in the world than the message of liberation, if we understand the fundamental role of the pastor, or shepherd, as that of a protector whose "rod and staff" bring comfort to the sheep. A shepherd who makes common cause with the ravening wolves and lions that prey upon the sheepfold can hardly be counted a good shepherd. Elisha, in these stories of miracle and wonder, articulates in the prophetic message the claim of the word of the Lord upon the lives of the

2. Terence Fretheim, *First and Second Kings*, Westminster Bible Companion (Louisville, KY: Westminster John Knox Press, 1999), 146.
3. Kristin Saldine, "One Prophet, Two Bears and Forty-Two Boys: Prophetic Ethos and Biblical Satire" (unpublished paper, Princeton Theological Seminary, October 20, 1999), 11.

Exegetical Perspective

performed is quite understated. There is no outpouring of gratitude, no expression of awe and wonder, no reports that the prophet is attaining the ancient equivalent of rock-star status as he moves through the countryside. Perhaps this is because these stories are not intended to create a literary effect in the characters depicted but an actual effect in the minds and hearts of the people among whom the story is told. The audience, the community gathered around these stories, contains the hearts that will come alive with hope and the mouths that will pour forth praise.

Today's text opens with a man bringing a grain offering to the prophet. The man is not named, although he may have been a member of the prophetic guild charged with caring for the needs of the group and their leader. The identity of the one making the offering appears to be less important than the name of the town from which he comes.

Baal-shalishah has been identified with Kefr Tilt, sixteen miles north of Lydda. The land of Shalishah is mentioned in 1 Samuel 9:4–5 as a district of the tribe of Benjamin near Mount Ephraim.[1] The name of the town may be intended to highlight the power of the God of Israel over and against the power of Baal, god of the Canaanites. During a famine, the temptation to placate local gods associated with both weather and fertility would have been particularly strong. In the deep background of this story may lie the drama of seeing which god would act to save the people from hunger—Baal or YHWH? The contest between YHWH and Baal is an ongoing drama in the Elijah and Elisha cycles. Both cycles include stories that display God's power at work through the prophets to defy the power of Baal and the followers of Baal. The contest between gods is also, of course, a contest between rulers. The entire Kings cycle traces the struggle in Israel and Judah between rulers and ruling houses who remain faithful to the covenant with YHWH and rulers or ruling houses who permit the worship of other gods among God's covenant people. In the first section of 2 Kings, in which this story takes place, Elisha eventually anoints Hazael and Jehu as leaders for Israel and Syria. They, in time, overthrow the house of Ahab and Jezebel, which has continued to promote the worship of foreign deities among God's people. In this story, a simple geographic reference places the story in the context of that ongoing struggle.

1. Mordecai Cogan and Hayim Tadmoor, *II Kings* (New York: Doubleday, 1988), 59.

Homiletical Perspective

loaves and ears of grain and knows it is a drop in the bucket of what is needed. "How can I set this before a hundred people?" Common sense tells us that putting so little before so many will probably do more harm than good. But Elisha views the scene with a different set of eyes. He sees an opportunity for God's abundant blessings to be made known even in the midst of such need. He once again instructs the servant, but this time he includes the word of the Lord: "Give it to the people and let them eat, for thus says the LORD, 'They shall eat and have some left.'" We do not know whether the servant was inspired by the word of the Lord through the prophet, or merely acquiesces because he sees no other choice, but he places the food before the people.

They eat and there is food left over. The word of the Lord is true. There is no effort to explain the mechanics of how this happened, and to debate the question would miss the point of the text. What is clear is that in the midst of human need a man arrives generously offering the best of what he has. And the prophet, with the eyes of faith, offers it to the people of God. The result is beyond any reasonable human expectation, and that is the point. God is at work beyond our expectations.

This text does not candy-coat the reality of the world. There is no promise that people will never go hungry or that all suffering is immediately removed from our reality. What we are told is that God's abundance is capable of appearing in the midst of our need. In this case the human agents of God's working are one person's generosity and one person's faithful vision. By this example we are challenged to be present in the midst of human need and with our own generosity and faithful vision seek to meet that need. God may choose to use our actions as a conduit of divine blessing.

There is an absurdity to this text that cannot be overlooked. What we have received is a message that is countercultural to the rules of our world. The words of the servant live in the midst of our lives every day. "How can I set this before a hundred people?" We budget our resources and our time with a careful eye to the limitations we see present. We tell ourselves "there are only so many hours in the day" and "a penny saved is a penny earned." When we design our church budgets we are very careful to be prudent and make sure we can afford to pay for any program that is proposed.

We would never put Elisha in charge of deciding how much food is necessary for a potluck supper or deciding what we can afford to do as a congregation.

2 Kings 4:42-44

Theological Perspective

force behind these qualities. Within the overall scope of the passages, it is clear that the promise of God's abundance and faith in this promise allows us to offer our bounty to God and neighbor with confidence and hope.

The overall dynamic of this passage is consistent with Luther's theology in *The Freedom of the Christian*. For both Luther and the community of Elisha, the holy life is grounded in God's abundant love. This love comes first—it is the blessing of an ample harvest that leads to initial generous gift—and all human response in the passage, from the initial gift to the provision of the meal, springs from confidence in this abundance. Response, then, consists both of thanksgiving for God's love and in a love for neighbor that forms the body of this thanksgiving.

This dynamic embodies Luther's key insight into the nature of Christian life and ethics. Luther was clear that Christian acts that were not predicated on the prevenient love of God were fearful acts—acts attempting to earn God's favor because God could not be trusted. Luther's emphasis on faith in God was first a testimony to the character of God. God is trustworthy because God is loving. Conversely, for Luther, we can act in love only when that love comes as a response to God's love—only when our acts are acts of thanksgiving. If our acts initiate our relationship with God, then they are self-serving, crafted not to serve our neighbor but to assure our standing before God. But if our actions toward our neighbor are grounded in God's love, then they can truly be self-gift, recognizing that God has given us ourselves in love, so that we might share ourselves in return. In all of this, Luther with the author of 2 Kings offers us a theology that is fundamentally eucharistic.

STEPHEN EDMONDSON

Pastoral Perspective

people, contrasting the self-giving power of the Lord with the self-serving power of the current dynasty in the northern kingdom. We may discern in these ancient stories an element of that "ethical monotheism" that transformed religious faith from mere cultic observance to ethical commitment in the name of the Lord.

Elijah and Elisha placed their distinctive stamps on the faith of YHWH and defined what it means to apply the law of God to society, regardless of its implications on international security and the status of the powerful. They also largely set the standard for what it means to be a prophet and to speak as a prophet in the world of dynasties and empires. Indeed, the line of prophetic thought, whose deep springs are to be found in the absolute claim, "I am the LORD your God, who brought you out of the land of Egypt, out of the house of slavery; you shall have no other gods before me" (Deut. 5:6–7), and which culminates in the prophetic challenge of prophets such as Amos, "I hate, I despise your festivals, and I take no delight in your solemn assemblies. . . . But let justice roll down like waters, and righteousness like an ever-flowing stream" (Amos 5:21, 24), passes directly through Elisha's prophetic intervention in the lives of suffering people. This line of prophetic thought, we might add, runs beyond the Old Testament, through the words of Mary in the Magnificat (Luke 1:46–55) and the teachings of Jesus (Luke 6:20–26). These readings should affect our hearing of texts such as the Gospel reading for this week, as well as the Synoptic versions of the feeding in Luke 9:10–17, Matthew 14:13–21, and Mark 6:30–44. By attending to this long history we may respect the integrity of 2 Kings, while affirming a fundamental connection between the ministries of Elisha and Jesus, both of whom intervened in the lives of real people to provide for their material needs in the here and now.

MICHAEL JINKINS

Exegetical Perspective

The grain offering consists of twenty loaves of barley bread and "fresh ears of grain in a sack." The Hebrew word from which this translation derives, *besqlono,* appears nowhere else in the Old Testament. The Targum translation is "garment," the Vulgate "bag." Support for the current translation comes from the Ugaritic *Tale of Aqhat,* where the word *bsql* parallels the word *sblt,* "ears of grain."[2]

Elisha commands his servant to give the offering to the people to eat. The servant looks at the offering and at the crowd and sees only scarcity. "How can I set this before one hundred people?" The prophet looks at the same small offering and at the large crowd and sees not scarcity but an opportunity to bear witness to the reality and power of God's presence among them. God is present with God's people in ways not immediately obvious from a human perspective. What seems inadequate will prove abundant. "They shall eat and have some left," Elisha promises. According to the word of God, it is so.

For Christians, the most important connection for this story is not backward to Elijah, but forward to Jesus. There is an obvious parallel between this story and the feeding miracles of the Gospels. This text, in fact, is paired with a portion of the bread of life passage in John 6 in the lectionary for this week.

Even without making this New Testament connection, there is good news in this text. First, God will not leave us without a witness. When one prophet passes from the scene, God will raise up another. Through the prophets, God will be at work for the people's good in the midst of the common realities, although this work may not appear obvious at first. God's will for us is trust and abundance. We will have what we truly need and more besides. Second, in a world where the temptation to worship other powers is strong, God will reveal in the ordinary course of daily events that God is faithful to the covenant promises and that our faithfulness to the covenant will bring us blessing.

KAREN C. SAPIO

Homiletical Perspective

We very carefully do what we know we can do with the tangible resources before us. A character such as Elisha in our midst would appear to be reaching beyond the appropriate bounds of the resources before us and the expectations of what we believe we can accomplish.

What we fail to see is that Elisha is being prudent as well. He too is carefully measuring the resources before him when he instructs the servant to feed one hundred people with twenty loaves. He views another element in the equation that we often overlook. Elisha is able to recognize the presence and will of God as a resource upon which we can draw to respond to the needs of the people of God. Of course it is a specific gift of the prophet to see when and where God's blessing will come to bear. But we are challenged to put on the eyes of the prophet. We are called to reach beyond the common-sense measurements of the world. We are given the opportunity to recognize how God's abundant blessings are at work in the world, or could be, and how we can participate in them.

If we bring our firstfruits before the Lord, recognize the needs of the people, and keep a close watch on God's movement in our midst, who knows what will happen? God's abundant blessings just might burst in upon us, bringing more before us than we ever previously imagined possible.

DOUGLAS T. KING

2. Ibid.

Psalm 145:10-18

¹⁰All your works shall give thanks to you, O Lord,
  and all your faithful shall bless you.
¹¹They shall speak of the glory of your kingdom,
  and tell of your power,
¹²to make known to all people your mighty deeds,
  and the glorious splendor of your kingdom.
¹³Your kingdom is an everlasting kingdom,
  and your dominion endures throughout all generations.

The Lord is faithful in all his words,
  and gracious in all his deeds.

Theological Perspective

Psalm 145 speaks of the relationship between God and creation in very intimate terms. The Lord is gracious and merciful, slow to anger and abundant in steadfast love; upholds those who are falling, raises up those who are bowed down, satisfies the desires of all, and gives food in due season. Creation in turn—not just humans, but all God's works— gives God thanks, blesses, speaks of God's glory and power.

With what worldview, however, do modern-day readers—preachers and parishioners—come to this psalm, and how is their worldview challenged by it? Worldviews both integrate things we know, believe, and feel concerning the reality that surrounds us, and regulate the way we experience and perceive that reality. It is therefore good to reflect critically on our worldview and have it be confronted by Scripture.

Many modern-day readers will come to this psalm assuming what is called "the scientific world-view." While few will be able to articulate exactly what this worldview amounts to, the intuition underlying it seems to be that the universe is like a great machine proceeding according to the laws disclosed in science. Moreover, these laws are nonadjustable. Once in place, they proceed slowly but certainly, causally determining the state of the universe at any time.

Pastoral Perspective

Psalm 145 is a hymn of praise (in Hebrew, *tehillah*). As James Mays says, "The Talmud showed its estimate of the psalm's worth by saying, 'Everyone who repeats the *Tehillah* of David thrice a day may be sure that he is a child of the world to come' (*Berakot*, 4b)."[1] To repeat the hymn of praise every day requires giving voice to such praise on the best of days as well as in the darkest hours. On the days filled with blessing, praise easily rises up from the people of God carried by gratitude for God's faithfulness (v. 13), mercy, and steadfast love (v. 8). Yet, the psalm is not a psalm for these rich days of blessing only. The psalm is stitched together with the word "all." It is also composed in an acrostic, an artistic structure that begins the first line of the poem with *aleph* (the first letter in the Hebrew alphabet) and each subsequent line with the next letter in the alphabet. The intention is clear. The praise of the faithful is to be offered not simply in the best of times, but in all times and circumstances, because God is faithful in all times.

If praise offered on the richest days of blessing is rooted in the soil of gratitude, praise offered in the darkest hours springs from a confidence in God's

1. James L. Mays, *Psalms*, Interpretation (Louisville, KY: John Knox Press, 1994), 437.

^{14}The Lord upholds all who are falling,
  and raises up all who are bowed down.
^{15}The eyes of all look to you,
  and you give them their food in due season.
^{16}You open your hand,
  satisfying the desire of every living thing.
^{17}The Lord is just in all his ways,
  and kind in all his doings.
^{18}The Lord is near to all who call on him,
  to all who call on him in truth.

Exegetical Perspective

The Orderliness of Praise. Psalm 145, from which the reading for today is taken, is an acrostic psalm; each line of the poem begins with a subsequent letter of the Hebrew alphabet. From the *aleph* beginning the phrase "I will extol you" (*'aromimka;* v. 1) to the *tav* at the beginning of the last line "The praise of God may my mouth speak" (*tehillat YHWH yedabber pi;* v. 21), the psalm portrays its subject "from A to Z."[1] The acrostic psalms generally have a twofold effect: they emphasize the inclusiveness and the orderliness of their subject. Here in Psalm 145 the subject is the praise of God, and that praise is portrayed as overwhelmingly inclusive of all creation and as completely consistent with all of its parts. Since the psalm portrays the worship of God as consistent and orderly, an overview of the whole psalm is in order before turning to the specific reading for today.

The Outline and Dialogue of Praise. The lines of the psalm comprise two different types of statements: praises addressed *to* God and praises describing a quality or action *about* God. The broad outline of the psalm includes four panels. The first three panels are composed of multiple lines of praise to God,

1. The line that starts with the letter *nun* is missing from the Hebrew text, but is reproduced in the NRSV as v. 13b and is based upon many other ancient versions and translations.

Homiletical Perspective

"Dad, tell me a Tommy Papreck story." The phrase became a common one from my two girls as they prepared for sleep. My wife and I had come across an article about children's fascination with the stories of their parents' upbringing. According to the writer, children yearn to know and find security in the stories of their family origins. While thinking this might be an exercise in self-indulgence (I do resist stories where I am the hero), I have found instead that it became a time of their fascination about the events and stories that shaped their mother, father, aunts, uncles, and grandparents.

The writer's suggestion seems to have come true. The escapades of their father and the friends of his youth, Tommy Papreck, John Costanza, and Tim MacKimm, became for these two girls more than tales of young boys growing up in post–World War II suburban Chicago. They provided a window into their origins—a base, a context for knowing who they are and a foundation from which they can sense their own futures.

Psalm 145 is a psalm of community family storytelling. While categorized as a psalm of praise, it is praise founded in the stories of the community. "[T]he invocation to worship was based fundamentally upon a 'root experience' of liberation from bondage that was enshrined in the memory of

Psalm 145:10-18

Theological Perspective

While we may marvel at the clockwork precision of the universal machine, it can also leave us with a feeling of coldness, emptiness, and fear. "The eternal silence of these infinite spaces terrifies me," wrote Blaise Pascal, one of the first inhabitants of the scientific worldview.

To this experience, Christian theology responds with the doctrines of *creation* and *conservation*. These doctrines help us see that nature is no blind power, but that God is its author: God created natural substances and their accidents and gave them their causal powers. Moreover, God is involved with this natural world by upholding it from moment to moment. If God were to withdraw this conserving power, the world would at once disappear, as the image on your television screen disappears once you hit the off button on your remote control. Both the doctrine of creation and the doctrine of conservation thus give meaning to an otherwise empty causal nexus. They explain that this world is neither blind nor empty but was designed by a God who continuously holds it in the hollow of God's hand. While science can teach the "how" of our universe, faith teaches us the "why." We may read Psalm 145 as an expression of that belief.

However, it would not be enough to read this psalm as an expression of the "why" of creation. Some would indeed prefer to leave it to that; these are theologians and believers who see no particular problem with combining the scientific worldview with the doctrines of creation and conservation, but who do see a problem with a third doctrine, that of *special divine action* within the causal nexus of the universe. In their view, God and religion are useful to give meaning to an otherwise empty universe, but there is no place for an additional divine action within this world. Such action is excluded, so the idea seems, by the very same causal nexus established and upheld in creation and conservation. Why? Because special divine activity would be incompatible with the laws of nature as disclosed by science.

If that is the view of the world we hold, we will have a hard time with the lectionary readings for this Sunday. We could try to read Psalm 145 as no more than a song about God's creation and conservation, but in the context of the lectionary, that is not good enough. The lectionary frames this psalm with two Bible stories that speak of God's "giving food in due season" (v. 15)—not just of God's conserving the causal nexus of creation, but actively being involved in this nexus—feeding a hundred hungry prophets with twenty loaves of barley and fresh ears of grain,

Pastoral Perspective

unfailing goodness even when that is not immediately visible. The faithful confession of the psalmist is that God is King. The heart of the psalm speaks of God's kingdom four times (vv. 10–13). Praise is the act of proclaiming God's sovereignty. The sovereignty of God is not limited to the mountaintop moments of happiness and comfort. The power of God is known by the fallen and the bowed down (v. 14). God's power is known as gracious love. The psalmist, in gratitude and faith, proclaims God's faithful love for all.

As the Talmud instructs, praise borrows language from the world to come, or the "kingdom," as the psalmist describes it. Praise offered every day by God's children reveals something of the world to come. The psalmist invites all to live in this new world, where God's power is demonstrated as gracious love. The world is reshaped so that those who are bowed down are raised up and those who are falling are lifted up (v. 14), and those who hunger for life are nourished (vv. 15–16).

This new world is voiced in eschatological tones, but the psalmist is not dreaming of heaven or solely of some time in the future. The salvation of God (v. 19) is known by God's faithfulness in the present. As Richard Foster once said, "The real issue [with salvation] is not so much us getting into heaven as it is getting heaven into us."[2] Those who voice the *Tehillah* daily are children of the world to come. The Talmud does not promise that they *will be* children of the world to come, but rather, like Jesus' present-tense blessing in the Beatitudes, that all who praise God in all circumstances *are* children of the world to come. The hymn of praise is the highway on which the world to come journeys toward us. Those who cry out to God know God's salvation or abundant life.

The salvation of God (v. 19) is not a reward for faithful praise. Those who confess the reign of God in every circumstance do not speak of reward, but know themselves to be connected to the King.

On a Sunday afternoon during my high school years, I was driving home from my part-time job selling shoes at a local mall. It was spitting rain, as it had all day. The way home required a ten-minute trip on the interstate. As quickly as these things always happen, two cars in front of me collided, resulting in a collection of swerving and braking, and a few horns honking. I ended up number three in a four-car pileup that brought the interstate to a halt. No one was hurt, at least not physically. Soon

2. Richard Foster, "Salvation Is for Life," *Theology Today* 61 (2004): 299.

each of which is rounded off with one or two lines of praise about God. Thus, the first panel includes the praises to God in verses 1–2, which is then rounded off with the praises about God in verse 3. The second panel includes the praises to God in verses 4–7, which are rounded off with the explication about God in verses 8–9. The third panel—which coincides with the beginning of the reading for today—includes the praises to God in verses 10–13a, which are rounded off with two statements about God in verses 13b–14. The fourth panel is organized as the inverse of the third; it begins with two statements to God in verses 15–16 and culminates in four statements of praise about God in vv. 17–20. The psalm concludes with verse 21, which serves as a parallel with the opening line, both of which describe the psalmist's own praise of God, with an emphasis on blessing the divine name "forever and ever" (vv. 1, 21).

The Wide Scope of Praise. Although the psalm is organized as an acrostic and even though its dialogic format between praise to God and praise about God is clear, it is by no means static in its reflection of the blessing and worship of God. The psalm moves from its initial panel through each of the remaining panels, growing in its implications about the realm and reach of God. The first panel (vv. 1–3) focuses upon the psalmist himself and his or her own individual praise of God's name. It ends, however, with the acknowledgment that God's greatness is larger than one person can discern: "his greatness is unsearchable." The second panel (vv. 4–9) widens the source of the praise to include multiple generations and widens the scope of the praise to include the glorious splendor of God's majesty and God's abundant goodness. The panel concludes by widening the scope even further, including all people and, indeed, all that God has made.

The Ever-Widening Scope of Praise. Beginning in verse 10, with the third panel, the source and effect of praise widen even further. The psalmist calls for all God's works and all God's faithful ones to join in the blessing of God. This invitation is addressed to all humanity (*libney ha'adam*) and focuses upon God's glorious reign and power. Moreover, God's reign is expansive not only spatially, but also temporally: God's "dominion endures throughout all generations" (v. 13). The closing acclamation praises God for who God is ("faithful in all his words and gracious in all his deeds") and for what God does

the people," writes Bernhard Anderson. "Israel's praise is a reflex to the prior action of God that moves the people, as one psalmist testifies, to seek God's 'face' (Ps. 27:8) in worship."[1]

Because of the stories of our fathers and mothers, Abraham and Sarah, Jacob, Rachel and Leah, Moses and Miriam, we know we have a future. Because of these "root experiences," we know of God's power and splendor. We know that God is faithful in word and merciful in deed. Our father was a wandering Aramean led by God. Our ancestors were slaves who were brought out and exiles who were led home through the mighty work of God. Ours is a tradition of telling stories that lead to hope and praise.

Many articles on leadership say how important it is for community leaders to be bearers of community stories. We are to be vision carriers, keepers of the flame, who remind people again and again of who they are and from where they have come. We are the ones who "enshrine" the stories in the memory of the people. It is our telling of the stories that can lead us to praise.

In preparation for the sermon, the preacher might ask, in what chapter is my community at this time? Is this a period when the praises come easily, and for the right reasons? Is this a period when the congregation is singing, "How long, O Lord?" What stories are appropriate for the chapter the congregation is in? Is this a period when our imagination needs to be expanded, stretched, broadened? What stories of our congregational ancestors might be available to speak to this chapter? What biblical stories might connect to this time and help us to see that our sojourning ancestors have passed this way before? Which stories can bring us to the place of trust and praise? Where has God brought us out? Where have we seen the faithfulness and mercy of God?

When seeking to proclaim the faithfulness of God, we are likely to encounter the response: "If God is faithful, why does such pain exist?" The experienced reality of pain and suffering in the world often creates a sense of dissonance, a sense of contrariness, to such proclamations of faithfulness and praise.

This is where narrative can free us from an either/or response to this question. The narrative allows us to experience tangibly, incarnationally, a story that is large enough to encompass the existential paradox of pain and faithfulness. It is Job

1. Bernhard W. Anderson, *Out of the Depths* (Louisville, KY: Westminster John Knox Press, 2000), 33.

Psalm 145:10-18

Theological Perspective

and feeding a five-thousand strong crowd with five barley loaves and two fish. This is more than God's giving meaning to an otherwise empty and random world; this is God "satisfying the desires of the living" (v. 10), more than natural causation can do.

The intimate relationship that Psalm 145 suggests between God and creation led our medieval theological predecessors to develop a model that still makes sense in the context of contemporary scientific findings. They believed in the idea of double causality: every natural effect is produced both by God and by created substances, so that the latter determine the specific nature of the causal act only if God cooperates with them. For example, when you put a kettle with water on the fire and the fire heats up the water, this happens only because God causally cooperates with the fire to produce heat. As far as we know, God very often does cooperate with nature's causal powers. But sometimes God does not. Then the fire flares up, but no heat is produced, and the young men leave the furnace of blazing fire unharmed (Dan. 3). Sometimes God produces by God's own causal powers, accelerating what would take natural powers a season, as when a few loaves feed a whole crowd.

What is interesting about the medieval model is not just its attempt to bring scientific knowledge and religious belief into one coherent picture, but also its understanding of a world in which God, as it were, walks in and out. Divine miracles are not seen as rare exceptions in a machine that otherwise continues without much input from God. No, with everything that happens God is intimately involved. God just works in different ways. Sometimes, when needed, God provides food by immediately causing it to appear. At other times, when our needs are less pressing, God takes the time of the season. In either case, "the LORD is near to all who call on him" (v. 18).[1]

EDWIN CHR. VAN DRIEL

Pastoral Perspective

we were surrounded by flashing blue lights and officers with notepads. These were the days before cell phones, so I asked a police officer if I could walk down the exit ramp to a gas station and call my mother. I walked to the gas station and put a dime in the pay phone. She answered.

"Mom," I said. That is all I said. I do not know how moms can tell, but with no more than one word, they can tell that trouble has come. She said, "Tell me where you are; I will be right there." I do not know what I expected her to say. Perhaps she would tell me to be more careful. Perhaps she would remind me of what was going to happen to my auto insurance. Perhaps she would rehearse how the weather conditions meant that I should have been driving more carefully. But it was not time for those conversations. She simply said, "Tell me where you are; I will be right there."

To repeat the *Tehillah* every day requires the children of God to give voice to praise on the days of richest blessing as well as the days of journey in the dark valley. Particularly when we have fallen or the powers of the world have bowed us down and we hunger for a life that nourishes the soul, praise uttered in these harsh times does not fall to the floor as empty words, but rests in the ears and heart of the Sovereign One. The psalmist promises, "The LORD is near to all who call on him." My God the King says, "Tell me where you are; I will be right there." In the presence of the King, God's children know they are children of the world to come.

TOM ARE JR.

---

1. A helpful book on these matters is John Polkinghorne, *Science and Providence: God's Interaction with the World* (West Conshohocken, PA: Templeton Foundation Press, 2005).

Exegetical Perspective

("upholds all who are falling, and raises up all who are bowed down"). The predominant word throughout the third panel is "all" (*kol*), which appears seven times in six lines.

The Inclusiveness of God's Reign. The invitation addressed to all humanity to praise God in the previous panel (v. 12) finds its response in the final panel, where God's regal relationship with all people is made explicit. The six lines of the final panel form an *inclusio* relationship with each other. As a response to the message about God's provision in panel three, here in panel four every living thing looks (*yesabberu*) to God for sustenance (v. 15). In its parallel line in verse 20, it is God who watches (*shomer*) all who love God, and withholds sustenance from the wicked. In verse 16, God opens God's hand and satisfies the desire of all living things. Likewise, in verse 19, God fulfills the desire of all who fear God and rescues them. The central two lines of the panel, verses 17–18, proclaim God's justice, faithfulness, and nearness to all who call out for help. Throughout the final panel, again the predominant word is "all" (*kol*), now found eight times in six lines.

The Communicability of Praise. The final line of the psalm, verse 21, parallels the first line, but with an important difference. In verse 1 the psalmist describes his desire to extol God, whom he calls "my God and King," and conveys his need to bless "your name" forever. The first line is, therefore, a personal expression of praise from a singular individual, spoken directly to God with whom he has a personal relationship ("my God"). Through the gradual widening and extending of God's praise throughout the psalm, however, the final line likewise broadens the implications for praise. Although the individual psalmist still speaks "the praise of the LORD," the result is no longer simply his own blessing of God's name. As a result of the psalmist's praise—now broadened and deepened by means of the psalm—"all flesh" joins in the chorus and blesses God's holy name forever and ever.

ROY L. HELLER

Homiletical Perspective

proclaiming from the desolation of his loss, "I know that my redeemer lives" (Job 19:25). He proclaims it with conviction, apart from any tangible signs. Even as the "things" of his life are restored, they do not replace what he has lost. Nothing can. His statement is one found in the soul, not in things. How can we say, "We know that our Redeemer lives" from the desert? How can the community practice its narrative enough that belief in the faithfulness of God is part of our spiritual DNA, our communal genetics?

What is it about gratitude that generates more gratitude? There is something contagious about thankfulness. We hear of its health benefits, and we know intuitively of its ability to generate life within us. What does it take to create a culture of gratitude, a culture of praise? How might the sermon be the avenue of thankfulness that elicits praise? How do we tell the stories that "enshrine memory," that enshrine the acts of God in us?

When I was doing a unit of clinical pastoral education, one of the wards to which I was assigned was for persons with strong manifestations of schizophrenia. We offered Holy Communion each week, and the homily was always a challenge for me. How does one offer reflections to persons whose minds regularly race from one thing to another? One week the text was Paul's words about the body of Christ and our spiritual gifts. This preacher was filled with gratitude (rooted in cowardice) that it was Chaplain Randy Pumphrey's week to preach. Randy began to move about the room and mention various acts that the residents had done on behalf of others on the ward. After offering these observations he said, "And that is how you are the body of Christ." I was transformed. He had recalled the acts of the people in a way that allowed them to see their participation in the mighty acts of God.

How do we as preachers do that for our respective communities? How do we see the mighty acts of God in the people around us and recall them in a way that elicits the praise of God? This is our legacy and privilege as preachers: to tell the stories, to enshrine memory, and to elicit praise for the faithfulness of God.

TODD M. DONATELLI

Ephesians 3:14-21

¹⁴For this reason I bow my knees before the Father, ¹⁵from whom every family in heaven and on earth takes its name. ¹⁶I pray that, according to the riches of his glory, he may grant that you may be strengthened in your inner being with power through his Spirit, ¹⁷and that Christ may dwell in your hearts through faith, as you are being rooted and grounded in love. ¹⁸I pray that you may have the power to comprehend, with all the saints, what is the breadth and length and height and depth, ¹⁹and to know the love of Christ that surpasses knowledge, so that you may be filled with all the fullness of God.

²⁰Now to him who by the power at work within us is able to accomplish abundantly far more than all we can ask or imagine, ²¹to him be glory in the church and in Christ Jesus to all generations, forever and ever. Amen.

Theological Perspective

The Confession of 1967 of the Presbyterian Church (U.S.A.) is based on 2 Corinthians 5:18–19 and the theme of reconciliation. It is divided into three parts, and reflects a Barthian approach to theology. The first part describes God's work of reconciliation in Jesus Christ. The second part describes the ministry of reconciliation to which the church is called because of what God has done in Christ, and also describes the equipment Christ gives to the church "as means of fulfilling its service of God" in the world. The brief third part describes the church's hope for the fulfillment of reconciliation in the kingdom of God, and concludes with the last two verses of our text, Ephesians 3:20–21, the ascription of praise to the God who "is able to do far more abundantly than all we ask or think."

It is appropriate that the Confession of 1967 concludes by quoting Ephesians 3:20–21, because both documents affirm the inseparability of worship and discipleship, of theology and ethics. Worship and discipleship are distinct, but they are also inseparable. The Christian tradition has long known that how one lives in relation to God is inseparable from how one lives with one's neighbors. The inseparability of the first table (the first four commandments) of the Ten Commandments from the second table (the last six commandments) and

Pastoral Perspective

Our lection begins with these words: "For this reason I bow my knees before the Father, from whom every family in heaven and on earth takes its name." Which begs one to ask, for *what* reason? Even with the *lectio continuo* of these summer readings from Ephesians, 3:1–13 is omitted from the lectionary. Reading back through these beautiful verses, we discover how Paul[1] revisits the theme from the prologue: God's will to include the Gentiles in salvation. That mystery is now revealed. Because of Paul's trust in God's purpose, he is confident, and perceives even his sufferings as being for the glory of this church. Indeed, he is a prisoner for Christ Jesus for the sake of "you Gentiles" (3:1).

"For this reason I bow my knees before the Father *(patēr)*, from whom every family *(patria)* in heaven and on earth takes its name." Paul is filled with joy and gratitude that all followers of Jesus Christ are part of God's own family—there is no "us" and "them," insider and outsider. All are part of the family of God.

He then begins a poignant prayer, a prayer that could be offered by all pastors who love their people. You could say Paul's hope is that they would be taken

1. Questions of the authorship and audience of Ephesians remain. For the purpose of this reflection, I refer to the author as Paul and his audience as the church in Ephesus.

Exegetical Perspective

With this passage, the author reaches the end of the first section of the letter, which has, as some of Paul's other letters, concerned mainly doctrinal or theological discussions. That exposition runs until 3:13. After our concluding passage (3:14–21), the author turns, in the second half of the letter (4:1–6:20), to an application of these theological points, admonishing his readers about how to lead lives worthy of the faith they have espoused.

In this concluding section, the author completes the prayer with which he begins the letter (1:15, 17) but which quickly becomes an exposition of the faith his readers have accepted. A doxology completes this section (3:20–21; see Rom. 11:36 for a similar doxology interposed between exposition and admonition).

The phrase "for this reason" can look either backward or forward. In this case it probably looks forward to the purpose clause that follows (*hiva*, "in order that"). This same phrase introduced the chapter (3:1) but was not followed there by a clearly stated reason. Perhaps the repetition of this phrase here indicates this is the reason Paul had in mind when he wrote the phrase in v. 1.

The word *patria* (v. 15, NRSV "family") is rare in the NT. Normally it means "tribe" or "lineage" (cf. Luke 2:4), but it also has the sense of "extended

Homiletical Perspective

Imagine a sermon in the form of a prayer. Here, in the midst of this letter to the infant church in Ephesus, Paul prays. He prays for the congregation. He knows that he cannot give the congregation what it needs in order to be sustained in the face of the struggles that lie ahead. He knows too that being the church is not a self-help project. The church must learn to rely upon God, not itself. Perhaps the sermon will take its shape from the shape of this text, describing the prayer that the preacher has for the congregation.

When a text begins, as this one does, with "For this reason . . . ," the preacher needs to read back in order to locate the passage within the logic of the letter. This passage follows on Paul's description of his ministry to the Gentiles. He is a messenger of the "boundless riches of Christ" (v. 8) to those who were once beyond the pale. This is "the plan of the mystery hidden for ages in God who created all things" (v. 9). This description of the outreaching mission of God that gives Paul his vocation concludes with the apostle bowing his knees "before the Father, from whom every family in heaven and on earth takes its name" (v. 14).

This suggests a dramatic beginning for the sermon. The preacher turns in awe to the God met in Jesus Christ, acknowledging the One who is the

Ephesians 3:14-21

Theological Perspective

the inseparability of the first three petitions of the Lord's Prayer from the second three demonstrate that theology and ethics are bound to one another in the core texts and faith of the Christian tradition.

Our text from Ephesians 3 is a prayer that serves as a hinge between the first three chapters of Ephesians—its descriptions of what God has done by gathering up all things in Christ (1:10), breaking down the dividing wall of hostility, and creating in Christ "one new humanity" (2:14–15)—and the last three chapters of the epistle, which instruct readers about what they are to do in response. They are "to lead a life worthy of the calling to which [they] have been called" (4:1). Prayer stands at the intersection of reflection on what God has done (reflection that can take the form of theology) and obedient discipleship in God's world.

The writer of Ephesians tells us there is a reason why he (or she) kneels before the Father, presumably the same reason mentioned at the beginning of the chapter (3:1). What brings the writer to his knees is the mystery to which he has several times alluded (1:9; 3:3, 4, 5, 9)—the mystery of God's will, the mystery that in Christ Jesus there is now peace between God and those previously estranged from God and peace between those previously hostile to one another, the mystery of the wisdom of God made known in the boundless riches of Christ. The writer does not believe this mystery that evokes prayer and worship can be discovered or known; it can only be received (made known) by revelation.

How does one know by means of revelation? This is not how we usually use the words "know" and "knowledge." When I say that I know something, I usually mean I am the subject of this activity, the one who knows, and what I know is the object apprehended by me. Revelation stands all this on its head. In revelation I am not the one who knows, but the one who is known, and what I know is the experience of being known by someone other than myself. This is a peculiar form of knowledge, a form of knowledge the writer describes by means of the term "revelation," which, among other things, suggests this knowledge is a gift and not a discovery, and that the Spirit and not the individual is the primary agent in this disclosure. As H. Richard Niebuhr put it, "Revelation means the moment in our history through which we know ourselves to be known from beginning to end, in which we are apprehended by the knower; it means the self-

Pastoral Perspective

over by Christ. He prays that they will be strengthened in their *inner being*—from the inside out—by the power of God's Spirit. This is not a matter of becoming stronger in themselves, but by having Christ dwell in their hearts. He then switches the metaphor from buildings to botany, describing their need to be rooted and grounded in love. He prays for their comprehension of that which is beyond all knowledge, the vastness of the love of Christ, so they may be filled with all the fullness of God.

The issue is letting Christ in to change us. Having Christ dwell in our hearts is akin to having a new person move into your household. If they're just visiting, it is all rather easy; you simply offer hospitality and try to practice good manners. But if someone moves in to stay, everything changes. At first you might try to hold on to your familiar patterns and routines, and the new member may work hard to accommodate you and stay out of the way. But eventually they make their mark. Conversations change. Relationships realign. Household tasks increase and responsibilities shift. So it is when Christ moves in to the hearts of Christians. This isn't merely tweaking old patterns; everything changes.

Eugene Peterson's paraphrase in *The Message* captures this sense: "that Christ will live in you as you open the door and invite him in."

Writer Anne Lamott tells of her profound experience of Christ indwelling in her. She was unmarried, pregnant, and decided to have an abortion. She coped with the pain in her usual way, by smoking dope and getting drunk. When she started hemorrhaging a week later, she sobered up fast.

It was that night she became aware of someone in the room with her. She writes, "The feeling was so strong that I actually turned on the light for a moment to make sure no one was there—of course, there wasn't. But after a while, in the dark again, I knew beyond any doubt that it was Jesus." What she felt was appalled. In her circle of family and friends, nobody was a Christian. They were all like the Ephesians: worldly, sophisticated, and in need of no one but themselves. But Jesus remained in the corner, "watching me with patience and love, and I squinched my eyes shut, but that didn't help because that's not what I was seeing him with."

She had been going to church for some Sundays, drawn in to a funky little church mostly by the music. The next Sunday she went back. She could not escape the feelings. "It was as if the people were

Exegetical Perspective

family." Some have suggested this refers to the fact that in NT times the father decided the names of all his children. Thus, God who names all peoples is the Father of all. Or perhaps here the reference is to the normal ancient practice of the father exercising primary control in the family. Then it would mean all benevolent authority that exists draws its origin and inspiration from the way God rules over the whole creation (heavenly and earthly "families"), that is, in love (v. 17). This would then reflect the general tenor of the whole passage, which is based on the power and authority of the God who in the Son acts benevolently toward human beings.

On "the riches of his glory" (v. 16), see Romans 9:23, which also refers to God's action toward his creatures. The reason Paul bows his knees to God in supplication is to ask that the gracious God may empower his readers' inner selves ("your inner being") through the Holy Spirit in order that Christ may indwell their hearts through their faith (on "inner self," cf. Rom. 7:22). For the people of NT times, the "heart" was the seat of intelligence and thought. Contrary to our culture's use of this metaphor, the heart was where thought, rather than emotion, originated. Emotions were regarded as centered in the area below the "heart"; the Greek word for feeling compassion derives from the term for "inward parts" (cf. the term "the bowels of compassion" in some older translations).

Since divine love is the basis for their lives ("rooted and grounded in love"), the reason for Christ to indwell them is that they may understand what the dimensions of that life-controlling love truly are, namely (v. 19), that it is a love that is unavailable to, and hence superior to, knowledge (cf. 1 Cor. 13:2). No one is able, in other words, to reason the way to knowledge of the kind of love God grants to those who are filled and controlled by faith in Christ.

The word "saints" or "holy ones" (v. 18) is the regular word Paul uses for baptized Christians, independent of their individual actions. He can even address the wayward Corinthians as "saints" (1 Cor. 1:2). The word is thus the equivalent of "Christians" or "believers," and reflects the word *patria* at the beginning of our passage (v. 15); both words refer to the family of Christian believers. To believe in Christ is to be a saint; it is then up to those saints to live lives that accord with their status. Hence the division of the letter—first the affirmation that the addressees are saints (chaps. 1–3), then admonitions on how to live accordingly (chaps. 4–6).

Homiletical Perspective

namesake of every human family. The theme running through Ephesians continues here. There is no nation, clan, or family—no person—who is beyond the love of God. This may seem an obvious claim in a church on a Sunday morning. But it may still be difficult for the congregation to believe. Even on a sunny summer morning, the gathered congregation brings together people with a myriad of secret hurts, private shames, and lost hopes. The congregation itself may be struggling to trust in God as it grays and dwindles. So the turn to God is made because only God can help. And God's help is needed now.

The sermon, like the prayer offered in this text, may now move in three parts. Paul intercedes twice for the congregation—once for its heart and once for its mind—before he offers a remarkable benediction. Paul begins by praying for power in the congregation's inner being. He longs for Christ to live in the hearts of the congregation as it is "being rooted and grounded in love" (v. 17). In praying for inner strengthening and for Christ's indwelling, Paul knows that the church is at risk. Instead of warning the congregation to be on guard lest it lose faith, he turns to God and asks for the power that is needed in the church. A sermon that takes its lead from Paul will name the places where the congregation needs strengthening in its "inner being" (v. 16). This longing for a life "rooted and grounded in love" is a way of confessing the truth—to God and to one another—that we are at risk of living a life together that is rooted and grounded in fear and self-preservation rather than in Christ.

Now the sermon can shift from a prayer for the congregation's heart to an intercession for its mind: "I pray that you may have the power to comprehend ... to know the love of Christ that surpasses knowledge" (vv. 18–19). This love, says Paul, is cosmically immense: "what is the breadth and length and height and depth" (v. 18). If the first intercession in this sermonic prayer is that the congregation experience the love of God in its heart and soul, then the second intercession is that the church comes to grasp in its intellect that this grace is utterly massive and awesome beyond adequate imagining. The preacher will struggle all week to find the words that will press the Sunday school language of "Jesus loves me" deeper, breaking this love open so that the sermon is not simply proclaiming a greeting card faith of clichés and platitudes. Perhaps the pastor knows the lifelong struggle of some in the

Ephesians 3:14-21

Theological Perspective

disclosing of that eternal knower."[1] In Ephesians what Christians know is "the boundless riches of Christ" (3:8)—boundless in that the breadth and length and height and depth (i.e., the limits) of God's grace in Jesus Christ are nothing less than the fullness of God, a boundlessness that is beyond the human imagination, but a boundlessness that includes and reconciles all things. Hence, the writer prays that his readers "may have the power to comprehend" and "to know the love of Christ that surpasses knowledge" (3:19).

How can one know that which surpasses knowledge? If knowledge is limited to what reason can affirm, how can reason know that which is beyond the limits of reason? That would appear to be impossible. As Immanuel Kant has taught us, if there are limits to what reason can know, then whatever is beyond those limits cannot be known by reason. Reason is not, however, the only human faculty that "knows." The heart has its reasons and its own knowledge as well. What is known in revelation, according to Ephesians, is "the love of Christ that surpasses knowledge" (3:19). It surpasses knowledge in that it dwells not only in the intellect but also (and perhaps primarily) in the heart. The boundless riches of Christ are made known by the Spirit, and when that happens, Christ "dwell[s] in your heart through faith, as you are being rooted and grounded in love" (v. 17). It is in this sense that Christian knowledge is always something more than belief, something more than what the intellect can affirm. The heart has its reasons the mind does not fathom, or as Ephesians puts it, for those in whom Christ dwells there is a "power at work within us . . . able to accomplish abundantly far more than all we can ask or imagine" (v. 20). It is in response to this One who is not only at work within us, but also at work in the breadth and length and height and depth of creation, that Christians are driven to their knees in worship.

GEORGE W. STROUP

Pastoral Perspective

singing in between the notes, weeping and joyful at the same time, and I felt like their voices or *something* was rocking me in its bosom, holding me like a scared kid, and I opened up to that feeling— and it washed over me."

When she got home to her houseboat, she opened the door, hung her head and said to Jesus, "F— it: I quit." She actually said this out loud: "All right. You can come in."[2]

We pastors should not be under the illusion that because worshipers are in church, they have let Christ live in them. We cannot assume they have tasted the breadth and length and height and depth of the love of Christ. Even if the persons in the pews have let Christ into their lives, they may merely be offering a grudging guest room or a couch. In J. K. Rowling's Harry Potter novels, Harry's aunt and uncle relegate their poor nephew to a cramped cupboard under the stairs. How much room are we willing to give up? For Christ? For others in "the family"?

Paul's prayer is full of hope for something different: for Christ to take over these people, and strengthen them by God's own Spirit. His prayer is for both power and love; power to comprehend the depth and breadth of Christ's love, and so be filled with the fullness of God.

How fitting that our passage ends with doxology. Paul's praise is grounded in gratitude for the power at work within us that can accomplish abundantly far more than we can ask or imagine. Beyond our small hopes, beyond our small lives, beyond our meager imaginations, God is at work, fulfilling the plan laid out for all eternity. To God be the glory.

KAREN CHAKOIAN

---

1. H. Richard Niebuhr, *The Meaning of Revelation* (New York: Macmillan, 1962), 154.

2. Anne Lamott, *Traveling Mercies: Some Thoughts on Faith* (New York: Pantheon, 1999), 48–50.

Exegetical Perspective

There has been considerable discussion regarding the difficulty of determining to what the four dimensions of breadth, length, height, and depth refer. Perhaps the best suggestion, adopted above, is to connect them to the love of Christ in the following verse, which would then give the meaning that we are to comprehend (*katalabesthai*, v. 18) and to know (*gnōnai*, v. 19) the love of Christ, which surpasses even our ability to know it. The oxymoron contained in knowing something that is inherently beyond knowledge points further to the surpassing love of Christ. Only when Christ dwells in our hearts through faith, leading us to be rooted and grounded in love (v. 17), do we have the ability even to be aware of that love that is in fact beyond any ability of humans to know. The fullness of God's grace that is to fill us (v. 19b) can be received, but it cannot be fully understood.

This doxology (vv. 20–21) mirrors the doxology with which the letter began (1:2–3), thus rounding out the first section of the letter. This concluding doxology reflects the theme of God's all-surpassing power, namely, in this case the power to accomplish more than his family could ask, or even imagine. Such power and benevolence through Jesus Christ represent a divine glory that is eternal.

An example of the importance of the church for our author is the fact that in the concluding words of this doxology (v. 21), God's glory reflected in God's Son is also reflected in God's church. This doxology thus solves the problem concerning the location of the "heavenly places," a phrase found in the opening doxology (1:3). Here it becomes clear that the church is where Christians are blessed in Christ "in the heavenly places," not in some mystical realm or paranormal experience.

Our passage thus begins with an act of worship (kneeling) and ends with a doxology—a fitting form for a description of the benevolent power of a God whose generosity is not limited by human inability to ask for or understand it.

PAUL J. ACHTEMEIER

Homiletical Perspective

congregation to understand and believe in God's love for all people. Now instead of trying to convince or explain the love of God, the preacher can confess to the congregation that only God can answer this prayer for understanding. Like Paul, the pastor longs for the congregation to be "filled with all the fullness of God" (v. 19).

Is this asking too much? Is it possible that a congregation with all its weaknesses and troubles and fears and misunderstanding can be filled with God, indwelt by Christ? Paul knows that the congregation is wondering how this prayer can possibly be answered. The preacher will want to name the same wondering in the present context. It is the reason that the sermon rightly ends where Paul ends this text—focused on God: "Now to him who by the power at work within us is able to accomplish abundantly far more than all we can ask or imagine, to him be glory" (vv. 20–21).

Paul gives the preacher the words to testify that God is already at work in the congregation. This massive, holy power is present even in our fumbling attempts to live faithfully, lovingly, and courageously in the face of our troubles. Our daring prayers to be strengthened in faith and to comprehend God's grace are not asking too much. In fact, God is able to "accomplish abundantly far more than all we can ask or imagine" (v. 20)! In announcing this gospel truth, the preacher may well discover that the very thing that has been prayed for has been given. The congregation rises stronger in faith, grounded more firmly in love, and more deeply filled by the fullness of a God who answers prayer.

EDWIN SEARCY

John 6:1-21

¹After this Jesus went to the other side of the Sea of Galilee, also called the Sea of Tiberias. ²A large crowd kept following him, because they saw the signs that he was doing for the sick. ³Jesus went up the mountain and sat down there with his disciples. ⁴Now the Passover, the festival of the Jews, was near. ⁵When he looked up and saw a large crowd coming toward him, Jesus said to Philip, "Where are we to buy bread for these people to eat?" ⁶He said this to test him, for he himself knew what he was going to do. ⁷Philip answered him, "Six months' wages would not buy enough bread for each of them to get a little." ⁸One of his disciples, Andrew, Simon Peter's brother, said to him, ⁹"There is a boy here who has five barley loaves and two fish. But what are they among so many people?" ¹⁰Jesus said, "Make the people sit down." Now there was a great deal of grass in the place; so they sat down, about five thousand in all. ¹¹Then Jesus took the loaves, and when he had given thanks, he distributed them to those who were seated; so also the fish, as much as they wanted. ¹²When they

Theological Perspective

The Trouble with Miracles. One of those "cute" prayers of children asks, "Dear God, how come you don't do any miracles now?" The Gospels seem to abound in miracles attributed to Jesus—two of the best known are given, in this passage, the special "spin" that we recognize as Johannine: the feeding of the five thousand and walking on the water. Such accounts seem to have impressed the premodern mind. The "argument from miracles," one of the traditional ways of demonstrating the existence of God, was applied by believers to the question of Jesus' identity: he must be divine because he is capable of these extraordinary feats, defying human comprehension. And of course the ultimate miracle, the resurrection, which the *earliest* Gospel (Mark) treats more as a concealing than a revealing—more as conundrum than clarification—is seen in popular religion as the final proof of Jesus' divine origin and nature. The author of John's Gospel cannot be accused of cheapening the miraculous in this way, but he does intend throughout his account to reinforce, in whatever ways open to him through the common tradition, his initial assertion that Jesus Christ is the very *Logos* ("Word") of God.

While appeal to the miraculous element was undoubtedly a natural—and even a necessary—aspect of the apologetic of the pre-Constantinian church, which had no external authority for its

Pastoral Perspective

Imagine that Jesus has posed his test (vv. 5–6) in a contemporary congregation. One might expect the trustees to echo Philip's money-management concern, pointing out that the congregation does not take in enough revenue to support such a project. The outreach committee might reinforce Andrew's position, stating that the congregation has earmarked only a small percentage of its income for mission giving and the proposed project's needs far exceed the allocated amount. The groups responsible for discipleship and worship may not even offer an opinion, as they are busy preparing for a fast-approaching religious festival. The building and grounds committee may assist with seating everyone on the lawn, although some members might worry about the effects of this event on the property's landscaping. It is likely that none of the congregation's boards or committees would expect to participate in a miracle, as that is not what they signed on for. They serve out of a sense of duty, or because they enjoy the work, or to contribute to a cause larger than themselves. They identify a few reasonable goals, set some workable plans in motion, and carry out their endeavors with the resources at hand. Their work together is not viewed as a venue for God's glory and mercy to break forth in the world, but as a means to facilitate the congregation's

were satisfied, he told his disciples, "Gather up the fragments left over, so that nothing may be lost." ¹³So they gathered them up, and from the fragments of the five barley loaves, left by those who had eaten, they filled twelve baskets. ¹⁴When the people saw the sign that he had done, they began to say, "This is indeed the prophet who is to come into the world."

¹⁵When Jesus realized that they were about to come and take him by force to make him king, he withdrew again to the mountain by himself.

¹⁶When evening came, his disciples went down to the sea, ¹⁷got into a boat, and started across the sea to Capernaum. It was now dark, and Jesus had not yet come to them. ¹⁸The sea became rough because a strong wind was blowing. ¹⁹When they had rowed about three or four miles, they saw Jesus walking on the sea and coming near the boat, and they were terrified. ²⁰But he said to them, "It is I; do not be afraid." ²¹Then they wanted to take him into the boat, and immediately the boat reached the land toward which they were going.

Exegetical Perspective

In today's reading (6:1–21), we encounter two of the better known—yet too often separated—miracle stories of Jesus: his feeding of the five thousand (vv. 1–15) and his walking on water (vv. 16–21). These stories were important for the early church. Indeed, the feeding narrative is the only miracle story that all four Gospels record, and accounts of Jesus' walking on the sea follow this narrative in all of the Gospels except Luke (see Matt. 14:13–33; Mark 6:35–52; Luke 9:10–17). The inclusion and coupling of these miracles in such diverse traditions ought to give modern interpreters cause to look more closely at these texts and their relationships. Indeed, for John, these revelatory stories unveil key aspects of Jesus' divine character and purpose.

These two passages follow the traditional four-part pattern for miracle stories: setting (vv. 1–4, 16–17), problem (vv. 5–9, 18), miracle (vv. 10–13, 19–20), and aftermath (vv. 14–15, 21). Interestingly, this pattern is more customary of the Synoptics than John (cf. 2:1–12; 4:43–54).

The Miracle of the Feeding (vv. 1–15). The pastoral setting of this passage stands in stark contrast to the preceding account of Jesus' ministry in Jerusalem. There, the Jewish leaders sought to kill Jesus because he healed on the Sabbath and called God his Father

Homiletical Perspective

There was a time when knowledge was power. It was assumed that if a person had the right data and the correct information, he or she could "objectively" use that knowledge to make the world a better place. During the age we call modernity, knowledge was the solution to all the problems that plagued humankind. It provided power over the world—and when used "objectively"—this power seemed limitless.

Now there is another reality, namely that of knowledge as powerlessness. What a strange irony that with the advent of the information age, wherein knowledge is everywhere, passivity is pervasive. The electronic media bring into our lives knowledge about weather, economics, politics, wars, famines. People "channel surf," going from a documentary on World War II to a reality show to a game show or sports event. If this is not enough, while we are watching one event, words are scrolling beneath the picture giving the facts about another.

In the face of all of this knowledge, it is common to find paralysis instead of empowerment. When faced with crises, famine, or AIDS in Africa, there is the temptation to ask, "In the face of so much, what can we do?" Rather than moving toward action, we are tempted by inertia. The pursuit of trivia is more appealing than the pursuit of answers to problems and solutions to crises. Knowledge thus becomes

John 6:1-21

Theological Perspective

claims; and while such an appeal might still, throughout the medieval and even the Reformation periods, carry a certain weight with ordinary—and even well-educated—people, it clearly does not impress the post-Enlightenment mind. And with very few exceptions, the protestations of "true believers" notwithstanding, most of us bring precisely that "mind" to our reading of ancient texts. Beyond failing to impress, the miracles of the Bible frequently repel belief today, or are subjected to the apparent need of contemporary homo sapiens to "joke" about once-sacred things—as in *Jesus Christ Superstar*, when Herod invites the holy "Superstar" to "walk across my swimming pool."

That is one aspect of what is wrong with appeal to the miraculous today: it does not work! In fact, as an apologetic it is more apt to reinforce doubt than encourage faith. But the trouble with miracles, used for apologetic purposes, is more subtle than that. When such attention is paid to these extraordinary "occurrences," the *truly* miraculous is obscured. For what is truly *wonder-full* in biblical terms is not that a (seeming) human could multiply loaves and fishes in so astounding a manner but that this ("truly human"[1]) human being could represent, by his words and deeds, such a sign of hope and healing that hundreds of needy people would follow him about, and feel that their hunger for "the bread of life" had been assuaged. What is truly awe-inspiring is not that someone could walk on the surface of the water without sinking, but that his presence among ordinary, insecure, and timid persons could calm their anxieties and cause *them* to walk where they feared to walk before—in the end, all the way to their own Golgothas. What is genuinely miraculous is not that a dead body should come to life again, but that through the journey with the crucified one, the disciple community was enabled to find hope on the far side of despair, faith that could live with doubt, and the courage to live beyond the sting of death. In other words, when the miraculous is identified too exclusively with those literally *incredible* things, the wonder of divine grace that permeates *the whole of life* is deprived of a witness. Then not only little children but every one of us wonders, "Dear God, why don't you do miracles any more?"

On the Other Hand . . . The foregoing seems to me both true and in need of being said today. In

Pastoral Perspective

survival as an organization. Their expectations and activities have lost their prophetic edge.

How would a congregation's work together be different if its members deliberately shared in Jesus' goal of revealing God's power through each act of ministry? Would members construct their worship and outreach activities differently if pointing to Christ's abundance in response to human hungers was their ongoing mission? This story suggests that the focus of ministry is not simply what good people decide is reasonable to undertake in order to meet basic needs. Instead, ministry is about multiplying resources so that what might have been a social handout becomes a revelation of amazing grace. Ministry should leave people exclaiming that prophets of transformation are active in the world, bringing hope to souls weary of oppressive social systems and values.

One popular interpretation of verses 9–13 is to explain the abundance of food generated in terms of people's deciding to share hidden stashes of provisions with their neighbors after being shamed by a young boy's willingness to give up his loaves and fish. While such an interpretation may explain what happened, it diminishes the formative potential of the story by downplaying the miraculous aspect. Instead of fostering an exploration of God's ability to act in surprising ways and transform human expectations, the shame-based version of the story focuses on the ability of persons to solve their own problems and justifies shaming as a means of motivating proper human behavior. God is no longer a miracle-worker unbounded by human laws, but a social manipulator who reminds people to share. Behavioral modification replaces amazing grace as the core of the story, and God is reduced to a divine therapist counseling charity among a greedy people who already know better. Can God not be much more in our lives than an omnipresent social worker reminding us of our duties?

Verse 15 invites reflection on how congregations might respond to social accolades that come their way because of ministries of abundance. The temptation in times of religious decline is to use good works as marketing tools, with the hope that coverage of activities in the local newspaper will generate interest among prospective members. Pastors and lay leaders may relish acknowledgment of their value and worth in the community as agents of transformation. Jesus models a different response to social approval, though. He withdraws from the public limelight to reflect in solitude on his ministry.

---

1. The Formula of Chalcedon insisted on it: he was *vere Homo*—truly and fully human!

Exegetical Perspective

(5:15–18). Now, on the other side of the Sea of Galilee, which is called the Sea of Tiberias only here in the Scriptures and serves as no small reminder of earthly rulers and their kingdoms, Jesus faces a different problem: many people are following him because they want to see more of his miraculous healing power (vv. 1–4).

Jesus surveys the crowd, lifts his eyes as from prayer, and speaks with his disciples (vv. 5–9). He asks Philip how they may feed the crowd—a "test" question showing that Jesus sees more than a crowd of people; he sees their need. Philip also sees their need and has even calculated that more than six months' wages would be necessary to buy bread for everyone just to have a taste. Andrew recognizes the emerging problem too and has been among the people, taking inventory of their resources. The only food he has uncovered are a boy's five barley loaves and two dried fish—traveling food of the poor. Andrew then asks the critical question, "What are they among so many?" In other words, how can the tremendous need before them be met by so small an offering?

Jesus takes the initiative to feed the hungry (vv. 10–13). The disciples follow his instructions and seat the people in the grass. Jesus then takes the boy's offering, blesses it, and distributes it to the crowd (in the Synoptics, the disciples help distribute the food). Whether the miracle is a supernatural multiplication of the food or the unleashing of compassion and generosity among the people is not altogether clear. The text is explicit, however, that Jesus causes everyone's hunger to be satisfied and twelve baskets of leftovers are collected (cf. Exod. 16:14f.), indicating the character of this new community where "leftovers"—both food and people—are neither insignificant nor abandoned.

In the aftermath, the people declare that Jesus is "the prophet who is to come into the world" (v. 14) and they want to make him king. Jesus, however, withdraws to the mountain by himself (v. 15), distancing himself from their plans to establish their own king and kingdom. They recognize him, but their recognition is at best partial and incomplete.

According to John, this incident occurs during Passover, the Feast of the Unleavened Bread, which celebrates God's deliverance of Israel from captivity in Egypt. God made it possible for the people to share a new life together with God in their midst. John's observance of the time suggests the exodus as the appropriate lens for viewing the feeding. The people, however, do not fully understand either the significance of the moment or Jesus' identity. They

Homiletical Perspective

escape from reality and does not empower but entertains.

The Gospel of John is all about knowledge as power. It is about the way, the truth, and the life. It is a knowledge that refuses to be objectified and controlled. It is not a knowledge that entertains or provides a satisfying experience. Rather, it is knowledge of a different kind, one that is expressly relational and deeply passionate. It is a knowledge that grounds the knowing event in the triune life as revealed in the incarnation of Jesus. "In Christian tradition," notes Parker Palmer, "truth is not a concept that 'works' but an incarnation that lives."[1]

The feeding of the multitude as portrayed in the Gospel of John addresses the temptation to shrug one's shoulders in the face of human need. It shows the finitude of human knowledge and points toward "the incarnation that lives." Here is a paralyzing situation. There is overwhelming need and few resources. Surveying the great crowd, Jesus asks a question that tests the limits of the disciples' knowledge: "Where are we to buy bread for these people to eat?"

When faced with this question, the disciples speak the despairing truth: "Six months' wages would not buy enough bread for each of them to get a little." Andrew, looking at the meager bread and fish, provides the final resounding rhetorical question: "What are they among so many people?" At the end of knowledge stands Jesus. For the text, the end of human knowledge is the beginning of love's knowledge, and that is enough to feed a multitude with much left over.

Our congregations are filled with people who have grown accustomed to facing overwhelming need: Katrina, tsunamis, and on and on. It is easy to look at the sheer magnitude of need and in light of small resources ask, "What are they among so many?" It is easy to come to the end of knowledge and in that place to despair.

In the "prayers of the people," we place before the Lord the great needs of humanity. We may find echoing back the words, "What do you have?" Whatever we have is not enough. Yet, as this text points out, the "not enough" is not the final answer. When placed in the hands of Jesus, human weakness and finitude become more than enough.

In 1946, when Agnes Gonxha Bojaxhiu (Mother Teresa) came face to face with the masses of

1. Parker Palmer, *To Know as We Are Known: A Spirituality of Education* (San Francisco: Harper & Row, 1983), 14.

John 6:1-21

Theological Perspective

theology, however, even the truest and most necessary observations require caveats. However true it is that the significance of Jesus Christ ought not to be based on extraordinary signs and wonders, it is also true that, in pointing out such a truth, we should avoid falling into the camp of the skeptics and superrationalists who see nothing unusual, nothing to wonder at, either in religion or in life; for whom, so to speak, the world is so utterly flat that there are no surprises as one makes one's rather smug way through it!

For instance, it was fashionable for Christian intellectuals in the wake of that same Enlightenment (whose overall effect on Western humanity Christians should certainly respect), to "explain" the miracles as purely "natural" occurrences. The feeding of the five thousand, for instance, might be explained thus: the generosity of the little boy who had fetched his lunch that day encouraged others with secret stashes of food to contribute it to the commonweal. Or Jesus did not really walk "on" the water but "by" it—since the Greek *epi* could mean either. And so on.

These modern explanations were often so ingenious as to seem marvels in their own right! But they were shallow and futile, in fact. To begin with, they did not mitigate the skepticism of the doubters. Nor did they eliminate the miraculous from the text: we cannot escape the biblical belief in a transcendent dimension, which in a prescientific culture could be allowed the kind of free range that moderns can only find excessive. But the caveat goes deeper than that: for the *habit* of "explaining everything," surely one of the more dangerous as well as pretentious adventures of the modern spirit, ends—*and has ended!*—in a culture that has all but lost the capacity to wonder. A people grown skeptical about the extraordinary is likely to miss the extraordinary *within the ordinary*. Elizabeth Barrett Browning said it best:

> Earth's crammed with heaven,
> And every common bush afire with God;
> And only he who sees takes off his shoes—
> The rest sit round it and pluck blackberries.[2]

DOUGLAS JOHN HALL

Pastoral Perspective

Faith communities also need to balance periods of intense social ministry with times of internal reflection on God's call. Spiritual introspection in response to social approval helps congregations remain faithful to Christ when alternative interpretations of their work threaten to overwhelm their true purposes. Ignatius of Loyola developed a set of spiritual exercises to assist individuals in regular examinations of conscience so that each person might learn "to desire and elect only the thing which is more conducive to the end for which I was created," which is "to praise, reverence, and serve God our Lord."[1] Congregations can modify Ignatius's approach, developing a communal process of evaluation and discernment that examines their ministries for congruence with the church's created end as a reverent and exuberant servant of God.

The "Jesus walking on water" story in verses 16–21 may be read as another cautionary tale for congregations that mistake Christ's desire to accompany them in their work for a threat to their activities. The problem lies not in the disciples' desire to have Jesus join them on their journey (v. 21), but in their inability to recognize Jesus as he approaches their location (v. 19). They regain spiritual companionship only by listening to Jesus' declaration of identity and invitation to reject fear (v. 20). Congregations that do not take time to look and listen for where God has come to meet them run the risk of laboring alone in the midst of social turmoil. They may assume that God has withdrawn to a distant place and left them to accomplish by themselves whatever ministries they deem appropriate. They may perceive divine attempts to join them in their work—such as some members' questions about mission and purpose or others' suggestions for a new strategy or direction—as potential assaults on a ministry plan already contending with the buffeting winds of social change and acceptance. Only by opening their hearts and minds through spiritual practices designed to seek God's face and hear God's voice will they be able to recognize salvation and spiritual guidance when it enters their lives in moments of communal discernment.

KAREN MARIE YUST

---

2. Elizabeth Barrett Browning, *Aurora Leigh*, bk. VII, line 820.

1. Quoted in Karen Marie Yust and E. Byron Anderson, *Taught by God: Teaching and Spiritual Formation* (St. Louis: Chalice, 2006), 143.

Exegetical Perspective

see in Jesus the fulfillment of Deuteronomy 18:15–18, and they may connect this feeding to Elisha (2 Kgs. 4:42) and even Elijah (Mal. 4:5), but the significance of this feeding miracle runs deeper. God promised the arrival of a Messiah who would satisfy the people's needs for food and justice (see Pss. 37:19; 81:10, 16; 132:15–17; Ezek. 34:15–16), even as he inaugurated a new exodus into the freedom of God's rule (see Isa. 40:3–11; 49:8–13; etc.). So when the people move to make Jesus a king rather than worship him as Lord, he slips away.

The Miracle of Walking on the Sea (vv. 16–21). Luke may not have considered this mysterious sea crossing an essential element of the gospel, but the other evangelists did and they coupled it with the feeding narrative. Details vary, such as the disciples' destination and responses. In Mark, for instance, the disciples do not understand and their hearts are hardened (6:52); in Matthew they worship Jesus as the Son of God (14:33); and in John they move from fear to joy (v. 21). Still, each Gospel asserts that Jesus joined his disciples on the sea to bestow calm and peace. Jesus also made himself known to his frightened disciples as "I Am" (*egō eimi*, v. 20). Such a declaration is not necessarily revelatory and could be a simple self-identification.

But John's penchant for "I Am" sayings suggests that if the disciples do not assign revelatory significance to this identification at the time (which is most clearly the case in Mark), they do later. Certainly, there is scriptural warrant for understanding the event in such terms (see Pss. 89:8–9; 107:28–32; etc.), and exodus connections may also be possible (see Exod. 14:21; Ps. 77:18–19; etc.). John's account of the disciples' reception of Jesus into the boat, however, is perhaps most revelatory, for John often uses the verb "to receive" (*lambanein*) in terms of believing that Jesus is the Son of God (see 1:12–13; 3:27–36; 5:43; 7:39; 12:48; 13:20; etc.). For John, such trust and reception on the dark and wind-tossed sea is followed immediately by calm and joy.

ROBERT A. BRYANT

Homiletical Perspective

suffering and dying in Calcutta, she experienced what she called the "call within the call," namely, to serve those suffering the most. Certainly her knowledge or her wealth or her wisdom would not be enough to fulfill a calling to the poorest of the earth. Yet love's knowledge fueled the passion of that call, and with that passion she began the Missionaries of Charity, a small order of thirteen members. In the ensuing decades, the order grew to thousands of members giving care in many orphanages and charity centers. Love's knowledge multiplies the meager resources and makes a way forward when knowledge comes to its end.

In 1976, when Millard and Linda Fuller began Habitat for Humanity International, there were few resources and a great need for affordable and decent housing for the working poor. With a few tools and a small group of volunteers, it would have been easy to ask, "What are they among so many?" Yet the passion for justice grounded in the incarnation of Jesus compelled them forward. Today Habitat for Humanity serves as a clear testimony to the multiplying power of love's knowledge.

All around us are those with knowledge of human need but with few resources. There are countless small congregations. There are people on limited incomes. There are those with physical or mental handicaps. In the face of it, all these resources are like a drop in the bucket. Yet, as this passage vividly portrays, in the hands of Jesus, little can become much, the few can become the many, and the weak can become strong.

This text closes with a couple of incidents that give warning to those who wish to control the world or manipulate this power. Jesus' refusal to "be taken" by force and made king and his refusal to allow the disciples to take him into the boat make clear that Jesus is not a concept that "works" for humanity, but an incarnation that lives among us. This incarnation will not be co-opted by human desire, no matter how sincere or lofty the goals.

CHERYL BRIDGES JOHNS

Exodus 16:2-4, 9-15

²The whole congregation of the Israelites complained against Moses and Aaron in the wilderness. ³The Israelites said to them, "If only we had died by the hand of the LORD in the land of Egypt, when we sat by the fleshpots and ate our fill of bread; for you have brought us out into this wilderness to kill this whole assembly with hunger."
⁴Then the LORD said to Moses, "I am going to rain bread from heaven for you, and each day the people shall go out and gather enough for that day. In that way I will test them, whether they will follow my instruction or not." . . .

⁹Then Moses said to Aaron, "Say to the whole congregation of the Israelites, 'Draw near to the LORD, for he has heard your complaining.' " ¹⁰And as Aaron

Theological Perspective

God "tempts" no one, contends the author of James, but is instead the source of "every generous act of giving, with every perfect gift" (Jas. 1:17). Nevertheless, God's gifts and giving, especially when they come with restrictions or instructions, may become either occasions for testing or the material of temptation. Eden is archetypal, of course, while the teaching of James may serve as both benediction and forewarning: "one is tempted by one's own desire . . . and when that desire has conceived it, gives birth to sin, and that sin, when it is fully grown, gives birth to death" (1:14–15).

Exodus 16 is illustrative. The narrative affirms that the gifts of God, manna and quail, are graceful provisions; but with them comes a kind of *torah*, explicit guidance for the ways and means by which Israel may receive the gifts, and an implicit caveat. God gives, to be sure, but the gift is to "test" the sojourners as to "whether they will follow [the Lord's] instruction or not" (v. 4).

Conversely, times of testing and temptation, including the near certainty of death, may become gifts—moments of unique intimacy with the Divine. The prophets Hosea (2:16–20; 11:1; 13:4) and Jeremiah (2:1–3) regard the sojourn as a time of singular blessing, the veritable honeymoon of YHWH's marriage to Israel. The manna and quail

Pastoral Perspective

The Ngambaye people of Chad have a saying that "one day of hunger can make a wife leave her husband's house."[1] Ignoring the pain of others can lead to disaster. Suffering alters people's perceptions and changes their behavior. The descendants of Abraham, Isaac, and Jacob are released from oppressive treatment in the land of Goshen, but the discomforts they find in the wilderness make their lives in Egypt seem luxurious in comparison. Retrospection renders almost any experience less onerous. Present pain cries out for attention. The Israelites point the finger at Moses, as mutinous sailors on a ship point to the captain. He led them into this predicament.

It should come as no surprise to a pastor that suffering in the congregation leads to grumbling against congregational leaders as well as God. People crave attention when their world is falling apart. Their cries are meant to be heard, especially by the person who can make a difference. To bring their pain to the attention of Moses is an indication that the Israelites have some hope for better treatment from God. Moses is the advocate for the beneficent nature of God. Did not Moses declare that the God

1. Abel Ndjerareau, *Africa Bible Commentary* (Nairobi, Kenya: Word Alive Publishers, 2006), 106.

spoke to the whole congregation of the Israelites, they looked toward the wilderness, and the glory of the LORD appeared in the cloud. [11]The LORD spoke to Moses and said, [12]"I have heard the complaining of the Israelites; say to them, 'At twilight you shall eat meat, and in the morning you shall have your fill of bread; then you shall know that I am the LORD your God.' "

[13]In the evening quails came up and covered the camp; and in the morning there was a layer of dew around the camp. [14]When the layer of dew lifted, there on the surface of the wilderness was a fine flaky substance, as fine as frost on the ground. [15]When the Israelites saw it, they said to one another, "What is it?" For they did not know what it was. Moses said to them, "It is the bread that the LORD has given you to eat."

Exegetical Perspective

The Context. Exodus 15:22–18:27 describes events that took place in the wilderness between the time that the children of Israel left Egypt and their arrival at Mount Sinai. Having left the pleasant oasis of Elim, the Hebrews now experience a shortage of food, water, and life support. As a result, popular discontent erupts, and Moses and Aaron face harsh accusations of grumbling Israelites. Those doing the grumbling are not merely a malcontent and murmuring mob but "the people" Israel. This chapter proclaims how the Lord responds to their physical and spiritual needs.

Theological Interpretation. Despite their many geographical and chronological references, the books of Moses do not provide a detailed itinerary of the journeying of the Israelites through the wilderness. There are several literary, historical, and geographical questions about the biblical witnesses. Some scholars assume that various sources are brought together in a long and complicated process of editing and redactions. Those complexities make preachers cautious about taking an easy or naive route in dealing with the historical and geographical issues of Israel's wandering in the wilderness.

On the other hand, even though there are exegetical problems, they do not serve as

Homiletical Perspective

This text needs amplification beyond the usual finger pointing at the Israelite community. Instead of considering our wandering foreparents in the faith to be "whiners" and "complainers," it is better to take a more compassionate look at their situation and their evolving relationship with YHWH.

Another trap to avoid with this passage is any naturalistic explanation of the quail and manna. Dwelling on the migratory patterns of quail, or the sources of manna and its nutritional makeup, will little help to deepen faith or be spiritually satisfying. What is important here is that God— once again—heard the people's cries and responded to their need, whether it was real or whether it was a misperception caused by panic. The fact that God listens is so glorious that God even appears to the people in a cloud with promises of blessing![1]

An immediate question on the part of the hearers arises as the passage is read. Right away, the

1. Bruce Feiler, *Walking the Bible: A Journey by Land through the Five Books of Moses* (New York: Harper Perennial, 2005), 287. "I was less inclined to accept a sterile, naturalistic explanation for every event. . . . I was more interested in how the writers took possibly factual occurrences and shaped them with spiritual objects. To overlook those objectives was to overlook the stories' undeniable source of power. . . . In the case of the quail, that meant going back to the Bible and noticing that the text implies that the deluge wasn't entirely natural, and that God played a pivotal role."

Exodus 16:2-4, 9-15

Theological Perspective

are God's providential, if peeved, response to the emergent and legitimate need of the people (v. 11). The provision is surely premeditated—God has planned to provide for the newly liberated people (v. 15)—but their hurry and murmuring has ruined the party.

The entire text is rich, speaking in many voices around the pattern of gift and (sometimes reluctant) obedience. Not least, Sabbath and its restrictions are given shape even before their legal institution (16:5, 22–26, 29–30). The theme of Sabbath has already been sounded in the creation narrative's overture, of course, and therefore anticipates the rhythm of Israel's faithfulness in the wilderness and beyond.

The history of interpretation and proclamation of Exodus 16 evidences a variety of approaches to the narrative, but three basic ones. The text is often moralized, with Israel held up as a bad example. Faithless, ungrateful, and forgetful, the "people of memory" suffer a heat-induced amnesia, about both who their deliverer is (not Moses, contrary to verse 3, but God), and where the promise of their life and identity lie (not behind them but before them). Accordingly, Israel's attitude and behavior becomes the "not this" for faithful, obedient people.

The text is just as often spiritualized, or even allegorized, with Israel representing any or all of God's children who—in their various isolations or configurations—find themselves between places, in a real or metaphorical wilderness. God graciously provides the bread they need as they journey through the barren wastes toward whatever might connote the land of promise. A cousin to this reading is typology, by which the dynamics of faith or faithlessness are discerned in the discrete history if Israel and applied in the new history of the church.

A more rationalistic approach to the text sets about to explain the divine generosity in terms of natural phenomena. Mystery-less messages may follow: God has created the world in such a way that provision and resource are all around us; therefore we must work together to maximize these benefits for others.

The sweep of the exodus narrative itself compels the theological affirmation—which indeed is the comprehensive doxology of all Hebrew and Christian Scripture—that God is the patient (if sometimes impatient!) provider of every good and perfect gift. These gifts include freedom, food, and water; deliverance, protection, and haven; presence, guidance, and regulation. God hears the prayers and interrupts the misery of the chosen people to provide even for those

Pastoral Perspective

of their ancestors had said, "I know their sufferings, and I have come down to deliver them from the Egyptians" (Exod. 3:7, 8)?

God responds to grumbling with compassion. A pastor visits congregational members at times of illness and personal loss to proclaim that God is aware of their pain, is listening to their cries, and offers comfort and hope. In sermons based on this passage, the preacher can proclaim the good news of a loving God who comes down in desperate and painful situations. Together, preacher and people can anticipate the benevolent care of God.

The Israelites understand that every experience of life has its source in the God who has called them. Their comment, "If only we had died by the hand of the Lord in the land of Egypt," acknowledges that God is in charge. Life and death belong to the Lord. But the people have only a limited knowledge of the kind of love that God wants to offer them in personal and daily provision for their needs. They are just beginning to experience the steadfast love and faithfulness (ḥesed) of God. Pastors can expect the same of their congregation. People grow in their understanding of the love of God, and their relationship with the Lord deepens throughout their spiritual journey. Their faith in the love of God wavers as they encounter various trials and temptations. No one can walk in complete trust, because no one has full knowledge of God. In fact, the Scriptures indicate that the purposes of God are to "test" the people in order to increase their knowledge of God's love and faithfulness.

Moses, their religious leader, gets angry and frustrated. He might have preferred that the people become ascetics and learn to live with the scarcity in the desert, but God's pastoral care is one of bountiful provision in time of need. The Israelites expect death, and hope only for a safe return to Egypt—the former things—but God moves them forward and lavishes upon them in daily provision. The manna in the wilderness is followed by quail and water in abundance. God's action far exceeds their expectation. The good news is that the people of God can dream and hope for great things from a God who loves and cares for them.

The giving of manna and quail on a daily basis with no need for stockpiling is a means for God to teach the people to trust that divine blessings will come regularly. But there is another form of nourishment that God offers to the Israelites. God instructs Moses to have a portion of the manna placed before the covenant of God, where the people

Exegetical Perspective

insurmountable obstacles to preaching this text. Preaching from Exodus proceeds out of the conviction that this book is Torah, instruction. Interpreted from that theological point of view, the narrative of Exodus 16 can be read as representative of the type of crisis that faith faces whenever God's people move from bondage to well-being. In that context, the (different) witnesses of this chapter all point to the salvific actions of the Lord on behalf of the community of faith. The wandering in the wilderness is for Israel the place to knock down the mental frame of being oppressed and to pick up the life of liberty. Here is an opportunity to lay aside the habits of darkness and put on the armor of light (Eph. 5:8; Rom. 13:12).

Israel's Grumbling (vv. 2–4). The hardship of life in the wilderness arouses nostalgia for life in Egypt. The house of bondage is depicted as a luxurious holiday place (see Num. 11:4)! In Egypt the Hebrews at least had food, drink, and lodging. Now, in the desert, these benefits seem to outweigh the disadvantages of slavery. The grumblers prefer dying at an old age as slaves to a premature death by starvation in freedom. The complaints may be understandable from a psychological point of view. People are almost instinctively inclined to forget the troubles of the past when they face new difficulties in the present. But Israel's reaction is nevertheless blasphemous. The verb "to complain" means something like "to grumble" or "to express resentment." The verb is used five times in this chapter, three times explicitly "complaining against the LORD." The use of this verb thus questions the very core of God's election and liberation of Israel.

The Lord's Response (vv. 9–12). Moses instructs Aaron to assemble the people "to draw near to the LORD," a technical term referring to an encounter at the sanctuary. While Aaron was still speaking, the glory of the Lord appeared in a cloud, the symbol of the Lord's active and dynamic Presence during the period of the wilderness. The "glory of the LORD" (*kabod*) is equivalent to "weight," "honor," "splendor."

In his address to Moses, the Lord affirms that he has heard Israel's murmuring and complaining. The Lord does not become furious but responds in a remarkable way, promising meat in the evening and bread in the morning. The grumbling of Israel is met in order that they may know the Lord. The verb "to know" is a key term in the narrative of the book of

Homiletical Perspective

"wilderness of Sin" can lead listeners to wonder if this place's name indicates that the Israelites were doomed to sin while passing through. A quick explanation of the name (Sin is a short form of the word Sinai[2]) will help to keep the congregation from jumping to the hasty and incorrect conclusion about the place or the behavior of the people.

The stage is set now to see the Israelite community six weeks into their journey out of Egypt. Although some commentators argue that their food situation was not so dire,[3] empathy with the sojourners is in order. This sermon will be preached in the midst of the abundant summer harvest and the convenience of 24-hour grocery shopping, so the preacher may need to work to shake the people out of their complacency in taking food for granted. The real worry of so many around the world about where the next meal is coming from should not be dismissed.

Furthermore, how many would want to set off on a long desert march only to run out of the unleavened bread, with animals and grain used for sacrifice rather than three square meals, without any survival instructions, and led by two brothers whose leadership abilities are in the early stages of formation. Who would *not* panic?

So, rather than casting the people in a bad light as complainers, it is more helpful to have the congregation have a concern for them. If not, the preacher will be hardening their hearts to become like Pharoah. If the congregation cannot be empathic with the threat of starvation for the Israelites, how will they be sensitive to the plight of millions of people worldwide who go hungry or who are undernourished? Condemning the ones in need of food isn't tolerable in this passage or within our contemporary society. This story emphasizes that food security is a priority for God.

Therefore, one direction this sermon might pursue is God's and our ability to respond to the plight of poor and hungry people. How can we provide for food delivery systems in our own day that are as effective as the quail and manna God provided in the wilderness?

It is also important to take into consideration that this desert relationship of only six weeks is evolving between the Israelites, their leaders, and God. Many sermons are preached about the uncertainty felt by the people during their pilgrimage, but it is

2. William H. Propp, *Exodus 1–18*, Anchor Bible (Garden City, NY: Doubleday, 1999), 592.
3. Ibid., 593.

Exodus 16:2-4, 9-15

Theological Perspective

who neither expect it nor recognize it for what it is. If the new Pharaoh does not know Joseph, God still does. If stammering Moses is an exile—and justifiably so—God is free to call even this murderer and coward to become a mighty instrument of divine freedom and justice. If Pharaoh's hard heart leads him to say, arrogantly, "They are astray in the land; the wilderness has closed in on them" (14:3 Tanakh), the alternative proclamation is that the wilderness is a table prepared for the elect, a track wide enough for pilgrimage.

Today we stand at the end of the beginning, in between the exodus itself and Sinai—which is to say, between the deliverance of the people and the constitution of the nation. We find ourselves, then, in a kind of wilderness within the wilderness. If the theological affirmation is God's provision, the corresponding anthropological confession is that those for whom provision is provided are often petulant and rarely satisfied.

Israel, typifying all humanity, gainsays both its salvation and its heroes. Israel forgets the horrors of its slavery when new challenges arise, and looks longingly back to its captivity. Elie Wiesel has pointed to the episode in Exodus 2:11–14 as emblematic. Moses rescues a Hebrew slave from an abusive Egyptian by killing the captor. Next day, the very same Hebrew repudiates his champion with a slur. This basic pattern of the deliverer's intervention and the delivered's repudiation of his deliverer will characterize the entire wilderness sojourn.

Also of interest in and around this lection is the matter of God's presence among the Israelites. If God's *provision* for the sojourners is apparent day by day, whether in daily bread or daily work (the gathering of the quail, the harvesting and preparing of the manna, constitute the nation's first vocation on the other side of slavery), God's *presence* is more mysterious. As the Israelites "turned toward the wilderness, there, in a cloud, appeared the Presence of the Lord" (16:10 Tanakh). This lection leads us to the familiar unknown—to the grace and giving, to the guidance and demand—to the mysterious presence of the God whose gifts are not limited to meat and bread.

THOMAS R. STEAGALD

Pastoral Perspective

can see it when they worship (Exod. 16:32–34). This object of remembrance ritualistically enhances the memory of the people about the ḥesed of God. Likewise, in the church, the congregation prays, "Give us this day our daily bread" in expectation of God's ongoing provision. The ritual of worship nourishes God's people in the knowledge that God is with them and will provide for their needs.

Do people need a constant reminder of the goodness of God? This passage indicates that they do, and God does not hesitate to offer what is needed for spiritual development as well as physical nourishment. People call upon God in their time of need as they trust God's bounty through personal knowledge or previous experience. Paul the apostle of Jesus Christ recounts the need of God's people to hear and believe. "How are they to call on one in whom they have not believed? And how are they to believe in one of whom they have never heard? And how are they to hear without someone to proclaim him? And how are they to proclaim him unless they are sent?" (Rom. 10:14–15a). The ultimate provision of the triune God is that the Father sends the Son in order that humanity may experience the fullness of God. Jesus Christ is the bread of life, the true manna, which comes down from above. He is the ultimate provision for human beings in life and in death. God in Christ is the comfort they need to walk in faithfulness while journeying on earth, and he is the gift that insures that they will live eternally with God.

God's benevolence never ends. The Father and the Son send the Holy Spirit to provide the power for people to believe and the impetus to share the knowledge they have received. As the preacher proclaims the goodness and love of God in Jesus Christ, the Spirit informs the believers, nourishes and sustains them with the bread of life, and sends them into the world with the knowledge of the bounty of God's goodness that can be shared with others.

SUSAN E. VANDE KAPPELLE

---

1. *Messengers of God* (New York: Random House, 1976), 201.

Exegetical Perspective

Exodus. The usual rendering of the Hebrew original hardly does justice to the richness of its semantic range. In the Old Testament context, knowledge is not essentially or even primarily rooted in the intellectual activities of a human being. Rather, it is more experiential and embedded in the emotions. It therefore encompasses qualities such as intimacy, concern, communication, mutuality, and contact. "To know the Lord" means to witness or to experience the display of the active, salvific, and dynamic divine Presence.

The Gifts of the Lord. There are all kinds of explanations that make the appearance of the quail and the manna understandable and rationally acceptable. But those naturalistic explanations do injustice to the theological proclamation. "The gift of manna is above all a gracious sign of God's care which sustains a rebellious, murmuring people and seeks to point them to an apprehension of the real meaning of provision through this divine favor."[1]

The institution of the Sabbath is woven together with this narrative. The Lord provides Israel with food under wholly new terms and completely different conditions from those in Egypt. Life is no longer under the oppression of fear and anxiety but under the "regime" of freedom (Gal. 5:1). The place of shortage, threat, and death is redescribed, rearranged, and even re-created by the Lord to a place of abundance, promise, and life. The place that was thought to be a place of death, thirst, and enemies can become the locus of the glory of the Lord; the wilderness turns out to be more brilliant than Egypt.

New Testament Context. There are several implicit and explicit references to the manna tradition in the New Testament, of which John 6:31–58 is the most extensive and profound. Jesus is identified as the bread of life who feeds our hearts and minds unto the hope for "the last day." The New Testament's christological interpretation of the manna is not a strict "literal" or "historical" interpretation, but remains within the borders of the central theological theme of "heavenly bread which brings life to those who eat."

REIN BOS

Homiletical Perspective

interesting to contemplate God's own uncertainty. This budding desert interaction between the Creator and the creatures reminds us of that between parents and a newborn. The long-awaited baby has arrived, but working out the feeding schedule takes some trial and error. It is a good thing that the baby cries to let the neophyte parents known when food is needed, and it is easy to imagine God fretting about care and feeding, now that the delivery/exodus has happened.

Because it is early in Israel's relationship with God, it is not difficult to grasp how the mutual testing described arises. YHWH tests the people to see if they will continue to follow directions on harvesting the exact amount of manna. And Israel tests YHWH to see if YHWH will provide according to their needs. Of course, since the Israelites and their leaders have followed YHWH's lead up to this point, we wonder why YHWH lacks trust in them. Or, since Yahweh has heard and responded to their need, we also are led to wonder why the people might lack trust in YHWH's providence. Both the Israelites and YHWH doubt the other's faithfulness. The existing covenant seems shaky; the need for a new, stronger covenant (or covenants) is foreshadowed.

This foreshadowing, of course, provides the preacher with a way to connect to New Testament allusions to Jesus as manna, the one who feeds and satisfies both body and spirit. The church receives the sign of his new, ultimate covenant in the sacrament. God in Christ has passed the test of faith, but the church is being reexamined every day. Will we trust God's steadfast love and care? Will we respond to God's direction in our lives? Will we be Christ's body for others?

The preacher is obligated to turn the tables in this passage, so that the congregation is not blaming the Israelites, but is motivated toward self-examination of its own trust in God, its own depth of compassion, and its degree of advocacy for those in need.

DEAN MCDONALD

---

1. Brevard S. Childs, *Exodus: A Critical, Theological Commentary*, Old Testament Library (Philadelphia: Westminster Press, 1974), 303.

Psalm 78:23-29

²³Yet he commanded the skies above,
  and opened the doors of heaven;
²⁴he rained down on them manna to eat,
  and gave them the grain of heaven.
²⁵Mortals ate of the bread of angels;
  he sent them food in abundance.
²⁶He caused the east wind to blow in the heavens,
  and by his power he led out the south wind;
²⁷he rained flesh upon them like dust,
  winged birds like the sand of the seas;
²⁸he let them fall within their camp,
  all around their dwellings.
²⁹And they ate and were well filled,
  for he gave them what they craved.

Theological Perspective

In Judeo-Christian tradition, memory is viewed as a source of life and continuity, grounding current experiences and directing what is yet to be discovered. Although we tend to think about time in terms of past, present, and future, the Judeo-Christian cosmology keeps a continuum between memory, experience, and expectation.

While a linear and progressive interpretation of God's journey with us leads us to think in terms of old vs. new, tradition vs. modernity, and backward vs. progressive, the faith community's memory, experience, and expectation intersect and enrich each other. They serve as correctives and clarifiers, propelling us to live the life of faith in a wide band of faithful ancestors, vibrant cobelievers, and imaginative innovators. Time is a *continuum* of interrelated events and experiences that reveal to us the eschatological character of the Judeo-Christian tradition, of God's activity in the universe and for God's people. This text is a reminder, an exercise in memory, of God's wondrous deeds in the cosmos—in creation and beyond what our senses register.

Earlier in the same psalm, the psalmist claimed this continuum by reminding the community:

I will open my mouth in a parable;
  I will utter dark sayings from of old,

Pastoral Perspective

In the Gospels of Matthew, Mark, and Luke, Jesus' "test" or "temptation" in the desert begins with a devilish idea. Jesus has just been baptized on the wild banks of the Jordan. God has just named him "my Son, the Beloved." Now the devil, ever the daring opportunist, calls that name directly into question: "If you are the Son of God," he purrs, "command these stones to become loaves of bread" (Matt. 4:3). Jesus answers by quoting Deuteronomy. "It is written, 'One does not live by bread alone, but by every word that comes from the mouth of God.'" Typically, Christians interpret this answer as an admirable feat of stoic piety: stoic, because Jesus refuses to satisfy his own hunger, and pious, because he does so by quoting holy writ (Matt. 4:4; Deut. 8:3). But as Matthew's version of the story goes on to make clear, even the devil can cite Scripture in an argument (Matt. 4:6), and though self-discipline is certainly part of Jesus' response, he is up to something here much more interesting than mere restraint. By citing Deuteronomy, he employs a crucial form of pastoral imagination, interpreting the world through the stories he grew up hearing and the songs he grew up singing—including, we may imagine, Psalm 78.

Here in the midst of an epic overview of Israel's sacred history, the psalmist briefly recounts the story

Exegetical Perspective

History Lessons. Ancient Israelites, like Americans today, looked to their history for inspiration, consolation, and challenge. Israelites did so with perhaps greater fervor because of their conviction that their history revealed God's ways and character with special clarity. It is not surprising, therefore, that a favorite kind of literature in the Old Testament is history (though differing somewhat from our notion of history). A few psalms detail the whole history (e.g., Pss. 44, 78, 105, 106, 135, 136) and others only incidents (e.g., Pss. 45–48, 68, 74, 89, 132). Such psalms presuppose that worshipers knew the main narrative and appreciated elaborations and variations. The narrative usually fitted the incident in the covenantal relationship and presumed that divine interventions were done out of justice and loving kindness (*ḥesed*). Even chastisements could be signs of love, for they were meant to turn the people from the wrong path. People learned new things about their Lord by looking at the Lord's ancient deeds.

Of all the historical psalms, Psalm 78 is the most detailed and comprehensive, exceeded in length only by Psalm 119. Its many verses teach an important lesson about what God is doing in the world. Though its message might appear somber at first reading—Israel's rebellions and God's punishment in response—its intent is positive. Each of the two

Homiletical Perspective

This small passage from the majestic Psalm 78 appears in the midst of a much longer rehearsal of Hebrew salvation history in versical form. Each verse, coming quickly and clearly, is the psalmist's interpretive summary of vast events that are detailed elsewhere in the Scriptures. The preacher, then, must discern how this small nugget of the psalmist's review might relate to his or her own context.

One principle clearly behind the psalmist's review is that YHWH is in charge. The Lord is in charge, no matter how the people of God have acted. YHWH is in command even while God's people wander in hunger and thirst and disbelief. The preacher might note her own community's doubt and hunger this week. What kinds of "wandering" has the preacher noticed lately? Every person, and every community, has components that do not yet seem to be guided by God. What does YHWH need to be in charge of?

The preacher might legitimately take this piece of Psalm 78 as a reminder that YHWH is in charge even during our wandering. In fact, YHWH might be said to have called the Hebrews into their wandering in the wilderness. Might some of the wandering in your community actually have been invited by God?

This psalm's claim is that, beyond our human actions, YHWH actually commands the natural

Psalm 78:23-29

Theological Perspective

things that we have heard and known,
   that our ancestors have told us.
We will not hide them from their children;
   we will tell to the coming generation
the glorious deeds of the LORD, and his might,
   and the wonders that he has done. (Ps. 78:2–4)

Throughout the psalm, we find a juxtaposition of God's marvelous acts of liberation and redemption and the people's fragmented obedience to God's law and will. God's redemptive acts counteract people's sinful demands and rebellion (vv. 9–20). The psalm also includes the Lord's rage, though it is softened by God's love and grace for the fragmented community. God loves God's people.

Knowing that God has been the deliverer from bondage in Egypt, Israel is sent on a path of uncertainties. Yet God expects Israel to trust and to live under the guidance of its deliverer. But memory of the liberation from Egypt runs thin. The psalmist reminds the people that, despite the memories that incite them to rebel against the Lord, the Lord is faithful. In another cosmic miracle—the feeding of the Hebrews in the desert—the people are more than satisfied. "And they ate and were well filled, for he gave them what they craved" (v. 29).

We have been robbed of the cosmological dimension of our faith, of God's mysterious works beyond the senses. Modernity dulls our religious imagination, removing enchantment and awe from our lives. In their place, we are offered a worldview that asks us to prove everything—what Max Weber calls a "disenchantment" outlook. Miracles do not happen for most of us. If they do, we keep them private.

Yet the psalmist's description of God's provision for Israel is cosmic. God commands the skies, opening the doors of heaven to give people the bread of angels. God causes the winds to blow, bringing nourishing rain to Israel. These cosmic events show God's sovereignty over creation, even as they show creation to be a medium for God's giving of life.

Heaven, earth, wind, and lesser creatures participate in God's life-saving actions. It rains in the desert, and food abounds. In a place of probable death and despair, the people experience life and hope. God's new but temporary order for the people of Israel brings to memory the liberation from Egypt. It offers them a fresh experience of that historical event with cosmic implications. Once again, memory, experience, and expectation ground Israel's faith, yet Israel fails to trust, due to its narrow, immediate outlook.

Mission trips to unfamiliar settings—places often described as "deficient," "lacking," or "undeveloped"

Pastoral Perspective

of God providing the Israelites with manna and quail in the wilderness (Ps. 78:23–29; Exod. 16; Num. 11). As a whole, Psalm 78 is meant to instruct all ages—but particularly "children" and "the coming generation"—about both "the glorious deeds of the LORD" and the inglorious deeds of Israel (v. 4). The "glorious deeds," the psalmist explains, are told so that children "should set their hope in God," and the inglorious ones so that children "should not be like their ancestors, a stubborn and rebellious generation" (v. 8).

This sharp contrast between divine glory and human corruption heightens the psalm's key theme: the grace of God toward an utterly undeserving people. Accordingly, the psalm's account of the miraculous manna and quail is immediately preceded by a vivid portrait of Israel's ingratitude. Just freed from slavery in Egypt, the Israelites "tested God in their heart by demanding the food they craved. They spoke against God, saying, 'Can God spread a table in the wilderness?'" (vv. 18–19). God had delivered them with a mighty hand, but they "did not trust [God's] saving power" (v. 22). Against this backdrop, the manna and quail—"bread of angels" and birds as numerous as "the sand of the sea"—emerge as divine gifts of dazzling, even overwhelming generosity.

Thus the whole force of Psalm 78:23–29 depends on its opening word, "Yet." Our ancestors did not trust in God—yet God trusted in them nevertheless, graciously providing "food in abundance" (v. 25). And so if the "children" who hear Psalm 78 are to be inspired to "set their hope in God," then the song's underlying pastoral message is this: not even Israel's mistrust, and so not even our mistrust, can thwart divine grace. We may and do reject God, but with a fierce and dogged love, God rejects our rejection, and indeed "spreads a table in the wilderness" (Pss. 78:19; 23:5). Therefore, you children of the Most High, no matter what your failure or predicament, hope in God! Mistrust is no match for love!

In this way, the psalmist testifies that genuine human hope is grounded in communal history and memory: the memory of God's tenacious hospitality, and the memory of humanity's bedeviling penchant for mistrust. If together we remember both of these things—compactly enshrined in the iconic, short-hand story of the manna and quail—then we will more likely be ready to face our own trials in the desert with grace and aplomb. And if we want our children to be likewise graceful and upright, then we will tell them the old stories whenever we can. Put

Exegetical Perspective

series of rebellion and punishment ends with a fresh offer of grace.

The Outline of the Psalm. There are two parallel narratives, which are meant to be contrasted, one playing off against the other. In the *introduction* (vv. 1–11) the speaker promises to reveal the meaning of the national traditions so that hearers might properly respond now and avoid the folly of earlier generations.

First recital	Second recital
Red Sea and wilderness (vv. 12–31)	*From Egypt to Canaan* (vv. 40–64)
Gracious act (vv. 12–16)	Gracious act (vv. 40–55)
Rebellion (vv. 17–20)	Rebellion (vv. 56–58)
Divine anger and punishment (manna and quail, vv. 21–31)	Divine anger and punishment (destruction of Shiloh, vv. 59–64)
God's readiness to forgive and begin anew (vv. 32–39)	God's readiness to forgive and begin anew (vv. 65–72)

To the author, the national traditions—the exodus and the journey through the wilderness—form a pattern: God's gracious act, Israel's rebellion, God's wrath and punishment, and then readiness to forgive and begin anew. The pattern is established in the first recital, "The Red Sea and wilderness" (vv. 12–31), so that by the time worshipers come to the second part, "From Egypt to Canaan" (vv. 40–64), they are able to fit the pieces into the pattern.

Who is the speaker and what is his authority? The language suggests the psalmist interprets the tradition in the name of Moses as explained in Deuteronomy: "I will raise up for them a prophet like you from among their own people; I will put my words in the mouth of the prophet, who shall speak to them everything that I command" (Deut. 18:18–19; cf. Deut. 5:1–6:3). The purpose and date of composition can be discerned from hints in the psalm. The psalm tells us that God's gift provoked the people to rebel, with the inevitable result that the Lord became angry and punished them, turning the very gift into an instrument of punishment. But the rebellion does not the end the relationship of God and people, "yet he, being compassionate, forgave their iniquity and did not destroy them" (v. 38). At the end of the second recital of gracious act, rebellion, and punishment (vv. 40–64), the destruction of the northern shrine

Homiletical Perspective

rhythms of the earth too. In this interpretation, what might seem like random events of weather—events of the skies, the rain, and the wind—are actually woven into a pattern of divine authority.

Consider that YHWH "opened the doors of heaven" (v. 23). Our common understanding of the words "heaven" and "abundance" is that both words mean "unlimited supply." So it is that some Christians imagine streets of gold and harvests of overflowing baskets of fruit in the kingdom of heaven. However, this psalm reminds us that heaven's abundance does not mean "unlimited supply" at all.

Rather, the word "heaven" might mean only "supply," not "oversupply." At verse 29 ("They ate and were well filled"), what is not said explicitly, but what is surely remembered, is that this food occurred only daily. The Lord did not provide enough for the people to store up as oversupply, nor did the Lord provide too much of a good thing. There was a daily allocation, and God's people were strictly prohibited from stocking up. The Lord provides neither too little, nor too much. The Lord provides enough, not more than enough.

Consider the words of eucharistic administration in some Christian churches: "the bread of heaven." That morsel is not an entire loaf of bread; it is not oversupply. It is simply "enough" bread. Thus, part of living in heaven is being satisfied, even abundantly satisfied, simply by living within one's means.

The preacher might take this opportunity to remind hearers of our human stewardship of the earth. Food in abundance is actually only our daily supply, not an oversupply. We do not need to be overusers of the earth and overstockers of the fruits of the earth.

Like much of the Psalter, this passage relies upon earthy and fertile images, images often unavailable to the urban hearer. Most of us do not harvest our own food, whether it comes miraculously as manna or whether we have to reap and sow from gardens. But when we remember that YHWH "rained down on them manna to eat" (v. 24), we might ask, "What rains down upon God's people today?" We speak of havoc raining upon us, or abuse, or even terror. God's rain is the opposite; it is nourishing. It is food in abundance. Here the preacher might enjoy some wordplay between "rain" and "reign." God "reigns" by "raining" upon us our daily bread.

At verse 29, God gave the people what they "craved." Craving has come to be a tough image in today's times. Some of us know that cravings are

Psalm 78:23-29

Theological Perspective

—have a way revitalizing the faith of many church people, who often respond to these experiences by saying, "I love the passion of those Christians" or "I've been blessed more than I have blessed." Such words point to a vitality of faith discovered in these new places. Though many who go on mission trips struggle to be open to those whom they serve, they often falsely see the places of mission as "backward" and their own environment as "progressive." They discover, however, that the faith of the Christians in the "backward" setting can actually be a fountain of hope. An enchanted worldview still exists in many of these places, where the cosmic breaks into the ordinary on a regular basis, giving fresh vitality to the community. God is not compartmentalized, but rather is integrated into the daily life of people. Missioners often find their own capacity for awe, mystery, and enchantment revitalized. When they return home, they want to kindle this fire.

Perhaps what they have experienced is not so much the simplicity of the faith of the people they have come to serve as the tangible cosmic presence of God in those people's lives—in their closeness to nature, in the reciprocity between nature and the human community. Suddenly, the cosmic has become an intrinsic dimension of their own faith.

Natural disasters in the early part of the twenty-first century raise questions about the integrity of creation. Tsunamis, hurricanes, droughts, and earthquakes remind the faithful of the painful and ambivalent state of creation. Whether created by humans or brought on by the natural course of events, these disasters remind us the cosmos itself seeks liberation. The apostle Paul reminds the Christian community that the cosmos is also in need of redemption. God's cosmic miracles in the psalm can be placed next to Paul's words in Romans: "We know that the whole creation has been groaning in labor pains until now; and not only the creation, but we ourselves, who have the first fruits of the spirit, groan inwardly while we wait for adoption, the redemption of our bodies" (Rom. 8:22–23).

Just as Israel struggles to be faithful and fails, so does creation. The psalmist brings to memory God's cosmic grace, letting us know about our intertwined relationship with the natural world. God's cosmic grace and salvation for us, despite our failure to be faithful, may come in the unexpected experience of cosmic reconciliation.

CARLOS F. CARDOZA-ORLANDI

Pastoral Perspective

an image of the manna and quail at our children's fingertips, the psalmist insists, and they will be better prepared for their own wilderness wanderings, their own tests, and their own demons.

One such child was Jesus of Nazareth. As he began his adult ministry, wet from baptism but alone in the desert, he recognized his pilgrimage as a contemporary version of Israel's so long before, with the same fundamental themes at stake: human trust and divine generosity. His answer to the devil's proposal, then, citing Deuteronomy 8:3 (itself a reference to the stories of the manna and quail in Exod. 16 and Num. 11), has a twofold effect. First, it exposes the proposal as an attempt to exploit human mistrust ("Can God spread a table in the wilderness?"). Second, it proclaims the good news that God does and will provide "food in abundance"—not only the bread of the baker's oven, but "the bread of angels" too—indeed, the nourishment of "every word that comes from the mouth of God" (Ps. 78:19, 25; Matt. 4:4; Deut. 8:3).

In other words, precisely because he had learned so well the stories passed on in such songs as Psalm 78, Jesus could see the devil's "test" clearly, interpret it decisively, and then speak directly from within a stream of tradition that was centuries old. Put another way, Jesus engaged and interpreted reality *through* Scripture, which is to say, in terms of the sustaining narratives passed on to him by his ancestors. Because they preserved these stories, because they vowed, speaking of their own ancestors, "We will not hide them from their children" (Ps. 78:4)—because generations did these things, the fully human "Son of God" could learn and live into his name. In him, Christians pray, all human "children" may do the same, each one a beloved son or daughter of God, each one a pilgrim in a desert blanketed by grace.

MATTHEW MYER BOULTON

Exegetical Perspective

(Shiloh) and its dynasty in verses 59–64 does not spell the end of the northern kingdom as the Lord's people. The Lord gives them a second chance—accept Zion as the shrine and the dynasty of David. This appeal situates the poem in a time when the southern kingdom made an outreach to the north. Such invitations were made twice in Israel's history. King Hezekiah (715–687 BCE) announced to the North: "Do not be like your ancestors and your kindred, who were faithless to the LORD God of their ancestors, so that he made them a desolation, as you see. . . . For the LORD your God is gracious and merciful, and will not turn away his face from you, if you return to him" (2 Chr. 30:7, 9). King Josiah (640–609 BCE) made similar overtures a century later. Though it is uncertain under which king the psalm was composed, the psalm appeals to *all* Israelites to unite as one people under the Davidic king.

Surprisingly, the lectionary quotes only verses 23–29, the divine gifts of manna and quail. It leaves out verses 17–22, the people's contemptuous words and the ensuing divine wrath that turned the quail into poison and slew the strongest among them (vv. 30–31). Though editing out the punishment from a deliberately linked sequence of sin-punishment-grace might seem outrageous to us, there is some warrant for it in the biblical traditions about the quail. In Exodus 16 and Numbers 11, God gives the people manna and quail, but Exodus 16 says nothing about the quail being poisonous. There was obviously more than one tradition about the manna and the quail, and Psalm 78 chose one tradition to make the point that even the noblest of divine gifts can be abused if one does not receive it with gratitude and faith. Divine gifts can turn into means of punishment, for example, Samson's abuse of his leadership gifts, Jeroboam's abuse of the kingship (1 Kgs. 11–12), and, in the New Testament, the abuse of wrongly receiving the Eucharist (1 Cor. 11:29–30; "For all who eat and drink without discerning the body, eat and drink judgment against themselves").

Though not mentioning divine wrath and punishment, Psalm 78 is a good accompaniment to the reading from Exodus 16, which uses the pure grace tradition of the manna and the quail. In their lectionary context, the verses show the utter gratuity and generosity of God's gifts of food—bread from heaven (not from the earth) and birds falling from the sky (without humans having to hunt them).

RICHARD J. CLIFFORD

Homiletical Perspective

actually addictions. "To crave" comes from an old English word, "to beg." Begging lowers us, as if we were dogs, needing to be fed by someone else each day, at the mercy of our masters. The Hebrew word here is connected with "lusting after," another form of addiction. So it is that an addiction puts us at the mercy of a lower god.

The preacher probably does not want to say that God feeds our addictions. In the mysterious activity of God, however, God sometimes seems to give us what we ask for, even when it is the wrong thing. Does God feed our addictions? After all, a previous portion of Psalm 78 (v. 18) has already reminded us that the people's craving was really how they were "testing" God. Psalm 106:15, after another description of the people's cravings (at Ps. 106:14) actually says that God gave them what they asked, but "sent a wasting disease among them" (NRSV). Another translation says that God "sent leanness into their soul" (*Book of Common Prayer*).

Thus, Psalm 78:29 might also be a disconcerting signal of how God deals with both material and spiritual needs. If people insist upon craving, if they insist upon feeding their addictions, God might satisfy physical appetites while also sending an even deeper emptiness into their souls. The point here is that the satisfaction of hunger, or the satisfaction of any addictive cravings, is not finally what God's people need.

Perhaps the final word here is how God delivers spiritual sustenance through even the smallest morsels of physical sustenance. But that small morsel is meant to instill divine trust. We are never meant to be addicted to an oversupply of God's provisions. God does not feed addictions; God feeds needs. We are meant to recognize in God's small, daily provisions a source of eternal care and grace. It is trust in God, not the oversupply of provisions, that gets us through the wilderness.

SAM CANDLER

Ephesians 4:1-16

I therefore, the prisoner in the Lord, beg you to lead a life worthy of the calling to which you have been called, [2]with all humility and gentleness, with patience, bearing with one another in love, [3]making every effort to maintain the unity of the Spirit in the bond of peace. [4]There is one body and one Spirit, just as you were called to the one hope of your calling, [5]one Lord, one faith, one baptism, [6]one God and Father of all, who is above all and through all and in all.

[7]But each of us was given grace according to the measure of Christ's gift. [8]Therefore it is said,

"When he ascended on high he made captivity itself a captive;
he gave gifts to his people."

[9](When it says, "He ascended," what does it mean but that he had also descended into the lower parts of the earth? [10]He who descended is the same

Theological Perspective

This rich but dense passage from Ephesians focuses on three theological themes: the centrality of Christ, the unity of the church, and the ongoing sanctification of believers.

Paul begins by reminding his readers that he is "the prisoner in the Lord," just as are all the baptized. Christ is the head and the cornerstone. Christ is the giver of our various gifts: "The gifts he gave were that some would be apostles . . ." (v. 11). Thus, one's individual ministries come from Christ, just as one is called to imitate Christ. This is a crucial point for the early church. When Christ is truly placed at the center, no one can claim self-serving authority or make theological claims contrary to what has been revealed of the nature of Christ. Moreover, Paul reminds us that Jesus is the Lord of all in his claim that "who descended is the same one who ascended far above all the heavens, so that he might fill all things" (v. 10). This descent can be read as either the incarnation or Christ's descent to Hades, but either way it indicates that Christ is in all and above all. Thus the cosmos is unified by the indwelling of Christ, and his followers are to grow in an awareness of that unity as well as to work for its full manifestation on earth.

"One" is a refrain throughout the passage, repeated seven times: one body, one Spirit, one hope, one Lord,

Pastoral Perspective

Why Do Preachers Say What We Say? The very existence of this passage occasions a reality check for preachers. It forms a link between a sophisticated theological treatment (chaps. 1–3) and the practical remainder of Ephesians by underscoring the goal of the letter, which is the advancement of unity, love, maturity, and the church's ultimate goal of growth "into" Christ. Preachers can benefit from probing their consciences about motivations. On the deepest level, what drives the content and shapes the rhetoric of a sermon?

Distinguishing Love and Niceness. This passage has been repeatedly used to stifle prophetic voices. This is perhaps explainable, because the human tendency is to hear all critical words as "unloving," or to hear perceived new paths for the church's growth into Christ (v. 15) as the underhanded behavior described in verse 14. Love and niceness are different categories. Given the goal of the passage, perhaps the communal test for prophecy ought to be the pragmatic test of what builds the church in its identity and mission, not a subjective reaction to what is critical or new.

The Letter's High Goal. In an age of mission and vision statements, how will people today understand "the calling to which you have been called"?

one who ascended far above all the heavens, so that he might fill all things.) [11]The gifts he gave were that some would be apostles, some prophets, some evangelists, some pastors and teachers, [12]to equip the saints for the work of ministry, for building up the body of Christ, [13]until all of us come to the unity of the faith and of the knowledge of the Son of God, to maturity, to the measure of the full stature of Christ. [14]We must no longer be children, tossed to and fro and blown about by every wind of doctrine, by people's trickery, by their craftiness in deceitful scheming. [15]But speaking the truth in love, we must grow up in every way into him who is the head, into Christ, [16]from whom the whole body, joined and knit together by every ligament with which it is equipped, as each part is working properly, promotes the body's growth in building itself up in love.

Exegetical Perspective

Epistles often contain moral exhortation that stems from proclamation, and Ephesians is no different. In Ephesians 4:1–16, the author transitions from proclamation about Christ's work on behalf of the church to practical ethical implications. That this passage begins with "therefore" indicates that it is the logical outcome of the convictions stated in the preceding passage, indeed in everything that comes before. On account of love, God has saved us (perfect tense) by grace through Christ, so thoroughly that we can say that we have already been raised with Christ and sit with him in the heavenly places (2:4–9). God has created us for good works and has gifted us with the Spirit, who empowers us to do good works that glorify God. "The indicative implies the imperative," as the saying goes. Because God has accomplished our salvation, then we should behave in certain ways.

What would our author have us do? In a phrase, "Grow up!" Growing up may require standing down because mature Christians are more concerned about *unity* than personal triumph. Notice all of the ways the author makes this point. First, he uses the language of "unity" (*henotēs*) and "one" (*heis*) extensively throughout the letter, with the heaviest concentration appearing in our passage. Twice he speaks of the "unity" (*henotēs*) of the spirit (4:3, 13).

Homiletical Perspective

It is a shame that the lectionary appoints a text like this one for Ordinary Time when it doesn't have the best chance of getting the hearing it deserves. Here is an extraordinary text that has startling relevance for congregations who are asking some basic questions about Christian identity and purpose. To bypass this ancient text is to miss the opportunity it affords to address some vexing issues for ministry in this time, this place. The fractious church's need to hear grace notes and exhortations on the themes of unity and diversity is acute, as is its hunger for doxology and direction. The human community is in desperate need of communities of faith where belief and practice are congruous. The text appointed for today lies at the heart of an expansive vision for Christian community as expressed in this widely circulated communiqué from a devoted disciple of the apostle Paul.

At first glance, the richness of texts from Ephesians as resources for contemporary preaching may not be apparent. When you read the first part of the letter aloud with clarity and intention, you can almost hear trumpets and brass in the background as a "cosmic Christ" makes an appearance. Some may be inspired by the writer's triumphalism and will find themselves cheering in the stands. Others, particularly those who are committed to deepening dialogues with persons of other faiths, may be put

Ephesians 4:1-16

Theological Perspective

one faith, one baptism, one God and Father of us all. The principal mark of the church is unity, and the calling of Christians is to build up the body of Christ in all that they do. The ecclesiology proclaimed here is that Christ's church is to be unified. The metaphor of the body is organic and dynamic, not static or rigid. The body of Christ is always living into its calling, but the vision of unity is clear.

While the passage affirms the diversity of individual gifts, it asserts that these are always to be used for the good of the whole "to equip the saints for ministry." The equipping is not about accumulating skills or knowledge. Rather the word "equip" comes from the Greek noun *katartismos* meaning "the setting of a bone." Its derivation is from a verb meaning "to reconcile," "to set bones," "to restore," "to create," "to prepare."[1] To grow in one's ministry, therefore, is to align oneself with God's intentions, both individually and corporately, and to avoid being "tossed to and fro and blown about by every wind of doctrine" (v. 14). Again this alignment applies both to individuals and to the corporate church.

Accordingly, as a person grows into the likeness of Christ, his or her ministry adds to the growth of the body of Christ. There is a mutuality between the individual and the corporate. I can become my true self only in relation to you. Moreover, as a follower of Jesus aligns his or her life with God's purposes, he or she grows into becoming a disciple, and this individual transformation aids in the corporate transformation of the world into the kingdom. We are to build up "the body of Christ, until all of us come to the unity of the faith and of the knowledge of the Son of God" (4:12–13).

This admission that we live in time indicates that sanctification is ongoing. Paul writes these assurances to these early Christians: "But speaking the truth in love, we must grow up in every way into him who is the head, into Christ" (v. 15). We are all pilgrims on the way. We journey toward Christ as we journey with Christ. As Thomas Merton says, "In one sense we are always traveling. . . . In another sense we have already arrived."[2] Or as Boethius says, "To see Thee is the end and the beginning / Thou carriest us and thou dost go before / Thou art the journey and the journey's End."[3] Christ is the means

---

1. Markus Barth, *Ephesians 4–6* (New York: Doubleday, 1974), 439.
2. Thomas Merton, *A Thomas Merton Reader* (Garden City, NY: Doubleday, 1974), 513.
3. *The Oxford Book of Prayer*, ed. George Appleton (Oxford: Oxford University Press, 1988), 7.

Pastoral Perspective

Ephesians claims much territory, including but also transcending personal salvation. In the first three chapters the epistle lays emphasis on the reconnection in Jesus Christ of all the world, which always tends to be "divided into two kinds of people," in this instance, divided into Jews and Gentiles. Chapters 4 and 5 understand Christ's followers to be bound by the highest standards of individual and corporate morality. The calling in general terms can seem to be nothing less than the ongoing reconciliation of all humanity to God and each other in Christ, into whom we ceaselessly grow. Ephesians balances knowing that this has already occurred in Christ's work with the realization that such reconciliation happens in infinite instances of humility, gentleness, and patient forbearance with others as the body articulates itself. The letter's writer will give some specific instances in passages that follow. For now, it is enough to ask whether our personal lives and communal mission statements contribute to the realization of the epistle's high goals.

A Sevenfold "One." Ephesians, often understood to be a kind of circular letter written by an associate or student of Paul's, assumes and addresses the human tendency toward division by using the word "one" seven times in two verses. There must have been a divisive energy in the communities the writer knew that he wished to redirect. The sevenfold emphasis on oneness—which the text speaks of a foundational work of God, not a human construct—is a given to which we are called to yield. As churches work toward (or around) the realization of the unity that God has created, the question repeatedly arises: which of our own preferences do we value more highly than the experience of this God-given unity? To what degree do we desire less unity than God intends? The community envisioned in Ephesians challenges entropy itself. Things and people do not have to move apart for chaos to enter.

A Test for Any Ecclesiology. "But," the writer continues after reflecting on essential unity, charisms are distributed individually in the one body. In a difficult passage (vv. 8–10), the writer asserts that the risen Christ is the source of all gifts. In verse 11, some of those gifts sound to many ears like those of office holders. Readers of this series represent many ecclesiologies. Some will see a straight line from verse 11 to the letters of Clement, Polycarp, and Irenaeus and right on through to the monarchical episcopate. Others may not see any kind of "office"

Through the cross, Christ has unified ethnic groups so that peace should ensue and hostilities cease (2:14), creating what Ephesians calls "one new humanity" (2:15), which has singular access to God through one Spirit (2:16). The author borrows liturgical language to express eloquently this unity: one body, one Spirit, one hope, one Lord, one faith, one baptism, one God who is the parent of everyone.

Second, unity is emphasized through "peace" language. Chapter 2, which also speaks of unity, names Christ as our peace (2:14), as one who makes peace between previously irreconcilable groups (2:15), and who proclaims peace to those both near and far (2:17). Therefore, we are called to make "every effort to maintain the unity of the Spirit in the bond of peace" in 4:3. The author closes the letter with these astounding words: "As shoes for your feet put on whatever will make you ready to proclaim the gospel of peace" (6:15). The gospel and peace travel as a unit. In his greeting (1:2) and in his farewell (6:23) the author says, "Peace." These are not throwaway words: concern for "peace" frames the entire epistle.

Third, the author fleshes out the theme of unity with the metaphor of the church as a body. This image is familiar (see 1 Cor. 12, Rom. 12, and Col. 2:19; 3:15). Christ is the head and the body is unified, composed of individual parts "joined and knit together by every ligament" (v. 16). Growth depends on each part working properly. If one part fails to function, growth is stunted. The author does not envisage numerous bodies with individual growth patterns, as in a school of fish or a gaggle of geese. There is only one body: it can grow, stagnate, or die, depending.

Fourth, the author stresses unity by employing familial language depicting God as a parent and, in various ways, believers as children. Positively, we are beloved children (5:1); but we are called to be mature, not children of this undiscerning age, prone to credulity and innocent of solid conviction.

So, clearly the main thrust of our passage points to concern for unity as the hallmark of Christian maturity. But the author also insists that mature Christians understand that they have been especially equipped for ministry. They do not need to imagine themselves as pan-gifted, and there is no reason to compete with one another. Our job is simply to recognize our particular gifts and use them for the development and augmentation of the body (4:11–14).

Mature Christians speak truth in love because it promotes growth (4:15). Some find it easy to speak

off by it and will find themselves looking for some other source for preaching. Then, here at the outset of this passage (v. 1), there is this troubling word— "worthy." In a culture where self-esteem is a highly prized commodity and resource for making it in a competitive world, who needs a word like "worthy," tinged as it is with judgment? Stay with reactions like these, for there is much here in this text to encourage the building up of an inclusive, distinctly Christian community where everyone is worthy of God's abundance and that shows forth this abundance in the way it lives out divine life.

As the writer sees it, the situation of the fledgling church is precarious. There has apparently been a takeover movement by Gentiles who neither know nor care much about Israel and her place in salvation history. Her traditions and practices are odd and strange to those of pagan heritage and are being dismissed as archaic and increasingly irrelevant to "real life." Moreover, these "new" Christians are (in the eyes of their Jewish brothers and sisters) too enamored with the easygoing morality of the dominant culture, calling it "freedom in Christ" and citing the rabbi and Christian apostle Paul as their justification for offensive practices. To address this, and to correct misinterpretations of Paul, this writer presents a vision of what God is up to in the community. Something new is clearly happening in the convergence of radically different traditions of religious experience that can be attributed to the ongoing work of Christ. The writer of this epistle aims to spell that out.

God is at work in Christ throughout the first three chapters, revealing, choosing, adopting, sacrificing, and blessing in order to bring differing communities together into a new, unified body in the face of pronounced and pervasive evil. The claim is bold and remarkable, that through the death and resurrection of Christ warring religious cultures, passionately divided by heritage, traditions, moral codes, and behaviors, have collided and now converged into a newly created order, a community that knows no barriers of race, class, or gender. Christian preaching within cosmopolitan, pluralistic contexts like ours will be enriched when it places visions like this on the horizon of the baptized.

Here at verse 1 is a hinge in the letter. The writer turns from laying out a grand vision of what God has done in Christ and what is given to and through the church, to answer the inevitable pressing question: "So what?" "How does this lofty vision play out in congregational life?" The writer of this text points out

Ephesians 4:1-16

Theological Perspective

and the end. He enables individuals to grow, and he is the fulfillment of that growth. To speak "truth in love" is to draw near to the source of truth.

The exhortation of the passage, therefore, is to encourage the listeners to accept their calling willingly, aware of the sacrifice that such a calling entails. They are called to "lead a life worthy of the calling to which you have been called" (v. 1) by "bearing with one another in love" (v. 2). To bear with one another is to sacrifice for the other. It is to help carry the other's burdens. Love is not an emotion; love is an act of the will. Paul is not calling for the early Christians to feel warmly toward one another, but to act according to their calling. They are to do love by serving one another. The church is called to be a new community based not on the divisions inherent in the existing social order but on the new humanity in Christ. The social hierarchy has been replaced by the body of Christ. In this new order, all members are essential, and all members are connected. Love, therefore, is neither theoretical nor abstract but is the glue of community; it is what knits the body together.

The tools for this body are humility, gentleness, and patience. Humility keeps us grounded in the reality of who we are as creatures formed from the dust by God. Gentleness reminds us of our corporate identity. Because we are essentially part of the body, we are called to build up the body by attending to one another. Finally, we are patient because we live in time. The kingdom of God is a gift from God, not a work achieved by humans. The Christian life is one of expectation for the new Jerusalem which gives us hope in the here and now. Jesus' yoke is easy because he bears it with us and because as we take it upon us and bear one another's burdens, we come closer to him.

G. PORTER TAYLOR

Pastoral Perspective

implied in the verse at all, focusing instead on function.

Notwithstanding our various churchly presuppositions, all can agree that what begins as a statement of circumstance in verse 11 completes with a statement of purpose in verse 12. However the several official ministries in the church are understood, their purpose is to equip the "saints," the holy people of God. Those saints are to be equipped for servanthood and for the overall building of the body of Christ. Their great variety is for a common aim: the corporate body as well as "all of us" individually are to come to unity of faith, knowledge of Christ, and maturity. The measuring stick for maturity is Christ. The passage sets a test for any ecclesiology: in the long run, does it empower and equip all the baptized? It is best not to ask that question about any organization or cultural setting other than one's own, at least at first.

"Until" is the lead word in verse 13; verse 15 speaks of growing "into him," and verse 16 imagines the body "building itself" in love. Such language suggests an early perception that while the church may in one sense be waiting for Christ, there is a parallel (or perhaps subsequent) "eschatology," for lack of a better word, that understands us individually and corporately as moving toward and into Christ. A challenge for preaching is to assist hearers in recognizing and valuing that movement in themselves and in the body of which they are a part. Is it too much to say that the humanity reunited in Christ is the one species that is invited to participate in its own evolution?

In that very regard, the least inviting verse for some will be verse 14, which is still applied to reject or punish the ideas and actions of others. Is a minority application of the text possible in which we conclude that mature Christians know that different trends in thought, along with deceit and empire building, are always with us, and that equipped with knowledge of this inevitability, they are not shaken? Such persons stay focused on their own commitment to giving their witness to truth in love and to participating in the maturation of the body. The author of Ephesians has been doing just that: demonstrating the behavior he endorses.

PAUL V. MARSHALL

Exegetical Perspective

truth, to set us straight on "how it is," to throw in their verbal grenades and then feel deserving of a spiritual Purple Heart for braving such enemy territory to deliver truth. Some people speak truth, but without love. They want to show off or one-up another. This is not good enough. William Sloane Coffin tells this story: "I remember several years ago a freshman asking if he could give me some advice. 'Go ahead,' I said. 'Well, Sir, when you say something that is both true and painful, say it softly.' Say it in other words to heal and not to hurt. Say it in love."[1] Others excel in a type of "love" that produces only warm feelings and smiles and, therefore, can neither broach nor tolerate truth. In that case, truth and love are opposing forces, and truth must lose. This also is not good enough. Our author insists that truth and love are symbiotic. Christians are neither to thrive on conflict nor to avoid it when it might reveal difficult truths.

Love and truth are favorite themes of Ephesians. Christian love is marked by lowliness, meekness, patience, and forbearance (4:2). The key to our passage is to speak truth in love in order to grow in love—the perfect cycle. We are rooted and grounded in it (3:17). We love sacrificially, not egotistically, because that is what God (2:4) and Christ do (3:19; 5:2). As Ephesians begins and ends with peace, it begins and ends with love (1:4; 6:23). The "gospel of your salvation" is called "the word of truth" (1:13). Half of the occurrences of the word "truth" are in our passage. "Truth is in Jesus" (4:21). Truth and holiness attend one another. We speak truth to one another *because* we are intimately related. We are to fasten "the belt of truth around [our] waist" (6:14), donning it daily.

JAIME CLARK-SOLES

Homiletical Perspective

that unity is not just a given but is also a goal for the community in living out its ethic. Unity is not just something Christians passively accept or reject—it is something we choose to do. The maintenance of unity requires "every effort" (v. 3) on the part of the baptized to create spaces of grace where diversity in life and practice is honored. "Diversity" here is not just a slogan or catch phrase that one would slap on a church sign or bumper sticker. It refers to the recognition, acceptance, practice, and celebration of gifts given to the community "for building up the body of Christ" (v. 12).

Unity for this writer does not mean uniformity. This is an appropriate word for the church today. To counter perceived threats from moral relativism and secularism many in religious bodies have heightened pressure on adherents to conform to doctrinal, moral, and even political correctness in interpretation and behavior to mark that community's witness or presence in humanity. Sometimes correctness is confused with maturity. The preacher might wonder aloud in the sermon how some of those pressures from within and without have affected the congregational life the preacher shares with his or her listeners. In what ways, the preacher might ask, has this community of faith resisted those pressures and celebrated the varieties of gifts present in the community? Celebrating the gifts given to particular congregations goes beyond noting the number of "professional Christians" that arise from their number to become "apostles, prophets, evangelists, pastors and teachers" (v. 11). Many bulletins list "All the members of the congregation" as "Ministers." It's clever, but what does it really mean? A sermon that would address that matter would do well to take seriously what this text says about unity in diversity and the generosity of God's gift giving through Christ for the building up of Christ's own body. "Christ's body" is that place at the intersection of divine and human life where sovereignty, brokenness, and communion are held together in God's grace.

RICHARD F. WARD

1. William Sloane Coffin, *Credo* (Louisville, KY: Westminster John Knox Press, 2004), 152.

John 6:24-35

24So when the crowd saw that neither Jesus nor his disciples were there, they themselves got into the boats and went to Capernaum looking for Jesus. 25When they found him on the other side of the sea, they said to him, "Rabbi, when did you come here?" 26Jesus answered them, "Very truly, I tell you, you are looking for me, not because you saw signs, but because you ate your fill of the loaves. 27Do not work for the food that perishes, but for the food that endures for eternal life, which the Son of Man will give you. For it is on him that God the Father has set his seal." 28Then they said to him, "What must we do to perform the works of God?" 29Jesus answered them, "This is the work of God, that you believe in him whom he has sent." 30So they said to him, "What sign are you going to give us then, so that we may see it and believe you? What work are you performing? 31Our ancestors ate the manna in the wilderness; as it is written, 'He gave them bread from heaven to eat.'" 32Then Jesus said to them, "Very truly, I tell you, it was not Moses who gave you the bread from heaven, but it is my Father who gives you the true bread from heaven. 33For the bread of God is that which comes down from heaven and gives life to the world." 34They said to him, "Sir, give us this bread always."
35Jesus said to them, "I am the bread of life. Whoever comes to me will never be hungry, and whoever believes in me will never be thirsty."

Theological Perspective

What makes a perspective on a text "theological" is not the imposition of a prior scheme of thought or predictable pattern of interpretation but the expectation of hearing a word from God. Approached in this manner, the testimonies of Scripture both question their hearers and provoke their hearers in turn to question them. Nowhere is this more strikingly evident than in the readings from John 6.

What Are We Hearing in This Text? As every preacher knows, waiting upon a recalcitrant lection when a sermon deadline is looming poses the fiercest temptation to skip from a text to a more conveniently manageable pretext, thereby revealing that a short-circuiting of attention has occurred. Listeners to sermons also need time to attend to the text's particularity before first being told what they are supposed to hear in it, or "what all this means for us today."

Notice that John 6:24–35 begins with a situation in which Jesus reportedly is not where a lot of people who are said to be looking for him expect him to be. The setting, we have earlier been told, is "festival" time (v. 4), with "a large crowd" following Jesus and his disciples. Preceding verses have recounted Jesus' feeding of "about five thousand" (vv. 1–14), and this event sets the context for what now follows.

Pastoral Perspective

There was a name in nineteenth-century China (and perhaps all over Asia) for persons who came to church because they were hungry for material food. They converted, were baptized, joined the church, and remained active members as long as their physical needs were met though the generosity of the congregation. But once their prospects improved and they and their families no longer needed rice, they drifted away from the church. Hence missionaries called them "rice Christians." That name calls to mind those who flocked to the churches in East Germany and Romania just before the liberation of eastern Europe—when the church was manifesting courage, and pastors were speaking out against Communist regimes. The people came to cheer the church on, and to join the congregation in its opposition to the tyrannical state. But after liberation from the heel of the Soviet boot and local dictators, the crowds dispersed and the churches began to look as straggling and abandoned as they had before the stirrings of political liberty took hold.

The crowds that followed Jesus to Capernaum to find him after he fed the five thousand in the wilderness are like those who see faith and church membership instrumentally, as something they can choose for themselves to use for their own needs or to pursue their own interests. Christians like the rice

Exegetical Perspective

In the Gospel of John, people come to Jesus again and again, seeking to understand him. The question of his identity, who he is and where he came from, is the central theme. No other document in the New Testament is more explicit in its answers to that question, yet those answers remain ironic or paradoxical, as often repelling as persuading the men and women with whom Jesus speaks. In the sixth chapter we see first "the crowd," then the disciples, trying to grasp the enigma of Jesus by using the best tools their religion supplies: the evidence of miracles, tradition, and Scripture. Yet each of these tools shatters when confronted with this One who seems to belong to another world.

Miracles, in the Fourth Gospel, do not easily bring faith to those who witness them, but more often confusion, division, and hostility. This Gospel calls them "signs," but if they are symbolic markers pointing toward truth, it is by a winding and ambiguous path. When this Gospel retells one of the stories of Jesus' miraculous acts that were so rich a part of the lore about him, it does so only to set the stage for Jesus to talk about himself in words that are often puzzling and challenging—to the characters in the story and to ourselves. As the Jesus in this Gospel seems to play verbal tricks on those who try to understand him, so the writer plays tricks on us as we struggle along with them.

Homiletical Perspective

Jesus is more difficult to comprehend than he ought to be. We believe Jesus to be the full revelation of God, but that revelation, particularly in the Fourth Gospel, does not come to us directly, straightforwardly, or unambiguously. At the beginning, we were told that Jesus is the light of God shining upon us in such a way that we "saw his glory" (1:14). Yet we were also told that we "love darkness rather than light" to the extent that we did not receive the light when it dawned upon us (3:19).

Seen from one angle, the Gospel of John is a veritable symphony of incomprehension. In chapter 6, these crowds who clamor after Jesus just do not get it. Of course, in this Gospel, those closest to Jesus do not get it either. As chapter 6 begins, we are told that Jesus is successful in attracting great multitudes. Yet immediately John warns us not to get too excited by the big numbers. They are attracted to Jesus, not for any of the right reasons, but merely due to his miraculous work (6:2). The reaction of the crowds is, in the Fourth Gospel, a clear indication of how widespread is the popular misapprehension of Jesus. The Christ has "come to them" (6:17), but he has not yet truly appeared to them, at least not appeared in a form that they can understand.

These crowds just do not get it. They did not get it when Jesus talked about the "temple" (2:19–21),

John 6:24-35

Theological Perspective

The keynote may be detected in 6:12, where the word "satisfied" in the account of the feeding of the five thousand by Jesus suggests not only a *filling* but also a *fulfilling* of their hunger. Parallels in the three other Gospels emphasize the point (see Matt. 14:13–21, Mark 6:32–44, and Luke 9:10–17). The literal, ordinary sense of "filling up" and "being full" thus takes on an extraordinary depth of further significance that has been remarked upon throughout Christian history. Augustine, for example, described the signification of the things recounted in John 6 as *in magno sacramento,* "a grand symbolism."[1]

Yet it is precisely this extraordinary added significance, not to be mistaken for an immaterial spiritualization, that is reportedly missed by the crowds' demands on Jesus. Having first attempted to "force" him to be their king according to their preconceived notions (v. 15), they now question why Jesus and the disciples are no longer around where and when they want to find them. "Rabbi, when did you come here?" is the first thing we are told that they say to Jesus upon discovering that he has subsequently gone to Capernaum. By this hint of reproach the passage discloses a total lack of awareness on the crowds' part of what has just been happening. As far as the events narrated in the preceding verses are concerned—a rough night at sea and a crossing of the waves to Capernaum, with the disciples in the dark until Jesus himself comes to them on the water in their terror (6:16–21)—the crowds, so we hear, see none of this, "neither Jesus nor his disciples." Their sense of location is thus called into question.

The response of Jesus to those who demand to know his whereabouts is to probe instead what they are really seeking. Are they after him to have their "fill of the loaves" but not the fulfillment of their lives? Chrysostom, the "golden tongued" preacher of antiquity, thought so. "By His words to them He was all but saying this, 'It is not the miracle of the loaves that has struck you with wonder, but the being filled.'"[2]

Having their purposes thus challenged, those questioned in turn ask to know from him what works they must perform, what sign he will give them, what work he is now doing in their midst. Not

Pastoral Perspective

Christians of the nineteenth century and expedient Christians of eastern Europe are not a new problem, but are as old as the gospel itself. (See in Acts 5 the story of Ananias and Sapphira.)

Indeed, the crowds of people who followed Jesus to Capernaum wanted to make him king, which was the reason he went away from them. These were the ones who saw the feeding miracle as an end in itself, rather than as the sign it was meant to be, something that pointed them to faith in the living God and in the Son whom God had sent. Jesus told them they were not to work for the food that perishes, but were to perform the works of God that lead to eternal life.

In John's account, those who hear this teaching are still hung up on physical manifestations, upon that which satisfies their own experience. This is why they ask the Messiah for another sign. They have had a sign, and still they do not believe. Moses, Jesus reminds them, did not give the bread that came from heaven. It was God who gave the bread that satisfied their hunger for one day only. The same God now gives them bread from heaven that will satisfy forever. In response to his teaching, they ask him for this bread. Jesus says he is the bread of life who will satisfy hunger and quench thirst forever.

Too often, we forget how to pursue what really matters. We are accustomed to inviting people into the community of faith for all the wrong reasons: for the "right" kind of worship; for political engagement on behalf of the poor and downtrodden; for the sake of a Christian America; for a strong youth and family ministry; for the opportunity to practice mission in a downtown location, or to go on mission trips to Africa or Central America. Yet what we have to offer—in Christ and by Christ and because of Christ—first and foremost is "soul food," which lasts forever and does not change with the changing circumstances of the church or the world. It is soul food that we desire, and soul food in which we will rejoice, long after our bellies are full of rice and our lives know justice in a free society.

We North American Christians have preached a broken, truncated gospel. We have been good marketers rather than true witnesses. We have bought into a culture that rewards consumers and addresses their needs, instead of proclaiming a gospel that offers us faith in the only begotten Son, who gave his life for the sins of the world—and who is lifted up so that all who believe in him have everlasting life. He is the bread of life. Those who come to him will never be hungry, and those who put their trust in him will never thirst.

---

1. *Saint Augustine: Tractates on the Gospel of John 11–27,* trans. John W. Rettig, in *The Fathers of the Church,* vol. 79 (Washington, DC: Catholic University of America Press, 1988), 246.

2. *Saint John Chrysostom: Commentary on Saint John the Apostle and Evangelist, Homilies 1–47,* trans. Sister Thomas Aquinas Goggin, S.C.H., in *The Fathers of the Church,* vol. 33 (Washington, DC: Fathers of the Church, Inc., 1957), 443.

Exegetical Perspective

At first we feel superior; because we know the story, we marvel at the obtuseness of some of their questions ("Rabbi, when did you come here?" "What sign are you going to give us?"). But then even those with whom we are led to identify, those who believe in Jesus, those whom he calls his friends, also fail to understand and will fail to stand by him in his darkest hour. Like them, we find this Jesus hard to follow. The crowds who cross the sea in the morning, "looking for Jesus," have seen the miracle of the bread and—though only the disciples have witnessed the miraculous crossing by Jesus—dimly sense this second sign. We the readers have seen both, but we too are put on the spot as the dialogue begins.

A day earlier, the people who "saw the sign that he had done" acknowledged that Jesus was "indeed the prophet who is to come into the world" and wanted to make him their king (vv. 14–15). But now Jesus, ignoring their shallow question (v. 25), declares that they have seen no sign at all but have followed him only because their stomachs were filled (v. 26). A few verses later, the evangelist shows us that Jesus is right about their dullness. When he offers them life-giving bread from heaven, they respond, "Sir, give us this bread always" (v. 34), as the Samaritan woman replied when he offered water of eternal life, "Sir, give me this water, so that I may never be thirsty or have to keep coming here to draw water" (4:15).

"Food that perishes" (v. 27) underlines the all-too-familiar longing for a religion of convenience, faith that satisfies our wants, rather than working for "the food that endures." The phrase anticipates the comparison of Jesus' work with the manna by which ancient Israel was fed in the wilderness, a comparison that the interlocutors will introduce in verse 31 and that is carried further in our Gospel lesson for next Sunday (vv. 49–51) and the Sunday after (v. 58). Jesus' allusion is to a detail in the biblical account: the manna did not "endure," but spoiled—"perished"—if anyone tried to keep it overnight (Exod. 16:19–21).

The religion of convenience typically thinks of the relationship with God as a kind of lobbying on the grand scale: a case of *do ut des*, "I give so you will give," as ancient Roman law put it. So the people now piously ask Jesus, "What must we do to perform the works of God?" (v. 28). For the reader who has paid attention, however, the question signals one of those recurring themes that reverberate through this Gospel. The "works of God" are, on one level, the miraculous deeds that Jesus performs, equivalent to his "signs" (5:19–23). At a deeper level, they are the

Homiletical Perspective

did not get the meaning of "new birth" (3:3–4), "water" (4:7–15), and now they do not get this talk about life-giving bread. They hear Jesus on "bread," and they immediately assume he is talking about grub. Jesus serves them by miraculously feeding them; they attempt to make him king (vv. 14–15). They just do not get it.

Jesus does not shrink from noting their incomprehension. The people are looking for Jesus, but Jesus dismisses their searching saying, "You look for me because you do not know who I am" (6:26). They are deficient in vision. In all this section, verse 29 is a key. The crowds lack "faith," which in this context surely means that they need faith in the one whom God has sent, the Word made flesh (John 1). Alas, their faith is in their idea of a Savior. By rejecting their attempt to make him king, Jesus is critiquing and rearranging their idea of reign, just as he has attempted to reframe and redefine their notions of temple, birth, water, and life.

With this, Jesus launches into an ambiguous and far from obvious explication on something called food of eternal life. With focus upon bread and food, this most incarnational of Gospels again reframes our notions of spiritual. In this Gospel, indeed in this faith, the spiritual is incarnational, tied to the stuff of this life, present, here, now. When the church following this one who is the Bread of Life wants to get especially spiritual, we do so at a table, with eating and drinking of bread and wine.

This is one of the reasons why we preachers find the Fourth Gospel to be a challenge. We think we are communicators. Our job is to communicate the gospel, to help our Sunday hearers "get it." The purpose of a sermon is to make the gospel fully accessible to all the hearers, without risk of confusing anybody. We simplify the complex and make fully apparent the difficult and the ambiguous. If we are not careful, we will blasphemously imply, "Here is what Jesus was trying to say to you if he were as skillful a communicator as I."

Jesus, at least in this pericope, risks ambiguity, metaphor, and "thick" communication. He is not trying to obfuscate the truth but rather to reveal a difficult, counterintuitive, countercultural truth. "Faith," as the word is used here, means more than clarity about the facts, belief in a set of propositions. Faith means encounter with a person, one who is "the way, and the truth, and the life" (14:6). The one who speaks to us in this peculiarly metaphorical way is the one who desires not only that we think about

John 6:24-35

Theological Perspective

surprisingly they frame their inquiries in terms of what is already familiar to them of Moses in times past: "Our ancestors ate the manna in the wilderness; as it is written, 'He gave them bread from heaven to eat'" (v. 31; cf. Exod. 16:15). In Jesus' reply we hear a striking shift of tense from past to present. It is not who "gave," in the sense of whose earthly giving of manna from heaven happened in the past, but who now "gives" the bread that is coming down from heaven and granting life to the world. Not what passes away but what is coming to pass alone can satisfy: "I am the bread of life" (v. 35). And God's work is that belief occur in the one whom the Father in heaven has sent with his own seal to give "the food that endures for eternal life."

The last words from the crowd, as here rendered, sound remarkably expectant and considerate, perhaps even approaching prayer: "Sir, give us this bread always" (v. 34).

What Would a Faithful Hearing Be Today? "Christ does not reply to the question put to him," writes John Calvin, when we seek "in Christ something other than Christ himself."[3] Yet the questioning of Jesus, misdirected as it is, is not disregarded in this passage but used to disclose a more confounding truth. The very signs the crowds look for obscure what is already there for them of life-and-death significance. The demands they make are overtaken by the bread of life that they are given. The works they insistently ask about performing mistake the work God is performing of bringing them to life in faith. What Jesus here saw before him, Martin Luther (1483–1546) in a sermon surmised, were "uncouth and coarse people who were interested solely in eating and drinking."

However uncouth and coarse, a misplaced confidence is shown to pervade their quest. And yet it is precisely with these that the Jesus of John's Gospel engages in such a way that they are led to prayer.

CHRISTOPHER MORSE

Pastoral Perspective

This is a hard saying for those who have everything and who need nothing—except to be transformed by faith in Jesus. Most of what we celebrate and espouse in First-World Christianity is merely instrumental in nature. This is more subtle and more deadly than becoming rice Christians or enthusiasts for faith that leads to political liberty. Perhaps the most startling place for us to end is where the text begins: "Rabbi," the crowd asks Jesus, "when did you come here?" It is a play on words. On the surface they want to know when he came (geographically) to where they discovered him.[1] But they also mean (even without knowing, as is typical of John) that they want to know when the Son of God came here to earth. He came from God, and he came to do the work of his Father, to give his life for the sake of the world, so that those who trust in him might receive everlasting life. Do we believe the good news—not caring whether believing brings us material prosperity or personal happiness—for that new, transformed life along the way? Let us stop making rice Christians.

O. BENJAMIN SPARKS

---

3. John Calvin, *The Gospel according to St. John, Part One 1–10*, in *Calvin's New Testament Commentaries*, trans. T. H. L. Parker (Grand Rapids: Eerdmans, 1961), 152.

1. Gerard S. Sloyan, *John*, Interpretation (Atlanta: John Knox Press, 1988), 67. Also consulted: Lesslie Newbigin, *The Light Has Come, An Exposition of the Fourth Gospel* (Grand Rapids: Eerdmans, 1982) and Walter Brueggemann et al., *Texts for Preaching, A Lectionary Commentary Based on the NRSV—Year B* (Louisville, KY: Westminster John Knox Press, 1993).

Exegetical Perspective

whole of his mission in the world, which he must "complete" (*telesthai*), ultimately on the cross (4:34; 5:36; 17:4; 19:30; cf. 14:9–12). For those who come to him, Jesus here defines "the work of God" as faith in himself, God's envoy in the world (v. 29)—an astonishing claim. If we put ourselves in the place of the questioners, we hear a demand for unconditional commitment. Faith in Jesus, in this Gospel, entails alienation from "the world" (17:14, 16)—in practical terms, alienation from the majority community and total allegiance to a sect that is despised and even persecuted (16:1–4). No wonder they insist, as we would, on proof that he is who he says he is. And, in a community faithful to Israel's history and Scriptures, what proofs count more than miracles, tradition, and the Bible?

So the questioners demand a sign from Jesus, a "work" (v. 30, *sēmeion, ergazein*)—but, ironically, it is precisely the sign he already did, for the story of the miraculous feeding has been told in such a way that the knowing reader understands it to echo the miracle of manna, and that is just the tradition that the questioners here invoke (v. 31), quoting Scripture to nail down their point (Ps. 78:24; cf. Exod. 16:4). In reply, Jesus gives them a lesson in interpreting the Bible. The subject of the sentence, he says, is not Moses, but God, and the tense needs to be changed to the present: Do not read, "Moses gave . . . ," but "God is giving . . ." (v. 32). And then the ambiguous explication, "For the bread of God is that which (or, he who) comes down from heaven" (v. 33, see text note). Verse 35 resolves the ambiguity, in one of the dramatic "I AM" sayings of this Gospel, "I am the bread of life." That breathtaking claim opens the next step in this controversy, which leads on to the decision of faith or rejection.

WAYNE A. MEEKS

Homiletical Perspective

him but that we feed on him, ingest him, implying that we could starve to death without him.

The truth being communicated here is so peculiar that mere surface comprehension, mere intellectual assent, is inadequate to the truth under consideration. Therefore our speech in interpreting Jesus' speech ought to be metaphorical, assertive, declarative, rather than analytical. When John Calvin was asked to explain the Eucharist, he said that he would "rather experience it than to understand it." Actually to feed upon the truth who is Jesus Christ, to find primary sustenance in him, is better even than to understand him.

Furthermore, we are modern people who believe that we have an inalienable right to comprehend everything. One of the promises of modernity was that anyone—regardless of character, talent, or experience—could "get" any idea, provided the proper intellectual methodology was utilized in thinking about the idea. Comprehension is a democratic right. But what if the idea we are attempting to think about is related to "the way, the truth, and the life"? What if the kingdom under consideration is "not of this world" (18:36), the bread being considered is "from heaven" (6:33, 50–51, 58) rather than from here? What if we have a truth here that we are unable to "get"? It may be a truth that must be given. We "get it" as a gift, rather than as our epistemological achievement.

This is the second of five Sundays on this section of John's Gospel. For the next three Sundays the lectionary helpfully follows a progression of ideas on Jesus as the bread of life. This explication on bread of life begins with frank admission that there is a good chance that whatever we think about this subject, we may not get it. Encounter and comprehension of the Word made flesh takes time, humility about what we can and cannot know, and a worshipful willingness to be taught by a Savior who does not come naturally.

Let's eat.

WILLIAM H. WILLIMON

1 Kings 19:4-8

⁴But he himself went a day's journey into the wilderness, and came and sat down under a solitary broom tree. He asked that he might die: "It is enough; now, O LORD, take away my life, for I am no better than my ancestors." ⁵Then he lay down under the broom tree and fell asleep. Suddenly an angel touched him and said to him, "Get up and eat." ⁶He looked, and there at his head was a cake baked on hot stones, and a jar of water. He ate and drank, and lay down again. ⁷The angel of the LORD came a second time, touched him, and said, "Get up and eat, otherwise the journey will be too much for you." ⁸He got up, and ate and drank; then he went in the strength of that food forty days and forty nights to Horeb the mount of God.

Theological Perspective

Teachers of writing generally agree that abstract concepts do not carry much freight in the crafting of fiction. The same may be said of nonfiction—also of opinion and punditry—and, perhaps most especially, of academic theology and preaching. In sum, abstracts such as "love," "anger," "despair," and "hope" are shapeless and fuzzy, without clear definition or content. Good writers, then, will endeavor to show through the emblematic experiences of their characters what these and other abstract words might mean (if only to them). The undeniable power of such work evidences a dark side, however. When life experience is granted unchallenged authority to define all terms, then history is trumped in favor of response, and reinterpretation of sacred texts emerges as the heart of the exegetical enterprise.

Conversely, biblical materials in general and prophetic narratives in particular—not least, this familiar passage regarding Elijah—evidence a different form of testimony. The text uses "concrete" words, and specifically words that have a given historical import—"forty days and forty nights," "broom tree," "a baked cake," "a jar of water," and "the journey" to the "mountain of God"—to interpret the experience, providing this story with an evocative foundation and shape. They suggest a

Pastoral Perspective

Fleeing the wrath of Jezebel, the prophet Elijah experiences the pain of isolation. As a reflection of the loss of his support systems, he sits under "a solitary broom tree." The limited shade of this desert bush does not generate much comfort. Elijah asks God to take his life. How does God respond to Elijah?

Thoughts of death, loss of interest in former activities, fatigue, and feelings of hopelessness are all signs of depression; and Elijah is a likely candidate. Depression is found in every community and in the pews of faithful congregations. Like Elijah, many would cry, "Now, O LORD, take away my life." Elijah recognizes that his existence is a gift of God and that his life is in God's hand. For Elijah and others in dire circumstances, death is often considered to be the best form of redemption that God can offer. Death at the hand of God is more appealing than the revenge that Jezebel has promised. Perhaps Elijah believes his work for God is complete, and in exhaustion he seeks the peace of death. There is also the possibility that Elijah or anyone who experiences depression harbors guilt for previous actions or for failure to act. Careful attention to the condition of depression is a concern for any congregation, and a sermon on this passage can provide a lesson on how to care for those who are depressed.

Exegetical Perspective

The Context of 1 Kings 19. This text is part of the stories about Elijah the Tishbite (1 Kgs. 17–19, 21 and 2 Kings 1–2), the great prophet of Israel. He is on the run, which is remarkable because, in the previous chapter, he won a great victory over the prophets of Baal on Mount Carmel. Elijah had taunted the prophets of Baal to prove that their god was real. They ranted and injured themselves to incite Baal to act, but nothing happened.

Then Elijah built an altar and prepared a sacrifice. He had put water all over and around it. Then he prayed to the Lord. Immediately the fire fell from heaven and consumed everything. When the Israelites saw it, they fell on their faces and shouted, "The Lord indeed is God" (1 Kgs. 18:39). The prophets of Baal were seized, and the echo of Elijah's bold actions against apostasy can still be heard in the New Testament Apocrypha and Pseudepigrapha, where he is portrayed as a model of piety and righteous zeal for the Lord.

When King Ahab reported this event to his wife Jezebel, she became furious and promised to kill Elijah. And while the names of Ahab and Jezebel are not mentioned in today's reading, Israel's king and queen are the ominous threats in the background. This has a clear political element. Elijah was a constant menace toward the royal house. He killed

Homiletical Perspective

This passage continues the theme from the previous week; God's miraculous feeding of those fearful and despairing in the wilderness.[1] Here Elijah, escaping Jezebel's contract on his life, ends up safely in the desert near Beersheba, south out of her jurisdiction. Having left his servant behind, he asks God to end his life, for he thinks he is a failure as a prophet. His heroic success on Mount Carmel and the killing of the prophets of Baal in the Kishon Valley seem to count for nothing now that he is alone with himself in hiding.

High drama precedes this short interlude of a text, and the story line that follows this text is the familiar, dramatic confrontation between God and Elijah on Mount Horeb. The congregation may be so familiar with the exciting stories that bookend today's lesson that they find this quiet text rather dull in comparison. Because the lesson is not contained in the Episcopal lectionary, some will never have heard it before. The preacher is required to set it in context and demonstrate how important it truly is.

In this passage Elijah "wrestles" psychologically with God and God's demands on him, not physically as Jacob did. So, despite the fact that today's story

1. It is a counterpoint too of the story in 1 Kings 17 in which God, through Elijah, miraculously provides food for the widow in Zarephath, saving her and her household from famine.

1 Kings 19:4-8

Theological Perspective

peculiar lens through which to examine and understand the experiences of the characters. The language helps to make connections with other episodes in the great drama of God and the people, offering entry into the discrete richness of both this specific story and also the larger narrative.

This schema is not pristine, of course. For example, the biggest word in 1 Kings 19, "wilderness," is given shape and content by the experience of the Israelites' sojourn after the exodus. But "wilderness," in turn, will provide a powerful opportunity for God's people to reflect on their own subsequent experiences of wandering and redemption, geographic or otherwise.

In this lesson from 1 Kings we discover ourselves, with the prophet, in the middle of an ongoing story with obvious allusions to the exodus and early portions of the wilderness sojourn. If God's provision is one obvious affirmation of both stories—specific and quantifiable—there is also an even more powerful theological motif: the mysterious and unexpected presence of God. As the Israelites "turned toward the wilderness and there, in a cloud, appeared the Presence of the Lord" (Exod. 16:10 Tanakh), Elijah went into the wilderness to experience the presence, provision, and voice of God in ways just as surprising: first, in the ministry and voice of an angel (v. 5), and ultimately in "a soft murmuring sound" (1 Kgs. 19:12 Tanakh). Elijah's "personal experience," then, is placed in context and defined by the prior, corporate experience of the liberated slaves. His experience will in turn add evocative and sticky connotation to Scripture's big words and phrases, helping readers and hearers, interpreters and preachers, to engage and even in some fashion to appropriate this episode in the life of Elijah as their own.

The backdrop of our lesson, so much like the stories of the exodus, is the ongoing war of God through the persons and work of the prophets against idolatrous royalty and their minions. If the plagues are the weapons of choice of God and Moses in the protracted battle against Pharaoh, then apocalyptic fireworks win the day against Ahab and, more particularly, against Jezebel and her imported priests of Baal. In each battle God humiliates the usurpers and pretenders—there is, quite evidently, no God but God.

But if at the Reed Sea and on Mount Carmel God is fighting against "other gods," in the wilderness stories that follow these victories, God is contending for the hearts of the faithful. The latter battles are

Pastoral Perspective

Is Elijah's condition caused by his own sin? Evil as punishment for misbehavior is a predominant belief among the people of God. We can imagine his friends, if any were available, coming to Elijah as they did to Job with a prevailing position of sympathy, but ultimately asking the condemning question about how he has slipped and fallen from the grace of God. Elijah could reply like Job that he has done nothing wrong. Elijah is a faithful servant of the living God. In the prophetic office, Elijah has known the Lord's provision in drought and famine. He speaks God's word to the weak and the powerful. On Mount Carmel, God answers Elijah's prayer for a resounding victory for the God of Abraham, Isaac, and Israel over the false god Baal. At his command, hundreds of the prophets of Baal and Asherah are massacred. Elijah proclaims the end of the drought previously brought on by the hand of the Lord.

Perhaps this faithful servant is experiencing burnout. "I am no better than my ancestors," he confesses. Even without blatant personal sin, Elijah sees no good in his life. Service to God has not brought him to a meaningful place in a congregation of the faithful. He assumes that he can be of no further service to the Lord. And what good is life without meaningful purpose?

Another possibility is that Elijah is overcome by the magnitude of evil around him. Jezebel convinces her husband, King Ahab, to lead the people of Israel away from YHWH to the worship of Baal. When Elijah confronts the prophets of Baal, orchestrates the victory of God on Mount Carmel, and orders their execution, Jezebel is furious. She swears revenge and promises to kill him. Elijah is now in a state of living death. Jezebel's power diminishes Elijah by isolating him from his people and turning him into a victim. His choices are limited, because he believes that he is the only remaining prophet of YHWH. Feeling the hopelessness of his situation, Elijah flees into the wilderness and seeks an end to his life.

In every situation God makes redemption possible. Whether the redemption needed is for individuals whose offenses estrange them from God, others, and themselves or for individuals who suffer from the sinful actions of others, God breaks the power of evil and offers new life. Elijah's story reveals the redemption that God brings to those who are trapped in depression. In response to an individual who has lost hope and direction for life and who has a poor sense of self-worth, God acts with compassion.

Through God's loving action, Elijah experiences redemption. An angel provides food and water to

the prophets of Baal, undoubtedly strong supporters of the crown, especially of the queen. Such an affront could not go unanswered. The threat also has a theological or religious ingredient. Elijah made the prophets of Baal, and therefore Baal himself, look like fools. As a result, Elijah was deemed a criminal and enemy of the state. He had to flee for his life, out of the territory of Jezebel and Ahab (1 Kgs. 19:3; cf. Amos 7:12). He fled south, to Beersheba in Judah. There he left his servant and went on farther south alone, a day's journey in the wilderness. Elijah was a hunted man.

Today's reading has two parts. In the first part Elijah expresses his despair. In the second part an angel of the Lord twice brings food and drink. The story may draw on material from independent sources, but the result is a literary unit with its own coherence.

Elijah Expresses His Despair (v. 4). The first part makes clear that Elijah did not find a safe haven south of Beersheba. The wilderness is a dangerous place with little to support life. Elijah has experienced that before (1 Kgs. 17:1–7), but this time it is even more dangerous, because now the prophet is completely worn out, distressed, and dismayed. He is at the end of his tether and falls asleep.

He cannot escape the heat of the sun or the despair of his heart. The Hebrew says explicitly that Elijah sat under "one" (and not "a") broom tree. This species of shrub does not necessarily grow solitarily. But for the lonely prophet, the lonely broom tree reflects his situation of isolation, depression, disillusion, and sense of futility. The text provides a number of explicit symptoms of the prophet's "burnout." Ignoring Obadiah's hundred prophets (1 Kgs. 18:1–6), ignoring the jubilee of the people (1 Kgs. 18:39), the prophet can see only the darkest side of the situation. He cries out "It is enough," and uses a simple imperative verb: "take away my life."

Offer of Food and Drink (vv. 5–8). The second part starts while the prophet is asleep. Perhaps this is a dream. But in that case, the dream has such an impact that Elijah reckons it as a dynamic and effective disclosure of the Lord's presence. Sleep can be a moment of the appearance of God's presence (Pss. 4:9; 127:2).

The angel of the Lord touches him, commands him, and feeds him. The messenger provides Elijah with food, warm bread, and water. Although Elijah asks to die, the messenger of the Lord brings life. He

isn't especially thrilling, it is more accessible to the preacher and the congregation who share familiar feelings of failure, despair, and fear. It is easier for us to relate to Elijah on the lam than Elijah slaughtering his enemies or speaking directly with the Lord, like Moses, on the mountaintop.

The preacher will want to explain what leads up to this despairing scene in order for the congregation to understand the sudden change in Elijah's confidence. Rather than considering himself a victor, he asks God to take away his worthless life. Elijah exhibits some of the characteristics that mark battle-worn soldiers who suffer from PTSD, post-traumatic stress disorder. Violence on the battlefield wreaks havoc, even with the so-called winners.

His thoughts of suicide need to be named for what they are, because undoubtedly there are listeners in the congregation who contemplate the same for themselves. Suicidal ideations are frightening and alienating. The preacher has an opportunity to talk freely about how awful depression is, and then tell of the hope treatment offers.

Due to the nature of their vocation, prophets are placed in the midst of the tension between the holiness of their God-given message and their own sense of unworthiness. Listeners need to understand just how difficult is the role of the prophet. God understands.

God has compassion on Elijah and sends an angel to minister to him. He is not left alone, his life is not taken. Rather, he is fed and given rest—perhaps suggesting to us the words of Jesus, "Come to me, all you that are weary and are carrying heavy burdens, and I will give you rest" (Matt. 11:28). God's ministry of angels takes a variety of contemporary forms, of course, from loving friends to specially trained therapists. Fortunately, Elijah demonstrates strength as he cries out to the Lord, the one who listens. He also allows himself to be cared for. Elijah refuses to life a live of quiet desperation.

Another way to shape the sermon might be to stress the need for time away, because, as Alice Walker writes, "wisdom requests a pause."[2] Flight from all that is death dealing is needed to reorder our lives in communion with God. Elijah had to pause and let go of his fear before he could embrace the transition to what was next in his life.

2. In Alice Walker's essay entitled "All Praises to the Pause, the Universal Moment of Reflection," in *We Are the Ones We Have Been Waiting For: Light in a Time of Darkness* (New York: New Press, 2006), she goes on to say, the "pause is the moment when something major is accomplished and we are so relieved to finally be done with it that we are already rushing, at least mentally, into The Future. Wisdom, however, requests a pause. If we cannot give ourselves such a pause, the Universe will likely give it to us" (p. 49).

1 Kings 19:4-8

Theological Perspective

not won by plagues or dramatic demonstrations of power—nor, as it turns out, by fire, wind, or earthquake—but rather by the ministry of angels, the gift of food, and the still, small voice. In the lesson before us we see the aftermath of the first battle (God against Baal) and the first engagements of the second (God for Elijah).

Though he has called fire from heaven, Elijah himself quickly melts in the heat of Jezebel's rage. He fears for his life, leaves both Carmel and his servant, and goes into the wilderness where he prays to die. His response is at once incomprehensible—he has just invoked God with effect against 400 prophets, so why is he afraid of this witch queen?—and at the same both vocationally (see Jonah 4:3) and anthropologically authentic. "I am no better than my ancestors," he says (19:4). We may take him to mean at the very least that he is no *different* from the Israelites who soon after their dramatic deliverance from Pharaoh and Egyptian slavery longed for death. But God provides life for Elijah instead, much as God provided manna and quail for his ancestors. Like the Israelites, Elijah experiences God's provision in spite of himself.

The same might be said of Jesus' providing bread for the multitudes in John 6:21. There is gracious provision even when the beneficiaries neither ask nor understand. Typologically, however, the Elijah story is more attuned to Mark's account of Jesus' temptations. Unlike Matthew and Luke, Mark gives no specific content to the tests but his conclusion is evocative: "[Jesus] was in the wilderness forty days . . . and he was with the wild beasts; and the angels waited on him" (Mark 1:13). The story of Elijah, following the story of the Israelites, anticipates (for Christians) the stories of Jesus, giving us the means for a kind of mutual interrogation between the stories and our own pilgrimage of faith.

The "wilderness" is a place of both giving and testing, a season of provision and obedience, a time of physical weakness and even despair, but also an occasion of spiritual strengthening and vocational redefinition. The words of God, as much as manna or cakes, are a feast for the famished faithful and a means for reinterpreting their experience so that the battle against idolatry and presumption, whether it occurs in the palace, on the mountain, or in the heart, may continue.

THOMAS R. STEAGALD

Pastoral Perspective

rebuild Elijah's strength. God's messenger also directs Elijah to sleep and offers another portion of food and rest on the second day. Then God takes him on a spiritual journey—a forty-day trip to Mount Horeb. Elijah knows that his journey is like the forty days Moses experienced on that same holy mountain in preparation for receiving the tablets of the law (Exod. 24:18). God honors Elijah by comparing him with Moses, the great leader of the Hebrew people. The journey ends in a cave, perhaps the same cleft of the rock from which Moses was able to see God. The redemption of Elijah takes time. It requires compassionate nurture and the recovery of Elijah's sense of his value to God. Elijah's worth is not based on his performing great feats for God or dependent upon overcoming evil in his own strength. Elijah's worth is found in God's love for him and in the call of God upon his life. God's redemption leads to further prophetic service to God in Elijah's life.

God responded in the passion of Jesus Christ to redeem the world. For humans who must face death, Jesus offers his own death as a substitution. In Christ's atoning sacrifice, humanity is set free from the destructive force of evil and offered the love of God. The love of God's action in Christ can redeem every situation and reveal to humans their value to God. The resurrection of Christ inaugurates an eschatological new creation. Every individual redeemed in Christ has new value as a child of God and receives the attention and care of God through the community of faith—the family of God. Each is sent on a spiritual journey that leads to the holy mountain of God's glory. Human worth does not depend upon living a sinless life. It is the concrete love of God that provides humans with self-worth and meaning for life.

SUSAN E. VANDE KAPPELLE

bids the prophet rise and eat. Elijah receives from the angel what he himself gave to the widow in a previous chapter (1 Kgs. 17:12, 16).

Elijah's actions in verse 6 are all described with one-word sentences: he looked, he ate, he drank, he returned, he lay down. There is no elaborate dialogue; Elijah says as little as is needed.

Despite the fact that Elijah is fed, he is still exhausted and "returns" to sleep. The messenger of the Lord "returns" also. He touches Elijah again and directs him for the second time to rise and eat. Then the prophet starts to recover, so that he becomes strong enough for a journey to Mount Horeb.

This part of the scene has a remarkable parallel in wording in the scene portrayed in 17:12–16. In both chapters it is ultimately the Lord who provides food and life. Whether this provision involves a raven, a widow, or an angel, they are all "messengers" from the Lord, bringing the goods and support that make life possible.

Parallel between Elijah and Moses. The whole Old Testament makes a strong comparison between Moses and Elijah. This passage draws remarkable parallels between Elijah's wandering and Moses' sojourn on the Mount of God. First, we hear both Moses and Elijah pray that they may die and be released from their burdensome and apparently hopeless missions (1 Kgs. 19:4; Num. 11:11–15). Second, Elijah travels forty days and nights to Mount Horeb/Sinai (1 Kgs. 19: 5–8), the place where Moses received the tables of the covenant during a stay of forty days and nights (Exod. 24:12–18; 32:30–35; Deut. 9:8–10). Third, both Moses and Elijah ask for a special revelation in a moment when they are disheartened about their position (Exod. 33:12–23; 34:33–35). Finally, Moses is hidden in a "cleft of the rock" while the Lord passes by and his mercy and justice are proclaimed (Exod. 33:12–34:7). Elijah comes to a cave (1 Kgs. 19:9) where the Lord reveals himself in the quiet stillness (1 Kgs. 19:11–12).

REIN BOS

Furthermore, Elijah's movement toward Mount Horeb—where Moses earlier received the law during the time of transition when the Israelites fled from Egypt—reminds us of the command to "Remember the sabbath day, and keep it holy" (Exod. 20:8). The preacher, including the forty-day experiences in each of their stories, can highlight many prophetic connections between Moses and Elijah.

Still again, the story's emphasis on food might lead the preacher to consider the sacrament of Communion, and how it reunites us with God in Christ. Indeed, the lectionary pairs the many verses about bread in John's Gospel (John 6) with this text. Post-Communion prayers voice thanksgiving for the strength contained in the sacrament, but then the liturgy urges us to "go and serve the Lord" using the energy received for ministry in the world.

The repetition on the theme of feeding surely is to reinforce our faith in God's steadfast care for us. The more often we hear the variety of stories of how God provides nourishment, the more readily we can believe that God intends for all to be fed and made strong, and that we are to minister on behalf of those in need. God's grace multiplies miraculously, exponentially, as bread is broken and shared. It is a challenge for us to trust that there will be more than enough for everyone. God's economy of abundance collides with the conventional wisdom that holds tight to the myth of scarcity. This sermon can lift up a life-giving countercultural perspective to what Walter Brueggemann calls our "society of skimpiness": "Jesus offers an alternative to the anxiety that assumes we never have enough when he says, 'Therefore I tell you, do not worry about your life, what you will eat or what you will drink, or about your body, what you will wear'"[3] (Matt. 6:25).

DEAN MCDONALD

---

3. Walter Brueggemann, "Loves Abound—Dayenu!" *Bread,* September/October 1997.

Psalm 34:1-8

¹I will bless the LORD at all times;
  his praise shall continually be in my mouth.
²My soul makes its boast in the LORD;
  let the humble hear and be glad.
³O magnify the LORD with me,
  and let us exalt his name together.

⁴I sought the LORD, and he answered me,
  and delivered me from all my fears.
⁵Look to him, and be radiant;
  so your faces shall never be ashamed.
⁶This poor soul cried, and was heard by the LORD,
  and was saved from every trouble.
⁷The angel of the LORD encamps
  around those who fear him, and delivers them.
⁸O taste and see that the LORD is good;
  happy are those who take refuge in him.

Theological Perspective

According to Lawrence Sullivan in his book *Ichanchu's Drum*, religion has four main aspects: cosmogony (where does creation come from?), cosmology (what is the nature of creation?), anthropology (who are human beings?), and terminology or eschatology (where is life going?). This psalm text is about anthropology, and in particular it offers us a window into Judeo-Christian anthropology. Although at first the text seems to speak about God and God's character, it also points to the human condition of those who believe in God.

The psalmist invites readers to exuberant praise for God. Soul and body are to express praise for God's mercy and protection in all circumstances of life. "I will bless the LORD at all times; his praise shall continually be in my mouth" is the ultimate imperative of one who has seen or experienced the steadfast love and mercy of God. The invitation in verse 3, "O magnify the LORD with me, and let us exalt his name together," is an invitation to others who need to be persuaded and perhaps convinced that the community of faith's main mission is to exalt and glorify God.

The psalmist knows, however, that not everyone has an awareness of the true imperative of human beings to praise God. Consequently, the psalmist takes us through the journey of human conditions

Pastoral Perspective

The Psalter is a hymnal, and so, from a pastoral point of view, its songs are best understood as hymns that found and form communal life. Our ancestors have been singing these songs for thousands of years, but each psalm's intended function is the same as those of such newfangled tunes as "Abide with Me" and "Amazing Grace." They are meant to shape us as we sing. They are meant to place us in a particular situation or scene or stance, enjoy the company of others there, and depart the song as different people.

To assist with this formative training, whoever finally edited the Psalter as we have it saw fit to include an occasional introductory note, a so-called superscription (not printed in this volume) that frames the singing even before the musicians begin to play. In the case of Psalm 34, the editor attributes the song to David, that sweet and celebrated lyre player and singer of Israel, but also to a particular sequence of events in David's life. While fleeing the murderous Saul, David encounters the priest Ahimelech, the king Achish, and then the cave called Adullam (1 Sam. 21:1–22:2). In the superscription, this sequence is jumbled and conflated into a single episode. In other words, the editor conceives Samuel's narrative as we might a Broadway musical in which the hero David, having just evaded the king

Exegetical Perspective

What Is the Genre of This Psalm? Psalm 34 is a thanksgiving psalm, with features found also in Wisdom literature. It teaches in the style of Proverbs 1–9. For example, it designates hearers as "children" (lit. "sons") in verse 11 (cf. Prov. 1:8; 3:1; 4:1); it insists on fear of the Lord in verses 7, 9, 11 (cf. Prov. 1:7, 29; 2:5; 9:10; 15:33); and it promises that "life" results from obedience to the master's teaching in verses 12, 22 (cf. Prov. 4:4; 7:2; 9:6). It is also a testimony to deliverance. One scholar even classifies it as a testimony: "We should hardly call it a thanksgiving, since there is not one line addressed to Yhwh."[1] Biblical thanksgivings, however, can have a didactic style and also give testimony. One need not speak directly to God, for a thanksgiving is essentially a public report of how God rescued a person or persons from danger. One tells others so they too might appreciate and lend their own voices in praise of the Lord's kindness and power.

In the Bible, people do not simply say thank you to God; the Bible does not even have a word for "thank you." Instead, biblical authors tell others what God has done, in a sense giving the one thing God "lacks" on earth—the acknowledgment and love of

1. John Goldingay, *Psalms: Volume 1 (Psalms 1–41)* (Grand Rapids: Baker Academic, 2006), 477.

Homiletical Perspective

The preacher who seeks to use the Psalms as text and theme must draw upon his or her deepest poetic instincts. The psalms are poetry, and their words often lose their flavor when they are analyzed chemically before they are tasted.

Consider, first, what it is to "bless the LORD" (v. 1). There is no more powerful act we can muster than to bless someone. When we bless someone, we say holy and encouraging words to them; we bestow positive energy. The Latin word "benediction" has an informative etymology here. If *bene* means "good," and *dicere* is "to say," then "to give a benediction" is to speak good to someone. When we bless someone, we speak good words to them.

"Give me your blessing" was a common request of our ancestors in the faith. We tend to restrict the use of "blessing" to what a minister does at the end of a liturgical service and what we are supposed to do before we eat our food. Or we might say, "God bless you," after a sneeze. But what if we are meant to be blessing people regularly? What if fathers and mothers took it upon themselves to bless each other, and to bless their children, regularly?

Psalm 34, like many of the psalms, shows forth its power in its ability to bless; but, furthermore, it takes on the special task of blessing God. What can it possibly mean to "bless" God? The word "bless" can

Psalm 34:1-8

Theological Perspective

and requests for God's merciful and gracious deliverance. "I sought the LORD, and he answered me, and delivered me" (v. 4). "This poor soul cried, and was heard by the LORD" (v. 6). For those who wonder about the community's imperative, the psalmist highlights the nature and character of God as one who creates in the human being an imperative for praise and glory. Therefore praise is also a testimony, a biographical narrative of God's merciful acts in the life of the community.

Fear is a human condition, and the psalmist addresses it: "The angel of the LORD encamps around those who fear [God], and delivers them" (v. 7). Fear is an all too common term in early twenty-first-century American discourse. The events of 9/11, the subsequent terrorist attacks around the world, and the political instability of fragile non-Western democracies all seem to create the justification to respond to fear with vengeful violence.

This psalm can be a double-edged sword. On the one hand, we emphasize "the Lord encamps," and we create our safe space with segregation and so-called national security measures, shifting our imperative from praising God to protecting ourselves from others. Refuge is to be found, however, in God's deliverance, not in our own efforts for protection.

Why would those who have the power to segregate themselves need protection? If the anthropological imperative of the Judeo-Christian tradition is to praise God—for God is protector and delivers God's people from evil—then why would believers seek to protect themselves by their own resources?

On the other hand, the psalm can also be used as a personal, blinding shield when we face hardships and tribulations. Denial of life's tragedies (such as terminal illness, natural disasters, unexpected death) becomes an unconscious strategy to deny reality and, regretfully, to justify our denial of reality. The human condition is fragile. As a result, "the Lord encamps" becomes a language game, for frequently we do not experience the deliverance of God but, rather, miss it by focusing on our own human strengths. When we succeed, God is put aside, and *we* become the focus of our praise. When we lose and show our vulnerability, God is blamed, so that anger shapes our relationship with God.

The psalmist gives us a clue to our human purpose and condition as we explore the human imperative to praise God. In verses 17–18, the psalmist reminds us: "When the righteous cry for help, the LORD hears and rescues them from all their

Pastoral Perspective

and "escaped to the cave of Adullam," breaks into an original song of praise, thereafter preserved as Psalm 34. Or, perhaps better, the editor imagines David composing the song there in the cave, waiting for "his brothers and all his father's house" to arrive (1 Sam. 22:1).

Psalm 34 is a carefully crafted, elegant acrostic, each verse beginning with a successive letter of the Hebrew alphabet, ʾaleph to tav. In this sense, it is an example of lyrical virtuosity, harnessing the ecstasies of deliverance within a strict alphabetical pattern. But this craft has theological dimensions too. If the editor situates Psalm 34 in a particular moment of Israel's sacred history, the song's alphabetical framework suggests a poetic universality and wholeness, "A to Z," as we would say. In this sense, then, Psalm 34 may be taken as a paradigmatic form, a comprehensive pastoral model for what to do, not only after a narrow escape, but always and everywhere.

Accordingly, the song begins, "I will bless the LORD at all times; his praise shall continually be in my mouth." The Hebrew word here for "to bless" (*barak*) can also be translated "to kneel," and so in this opening lyric, doxology and deference coincide in the promised stance of perpetually blessing the Lord. But this blessing, it turns out, is not only for the Lord's sake, or even for the psalmist's. It is also good news for those nearby who need it most: "Let the humble hear and be glad. O magnify the LORD with me, and let us exalt his name together." In other words, Psalm 34:1–8 is a miniature sermon meant to hearten and rally the "humble" (*'anav*, a Hebrew term also translatable as "poor," "weak," or "afflicted"). Indeed, as the psalmist's own story goes on to make clear by implication, this is a sermon for those who are afraid (v. 4), ashamed (v. 5), distressed (v. 6), persecuted (v. 7), unhappy (v. 8), and vulnerable (v. 8). In this way, the singer's testimony is fundamentally evangelical (in the root sense of "bearing good news"), a case of one "poor soul" encouraging others (v. 6), and so inviting them into the celebrative song.

In pastoral life and work, a frequent topic of reflection and strategy is how to minister effectively to people beset by the sorrows that attend loss, suffering, and guilt, so much so that the very idea of ministry is sometimes reduced to "serving the sorrowful." But occasions of great joy also require wise guidance and sound communal forms. Psalm 34 provides an intriguing template for what to do in circumstances worth celebrating (an escape from a hostile king, for instance, but also a favorable

human beings. The report of deliverance thus enlarges the circle of those who revere the Lord. Praising is thus a form of giving thanks. It must be admitted, however, that the testimonial and didactic style are unusually pronounced in Psalm 34. That the psalmist here resembles the teacher in Proverbs is simply an indication that the psalmist knows how to teach in the traditional manner. In form, the poem is an acrostic, that is, each line begins with a successive letter of the Hebrew alphabet of twenty-two consonants (though there is some irregularity). The device provides unity and adds interest; the A-Z structure suggests completeness.

A Look at Verses 1–8. Verse 1a states the psalmist's intention to bless God ("I will bless"); it is immediately seconded and amplified by the parallel verse ("his praise"). For God to bless human beings is to bestow on them qualities they do not have and greatly need—health, wealth, children, loving spouses, standing in the community. But how can humans bless God? What can they give that God does not already possess? The answer is partially given in verse 2b: by boasting in the Lord (acknowledging God as one's strength), and by rejoicing in God. This is what the psalmist is eager to provide (v. 1) and will invite others to join in providing (vv. 2b–3). A thanksgiving psalm is not the record of a private transaction between an individual and the Lord. The psalmist is eager to be overheard and to have the song be sung by others. The people called to join in are called "the humble (*'anawim).* The word can be rendered "poor," "afflicted," or "lowly." The word refers to those in great need—from poverty or from some other affliction—who trustingly wait for the Lord to intervene on their behalf. Deliberately, the singer becomes a model for such people, "This poor soul cried, and was heard by the LORD." The singer was in the same situation (vv. 4b and 6) and had the faith and courage to cry for help. It is possible to paraphrase verse 3b: "May the humble hear my song and join with me in singing." Note that the verb "be glad, rejoice" (*samakh*) can refer to external expression of one's joyful state and thus can occasionally mean "to shout, make a joyful noise."

In verses 4–8, report, reflection, and exhortations alternate: report (v. 4), exhortation (v. 5), report and reflection (vv. 6–7), exhortation (vv. 8–9), reflection (v. 10). Verse 4 gives the reason for the song: the singer was rescued "from all my fears." "Fears" should be taken in an objective sense, of *what* one

mean "speak good words to," but this psalm provides another meaning: to magnify the Lord. To bless someone is to build them up, to magnify them (v. 3 says "magnify the LORD with me").

As large as God is, beyond our very comprehension, the psalmist still seeks to magnify God even more. Might it be that our blessing God actually magnifies our image of God? If our perception of God can be amplified, surely our perception of other people can be amplified. If we bless God and raise perceptions of God, surely we can bless other people and raise perceptions of them too!

While on the subject of "magnify" and "amplify," the preacher might well pause to consider what tendencies and events our culture specializes in amplifying. Do we emphasize good news or bad news? Do we magnify the unfortunate qualities of our colleagues or their encouraging qualities?

The great family-systems therapist Edwin Friedman has noted how sick systems (whether they be families or communities or churches) tend to increase anxiety. When conflicts, or even crises, occur, one sign of ill health is how the system amplifies anxiety, which then tends to build back upon itself. Friedman would claim that health emerges from a "non-anxious presence"; but that presence might be strengthened by an ability to magnify the Lord, to magnify the grace and peace of God. Thus Psalm 34 reminds us what is worth magnifying: God's presence, God's answers, and God's deliverance.

The psalmist invites us to exalt God's name "together." Bernhard Anderson has noted that this is an invitation for community to enter into blessing.[1] How powerful a community can become when it knows how to bless God together! It follows that the preacher might next use this text to consider what his or her community should be blessing.

There are many communities of faith today held together more by what they *condemn* together than by what they bless together. Is your community one that condemns together or one that blesses together? "Let us exalt his name together," is the hope of Psalm 34.

When the psalmist declares, "Look to him and be radiant," the images hearken back to the radiance of Moses. It was Moses whose face shone with glory after he had been in the presence of God. Can the preacher describe a radiant face she has seen lately?

In particular, however, the hearer is urged to "look to him" in order to be radiant. The Lord might

1. Bernhard Anderson, *Out of the Depths* (Louisville, KY: Westminster John Knox Press, 2000), 150.

Psalm 34:1-8

Theological Perspective

troubles. The LORD is near to the brokenhearted, and saves the crushed in spirit." The text suggests that the righteous who cry for help, the brokenhearted, and the crushed in spirit are the subjects of the Lord's deliverance. It is hard to determine in the text whether their conditions are externally imposed or internally generated. What we know is that believers are not to deceive themselves, claiming to be brokenhearted or crushed in spirit for the sake of segregating themselves from others. They are not to create their safe space and deny their vulnerability for the sake of preventing their shame. Deliverance can come only as we embrace our imperative to praise God, to "look to him, and be radiant; so your faces shall never be ashamed" (v. 5).

A distinguished Brazilian theologian was shot during a robbery in downtown São Paulo. After several days in the hospital, a fellow priest assured him that he was praying that God would deliver the theologian from his terrible pain. The theologian replied, "Do not pray for me. Pray for those whose lives are in constant peril in the *favelas* [poorer neighborhoods] of our city, suffering from the oppression and despair of lack of food, health care, housing—basic human needs." His fellow priest inquired, "But why should I not pray for you? You have suffered a tragedy, and you have been close to death."

"My esteemed brother," the theologian tenderly answered, "do not confuse the realities of life with the realities of a life strangled. I praise God for all God has given me, but I don't need to be delivered from this pain, because it nourishes my solidarity with those who suffer for no reason in this world."

As those in the Judeo-Christian tradition discover the character of God, they also discover the answer to the question "Who are we?" "My soul makes its boast in the LORD; let the humble hear and be glad. O magnify the LORD with me, and let us exalt his name together" (vv. 2–3). As we witness and testify to God's deliverance, we are launched to live our true human vocation. We are agents of praise—no less, no more.

CARLOS F. CARDOZA-ORLANDI

Pastoral Perspective

medical test result, a reconciliation between estranged communities, or a brand-new baby girl). As we have seen, since Psalm 34 frames all of human life doxologically, the question is not *whether* to "bless" God, but *how*. To this question of *how*, Psalm 34 implicitly provides a twofold answer: first, form your praise into a beautiful thing (if not an intricate acrostic poem, then a simple, lovely work of art nonetheless); and second, tell your artful story to the afflicted and afraid, so that they might "taste and see that the LORD is good" (v. 8). That is, the psalmist recommends that you transform your good fortune into compassionate, beautiful testimony for "the humble," lifting their spirits so that they too might join the celebration. This is the key, Psalm 34 suggests, to how joy is well done.

After all, this is exactly what David does in 1 Samuel 22. He is a shepherd—the good pastor—who knows his sheep. After his escape, some "four hundred" of his allies gather around him in "the cave of Adullam." But this band of resistance is composed, as Samuel tells it, of none other than "the humble." "Everyone who was in distress, and everyone who was in debt, and everyone who was discontented gathered to him" (1 Sam. 22:2). Perhaps this is why the Psalter's editor associates Psalm 34 with this episode in David's life. Enthralled by the joy of deliverance, David sings a song that tells his story in a way that heartens and rallies "the humble" around him in a widening chorus of praise. Christian churches should do the same. That is, we should gather together in our exilic caves, bless God and one another with beautiful testimonies, and then at last, there at the Table where Christ the shepherd—the good pastor—is host, "taste and see that the LORD is good" (Ps. 34:8).

MATTHEW MYER BOULTON

Exegetical Perspective

fears, not the emotion of fear. Exactly what the singer feared is left unspecified (as is often true in the Psalms) in order that the psalm may be used by others. Verse 4b, literally, "from all that he fears he delivers him," is echoed with only slight changes (in the Hebrew) in verses 6b and 17b, forming a thread through the poem. The repetition underlines the fact that one may attain intimacy with God, but never equality; one always stands in need of God's help. In verse 5, the psalmist does not say (as moderns are wont to do), "Look at me," but "Look to God." The psalmist is speaking to move others to praise and obey God, not to be the center of attention. The phrase "be radiant" (v. 5) occurs also in Isaiah 60:5, where it describes the faces of the people of Zion as they look at the nations bringing their treasures in homage; it refers to a bright and smiling countenance (Jer. 31:12). "Never be ashamed" (v. 5b) means that what one trusted has proved reliable.

"The angel of the LORD" (v. 7) is a member of the heavenly court. Such angels sometimes have a military function (as in Judg. 2:1–4; 6:11–22), and here the angel is a military escort for those who fear the Lord. The figure is a concrete way of expressing divine protection. Later belief in guardian angels comes from such passages as this. "Taste" is a metaphor for experience in Hebrew and in English. In Ezekiel 3:3, God tells the prophet, "Eat this scroll that I give you and fill your stomach with it. Then I ate it; and in my mouth it was as sweet as honey." The psalmist exclaims in Psalm 119:103, "How sweet are your words to my taste, sweeter than honey to my mouth!" Experience is the best teacher of the truth that God is a refuge. God will protect the poor, though mighty lions go hungry.

RICHARD J. CLIFFORD

Homiletical Perspective

be rather like the sun, our star, after all. It shines forth light that is then reflected. Those who look to God actually reflect God. The one who sees God is rather like the moon, then, or a planet, reflecting the light of the sun. Even if each of us reflects that light at a different angle, or with perhaps a slightly different hue, the light itself is the light of deliverance (vv. 4 and 6).

At verse 8, we finally have an image not of radiance and blessing, but of taste: "Taste and see that the LORD is good." Thus, this portion of the psalm (1–8) begins with praise in the believer's mouth and ends with an allusion to taste in the believer's mouth. Perhaps the way to taste of the goodness of God is, first, to speak of the goodness of God. When one speaks with the tongue, the tongue itself begins to taste of God's grace.

All of this is to say that the Psalms are not meant to be examined, analyzed, and therefore delivered over to rationality for their final authentication. Rather, the final authentication is in the tasting itself. The spiritual authority of the psalm (and of all the psalms) arrives in our very sensory experience of the grace of God.

The preacher would do well to speak as poetically as possible when dealing with the poetic images of this psalm. Denise Levertov, for instance, whose father was raised a Hasidic Jew and then became an Anglican priest, offers a taste of this sensory experience of grace in her poem "O Taste and See:"[2] The preacher might ask his or her congregation, "Where are the places in our community where we can actually taste God?"

SAM CANDLER

---

2. Denise Levertov, "O Taste and See," in *O Taste and See* (New York: New Directions Press, 1964).

Ephesians 4:25–5:2

25So then, putting away falsehood, let all of us speak the truth to our neighbors, for we are members of one another. 26Be angry but do not sin; do not let the sun go down on your anger, 27and do not make room for the devil. 28Thieves must give up stealing; rather let them labor and work honestly with their own hands, so as to have something to share with the needy. 29Let no evil talk come out of your mouths, but only what is useful for building up, as there is need, so that your words may give grace to those who hear. 30And do not grieve the Holy Spirit of God, with which you were marked with a seal for the day of redemption. 31Put away from you all bitterness and wrath and anger and wrangling and slander, together with all malice, 32and be kind to one another, tenderhearted, forgiving one another, as God in Christ has forgiven you. 1Therefore be imitators of God, as beloved children, 2and live in love, as Christ loved us and gave himself up for us, a fragrant offering and sacrifice to God.

Theological Perspective

At first glance, this passage looks like a list of rules for the new life of being a Christian. Echoing the Decalogue, Paul lists acts that are prohibited before he enumerates the behaviors Christians are to embrace. However, the key to the passage is at the beginning. The new believers are to "put off" or "strip away" the old self so that God can give them the new. This verb is also used in verse 22 of this chapter: "You were taught to put away your former way of life, your old self." This fundamental repentance and renewal comes at baptism and is a prerequisite to doing these tasks. The behavioral changes coming from that conversion is the theme of this section.

We go from the old self to the new creation in baptism. As we go under the waters of death, the old self is killed off and we are raised with Christ into newness of life. In the first liturgies of the church, the baptismal candidates faced the west and renounced the forces of darkness. They then turned to the east at sunrise and proclaimed their allegiance to the light of the world. They literally stripped off their old clothing and put on the new garments of being adopted by Christ as children of God after they were baptized. They were then brought into the community of faith.

In baptism the old self is killed off, and the new self is raised. The Episcopal liturgy expresses this

Pastoral Perspective

The passage lists virtues and duties that mark the transformed and transforming community. It begins with a gentle irony: we do not lie to ourselves, do we? Because "we are members of each other," we must be as truthful with each other as we are with ourselves. The call to truth as a hallmark of community is a call to honesty about the individual and corporate self.

Amazon.com currently lists more than forty thousand religious titles that touch on the subject of anger. That number testifies to the level of difficulty we have with this emotion. Each pastor knows the damage that suppressed and denied anger does, and each knows that there is no aggression quite like passive aggression. It is enough to say here that our passage acknowledges anger. "Be angry" (v. 26) is not an imperative; it is an acknowledgment that anger will be present. The ways to deal with anger without sinning begin with dealing with it today (before sundown). The demonic mischief that unresolved anger can wreak on the community puts it high on the writer's list of issues. The reconciled community must practice reconciliation especially when this frightening emotion is raised, and that reconciliation begins with naming it.

A similar concern for community drives the next instruction about stealing. Hearers will perhaps be

Exegetical Perspective

Ephesians 4:17–24, excluded from the lectionary, calls the Ephesian converts to discard their old nature and don a new one, moving from debauchery and dissolution to righteousness and holiness. Living into holiness involves specific kinds of behavior, namely, those that enhance relationships and enrich Christian community. If 4:1–24 provides the theological basis for unity, then 4:25–5:2 prescribes particular practices and prohibitions.

Ephesians 4:25 (which quotes Zech. 8:16) may strike us variously as idealistic, hyperbolic, scary, or excitingly challenging. "Let everyone speak the truth with their neighbor." Why would we risk such a thing? It is not polite behavior, it is a huge investment of time, and it is potentially troubling. The author insists that we need to speak truth because we actually are all part of one another. Not speaking truth to each other is tantamount to not speaking truth to ourselves, and vice versa. We could dispense with this verse as some sort of temporary insanity on the part of the author, were it not the case that he repeatedly returns to the themes of speaking truth (vv. 15–16, 21) and our connection with our Christian brothers and sisters. Without truth, authentic community fails.

Much has been made of verses 26–27 (which quotes Ps. 4:5), and many pastors have deployed this

Homiletical Perspective

If your congregation has not been singing "They'll Know We Are Christians by Our Love" for a while, this is a good time to dust it off and give it voice. You can think of that chorus as a musical midrash on John 13:35, but it picks up on some key themes in Ephesians—oneness in the Spirit, walking and working together "side by side," and praise for that unity as a gift of a gracious God. Singing a song or hymn like this is but one of a variety of gestures the body of Christ uses to perform its unity in sanctuaries set apart for worship. Many congregations join hands as they pray the Lord's Prayer together; some leave their seats to surround the Lord's Table where the elements of the messianic banquet are spread; many drink from what is a common "cup of salvation" and eat of a common loaf; and in some smaller congregations, members step into the aisles at the close of worship, encircling the sanctuary, and offer a choral benediction with joined hands upraised. Powerful moments these, especially when those congregations are made up of persons of different ages, races, genders, classes, theological positions, sexual orientations, or nationalities.

But are Christians these days known by the rare shows of unity in the liturgical assembly? In the public square, things seem different. Fault lines in the foundation of Christian unity show up all the

Ephesians 4:25-5:2

Theological Perspective

process in the following prayer: "We thank you, Father, for the water of Baptism. In it we are buried with Christ in his death. By it we share in his resurrection. Through it we are reborn by the Holy Spirit."[1] Because we are reborn, the habits of the old self have no dominion over us. The Holy Spirit enables the baptized to put off the "evil powers of this world which corrupt and destroy the creatures of God" as well as giving the inclination and will to "put your whole trust in [Jesus Christ's] grace and love."[2]

Therefore, the works described by Paul are not merit badges set out for us to achieve. Rather, they are marks of the new life given to us in baptism. If we are a thief, we are to turn away from stealing and turn toward "working honestly with their own hands" (v. 28). We are to strip away all "bitterness and wrath and anger and wrangling and slander, together with all malice" and instead we are to put on being "kind to one another, tenderhearted, forgiving one another" (4:31–32).

We are to do these things for at least three reasons. First, we are a new creation. We have come through the waters of baptism and are commanded not to go back to Egypt. Once the baptized person puts on the new white garment, the old clothes are cast away. In like manner, Paul is calling for the new Christians to remember who they now are in Christ and to focus on the way to life, instead of turning back to the ways of death. As we recollect what Christ has done for us, we remember the continuing work of the Holy Spirit, who enables us to stay focused on the light. God gives us the capacity to turn around as well as to refrain from turning back. Of course, we have free will, but we no longer make our choices alone. Again, the Episcopal baptismal liturgy reads: "by the sealing of your Holy Spirit you have bound us to your service. Renew in these your servants the covenant you made with them at their Baptism. Send them forth in the power of that Spirit to perform the service you set before them."[3]

Second, we are now part of the body of Christ, and that membership gives us strength to do what is set before us. As part of this body, we encourage one another and help one another to live out our baptismal promises. Paul says, "Let all of us speak the truth to our neighbors, for we are members of one another" (v. 25). That is, we all are in this enterprise of being church together. Therefore, we are to learn from each other and help each other.

Pastoral Perspective

startled to note that here honesty and hard work are not recommended to preserve the sanctity of private property. Former thieves are to invest their time and energy in self-support so that they may be in a position to join the community's care for the destitute. The work ethic itself is transformed into participation in Christ's ministry.

The contrast continues. We might cheer when thieves are told not to steal and then be surprised when they are told to do some positive good. Similarly, we can agree when Christians are told to cease speaking evil. The transformation of speech goes farther too and brings us back to the question of unresolved anger. For the author of Ephesians, truth is not sufficient warrant for speech. What is spoken is to be for building up, for occasioning grace. There is no one for whom these words do not represent a challenge and opportunity. That thought is perhaps best emphasized in terms of possibility. We all know in an instant how we are judged by the passage. Do we understand the power of the slightest of our words to be creative acts?

Isaiah 63:10 warns God's people that their rebellion has "grieved his holy spirit." The consequences Isaiah sees flowing from that act are terrible. Another translation of the Isaiah passage uses "afflicted" instead of "grieved." Either way, there is a sense of God's vulnerability that is appealed to here, whether or not there is a threat implied. How might the life of the contemporary Christian community afflict the Spirit? Both the ends and the means of our endeavors are questioned here.

The motivation for not grieving the Spirit is organic. Christians are to tell the truth to each other in verse 25 because they are members of each other. Similarly, here they are told not to grieve the Spirit because it is the Spirit that seals them. The seal (*sphragis*) of the Spirit appears in ancient baptismal texts; the Spirit marks us as Christ's property as surely as the tattoos of slaves or soldiers marked them. There is a contradiction in rejecting that which attaches Christians to their primary identity. "Brand loyalty" is more than a pun here; it is an existential position for those marked for Christ.

We tend to repeat ourselves when we are not sure that we are heard, and verses 31 and 32 expand on the thought of verse 26. The emphasis cannot be unintentional, and the echoes of situations in Corinth and Galatians are difficult to miss. The preacher's temptation to moralize here is strong, but is to be resisted. It is not pastorally useful to dwell on guilt here, although stocktaking is certainly called

---

1. *The Book of Common Prayer* (New York: Seabury Press, 1979), 306.
2. Ibid., 302.
3. Ibid., 309.

verse in premarital counseling for better or for worse: "Do not let the sun go down on your anger." The text does not say, "Do not be angry; anger is not Christian." Rather, it warns against the dangers that tend to accompany anger. Anger agitates us and agitation can cloud our judgment, making us susceptible to the wiles of the devil. According to Scripture, the devil traffics in deceit, leading people astray (into sin), and destroying relationships. Brief anger may bear fruit, but sometimes it is attended by enmity, self-righteousness, tearing one another down, haughtiness, and the hard, desiccated ground where we believe we are "right." This author never imagines that Christians are inoculated against sin. If they avoid it, it is through practice and the crucible of Christian community, not through conversion or some new state of "goodness."

Christian thieves must abandon their thieving (v. 28). All of the moral exhortation in Ephesians is directed to those who are already Christian; the author expresses no interest in modifying the behavior of unbelievers. Why should Christians give up thievery? So that one might escape a fiery eternal hell? Because it is debased or unjustifiable? No, because it does not allow for contributions to the needy. By now we should not be surprised by this reasoning. The author does not argue from the Ten Commandments or natural law or some such; rather he is acutely concerned about actively authentic, deep community where everyone contributes. Christians should have jobs primarily so that they can help those in need. The author challenges us to imagine what it would it be like if we made our decisions based not on whether choice A or B would bring us the best paycheck, highest status, and most comfortable life, but whether it would allow us to serve those in need.

Verse 29 is a literary thunderclap. Let no evil talk come out of your mouth? Only that which imparts grace to the hearers? I daresay that (a) it takes no great exegetical work to figure this out; (b) if we took this to heart, we would think before we spoke far more often; and (c) we would speak far less often. Again, it is tempting to write this author off as an extremely unrealistic stick-in-the-mud, but again, concern for evil speech runs throughout Scripture, particularly in the Wisdom literature of both Testaments (Jas. 3:5–10; Matt. 12:33–37; numerous times in Proverbs). Like the other behaviors spotlighted, speech matters, because it can either build or destroy community.

Verse 30 ups the ante regarding behavior— negative behavior not only harms the one doing it

time. The church is shaken regularly by scandal, ecclesial warfare, fear of the other, difference, and change. The pastor with an ear pressed down to the ground of congregational life hears the plates shifting underneath. The phone call complaining of a stance the church has taken, the angry tone of the one outvoted, or the diatribe by one threatening to withdraw a pledge on a "matter of doctrine" make liturgical hand-holding in worship seem silly and naive. So pronounced are these divisions that these gestures toward love and unity we Christians make in the relative privacy and safety of our sanctuaries come off as empty ones. The wags who watch us would hear our prayer that "all unity will one day be restored" and snicker.

The ethical practices that the writer of Ephesians proscribes in the appointed passage today can save our ditties of devotion to love and unity from becoming sentimental schlock. There is nothing wounding the body of Christ today that this writer has not already seen in an earlier version. Understandings of the Christ event born within Judaism and "pagan" cultic practices are in conflict behind this text, and the bitter fruit is evident: lying (v. 25); anger that festers in the heart (v. 26); stealing! (v. 28); evil talk (v. 29), bitterness, wrath, wrangling, and slander (v. 31), all of which grieve the Holy Spirit of God (v. 30). What a picture! Who would want to join First Church of Ephesus? If you were going to preach to a congregation like that, where such behavior was evident, what on earth would you say? What theme would you choose?

The writer chooses "forgiveness" as a theme. This is a word for the church, not just for individuals in it. For this writer, to be "forgiven" is to be "pardoned." God has done something "in Christ" that forgives or pardons all those who take this letter to heart, and in recognition of that action, recipients of God's forgiveness and pardon freely offer it to others in kind. This is harder to pull off than it first appears. The writer of Ephesians seems to be a lot clearer about what "sin" is than most contemporary Christians are. You have to reach back into the passage before this one to get the sense of what the author means by it. "They [meaning the "Gentiles"] are darkened in their understanding, alienated from the life of God because of their ignorance and hardness of heart" (v. 18). It is from this state of being in the world (insensitive, licentious, greedy, impure) that "they" are "forgiven" and set free to live a different way of life. The sign of this alternative ethic, at least according to this part of the text, is the

Ephesians 4:25–5:2

Theological Perspective

Christianity has yet to grasp the full implication of the incarnation: the Word has become flesh and dwells all around us. Paul is calling for these early Christians not merely to worship God in Christ, but through the Holy Spirit to imitate Christ in their own behavior, for the sake of the Christ's church and the sake of the world. They are to forgive as they have been forgiven. They must turn from wrangling and slander and turn instead toward kindness and forgiveness for Christ's sake. We imitate Christ in hopes that through the Holy Spirit we will grow into the likeness of Christ and that God will use us as instruments to bring in God's realm of peace, justice, and mercy.

Finally, Paul calls upon them not to "grieve the Holy Spirit of God" (v. 30). Christianity is an ongoing encounter with the living, loving God in Christ Jesus. The nature of love is to love and to grow in that love. No one willingly disappoints the beloved; certainly no one makes the beloved grieve. While this verse seems out of place in this catalog of forbidden and prescribed behaviors, in a certain sense it is quite fitting. We do not wish to do anything to grieve God, because of our love for God in Christ. Therefore, we joyfully turn toward those acts that bring God joy and away from those that do not, because our individual and corporate focus is to serve Christ by pleasing him.

Therefore, while at first glance this passage resembles a long list of prescribed and proscribed behaviors, in actuality it is centered on the converted life of the baptized.

G. PORTER TAYLOR

Pastoral Perspective

for. Instead, in consonance with the rest of the passage, the author repeats that it is precisely when aggression is the customary path (as with lying or stealing) that tremendous effort is required for reconciliation. In making it, Christians have the opportunity to participate in the work of Christ. The text warns against the vices that destroy the baptismal community and simultaneously holds up a difficult but transforming path.

A final motivation for inhabiting the virtues that protect and deepen community is the writer's understanding of Christ's work as sacrifice. The ancient world believed that offerings had an olfactory quality that pleased the deity. Christ's surrender to God was motivated by love, and Christians are here invited to follow suit, understanding their own lives as pleasingly sacrificial. There has been much quarreling in Christian circles over whether we have anything to offer God, whether Christians should ever speak of any sacrifice except that of Christ. One may wish to fence the word in such a way as to exclude the idea of sacrifice as motivating God to act or to be well disposed toward those who offer, but the idea of offering one's attitude and behavior from a desire to respond pleasingly to love of God seems inescapable.

Here Christians offer themselves in imitation of the divine rescuing love, the sacrificial love of Christ. Deliberate imitation sounds insincere or blameworthy in some ears. But putting on Christ and imitating God are phrases that Pauline thinking repeats out of the knowledge that we grow into the identities we choose to have. Only in the matter of the spiritual life does one hear the charge that actions coming out of a state one does not fully possess are phony. One would never argue with anyone's attempt to "become" possessed of the traits of a successful lawyer, rock star, or world leader. The invitation here is to assume the discipline of saint in a deliberate way. The text invites us to do what comes unnaturally as a means to making it natural, or second nature.

PAUL V. MARSHALL

Exegetical Perspective

and the Christian community to which he or she belongs, but it actually grieves the Holy Spirit. The Spirit is an essential part of the community: without the Spirit there could be no worship, no community, no virtue. Believers know this Spirit because the Spirit was active in our conversion and baptism, marking us as God's own with a view to the final glorious unfolding of the future that God has promised believers in Christ, what the author calls our "day of redemption." Ephesians is generally considered to exhibit a realized eschatology, as Christians have already been raised with Christ and seated with him in the heavenly places (2:6). So certain is this outcome that it can be spoken of in the past tense—this is the power of the gospel. Christians still reside for the moment, however, in a time when "the days are evil" (5:16) and the devil looks for opportunities (4:27).

Throughout our passage, the author has set up contrasts: avoid doing destructive behaviors (lying, stealing, evil speech); rather, do edifying behaviors (truth telling, working to contribute, edifying speech). Verses 31 and 32 follow suit: the former enjoins us to discard spiritual clutter to make room for the spiritual collectibles enumerated in the latter. The six discards cause discord: wrath, bitterness, anger, clamor, slander, and malice. They act as a suit of armor protecting the real flesh-and-blood us. But church is not a gladiatorial event. In contrast, kindness, tenderheartedness, and forgiveness facilitate unity and cooperation, the way a flesh-and-blood body works (4:15–16) or a healthy family. Armorless, we are more vulnerable, but we finally have a real shot at intimacy, at knowing and being known.

There is no doubt that intimacy will involve hurt; hence, the necessity for forgiveness. This theme runs through Scripture like a red thread. No meaningful relationship can function without it. Why should we forgive? We could make a list of possible psychological and sociological benefits, but it comes down to the fact that this is what God does in Christ (4:32). As God's "beloved children" (5:1), we do not just love God, praise God, worship God, thank God. We also aim to imitate God (5:1), minding and then closing the gap between God's behavior and our own.

To imitate God, only one thing is needful: kenotic love (5:2), love that sacrifices for the good of others. If we get that, we get it all.

JAIME CLARK-SOLES

Homiletical Perspective

virtue of kindness. The preacher would do well to follow this writer's lead—to offer this writer's view of "sin" and then set forth this ethical vision to the church both as a challenge and a rebuke to the culture it finds itself in. The practice of kindness draws one away from "hardness of heart" and into the "life of God."

Now then, is this "tenderheartness" the kind of soft, banal ethic that turns the Christian into "a nice person" who slips through a world of hurt barely noticed? Not if you see how the writer raises the stakes in 5:1. Here a bold statement, a command really, rises off the page and into our hearing: "Be imitators of God." *What?*

"Imitating God" means putting our focus on the *actions* that flow from God's character. Teachers in the world that the writer of this epistle inhabited thought human beings to be *mimetic* beings, that is, those creatures who felt the urge to *imitate* their vision of the real through their actions in art and culture. "Real life" was that which was being "shown forth" in all of its dimensions through the "actions" of the poets, the playwrights, the orators, and the actors. Actions deemed worthy of imitation were "grand" ones by noble, even heroic individuals played out on stages in front of the gods and the gathered community for the instruction of all.

The writer of Ephesians sees such an action performed by God in the person and work of Jesus Christ. It is a grand gesture of love played out on the stage of Creation for the instruction of the human community. Those who are baptized are called to be imitators of that action, not just in the sanctuaries we find ourselves in, but on the stage of a global village and on the front lines of human relationships.

RICHARD F. WARD

John 6:35, 41-51

³⁵Jesus said to them, "I am the bread of life. Whoever comes to me will never be hungry, and whoever believes in me will never be thirsty." . . .

⁴¹Then the Jews began to complain about him because he said, "I am the bread that came down from heaven." ⁴²They were saying, "Is not this Jesus, the son of Joseph, whose father and mother we know? How can he now say, 'I have come down from heaven'?" ⁴³Jesus answered them, "Do not complain among yourselves. ⁴⁴No one can come to me unless drawn by the Father who sent me; and I will raise that person up on the last day. ⁴⁵It is written in the prophets, 'And they shall all be taught by God.' Everyone who has heard and learned from the Father comes to me. ⁴⁶Not that anyone has seen the Father except the one who is from God; he has seen the Father. ⁴⁷Very truly, I tell you, whoever believes has eternal life. ⁴⁸I am the bread of life. ⁴⁹Your ancestors ate the manna in the wilderness, and they died. ⁵⁰This is the bread that comes down from heaven, so that one may eat of it and not die. ⁵¹I am the living bread that came down from heaven. Whoever eats of this bread will live forever; and the bread that I will give for the life of the world is my flesh."

Theological Perspective

With verse 6:41 the spotlight shifts from the questions of the crowds still looking to know Jesus' whereabouts to the complaint of those who are confident already in their knowledge of how Jesus is to be located. Theologically considered, what we hear in this account divides into two sets of issues that continue to provoke debate. The first appears with the words regarding Jesus, "whose father and mother we know" (v. 42), and the second with the statement that no one comes to Jesus, "unless drawn" (v. 44).

At the outset, the negative reference here to the complainers as "the Jews" must be set in context to counteract anti-Semitic impressions it may engender in hearers today. The opponents featured in John 6 are equally Jews; the opposition is between those excluded from the synagogue for following Jesus and those, designated by John as "the Jews," who do the excluding. "For the Jews had already agreed that anyone who confessed Jesus to be the Messiah would be put out of the synagogue" (9:22). For the writer of the Fourth Gospel, in the generation after the crucifixion, the life of Jesus Christ both "once was" and "now is." Both aspects are viewed together by what the New Testament scholar J. Louis Martyn has called "stereoptic vision" of one life then and now,

Pastoral Perspective

A recent document released by the Vatican to clarify Pope Benedict's encyclical *Dominus Jesus* stirred an international controversy because it appeared to restate a former Roman Catholic dogma that no one could be saved outside the church—that is, the Roman Catholic Church. Several Protestants and the religious leaders of other faiths squealed like stuck pigs. They loudly sounded off to the media, saying that this claim set ecumenical and interfaith relations back by a century or so. The Catholic Church replied, asserting that this is not a new teaching, and is no different from the ecumenical teachings of John XXIII and John Paul II.

Nor is that claim so different from what Jesus said when the religious leaders murmured against him for saying that he was the bread of life who had come down from heaven for the hunger of the world. Those religious leaders balked at such a claim for Jesus' origins; they believed it impossible for Jesus to have come down from heaven: "Is this not Jesus," they said, "the son of Joseph, whose father and mother we know?" They refused to countenance that a mere human being with a "known address"[1] could have

1. Lesslie Newbigin, *The Light Has Come, An Exposition of the Fourth Gospel* (Grand Rapids: Eerdmans, 1982), 82 ff.

Exegetical Perspective

As we saw last Sunday, Jesus challenges the crowd who come looking for him after the feeding miracle, seeming to mock both their incipient faith in him and their struggle to find in the story of Moses and the manna a key for understanding who he is. His startling announcement, "I am the bread of life" (v. 35a), sets in motion a rising tension, which will at last divide the crowd and even his disciples: a few will accept his radical claims; the majority will go away. His further promise (v. 35b) echoes his words to the woman at Jacob's well in Samaria (4:14) and anticipates his bold declaration at the Festival of Sukkoth in Jerusalem (7:37–39); it also echoes but revises the words of personified Wisdom in Sirach 24:21. But the promise is double edged: it is only for the one "who comes to me" and "believes in me." Jesus' remarks here seem calculated to make that belief as difficult as possible.

The paragraph omitted by the lectionary, verses 36–40, is pertinent to just this problem, for in it Jesus promises that "anyone who comes to me I will never drive away," though that seems to be just what he is doing throughout this chapter. These verses complicate rather than solve the puzzle, by introducing the theme that Jesus will "lose nothing" of what God has given him (v. 39). Now we see why

Homiletical Perspective

"I wish I could get you to pray the way that my dog goes after meat." That is what Martin Luther once said to his congregation. In our moderate, measured, middle-of-the-road, meekly Christian milieu, such talk seems carnal and crude, even for Luther.

One of the greatest contemporary impediments in comprehending this pericope is the widespread but clearly erroneous impression that Christianity is spiritual. "Spirituality" has been "in" for some years now. Apparently, many North Americans long to be lifted out of the muck and mire of the everyday. What is here, the stuff of ordinary life, is not enough for us. We want to rise above that, to go higher, to ascend. As modern, scientific people, we have learned so much about everything we can taste, and touch, and feel. In the process, the world got demystified, explained, unbearably flattened and figured out. We therefore long to peek behind the veil, to penetrate the less obvious. Was not this the great engine that drove classical Greek philosophy? Through thought, we can rise above the decay and death that plagues reality in this world and ascend toward some other ideal, eternal, spiritual realm.

In places, if you are not careful, the Gospel of John sounds as if it is attempting Greek philosophy. John begins with high-sounding talk of the Word,

John 6:35, 41-51

Theological Perspective

identifiably sent from heaven and currently taking place on earth.[1]

The complainers in this case exhibit no such vision. By highlighting their particular complaint, the evangelist calls the immediate generation of hearers facing divisions in their communities, and subsequent ones as well, to reflect on its due recognition. What then is there to recognize?

"Whose Father and Mother We Know." First, notice the contrasts between what we hear of the crowds in the previous lection (6:24–35) and what we are now told of the complainers. The crowds are depicted as outsiders, not only in physically being outside in the open fields and along the sea, but in their uninformed looking for Jesus and demanding to know what is going on with him. Their questions and exchanges with Jesus emerge, so to speak, in transit. The complainers in distinction are apparently within the synagogue at Capernaum (v. 59). As insiders they are familiar enough with rabbinic traditions to know when proper teaching about God's heaven is being violated. Their words resonate with the more settled confidence of already knowing how Jesus is to be known. His "father and mother we know." Yet in each setting, as John presents it, whether the focus is upon outsiders or insiders, a dramatic upset is created when Jesus enters the picture.

With respect to the insiders, what is there for them to complain about? Nothing, it would seem, so long as their way of locating Jesus and fixing his proper identification is not challenged. Their beginning with a familiar form of classification and attempting to explain Jesus' coming by means of it should hardly strike any of us as unusual. Knowing who one's parents are is certainly one way of providing identification. So is knowing what scholars call "the historical Jesus" by first agreeing upon what may be counted as historical fact. Others equally confident of "the plan of salvation" may assert just as assuredly where Jesus belongs within it, as do defenders of set dogmatic traditions who know how Jesus is to be spoken of within them. In each instance it is the settled confidence in knowing how to situate Jesus that the arrival of his life-giving presence abruptly undermines. Starting from experience that is familiar and familial, how can Jesus be known to say, "I have come down from heaven"? Of these "murmurers" constricted by their familiar frames of reference,

Pastoral Perspective

come from God in a unique fashion, especially when his "lifting up" would be for the salvation of all who turned to him. After all, they had Moses and the prophets. Jesus responded to their question and complaints and said that no one comes to him—the bread of life—unless that person has been drawn to him by the Father. You just don't come to faith by yourself, through your own deduction, reasoning, and insight alone. You are wooed, invited, even cajoled. A well-known hymn puts forward that same claim as a gracious insight of faith:

> I sought the Lord, and afterward I knew
> He moved my soul to seek Him, seeking me;
> It was not I that found, O Saviour true;
> No, I was found of Thee.[2]

The church is thus confronted with not one but two offensive teachings in this text, as well as the companion teachings elsewhere in John 6: (1) No one comes to the Father (who is drawing people to himself for the healing of the cosmos—"God did not send the Son into the world to condemn the world") except through the bread of life. (2) And, adding insult to the injury of current, narcissistic cultural norms, no one comes to Jesus unless God wants that one to come.

How then does the church, to say nothing of citizens of the "unconverted" world, hear the gospel? If this text is preached in all its revelatory grace—discounting, as it does, not only works that lead to justification, but even a "decision for Christ" as a criterion for salvation—will anyone believe? Do I wait passively until my heart is "strangely warmed" by some spirit outside of and invasive of my own striving human spirit? According to Jesus, it is not my religious experience, my philosophical insight, the accident of my birth, my economic status—nor most of all, God help us, my *choice*—that puts me within the realm of light that is the presence of Jesus within the community of faith.

I am saved by grace alone. It is grace that opens my eyes to see my sin and my need of the living God who is made known to the world in Jesus the Christ, the bread of life, the one who, when I come to him, will never leave me hungry again. When—invited—I turn to him, I have my thirst quenched from a living stream.

We do not save anyone—only God does that. And we who have been invited and eat the living bread

---

1. On these points and other matters in John 6, see especially J. Louis Martyn, *History and Theology in the Fourth Gospel*, rev. and enlarged ed. (Louisville, KY: Westminster John Knox Press, 2003), 46 and 130ff.

2. Anonymous, "I Sought the Lord, and Afterward I Knew," in *The Hymnbook* (Richmond, Philadelphia, and New York: Presbyterian Church in the United States, United Presbyterian Church in the U.S.A., and Reformed Church in America, 1955), #402.

this Gospel emphasizes a detail of the feeding story, when Jesus orders the disciples after the feeding to gather all the crumbs, "that nothing may be lost" (v. 12). That in turn reminds us of the thematic statement in 3:16 and of the contrast between the "real bread" and the manna, which "perishes" (v. 27; the verb is the same). Implicitly, it also contrasts Jesus with Moses, who lost the generation who died in the wilderness (vv. 50, 58).

This theme recurs in the parable of the Good Shepherd (10:28), in the prophecy of the high priest (11:50), in Jesus' final prayer (17:12), and in the account of his arrest (18:9). The most important addition to the theme in this passage is identification of the promise that Jesus "will lose nothing" with the promise that he "will raise up" the believers "on the last day" (6:39–40)—a promise that was introduced at 5:24–29 and that will be dramatized in the story of Lazarus in John 11 (note esp. 11:25–26, 43–44). The stakes for believing or disbelieving are thus as high as possible.

Those who disbelieve are identified in verse 41 as "the Jews," or, more literally, "the Judaeans." This seems strange, for of course Jesus and his disciples are also Jews (note 4:9, 22). Indeed, in this Gospel the only Gentile characters are the Roman governor and soldiers; all the rest are either Samaritans or Jews. What can be the meaning of this odd stigmatization, which names "the Jews" as the enemies of the one who is called "King of the Jews"? Many scholars in recent years have found the answer in the experience of a special circle of early followers of Jesus. That group, facing threats and expulsion from their own Jewish community, struggled to understand their experience. Convinced that Jesus was the Messiah and that his coming brought to fulfillment promises embedded in Israel's Scriptures and traditions, they had difficulty understanding how so few could share their belief.

For explanation, they turned both to the stories of Jesus so precious in their community's memory and to the traditional ways of interpreting the Bible, now radically transformed by being read through the lens of the Jesus story. Their situation and their interpretive response in many ways parallels that of another sect that had flourished only a few years earlier, the one known now from the Dead Sea Scrolls. Like that sect, the followers of Jesus find their experience mirrored in the story of Israel under Moses. As the Israelites "complained" against Moses (Exod. 16:2–12; Num. 11), so now "the Jews" complain against Jesus (John 6:41, 43). Both

the eternal Word, being the beginning of all things, light and life, the ultimate source and end.

Our selection opens with one of those wonderful "I am" statements. In a Gospel that at times appears cagey, evasive, and indirect, there are these moments when Jesus pulls back the veil and declares, "I am the way, and the truth, and the life," or here, "I am the bread of life." In being so direct, so declarative, Jesus provokes a crisis in our apprehension of him. Now there is no room for evasion on our part. A verdict is demanded. We are pushed to a decision: Is he really who he says he is?

The statement "I am the bread of life" also, by implication, raises questions about other possible nourishment. What the Bible names in places as "idolatry" could also be called attempts to seek sustenance in places other than with Jesus, who says he is the bread of life.

Note that Jesus says that he is the bread that originates "in heaven." Here is nourishment that does not originate "from earth," or from within our subjectivity, or from the fruits of human aspiration. It is bread that has "come down from heaven" (v. 41). Of course, Jesus' critics immediately react to his "I am" and "from heaven" with, "Is not this Joseph and Mary's kid? We know them! There're right here with us on earth."

In response, Jesus continues to claim his heavenly, divine origins, saying that no one can come to him except by being led to him by the Father (v. 44). No one can learn of him except by being taught by the Father. No one can see him except by revelation of the Father (vv. 45–46).

Whatever we need to comprehend Jesus, to come to Jesus, to see who he is and what he means, must come to us as a divine gift, through revelation, not through our earnest effort. Every preacher knows what it is like to preach a sermon on one subject, only to have someone in the congregation report having heard a different sermon! Every pastor knows that the most spiritually perceptive persons in the congregation are rarely the most intelligent or gifted. I call this an everyday experience of the working of the Holy Spirit. As Jesus says elsewhere in the Fourth Gospel, "The Spirit blows where it chooses" (John 3:8). Revelation is not containable, controllable by us, not programmed or predicted by us.

Perhaps this implies that at the end of a sermon on John 6:35, 41–51, if someone says, "I don't get anything out of all this talk about 'bread of life' and 'come down from heaven,'" the preacher is justified in saying, "If you get anything out of any talk from

John 6:35, 41-51

Theological Perspective

Augustine comments: "They had weak jaws of the heart, they were deaf with open ears, they saw and stood blind," not recognizing that what God gives is not what we make of things ourselves.[2]

"Unless Drawn." It is precisely the news of what God is giving them, and how radically this contradicts what they themselves are making of Jesus' arrival, that provokes the insiders at Capernaum. What John reports they hear from Jesus is that his presence among them is "the bread that comes down from heaven" that no one can come to "unless drawn by the Father who sent me." This kind of drawing clearly does not fit the picture they already have formed of him.

"See how he draws," exclaims Augustine, "Not by imposing necessity" but by grace enabling the "inner palate" of the soul to find its greatest "pleasure" and "delight" in partaking of the truth. It is not, Augustine cautions, for us to judge who is thus drawn and who is not, but rather to realize that our preaching is only noise to the ears unless listeners are drawn by the Father's love to hear it (pp. 260–64).

"As far as the manner of drawing goes," writes John Calvin, "it is not violent, so as to compel [us] by an external force; but yet it is an effectual movement of the Holy Spirit, turning [us] from being unwilling and reluctant into willing." Unlike the "manna from the sky" God gave through Moses, this coming of Christ reconfigures the relation of earth and heaven by conforming to no earthly background check, but by showing instead how near "heavenly life" is now to us, so "there is no need to fly above the clouds or cross the sea."[3]

With their presuppositions inadequate to account for Jesus' presence, the classifiers inside Capernaum's synagogue, like their counterparts ever since, are left with an unclassifiable promise by Jesus: "I am the living bread from heaven; whoever eats thereof will live forever."

CHRISTOPHER MORSE

Pastoral Perspective

and drink from the healing, life-giving stream can only bear witness. We may bear witness not to the predicament of faith, but to the abundance Christ brings to the hearts and lives of believers. "I came that they may have life, and have it abundantly" (John 10:10).

Then we can more adequately explain and defend the "exclusiveness" of the gospel, what has long been called the scandal of particularity, which is so starkly presented by Jesus in this passage. Far from denouncing Pope Benedict's claims about the church, all Christians may appropriately rejoice in his courage—speaking "God's truth" about salvation to a world of relativistic naiveté and shallow interfaith hypocrisy.

It is simply a fact that without the church— broken, divided, "by heresies distressed," filled (at least since the congregation is Corinth) with unending squabbles—there is no salvation. Without the church there is no witness to the Word made flesh, a witness found uniquely and with finality only in the Scriptures. The New Testament came from, grew out of, and is sustained by the church. Without the church's preservation of the Scriptures of the New Testament from which we Protestants preach most Sundays (and in whose authority we take great pride) there is no means of a witness to the imperishable, troubling, saving, and joyous gospel. "'Twas grace that taught me to fear and to believe."

Someone defended Pope Benedict's claim with these words: "unity based on a whitewashing of differences . . . is a façade and only stills fruitful dialogue."[3] Everyone, says Jesus, who has heard and learned from [God the] Father comes to me. There is no salvation outside the church. That is a refreshing, renewing word for our disjointed days.

O. BENJAMIN SPARKS

2. *Saint Augustine: Tractates on the Gospel of John 11–27*, trans. John W. Rettig, in *The Fathers of the Church* (Washington, DC: Catholic University of America Press, 1988), 79:259.
3. John Calvin, *The Gospel according to St. John, Part One 1–10*, in *Calvin's New Testament Commentaries*, trans. T. H. L. Parker (Grand Rapids: Eerdmans, 1961), 158, 164.

3. This quotation and other information from Father Jonathan Morris, "Document Released by Pope Stirs Catholic Controversy," FOX News, July 11, 2007.

Exegetical Perspective

complaints have to do with miraculous feeding in the wilderness, but their substance is different. The escapees from Egypt complain that Moses has led them from the safety of slavery to the dangers of freedom in an unknown land and an insecure future. The questioners of Jesus complain that he has made impossible claims about himself: "Is not this Jesus, the son of Joseph, whose father and mother we know? How can he now say, 'I have come down from heaven'?" (v. 42).

Jesus' reply begins his church's struggle to answer the question why so few of "his own people" (1:11) accept the radical new story proclaimed here as "good news." Jesus quotes Scripture again, "They shall all be taught by God" (Isa. 54:13), with the explanation, "Everyone who has heard and learned from the Father comes to me" (v. 45). The implication is that those who do *not* come are unteachable. Verse 46 then reminds us of what we were told at the beginning of this Gospel: *only* Jesus has seen God; *only* Jesus can reveal God (1:18). This is an answer that raises more questions than it solves, and the search for an answer continued long after this Gospel was written. The Gospel of John does not explain, but only challenges its hearers to be those who *do* learn and *do* come.

To that end, Jesus returns to the story of the manna. It is well and good to be taught through the Scripture and through the tradition, but finally one must not remain with the past but must decide about God's new action in the world. Those who ate the manna died without entering the land of promise (v. 49). Those who eat "the bread that comes down from heaven" *now* "will live forever." And, to put the ultimate test for understanding and faith, Jesus says, incredibly, "The bread . . . is my flesh" (v. 51). With that final allusion to the story of Moses' care for Israel in the wilderness (cf. Exod. 16:8; Num. 11:18), the stage is set for the debate in next Sunday's Gospel lesson, which asks what it can possibly mean to eat Jesus' flesh and drink his blood.

WAYNE A. MEEKS

Homiletical Perspective

Jesus or about Jesus, it is a gift!" Whatever we need in order to comprehend Jesus must come as a gift, insight not of our own devising. It must "come down from heaven."

Lest all this talk of "heaven" suggest that we are here dealing with ethereal, otherworldly fuzziness, Jesus compares his significance to that of everyday, mundane, bread. He may be "from heaven" but he is also that which has "come down." He is the Word, the eternal Word "made flesh."

Here, standing before us, in the flesh, is the fullness of God. If you have ever wondered just what God looks like, or how God acts, or how God talks, then wonder no more. In this faith, we do not have to climb up to the divine; God discloses, unveils, climbs down to us.

As Luther puts the practical, continuing consequences of the Incarnation:

> It is the honor and glory of our God . . . that, giving himself for our sake in deepest condescension, he passes into the flesh, the bread, our hearts, mouths, entrails, and suffers also for our sake that he be dishonorably handled, on the altar as on the cross.[1]

Let's admit it. There is something within us that likes our gods high and lifted up, distant, exclusively in heaven. We so want religion to be something spiritual, rather than something that is uncomfortably incarnational. Yet here we are with God-in-the-flesh before us saying, "I'm your bread; feed on me!"

Our hungers are so deep. We are dying of thirst. We are bundles of seemingly insatiable need, rushing here and there in a vain attempt to assuage our emptiness. Our culture is a vast supermarket of desire. Can it be that our bread, our wine, our fulfillment stands before us in the presence of this crucified, resurrected Jew? Can it be that many of our desires are, in the eternal scheme of things, pointless? Might it be true that he is the bread we need, even though he is rarely the bread we seek? Is it true that God has come to us, miraculously with us, before us, like manna that is miraculously dropped into our wilderness?

WILLIAM H. WILLIMON

---

1. Josiah Young, "Some Assumptions and Implications regarding John Wesley's View of the Trinity: 'The Root of All Vital Religion,'" *Quarterly Review* 18, no. 2 (Summer 1998): 142.

Proverbs 9:1-6

¹Wisdom has built her house,
  she has hewn her seven pillars.
²She has slaughtered her animals, she has mixed her wine,
  she has also set her table.
³She has sent out her servant-girls, she calls
  from the highest places in the town,
⁴"You that are simple, turn in here!"
  To those without sense she says,
⁵"Come, eat of my bread
  and drink of the wine I have mixed.
⁶Lay aside immaturity, and live,
  and walk in the way of insight."

Theological Perspective

Wisdom and teachers of wisdom are in short supply—which is not to say that there are not a gaggle of self-help gurus and countless New-Age coaches strategizing business, weight loss, and even romantic success. Scratch the surface of cyberspace or visit a local Barnes and Noble to find books offering the latest batch of timeless secrets or easy-to-follow maps to enlightenment (and countless treasures at journey's end!). To call these materials gnostic insults the historic heresy of Gnosticism, but the dynamic is much the same: somebody knows something the rest of us do not; we must come to that source, must pay one way or the other, and only then will receive the secret and its rewards.

The idea of wisdom as a free and fabulous banquet, as hospitable to the poor and simple as to the rich and cultured, is alien to gnostic teaching and practice. Accordingly, wisdom as the Bible understands it—beginning with the "fear of the Lord"—is not so evident in the marketplace of ideas. The recovery of biblical wisdom, however, whether in the form of a compelling dissent from the prevailing politics of self-help and self-aggrandizement, or in the patient and faithful proclamation that grows out of abiding biblical teaching, is an urgent need. It is also as difficult as it is urgent, if only because the church itself and its

Pastoral Perspective

The purpose of a proverb is to gain a hoped-for result through a verbal medium. The book of Proverbs includes sayings that are written down in order for the wisdom of the Hebrews to be passed on to successive generations. Since the book of Proverbs is directed at the young, sermons based on the text of Proverbs 9 can be a means for bringing youth into the faith community.

Rituals marking the transition from childhood to adulthood are found in every culture and religious tradition. The community and congregation recognize the conflict that rages in the heart, mind, and body of the adolescent during this difficult time of adjustment. This is not a time to leave a young person alone to make life-transforming decisions. Each culture seeks the best models and the most influential patterns to help young people through this metamorphosis. The wisdom of the congregation and the support of family in establishing child-to-adult rituals influence young people naturally to choose the way of their faith community and family.

To guide a child in making wise decisions for life, the Hebrew Wisdom literature offers the law of God. But this law is not merely words or rules to follow, but rather the offer of relationship. The Jewish rite of passage, the bar mitzvah or bat mitzvah, means "son of the commandment" or "daughter of the

Exegetical Perspective

The Context. The book of Proverbs is composed of collections of sayings, lectures, speeches, and admonitions. The book grew over time as a compendium of sayings about wisdom, generally meaning "masterful understanding," "skill," or "expertise." The wisdom tradition was shaped by the sages in the schools of court, the temple, and in the cities of ancient Israel and early Judaism. This tradition embodied what the "teachers" saw as the essentials of Jewish life that had to be transmitted, taught, and incorporated in the life of both individual persons and the community.

The first nine chapters of the book form a more or less coherent introduction to the rich diversity of sayings in chapters 10–31. In this introduction Woman Wisdom is personified as a guide (6:22), as a beloved sister or bride (7:4), and as a hostess (9:1–6). Woman Wisdom is portrayed "as a unique woman who wears the mantle of a prophet, carries the scrolls of wise men, and wears a goddess-like diadem."[1] Everything that is the opposite of wisdom, that which destroys and endangers life, is personified in the image of the "strange woman," a composite of different images and sayings all sharing the integral characteristic of "Folly."

Homiletical Perspective

By this Sunday, the preacher and the congregation may be sated by all the references to bread during the previous weeks. Therefore, this reading of "Wisdom's Feast" might make the preacher feel as if another big helping of more of the same has been put on his plate.

However, introducing Lady/Woman Wisdom to the congregation offers the possibility to divert from what could be the stale theme of bread, and to familiarize the people with a fascinating, and usually unfamiliar, character. Getting to know her is worthwhile, for she has much to offer, and she is eager to share it generously.[1] She is mature, experienced, perceptive, and she has excellent judgment. By contrast, her townspeople are described as callow, immature simpletons who are quite satisfied, thank you, to live unreflective lives.

Wisdom's widespread invitation reminds us of Jesus' parable of the Banquets (Matt. 22:1–14; Luke 14:15–24), although in this passage it is not clear if people heed her call or if, as in Jesus' story, they make excuses for not attending. Alluding to these parables sets the stage for the preacher to compare and contrast Wisdom's character with Jesus.

1. Bruce K. Waltke, *The Book of Proverbs*, New International Commentary of the Old Testament (Grand Rapids: Eerdmans, 2004), 85.

1. Michael V. Fox, *Proverbs 1–9*, Anchor Bible (Garden City, NY: Doubleday, 2000), 297.

Proverbs 9:1-6

Theological Perspective

servants are often ensnared by gnostic webs—whether in the form of "techniques" for ministry or in the stated goal of "success."

A brief, broad-stroked review is in order. In the early days of covenant history, the prevailing and operative theology was what scholars call Deuteronomic. God was present and active in the world, omniscient to enforce a basic and binding moral code, whether in the Law or otherwise. God rewarded the faithful, punished the wicked, and did so immediately. The world was predictable and orderly. "Wisdom," then, meant following the rules. Only the faithless, or gluttons for punishment, did otherwise.

With the exile came a radical reworking of Deuteronomic theology. Eventually called "apocalyptic," this theology still believed the world to be predictable and orderly but upside down. The righteous would suffer (not at the hand of God but of the wicked) while the evil prospered. There would come a day, some foresaw, when all would be put right again, but in the meantime the righteous had three choices: to oppose the wicked (at threat of imminent death), to collaborate (at threat of ultimate death or communal exclusion), or to maintain one's identity (eating kosher, worshiping underground) while trying to avoid notice (sometimes impossible, as in Daniel). Wisdom strengthened and guided those attempting the first or third strategies by recalling heroic examples of others who suffered unjustly, reminding the faithful of the eventual and eternal purposes of God.

After the rebuilding of the temple both theologies were extant, but neither proved entirely suited to the new circumstances of the people. Wisdom evolved as a third option. Such Wisdom discerns a certain unpredictability in the world: sometimes the righteous prosper, sometimes the wicked do. God is neither obviously nor immediately evident to bless or punish. Wisdom is not only an almanac for negotiating the world's tensions but a way to interrogate the ambiguities. Proverbs is Wisdom's literature.

In Proverbs, as in the rest of Scripture, we understand that God is one, God alone. And yet Wisdom is portrayed in Proverbs as God's consort and companion. Wisdom is God's first creation (8:25), who stands with and beside God as the balance of the world is created. Wisdom, in fact, is hailed both as a tool of God's creation and as an operative aspect of what has been created. Wisdom is created and timeless, numinous and practical,

Pastoral Perspective

commandment." This title rightly implies that the law of God is like a parent. The divine standards provide children guidance and strength for life. "Honor your father and your mother, so that your days may be long" (Exod. 20:12) guides young people to build good relationships with their parents. The child who thinks that surreptitious behavior can be kept to oneself is reminded in the concluding words of Ecclesiastes, "God will bring every deed into judgment, including every secret thing, whether good or evil." The child's response to God's law is a reflection of the child's relationship to family, the faith community, and God. The importance of the tradition, the family, and the learning of God's law weave together a cloth that is not easily torn by foolish actions or choices.

The writer of Proverbs creates a character, a personification of wisdom, to offer a winsome invitation to the young in order that they may choose the way of God. The message is clear in the ninth chapter of Proverbs that God cares about the outcome of the choices made by young people. The strong call of the woman of wisdom is the main focus of the chapter. The mimicking voice of the foolish woman that follows in a mumbling echo suggests that there is no real contest between the two. The wise woman has a well-kept house, built with a divine support structure. Her servants work faithfully to do her bidding. She is known in the city and prepares a great feast for all who come to her home. The personification of wisdom in Proverbs is not unlike a grandmother who keeps her house in order and offers a sumptuous feast that is familiar and welcoming to her young ones. She knows well the individual likes and dislikes of her grandchildren and can direct the attention of the youth to that which is most suitable for the building of faith and character. Ultimately, she offers the unconditional love of God. A grandmother's love and wise guidance have a firm grasp on the mind of the young. As children grow up to face various trials, hers is the voice of wisdom that surfaces from deep within. Focusing on the power and importance of God's way of love, rather than lifting up the negative choices that need to be avoided, is the work of the one who preaches on this passage.

Jesus Christ follows a pattern similar to the woman of wisdom as he prepares a household and a feast to welcome those who would come to him. Jesus does not condemn and threaten people with fearful and negative outcomes, but rather offers life and hope. He prepares a Passover meal for his

Exegetical Perspective

When the simple give ear to her call and enter her house on the high places of the town, they will discover that they have entered the realm of death and the dead. The personified Folly is thus portrayed as the opponent or nemesis of Wisdom. The description of Woman Folly as a harlot can be read as a warning against fornication, but it has also clear religious connotations. The prophets compare Israel's idolatry to harlotry (Hosea and Jeremiah).

The struggle between Wisdom and Folly runs through the first nine chapters of the book and is brought to a climax in Proverbs 9. This chapter is a well-designed poem that consists of three strophes. Woman Wisdom is the subject of the first strophe (vv. 1–6), Woman Folly of the third (vv. 13–18). The two poems enclose the second strophe—an instruction of Woman Wisdom, offering the final advice to those who want to learn life of her (vv. 7–12). The invitations of the two women are almost identically framed. In the first strophe, Wisdom offers her banquet of life to young Israelites who want to partake in her reward. Folly sits on the height of the city and tempts the youngsters to taste of her meal.

Preparation for the Meal (vv. 1–3). Woman Wisdom prepares a dedicatory feast and is portrayed as a noble hostess. The preparation for the banquet includes building her large house (v. 1), preparing an abundant banquet (v. 2), and issuing an open invitation (v. 3).

The slaughtering of the animals points to a festal banquet. The mixing of the wine has possibly to do with adding honey or herbs to make the wine spicier (see Song 8:2). The seven pillars may underscore that the house of Woman Wisdom is rather splendid, with ample room to seat at her table all who accept her invitation (cf. John 14:2). The concluding poem in the book, the praise of the capable wife who creates a great household (31:10–31), may allude to this house of Wisdom.

The efforts of Wisdom are contrasted by the laziness of Folly. She does very little; she only "sits" at the opening of her house (9:14). Folly is portrayed in a strongly negative way ("loud . . . ignorant and knows nothing"). Wisdom's antithesis is portrayed with elements of the adulterous woman (2:16–19; 5:1–23; 6:20–35; 7:1–27).

Invitation (vv. 4–5). Woman Wisdom and her maidens invite the "simple" and "those without sense" to turn aside to her house (v. 4) and to dine on her rich table (v. 5). The invitees are the same

Homiletical Perspective

Becoming too academic or long winded about their commonalities would be a mistake, however, because it would serve as a diversion from the main point of the text.

Similarly, informing the listeners about the ancient Greco-Roman world's salons, where food and philosophizing were shared and which serve as the model for the writer's description of this feast, makes for interesting background material but carries little message.

What is most important is the acknowledgment that here with Lady Wisdom, as with the host mentioned by Jesus, all of us can choose whether or not we will respond to God's invitation for a fulfilling, blessed life. This life is not one of faithful drudgery or morbid asceticism, but one of great satisfaction and happiness. God intends an abundant life for us. The wine at Wisdom's party is for enjoying, just like the new, improved wine Jesus provides when prompted by his mother Mary— another wise woman—at the wedding at Cana.

To some hearers, this will be a surprise. Their assumption is that the Christian life is one of somber responsibility, with no time for enjoyment. Preached toward the end of summer, the preacher could encourage workaholics to take time off before the fall start-up, or a visiting preacher could bless the priest/pastor on her well-deserved vacation.

But at a deeper level, before the eve of Labor Day is a good time for all to self-reflect, asking, "Am I pursuing the life of wisdom, or am I squandering my life on that which does not satisfy?" Or, for the gathered church to ask ourselves if we are embodying a mature faith, or if we have settled for less than we are intended to be. Is there evidence we are shrinking from our call? What choices will individuals or the community make in accordance to the kind of future, with or without God, that we envision? Are we walking in the way of insight? This fallow period near the end of summer can provide the time for self-assessment and recommitment to wise living, to choose to accept Wisdom's invitation into her wonderful home to feast at her rich table.

The Gospel lesson for this Sunday, John 6:51–58, contains Jesus' promise of eternal life for those who partake of his flesh and blood. Wisdom's Feast echoes that promise, making it clear that eternal life is about much more than life after death. Wisdom's banquet is happening now, as evidenced in the sacraments shared at the communion table.

The preacher would do well to make sure the congregation understands the ongoing nature of

Proverbs 9:1-6

Theological Perspective

sapiential and ethical—a wonder to be contemplated as well as a way to engage the world.

If Wisdom is mysterious, she is at the same time reliable. Wisdom is ineffable but also teachable. Her truth and instruction can never be entirely comprehended, and yet she is intimate with God and the world, her purposes apparent. Wisdom has content, but the mysteries of the world sometimes juxtapose her teachings.

Wisdom is both grace and faith. She is the gift of God to God's children, inviting them to learn her ways of life and peace. Wisdom is God's "torah" for all people, but she is also the pattern of faithful response to God. Wisdom, therefore, has both objective and subjective aspects, eternal dimensions that are at the same time quite temporal. Wisdom is, in sum, relational. It is a call and a way of relating to the world.

In the text before us we have the image of a great feast, a banquet, set in the house of Wisdom. Her house, built for her guests, has seven pillars—but whether this is to suggest the foundations of the earth or perhaps the temple is unclear. In any event, the slaughtering of the animals (v. 2) connects this house to the *cultus* and also to the traditions of Israel. Wisdom, therefore, is not disembodied (as all forms of Gnosticism inescapably are).

Wine for the banquet is "mixed," implying that wisdom's vintage is produced by the mixture of various fruits (theologies? commands?). All are invited. Any who desire Wisdom, who would lay aside immaturity and gain insight, are welcome to feast on the wine and bread of Dame Wisdom's table. To Christian ears the feast is almost eucharistic in tone, corresponding to Jesus' invitation in the Gospel lesson for today (John 6). As Jesus offers himself as the bread of life, as new and lasting manna, so too does Wisdom offer a pattern for living to those who seek to walk "in the way of insight" (v. 6).

The banquet of Wisdom is contrasted to the "fast food" offered by Dame Folly in verses 13–16. That quick and easy meal offers only ruin and destruction, whereas the feast of Wisdom offers life and health and peace. Wisdom, then, is this: getting one's fill of Wisdom.

THOMAS R. STEAGALD

Pastoral Perspective

disciples before his arrest and crucifixion. The table is set, and he welcomes them in the custom of the day by washing their feet. He knows the importance of caring for their physical needs as a means to help them learn the truth and find fulfillment for their spiritual needs from the witness of his life.

After eating the Last Supper with his disciples, Jesus promises that he goes to prepare a place for them. He calls to them, "Believe in God, believe also in me" (John 14:1b), and goes on to describe a house, a mansion in heaven in which they each have a special room. The call and promise of Jesus are a reflection of God's care that the disciples know from the history of their people. Like the call of the woman of wisdom, Jesus' call is to come in and sup with him, to make a home with him. The work of Christ from incarnation through ascension establishes a permanent relationship between humans and their heavenly Parent.

God cares about the decisions made by all people, young and old. In celebrating the Last Supper with the disciples, Jesus establishes a ritual that reminds them of the abundant life he offers them through his death and resurrection. When some of his followers encounter the risen Christ on the road to Emmaus and share another common meal with him, they recognize Jesus in the breaking of bread and say to one another, "Were not our hearts burning within us while he was talking to us on the road, while he was opening the scriptures to us?" (Luke 24:32). Holy Communion is a feast in the church that provides young people with a ritual that teaches them of the love of God in Jesus Christ. As young people choose the way of Jesus Christ and come to the Table, they discover they have a place at the Table of God. Jesus is clear that he will nourish them all through their lives, and he promises that they will be his friends forever.

SUSAN E. VANDE KAPPELLE

Exegetical Perspective

group that Woman Wisdom addresses in the previous chapter. The "highest places in town" (v. 3) point to the upper city, where the palaces and public places are situated.

"Eat of my bread and drink of the wine" is a metaphor for the acceptance of the teaching of Wisdom (cf. Isa. 55:1–3). Just as food and drink nourish physical life, the teaching of Wisdom feeds spiritual and ethical life. The invitation to the rich meal of Woman Wisdom stands in contrast to the meagre diet of the wicked. They eat the food of wickedness and drink the wine of violence (4:17).

Conclusion (v. 6). Wisdom tries to persuade her pupils by promising them life (v. 6a). "And live" makes clear that the stakes are high in accepting or rejecting Wisdom's invitation. It is in fact nothing less than a matter of life and death (see 3:18; 4:13; 5:6; 6:23; 8:32–35). This closing verse uses the sage's favorite metaphor of "way" for his teaching (cf. 1:15; 20–33). In this chapter life and death are set off starkly over against each other. This evokes the life and death choice of Deuteronomy 30:15–20. Using metaphorical language, the teachers of wisdom invite the unlearned to avoid the destructive entrapments of a foolish life. It is either-or, there is no escape or third way. Wisdom summons to a decision.

New Testament Context. The echo of the portrayal of Wisdom can be heard in the Gospel of John, where Jesus issues a comparable invitation (John 6:35–40). From that point of view, today's reading gained its place in a wide range of liturgical moments and contexts.[2] Especially in early Eastern Christianity, the text is given a eucharistic and christological interpretation. In the Byzantine liturgy it is read at the Holy Thursday celebration of the Lord's Supper. Theologians of the patristic period and the Middle Ages interpreted the personified Wisdom who builds a house for herself as an image of the incarnation, the divine Word who builds a body for himself. In that context, Proverbs 9:1–5 came to serve as a reading for the feasts of the Virgin Mary. This pericope served in later times also as a reading in the dedication for a new church.

REIN BOS

Homiletical Perspective

eternal life. As Moltmann wants us to realize, "Eternal life has nothing to do with timelessness and death, but is full-filled life" here on earth that makes us yearn it will never end. Living life to the fullest as disciples brings joy in the present and a hope for the future. Bill Coffin, in *Credo*, puts it this way, "We are on the road to heaven now if today we walk with God. Eternal life is not a possession conferred at death; it is a present endowment. We live it now and continue it through death."[2]

Preachers might want carefully to address the listeners' resistance to this message due to their misunderstanding of original sin. They learned from the creation story that unwise choices, against God's intentions, have led to our expulsion from the garden. It is understandable that they fear human corruption dooms us from ever experiencing the quality of eternal life spoken of in these passages.

Therefore the preacher cannot overemphasize that we are created in God's image, and that sacred nature is never lost though we often stray from it. The good news is that Christ graciously seeks the straying and lost in order to transform them into righteousness, capable of making decisions in keeping with the divine intention. This is no doom-and-gloom passage; it is meant to bring hope.

Furthermore, it would be important to dissuade any misconceptions or confusion with Lady/Woman Folly, whose banquet description follows on the heels of this text. Wisdom represents a synopsis of all the positive roles played by wives and mothers in Israelite society, even as Woman Stranger/Folly combines all male fears of female temptation into one figure.[3] Wisdom is wisdom; not folly or some evil temptress, as some might wrongly assume or fear. Too often biblical women unfairly are cast in a negative light, and it would be a shame for this to happen to Wisdom. Her banquet is not depraved; it is delightful.

Proverb's Wisdom offers the preacher an opportunity to explore a biblical character and passage that gives new and interesting material for thought and inspiration. This is a passage to be savored.

DEAN MCDONALD

2. Jürgen Moltmann, *The Coming of God*, trans. M. Kohl (Minneapolis: Fortress Press, 1996), 291. William Sloane Coffin, *Credo* (Louisville, KY: Westminster John Knox Press, 2004), 170.

3. Carol R. Fontaine, *Proverbs*, Women's Bible Commentary, expanded edition with Apocrypha, ed. Carol A. Newsom and Sharon H. Ringe (Louisville, KY: Westminster John Knox Press, 1998).

2. Richard J. Clifford, *Proverbs*, Old Testament Library (Louisville, KY: Westminster John Knox Press, 1999), 105.

Psalm 34:9-14

[9]O fear the LORD, you his holy ones,
   for those who fear him have no want.
[10]The young lions suffer want and hunger,
   but those who seek the LORD lack no good thing.

[11]Come, O children, listen to me;
   I will teach you the fear of the LORD.
[12]Which of you desires life,
   and covets many days to enjoy good?
[13]Keep your tongue from evil,
   and your lips from speaking deceit.
[14]Depart from evil, and do good;
   seek peace, and pursue it.

Theological Perspective

Jews and Christians believe that to be human is to live a life engaged in the praise of God. The human condition is transformed when it focuses on praise to the one true God. We shift our priorities from selfish human acquisition to compassionate simple lifestyles that help us be faithful to God. All of our actions and all of our thoughts—that is, our whole beings—seek to praise God. This condition of praise makes the worshiping community one that "has no want."

The psalmist reminds us, however, that praise to God as our human imperative has historical consequences for our lives and communities. Praise is not just an attitude or an aptitude. Praise requires a relationship defined by fear of the Lord and our lives' desires. The psalmist does not separate the practice of praise from a life of justice and peace (see vv. 11–14 in particular). The agency of praise is nourished by the good life, by a grateful life. But gratitude is defined not in terms of thanking God for things acquired, but rather in terms of living the faith in service to others. The psalmist encourages us to speak the truth, to do good, and to seek peace. Again, praise becomes contingent on believers' relationships with each other and with the world.

The NRSV translation of verse 10 reads, "[T]he young lions suffer want and hunger, but those who seek the LORD lack no good thing." However, the

Pastoral Perspective

When Franklin D. Roosevelt declared in his first inaugural address, "The only thing we have to fear is fear itself," what he was warning against was the cowardice that causes paralysis. In 1933, in the face of the Great Depression and the need for bold and decisive action, such cowardice was, he argued, his nation's chief adversary. Cowardice, however, is but one variety of "fear itself" among many. Seventy years later, people all over the world are consumed with another kind of fear, and indeed are variously engaged in an ongoing struggle against it: the so-called war on terror. Never in human history have so many human beings been gripped by so much fear, in all its varieties. And accordingly, never have so many been so critical—and indeed so fearful—of "fear itself."

As Psalm 34 opens, the psalmist seems to echo this critical assessment of "fear," summing up her situation this way: "I sought the LORD, and he answered me, and delivered me from all my fears" (v. 4). From a pastoral point of view, this reference to "fear" is both familiar and compelling, since human trouble can so often be traced to the various ways in which fearful people require pastoral reassurance and encouragement. Considered from this angle, the good news of the gospel is that God delivers us from "all fears," and so establishes a great reversal: fear becomes confidence, trust, faith. Thus the Christmas

Exegetical Perspective

The Genre of Psalm 34. Psalm 34 is a thanksgiving psalm, which in essence is a report to the community of the psalmist's rescue. One might say that the element of thanksgiving continues the drama of the lament, for it is the next stage if the lament (petition for rescue) has been heard. In praying for deliverance, psalmists sometimes promised to do certain acts if and when God answered their prayer. Sometimes it was a vow ("my vows I will pay before those who fear him," Ps. 22:25b), and other times it was telling others of the saving act ("in the midst of the congregation I will praise you," Ps. 22:22b). In a sense, a thanksgiving psalm is the record of such a public announcement. Such psalms might be described as verbal votive offerings, "posted" publicly so that others may learn that the Lord is active in the world, acting out of loving loyalty (*ḥesed*) for those who cry for assistance. Psalm 34 is unusual among thanksgivings in its strong casting of the psalmist in the dual role of subject of the rescue and proclaimer of the rescue. Since the psalmist is the one who received the divine favor, the psalm quickly turns into a testimony, a witnessing of the great deeds of the Lord.

Instructing the Community to Praise the Lord. Earlier in the psalm, the psalmist proclaims, "This poor soul cried, and was heard by the LORD, and was saved

Homiletical Perspective

At any given moment in a congregation's life, the preacher is speaking to people who are afraid, and we preachers ourselves are afraid of something. (Usually we are afraid either that we will utterly fail or that we have absolutely nothing to say.) Perhaps our fear, like that of everyone else in our congregation, is not apparent, not spoken, or not even acknowledged.

For those of us in fear, the words of Scripture that are more familiar to us might be, "Do not be afraid." They rattle around from Genesis (Gen. 15:1) through the Gospels (Luke 1:30) to Revelation (Rev. 1:17). The words "Do not fear" might be God's favorite phrase.

Thus, the natural question arising from both Psalms (e.g., 34:9) and Proverbs (e.g., 1:7) is: "Why are we also told to fear?" One strain of Christianity, not a very healthy one, grows by highlighting a negative fear of the Lord. Negative fear emphasizes judgment and terror. That fear sets a deep guilt into our souls, and it tends to feed on itself; thus the virus spreads.

Further, this negative fear focuses on need and scarcity. The fear which "suffer[s] want and hunger" (v. 10) believes that the love and grace of God has limits. It is a scarce thing, to be allocated carefully and meticulously. All too often, Christians have treated salvation itself as a limited commodity; one

Psalm 34:9-14

Theological Perspective

Spanish Popular Version of the United Bible Societies, which is based upon the ancient Greek translation of the Hebrew Scriptures called the Septuagint, equates the young lions with the rich. This version reads as follows:

Los ricos se vuelven pobres,	The rich become poor,
Y sufren hambre.	And go hungry.
Pero los que buscan al Señor	But those who seek the Lord
Nunca les faltará ningún bien.[1]	Want of no good thing.[1]

Theologically, this translation points to the relationship between those who are rich and self-sufficient, and those who are poor. Both the Hebrew and Christian Scriptures warn the community that attachment to money is, ultimately, idolatry. The text in Spanish refers to the suffering of the rich when they become what they never want to be: poor. Yet the psalmist emphasizes that seeking the Lord will ensure them of good things. Because the psalmist interlocks praise, plentiful life, and justice, we are called not to confuse material acquisition and capitalistic individualism with a simple lifestyle that gives us freedom to praise, live abundantly, and do justice. As a result, praise is not an isolated practice of faith communities but an expression of the historical relationship between who we are and how we live in this world.

The psalmist's call in verses 12–14 echoes Micah's words: "And what does the LORD require of you, but to do justice, and to love kindness, and to walk humbly with your God?" (Mic. 6:8). It also echoes the words of Isaiah when he defines true worship (Isa. 58:9–11):

> Then you shall call, and the LORD will answer;
> you shall cry for help, and he will say, Here I am.
>
> If you remove the yoke from among you,
> the pointing of the finger, the speaking of evil,
> if you offer your food to the hungry
> and satisfy the needs of the afflicted,
> then your light shall rise in the darkness
> and your gloom be like the noonday.
> The LORD will guide you continually,
> and satisfy your needs in parched places,
> and make your bones strong;
> and you shall be like a watered garden,
> like a spring of water,
> whose waters never fail.

The practice of separating worship from everyday demands for justice and peace is dualistic, and it

1. Translation to English is by the author.

Pastoral Perspective

angels sing, "Do not be afraid!" and Jesus remarks, "Do not fear, only believe" (Luke 2:10; Mark 5:36).

And yet, just a few lines later in Psalm 34, the singer proclaims, "O fear the LORD, you his holy ones, for those who fear him have no want," and then again, "Come, O children, listen to me; I will teach you the fear of the LORD" (Ps. 34:9, 11). Apparently, there is one fear from which God does not deliver the psalmist—or rather, one "fear" *to which* God delivers her. The "fear of the LORD" is a fear worth learning. To that end, Psalm 34:9–14 offers a compact curriculum.

The idea that a form of fear is worthwhile may seem counterintuitive at first, but upon closer inspection, we see that life-giving fears are at least as common in human affairs as death-dealing ones, and we spend a good deal of our time learning the former. As every parent knows, children must be taught a whole range of fears just to navigate the house and neighborhood safely, to say nothing of their need, as they grow older, to learn about the wolves that lurk in the forest. Likewise, every time we learn a new task (how to operate a machine, dance a new step, cook a new dish, or make a new friend), particular fears draw the outer boundaries within which the task is properly carried out. In this sense, fear walks hand in hand with wisdom. Learning to be wise involves learning when and how to be fittingly afraid.

Indeed, one way of reading Genesis 2 and 3—the mythical narrative portrait of what Christians call the fall of humankind away from God—is to hear God's remark ("of the tree of the knowledge of good and evil you shall not eat, for in the day that you eat of it you shall die," Gen. 2:17) less as a prohibition than as a wisdom teaching, a hospitable inculcation of fear provided for the sake of humanity's well-being (akin to a parent's instruction to a child, "Do not drink from the containers in the cabinet under the sink!"). Later, however, this instruction is mistaken by the man and woman as a rule imposed against their best interests (Gen. 3:4ff.). In other words, human beings mistake a good fear for a bad one, disregard the divine counsel, and so "fall" into disobedience, danger, and shame. Thus salvation, reversing this disaster, is a life-giving "rise" into obedience, safety, and dignity. This means learning anew the differences between death-dealing and life-giving fears. For the psalmist, "the fear of the LORD" is the key fear worth learning, the one that gives life and guards it. Hence Psalm 34's brief, threefold curriculum.

from every trouble" (v. 6). This assertion propels the psalmist into the role of witness and testifier to how God works in the community. The prayer for help and subsequent deliverance endow the psalmist with the authority to teach others or, more accurately, to testify to others what God has done. The psalmist's knowledge of God as a saving God is not theoretical, but comes out of personal experience. The experiential tone is conveyed in the exhortation that immediately follows: "O taste and see that the LORD is good." Taste is a metaphor for personal experience, as in Psalm 119:103, "How sweet are your words to my taste, sweeter than honey to my mouth!"

The second exhortation, "O fear the LORD, you his holy ones" (v. 9, cf. v. 11) requires comment, for "fear of the LORD," though traditional, is an unsatisfactory translation of a Hebrew phrase best rendered "revering YHWH." One problem with the traditional translation is that "LORD" is a *title* and thus slightly less personal than YHWH, which is a *proper name*. We must say immediately that "LORD" is the traditional Jewish and Christian reverential substitute for the name YHWH and is rightly used in liturgy and public discourse. "Fear" is even more unsatisfactory, for the phrase does not mean "to be afraid of God," nor does it mean, as is sometimes said, reverence in general. The idiom "fear of [divine name]" is widely attested in the ancient Near East. In polytheistic cultures, fearing a god meant singling out the god for worship and for loyal service and obedience. To revere a particular deity invited that deity to look with favor on the client and to bestow blessings—healthy and long life, children, wealth, standing in the community, and protection from enemies. To paraphrase Psalm 34:9: revere YHWH alone by honoring and obeying only YHWH; be lovingly loyal to the God of your ancestors.[1]

Why does the psalmist exhort members of the community to revere YHWH? Because not to do so risks impoverishment. Those who take pride in their self-sufficiency and reliance on their own power ("the young lions" of v. 10) will be left to their own devices, whereas those who revere the Lord will lack nothing. Note that the psalmist is not giving a lecture, but sharing a genuine experience of the compassionate God and inviting others to join in a worshipful response.

With the exhortation "Come, O children, listen to me," the poet takes on the mantle of a teacher and

must be careful to do exactly the right thing (in cowering fear) in order to gain access to salvation.

However, when Scripture says, "Do not fear," the fear that is proscribed is exactly the sort of irrational terror with which some churches are obsessed. It is a fear that often overtakes the believer's life. It is related to anxiety and guilt, and often related to death itself.

But there is a "fear of the Lord" related to the positive force of God; it is respect for the positive mystery of God. This is the fear that Psalm 34 discusses. Rudolf Otto declared famously that the definition of the religious experience was *mysterium tremendum et fascinans* (roughly translated as a "tremendous and fascinating mystery"). To experience God is to be in touch with a tremendous mystery that does not drive us away, but fascinates and attracts us. This attractive fascination is awe and wonder.

This positive fear of the Lord does not focus on scarcity. This positive fear knows no limit to the grace of God. Those who seek the Lord "lack no good thing" (v. 10). Psalm 34:10 suggests that this "fear" is related to seeking; part of respect for the Lord is to seek after the Lord. Thus the preacher may remind us that "seeking" need not be a reason to feel guilty. Rather, seeking is actually the process that respects God. To honor and respect God might be to have the courage to search, to seek, to ask. "Fear" does not mean passive surrender and cowering; "fear" means seeking and pursuing.

Further, Psalm 34 reminds us that proper religious fear is related to ethical behavior. In the passage at hand, respect for the Lord is also related to goodness and peace. To seek after the Lord is to turn away from evil for the sake of the utter good. "Depart from evil, and do good; seek peace, and pursue it" (v. 14). One of the distinctive features of Christianity is its treatment of evil. Every religious tradition, in fact, wrestles with "the problem of evil." If God is both all-good and all-powerful, why does evil exist? No sensitive Christian escapes having to consider evil. Christianity is actually one of those religions that does acknowledge the existence of evil. For Christians, evil is not defined away as nonexistent or an illusion. Evil is real. Psalm 34:14 is our tradition's most powerful and succinct response to evil: "depart from evil, and do good; seek peace, and pursue it." The work we have to do is not speculating about evil's existence; the work we have to do is to meet evil directly and overcome it by doing the good.

In the end, how do believers know whether we are engaged in a respectful fear (of awe) or in an unhealthy

---

1. For a thorough and concise treatment, see Michael L. Barré, "Fear of God and the Worldview of Wisdom," *Bulletin of Biblical Theology* 11 (1981): 41–43.

Psalm 34:9-14

Theological Perspective

deceives us into faithlessness, making us idolaters of our own interests and securities. While the psalmist invites us to praise God, this praise is bound to our departing from evil, doing good, and pursuing peace.

The Christian tradition is rich in its practice of justice connected to praise. Hymns, prayers, Bible studies, and spiritual disciplines help us remain faithful by keeping our personal and communal devotion together with our daily commitment to meet the demands of justice and peace. As we seek to tear down the dualistic practice of separating worship from justice, we are reminded of Jesus' words in Matthew 7:22–23: "On that day many will say to me, 'Lord, Lord, did we not prophesy in your name, and cast out demons in your name, and do many deeds of power in your name?' Then I will declare to them, 'I never knew you; go away from me, you evildoers.'"

As the psalmist also reminds us, seeking a long and joyful life comes both from love and praise for God and from love and justice for the world. Our human condition, therefore, is always intertwined with the *imago dei*. We seek to praise God, and, in doing so, we seek and live a life of peace and justice.

A pastor in a Puerto Rican country barrio, or neighborhood, was called by her denomination to help out a church experiencing deep conflict, much of it over the nature of proper worship. A group of very spiritually oriented men invited her to climb a hill in back of the church with them to pray and to discern the will of God for their congregation. She recognized that these faithful men had a passion for worship and a desire to be in solitude in the beauty of nature, but she decided to invite them to have a different kind of experience.

"After we descend from the hill and before we share our experiences with the congregation, let's visit the capital's medical center so that we can serve those who are sick and suffering," she said. The men stared at her, puzzled. They ended up refusing her invitation, in fact not even ascending the hill to pray. They shied away from praise, thereby losing the opportunity to rediscover something of what it means to be human. Our humanity means that we must praise God, but this praise must heal, building a community that "has no want."

CARLOS F. CARDOZA-ORLANDI

Pastoral Perspective

First, like any good wisdom teacher, the psalmist sets the proper goal in clear view. The goal is not "obedience" per se, or piety, or praise. All of these have a place in the program, but the goal itself is quite different: "life" and "to enjoy [the] good" (v. 12). Second, since so much day-to-day human iniquity begins with speech (gossip, slander, and deception), the psalmist recommends that any effort to "turn from evil and do good" should begin there: "Keep your tongue from evil, and your lips from speaking deceit" (v. 13). Third, now specifying her instruction to "do good," the psalmist urges a vigorous life of making peace: "Seek peace, and pursue it" (v. 14). Thus according to Psalm 34, the abundant, joyful life begins by fasting from evil speech, and comes to fruition through peacemaking. This is what "the fear of the LORD" looks like, not only because God hates evil and loves the good, but also—and decisively—because evils cut us off from life and enjoyment, while genuine peacemaking, by contrast, immerses us in them.

In Psalm 34, "fearing the LORD" means neither to overestimate our ability to survive participating in evil (say, as we blithely gossip, thus cutting ourselves off from life and joy), nor to underestimate our ability to contribute to God's work of reconciliation and justice. "The only thing we have to fear," the psalmist might say, "is fearlessness itself"—since genuine human flourishing depends on the wisdom, obedience, and dignity involved in "fearing the LORD." This kind of fear leads not to cowardice but to courage, and so at last to freedom from fear in all its death-dealing varieties. As the old hymn puts it, "'Twas grace that taught my heart to fear, And grace my fears relieved."

MATTHEW MYER BOULTON

Exegetical Perspective

also the traits of Woman Wisdom in Proverbs 1:20–33; 8:1–36; and 9:1–6, 11. The resemblances to Proverbs 9:1–6, 11 are particularly striking (words identical to Psalm 34:11–15 are italicized): "*Whoever* (Ps. 34:12a) is simple, turn aside here . . . / *Come*, eat my food, / drink the wine I have mixed. / Leave behind simpleness and live, / walk on the path of understanding. . . . For by me will your *days* be made many, / and years of *life* will be added for you" (Prov. 9:4, 5, 6, 11, my translation).[2]

"Life" in this context is long life resulting from righteous conduct, the diametrical opposite of the brief life of the wicked who are cut off prematurely. In addition to shared vocabulary, Proverbs' exhortation to turn away from evildoing (Prov. 9:6, "lay aside immaturity") is equivalent to Psalm 34:14, "depart from evil." As in Proverbs 1–9, the audience is called "children" (lit., "sons, disciples"), somewhat misleading, because in Hebrew "sons" includes anyone who can profitably listen to a "master." Psalm 34:11–14, even the whole block of verses 11–22, could be inserted into Proverbs 1–9 without appearing out of place there.

Some differences between Proverbs and Psalm 34 should be noted, however, the chief one being the *source* of the teacher's authority. In Proverbs, the source of the father's authority is his position in the family (or the father and mother in Prov. 1:8 and 6:20), whereas in Psalm 34 it is the psalmist's transformative experience of the living God.

The psalm is especially appropriate as a responsorial to the first reading, Proverbs 9:1–6, because Proverbs 9 and Psalm 34 share a common vocabulary and perspective. Psalm 34 also points to the Gospel reading, the bread of life discourse of John 6:51–58, which itself is inspired by Proverbs 9.

RICHARD J. CLIFFORD

Homiletical Perspective

fear (of anxiety and terror)? At any given moment, we can be among those who simply cannot figure out our own fear. Should we be fearful or not? This question might be answered by the ethical behavior described in Psalm 34. Respectful fear consists of good behavior. It is to keep from evil and deceit.

The preacher might also point out that "seeking the Lord" is not an activity restricted to private religious experience. In this passage, to seek the Lord is to enter the arena of moral action and collective good. The question "which of you desires life?" is answered not by a new style of private prayer or individual practice. Rather, the question is answered by collective social good. The good life is not private; the good life is seeking peace and social good. Nor is the good life one of passive, noninvolved "self-liberation." The good life is one of action and involvement.

Finally, the preacher might note a connection between verse 13 here ("keep your tongue from evil, and your lips from speaking deceit") and verse 1: "I will bless the LORD at all times; his praise shall continually be in my mouth." What we speak really is important. We have choices between having our tongue speak evil and having our tongue speak praise.

It follows that to speak praise is also a way of fearing, that is, respecting, the Lord. At this point, fear does not seem to cause trembling at all. The fear of God that respects and honors God removes guilt, terror, and scarcity. It puts words of praise on the believer's lips (v. 1). It magnifies the grace and glory of God, without considering for a moment that God is limited!

SAM CANDLER

---

2. Richard J. Clifford, *Proverbs: A Commentary*, Old Testament Library (Louisville, KY: Westminster John Knox Press, 1999), 101.

Ephesians 5:15-20

¹⁵Be careful then how you live, not as unwise people but as wise, ¹⁶making the most of the time, because the days are evil. ¹⁷So do not be foolish, but understand what the will of the Lord is. ¹⁸Do not get drunk with wine, for that is debauchery; but be filled with the Spirit, ¹⁹as you sing psalms and hymns and spiritual songs among yourselves, singing and making melody to the Lord in your hearts, ²⁰giving thanks to God the Father at all times and for everything in the name of our Lord Jesus Christ.

Theological Perspective

While only six short verses, this passage contains several key theological themes. First, building upon the earlier imagery of the old self and the new, the writer casts the times in apocalyptic terms. Christians are to make "the most of the time, because the days are evil" (v. 15). Clearly the writer sees this as an apocalyptic age with the end time near. There is an urgency for the church to "redeem the time," as the passage is sometimes translated. Christians are to be in haste to participate in Christ's work on this earth. The word "time" here is *kairos*. This is much like the passage in Galatians: "So then let us not grow weary in doing what is right, for we will reap at harvest time, if we do not give up. So then, whenever we have an opportunity, let us work for the good of all, and especially for the family of faith" (Gal. 6:9–10). Having turned away from the old self to the new, Christians are urged to focus on that which builds up the body, with expectation of this realm coming to an end. Thus these Christians are urged to "not get drunk with wine . . . but be filled with the Spirit" (Eph. 5:17), both because this behavior harms the body of Christ by diminishing one of its members and also because it wastes the precious time left before Christ comes again.

A second theme is the corporate nature of the faith. The writer emphasizes the importance of the

Pastoral Perspective

Jesus sternly warns his disciples not to call anyone a fool. "You fool" amounts to the charge of being subhuman. Human beings want to be wise, not foolish, and yet we know wisdom itself is not innate, so we seek it. The suggestion in verse 15 that we might not be wise accordingly gets our attention by appealing to both our fear of being foolish and our desire to be wise.

Both testaments reject "worldly" wisdom and offer advice on how to be wise in a godly way. This passage repeats the exhortation. The mark of the wise, according to this passage, is using time wisely, and using it to change the world. "Making the most" of the time, or more familiarly, "redeeming" the time (v. 16) carries with it the urgency of a shopper snatching up a bargain. Grab it while you can, the writer urges here. We all know that time we do not use is lost, but once again in Ephesians the writer adds purpose to what might be merely a statement of the wrong to be avoided or the virtue to be acquired.

The phrase "because the days are evil" shifts the purpose of seizing the day from personal gain to Christ's purpose for the church. Christian language speaks of "evil days" in terms of systems of oppression that require resistance. More positively, there are many paths open to us for the transformation of the world before it is too late for millions,

Exegetical Perspective

The main themes in this passage include Christian wisdom, self-discipline, worship, and community identity and boundaries. The rather harsh words of 5:3–14 seek to draw a sharp distinction between children of light (Christians, led by the Spirit) and children of disobedience (non-Christians, dominated by the devil [2:2]). The author expects those outside the community to behave in ways that draw the wrath of God, but those within to live for God's pleasure. In our own context, quite different from this author's, we have learned the danger of denigrating those outside our communities: not only does it harm others, but it also tempts us down the path of self-righteous arrogance. Drawing deep lines in the sand demarcating "us" and "them" and then derogating "them" precludes us from seeing that we *are* them and they *are* us.

While we may question the applicability of the author's strict anthropological dualism, we can appreciate his insight that communities do need boundaries of some sort if they are to have an identity that helps to shape their members. Fortunately Christians have many of these tools ready at hand, thanks to our ancestors in the faith. Already by the time of Ephesians this was so. In that letter we find our Scriptures, our hymns, our spiritual odes, our Spirit-filled, Spirit-led liturgy. No

Homiletical Perspective

"Formation" is a word enjoying currency in both the church and the seminary. It is usually paired with the word "spiritual" to describe a way to live, move, and have our being within a Christian identity. It tries to catch the idea that conversion is a lifelong endeavor for both the individuals and the communities that call Jesus Christ "Sovereign." You can find *spiritual formation* now in the job descriptions of some ministers, in the church's programs of retreats and adult education, and even in the curriculums of the theological school. Some lift an eyebrow of suspicion when the words appear in conversations about living the Christian life. They fear a return of quietism, the equivalent of "whatever" in the religious life, and therefore empty of accountability or ethical merit in the public square. Many fear that in all the push toward "formation," the church is "in retreat" all right, but in flight from its responsibilities to offer a prophetic word in the marketplace. But for others, *spiritual formation* describes an integrated religious life, with balance between contemplation and action, firmly rooted in God's vision for all humanity, and particularly for those who are "in Christ." To retrieve this deeper, richer set of meanings for this popular but potentially vacuous construct, the preacher is on the lookout for those biblical texts that will give *spiritual formation* depth, shape, and definition. You

Ephesians 5:15-20

Theological Perspective

community worshiping together. They are to "be filled with the Spirit, as you sing psalms and hymns and spiritual songs among yourselves" (vv. 18–19). True worship does not come from an artificially induced frenzy, but from a community being infused with the Holy Spirit. The passage is not primarily focused on the importance of worship; nevertheless, worship is at the core of who we are as Christians and a principal means of being transformed into the likeness of Christ. One of our primary obligations is to praise God. Indeed the primary focus of worship services is praise.

Worship of God redeems the time. It orients the person to the Almighty and keeps his or her life in right relation, which is what it is to "equip the saints" (4:12). Paul urges his listeners to be "singing and making melody to the Lord in your hearts" (5:19), which can be translated, "sing and play to the Lord from your heart."[1] That is, we are to bring the center of the self into our worship. We are to worship God from the core of our being. Paul is calling for authentic worship, which begins in one's heart, that is, in the center of one's being.

Worship also depends upon the connection the person has to the body of Christ. We experience the body as we worship in the body. This passage underlines the corporate nature of our existence and our salvation. We are connected with one another. The South African concept of *ubuntu* says this most clearly. Archbishop Desmond Tutu defines it:

> It is to say "My humanity is caught up, is inextricably bound up, in yours." We belong in a bundle of life. We say, "A person is a person through other persons." It is not "I think, therefore I am." It is rather: "I am human because I belong. I participate. I share." A person with *ubuntu* is open and available to others, affirming of others, . . . for he or she has a proper self-assurance that comes from knowing that he or she belongs in a greater whole and is diminished when others are humiliated or diminished, . . . or treated as if they were less than they are.[2]

Therefore, I can be I only in relation to you. We become persons as we engage others and, therefore, cannot be fully human by ourselves. Human beings are interdependent and communal.

Finally, we are called to give thanks always and everywhere. Give "thanks to God the Father at all

1. Markus Barth, *Ephesians 4–6* (New York: Doubleday, 1974), 583.
2. Desmond Tutu, *No Future without Forgiveness* (New York: Doubleday, 1999), 31.

Pastoral Perspective

and too late for the species. There is reason to believe that the planet itself is in danger, and even the United Nations has begun to enlist a worldwide effort to eradicate poverty, ignorance, and oppression (in the Millennium Development Goals). Do we share the urgency felt in the passage?

A vision of world transformation is daunting. Who would not run from it or from the other challenges of life? We routinely speak of "self-medication" as the attempt to blot out the unpleasant realities of life, and the writer prohibits escape into alcohol. The problem in this passage is that the drunkard or other addict not only is useless to the cause, but also misses real ecstasy, the kind that empowers Christlike action for the good of the world, being "filled with the Spirit."

This passage in Ephesians is neither a temperance lecture nor a dissertation on church music: it wants us to seek the Spirit. The singing of the three types of music the writer names is meant to shape the heart at the very least, and to open channels for the Spirit at the most. In our century this assertion is obvious: we know that our neural activity and experience change when we are involved in song, and we also know that a special state is available to us in certain kinds of meditative chant or prayer. In Acts 16, it was in the middle of the prayer and song of Paul and Silas that the earthquake came. In many smaller ways there are testimonies to song as the gateway to unanticipated blessing.

Not all Christians are comfortable with the mention of ecstasy, but in this text we are confronted with it nonetheless. External manifestations of the Spirit's presence, alarming as they are to many, are not the point. The text is looking to the transformation effected in singing hearts. The ecstasy will come on God's terms and make us useful.

The practical wisdom—is there another kind?—of the text asks us to open our experience to the Spirit with the goal of shaping our attitudes. A great deal of grant money and clinical experience has gone into recapturing a theme already present in Paul and those who wrote in his school: we shape our experience by what we bring to it, how we receive it, and how we are in the habit of responding to it. To a significant extent, mood is what we make it.

In its alternative to useless anesthesia, the text urges that the singing heart also be a thankful heart, "at all times and for everything" (v. 20). Here eyebrows may incline. Preachers are caught between the heartwarming stories of concentration camp survivors who forced themselves to be thankful for

Exegetical Perspective

doubt we need to allow our particular sociocultural contexts to inform how we employ our inherited gifts, but the language of Scripture and songs is our "primary language" spoken at home (by which I mean church). We learn other languages that help us navigate the wider world, but when the day is over, we come home, change into comfortable clothes, let our hair down, and put on our spiritual slippers, reverting to our primary language. Recently my nine-year-old asked with exasperation, "Mom, can you go one minute without being biblical?" Within five minutes she herself had analogized something to Scripture, causing me to turn the question back onto her (against the advice of the author of Ephesians, who doubtless would deem sarcasm unedifying). Scriptural language is good language that has transformed and sustained people worldwide for centuries in a way that no other language has. We seek to add our gifts to the treasure chest as it gets passed down to the next generation (gifts such as inclusive language, hymns from the global church, the testimony of modern saints), not simply to replace the old with the new.

Notice, for example, that our author frequently cites Scripture (4:8, 26; 5:31; 6:2f.) and pieces of Christian liturgy (4:4–6; 5:2, 14) while, unbeknownst to him, he is composing a work that will, in time, become Scripture. Given that he writes primarily to Gentiles, you might expect him to avoid reliance upon the Hebrew Bible to make his case. But if the Ephesians are going to be Christian, they will need the deep well of Scripture at their disposal to help them frame and narrate their lived reality. When exegesis and sermons do not quite hit the spot or reach down to that inarticulate space, the hymns and spiritual odes are there to signify ineffable truths. They glue the pieces back together, reminding us of where we have been (v. 8, "for once you were darkness, but now in the Lord you are light"), where we are now and by whose grace this is so, and of course where we are headed (a day of redemption). There is wisdom in the church hymnsing.

Brilliantly our passage juxtaposes two apparently incongruent facts that mark our daily existence, just as they did that of the Ephesians: at one and the same time, the author declares that "the days are evil" (v. 16) *and* enjoins us "always and for everything give thanks to God in the name of Jesus" (v. 20, my translation). Has he forgotten by verse 20 what he declared in verse 16? No more than we have forgotten the prayers of the people by the time we sing the doxology. Indeed, we know this world of

Homiletical Perspective

can find one here in this brief exhortation from Ephesians.

For one to be "spiritually formed" as a Christian believer, one is to be mature in one's faith and to be concerned about developing character as a human being. Claiming oneself to be "formed" or "mature" is the height of hubris, so we think of ourselves as being in a process of or on a journey toward maturity. Think of these few verses as but one signpost on that path that provides *spiritual* direction.

To see more clearly what the writer is up to at this point in the letter, go back to Ephesians 4:1. There the writer started taking an extended respite from offering a doxology for what God has done in Christ to bring God's household together, to give direction to the congregants for how they are to live out this new expression of faith. The writer is like the preacher who finally hears the plea from the parishioners in the pew: "So what does all this hand raising and clapping in worship mean for the living of my life?" "Very well, then," says the writer, "here is what you do," and now some "musts" and "oughts," along with clusters of imperatives, come clunking into the text of the letter wearing heavy boots.

The preacher can follow the lead of the writer in this section by telling us what time it is. The perspective of the writer is clear: "the days are evil" (v. 16), so " make every moment count" (v. 16 CEV). Now the writer doesn't indicate the sense in which "time" is used, so there is room for the preacher's interpretation. Are we living in the end times? Or is this a particular moment in time, say in our nation's history or in the life of our church? In whatever sense you have it, there is a particular urgency in the way we live *right now*. The preacher won't have to do much work to convince the listener that the times are evil. In fact, the preacher needs to take the lead of the text and name some specific things that makes the time "evil." However, it would be easy to get stuck here and start preaching an "ain't-it-awful" sermon that features a display of the preacher's favorite axes, ready for the grinding stone. Rather, the preacher works to find the path through this brief text that will leave the congregation in a place of light rather than in the darkness of helplessness and despair. Remember, we are trying to help the congregation understand how to make "every moment count" in "evil" days like these.

First, says the writer, we need to be "careful" or "cautious" (v. 15). Careful? Of what? What is the writer afraid might happen if the church is not cautious? Look through this small window of a text,

Ephesians 5:15–20   353

Ephesians 5:15-20

Theological Perspective

times and for everything in the name of our Lord Jesus Christ" (5:20). This attitude of thanksgiving requires a radical openness to existence. We are to receive the day the Lord has made, certain that God is in it. Paul certainly distinguishes between the forces of darkness and the forces of light, but he refuses to limit God's sovereignty or God's presence. This is not a gnostic world; rather, it is God's world and God is in all of it.

Thus we are to emulate the psalmist and "taste and see that the LORD is good" (34:8). In his book *Dark Night of the Soul* Gerald May writes,

> I must confess I am no longer good at telling the difference between good things and bad things. Of course, there are many events in human history that can only be labeled as evil, but from the standpoint of inner individual experience the distinction has become blurred for me. Some things start out looking great but wind up terribly, while other things seem bad in the beginning but turn out to be blessings in disguise. . . . I also feel that the dark night of the soul reveals an even deeper divine activity: a continually gracious, loving, and fundamentally protective guidance through all human experience—the good as well as the bad.[3]

What matters is not whether we think an event is good or bad; what matters is our discovering God's "protective guidance" in it. We do that only by tasting the life given to us and giving thanks to the Creator who is the giver of all things. The days may be evil, but our lives are not evil, and the One who gives of life is not evil but good. The attitude of thanksgiving and a discipline of giving thanks in worship keeps our orientation to God on the right keel.

G. PORTER TAYLOR

Pastoral Perspective

everything and the sheer impossibility of being thankful for the horrors of Rwandan genocide or for 9/11 and the unspeakable policies and actions that flowed in reaction to it. This small verse may occasion a useful crisis for preacher and listener. The days are often evil. Do Christians give thanks for them, in spite of them, or as a path through them?

It has been suggested that this passage intends that thanks be given for everything good, if people were only wise enough to recognize the goodness. Others take the passage to mean total submission to the working out of God's will, their thanksgiving an act of trust that all things do indeed work together for good, at least for those who love God. There seems to be no resolution for the stress this verse occasions, leaving readers with the continuing effort to give thanks not as we ought but as we are able. At the very least, the text pushes us to make the effort toward gratitude. Leaving the great imponderables unanswered, it seems more important to suggest that there is much for which thanks are left unoffered, and that our spirituality is the weaker for the omission.

The overall thrust of this passage is the exhortation to put ourselves where the wisdom is, to court the experience of the Spirit through abstention from what dulls the senses and through disciplined courting of ecstasy in song and thanksgiving. For the overwhelming majority of the world's Christians, the chief act of their worship is the great corporate act of thanksgiving, the making of Eucharist. Countless times each week they pray words similar to these: "It is right, and a good and joyful thing, always and everywhere to give thanks to you." The passage before us reminds us that, like all good ritual, the pattern of words and actions we use in worship are meant to shape our individual and corporate lives. The passage before us informs those words and urges the practicality of inhabiting them.

PAUL V. MARSHALL

---

3. Gerald May, *The Dark Night of the Soul* (New York: HarperSanFrancisco, 2004), 1–2, 12.

Exegetical Perspective

which he speaks, and if the language that we give our people is going to be at all useful, it has to cover the whole range of human experience, from realism to hope. Ephesians does this especially well.

Not only do our language and our liturgy define us, but so does our behavior. Markedly, self-discipline and self-control rank high on this author's virtue list. The mouth should be used for thanksgiving (*eucharistia*: vv. 4, 20), not slander, deceit, or silly talk (v. 4). Again, although we would certainly agree that thanksgiving is a key identity marker for Christians, we might find our author a bit too dour at times. He eschews banter, levity, indulgence, and any loss of self-control, be it covetousness (vv. 3, 5) or drunkenness (v. 18). He is a straitlaced kind of guy whose partygoing is confined to the church community. I suspect 1 Corinthians 9:19–23 made him cringe.

Our author despises stupidity and uses at least three different words to say so in chapter 5. Christian morality is often referred to as "walking" a certain way, though translators often render it as "living" (see 2:2, 10; 4:1, 17; 5:2, 8, 15). Living Christianly does not come naturally. Its features require discernment and wisdom, because Christians live in a world ruled by Satan, powers, and principalities, all of which constantly aim to trip us up if not fell us (2:2; 4:27; 6:10ff.). Since the author commands the reader to understand God's will, it follows that God's will is discernible. Traditionally, it is the role of Lady Wisdom to reveal God's will to human beings. Proverbs 8 pellucidly exemplifies her destiny. She cocreates the world with God; she offers human beings wisdom. Some accept it and thrive; others refuse her offer with calamitous effects. Christian wisdom is tricky business, however, because it is counterintuitive. Paul already noted this eloquently in 1 Corinthians 1:18–25: God's wisdom appears foolish to human beings, but it is the world's so-called wisdom that turns out to be moronic. According to Ephesians, we are susceptible to powers that cloud our vision and deceive us into thinking wrongly. Life in a well-defined Christian community, regular worship, training in the church's tradition, and the indwelling of the Spirit bulwark the church against such forces and train her up in the ways of Lady Wisdom.

JAIME CLARK-SOLES

Homiletical Perspective

and you can see some behaviors that are of concern to the writer. Drunkenness! (v. 18) Pardon me, but *is that all?* So is the preacher's sermon going to turn out to be about behaving ourselves at happy hour or the cocktail reception before dinner, and that's it? No, the deeper concern for this writer should be that of the preacher—*that the church of Jesus Christ would be so foolish as to miss what the will of God for it is.* The times are so urgent, so pregnant with possibilities for redemption and transformation, that the church cannot afford to miss its vocation. That is the key to the church acting wisely. When the church is acting contrary to its vocation, it is acting foolishly.

The preacher can underscore this point by exploring the value of drunkenness, not as a particular behavior, but as a metaphor. When the church is out of touch with its vocation, it moves through these evil times as one who is intoxicated— satiated and reeling, engaging in regrettable behaviors. If a quest for spiritual formation and maturity in the church displays a desire for balance and integration, drunkenness is the condition of being unfocused, off balance, and out of kilter with "what God wants for you" (v. 17 CEV).

So how do we fill in the blank: "The church's vocation is_____"?

Imagine the church's vocation as a great series of interpretive images set in stained glass and put on display. Within that display we see an image found in this little blip of a text from Ephesians. Here is the church "filled with the Spirit" (v. 18). And what does that look like? A group of folks like you and me, on the path toward formation and maturity, "singing psalms and hymns and spiritual songs" that rise out of grateful hearts.

RICHARD F. WARD

John 6:51-58

⁵¹"I am the living bread that came down from heaven. Whoever eats of this bread will live forever; and the bread that I will give for the life of the world is my flesh."

⁵²The Jews then disputed among themselves, saying, "How can this man give us his flesh to eat?" ⁵³So Jesus said to them, "Very truly, I tell you, unless you eat the flesh of the Son of Man and drink his blood, you have no life in you. ⁵⁴Those who eat my flesh and drink my blood have eternal life, and I will raise them up on the last day; ⁵⁵for my flesh is true food and my blood is true drink. ⁵⁶Those who eat my flesh and drink my blood abide in me, and I in them. ⁵⁷Just as the living Father sent me, and I live because of the Father, so whoever eats me will live because of me. ⁵⁸This is the bread that came down from heaven, not like that which your ancestors ate, and they died. But the one who eats this bread will live forever."

Theological Perspective

To preach on matters of less than life and death is not to preach the gospel as John presents it. This point is made explicit in today's lection. The crucial subject at stake—so we hear in Jesus' words at the start—is "the life of the world." The equally crucial assurance conveyed is that this life is not our production but his gift. "The bread that I give for the life of the world is my flesh" (v. 51). Sustained by these two claims of life and gift, a lively, but never deadly, seriousness attends the preacher's call to faithful proclamation.

Yet immediately upon hearing such life-giving claims, the passage diverts our attention to disputed territory. First "the Jews" are said to have "disputed among themselves"(v. 52). Then "many of his disciples" find Jesus' teaching "difficult," even to the point of questioning its acceptability (v. 60). Finally, many of these followers reportedly "turned back and no longer went about with him" (v. 66). With such a drastic change of scene, what is the problem? As is characteristic of the Johannine writings, the focus centers upon Jesus giving bread for the life of the world in his "flesh." Thus the consternation and dispute, "How can this man give us his flesh to eat?" (v. 52).

A too-ready response with textbook answers from later eucharistic doctrines about sacramental presence domesticates the consternation as enacted

Pastoral Perspective

Over many years of preaching the lectionary, my friends and I have more than once shamefully confessed to each other that when this text appears as the Gospel reading, we choose from the Epistle or the Old Testament. These are shocking words for modern sensibilities ("unless you eat the flesh of the Son of Man and drink his blood, you have no life in you," v. 53). They shock and surprise not only in the "cannibalistic" metaphor of Jesus, but also, again, in the exclusivist claim—apart from the Lord's Supper, apart from this church banquet, you have no life in you. Jesus enlarges this claim to say that this meal is the gateway—not only to life now, but eternal life. "The one who eats this bread will live forever" (v. 58).

There are rich possibilities here, once the preacher gets past the eating of the flesh and the drinking of the blood of Jesus. The most direct way is to treat this confrontational metaphor as John's symbolic "institution of the Lord's Supper." There is no last Passover in John's Gospel. It is alluded to in John 13, but does not fit chronologically (as it does in the Synoptics), since in John, Jesus was crucified on the day of the slaughter of the lambs for Passover. Seeing this passage as "John's Eucharist" is undergirded by the language of Jesus in the feeding of the multitude that introduces this teaching: "Then

Exegetical Perspective

Jesus' claim that he *is* the "bread that comes down from heaven" is provocative enough. Now he puts the claim even more outrageously: "The bread that I will give for the life of the world is my flesh" (v. 51). This turns the "complaining" of the Jews into a dispute among themselves. "How can this man give us his flesh to eat?" (v. 52). Again, there is a hidden allusion to the story of the "craving" of the Israelites in Moses's time, when they demanded flesh to eat (Num. 11:13). The allusion is clearer in many of the ancient manuscripts of John 6:52, which omit "his" to read, "How can this man give us *the flesh* to eat?" Jesus' reply, underlined by the solemn formula *amēn, amēn*, does not make it easier for the questioners to accept what he is saying: "Very truly, I tell you, unless you eat the flesh of the Son of Man and drink his blood, you have no life in you" (v. 53). It is absurd enough that he promises to give his own flesh instead of the flesh of quails; now he speaks of drinking blood. Even leaving aside the cannibalistic sound of it, the notion transgresses one of the most fundamental taboos in the food laws of Israel (see, e.g., Lev. 17:10–14; Deut. 12:16, 24).

Of course Jesus is not speaking literally of eating his flesh and drinking his blood; he refers, first of all, to the bread and wine of the Eucharist. The Gospel of John is written for insiders, for the beleaguered

Homiletical Perspective

More bread.

A few years ago my wife Patsy and I enjoyed a wonderful Canadian movie, *The Gospel of John*. The movie goes through the Fourth Gospel, word for word, start to finish, in about three hours. We loved the movie. We both found it beautiful and engaging. When I mentioned the movie to a friend of mine, he said that his wife looked at him midway through the film and asked, "Will Jesus ever shut up?"

John's Gospel is noted not only for its poetry, its high Christology, and its rich metaphorical imagery, but also for its redundancy. Here we are again, one more time with Jesus as the bread of life, the eternal bread come down from heaven (6:51). *John's repetitiveness can best be seen as a sign that what is being said is important.*

It is also a sign of the difficulty of what is being communicated. It is as if, in this sixth chapter, Jesus knows that what he is talking about is against our natural inclinations, against our accustomed means of making sense, so much so that he must be redundant and repetitive, in order to keep hammering upon our cognitive defenses until we comprehend that when he says "bread," he is not talking about flour, water, and yeast; he is talking about something that has "come down from heaven" (v. 51). Jesus always has more to say in John's Gospel

John 6:51-58

Theological Perspective

in this text. Theological commentators on this passage as divergent in their interpretations as the least allegorical John Chrysostom of the Eastern church and the most symbolic Huldrych Zwingli of the Swiss Reformation appeal to John 6 as a key text in referring to Holy Communion.

A notable exception is Martin Luther (1483–1546), whose comment on the words of Jesus in verse 51 is, "This cannot be applied to the Sacrament."[1] Rambunctious in tone, graphic in detail, geared directly to his congregation, Luther's preaching on this scriptural passage deserves mention. The reason Jesus speaks of "eating" and "drinking" his "flesh" and "blood" when calling his hearers to believe in him, Luther states, is that he wants people who are already familiar and preoccupied with eating and drinking to recognize by comparison what his words surely do *not* mean. They are "to investigate what He was driving at with this peculiar speech. What could He mean? Is one man to devour the other? Surely this cannot be the meaning. Then let them deliberate and reflect on the matter, and ask what He did mean." In gist, Luther argues that when Jesus in verse 51 speaks the words, "*My* flesh," it is the "*My*" that defines the "flesh," not the reverse. This is not "the sort of flesh from which red sausages are made," "not flesh such as purchased in a butcher shop or is devoured by wolves and dogs," "not veal or beef found in cow barns." And to those hearers of verse 53 who may object that there is other bread of life from heaven to feed upon, that need not come from him, saying in effect, "Wittenberg beer quenches the thirst, but Annaberg beer does so too," let them be advised by this Gospel, "If you do not drink Wittenberg beer, you will find no other beer to slake your thirst." "Arians," Luther considers those who so object, because their objection implies that the life in flesh and blood Christ gives us of himself is somehow less than the eternal life of God. "I am directing this against the Arians, the Sacramentarians, and other schismatic spirits and fanatics," he concludes, "who do not understand this text."[2]

Equally graphic in his own way is Chrysostom's homily on this passage, which, unlike Luther's sermon, does draw connections between the sacrament and Jesus' flesh and blood referred to in the text. It is "characteristic of those who greatly love," he remarks of verse 53, that Christ "brought

1. Martin Luther, *Luther's Works*, vol. 23, *Sermons on the Gospel of John, Chapters 6–8* (St. Louis: Concordia Publishing House, 1959), 118.
2. Ibid., quotes in order from pp. 43, 119, 123, 137, and 147.

Pastoral Perspective

Jesus took the loaves, and when he had given thanks, he distributed them" (6:11).

One avenue of interpretation is to take the institution of the Lord's Supper as Jesus' gift to the church (and through the church to the whole cosmos) for life abundant now, and for life with God everlasting. There is a wonderful prayer in *Worship Now*[1] attributed to George Macleod, founder of the Iona Community, in which he evokes the Creator in these words: "The morning is yours, rising to fullness; the summer is yours, dipping into autumn; eternity is yours; dipping into time." This prayer of adoration leads into a confession that precedes a celebration of the Eucharist. Tellingly, especially for this text, the confession of sin includes not only the scars on our hearts and consciences, but also nature "red as well as green:" the thorn on the rose and "lambs, once frolicking, now grown sheep, led off to slaughter."

If these shocking words of Jesus mean anything in the life of the church, then at the least they mean that when we eat and drink at the holy Table, eternity has broken into time in a unique, unrepeatable way. Eternity keeps on dipping into our time. Our memorial feast of bread and wine joins us with the living Christ, who is forever—and thus joined to him, we are forever. We who belong to (and with) Christ in this feast are in a community that is eternal—made so not by any human doing or by any ecclesiastical accomplishment, but only by the action of the One who laid down his life for the sins of the cosmos. "O Lamb of God, you who take away the sins of the world, have mercy upon us." It is the feast of the Lamb, who once announced the frolicking of abundant life, led off to slaughter for the world's sake. The very first time Jesus appears in the Gospel of John, John the Baptizer declares: "Here is the Lamb of God who takes away the sins of the world" (1:29).

Another avenue of interpretation is found in the little word "forever." The hymns of the church are full of the words "forever" and "eternal." The assaults of current events and history proclaim that all is transient, passing, and doomed to nonexistence. And so there are always human attempts to make our own lives eternal, our nation infinite, and our causes everlasting. It is part of human nature, our inborn hubris that makes us try as we might to spread concrete over contingency.

One recent attempt at making eternal what is merely temporal comes from the same U.S.

1. *Worship Now* (Edinburgh: St. Andrew Press, 1978), 64.

little group of believers whose allegiance to Jesus has brought them to the crisis of separation from their neighbors and families, "the Jews" who now hate them. When these believers hear this Gospel read to them, they know the story well. They have heard the echoes of the liturgy of the Lord's Supper from the beginning of chapter 6, echoes that are found in all four Gospels' accounts of the miraculous feeding.

Yet, oddly, this Gospel does not describe the Last Supper of Jesus with his disciples, though it presupposes our knowledge of it (chap. 13). The effect of this omission is to force us to think again about the meaning of that sacrament. When we eat the bread and drink the cup, we do not just repeat a ritual for which Jesus, "on the night when he was betrayed," set the example. Rather, we "proclaim the Lord's death until he comes," as the oldest extant report of the Last Supper tells us (1 Cor. 11:23–26). In John's Gospel, not only is the miraculous feeding a "sign" pointing toward the Eucharist, as it is in all the Gospels; in Jesus' words both it and the Eucharist become signs pointing to his own death.

The conundrums posed by Jesus in this controversy are characteristic of the style of this whole Gospel. As Nicodemus, "a leader of the Jews," asks, "*How can* anyone be born after having grown old?" (3:4), now "the Jews" ask, "*How can* this man give us his flesh to eat?" (6:52). These questions are like riddles whose answers are obvious to the insider, but opaque to the outsider. The answer to the riddle is this: the way Jesus will give "bread" or "flesh"— that is, the way he will give *himself*—"for the life of the world" (v. 51) is to be "lifted up" on the cross.

This is the strange paradox that is the center of this riddling, ironic narrative. The eternal Wisdom and Word of God came down from heaven and "became flesh" (1:14) in order that he, as flesh, could give himself for the world's life. The believers who speak in this Gospel have "seen his glory" (1:14), but only in the form of a paradox. His signs "reveal" it, for those in on the secret, but the event of his glorification must wait through the entire narrative for the coming of his "hour" (2:4, 11; 4:21, 23; 5:25, 28; 7:30; 8:20; 12:23; 13:1; 17:1; cf. 16:21, 25, 32). Like Moses's bronze serpent, Jesus must be "lifted up" for the life of those who believe (3:14–15). As the unique Son he must receive again the "glory" that he had before the world began (17:5). And that glorification, that exaltation—the way the one who came down from heaven returns to the Father—is precisely his being lifted up on the cross (note esp. 12:32–33).

as he beckons us toward a thick, multilayered world where there is always more than meets the eye. As modern people, we are conditioned to live in a flattened, demystified world that is only what we can see or touch. The modern world loves "this is only . . ." statements: this is only bread, this is just another day at the office, this is only a Jew from Nazareth.

The Fourth Gospel tries to train us limited, modern people in the expectation that now the Word has become flesh, we may expect more.

The thick reality being communicated here is incarnation. We were warned upfront in this Gospel. The Word has become flesh and moved in with us (John 1). Incarnation is so against our natural, normal, widespread expectations for what is spiritual and religious that we must have Jesus reiterate to us that "flesh" (life in this world) is where this God deems to meet us. It is as if, throughout this sixth chapter, Jesus has been gradually, patiently raising the bar on incarnation. He is not only a gifted teacher, a compassionate healer, a worker of miraculous signs and wonders. He is also our "bread." He is "bread" "come down from heaven." He is "flesh" that is to be eaten, "blood" to be drunk.

At this point incarnation becomes not only vivid but also repugnant. We eat "flesh" to survive. "Blood" is the essential stuff of life itself. Levitical law forbids observant Jews from drinking the blood of a slaughtered animal, so the image is particularly repugnant in context. But in verse 53 Jesus really presses the image by saying that the flesh and blood of "the Son of Man" must be ingested—indeed, such repugnant eating and drinking is linked to being raised up on the last day (v. 54). We are thus encouraged not simply to follow Jesus, which is difficult enough in itself, nor simply to be with Jesus, but we are to "consume" (v. 57, my translation) him.

Those of us who have been conditioned to think through cool, detached, distant, and dispassionate consideration will find it strange to be told that if we are to think about the Word made flesh, we must think through ingestion, consumption, and intimate, deep engagement. The metaphor reminds one of Paul's claim of "no longer I . . . but . . . Christ who lives in me" (Gal. 2:20). There is no knowing who the Christ is without visceral, total engagement. We will not be able to comprehend him by sitting back, comfortable in the pew, and coolly considering him as if he were an abstract, disembodied idea. Incarnation means that we must get up, come forward, hold out empty hands, sip wine, chew bread (the verbs in the Greek here move from polite ones about eating

John 6:51-58

Theological Perspective

his body down to our level, namely, that we might be one with Him as the body is joined with the head." The point is that the literal reality of this condescension of love makes it possible to do more than just "look upon" or "observe" him. Rather, it is for those Christ feeds to "fix their teeth in His flesh and to be commingled with Him," that is, in short, "to fulfill all their love." As with the feeding of the multitude, in the case of loaves that come from heaven, "it is not possible to find their limit or end." Only those who so eat his flesh and drink his blood, partaking of his flesh as "true food" and his blood as "true drink" (v. 55) will have the life in them to "come back from that table like lions breathing out fire, thus becoming terrifying to the Devil."[3]

Where then in this disputed territory does this lection leave its hearers? No hearer can speak for another. But between the venerable Chrysostom's insistence that no limits or end can be imposed upon love's condescension in Christ to our bodily level, even to the fixing of our teeth in his flesh as a commingling with heavenly love, and Brother Martin's reminder that this flesh is not the sort from which red sausages are made, we at least are beckoned to a major theme of Johannine testimony, and other Gospel traditions as well. The life stronger than death that God gives to the world in what happens with Jesus Christ always comes to us *en sarki* (1 John 4:2), "in the flesh" and blood sufferings of the present time. But this coming of bread from heaven is never recognized, as Paul puts it, *kata sarka* (2 Cor. 5:16), to be regarded "according to the flesh" from a spectator's point of view.

CHRISTOPHER MORSE

Pastoral Perspective

government that initially called our response to the terrorist attacks of September 11, 2001, Operation Infinite Justice. The Pentagon quickly changed that name to Operation Enduring Freedom when they realized that their first choice was blasphemous in the eyes of American Muslims.

Now we have been given a postage stamp called "Forever." The picture on the first-class-mail stamp, unveiled in March 2007, is of the Liberty Bell in Philadelphia. Postmaster General John E. Potter said the bell was selected because of its powerful symbolism.[2] No one protested. There were apparently no outcries from the World (or the National) Council of Churches, the National Association of Evangelicals, *The Christian Century*, or *Christianity Today*. The church just trudges along, eating the bread of eternal life, not noticing the claims made by merely human, contingent institutions for that which—however long lived—is temporal. While all Christians in the United States may appropriately attribute to God's providence some of the freedoms we enjoy as citizens, all Christian should also be vigilant, lest the freedom we enjoy and the protection we expect are defeated by our own overweening, ignorant pride.

Every flag of every nation, every symbol of every nation, every army and every congress or parliament of every nation will (we can depend upon it) be relegated to history's garbage dump in the long haul. But the holy, universal church, eating the flesh of Jesus and drinking the blood of Jesus (in cathedral, in grass hut, in suburban splendor, or in city storefront) is forever.

O. BENJAMIN SPARKS

3. *Saint John Chrysostom: Commentary on Saint John the Apostle and Evangelist, Homilies 1–47*, trans. Sister Thomas Aquinas Goggin, S.C.H., in *The Fathers of the Church*, vol. 33 (Washington, DC: Fathers of the Church, Inc., 1957), 468, 448, and 469.

2. *The Richmond Times Dispatch*, March 27, 2007, p. B7.

Exegetical Perspective

As even many disciples will observe, "This teaching is difficult" (6:60). Those who accept it commit themselves to a life of irony, to seeing the world strangely, to a permanent skepticism about what seems only common sense to most of those who are comfortable in that world. They will be tempted to hate the world that hates them (1 John 2:15; 5:19). A persecuted sect is tempted to define itself *against* the outsiders. Yielding to that temptation would mean not only to give up on the others, hating the world that, John's Gospel tells us, God continues to love, but also to accept a negative identity for one's own group.

The history of the Christian movement, alas, reveals how powerful that temptation has often been. Once the followers of Jesus were no longer a tiny sect within the larger Jewish communities, their stories took on new meanings. Their identification of their enemies as "the Jews" had a different resonance when used by communities that were themselves mostly Gentile, and when those communities became the beneficiaries of imperial power, rather than its victims, that resonance could become deadly. The history of Christian anti-Judaism hangs over every modern reading of the Gospel of John, requiring that we ask—in the context of the whole canon of Scripture and the whole story of God's love for the world epitomized for many by a verse from this very Gospel—how its sectarian telling of the story can be made liberating rather than confining. The challenge this Gospel puts to us is to allow its paradoxes to make us, as Jesus made his disciples, "not belong to the world" (17:16), while, precisely by means of this skeptical estrangement, to manifest in that same world the strange truth of God's love.

WAYNE A. MEEKS

Homiletical Perspective

and drinking to more visceral verbs of chewing and gulping).

Our Muslim friends are willing to walk with us along many mutual paths of ethics or noble ideas about the holiness and righteousness of God. But here at the incarnation, in this talk by Jesus of flesh and blood, eating and drinking, they part company. Islam finds the notion of God Almighty becoming our flesh, our blood, fully divine and fully human, a repugnant, self-contradictory notion.

Ah, wouldn't the Christian faith be easier if it were a matter of mere belief or intellectual assent! No, today's rather scandalously carnal, incarnational gospel reminds us that Jesus intends to have all of us, body and soul. His truth wants to burrow deep within us, to consume us as we consume him, to flow through our veins, to be digested, to nourish every nook and cranny of our being.

I have a friend who teaches theology at Oxford. He says that his toughest task is to ask and answer the question, "What is theology about?" His students tend to respond that theology is about spiritual matters, or about religion, or deeper meaning in life, et cetera. No, he instructs them, theology (at least Christian, incarnational theology, theology in the mode of the sixth chapter of the Fourth Gospel) is about *everything*. Jesus has come down from heaven with the intention of taking it all back. He wants all of us, and he wants us to have all of him.

This God is so scandalously, intimately available to us. Who ever knows this, knows how to live forever.

WILLIAM H. WILLIMON

PROPER 16 (SUNDAY BETWEEN AUGUST 21 AND AUGUST 27 INCLUSIVE)

Joshua 24:1-2a, 14-18

¹Then Joshua gathered all the tribes of Israel to Shechem, and summoned the elders, the heads, the judges, and the officers of Israel; and they presented themselves before God. ²And Joshua said to all the people, . . .

¹⁴"Now therefore revere the Lord, and serve him in sincerity and in faithfulness; put away the gods that your ancestors served beyond the River and in Egypt, and serve the Lord. ¹⁵Now if you are unwilling to serve the Lord, choose this day whom you will serve, whether the gods your ancestors served in the region beyond the River or the gods of the Amorites in whose land you are living; but as for me and my household, we will serve the Lord."

¹⁶Then the people answered, "Far be it from us that we should forsake the Lord to serve other gods; ¹⁷for it is the Lord our God who brought us and our ancestors up from the land of Egypt, out of the house of slavery, and who did those great signs in our sight. He protected us along all the way that we went, and among all the peoples through whom we passed; ¹⁸and the Lord drove out before us all the peoples, the Amorites who lived in the land. Therefore we also will serve the Lord, for he is our God."

Theological Perspective

From many theological themes here, let us emphasize one for congregational life in our time: the renewal of our covenantal relationship with God in worship, the affirmation of our identity as the people of God, and the faith commitment of service and obedience to God.

At the threshold of entering the promised land and with the promise of a future home, Joshua becomes like Moses (Exod. 20; Deut. 5; Deut. 6:20–24; Deut. 26:5–9). He reminds the people of the miracles by which the Lord gave birth to Israel in the call of Abraham and Sarah and especially calls to mind their deliverance through the plagues of their Egyptian slave masters and escape from their chariots and horsemen, through the sea and out of the darkness the Lord put between the Israelites and the Egyptians (v. 7). With this affirmation of what the God of Israel had done, Joshua, like Moses before him, addresses the people with the imperative to fear the Lord, to serve him, and to forsake the other gods of ancient memory and now temptingly close at hand. "Choose this day whom you will serve," Joshua implores. Three times he repeats his imperative and claim with different nuance: first, the choice of the Lord above all other gods (vv. 14–15); second, the denial of their choice and service unless they recognize that God is jealous and holy, and so

Pastoral Perspective

The biblical story of Joshua is an exciting story of conquest, a testimony to faith, a statistical record, and a geography. It is also a theological and pastoral account of God's covenant with God's people.

After long years of wandering in the wilderness, the Israelites conquer the promised land. Bloody battles and numerous deceptions result in the Israelites' destruction of Canaanite power. The land is to be divided among the twelve tribes of Israel. In preparation for this historical event, Joshua gathers all the tribes at Shechem (a city of refuge that is not hostile to Israelites), bringing together the heads of the tribes, the judges of the people, and the officers of Israel. Then he brokers a relationship. "Long ago your ancestors . . . lived beyond the Euphrates and served other gods," he says (v. 2). "Now therefore revere the Lord . . . put away the gods that your ancestors served . . . and serve the Lord" (v. 14).

While the text presents this event as something that happened only once during the lifetime of Joshua, there is evidence that it was in fact a rite known and reenacted by the people of Israel. External evidence includes other reports of such events in 2 Kings 23 and Nehemiah 9–10 as well as a parallel account in Joshua 8.

The question of the people's allegiance arises in the midst of a crisis of choice between YHWH and the

362   *Proper 16 (Sunday between August 21 and August 27 inclusive)*

Exegetical Perspective

The book of Joshua belongs to a larger collection called the Deuteronomistic history, which includes Deuteronomy, Joshua, Judges, 1–2 Samuel, and 1–2 Kings. While some material may be quite ancient, the books were substantially edited into a consistent history of Israel, using the themes of the book of Deuteronomy—such as the importance of exclusive worship of YHWH and refraining from the worship of other deities—as a framework for understanding the past.

Just how many times the Deuteronomistic history was edited is a matter of scholarly debate. The material may have been compiled first under the reign of the Judean king Josiah to support his religious and political policies. A crucial redaction of the Deuteronomistic history took place in the exile, soon after Jerusalem in 587–586 BCE was defeated by the neo-Babylonians and many of its citizens were forcibly relocated to Babylon. Read in exile, these books would have explained Israel's and Judah's history as one of success when YHWH alone was worshiped and failure when the people turned to other gods.

This particular text would have spoken powerfully to an exilic reader. It explains that, right before entry into the land of Canaan, the wilderness generation entered into a solemn agreement with YHWH at the city of Shechem. There the people

Homiletical Perspective

The text before the preacher this week reaches a dramatic climax with words that have become familiar to many: "Choose this day whom you will serve. . . . But as for me and my household, we will serve the LORD" (v. 15). While familiarity with this phrase is not in and of itself a barrier to hearing the word of God from Joshua 24, the domestication of these words certainly is. These words of Joshua have found themselves neatly printed as artwork, stitched as needlepoint, and carefully encased in beautiful frames to be hung on walls in houses. There, rendered one-dimensional, they drip with a syrupy sentimentality that leaves little room for the hard, gritty edginess of these words. Quite literally, Joshua's "choose this day" has been domesticated. One of the challenges facing the preacher who takes up this text is how to recover the liveliness of these words.

Perhaps one place to begin is to consider how the text of Joshua 24 functions. Joshua 24 is the second of two farewell addresses offered at the end of the book of Joshua, undoubtedly evidence of the complex literary history of the book. What is preserved in chapter 24 is a well-formed covenant ceremony. Scholars have understood the form of Joshua 24 in various ways. William Koopmans argues that within Joshua 24 there is "a sufficient degree of poetic characteristics" to demonstrate that

Joshua 24:1-2a, 14-18

Theological Perspective

requires them to reject the idolatry of the nations (vv. 19–20); and third, the corporate accountability and their inclination of their hearts to the Lord (vv. 22–23). With the emphasis of these three reiterations, Joshua's sermon reminds the people of the same sequence of affirmation and command that Moses gave at Horeb (Deut. 5:6). The redemption from Egypt and the gift of land and promise come with the covenant obligation to choose, fear, incline the heart to, serve, and obey the Lord.

The threefold repetition in the litany of Joshua's charge and affirmation is the foundation for the people's worship. Joshua requires their public affirmation of loyalty to the Lord as witnesses against themselves (v. 22); he makes a covenant with them "that day" (v. 25); he writes the words in the book of the law of God (v. 26); and he sets the large stone of witness under the oak in the sanctuary of the Lord at Shechem, where he calls the people and himself to account (v. 27). These features are components of the worship of Israel in which they affirm the choice of the Lord who delivered them and the remaking of the remembered covenant for the new day of land and promise. They mark the choice and renewal in their mutual accountability of witness against themselves, in the hearing of the words, the writing of the book of the law of God, and with the stone of witness in the sanctuary.

For an example from recent time of Joshua's covenant renewal and call to obey God, we could remember the Theological Declaration of Barmen (May 29–31, 1934). Karl Barth, the Reformed theologian, was teaching at the University of Bonn (1930–35) when Adolf Hitler, head of the National Socialist Party, was named as chancellor of Germany on January 30, 1933. Well before, in November 1931, reflecting on the chaotic situation, Barth wrote to his friend Eduard Thurneysen in Switzerland that the German political situation was "like sitting in a car which is driven by a man who is either incompetent or drunk."[1] Barth recalled that he wanted "to urge the students for whom I was responsible to keep on working as normally as possible in the midst of the general uproar." "I also felt," he said, "it my duty to join in helping the Evangelical Church to carry on its work in the changed national situation, in other words to maintain the biblical gospel in the face of the new regime and the ideology which had now become predominant." In the first days of the Third

1. Eberhard Busch, *Karl Barth: His Life from Letters and Autobiographical Texts* (Philadelphia: Fortress Press, 1976), 217.

Pastoral Perspective

gods of the ancestors. Behind this crisis lies the old perspective that deities are limited geographically and that every land has its own gods. Joshua challenges the community to renounce allegiance to all these gods for the one God YHWH. Thus the centerpiece of this covenant ceremony reflects the first commandment, in which loyalty to YHWH is complete.

What does it mean to leave behind the ancestral gods and serve the one God YHWH? This movement may not be easy as one might imagine. How we long to serve the gods of our ancestors, the gods on the other side of the river where we remember life was better! In the 1950s, the television show *Leave it to Beaver* characterized such a life. Nuclear families prospered through the support of their fathers. Tidy homes flourished with abundant food, lovely flowers, and all-around happiness. Mothers were beautiful from morning to night. Those were the days when safety and plenty reigned. The gods of order and abundance held sway. America watched over and protected all the inhabitants of the land. All was right with the world.

The ancestral gods of the Israelite people provided many of the same benefits. Tied geographically to the land they protected, these gods guaranteed security and abundance to all who lived within their embrace. As the people discovered while they were wandering in the wilderness, slavery did not seem too high a price to pay for safety and prosperity.

The place of belonging, even if it is in bondage, may be better than wandering about, unsettled, homeless, hungry, and unknown. It would be difficult for the people to face a future in a new land with different promises, different expectations, different dreams, and a new understanding of God.

The covenant with YHWH is different from the worship of the ancestral gods. This one God is not simply a god of the land, of place, of prosperity. This one God is a God who travels with God's people. YHWH is not tied to the land, to any place or sanctuary. This God makes a different kind of promise to the people. This God promises to accompany the covenant people no matter where they go. This God will be with them not only in their prosperity but also in their suffering and in their trials. This God does promise security and abundance. This God promises to be present through all that life brings.

For a battle-worn, world-weary, wandering community, this is a different kind of promise from a different kind of God. Through it, they glimpse the

willingly chose to worship YHWH alone and to renounce the gods of the land they were entering.

The gravity of their decision is clearly indicated in verses 20–28, beyond the lectionary boundaries. Even though the people were warned of the dire consequences for their likely failure, they decided to join Joshua in pledging exclusive allegiance to YHWH. For a reader in exile, such warnings would have foreshadowed their own plight ("If you forsake the LORD and serve foreign gods, then he will turn and do you harm, and consume you, after having done you good," v. 20). The warnings would have also named idolatry as the reason for Jerusalem's fall. When read in light of the warnings of verses 19–24 and their realization in the experience of exile, the people's simple promise in verse 18 takes on a more poignant, even tragic, tone.

Within the book of Joshua, the covenant at Shechem belongs to the concluding chapters of the book. After an introduction (chaps. 1–5), narratives of the conquest of Canaan (chaps. 6–12), and the details of tribal land allotments (chaps. 13–22), the narrative turns to the farewell speech of Joshua (chaps. 23–24), given "a long time after" these earlier events (23:11). Joshua's instructions outlining how the people are to behave upon entering the land serves as the culmination of the book; they are the conclusions that the people should draw from their prior experiences, how they should live in response to what has happened in the exodus experience and in the wilderness.

The beginning of the speech in chapter 23 rehearses many of the classic themes of the Deuteronomistic history. The people should not mix with the inhabitants of the land; they should love and worship YHWH alone; and they will receive "bad things" (23:15) from YHWH should they fail to live up to their promises. Frequent is the reminder that if the people serve other gods they will perish from the land YHWH is about to give them.

Chapter 24 falls into five parts.
1. Verses 1–13 serve as the preamble to what follows. They recite YHWH's past acts of graciousness to the people, starting with the choice of Abraham and continuing through the people's experience in Egypt and the wilderness. Credit for the people's success belongs exclusively to YHWH (v. 13). Important within this recital is the shift that occurs in verse 5. The narrative speaks not only about the ancestors but also claims that YHWH brought "you," this new generation born in the wilderness, out of Egypt.

it is a "carefully composed poetic narrative."[1] Others have considered the way in which OT narratives might very well be considered as drama plays to be performed for subsequent generations.[2] One very likely possibility is that Joshua 24 consists of a carefully constructed liturgical form that is taken up by Israel at various points in Israel's history. The people assemble (v. 1), the word of God is proclaimed (vv. 2–15, "This is what the Lord, the God of Israel says . . ."), the people respond (vv. 16–24), the covenant is symbolically enacted (vv. 25–27), and the people are sent out (v. 28).

Whether we are to consider the older covenant tradition when there is a crisis for Israel within the land, or the final editorial stage in the time of Babylonian exile, it is clear that Israel is summoned and assembled to discern the promise of God in various experiences of life. I would argue that in its liturgical form this text was taken up by Israel on numerous occasions. What is at stake is the reappropriation of the promise of God in the midst of shifting circumstances. Such appropriation is done within the context of worship. The function of Joshua 24, then, extends beyond the crisis for Israel in the land and offers the occasion for the people of God to hold the memory of God's promise up against the world in which they live, to discern the promise of God, to choose. Such moments are understood as a gift in which the good news of God might be received.

The preacher's task, however, is not merely to explain the text of Joshua 24 and its literary history or form, but to facilitate the church's own discernment or choosing. The question before us is, How does the text of Joshua 24—its language, imagery, and narrative movement—provide the substance for the church's discernment of the promises of God in the midst of the competing allegiances of the world in which the church exists? Is it possible that while the church still bears the name of God, its allegiances are always confused and therefore in play?

One way the sermon might function in this way is by creating a present-tense fusion of the language, imagery, and narrative movement of Joshua 24 with the world inhabited by the listening community. This is something quite different from a homiletic structure that would explain the text and then seek to make applications. Rather, the preacher might

---

1. William T. Koopmans, *Joshua 24 as Poetic Narrative*, JSOTSup 93 (Sheffield: Sheffield Academic Press, 1990), 267.
2. For example, Thomas A. Boogaart, "History and Drama in the Story of David and Goliath," *Reformed Review* 38 (1985): 204–14.

Joshua 24:1-2a, 14-18

Theological Perspective

Reich, Barth gave a lecture, "The First Command-ment as a Theological Axiom,"[2] in which he main-tained that the basis for all pastoral and theological work was that "other gods" were all the "other authorities which for some reason are thought to be important."

Reclaiming the First Commandment, Barth went on to join the Confessing Church movement and became the decisive influence on and writer of the Declaration. Its first article affirms "Jesus Christ, as he is attested for us in Holy Scripture, is the one Word of God which we have to hear and which we have to trust and obey in life and in death." And with the affirmation comes also the repudiation of "other gods": "We reject the false doctrine, as though the church could and would have to acknowledge as a source of its proclamation, apart from and besides this one Word of God, still other events and power, figures and truths as God's revelation."[3] For its day the credo of those at Barmen gave a way to work in the uproar and spoke a word of loyalty and obedience to the Lord to the churches.

In our own day of global political uproar, the preacher on this text will be looking for a fresh response to Joshua's sermon for renewal of the people, in covenanted, responsive obedience to God "above all earthly powers." Like Joshua, the covenant renewal will remind the people of the unique miracles of the Lord for the people and issue a call to forsake the false gods and insecurities in our common life, such as the love of North American wealth, the fear of terrorism, the trust in military force instead of the other choices required for building up alienated and oppressed people. We all need to rediscover Joshua's way of single-minded loyalty to the Lord, the obedient refusal to give ourselves over to the temptations of compromise with the great wealth, powers, and fears that enthrall most people and all nations today.

CHARLES E. RAYNAL

Pastoral Perspective

one God who is present with them in birth, in death, in humiliation, in joy, in wandering, and in arrival. This God delights in the people and desires more than safety and plenty for them. This God desires for them new life.

The invitation to this covenant requires that these people will be loyal and faithful to this God who is with them. This covenant requires loyal relationship through all the vicissitudes of life, instead of looking for the god who will deliver the best benefits. While the preacher may note several ways into the passage, here is an obvious pastoral opening: what are the names of the ancestral gods still worshiped in his or her own congregation? What benefits have these gods provided in the past? What losses might result from deserting them for the one God who promises relationship instead of rewards?

As the fantasy life portrayed in *Leave it to Beaver* illustrates, nostalgia may be one of the best ways to sniff out these gods. When people reminisce about "the old gods"—the ones who presided over the ways things used to be—what do they say they miss? By contrast, the passage from Joshua asks the people to leave the old gods on the other side of the river in favor of the one God who is with them no matter where they go.

In Joshua, at least, the covenant is made. God chooses the people and the people promise to be faithful to the covenant. Recognizing the one God who has been with them all the way, they declare, apparently in unison: "Therefore we also will serve the LORD, for he is our God" (v. 18).

SUSAN HENRY-CROWE

2. In *The Way of Theology in Karl Barth*, edited by H. Martin Rumscheidt (Allison Park, PA: Pickwick Publications, 1986), 63–78.
3. *The Book of Confessions* (Louisville, KY: Office of the General Assembly, 1999), 249. The entire Declaration is found on pages 247–50.

These verses continue to shift from "the ancestors" to "you," as the present generation is grafted onto the story of the ancestors. The old story becomes theirs. (Although the lectionary omits this crucial rehearsal of the saving acts of YHWH, vv. 17–18 will later provide a brief review of YHWH's deeds.)

2. Verses 14–18 explain how the people should respond to their history. Having been reminded of the faithfulness of YHWH, they are "therefore" confronted with a decision: will they enter into an exclusive relationship with the one who has already acted to save them, or will they serve the new gods of the land they are about to enter? As in the covenant treaties of other ancient Near Eastern cultures, allegiance is expected as a response to gratitude.

3. The lectionary ends the pericope prior to Joshua's questioning in verses 19–24 of the people's ability to serve YHWH. These verses stress that while choosing to serve the God who has already saved might be a logical thing to do, it is also a risky, dangerous choice. As the Old and New Testaments make clear, human actions have consequences.

4. Verses 25–28 describe the ceremony by which Joshua and the people solemnize their promise to serve YHWH alone.

5. Verses 29–33 complete the book of Joshua. The old leadership comes to an end as Joshua and the priest Eleazar die and the bones of Joseph are relocated to the land.

In literary context, then, the pericope at hand serves as the culmination not only of the book of Joshua but of the wilderness experience. The book of Judges begins the next chapter of the Deuteronomistic history, relating the story of how well (and how poorly) the new generation, having promised to worship YHWH and remain distinct from the inhabitants of the new land, will live out their promises.

Those who read this story in the literary context of the broad sweep of the Deuteronomistic history know that the people will fail to keep this promise. Those who read it in the historical context of the exile know that it was, in retrospect, a naive promise. And yet, in the story itself, as risky and as doomed to failure as the promise to love God alone is, it is really the only choice that a grateful heart and mind can make.

JULIA M. O'BRIEN

begin by allowing Joshua and his assembly to be present to us. Joshua summons all of us to Shechem on this day. We find our place alongside these elders, leaders, judges, and officials, and not only those, but countless others who have been called to this solemn assembly. We are all here telling stories of inclusion and exclusion, stories of place and no place, stories of land and exile, of the hand of God in all of it. We are discovering along the way just how tenuous our devotion has become.

The sermon's fusion will allow the preacher to interpose the language of "foreign gods" with other ways in which our allegiances are compromised. For example, it is possible that the experience of abundance and prosperity may very well be the occasion for the distortion of God and the pursuit of self-interest. When this is the case, we do well to discern those ways that we have constructed other gods who exist to protect, preserve, and defend our abundance and prosperity.

We do well to give some attention to other ways in which our own forms of religious devotion have been subtly co-opted by the spirit of the age. Have cheap substitutes for God been fashioned in the spirit of national interests? Have some therapeutic notions of God, as the one who exists to meet our individual needs, domesticated the Almighty? Has the experience of disequilibrium created by an ever-changing world led to simplified ideological versions of God that rob both life and the divine of mystery?

Just as the liturgical form of Joshua 24 moves from assembly to proclamation to covenant making and sending, the sermon can draw the listening community into a moment in which the covenant questions of Joshua 24 emerge as real questions for our time and place.

STEPHEN C. JOHNSON

Psalm 34:15-22

¹⁵The eyes of the LORD are on the righteous,
  and his ears are open to their cry.
¹⁶The face of the LORD is against evildoers,
  to cut off the remembrance of them from the earth.
¹⁷When the righteous cry for help, the LORD hears,
  and rescues them from all their troubles.
¹⁸The LORD is near to the brokenhearted,
  and saves the crushed in spirit.

¹⁹Many are the afflictions of the righteous,
  but the LORD rescues them from them all.
²⁰He keeps all their bones;
  not one of them will be broken.
²¹Evil brings death to the wicked,
  and those who hate the righteous will be condemned.
²²The LORD redeems the life of his servants;
  none of those who take refuge in him will be condemned.

Theological Perspective

This psalm is identified as a thanksgiving psalm because of its note of gratitude and joy in the divine majesty of God. The first verse sets the tone of confidence and praise, "I will bless the LORD at all times." Verses 15–22, however, contain themes of the suffering of the righteous and the frequency of affliction. Yet the note of thanksgiving continues because the nearness of God to the brokenhearted is affirmed. In spite of the bitter reality of suffering, the original theme of hope is not extinguished in this section. The final verse of the psalm states, once again, the steady confidence of believers, including those who suffer, of God's ultimate plan and purpose for them.

The section of verses on suffering and loss raises all the issues that immediately surface when bad things happen to good people. Where is God in the realities of suffering and evil? Or, perhaps, *who* is God in the realities of suffering and evil? These perennial questions have often produced a theodicy—a rational account of how it is possible to confess a good God and yet confront persistent evil. The painful questions of theodicy arise, of course, because of the incongruity of widespread suffering and faith in a good, loving God. The medieval theologian Boethius put the congruity in classic form with the pair of statements: Either God wishes

Pastoral Perspective

An old story about temptation—I have never identified its original source—involves a boy and a girl, dressed up for church in their Sunday best. All spiffy in their clean, pressed, tucked, and tidy clothing, the children were propped up to sit outside on the back porch stairs for just a moment. They were instructed not to move from the steps until their mother returned. The children sat and waited. Then the little boy moved and the little girl did not. Who was wicked? Who was righteous?

Human beings often operate with a mind-set that differentiates between people who are ill behaved and therefore evil, on one hand, and those who are well behaved and therefore good, on the other. When we think in terms of righteousness, we really have in mind the terms of self-righteousness—the habit of judging others according to our own terms and determining that some are better than others. For example, the meritocracy of college admissions and the state of the penal system in our country both reflect how shallowly we assess and how poorly we value each other as human beings in American society.

The terms we use to label the "good" and the "bad" in our world are quite different from the terms of righteousness and wickedness identified in Psalm 34. The righteous are those who seek the Lord and fear God, who do good, speak truthfully, and seek

Exegetical Perspective

Psalm 34 is a blend of thanksgiving (vv. 1–10) and wisdom instruction (vv. 11–22). In verses 1–10, the psalmist praises YHWH (the Lord), recounts that God delivered him, and boasts how YHWH saves those who share the psalmist's attitude toward God. For these people, YHWH delivers them from distress and protects them; those who fear YHWH lack nothing. The psalmist calls upon the audience to exalt YHWH with him (v. 3), but this call for thanksgiving shifts abruptly to an instructional setting: "Come sons, listen to me; I will teach you the fear of YHWH" (v. 11, my translation). From this point on, the psalmist discusses a frequent theme in Wisdom literature: the dichotomy between the life consequences of the righteous and the wicked. Although this mixture of thanksgiving and wisdom instruction is uncommon in the Psalms, the composer of Psalm 34 clearly indicates that the two are interrelated components of religious practice. Psalm 34 is an alphabetic acrostic poem; the first letter of verse 1 begins with the first letter of the Hebrew alphabet, and each successive line begins with the next letter of the alphabet (except for v. 22). By design, the composer communicates that worship and daily behavior are equally important.

Some of the categories in this psalm, which seem very general to contemporary readers, were quite

Homiletical Perspective

The language of this psalm could lead us to perpetuate attitudes of division: us vs. them. In the psalm, the righteous ones are set in contradistinction to the evildoers, and the Lord is clearly on the side of the righteous. The psalm says that God will hear the righteous; God will rescue them and will redeem them (vv. 17, 22). The evildoers, by contrast, are silenced before God. They will not be remembered, and they will be brought to death (vv. 16, 21). These verses, from the latter section of the acrostic psalm, describe human reality according to categories: the righteous and the wicked, the blessed and the cursed, the favored and the condemned.

These fixed oppositional categories are familiar language to our ears. This is the language of world news—or at least the news in the United States. World leaders have used this exact language, as if quoting directly from this psalm, to describe certain peoples as the enemy, as evildoers. Whole nations and races are categorized by labeling some as righteous and others as unrighteous. This language permeates the media. It comes to us in the headlines that pop up from our Web site connections as well as those that scroll below the newscasts. We are shaped to think that there are two kinds of persons, the good and the evil. There are only two categories and therefore everyone is either this way or the other

Psalm 34:15-22

Theological Perspective

to prevent evil but cannot, in which case God is just but not omnipotent, or God can prevent evil but does not want to, in which case God is omnipotent but not just. Either horn of the dilemma is unthinkable.

The effort to construct a coherent theodicy has challenged the finest theological and pastoral minds in the Christian tradition. These questions that arise from the depths of pain challenge many Christian affirmations, including the doctrines of God, creation, Christ, and humanity. One way forward is to avoid the tension of either—or as expressed in Boethius's categories. Karl Barth, for example, insisted that God is not to be understood as existing in the sort of contingencies that characterizes human existence. Rather, God "is absolute, infinite, exalted, active, impassible, transcendent, but in all this He is the One who loves in freedom, the One who is free in His love, and therefore not His own prisoner. He is all this as the Lord, and in such a way that He embraces the opposites of these concepts even while He is superior to them."[1] This means that the conflict that we seem to see between suffering and God's goodness is a conflict that is only apparent to us. In God's freedom, there is no dilemma, but rather a unity of love and purpose. Not all Christian believers are convinced by Karl Barth's approach to the problem of suffering. This is an area where, it seems, rational explanations falter or fail.

Instead of trying to explain suffering and evil, the psalms boldly express the reality of evil, and yet affirm believers' ongoing relationship with a faithful God. Many psalms contain words of struggle with suffering and affliction. The lament psalms especially include direct expression of lament, argumentation, weariness, and protest.[2] In contrast to much contemporary spirituality that conveys unrelenting optimism and cheer, the piety of the psalms is honest and direct, willing to play the entire scale of human experience and emotion, from the deep low to the exultant high.

The particular sort of theodicy that is expressed in the Psalms is not a philosophical or rational theodicy. It is, instead, a theodicy of relationship or, perhaps, a theodicy of identity. The theodicy of relationship can be seen in verses 15, 17, and 18, when the righteous are crying out in trouble and God both hears and helps. "The eyes of the LORD are on the righteous, and his ears are open to their cry"

1. Karl Barth, *Church Dogmatics*, IV/1 (Edinburgh: T. & T. Clark, 1956), 187.
2. Daniel Migliore and Kathleen Billman, *Rachel's Cry: Prayer of Lament and Rebirth of Hope* (Cleveland: United Church Press, 1999), 25.

Pastoral Perspective

peace. The wicked are those who do evil, hate the righteous, and cut themselves off from God. It is not our selves, our merits, or the other's demerits that are central to our identity, but God—God's care, God's purposes, and God's presence. Furthermore, the presence of God outlined in the final third of Psalm 34 is far more tender than any human self-righteousness we might extend to one another.

Here, in the poetry of the Psalms, God takes on human form in its most nurturing capacities. God's eyes gaze upon the righteous; God's ears are open to their cry. The face of the Lord, God's presence, shuns evil and spares our memories its mark. Hearing the righteous cry, God delivers them from their troubles. Those whose spirits are crushed, and the brokenhearted—for these God cares and tends. God keeps every bone of our bodies safe and ransoms the life of each servant. God hears, rescues, saves, and delivers. God's nurture is tender, loving care of our bodies as much as of our minds and souls. God's presence uplifts our spirits.

Such an image of God gives preachers a word to share in times of calamity and misfortune. In the wake of a tsunami halfway around the world or a disastrous hurricane on distant shores, where human will and human capacities to respond and provide care fail or reach their limits, God's will and God's capacities extend. God's steadfast mercy endures.

Such an image also provides Christians with a way of being in the presence of those who suffer, who are sad, who feel pain, face disease, or need care. To see and hear one another, especially when we cry out; to approach and be near to those who are broken in mind and soul; to lift up, to love, and to encourage those with crushed spirits; to tend to the bodies that need our care—all of this is the work to which God calls us.

Psalm 34 presents an intimate portrait of God's goodness, care, and justice experienced on a very personal level. This is a level at which God's people can extend care to one another, but it is not a level at which we may assume that everyone has experienced a relationship with God. On one hand, someone in recovery from addiction might identify so closely with this hymn of personal thanksgiving that its words and its spirit of grateful redemption might as well be their very own. On the other hand, a newcomer to the church who grapples with the evening news of genocide, civil wars, widespread disease, and political corruption might distrust the psalmist entirely, seeing no evidence that God keeps safe all our bones. As with any personal thanksgiving, Psalm 34 will neither

particular realties for the psalmist and his audience. First, the "righteous" and the "wicked" *both* refer to members of the community. The psalmist is not addressing a universal audience but specifically addresses an audience that worshiped YHWH. Second, performing "the good" (v. 14) and doing "evil" (vv. 14, 16) are in relation to a presumed understanding of what obedience to YHWH means, which the psalmist summarizes as "the fear of YHWH" (vv. 7, 9, 11; cf. Prov. 1:7). The concept of "fear" refers to proper behavior in an asymmetrical relationship where the party to be feared could wield more power (in social, economic, or religious terms) than the fearing party. In antiquity, not all humans were considered "created equal"; every society lived by formal and informal rules that accepted the superiority of some over others. To sustain social stability, there were expectations placed on both superior and inferior members of society, and analogous expectations were assumed in the relationship between YHWH and ancient Israel. Ancient Israel's proper posture was to accept the authority of YHWH, whether expressed in the form of a test (e.g., Gen. 22), a contract (e.g., Deut. 10:12), or a general reference to that which constituted the relationship (e.g., Prov. 1:1–7; Ps. 19:7–10). This notion of fear, then, is a positive one; it simply describes appropriate Israelite behavior.

Given the power that YHWH possesses, there could be benefits to this relationship *or* serious consequences. For those of the community who fear YHWH, *their* cries will be heard (v. 15). Whenever they encounter distress, YHWH will respond to their pleas (vv. 17–10) and will "redeem" them (v. 22). In the ancient setting, "redemption" referred to the act of a superior party delivering an inferior party from difficult obligations, which usually involved payment or labor. YHWH, then, rescues the righteous from hardship. In addition, the psalmist uses the terms "poor" (v. 6), "the brokenhearted," and "the crushed in spirit" (v. 18) to refer to the righteous. The concept that YHWH would heed the cries of the wicked is unthinkable to the psalmist and his audience. Psalm 34, in part, is a statement of YHWH's might, so to declare that YHWH fails to exhibit power against human insubordination would assign weakness to Israel's deity.

For those who do not fear YHWH, their future is described in very stark terms: "The face of YHWH is set against evildoers, to cut off the remembrance of them from the land" (v. 16; my translation). Those who transgress from appropriate behavior will be

way. This is the language of dichotomy. It is language of binary opposites.

In the church what are we left to think? We want to think that if we are the ones studying this text and hearing it in the form of proclamation then surely we are on the Lord's side. This reasoning is evident among those who equate gospel living with having a good salary and enjoying an enviable lifestyle. Yet this reasoning can lead to an erroneous understanding of the life of faith, namely, that the redeemed ones are fixed for life and should simply enjoy the blessings of God. This is the type of reasoning that smugly claims a prime spot on the continuum of salvation/damnation and suggests that Christians are those who may enjoy life in a carefree manner.

Yet the psalmist says that the righteous ones of God suffer. Even though the psalm gives an account of both categories of people, the redeemed ones do not live a carefree life. They are described as "brokenhearted" (v. 18), as having "troubles" and "afflictions" (vv. 17, 19), even as they "cry for help" (v. 17). Suffering does not make it so easy to have bragging rights. The suffering of the righteous makes it more difficult to say that the lifestyle of the righteous ones is superior to that of the evildoers.

This is a psalm of thanksgiving. It begins with words of praise and blessing toward God. Yet it is also a psalm in the tradition of Wisdom literature. It teaches about having "the fear of the LORD" (v. 11), which, rather than actual fright, means trusting in and depending on God. The section of the psalm assigned for this lection responds to verse 12, "Which of you desires life, and covets many days to enjoy good?" These words set out the choice for our lives: do we wish to live trusting God to be present in our midst, or do we work to separate ourselves from God, following paths of hatred and death?

According to the arrangement of the Revised Common Lectionary, the psalm is intended to be the congregation's response to the first reading. That reading for this Sunday is Joshua 24:1–2a, 14–18, a reading that includes the well-known words from Joshua to "choose this day whom you will serve" (v. 15). The psalm builds on this tension. Which path do we choose, the path of life or the path of death? The covenant-making ceremony in Joshua is a decision to choose the path of life, with all the weight that accompanies a momentous act of ratification. The people are asked to make public vows again, consecrating their choice to live for the Lord. The psalm further intensifies that moment and brings that intensity to our feet: whom do *we*

Psalm 34:15-22

Theological Perspective

says verse 15. The suffering is acknowledged, not repressed, but it is seen in the broader context of God's connection to the people. God's ears and eyes are open. This same theodicy of relationship is seen in verses 17 and 18. God is *near* to the broken-hearted; the relationship of closeness and connection forms the frame of the affirmation that God "saves the crushed in spirit" (v. 18).

The theodicy of identity can also be seen in the entire section. It is the *righteous* who cry out for help. This word implies an identity, a designation that places those who suffer in the context of God's redemptive purposes. "When the righteous cry for help, the LORD hears, and rescues them from all their troubles," says verse 17. The righteous are identified here as the recipients of God's compassionate hearing and saving actions. In spite of sufferings that continue and persist (v. 19), the righteous assert their expectation of God's rescue. Although the statements in this section would seem to be a contradiction—that the afflictions are many, yet God protects and rescues the righteous from harm—they portray a firm sense of identity. No attempt is made in this psalm to explain the contradiction of affliction and divine protection. The paradox remains. Yet the affirmation of faith also remains. Although the righteous suffer, they belong to God. That foundational fact gives rise to the hope of restoration.

These verses form a theology of life before God in the middle of all the painful realities of the world. They are vitally connected to the first fourteen verses of the psalm and cannot stand alone. Those first verses "bless the LORD" and counsel a life of obedience and worship. They invite an intimate connection with God, to "taste and see that the LORD is good" (v. 8). The capacity to suffer and yet be filled with hope for a restored tomorrow is given its context in the God of steadfast love and tender mercies.

LEANNE VAN DYK

Pastoral Perspective

articulate the experience of everyone nor satisfy the observations of all people who seek God. Some pastoral imagination, or even evangelical sensitivity, may open the pastor's heart and the people's ears to hear God's call, feel God's presence, and see God's purposes, just as we are seen and heard by God.

Whether rejoicing in a moment of thanksgiving for deliverance or grappling with God in the midst of human suffering and injustice, any listener will recognize that the psalmist speaks plain truths. The righteous do cry; the good have many troubles; people do evil and its memory is hard to bear; we are captives in need of ransom. Even those near to God are brokenhearted and have crushed spirits, and yet they trust and believe anyway. The challenge is to discern the face and form of God caring for us and place our trust there, where the righteous will be safe. Where we can see the face of God, the wicked cannot be present, because God has turned his face from them.

When the mother of two small children turns away for even a moment, we can expect anything. On the face of it, we might name the little boy in the opening story as wicked and the girl righteous—until we discover that he resisted temptation sixteen different ways before moving from the steps while she never faced temptation for even an instant. Where God shows God's face, we can expect everything. The God revealed in Christ gave himself so that we might be righteous, neither on our own merit nor because we are worthy, but for God's tender mercy's sake. Bones broken, crying out, spirit gone, slain by evil, God's servants are yet ransomed by God and delivered from all their troubles. With ears, eyes, face, and every bone restored, the Spirit of righteousness is born.

ALLISON READ

Exegetical Perspective

removed from the community, and their presence will be erased from the community's memory (cf. Exod. 31:12–17; Lev. 20:3). For this reason, the "wicked" bring death upon themselves (v. 21). This effect is a communal one, and so the translation of "land" better conveys the significance of such a consequence from ancient Israel's perspective. The punishment is a removal from the community, whose identity is deeply intertwined with a particular land (esp. the concept of land in terms of YHWH's gift).

Since most Israelite wisdom teachings relate primarily to men (e.g., Prov. 1–9), the psalmist's call to the "sons" (*banim*, v. 11) and his use of standard wisdom instruction makes it likely that this psalm was composed with a male audience in mind. In ancient Israelite religious practice, however, this psalm may have been proclaimed to a mixed audience, and certainly obedience to YHWH also applied to women. Given the nature of specific gender roles in antiquity, one must assume that practically speaking, "fearing YHWH" did not mean the same thing for females as it did for males. For example, there are more records of remembering the men of ancient Israel (e.g., in genealogical lists) than the women, so the threat of having one's remembrance cut off from the community may have signified different realities for women and men.

The severity of the psalmist's teaching does not supplant other perspectives in the Old Testament. Ancient Israel also perceived YHWH as forgiving, even for those who acted in "wicked" ways (e.g., Ezek. 37; Jer. 31). Psalm 34 presents a clear distinction between good and bad behavior for instructional purposes; the psalmist urges the audience to carefully discern how to conduct their lives. Righteousness is a way of life, and one must persist on this path (vv. 12–14); likewise, wickedness is the incessant action of living in contradiction to the relationship between YHWH and ancient Israel. Any behavior that stands in contrast to fearing YHWH is equivalent to hating the obligations of this relationship (v. 21; cf. Prov. 8:13). The psalmist tries to convey how serious a choice it is to commit to this relationship, but he also sings about the joys that this relationship brings: "O taste and see that YHWH is good!" (v. 8).

PATRICIA D. AHEARNE-KROLL

Homiletical Perspective

choose? In our choosing we become known as one type of people or the other, the righteous or the unrighteous.

In the language of the psalmist, we are asked about our place of refuge. We are asked about our place of safety, of hiding, of restoration. We are asked to identify where we go when all of life is against us. In the language of the psalmist, we are told that God rescues us and keeps our very bones. The part of us that is our physical foundation—needed twenty-four hours each day of our lives—is undergirded by God's continuous holding.

The psalm at first glance could seem like an incendiary for name-calling and pointing fingers. Instead it brings grace and a question. For while we claim ourselves to be, by the Triune God's grace, among the redeemed, we also know that we continue to act in accord with death-dealing ways. Set before us is the daily choice of our baptismal turning: whom will we serve this day?

The preacher may choose to work with the psalm alone, exploring the ways that we live categorically divided lives, interpersonally and internationally as well as theologically. The preacher might also look at the theological complexities that come with deeper attention to the structure of the psalm and the connection of verse 12 to the appointed verses. This psalm is about more than two categories of people. The preacher might also explore the connections between all the lections for the day, tracing the recurring emphasis on choosing between life and death. It is important to remember that righteousness carries with it a sense of communal well-being. The intention of this text, then, is not to divide people but instead to summon them to right living in community.

JENNIFER L. LORD

Ephesians 6:10-20

[10]Finally, be strong in the Lord and in the strength of his power. [11]Put on the whole armor of God, so that you may be able to stand against the wiles of the devil. [12]For our struggle is not against enemies of blood and flesh, but against the rulers, against the authorities, against the cosmic powers of this present darkness, against the spiritual forces of evil in the heavenly places. [13]Therefore take up the whole armor of God, so that you may be able to withstand on that evil day, and having done everything, to stand firm. [14]Stand therefore, and fasten the belt of truth around your waist, and put on the breastplate of righteousness. [15]As shoes for your feet put on whatever will make you ready to proclaim the gospel of peace. [16]With all of these, take the shield of faith, with which you will be able to quench all the flaming arrows of the evil one. [17]Take the helmet of salvation, and the sword of the Spirit, which is the word of God.

[18]Pray in the Spirit at all times in every prayer and supplication. To that end keep alert and always persevere in supplication for all the saints. [19]Pray also for me, so that when I speak, a message may be given to me to make known with boldness the mystery of the gospel, [20]for which I am an ambassador in chains. Pray that I may declare it boldly, as I must speak.

Theological Perspective

The writer of the letter to Ephesians gives several pieces of advice on how to live the new Christian life, as distinct from the old pagan life (4:17–6:9). In this text (6:10–20), the writer gives advice on Christian spiritual warfare. This reflects early Christian pacifism, in which they do not take up arms against the "enemies of blood and flesh" (6:12). Multiple images are used of weapons and references to "the wiles of the devil," struggles "against the rulers . . . authorities . . . cosmic powers . . . [and] the spiritual forces of evil in the heavenly places" (6:11, 12). In the Christian tradition, the notion of warfare against spiritual forces has been often shifted to justify wars against particular others, who are named "enemies of God" and "forces of evil." A theological reading of this text thus requires twenty-first-century preachers to think carefully about the metaphors of spiritual warfare.

In its original context, the community of Christians, called "Ephesians," may have lived somewhere in Asia Minor during the first two centuries CE. They were religious minorities in the Roman Empire. Christianity was illegal until 313. Though this letter does not mention a particular persecution, these Christians faced daily harassment and discrimination from their neighbors and possible suppression by the authorities. If they were in fact in Ephesus, they may have been taken to worship the emperor at the newly

Pastoral Perspective

Americans tend to value flexibility. "Bend!" "Swim with the stream." "When in Rome, do as the Romans do." "Don't get stuck, go with the flow," we counsel ourselves. It is this attitude that makes this passage of Scripture so difficult for us, because here Paul counsels that we stand firm: "Put on the whole armor of God, so that you may be able to stand against the wiles of the devil" (Eph. 6:11). This is the opposite of going with the flow.

Paul does not encourage conformity. If Paul were interested in conformity, he would have encouraged the Christian church to blend with conventional morality and wisdom. Indeed, Paul's counsel can make one unpopular. Yet even when the stance is unpopular, still Paul counsels us to stand firm on our convictions and not be given to whim. Who can do this? Who can stand on convictions when the tide of popularity turns against us and strong winds of criticism blow? Is this all about lone individuals standing rigidly and resolute? No. Paul is talking about Christian identity and the roots of our common faith. In order to stand firm, we have to be nurtured in a tradition, a faithful community, and grow deep in its rich soil.

There is a difference between being stubborn and standing firm. Paul is not asking us to be stubborn, wedded to an opinion, rooted in prejudice, or

Exegetical Perspective

The Imperatives and the Reason for the Imperatives (vv. 10–12). These verses form the climax of the letter, and the word "finally" (v. 10) connects them with what has preceded. It is no surprise that Paul warns of spiritual battles at this point. First, this passage follows his exhortations to slaves and masters not to deal with one another according to the schemes of the powers, but with "sincere hearts," honoring Christ. Secondly, spiritual warfare has been a major concern of this letter (1:21; 2:2; 3:10). The Ephesians are to be strong against the devil's wiles (4:27; 6:11).

Paul's imperatives to "be strong" in the Lord and "put on" the armor of God expose the inadequacy of any human resources for spiritual battle. The struggle is not with "flesh and blood," but with the powers (6:12). Walter Wink says that Ephesians 6:12 is "the *locus classicus* for the demonic interpretation of the powers." He goes on: "So formidable a phalanx demands spiritual weaponry. . . . It is the suprahuman dimension of power in institutions and the cosmos which must be fought, not the mere human agent."[1] Without rejecting Wink's view of the powers as anticreation forces hidden within corporate entities, N. T. Wright, though not advocating Satan as

1. For Walter Wink's discussion of Eph. 6:10–17, see *Naming the Powers*. vol. 1 in *The Powers* (Philadelphia: Fortress Press, 1984), 85–87; quotation from 85–86.

Homiletical Perspective

This classic text enjoys what Fred Craddock calls the power of the familiar. Many Christians fondly recognize this passage and have internalized its vital imagery already. The passage contains not only a metaphor but also an extended analogy of the armor of a Roman soldier. A touch of creativity might lead to a bulletin insert picturing this armor of a Roman soldier. One could be slightly more daring and insert a contemporary sports uniform. For a "straightaway" sermon to work, it is imperative that the "armor" be quite existential, offering the hearer insight on how to survive in a secular society.

Some Christians have shied away from the text, however, as being too dependent upon outmoded thought. Indeed, barriers to the language of powers and principalities likely lurk among hearers. Allowing the congregation to share in a journey of discovery may assuage at least part of this hermeneutical difficulty. During a stint when I was preaching in New York City, in the days when you could go over to Union Seminary on Sunday night and drink hot chocolate and sing freedom songs, I began to hear about this exceptionally insightful lawyer by the name of William Stringfellow. Soon I was reading *Free in Obedience,* in which Stringfellow tells of lecturing on the biblical idea of "powers and principalities" to divinity students at Harvard. They

Ephesians 6:10-20

Theological Perspective

constructed temple of Domitian to test their allegiance. Ephesus was also a thriving commercial city and the cultic center of goddess Artemis. New Christian converts continued to use their Greco-Roman Platonic cosmology to understand their new religion. The letter writer portrays the resurrected Christ being "seated . . . in the heavenly places, far above all rule and authority and power and dominion" (1:20–21), foreshadowing the future icon of Christ *Pantokrator* (triumphant ruler of the universe). The church is understood to be raised up with Christ in heavenly places (2:6). Between the heavens and the earth, spirits and powers swirl. However, while they grow spiritually into such a dwelling place for God (2:22), Christians must go through transformation. They must shed their former pagan selves and licentious lifestyle (2:3; 4:17–19; 5:3–5), and put on their new selves of godly righteousness and holiness (4:22–24). Christian individuals, households, and communities become morally exemplary, living in love, forgiveness, and thankfulness.

To live such a Christian life in the predominantly pagan world posed challenges to the "Ephesians." One of the major challenges that these early Christians experienced in their transformation concerned power. Roman civilization was built on militarism. Yet Christians were called not to bear arms against any human agents, because their battle was a spiritual one. Their true enemies were sin, evil, and death, forces that constantly waged war in their inner spirit and at the cosmic level. In this spiritual warfare God in Christ through the Spirit supplies to Christians power and strength (1:19; 3:16), and Christians are "to be strong in the Lord and in the strength of his power" (6:10).

Theologically, if this message was understood, we Christians would be exemplary peacemakers. But the history of the Christian church reveals a bewildering array of Christian violence, in which the rhetoric of spiritual warfare against the dark forces of evil became literal warfare. No early Christians took up weapons against their persecutors, and many died as martyrs. Yet by 325, when Christianity became legalized, Christians persecuted "other" Christians. In the process of establishing Nicene and Chalcedonian standards of our faith, the "orthodox" Christians brutally punished the "heretics." At the third ecumenical council at Ephesus in 431, two parties of Christians (later Monophysites and Nestorians) confronted each other bitterly, calling each other tools of the devil because they had different understandings of the person and nature of Christ. In medieval Crusades, European

Pastoral Perspective

closed-minded. But he is asking us to stand in something that is not transient, something that is transcendent and renewing. This means being willing to be humble and to risk being unpopular, even to suffer ridicule, if not worse, as a faithful person in the community of faith. A stubborn person will not listen to ideas that differ from his or her own. A stubborn posture rejects alternatives out of hand and refuses, regardless of the situation, to change one's position. Stubbornness is not self-or-other discerning. It is not informed, and it does not grow. It is enshrined in a closed circle of certainty and becomes fearful, boisterous, and one-dimensional. The stubborn heart and mind are impervious to reason and may constitute one way to hide insecurity.

Standing firm is different. Standing firm means that one is willing to debate, listen, and consider alternatives in order to reach a beneficial goal, while at the same time not sacrificing basic principles. Martin Luther King Jr. stood firm on nonviolence. Margaret Sanger, the twentieth-century suffragette, stood firm on women's rights. Nelson Mandela stood firm and resolute against apartheid. Representative Barbara Lee stood firm against the war in Iraq. Robert Sobukwe stood firm as he faced the evils of imprisonment under apartheid. All stood firm against injustice. The lesson we draw from them is that to have a strong ego, a concern for justice and compassion, is to be grounded in the convictions of the community and open to critical evaluation. This is how we stand firm, as Paul counsels.

Søren Kierkegaard said, "Purity of heart is to will one thing." One can do this, staying focused and having singleness of purpose, without being stubborn about it. Paul is not asking us to get stuck on one strategy, idea, or position. He has in mind a larger goal, a bigger picture of God's wider mercies. He is not counseling stubbornness, tunnel vision, or a siege mentality.

"I am too blessed to be stressed," are words that some of the faithful have used. Paul's words, "put on the whole armor," prepare us for struggle. Stress and anxiety come when one prepares to engage things that really matter. No one in his or her right mind prepares for struggle without forethought. We want to know what we are up against so that we can prepare appropriately and engage the struggle successfully.

Standing firm gives the struggle purpose and us meaning. In the midst of controversy we may ask, "Is the price to be paid worth the struggle?" Sometimes, in the midst of struggle and fatigue, we may find our

"personal" in the same way that God or Jesus is personal, prefers to label this negative force as "subpersonal" or "quasi-personal."[2]

Paul declares Christ's victory over the powers, but Paul is a realist. The Ephesians are in the position of "already/not yet." Already they have triumphed in Christ, but they are not yet beyond the battle. They wrestle with the powers in the confidence of Christ's triumph.

Fit for Battle (vv. 13–17). This is strange armor: truth (belt), righteousness (breastplate), gospel of peace (shoes), faith (shield), salvation (helmet), and Spirit/Word (sword). These weapons are meant for war!

Paul uses the stem "stand" four times in verses 11–14. The use of "stand" does not suggest passive resistance. The sword is clearly an offensive weapon. Wink notes that "'stand" (vv. 11, 14) has the sense of the "drawing up a military formation for combat"; in verse 13 it refers to the triumphant stance of the victor.

"Stand *therefore* (v. 14, my translation) . . . *having girded* yourself with truth and *having put on* breast-plate of righteousness . . . *having shod your feet* in readiness for the gospel . . . and *having taken* the shield of faith." The underlined words are aorist, past participles. They indicate the preparation necessary to heed the imperative, "Stand!"

"Therefore take up the whole armor of God, so that you may be able to withstand on that evil day, and having done everything, to stand firm" (v. 13). In view of the fact that the days are evil, Paul has instructed the Ephesians literally to "buy up the time because the days are evil" (5:16, my translation), that is, they need to be prudent and aggressively enter the market and challenge the hold of evil in the marketplace of life. Paul is challenging his readers to take the fight to the enemy. The church is a phalanx penetrating the powers of darkness as a wedge of light (cf. 5:8–14).

There is another imperative, followed by participles. "Receive/take" (v. 17, my translation) the helmet of salvation [the victory over the powers] and the sword of the Spirit, the Word of God [for combat], "*praying* (v. 18, my translation) and *keeping alert*." In this case, the participles are in the present tense, calling for ongoing prayer and focus in the face of the continuing battle. The sword of the Spirit

2. N. T. Wright, *Evil and the Justice of God* (Downers Grove, IL: InterVarsity Press, 2006), 111, 114.

found the terminology archaic, he says. But when he addressed students in the business school, who had done time tithing daily at the church of realism, they recognized the language immediately.

In Stringfellow's vision, one finds creatures who are fallen, who thrive on chaos, who do not foster life but dehumanize. Theologians in the beastly Nazi era such as Barth, Heim, and Bonhoeffer named the powers and principalities; they were joined later by the careful explorations of Walter Wink and Jacques Ellul and the creative insights of Marva Dawn and Charles Campbell. These theological visionaries influence us to see life at great depth, and could be figuratively invited to the chancel to speak in their own voices.

When the biblical image of the powers and principalities is recovered from the dustbin, it shines a revealing light on the modern landscape. We discover the frequent fallenness of money, sex, fashion, sports, and religion in our culture. We are told that new fortunes are to be made while the military spending boom lasts. We learn that investing in the stocks of companies that market to human vices can earn us higher returns. What should a Christian's 401(k) or 403(b) look like?

In unmasking the powers, one thinks of segregation, apartheid, fatalism, the Mafia, addiction, bondage of the will, totalitarian states, a celebrity culture of glamorized Bad Girls and Boys, serfdom in the medieval period, attempted bribery of legislatures through large campaign contributions, and genocide. Depersonalization creates a long gray line of faceless folk who think of themselves as no more than a Social Security number. One thinks of Nazi philosophy, unbridled nationalism, violence, hunger, racism, obscenity, addiction, brothels in Mumbai, nuclear weapons, and tobacco companies. In the movie *Chocolat*, the indentured priest must submit his sermons for approval to the man of the manor. Later the priest insists upon the independence of his pulpit. Only then can the church stand against the principalities and powers. In this light, the Pauline vision is realistic and illuminating. One could preach a sermon on the unmasking of the powers through a series of discoveries entered into by the congregation on one or more of the realities listed above.

Drawing from the world of rhetorical criticism, which identifies Ephesians 6:10–20 as a peroration (Aristotle, *Rhet.* 3.19), one could make a rousing call to the congregation to resolve to live out the Christian life in a hostile environment. In Greek literature, generals rallied their troops with

Ephesians 6:10-20

Theological Perspective

Christian soldiers slaughtered Jews, Muslims, and "heretics" (i.e., the Eastern Christians), believing that they were slaughtering the forces of evil. In 1492 devout Catholic Iberian crowns sent Columbus to "discover" the world while expelling God's enemy, that is, Jews and Muslims, from their domain. Likewise, Protestant Reformers approved the state right of execution of those whom the church perceived as the enemies of God, including "Turks," "Jews," "Christian heretics," and "witches." In the ensuing years, Christian Europe justified the conquest, colonization, and forced Christianization of those dark "savages" of the Americas, as well as the enslavement of some Asians and numerous Africans using the similar rhetoric.

According to historian Kathleen E. McVey, the church's three basic positions about war—pacifism, just war, and holy war—are all based on the biblical interpretation of spiritual warfare against the powers of "this present darkness" (6:12).[1] With McVey, we learn: "Historical study undermines the illusion, perhaps still widespread among Christians, that theirs is a history of peace while others, such as Muslims, have 'lived by the sword.'"

More positively, there are examples of Christians who have taken up the "warfare of peace." Christians in the French village of Le Chambon sur Ligno hid and protected 5,000 Jewish children in World War II. Martin Luther King Jr. preached the "more excellent way" (1 Cor. 12:31) of love and nonviolent protest.

The message to the Ephesians is clear that in the middle of our fierce fighting, Christians bring the gospel of peace (6:15), and "the whole armor of God" is only for their protection (v. 13). The only offensive gear is the "sword of the Spirit, which is the word of God" (v. 17). The writer transforms common idioms of military warfare into new Christian terms of spiritual warfare. Confident in the great power of God (1:19), giving up weapons of destruction, Christians are to move forward, in whatever good shoes they have (6:15), in proclaiming the gospel of peace.

Where do you see the spiritual darkness operating against God's power of love in today's world? In our own minds, or in the embodied "others"? Can Christians be extremists of love, peace, and boldness (6:20) in bringing peace in these present evil days (5:16)?

HARUKO NAWATA WARD

Pastoral Perspective

strength renewed. We may find ourselves assessing and reassessing our situations and coming to new resolve. Surely, during the twenty-seven years of his incarceration, Nelson Mandela became discouraged. But he found strength to hope. He stood firm in his convictions. Such spiritual struggle requires discipline. We must prepare ourselves inwardly and prayerfully for the outer struggle. The outer struggle, the struggle against the principalities and powers, will test again and again our inner resolve. God never ceases to offer fresh opportunities to assess our situation, to grow and deepen our sense of commitment in community.

Struggle can be part of the process of faith development where spiritual growth, deepening into a mature faith, is valued. Struggle may also be seen as a resource and as opportunity for spiritual growth where followers of the Way stay alert to evil, pray, nurture one another's growth, and hold one another accountable.

God's rich mercies and spiritual resources are found among people and in nature. Spiritual resources enable us to stand firm and endure in the struggle—against systemic forces, "the principalities, . . . the powers, . . . [the] rulers of this present darkness" (6:12 RSV). Among these spiritual resources are "truth, . . . righteousness [or right relations], . . . the gospel of peace, . . . and faith" (6:14–16). These resources may be found in the living expressions of people, in the divine-human relationship, and in the natural environment. Ideally, God, self, others, and nature are kept together in struggle. Spiritual resources indwell the personality as well as relations between people. Spiritual growth may be seen in hope and resiliency, in faith and doubt, in prayer and play. Spiritual resources are expressed in music and through the arts. Such expressions are at the heart of pastoral care for faith communities, where individuals find imaginative and bold faith for today and bright hope for tomorrow. Expressions of rich spiritual resources can be seen in the wonders of nature, in acts of boldness and justice among the people, and in the compassion and courage of the community of the faithful.

ARCHIE SMITH JR.

---

1. Kathleen E. McVey, "What Then Shall We Do? Pacifism, 'Just War,' and 'Holy War' in Western Christianity," in *Breaking Silence: Pastoral Approaches for Creating an Ethos of Peace*, ed. Chad R. Abbott and Everett Mitchell (Longmont, CO: Pilgrims Process, 2004), 217–36; quotation on 233.

is the word of God. Gordon Fee observes that the term used here for "word" emphasizes the word that is spoken, inspired by the Spirit—it is the proclamation, not the book.[3]

Prayer in the Spirit (vv. 18–20). Putting on the whole armor of God is linked to evangelism. Prayer is vital in this work. The church has been created to proclaim the mystery of the gospel to the world and to the powers (3:10). The mystery begins with Israel as a "peculiar" people (2:12). It discloses God's plan "to gather up all things in [Christ], things in heaven and things on earth" (1:10); it is demonstrated in making one people of Jew and Gentile. Anyone making such "offensive" proclamations will be confronted by the powers. It takes courage—and prayer—for anyone publicly to preach the offense of the gospel in a multicultural setting such as Paul's.

What Paul means by "praying in the Spirit" can lead to a lengthy discussion. One thing is clear: the role of the Spirit—praying in the Spirit—is indispensable in confronting the powers (and indispensable in the life of prayer). In his struggle with the powers, Paul undoubtedly lifted up inarticulate groaning (Rom. 8:26), resorted to "speaking in tongues," and prayed with his "mind" (1 Cor. 14:15). Paul openly spoke of his weakness and fears in proclaiming the mystery of God. Yet he knew that his proclamation was "a demonstration of the Spirit and of power" (1 Cor. 2: 3–4). Evangelism is serious business, and the powers do not give in easily. Prayer—prayer in the Spirit—is crucial.

The urgency for such prayer is underscored by Paul's fourfold use of "all" and also found in repeated words for prayers. An ambassador of the mystery could end up in chains! Paul, in prison, asks for prayer in the Spirit in his behalf (and the other saints!) that "I may declare the mystery *boldly* as I must" (v. 20). The Ephesians are to take on the enemy by Spirit-empowered proclamation and by Spirit-inspired prayer. Gordon Fee concludes, "Thus, the final word in this letter is a word of evangelism. And prayer in the Spirit is not merely so that God's people will stand against the foe, but so that Paul will be bold to make Christ known."

"Let anyone who has an ear listen to what the Spirit is saying to the churches" (Rev. 2:7).

AARON L. UITTI

perorations to do battle against daunting enemies. The preacher could form an inspiring exhortation for "resident aliens." Since a peroration often includes recapitulation, prior themes of Ephesians could be highlighted and lifted up. Such a closing may give some hearers a satisfying sense of completion, an enlarged sense that something worthy has been brought to the congregation. This type of conclusion may not play as well with postmoderns, however.

Critical scholars suggest hypothesized settings in the life of the text. If Ephesians 6:10–20 originally functioned in a baptismal context, with parallels to putting on the new humanity (4:24), a sermon might be designed as teaching for baptismal candidates. Since Paul spent tumultuous times in Ephesus (Acts 19) and our text is so martial in metaphor, one could read this passage in the context of persecution, inviting solidarity with persecuted people elsewhere in the world. Or if one finds a crisis of confidence in the epistle, one might strengthen hearers to fearless living out of Christian existence in the midst of a hostile world. Another promising strategy might be to reflect on each division of the larger text in terms of the church standing against the powers (vv. 10–13), equipping the Christian vocation for the real world (vv. 14–17), and/or praying in the Spirit for fellow Christians (vv. 18–20).

Just one day after France surrendered to Nazi Germany, a pastor preached to a small village congregation with a prophetic vision that "The responsibility of Christians is to resist the violence that will be brought to bear on their consciences through the weapons of the spirit."[1] These Huguenots would provide sanctuary for 5,000 Jews. They discovered the Pauline "weapons of the Spirit." Christians can be awakened to weapons of the Spirit such as prayer (v. 18), Christian truth (v. 14), and the Spirit (v. 17b). How can the weapons of the Spirit enumerated in this text become life giving? From Christian worship one could draw upon preaching that names the powers and declares the victory (Col. 1:16; 2:14–15), offering that defeats the negative power of money and furthers the Christian mission, and/or spiritual gifts that Christians can employ against the powers (Gal. 5:22–23).

The most potent idea to take away from this text may be the gathered community's heightened awareness of the "weapons of the spirit" available to the Christian church.

PETER RHEA JONES

3. For Gordon Fee's comments on Eph. 6:10–20, see his *God's Empowering Presence* (Peabody, MA: Hendrickson, 1994), 728–32.

1. *Weapons of the Spirit*, prod. and dir. Pierre Sauvage (First Run Features, 1989, videocassette), cited by Charles Campbell, *The Word before the Powers* (Louisville, KY: Westminster John Knox Press, 2002), 1.

John 6:56-69

⁵⁶"Those who eat my flesh and drink my blood abide in me, and I in them. ⁵⁷Just as the living Father sent me, and I live because of the Father, so whoever eats me will live because of me. ⁵⁸This is the bread that came down from heaven, not like that which your ancestors ate, and they died. But the one who eats this bread will live forever." ⁵⁹He said these things while he was teaching in the synagogue at Capernaum.

⁶⁰When many of his disciples heard it, they said, "This teaching is difficult; who can accept it?" ⁶¹But Jesus, being aware that his disciples were complaining about it, said to them, "Does this offend you? ⁶²Then what if you were to see the Son of Man ascending to where he was before? ⁶³It is the spirit that gives life; the flesh is useless. The words that I have spoken to you are spirit and life. ⁶⁴But among you there are some who do not believe." For Jesus knew from the first who were the ones that did not believe, and who was the one that would betray him. ⁶⁵And he said, "For this reason I have told you that no one can come to me unless it is granted by the Father."

⁶⁶Because of this many of his disciples turned back and no longer went about with him. ⁶⁷So Jesus asked the twelve, "Do you also wish to go away?" ⁶⁸Simon Peter answered him, "Lord, to whom can we go? You have the words of eternal life. ⁶⁹We have come to believe and know that you are the Holy One of God."

Theological Perspective

This text addresses two key Christian doctrines, (1) God and (2) the person and work of Jesus Christ, from a uniquely Johannine theological perspective. John's claim about the first doctrine, the doctrine of God, is that the divine life is eternally communal. John's claim about the second doctrine, the person and work of Jesus Christ, is that the Christian belief in Jesus as the Christ is based on the principle of incarnation, the divine indwelling among the human. The Gospel of John as a whole is concerned with the mystery of the person of Jesus as the Christ and how Jesus serves as the ultimate means of access to God through multiple approaches of understanding: the man sent from heaven, the Holy One of God, the bread of life, the path, the doorway, and the lamb of God, to name several. Chapter 6 is roughly divided into two parts: the miracle stories of verses 1–21, and the discourse and dialogues that seek to explain the meaning of these miracles in verses 25–71. This division itself shows something of John's preference for complementary dyads: miracle and discourse, sign and word, human and divine, flesh and spirit. In John, signs are primary sources of revelation about the truth of who Jesus really is, but the signs by themselves are not enough. Believers must come to understand the truths that the signs reveal in order for them to be effective in the

Pastoral Perspective

"Those who eat my flesh and drink my blood abide in me, and I in them." Our passage today begins with rather shocking words, a disturbing image. The image would have been upsetting to the Jewish audience who heard Jesus' words. Pagans ate flesh with the blood still in it, but *not* the children of God. Today Protestants in particular may be so jarred by "flesh eating" and "blood drinking" that they tune out the more important words, "Abide in me." Jesus is inviting the disciples to be at home in him, just as he is at home in God. College students miss the smell of their closets and yearn for home. The elderly in nursing homes miss the sight of their collectables gathering dust on the shelf and yearn for home. Soldiers in Iraq miss the quiet of a lazy afternoon uninterrupted by gunfire and yearn for home. Out in the world we must fend for ourselves in an often hostile environment. Whether we are college students coping with a new adult identity or soldiers facing the brutality of war, the world is a place where fear often reigns. Home is the promise of safety, of security; a place where fear does not have the upper hand.

Jesus goes on to explain that the bread that he is offering is far greater than the manna that sustained the people's ancestors in the desert. After the people ate the manna, they died. In verse 58, Jesus tells his

Exegetical Perspective

The long discourse on the bread of life is set near Passover (6:4) and is built on the double miracle of the feeding of five thousand men in the wilderness and Jesus' walking on the lake. The first miracle is reminiscent of the significance of bread both in the exodus story and in the reliving of that story in the annual Passover Seder. The possibility that Jesus will be mistakenly viewed as a second Moses, providing manna for Israel in the wilderness, is countered by the second miracle. The story of Jesus walking on the water points to the mystery of his supernatural origin. He is not just Messiah (vv. 14–15) but much, much more: he is the Word of God incarnate (1:14).

To grasp the significance of the Gospel lesson we must go back to verse 51, which summarizes the preceding part of the discourse: Jesus is the living bread that came down from heaven to provide eternal life to those who eat it. Because of the danger that someone will mistakenly suppose that Jesus is simply a heavenly messenger who brings new spiritual ideas, the last clause of verse 51 drops a bombshell: "And the bread that I will give for the life of the world is my flesh." Note the future tense. He has not already dispensed this bread through his preaching and teaching. The saving bread is somehow related to his crucified flesh.

Homiletical Perspective

For the preacher who has followed the sequence of Gospel lectionary readings in the preceding weeks, this final passage from the sixth chapter of John poses several challenges and opportunities. These verses allude to numerous themes that recur throughout this remarkable chapter: Jesus is the bread of heaven who offers eternal life; Christ's body and blood recall the eucharistic meal; his relationship with the Father is highlighted; and many turn away from Jesus' teaching. A new element is introduced when Jesus presses his closest disciples to decide if they wish to turn away from following him, also. The preacher may want to include verses 70–71, since these continue the theme of Jesus' rejection and his awareness of the one who would betray him.

Theologically, this text raises several challenges for the preacher, who must decide which issues to address and which to set aside. For example, it may or may not be of great significance for the congregation to wrestle with the meaning of Jesus' comment that "no one can come to me unless it is granted by the Father" (v. 65). Whether we interpret this to mean that God determines ahead of time who will be given the gift of faith or, conversely, if we place the emphasis on our own response-ability in choosing to follow Jesus Christ, both God's initiative and our response are essential to Christian discipleship. Another potential

Theological Perspective

transformative process of salvation. For that to happen, however, the signs need to be interpreted and thus the dialogue and discourse sections serve to show the reader (hearer) how Jesus is both the sign and the interpreter.

This particular passage is widely known as John's eucharistic discourse, since it is the clearest reference that John makes to the ritual practice of the Eucharist. For John, Jesus has identity (communion) with God as the one sent from heaven; seen here as the bread of life, the gracious gift of manna becomes truly personal. John's view of the Eucharist varies from the Synoptic understanding by tying the ritual not directly to Jesus' death but rather to his life. The Eucharist is the gift of life, since the "bread" references of this passage are part of the explanatory discourse of the miraculous feeding earlier in the chapter, as well as an echo of the salvation story of the manna in Exodus 16. Here Jesus is the new manna giving life to his believers as God gave it to the Israelites in the wilderness. John's Eucharist theology is unabashedly life affirming: Jesus saves life by giving life. Creating is the means of redeeming. The mystery of the incarnation is seen through the metaphor of eating and drinking, a eucharistic view of not only the incarnation of Jesus, but of what it means to be human in an incarnational way. The language of flesh and blood emphasizes embodiment. Flesh and spirit belong together according to God's intended plan for creation, and only by their union is true (eternal) life possible.

Yet John acknowledges that it is not that easy to do. In verse 60 we see that this teaching about eating flesh and drinking blood is so hard to accept that many disciples end up leaving the Jesus movement altogether. Verse 63 points us to John's solution to the problem: a proper understanding of incarnation. The issue at stake is how often we confuse the body as flesh *without* spirit with the body as incarnate, flesh *with* spirit (enspirited or literally, inspired). What John wants us to consider are our misunderstood ways of consumption. We "eat up" the world without appreciating how God has infused creation with the Spirit; thus we use and discard it in crude and materialist ways. The ethical imperative at the heart of John's incarnational theology of the Eucharist is clear. Will we treat the world around us as incarnational or simply as material? To do the former requires faith. Keeping the flesh together with the spirit requires us to live deeply, appreciating our interdependence and interconnectedness with the Creator, the creation, and our fellow creatures. By

Pastoral Perspective

disciples that if they eat the bread that he is offering, they will live forever. Is Jesus offering immortality? We are reminded of the story of the Samaritan woman in John 4. In verses 13–14, Jesus says, "Everyone who drinks of this water will be thirsty again, but those who drink of the water that I will give them will never be thirsty." Jesus uses these familiar symbols of bread, wine, flesh, blood, and water to teach about the gift of life, eternal life—not immortality, but a way of living that deprives fear of having the upper hand.

The disciples have now been offered this great gift. They have yearned for home, and they are at the doorstep. Surely they will embrace Jesus and walk through the door. But no, many of disciples complain that the teaching is too difficult (v. 60). Jesus asks them if he offends them (v. 61). He reminds them that the spirit gives life and his words "are spirit and life" (v. 63). And yet there are many who will not believe, many who refuse the safety, the security of home. The very thing they have yearned for is being offered them, and still they turn away from the gift.

Why on earth would some of the disciples walk away from the chance to abide in God, to dwell in Jesus and Jesus in them? Why would they not want to "go home"? Are we so different? Why is it so difficult to accept spirit and life? We yearn for home because we are afraid. Fear is a powerful motivator. We like to think we are in control of our lives, of our destiny. When things are spinning out of control in my world—deadlines looming, neighbors needing, a chronically ill child—I stop and clean my house. I do not have control over the other, but I can bring order to the chaos of my kitchen!

Our culture tells us that we are in control of our lives, our destiny. If we work hard, we will be rewarded with material gain. We feel good about ourselves when we are successful, when we have a good job, a clean house, children who make good grades. We attend the right church, we live in the right region of the country, we vote for the correct politician. We wake up with a full "to do" list, and we go to bed with it incomplete. Our job, our gender, or our sheer business makes us more valuable than our neighbor. There is little time for watching a sunset or playing with the kids, let alone reaching out to the homeless woman on the street corner.

My theologian sister says that we prefer religion to God. We, like the disciples, are offended by Jesus' offer of spirit and life. We feel good about serving in the soup kitchen, but we refuse to forgive our pew

Exegetical Perspective

It is often assumed that verses 51–58 allude primarily to the Eucharist. Indeed, it is sometimes conjectured that these verses constitute an insertion in a discourse that originally had nothing to do with the Eucharist. Since this conjecture can be neither proved nor disproved, it is best to deal with the chapter as we have it. There can be little doubt that there are allusions to eating the bread and wine of the Eucharist in these verses, but it is more satisfactory to treat these as metaphors for something else.[1] For John eating the bread and drinking the wine are metaphors for taking into one's body, mind, and soul the climax of the incarnation in the death of Jesus.

As is typical of dialogues in the Fourth Gospel, Jesus' hearers completely misunderstand verse 51. They dispute (literally: fight) with one another over the question, "How can this man give us his flesh to eat?" (v. 52). The outrageous scandal posed by verses 51–52 is greatly intensified in the following verse: "Amen, amen I say to you, unless you eat the flesh of the Son of Man and drink his blood, you do not have life in yourselves" (v. 53, my translation; John's doubled *amen* marks a specially important statement from Jesus). Cannibalism was no less offensive in that day than in our own. Furthermore, to Jews it was unthinkable to drink animal blood, a capital crime according to the law (Lev. 17:12–14). How much more scandalous to drink human blood! The writer is not content to leave the matter so; he reinforces the scandal over and over again in the following verses.

To understand the meaning of the "flesh" of Jesus that he will give for the life of the world, we must ponder what appears to be a contradiction in verse 63, "It is spirit that gives life; the flesh is useless [literally, "profits nothing," as in Gal. 5:2]. The words that I have spoken to you are spirit and life." Translators differ concerning whether to capitalize "spirit" in this verse. The NRSV and the REB follow the KJV in using lower case in both instances. The NIV parts company with them, reading instead: "The Spirit gives life; the flesh counts for nothing. The words I have spoken to you are spirit and they are life," with the marginal reading "Spirit" for the second instance. The paraphrase of the CEV sides with the NIV: "The Spirit is the one who gives life! Human strength can do nothing. The words that I have spoken to you are from that life-giving Spirit." As these differences in translation suggest, it is

---

1. James D. G. Dunn, "John VI—A Eucharistic Discourse?" *New Testament Studies* 17 (1971): 336.

Homiletical Perspective

problem arises as we seek to understand what Jesus means by saying, "It is the spirit that gives life; the flesh is useless" (v. 63a). The apparent dichotomy between spirit and flesh deserves careful attention, lest we end up simply opposing the material world to the spiritual and ignore the fact that in Jesus Christ we encounter the flesh and spirit working together for the fulfillment of God's will. This is not an invitation for the church to name the many ways the material world may be opposed to God (however real the opposition may sometimes be), but an opportunity to consider the temporal nature of the world we inhabit (see also Isa. 40:3).

While recognizing the importance of these questions for the life of faith, there are at least three compelling insights that arise out of this text and may be of particular interest to contemporary worshipers. First, this passage will not let us forget how strange the message of Christian faith really is. Eat his body? Drink his blood? With just a few words, Jesus manages to offend other Jews and alienate everyone else. He gathers great crowds around him but little by little, as they listen to his message, the people turn away until only a few of his closest disciples remain.

The more we realize that faith calls us to consume the body and blood of Christ, to embrace his death and resurrection and to emulate his manner of living and dying for others, the more difficult the journey of faith becomes. There may be a word of comfort here for congregations who strive to be faithful disciples yet experience declining attendance and church membership. This passage is not intended to reinforce our complacency or discourage us from witnessing the gospel of Jesus Christ to others. But it will help us remember that our calling is a strange and difficult one. It is more than skin deep, reaching beneath the surface of our lives and into our workplaces, bank accounts, family relationships, eating habits, daily schedules, and all the other ways we choose to live and die for Christ and our neighbors.

A second insight that arises out of our encounter with this text is found in Peter's confession of verses 68–69. When Jesus asks the Twelve if they also want to turn away from following him, Peter answers with a question of his own: "Lord, to whom can we go?" We could interpret this as either an expression of despair or an expression of exultation. Where else do we have to go? Surely, there were many places Peter and his friends could have turned. There were business prospects, family commitments, the comforts of home, and the search for social status

John 6:56-69

Theological Perspective

inviting us to eat and drink of his whole person, Jesus challenges us to risk living incarnationally, becoming whole in both flesh and spirit, as the means of our salvation.

This text provides a means of seeing the faithful life as a spiritual practice of "incarnational abiding." John's eucharistic theology is offered as means of helping to draw the believer into deeper relationship with Jesus and thus also with God the Creator through a spirituality of abiding, or being with/in. This then raises even more difficult practical questions for the believer: what does it actually look like to abide? John suggests that we abide with God by abiding with Christ, and we abide with Christ by truly abiding with ourselves, in other words, by not separating our flesh and spirit from each other.

In verse 69 we see how belief and knowledge are contingent upon each other. We have knowledge of God through belief in Jesus and his identity with God. In the same way, there is an interdependent relationship happening in John's Eucharist that necessarily links the relationship between Jesus and God and the relationship between Jesus and the believer through the power of the Holy Spirit. The metaphor of corporeal consumption in this passage, interpreted ritually in the Eucharist, reveals John's theological understanding of God as the divine community reflected in the mutual indwelling of the Father and the Son, Christ and God, Jesus and believer, and believer and God, all through the power of the Spirit. Just as Jesus is the incarnation of God, so we as believers are invited to be part of that divine body, to be the incarnation of Christ in and to the world. Perhaps then there is a vocational reading of Jesus' language regarding "abiding": to choose, by the gift of faith given by God, to accept God's call to become part of the divine life as it is in its eternal fullness, both body and Spirit.

LOYE BRADLEY ASHTON

Pastoral Perspective

mate for his addiction. We feel righteous when we teach Sunday school, but we are annoyed by the coos of the baby in worship. We make religion about the rules because we can control the rules. We can amend books of order, we can use Scripture to oppress, and we can punish the rule breakers—much easier than compassion and forgiveness.

In verse 67, we learn that twelve disciples remain by Jesus' side. He asks them if they too want to go away. Simon Peter answers him, "Lord, to whom can we go? You have the words of eternal life. We have come to believe and know that you are the Holy One of God" (vv. 68–69). In that moment, Simon Peter realizes that despite the startling images, despite the hard path, he is ready to give up some control in order to go home, in order to accept the gift of life.

In the moment that we choose to eat Jesus' flesh and drink Jesus' blood—and we truly abide in him and he in us—we choose life. We give up the notion that we are in control. Fear truly no longer has the upper hand. We understand that we are no better than any other child of God because of our denomination, our skin color, our gender, our job. We turn over to God that which we fear most, trusting that we are loved. When we can accept the love of God that is pure grace, love flows from us and we love others. We do forgive our pew mate for his addiction. We stop in real conversation with the homeless woman on the street corner. We value the baby fussing during worship. We suddenly prefer God to religion.

AMY C. HOWE

impossible to know exactly what is meant here. The ambiguity may be intentional: perhaps we are to think both of the basic dualism of "spirit" and "flesh," that is, spiritual matters and worldly matters, as in 3:6, and the contrast between God's Spirit and human resistance to that Spirit (as in the opposition of "the works of the flesh" and "the fruit of the Spirit" in Gal. 5:16–23).

One way of reconciling the useless flesh of verse 63 with the indispensable flesh of verse 53 is to relate both to the Eucharist. While the verses about eating Jesus' flesh and drinking his blood inevitably recall the Eucharist, we must remember that John downplays the importance of this central rite: he devotes five chapters to the Last Supper but omits the cup and bread sayings. Here in chapter 6 he may be warning his readers that participation in the Eucharist is no guarantee of eternal life; merely eating the flesh of the Son of Man in this way profits nothing. What is required is believing.

Faith is a central concept for John, but the noun itself never occurs. The verb "believe," however, occurs more than eighty times, more often than in all the letters of Paul taken together. John stresses that faith is not something you have but something you do. Sometimes "believe" is used absolutely, as in verse 64 (and v. 47), without any indication of the content of faith. This shorthand expression is amplified only slightly in the phrase "believe in him" (vv. 29, 40; see also 3:16) or "believe in me" (v. 35). In the Fourth Gospel, believing in Jesus means accepting the gospel of the incarnation: in him the Word became flesh and lived among us (1:14), and through the death of this Lamb of God the sin of the world is taken away (1:29). The scandalous ideas of eating his flesh and drinking his blood are probably drawn from eucharistic practice, but they are here merely metaphors for incorporating at the center of one's being the saving death of the incarnate Word.

DOUGLAS R. A. HARE

that called for their attention. There is always another dollar to be earned, another purchase to be made, another relationship to explore, another position to pursue, another enemy to withstand, another grief to mourn, another country to explore.

But Peter knew what he had found. In following Jesus, he came to recognize that Jesus was the Holy One of God, who alone possessed the words of eternal life. Sometimes the last choice is the best choice—it just takes a while to see it. When my grandmother immigrated to the U.S. from Italy, she had high hopes for her children's prosperity in the land of plenty. Yet she often puzzled over what she saw as the pursuit of happiness. Pointing to the loaves of bread at the local supermarket, I remember her asking, "Why do people eat-a these things? They have-a no taste." She used to say that life was too short to eat anything but good bread, to drink anything but good wine. Little wonder we spent nearly every Saturday of my childhood making our own bread, pizza, and pasta for our family. Why settle for bread that is not bread, for life that is not life?

Finally, there is another point worth pursuing in this text. This is the first time in the Gospel of John that Jesus' closest disciples are named "the twelve" (v. 67). Their decision not to turn away but to walk forward with Christ draws them together as a community of faith. It is not any particular creed, mission statement, style of worship, or service program that unites them as the body of Christ. It is their professed willingness to follow Jesus Christ that renders them a community of faith. What a blessed word to remember as we agonize over mission statements, budget priorities, worship attendance, or other preoccupations of churchly life. It is our commitment to follow Christ alongside others that makes us the people of God.

DAWN OTTONI WILHELM

Contributors

Paul J. Achtemeier, Jackson Professor of Biblical Interpretation Emeritus, Union Theological Seminary, Richmond, Virginia

Efraín Agosto, Professor of New Testament, Hartford Seminary, Hartford, Connecticut

Patricia D. Ahearne-Kroll, Assistant Professor, Religion Department, Ohio Wesleyan University, Delaware, Ohio

Stephen P. Ahearne-Kroll, Assistant Professor of New Testament, Methodist Theological School, Delaware, Ohio

Tom Are Jr., Senior Pastor, Village Presbyterian Church, Prairie Village, Kansas

Loye Bradley Ashton, Assistant Professor of Religious Studies, Tougaloo College, Tougaloo, Mississippi

Steven Bishop, Assistant Professor of Old Testament, Episcopal Theological Seminary of the Southwest, Austin, Texas

Rein Bos, Pastor, Protestant Church of the Netherlands, Utrecht, Netherlands

Matthew Myer Boulton, Assistant Professor of Ministry Studies, Harvard Divinity School, Cambridge, Massachusetts

Walter Brueggemann, Professor Emeritus of Old Testament, Columbia Theological Seminary, Decatur, Georgia

Robert A. Bryant, Associate Professor of Religion, Presbyterian College, Clinton, South Carolina

Eberhard Busch, Professor of Theology, University of Göttingen, Friedland, Germany

Sam Candler, Dean, The Cathedral of St. Philip, Atlanta, Georgia

Carlos F. Cardoza-Orlandi, Associate Professor of World Christianity, Columbia Theological Seminary, Decatur, Georgia

Karen Chakoian, Pastor, First Presbyterian Church, Granville, Ohio

Jaime Clark-Soles, Associate Professor of New Testament, Perkins School of Theology, Southern Methodist University, Dallas, Texas

Richard J. Clifford, Dean and Professor of Old Testament, Boston College School of Theology and Ministry, Chestnut Hill, Massachusetts

Andrew Foster Connors, Pastor, Brown Memorial Park Avenue Presbyterian Church, Baltimore, Maryland

Richard S. Dietrich, Minister, First Presbyterian Church, Staunton, Virginia

Todd M. Donatelli, Dean, The Cathedral of All Souls, Asheville, North Carolina

James O. Duke, Professor of the History of Christianity and History of Christian Thought, Brite Divinity School of Texas Christian University, Fort Worth, Texas

Mark D. W. Edington, Epps Fellow and Chaplain, Harvard College, Cambridge, Massachusetts

Stephen Edmondson, Rector, St. Thomas Episcopal Church, McLean, Virginia

Mark Barger Elliott, Senior Minister, Mayflower Congregational Church, Grand Rapids, Michigan

Wendy Farley, Professor, Department of Religion, Emory University, Atlanta, Georgia

Michael H. Floyd, Professor of Old Testament, Centro de Estudios Teológicos, Santo Domingo, Dominican Republic

Garrett Green, Professor Emeritus of Religious Studies, Connecticut College, New London, Connecticut

Douglas John Hall, Emeritus Professor of Christian Theology, McGill University, Montreal, Quebec, Canada

Paul L. Hammer, Professor of New Testament (retired), Colgate Rochester Crozer Divinity School, Rochester, New York

Douglas R. A. Hare, William F. Orr Professor of New Testament Emeritus, Pittsburgh Theological Seminary, Pittsburgh, Pennsylvania

J. Barney Hawkins IV, Executive Director of the Center for Anglican Communion Studies and Professor of Parish Ministry, Virginia Theological Seminary, Alexandria, Virginia

Peter S. Hawkins, Professor of Religion and Literature, Yale University Divinity School

Roy L. Heller, Associate Professor of Old Testament, Perkins School of Theology, Southern Methodist University, Dallas, Texas

Susan T. Henry-Crowe, Dean of Cannon Chapel and Religious Life, Emory University, Atlanta, Georgia

Amy C. Howe, Parish Associate, Evergreen Presbyterian Church, Memphis, Tennessee

Michael Jinkins, Academic Dean and Professor of Pastoral Theology, Austin Presbyterian Theological Seminary, Austin, Texas

Cheryl Bridges Johns, Co-Pastor, New Covenant Church of God, Cleveland, Tennessee

Stephen C. Johnson, Assistant Professor of Preaching, Abilene Christian University, Abilene, Texas

Peter Rhea Jones, Professor of Preaching and New Testament, James and Carolyn McAfee School of Theology, Mercer University, Atlanta, Georgia

Douglas T. King, Associate Pastor, Brick Presbyterian Church, New York, New York

Cynthia Briggs Kittredge, Ernest J. Villavaso Jr. Associate Professor of New Testament, Episcopal Theological Seminary of the Southwest, Austin, Texas

Emmanuel Y. Lartey, Professor of Pastoral Theology, Care and Counseling, Candler School of Theology, Emory University, Atlanta, Georgia

Michael L. Lindvall, Senior Minister, Brick Presbyterian Church, New York, New York

Jennifer L. Lord, Associate Professor of Homiletics, Austin Presbyterian Theological Seminary, Austin, Texas

Bert Marshall, Regional Director, Church World Service, Ludlow, Massachusetts

Paul V. Marshall, Bishop, Episcopal Diocese of Bethlehem, Bethlehem, Pennsylvania

David W. McCreery, Professor of Religious Studies, Willamette University, Salem, Oregon

Judith M. McDaniel, Howard Chandler Robbins Professor of Homiletics, Virginia Theological Seminary, Alexandria, Virginia

Dean McDonald, Director, Cathedral College of Preachers, Washington, D.C.

John T. McFadden, Chaplain, Goodwill Industries of North Central Wisconsin, Appleton, Wisconsin

Donald K. McKim, Executive Editor of Theology and Reference, Westminster John Knox Press, Germantown, Tennessee

Wayne A. Meeks, Woolsey Professor Emeritus of Biblical Studies, Yale University, New Haven, Connecticut

Deborah Anne Meister, Rector, Christ Church, New Brunswick, New Jersey

Mark Miller-McLemore, Assistant Professor, Practice of Ministry, Vanderbilt University Divinity School, Nashville, Tennessee

Christopher Morse, Dietrich Bonhoeffer Professor of Theology and Ethics, Union Theological Seminary, New York, New York

D. Cameron Murchison, Dean of Faculty and Executive Vice President, Columbia Theological Seminary, Decatur, Georgia

Julia M. O'Brien, Professor of Old Testament, Lancaster Theological Seminary, Lancaster, Pennsylvania

V. Steven Parrish, Professor of Old Testament, Memphis Theological Seminary, Memphis, Tennessee

Robert Warden Prim, Pastor, Nacoochee Presbyterian Church, Sautee-Nacoochee, Georgia

Neta Lindsay Pringle, Interim Pastor, The Presbyterian Church at Woodbury, Woodbury, New Jersey

G. Lee Ramsey Jr., Professor of Pastoral Theology and Homiletics, Memphis Theological Seminary, Memphis, Tennessee

Charles E. Raynal, Director of Advanced Studies and Associate Professor of Theology, Columbia Theological Seminary, Decatur, Georgia

Allison Read, Chaplain, Trinity College, Hartford, Connecticut

Leanne Pearce Reed, Pastor, Montevallo Presbyterian Church, Montevallo, Alabama

Stephen Breck Reid, Professor of Christian Scriptures, George W. Truett Theological Seminary, Waco, Texas

Matthew S. Rindge, PhD Candidate in New Testament, Graduate Division of Religion, Emory University, Atlanta, Georgia

John Rollefson, Pastor, Lutheran Church of the Master, Los Angeles, California

Iwan Russell-Jones, TV Producer, BBC Wales, Cardiff, Wales, United Kingdom

Kristin Emery Saldine, Assistant Professor of Homiletics, Austin Presbyterian Theological Seminary, Austin, Texas

Don E. Saliers, William R. Cannon Distinguished Professor of Theology and Worship Emeritus, Candler School of Theology, Emory University, Atlanta, Georgia

Karen C. Sapio, Pastor, Claremont Presbyterian Church, Claremont, California

Clayton J. Schmit, Arthur DeKruyter/Christ Church Oak Brook Associate Professor of Preaching and Academic Director of the Brehm Center for Worship, Theology, and the Arts, Fuller Theological Seminary, Pasadena, California

Edwin Searcy, Minister, University Hill Congregation, Vancouver, British Columbia, Canada

Archie Smith Jr., James and Clarice Foster Professor of Pastoral Psychology and Counseling, Pacific School of Religion, Berkeley, California

O. Benjamin Sparks, Pastor, Honorably Retired, Richmond, Virginia

Thomas R. Steagald, Pastor, First United Methodist Church, Stanley, North Carolina

John K. Stendahl, Pastor, The Lutheran Church of the Newtons, Newton, Massachusetts

Chandler Brown Stokes, Pastor, First Presbyterian Church, Oakland, California

George W. Stroup, J. B. Green Professor of Theology, Columbia Theological Seminary, Decatur, Georgia

Nibs Stroupe, Pastor, Oakhurst Presbyterian Church, Decatur, Georgia

G. Porter Taylor, Bishop, Episcopal Diocese of Western North Carolina, Asheville, North Carolina

Eugene TeSelle, Professor Emeritus, Vanderbilt University Divinity School, Nashville, Tennessee

Mary Douglas Turner, Associate Rector, Bruton Parish Episcopal Church, Williamsburg, Virginia

Aaron L. Uitti, Rector, Episcopal Church of Saints Peter and Paul, Marietta, Georgia

Susan E. Vande Kappelle, Pastor, Fourth Presbyterian Church, Washington, Pennsylvania

Edwin Chr. van Driel, Assistant Professor of Theology, Pittsburgh Theological Seminary, Pittsburgh, Pennsylvania

Leanne Van Dyk, Dean and Vice President of Academic Affairs, Western Theological Seminary, Holland, Michigan

Haruko Nawata Ward, Associate Professor of Church History, Columbia Theological Seminary, Decatur, Georgia

Richard F. Ward, Associate Professor of Preaching and Performance Studies, Iliff School of Theology, Denver, Colorado

Jo Bailey Wells, Associate Professor of the Practice of Christian Ministry and Bible; Director of Anglican Episcopal House of Studies, Duke Divinity School, Durham, North Carolina

Dawn Ottoni Wilhelm, Associate Professor of Preaching and Worship, Bethany Theological Seminary, Richmond, Indiana

William H. Willimon, Bishop, North Alabama United Methodist Church, Birmingham, Alabama

Judith Hoch Wray, Director, Faith Empowerment Institute; Pastoral Associate, Park Avenue Christian Church (Disciples of Christ), New York City, New York

Karen Marie Yust, Associate Professor of Christian Education, Union Seminary–Presbyterian School of Christian Education, Richmond, Virginia

Randall C. Zachman, Professor, Department of Theology, University of Notre Dame, Notre Dame, Indiana

Beverly Zink-Sawyer, Professor of Preaching and Worship, Union Seminary–Presbyterian School of Christian Education, Richmond, Virginia

Scripture Index

Author Index

Mark D. W. Edington	Proper 7 G TP, Proper 8 G TP, Proper 9 G TP	Stephen C. Johnson	Proper 16 OT HP
		Peter Rhea Jones	Proper 16 E HP
Stephen Edmondson	Proper 10 OT TP, Proper 11 OT TP, Proper 12 OT TP	Douglas T. King	Proper 10 OT HP, Proper 11 OT HP, Proper 12 OT HP
Mark Barger Elliott	Proper 4 E HP, Proper 5 E HP, Proper 6 E HP	Cynthia Briggs Kittredge	Proper 4 E EP, Proper 5 E EP, Proper 6 E EP
Wendy Farley	Proper 4 G TP, Proper 5 G TP, Proper 6 G TP	Emmanuel Y. Lartey	Day of Pentecost G PP, Trinity Sunday G PP, Proper 3 G PP
Michael H. Floyd	Day of Pentecost NT EP, Trinity Sunday OT EP, Proper 3 OT EP	Michael L. Lindvall	Proper 7 G PP, Proper 8 G PP, Proper 9 G PP
Garrett Green	Proper 7 E TP, Proper 8 E TP, Proper 9 E TP	Jennifer L. Lord	Proper 16 PS HP
		Bert Marshall	Proper 4 OT HP, Proper 5 OT HP, Proper 6 OT HP
Douglas John Hall	Proper 10 G TP, Proper 11 G TP, Proper 12 G TP	Paul V. Marshall	Proper 13 E PP, Proper 14 E PP, Proper 15 E PP
Paul L. Hammer	Day of Pentecost G EP, Trinity Sunday G EP, Proper 3 G EP	David W. McCreery	Proper 4 OT EP, Proper 5 OT EP, Proper 6 OT EP
Douglas R. A. Hare	Proper 16 G EP		
J. Barney Hawkins IV	Day of Pentecost E PP, Trinity Sunday E PP, Proper 3 E PP	Judith M. McDaniel	Day of Pentecost G HP, Trinity Sunday G HP, Proper 3 G HP
Peter S. Hawkins	Proper 7 E HP, Proper 8 E HP, Proper 9 E HP	Dean McDonald	Proper 13 OT HP, Proper 14 OT HP, Proper 15 OT HP
Roy L. Heller	Proper 10 PS EP, Proper 11 PS EP, Proper 12 PS EP	John T. McFadden	Proper 7 E PP, Proper 8 E PP, Proper 9 E PP
Susan T. Henry-Crowe	Proper 16 OT PP	Donald K. McKim	Day of Pentecost NT TP, Trinity Sunday OT TP, Proper 3 OT TP
Amy C. Howe	Proper 16 G PP		
Michael Jinkins	Proper 10 OT PP, Proper 11 OT PP, Proper 12 OT PP	Wayne A. Meeks	Proper 13 G EP, Proper 14 G EP, Proper 15 G EP
Cheryl Bridges Johns	Proper 10 G HP, Proper 11 G HP, Proper 12 G HP	Deborah Anne Meister	Proper 4 PS HP, Proper 5 PS HP, Proper 6 PS HP

Mark Miller-McLemore	Day of Pentecost PS PP, Trinity Sunday PS PP, Proper 3 PS PP	Don E. Saliers	Proper 4 G PP, Proper 5 G PP, Proper 6 G PP
Christopher Morse	Proper 13 G TP, Proper 14 G TP, Proper 15 G TP	Karen C. Sapio	Proper 10 OT EP, Proper 11 OT EP, Proper 12 OT EP
D. Cameron Murchison	Proper 4 PS TP, Proper 5 PS TP, Proper 6 PS TP	Clayton J. Schmit	Day of Pentecost E HP, Trinity Sunday E HP, Proper 3 E HP
Julia M. O'Brien	Proper 16 OT EP	Edwin Searcy	Proper 10 E HP, Proper 11 E HP, Proper 12 E HP
V. Steven Parrish	Proper 4 PS EP, Proper 5 PS EP, Proper 6 PS EP	Archie Smith Jr.	Proper 16 E PP
Robert Warden Prim	Day of Pentecost PS EP, Trinity Sunday PS EP, Proper 3 PS EP	O. Benjamin Sparks	Proper 13 G PP, Proper 14 G PP, Proper 15 G PP
Neta Lindsay Pringle	Proper 7 PS HP, Proper 8 PS HP, Proper 9 PS HP	Thomas R. Steagald	Proper 13 OT TP, Proper 14 OT TP, Proper 15 OT TP
G. Lee Ramsey Jr.	Day of Pentecost NT HP, Trinity Sunday OT HP, Proper 3 OT HP	John K. Stendahl	Proper 4 E PP, Proper 5 E PP, Proper 6 E PP
Charles E. Raynal	Proper 16 OT TP	Chandler Brown Stokes	Proper 7 PS PP, Proper 8 PS PP, Proper 9 PS PP
Allison Read	Proper 16 PS PP		
Leanne Pearce Reed	Proper 7 OT HP, Proper 8 A HP, Proper 9 OT HP	George W. Stroup	Proper 10 E TP, Proper 11 E TP, Proper 12 E TP
Stephen Breck Reid	Proper 7 OT EP, Proper 8 A EP, Proper 9 OT EP	Nibs Stroupe	Proper 4 G HP, Proper 5 G HP, Proper 6 G HP
Matthew S. Rindge	Day of Pentecost E EP, Trinity Sunday E EP, Proper 3 E EP	G. Porter Taylor	Proper 13 E TP, Proper 14 E TP, Proper 15 E TP
John Rollefson	Proper 4 OT PP, Proper 5 OT PP, Proper 6 OT PP	Eugene TeSelle	Proper 4 E TP, Proper 5 E TP, Proper 6 E TP
Iwan Russell-Jones	Day of Pentecost PS TP, Trinity Sunday PS TP, Proper 3 PS TP	Mary Douglas Turner	Proper 4 PS PP, Proper 5 PS PP, Proper 6 PS PP
Kristin Emery Saldine	Day of Pentecost NT PP, Trinity Sunday OT PP, Proper 3 OT PP	Aaron L. Uitti	Proper 16 E EP